1986

A HISTORY OF
JEWISH PHILOSOPHY IN
THE MIDDLE AGES

A HISTORY OF
JEWISH PHILOSOPHY
IN THE
MIDDLE AGES

COLETTE SIRAT

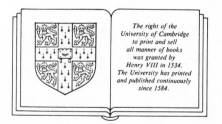

The right of the
University of Cambridge
to print and sell
all manner of books
was granted by
Henry VIII in 1534.
The University has printed
and published continuously
since 1584.

CAMBRIDGE UNIVERSITY PRESS

Cambridge

London   New York   New Rochelle   Melbourne   Sydney

EDITIONS DE

LA MAISON DES SCIENCES DE L'HOMME

Paris

Published by the Press Syndicate of the University of Cambridge
The Pitt Building, Trumpington Street, Cambridge CB2 1RP
32 East 57th Street, New York, NY 10022, USA
10 Stamford Road, Oakleigh, Melbourne 3166, Australia
and Editions de la Maison des Sciences de l'Homme
54 Boulevard Raspail, 75270 Paris Cedex 06

First published 1985

Printed in Great Britain by
the University Press, Cambridge

Library of Congress catalogue card number: 84-29343

British Library cataloguing in publication data
Sirat, Colette
A history of Jewish philosophy in the Middle Ages.
1. Philosophy, Jewish   2. Philosophy, Medieval
I. Title   II. La Philosophie juive au
Moyen-Age. *English*
181'.06   B755
ISBN 0 521 26087 6
ISBN 2 7351 0103 7 (France only)

UP

CONTENTS

ACKNOWLEDGEMENTS

I would like to express my gratitude to the librarians and custodians of Hebrew manuscripts to whose kindness and helpfulness I frequently had recourse, especially those of the Bibliothèque Nationale in Paris, and the National and University Library and the Institute of Hebrew Microfilms, both in Jerusalem. I would like also to thank the editorial board of *Kriat Sefer*, who are always ready to help me in bibliographical matters.

My thanks are due to the Press of the Centre National de la Recherche Scientifique for permission to use the French text as the basis for this book.

– To Professor L. Berman, Dr H. Ben-Shammai, Professor R. Loewe and Professor S. Pines for generously allowing me to use as yet unpublished articles and translations.

– To Ms M. Reich who prompted me to prepare this English edition, translated it from the French and helped me with her remarks. The bibliography has particularly benefited by her efforts.

– To Dr R. Williams for the kind and courteous help he gave during the preparatory stages of the publication of the present book and to Jane Hodgart for her careful editing and numerous questions.

– And finally to Professor S. Pines for his untiring patience during the revision of the book. The present text reflects his advice and valuable criticism.

PREFACE

This book was written as an introduction to the study of Jewish medieval philosophy. It is based on the texts themselves,[1] printed and in manuscript, presented and analysed in an attempt to elucidate their meaning and to situate them in their historical context.

In the first part of the book the Jewish authors are classed according to the currents of thought to which they belonged. From the beginning of the Middle Ages until about 1200, Jews in Islamic countries wrote in Arabic and participated in all the spiritual trends that stirred the Arab world. The change to Hebrew took place in Spain, during the twelfth century, with the Reconquista, when the vital centre of Jewish philosophy shifted to Christian Europe – Provence, Spain and Italy.

In the second part our authors are discussed within their centuries. Although this division is necessarily artificial, it nevertheless reflects a historical reality. Philosophy had become the framework of thought of whole classes of Jewish society. Writers abounded and the basic texts – Maimonides Abraham Ibn Ezra, Averroes – were known and used by all of them. The chapter on the thirteen century describes the period when Jewish thinkers, as well as Christian Schoolmen received and studied Greek and Arabic texts. 'Science', in Arabic, Hebrew or Latin garb, was considered by Jewish Philosophers the same, identical 'Science'. Towards the end of the thirteenth century and during the fourteenth, Jewish authors did not abandon the Arabic and Jewish philosophical texts that constituted the foundation of their thought, but they were aware of the problems being discussed in the universities. The Italians were the first to translate Latin texts into Hebrew, but during the second half of the fourteenth century translations of Latin works on logic and medicine appeared in Spain and Provence with increasing frequency.

The fifteenth century in Spain was one of physical and intellectual oppression, a century of inner withdrawal and of spiritual distress, which ended in the Expulsion of the Jews from the country. Meanwhile, around the Mediterranean, Jewish scholars, whether from necessity or out of intellectual curiosity began to use Latin and the vernaculars as their languages of literature and philosophy. But this is no longer part of the Middle Ages.

---

[1] Unless otherwise stated, translations from the original texts and from secondary material were made by the author and by the translator, and in most cases revised by Professor S. Pines.

ix

Preface

The book published here in English differs from that in French which I completed five years ago and which was published by the Centre National de la Recherche Scientifique in 1983. Numerous passages have been entirely recast, in order to make use of existing English translations of many texts, and to take into account the numerous studies that have appeared during the last five years. The transcription of Arabic and Hebrew names is a compromise between a scientific transliteration, which would have been unreadable, and current usage; in most cases, I used the transcription adopted by the Encyclopaedia Judaica. The bibliography has been especially prepared for the English edition.

Chapter 1

INTRODUCTION

What do we mean by Jewish medieval philosophy?

In modern times, the meaning of the word 'philosophy' has considerably changed; it has come to mean almost all systems of thought; we say Hindu philosophy, the philosophy of the Bible and, even, the philosophy of a certain way of life. During the Middle Ages, 'philosophy' had a signification both broader and more restricted. The word referred to the 'explanations of the world', the 'systems of thought' elaborated by the Greeks, which reached their culmination in the fifth and fourth centuries B.C. with Plato and Aristotle. Whatever importance accrued to their predecessors and successors, these two great figures dominated medieval philosophy. The philosophy of Aristotle (not the ancient but the medieval Aristotle) gave a total explanation of the world: that is to say, it comprised all the science known at the time, and the 'First Philosophy', called *metaphysics* (that which comes after physics), is the culmination of physical, biological, zoological, mathematical, etc. thought. Aristotle's cosmology, more or less harmonized with that of Plato, was, during the Middle Ages and at least until the fifteenth century, the 'Science'. The earth, which did not move, was considered to be the centre of the world; and the sublunary world, constituted of the four elements, was subject to generation and corruption. Around it, the celestial spheres moved in a circular 'perfect' movement; these spheres, one contained within the other, were made of a fifth element, the 'quintessence', and the stars were set in them. They were not subject either to generation or to corruption and were often compared to translucent diamonds. Each of these spheres was propelled both by its own movement and by that communicated to it by the highest sphere, which was the ultimate limit of the universe. Beyond this sphere there was nothing, not even emptiness,[1] and when in thought one had passed in review the celestial spheres, then the sublunary world, the earth and what is on it, one knew all things as completely as man's limited intellect could know them; one could learn no more about the physical world. There were, however, other domains of knowledge: the intelligible world, the world of intellects, the divine world, to the extent that man can understand it; a man who possesses Science in this sense was a 'lover of wisdom', a philosopher.

---

[1] In some neoplatonic systems it is said that the spiritual substance surrounds the corporeal substance, but this does not imply material localization.

In this closed world, things and beings were hierarchically disposed, that is to say, the world was conceived as a hierarchy of beings.

As Shakespeare said, in a well-known speech:

> The heavens themselves, the planets and this centre
> Observe degree, priority, and place,
> Insisture, course, proportion, season, form,
> Office, and custom, in all line of order ...:
> How could communities,
> Degrees in schools, and brotherhoods in cities
> Peaceful commerce from dividable shores,
> The primogenitive and due of birth,
> Prerogative of age, crowns, sceptres, laurels,
> But by degree, stand in authentic place?
>
> (*Troilus and Cressida*, I. iii)

From this it ensued that men aspired to the perfection of the superior degree, and, for the philosophers, the supreme aim of human destiny was to attain to the Active Intellect and to identify themselves with it: to be truly a man was to raise oneself above humanity and become pure intellect.

In the philosophical tradition God is perfection, that is to say, being perfect; He aspires to nothing, for every desire is the sign of a lack; He is the unmoving and eternal mover of the moving world of the spheres. This God of the philosophers has been very well described by Judah Halevi.

There is no favour or dislike in [the nature of] God, because He is above desire and intention. A desire intimates a want in the person who feels it, and not till it is satisfied does he become (so to speak) complete. If it remains unfulfilled, he lacks completion. In a similar way He is, in the opinion of philosophers, above the knowledge of individuals, for these change with the passage of time, whilst there is no change in God's knowledge. He, therefore, does not know thee, much less thy thoughts and actions, nor does He listen to thy prayers, or see thy movements. If philosophers say that He created thee, they only use a metaphor, because He is the Cause of causes in the creation of all creatures, but not because this was His intention from the beginning. He never created man. For the world is without beginning, and there never arose a man otherwise than through one who came into existence before him, in whom were united forms, gifts, and characteristics inherited from father, mother, and other relations, besides the influences of climate, countries, foods and water, spheres, stars and constellations. Everything goes back to a Prime Cause; not to a Will proceeding from this, but an Emanation from which emanated a second, a third, and fourth cause.

The Cause and the caused are, as thou seest, intimately connected with one another, their coherence being as eternal as the Prime Cause and having no beginning. Every individual on earth has his completing causes; consequently an individual with perfect causes becomes perfect, and another with imperfect causes remains imperfect, as the negro who is able to receive nothing more than the human shape and speech in its least developed form. The philosopher, however, who is equipped with the highest capacity, receives through it the advantages of disposition, intelligence and active power, so that he wants nothing to make him perfect. Now

2

these perfections exist but in a latent state, and require instruction and training to become active, and in order that this capacity, with all its completeness or deficiencies and endless grades, may become visible.

. . . A light belonging to the divine hierarchy and called the Active Intellect is conjoined with the perfect man. And this man's [passive] intellect is conjoined with the Active Intellect in such a conjunction and union that this individual considers that he is the Active Intellect, there being no differences between them . . . This degree is the ultimate end which the perfect man may hope for . . . The soul of the perfect man and this Intellect become one and the same thing. He pays no attention to the passing away of his body and his organs since he and this entity are one and the same thing. And his soul is in excellent state during his life, as he comes to belong to the company of Hermes, Asclepius, Socrates, Plato and Aristotle; nay he, they, and all those that [have attained] their degree as well as the Active Intellect are one and the same thing. This is what is called allusively and approximately Pleasure of God.

(*Kuzari* I, 4–6)

This God of the philosophers is essentially different from the God of the Bible. In the Scriptures God is a moral person endowed with will and decision. He says in Genesis: 'Let us make man in our image, after our likeness', and this man whom He created was given the commandments and the interdictions. From Genesis onwards God has directed the course of the history of the universe: the sun and the planets are subject to His decisions, and man also, who can please God, pray to Him and make Him retract His decisions. Moses speaks to God person to person; there is a dialogue. God is free to answer or not, but He remains present and even, for the prophets, visible and audible and often enough anthropomorphic: He shows Himself with the features of a 'powerful king', or else, He sends His angels.

God has made an alliance with the Jewish people; a chosen people, privileged by its closeness to God; God has given it, through the intermediary of Moses, His Law, the *Torah*, that is the five books constituting the Pentateuch; the other peoples are an instrument in the hand of God; He uses them to punish Israel and to bring it back to the right way. Even when, in the later prophets, the kingdom of God expands to include all humanity, His will remains incarnate in one text: the Bible. This book, revealed once and for all at Mount Sinai (a doctrine most probably admitted some centuries before the Christian era, although the biblical canon was finally established only later), contains all the divine commandments and prohibitions; and the *Torah*, considered as eternal truth, was to be for the Jews the criterion of all other verities: to rebel against it would be to rebel against God.

But the Bible itself is not monolithic; and as time passed and new problems presented themselves to human consciousness, it became necessary to find the answers to new questions in the revealed text itself. Fortunately certain verses of the biblical text can be explained in different ways.

We know that in legal questions the oral law referring to the written text has permitted modifications since a very ancient period. The extent of the oral tradition, which in the second century was committed to writing under the

3

name of the *Mishnah* and explained, commented-on and glossed to compose an enormous corpus that is still being amplified, attests to the difficulties incurred in responding to new situations while basing oneself on immutable texts; this literature shows how with the help of these same texts problems were resolved. The problem of finding a correspondence between a revelation that does not admit a change and a human world in constant evolution has similarly presented itself to the other religions based on revelation, Christianity and Islam, and it has been resolved, generally, in the same manner, that is, by an 'interpretation' of the revealed text; two meanings are discovered in it: the internal, esoteric sense, and the external sense. The internal sense, which has to be discovered by the intelligence, with the aid of the tradition, is evidently more flexible than the external, but it is based on it. It is related, for example, that Simeon of Emmaus, a Palestinian rabbi of the first or second century A.D., found an interpretation for each of the *et* (the particle that introduces the complement of the direct object) in the *Torah*. It is evident that the biblical text is not the source of the interpretation; it is only the written reference for it. We know the sentence: 'The Torah has seventy faces . . .'

Only interpretation, allegorical or symbolic, has permitted different systems of thought, whether philosophical, kabbalistic or ascetic, to remain within Judaism. As long as traditional texts were referred to in order to justify a philosophical doctrine, for instance the Aristotelian one adopted by Maimonides, one can speak of Jewish philosophy. Spinoza, whose philosophy is undoubtedly one of the most original of all those constructed by Jews, is certainly a Jewish philosopher; but his philosophy is not a Jewish philosophy even if his sources are deeply rooted in the tradition; for he rejected this tradition and did not wish it to form part of his system as he expounded it in the *Ethics*.

Maimonides on the other hand did not innovate very much in philosophical thought; he took over the 'philosophy', the 'science', as it was expounded by the Arab philosophers; but he wished to show not only that this philosophy did not contradict the revealed text but that the revealed text alludes and leads to it. Thus, Jewish philosophy does not signify a philosophy elaborated by a Jew; nor does it signify a philosophy of which the sources are Jewish, for, as we shall see, the philosophical current that arose in Greece some 2500 years ago remained more or less true to itself (except for the Mu'tazilite school, which is rationalistic in tendency without being properly speaking philosophical). This means that a given philosophy, appearing at a certain moment of human history, was brought into connection with the Jewish tradition, and the traits common to certain texts of the Hebrew heritage and to this system of thought were emphasized.

In speaking of Jewish tradition, we do not mean an 'essential' Judaism, the spirit of which has not changed since the revelation of the Law on Sinai. The Jewish tradition referred to by the Jewish philosophers may be one specific part of what we now call 'Jewish tradition'. For example, the Karaites rejected the entire oral tradition, but are, and thought themselves to be, Jewish thinkers. Nevertheless, not all philosophers who considered themselves Jews can be accepted as such. Abner of Burgos, when becoming a Christian, proclaimed himself to be a true Jewish philosopher, realizing the true essential aim of Israel; but we can hardly consider a Christian bishop to be a Jewish philosopher.

Thus the texts that constitute 'Jewish philosophy' are rarely purely philosophical; they are rather commentaries, either biblical commentaries, or commentaries on philosophical texts by Aristotle, Averroes and others. Among the several works of 'pure' philosophy we have the *Fountain of Life* by 'Avicebron', and the history of this celebrated text illustrates my meaning very well. During the thirteenth century a certain 'Arabic' philosopher was frequently cited by Christian authors, including Albertus Magnus and Thomas Aquinas; the influence of his book, the *Fountain of Life*, was considerable, but nobody knew what personage was hidden behind the name of Avicebron; the work was in Latin, but it was known that it was translated from Arabic. In 1846, the great Jewish scholar S. Munk, identified Avicebron as Solomon Ibn Gabirol, famous for his liturgical poems.[1] Apart from some references to the Sefer Yeẓirah (*Book of Creation*), no internal evidence or biblical allusion suggested that the author of the *Fountain of Life* was Jewish, and this is not surprising, for this book treats solely of philosophy, that is, of God, the relations of God with the world, of form and matter, and so on; but this God is not the God revealed in the Bible; it is the God of the philosophers who is too perfect to speak directly to men. Other works by Ibn Gabirol, such as *The Kingly Crown*, show us how the author brought this philosophy into harmony with the rabbinical tradition. These texts, the purely philosophical work and the poetical commentaries, taken in conjunction, form the Jewish philosophy of Ibn Gabirol. In any case, they allow us to integrate him into the history of Jewish philosophy.

Thus one can say that the history of Jewish philosophy in the Middle Ages is the history of the effort of Jews to reconcile philosophy (or a system of rationalist thought) and Scripture. According to the various philosophers, this effort was more or less successful; the different elements, philosophical or religious, assumed greater or lesser importance, but the harmonizing of these two systems of thought in one unique verity was the theme of almost all Jewish medieval philosophy. And when the accepted philosophy was called in doubt, this was in the name of reason.

---

[1] The identification had already been proposed by a Spanish scholar in the seventeenth century but this suggestion was not taken up by later scholars, including S. Munk, until his own discovery of the Hebrew fragments of *The Fountain of Life* by Shem Tov ben Joseph Falaquera.

Introduction

One cannot begin to discuss medieval Jewish philosophy without recalling that the first contact between Greek philosophy and biblical thought took place at Alexandria. Of this original encounter only the work of Philo has survived.

Philo lived in Alexandria at the turn of the first century. Alexandria was then a very large city, and a centre, perhaps the most important, of the Greek philosophical tradition. Unfortunately, we have hardly any direct attestation to the philosophical life of the time. Numerous schools existed; the Stoics and the Epicureans co-existed with the followers of the ancient schools: Platonists, Sceptics, Aristotelians; but of all that was said and written, nothing remains except citations in the Greek and Latin authors. Cicero has left us some Stoic and Epicurean texts, but it is difficult to identify them exactly; only the doctrines of Epicurus are sufficiently well known, thanks to the Latin poet Lucretius. This means that Philo is in a way the only important Greek witness of a long (from the third century B.C. to the second century A.D.), extremely rich and diversified period. He is a representative of Hellenic culture and also of Alexandrian Judaism. An important member of the community, he went to Rome as ambassador to the Emperor Caligula, in A.D. 40, to intercede on behalf of his co-religionists, and he has left us an account of this voyage in which he remarks that he was already old, thus leading us to suppose that he was born in about 20 B.C. This is more or less all that we know of his private life. He wrote a great deal: biblical exegeses, commentaries on certain biblical tales, a treatise about the Essenes, and also purely philosophical works such as the *Treatise On the Eternity of the World*.

He wrote in Greek, and it is not established that he knew Hebrew. He had, it seems, some knowledge of the ancient *midrashim*, but he quotes the Bible in the Septuagint version, of which it was said that it was made under divine inspiration, and which has survived, like the works of Philo himself, in the Christian tradition. For Philo was forgotten by the Jews, and his direct contribution to Jewish medieval thought is almost non-existent. Sometimes one finds translations of short passages from his works, especially among the Karaites, but there was no really direct or important influence. As we shall see, the first centuries of our era, during which the Christians, having divested themselves of particularist traditions, were engaged in conquering the Greco-Roman world with its own arms, were for the Jews centuries of elaboration of their own tradition. Philo, 'assimilated' Jew, had a very great influence on the Christian authors of the early centuries and on the later Christian literature, for he was, like them, inclined to the profane world, showing that the Bible was not opposed to Greek culture, and even that the two could get on very well together.

The presumed harmony existing between the teachings revealed in the Bible and the doctrines taught by pagan philosophy was explained by the ingenious theory that the wisdom of the Greeks and of other nations had its source among the Jews. The original works were lost in the Exile, but, through translation, the ideas in them were transmitted first to the Chaldeans and Persians and subsequently to the Greeks and Romans. In its essential points this notion was current among the Jews of Alexandria as early as the second century B.C., being found in Aristobulos of Paneas, an author quoted by Josephus and Eusebius. Pythagoras, it was supposed, studied under King Solomon; or, in another opinion, he was a disciple of the prophet Ezekiel. Socrates derived his philosophy from Ahithophel and from Asaph the Psalmist; Plato was a pupil of Jeremiah, and Aristotle studied under Simon the Just.

A number of medieval Jewish philosophers[1] echoed this theory and even stressed it, as we shall see.

It is very difficult to give a systematic account of Philo's thought, first because his treatises are chiefly commentaries, but also because he very often contradicts himself. Even for really important notions he has no consistent definitions, but rather multiple variations on a given theme. In effect, Philo's aim was not to construct a philosophy, but to show the convergence between the 'Law' (*Torah*) and 'a philosophy of nature', the syncretism of which did not unduly trouble him. In his own words (*De migratione Abrahami* 127–9) 'So Abram departed, as the Lord had spoken unto him' (Genesis 12: 4):

This is the aim extolled by the best philosophers, to live agreeably to nature; and it is attained whenever the mind, having entered on virtue's path, walks in the track of right reason and follows God, mindful of His injunctions, and always and in all places recognizing them all as valid both in action and in speech. For 'he journeyed just as the Lord spake to him': the meaning of this is that as God speaks – and He speaks with consummate beauty and excellence – so the good man does everything, blamelessly keeping straight the path of life, so that the actions of the wise man are nothing else than the words of God.

(The Loeb Classical Library, trans. F. H. Colson and G. H. Withaker, pp. 205–7)

Philosophy, virtue, wisdom are, in the final reckoning, synonyms of the 'commandments of the God of the Bible'. The apologetic intention is evident, but this is perhaps not the internal dynamic of Philo's thought: it is more a meditation on the biblical text with the help of all the intellectual instruments of a cultivated man of his period; these instruments, notions and ideas are not original, and philosophical allegory was applied to the Bible also before Philo, but the multiplication and variety of interpretations stemming from the Scripture was genuinely original. It was a meditation on the text but also a mystical experience.

On other occasions, I have approached my work empty and suddenly become full, the ideas falling in a shower from above and being sown invisibly, so that under

---

[1] The Jews, moreover, were not alone in these opinions. The Arabs (as, for instance, Averroes and the *Ikhwān al-Ṣāfā*) agreed with them as did also some Christian authors in the Middle Ages.

the influence of the Divine possession I have been filled with corybantic frenzy and been unconscious of anything, place, persons present, myself, words spoken, lines written. For I obtained language, ideas, an enjoyment of light, keenest vision, pellucid distinctness of objects, such as might be received through the eyes as the result of clearest shewing.

Now the thing shewn is the thing worthy to be seen, contemplated, loved, the perfect good, whose nature it is to change all that is bitter in the soul and make it sweet, fairest seasoning of all spices, turning into salutary nourishment even food that do not nourish. So we read 'The Lord shewed him a tree, and he cast it into the water' (Ex. xv. 25), that is into the flabby, flaccid mind teeming with bitterness, that its savagery might be sweetened away. This tree offers not nourishment only but immortality also, for we are told that the Tree of Life has been planted in the midst of the Garden (Gen. ii. 9), even Goodness with the particular virtues and the doings which accord with them to be its bodyguard. For it is Virtue that has obtained as its own the central and most honourable place in the soul.

(Ibid. 35–7, pp. 151–3)

What Philo contemplated during the mystical ecstasy was not God as a king in his palace, as Isaiah saw Him, nor as a majestic old man as He appeared to Daniel's prophetic vision: but rather as Idea and Light, something very close to the world of Platonic ideas, eternal archetypes of terrestrial things, which imitate the Ideas and are like a mirror reflecting them. God, for Philo, cannot have a human or any other form. The refusal of anthropomorphism is one of the fundamental themes of his thought, and it is also one of the central subjects of all Jewish medieval philosophy.

Between this God, who is pure intellect, and man, intermediaries are necessary; and here a particularly rich multi-faceted notion is interposed, allowing many exegeses. This is the Logos, the 'Word', the discourse.

The idea of the Logos of God, 'Law of the World' and 'Rule of the Universe', accords very well with the biblical vision: and another aspect, that of the intelligible world, is found in the *Midrash*, in the conception of the *Torah* that God is supposed to have contemplated during the creation of the world. If Philo's thought has survived it is because the Christians were convinced that Philo's philosophy proclaimed Jesus, son of God and incarnate Logos. In truth, Philo saw in the Logos not only the divine world, but also, sometimes, the elder son of God, standing opposite the world, designated as 'young son of God'. Did Philo have the idea that this Logos, multiform, had become incarnate and had taken human shape? It must be admitted that since clarity is not the most conspicuous quality discernable in Philo, one can perhaps, if absolutely necessary, deduce this from the text.

The problem posed by the biblical God's anthropomorphism was recognized at that period by Hellenized as well as by less 'assimilated' Jews. Thus, to Philo's notion of 'Logos' – Divine Word, addressed to man and heard only by the pure soul – corresponds the word *Memra* – 'Word', in the Aramaic paraphrase of the Bible, made in the second century B.C. by Onqelos (Targum Onqelos). In Philo as in the Targum the intention is the same: to obviate the anthropomorphism of the biblical text. Thus the phrases 'God descends, mounts, moves' are translated in Aramaic by 'The Glory of God descends, mounts, moves . . .'

Non-Hellenistic Judaism, faced with the problem of a non-corporeal God and His relation with the world, could not make use of Philo's writings, because his thought was too close to Hellenism for non-Greek-speaking Jews to benefit from it. And it was in rabbinical Judaistic circles that the philosophy reappeared, after Alexandrian Judaism had disappeared.

Up to the eleventh century rabbinical Judaism devoted all its energy to preserving and enriching a tradition that still remains the foundation of present-day Judaism. On the one hand the *midrashim* contain commentary and explication of the Scriptures, that is, the twenty-four books of the biblical canon (their committal to writing went on from the fifth to the twelfth centuries). On the other, the oral traditions codified in the second century A.D., the *Mishnah*, were commented on and expanded in the *Gemarah* (second to sixth centuries). The *Mishnah* and the *Gemarah* together form the Talmud, or more precisely the *Talmudim*, since the *Mishnah* was explicated both by the Babylonian rabbis (Babylonian Talmud), and by the Palestinian rabbis (Jerusalem Talmud).

The greater part of the texts collected in the Talmuds is concerned with the *halakhah*, that is, religious and civil, public and personal law; a smaller part consists of the *Aggadah* and has no legal authority. (The *Aggadah*, a collection of stories, maxims, parables and allegories, is also generously represented in the *midrashim*.) From the middle of the seventh century the great Babylonian academies of Sura and Pumbadita, under the authority of the Exilarch, a descendant of David, perpetuated and enlarged the talmudic tradition under the direction of the Geonim, whose renown spread through all countries of the Diaspora. They used to answer questions, as much on law as on theology, addressed to them by both the occidental and the oriental communities. In Palestine, the Patriarch (*Nasi*, Prince), who was also a descendant of David, enjoyed less authority on the intellectual level even if on the sentimental one he continued to be venerated.

Thus, between Philo's century and that of Saadiah, Jewish thought consisted mainly in reflection and elaboration of the written and the oral Law behind the shelter of barriers erected against the surrounding ambience, especially that of Greek thought. The Hellenic influence was nevertheless important in everyday life and theological questions could not be avoided, especially because of the proliferation of religious and philosophical sects; but the responses were made on a decidedly religious and rarely on a rationalist level, if one defines reason as the philosophers did. Moreover, an esoteric line of thought is apparent in the Talmud and in the gnostic *midrashim*.

The mysticism of the Sages of the Talmud and later of the period of the Geonim is that of the *Hekhaloth*, the divine palaces, and it is close to that of the Gnostics. Jewish mysticism developed during the Middle Ages in two main trends: Ashkenazi *Ḥassidut* and the Kabbalah. Two of the compositions committed to writing during the earlier talmudic period played some part in Jewish medieval philosophy. First, the *Sefer Yezirah*, the *Book of Creation*, written probably between the third and sixth centuries. The *Book of Creation* is very short and not very explicit. It describes the thirty-two ways of Wisdom through which God created the world – the ten *sefiroth* and the twenty-two letters of the Hebrew alphabet. The ten *sefiroth* are enumerated in chapter I: the word *sefirah* comes from the root *sfr*, 'tell', 'relate' and also 'count'. It is this last sense, it seems, that the author of the *Book of Creation* had in mind when he affirmed that the *sefiroth* are created forces (and probably not emanations of God), and that they play a decisive part in the order of the world:

Ten Sefiroth alone: they are measured by ten without end: the depth of the first and the depth of the last, the depth of good and the depth of evil, the depth above and the depth below, the depth of the east and the depth of the west, the depth of the north and the depth of the south. One Lord, God the Faithful King, rules them all from His Holy dwelling for all eternity.

(*The Book of Creation* I, 5, trans. I. Friedman, p. 1)

In chapter II the subject of the *sefiroth* is dropped and we find a description of the creation of the heavens and the earth by the combinations and permutations of the letters of the Hebrew alphabet. 'God drew them, hewed them, combined them, weighed them, interchanged them and through them produced the whole creation and everything that is destined to be created.' It was by contemplating the mystery of the letters and the *sefiroth* that Abraham had the revelation of Omnipotent God. It is most probably because of this conclusion that the book was sometimes called *The Letters of our Father Abraham*.

Because of its brevity, its density and its emphatic and esoteric style the *Book of Creation* gave rise to interpretations and commentaries throughout the Middle Ages.

The *Shiur Qomah* (*Measure of the Divine Stature*) (the final redaction of which G. Scholem dates from about the seventh century), describes the appearance of the body of the Creator and gives enormous estimates of the length of his various organs. At the same time it indicates the secret names of the various organs with the help of figures and configurations. This text, also very short, is at first sight anthropomorphic, for God is spoken of as if He were of human form, but what is really meant by these monstrous measurements is not clear. Perhaps the intention was to suggest the infinity of God and the impossibility of an anthropomorphic representation of the divinity. This *midrash* was to cause much embarrassment to medieval rational thought.

All this intense activity of rabbinical thought played a great part in the survival of the Jewish people; after the national catastrophes of 70 A.D. (the destruction of the Temple of Jerusalem) and 135 A.D. (when the last Jewish revolt against Rome was crushed), Judaism had to reinterpret the relation between man and God, since this relation no longer passed through the medium of the Temple and the sacrifices; and the Diaspora, which had existed long before the Christian era, was invested with a new religious meaning. All these misfortunes took on a moral and positive significance. Moreover, Judaism had to defend itself more and more energetically against the new religion that had sprung from it – Christianity[1] – and only rabbinical Judaism had enough internal strength not only to continue to exist but also to develop into a rich tradition.

Neither was the political conjuncture favourable to the reception of external influences; the fall of the Roman Empire and the great invasions were plunging the Roman world into chaos. The social and economic decline of the Roman Empire had impelled Jews to emigrate to Persian Babylonia, where Zoroastrian Sassanid rule was more merciful than Christian, and provided a refuge. With Constantine's conversion in 313, when Christianity became the official religion of the Roman Empire, and in 439, with Theodosius II's expulsion of Jews from important posts, the intellectual centre of Jewish life moved to Babylonia. The rivalry between the Patriarch in Palestine and the Exilarch in Babylon remained alive for a long time.

After the Islamic conquests and until about 1200, the Jewish world was divided into two communities.

(1) Judaism in northern Europe (France, England, Germany), immersed in a Christian environment not propitious to the development or the formation of external relationships, proceeded in the specifically Jewish direction that had characterized the elaboration of the rabbinical tradition; the activity of the Franco-Rhenian exegetic school, of which Rashi is the best known representative, owes comparatively little to the surrounding ambience, although the ascetism that is a distinctive feature of the Ashkenazi *Hassidim* (pietists) of Germany in the twelfth and thirteenth centuries had points of similarity with that of their Christian contemporaries; but this could have been the result of similar preoccupations rather than direct influence; such an influence, direct or indirect, was never recognized as such by the rabbis.

In Italy, Provence and Christian Spain, the social and intellectual ambience seems to have been more relaxed, although literary attestations to this impression are scanty. However, except perhaps in South Italy, relations between Christians and Jews never reached the symbiosis that seems to have existed in the Orient. In the Islamic countries, notwithstanding certain extremist movements, the Jewish communities were in a flourishing condition between 900 and 1200; Arabic and Jewish milieux were so close that Arabic

---

[1] Certain Jewish sects seem to have been much closer to non-Jewish thought than was rabbinical Judaism; but they have not survived. The only Jewish texts that have been preserved are those that were still in use in the Middle Ages. The Dead Sea manuscripts found at Qumran are a remarkable exception; other traditions resurfaced in Karaism, and some others have been preserved in Arabic works, but they are far from numerous.

became the literary language of the Jews. In Christian countries, Jews spoke the vernacular, and the erudite language was Hebrew.

(2) In the Orient, Arabic was not only the everyday language, but also the literary instrument of the entire cultural milieu. Although the classical works like the *Book of Beliefs and Convictions*, the *Kuzari* and the *Guide for the Perplexed* are generally studied in their Hebrew translations, almost all the great works of Jewish thought and all the scientific texts, until 1200, were written in Arabic. Until the end of the Middle Ages Jewish thought bears witness to the influence of the Islamic cultural environment.

Life in the Islamic countries was very different from that of Northern Europe. In Europe the Norman invasions had obliterated most of the Greco-Roman culture that had contrived to survive the great earlier Germanic onslaught; society was rural; there were few cities and villages lived at subsistence level; from the tenth to the twelfth centuries commerce was almost non-existent or was carried on for the benefit of kings and nobles. Only a few clerics could read and write. Only with the emergence of the first towns, still very small, did the cultural renaissance of the twelfth century begin.

In the Near East, on the contrary, the basis of Greco-Roman civilization, enriched by Manichaean and Zoroastrian oriental contributions, had survived in the Eastern Christian Empire as in the Muslim. There was no break in continuity between the last commentators on Aristotle and the first Byzantine or Arabic philosophers, for a great enterprise of translation made most Greek scientific works available to the Islamic world. These translations were carried out, broadly speaking, between 850 to 1050, generally by Christians (the most celebrated being Hunayn Ibn Isḥāq) under the patronage of the Caliphs; they were often made from a Syriac text. The first works translated were on medicine, astrology and alchemy, that is, scientific works of practical usefulness. Astrology was then a science, as we shall see later. Let us note here that when Latin translations of these Arabic versions began to reach Europe, the first to become known dealt with astrology; the unfavourable reputation of these works, of which some were erroneously attributed to Aristotle, was most probably the reason for the initial rejection of Aristotle's philosophy by the Church, which later became an ardent defender of this same Aristotle, but always maintained an extremely reserved attitude towards astrology. The interest naturally felt for the practical sciences, such as mathematics, medicine, astrology, etc., led to the study of science for its own sake, and to the translation of the whole corpus of Greek science and philosophy.

At the end of the ninth century the Jews began to participate in this great movement, favoured by a common language and culture. In the eighth and ninth centuries the social level of the Jews began to rise with the constitution of a class of merchants often engaging in international commerce, some among them being bankers like the Bnei Natira, whom we shall meet among Saadiah's partisans. An intellectual Jewish milieu emerged, comparable in every way to its Muslim or Christian homologues. Great cities were not lacking; Baghdad, founded at the beginning of the eighth century, was at the time of Harun al-Rashid perhaps the largest city in the world, and only Constantinople could compete with it in size and wealth. Islam was divided into sects and the dissensions between them were propitious to freedom of thought and discussion. Sects did not multiply in Islam only; this was also the period when Karaism appeared and flourished.

Founded by Anan in the middle of the eighth century, Karaism rejected the authority of the Talmud and the whole rabbinical tradition, and in consequence advocated the personal interpretation of the Scriptures. Ancient currents of thought, perhaps stemming from the Qumran sect, and probably other sources as well, met again in Karaism, whose vigour was such that rabbinical Judaism was imperilled. The polemics and discussions that took place in this extraordinarily variegated milieu between the representatives of the various religions and sects were bound to abut in a common criterion on which everybody could agree. This was 'reason', that is, certain scientific self-evident truths independent of any specific religion. But the definitions of 'reason' can differ considerably, and two main rationalist trends are distinguishable.

The first is connected with the traditional current of Greek philosophy and was rendered illustrious by very great names: Al-Kindi, Al-Fārābī. This was one of the links in the chain of philosophy which joins Greek antiquity to all later philosophy and which we shall study from chapter 2 onwards.

The second, also rationalist, is closer to Islam, and its preoccupations are often in the nature of apologetics: this is the *kalām* and especially the theoretic current of the Mu'tazilites. It remained limited to Islam and to Judaism both rabbinical and Karaite. Saadiah and the Karaites cannot be understood outside the Mu'tazilite spiritual current, and among the Karaites the Mu'tazilite influence became part and parcel of the sect's orthodox theology. In Islam Mu'tazilism lasted much longer than in rabbinical Judaism, where it flourished for only a few generations, and, vigorously combatted by the philosophers, especially Maimonides, soon disappeared, although some ideas, more or less separated from their context, remained alive in later Jewish thought.

For the sake of completeness, I should mention Sufism, a mystical movement that influenced some Jewish thinkers; however, in Jewish thought, its impact was more moral than intellectual. Some of the notions characteristic of Ismaili thought also became of central importance in the explication of Jewish history.

THE MUTAKALLIMŪN AND OTHER JEWISH THINKERS INSPIRED BY MUSLIM THEOLOGICAL MOVEMENTS

The Mutakallimūn are adherents of the *kalām*. *Kalām* designates a group of Muslim theological schools that developed from the eighth century onwards, arising, it seems, from dissensions between sects within Islam (the *kalām*'s relation with the *fiqh*, juridical science, was very close at the beginnings of the movement), and from discussions between Muslims and devotees of other religions under Muslim rule.[1] During the conquest, centres of still lively Hellenistic and Christian culture were absorbed into the new empire and the influence of currents of thought existing before Islam are felt in the *kalām*; the Muslim Mutakallimūn either availed themselves of arguments drawn from other schools, especially those of Christian theologians, or refuted them. They thought it necessary to expound and justify Islam as compared with other religions such as Christianity, Manichaeism, Zoroastrianism, but also to make a 'rational' conception of Islam prevail against the ideas of other Islamic sects. Controversy thus became a science, regulated and ruled by well-defined principles. In the history of ideas, the Mu'tazilite school was the most important of the sects of the *kalām*, and we shall find its conception of reason among Jews, Rabbanites as well as Karaites.

The Mu'tazilites were more or less in agreement on five principles,[2] of which the two first, Divine Justice (*'adl*) and Unification (*tawhid*) were so important to them that they called themselves 'people of justice and of unification'.

The proclamation of the unity of God, literally 'unification', is the first principle and defines God as a unique God, or rather, it defines what God is not. In effect, when we say that God is Knowing this does not mean that God and His Knowledge are two distinct entities, it means that God and His Knowledge are one and the same thing. The Knowledge of God is thus not

---

[1] The political factors that equally contributed to the formation of the *kalām* do not concern us here.

[2] (1) The proclamation that God is one, in the strictest sense of monotheism; (2) the justice of God; (3) belief and unbelief, and their definition; the promise and threat of God; (4) a neutral attitude on all that concerns the question relating to the superiority of one of the successors of the Prophet and the problems connected with this attitude and the sinfulness of man; (5) the advancement of good and prevention of evil and what should be done about them. Cf. *Encyclopaedia of Islam* s.v. Al-Mu'tazila.

comparable to ours, which is acquired and can exist, and afterwards disappear. To say that God is eternal and that the Knowledge of God is eternal, would suggest the existence of an eternal entity comparable to God, who would no longer be unique; in consequence, God and all his attributes must be one, in a perfect and indissoluble unity. Since God's attributes cannot be separated from the divine essence, the various words that we employ when we speak of God, saying 'God is powerful, God is wise, God is living' mean only that 'God is'.

The justice of God: this means that God's actions are always good; He could not be supposed to do evil. The good means what is morally beautiful, and evil what is morally ugly. God's commandments are not good because God has ordered them: God has ordered them because they are good. Divine justice is thus the boundary and limit of divine omnipotence, it is the necessity to which God conforms. In a way, God and man find themselves subjected to the same definitions of good and evil, but contrary to man, who has received free will, God chooses only the good, for He is just. Certainly, God has the power to do evil, but, because of His perfection, which excludes want and need, He does not perform it. God has created man for good and given him free will, so that he may gain his salvation; but He has also given him the means of distinguishing good from evil: reason. This immediate and spontaneous knowledge is the part of all sane men; one may therefore, relying on human reason, find the straight road and show it to others; in this sense, the Mu'tazilites place all men, even the prophets, on the same level. Man, responsible for his acts since he can choose between good and evil, should be rewarded for his good actions and punished for the bad, for God is just. All suffering is just, for if it does not come as punishment for faults committed, a recompense proportional to the suffering undergone will be enjoyed in the next world. For certain theologians, brute animals also will be compensated for their sufferings on earth.

With the unity of God is associated a question treated at great length by Muslims, that of the Speech of God (*kalām Allah*). If God is eternally one, what is the relation between God and His Speech, that is, the Koran, which appeared at a precise moment of history? Some Mu'tazilites give the following answer: when God wanted to make His Speech reach the prophets, He created it in a material substratum, and the Koran, 'direct' creation of God and at the same time multiple and temporal, is created on the lips of him who recites it.

However, for the Jews, God himself engraved the commandments on the Tables of the Law, and the 'written' character of the Bible is therefore too essential to permit them to adopt this kind of explanation.

Another question, concerning physics, is approached differently by Arab and Jewish Mu'tazilites: the world, for most Muslim Mu'tazilites, is constituted of indivisible corporeal atoms, which God at every instant maintains and organizes in bodies that appear to exist by themselves and to act one on the other; the causal relation between facts was denied; at every instant God creates new atoms or maintains them. With every atom of time, the world is created anew, and without God, it would be annihilated at every moment; no law of nature represents an obstacle to the divine will. This atomism was generally not adopted by the Jews,[1] who maintained the existence of the causal laws of nature.

From the outset the Jews made certain choices, associating some Mu'tazilite theses with other ideas stemming from Greek philosophy or even Christian theology, and harmonizing these various themes with the Jewish tradition.

There were numerous interactions between philosophy and *kalām*; however, one fundamental difference remains distinguishing between *mutakallimūn* and philosophers. The authors who will be discussed in this chapter have in common a certain definition of reason that is specifically Mu'tazilite, differing from that found in the Greek philosophical texts; it is not reason that attempts to distinguish between the true and the false; it is moral law that makes us say that a thing is good or bad, that makes us grateful to a benefactor and impels us to summon the wicked back to the right road. This moral law is universal and transcends races and religions. Every man recognizes its existence in himself and since this law also applies to God, we can be sure of the existence of a good God, in whom we may have confidence.

We shall see with Saadiah Gaon how this moral reason permits an explanation of God and the world that agrees remarkably with revelation. But let us first turn to David al-Mukammis whose work is the earliest of this school to have been preserved.

The Rabbanites

DAVID AL-MUKAMMIS

David (Dā'ūd) Ibn Marwān Al-Raqi Al-Shirazi, commonly called David al-Mukammis or David Ha-Bavli, lived between 820 and 890. Of his major work, written in Arabic and entitled '*Ishrūn Maqāla* (*The Twenty Chapters*) only part has survived, and it is as yet unpublished. Kirkisānī, a Karaite author of the tenth century, says of him:

Daūd ibn Marwān al-Raqqī, known as al-Muqammis, was a philosopher. Originally a Jew, he was converted to Christianity in Nisibis through the agency of a man named Nānā. This Nānā was greatly honored among the Christians, for he was an accomplished philosopher and practised surgery. Daūd al-Muqammis was his pupil for a great many years; he learned thoroughly the origins of Christianity and its mysteries and mastered philosophy. But [afterwards] he composed two books against the Christians in which he attacked them; these two books are well known. He also translated from among the books and the commentaries of the Christians a commentary on Genesis, called 'Book of creation' and a commentary on Ecclesiastes. (*Book of Lights*, trans. L. Nemoy, *Account of the Jewish Sects*, p. 366)

---

[1] Except in the eleventh century, with Yūsuf al-Baṣīr and his disciples, during the full flowering of Karaite Mu'tāzilism.

In another text, Kirkisānī confirms:

Dā'ūd ibn Marwān al-Raḳḳī, known as al-Muḳammiṣ, has written a fine book containing a commentary on Genesis, which he translated from the commentaries of the Syrians. But in some places he did not say all that needed to be said about the intended meaning of the Sacred Text, while in other places he was guilty of foolish verbosity for which there was no need. Another scholar of our own time also composed a fine book on this subject in which he followed a method similar to that of Dā'ūd. We shall extract the best part of both works and we shall add thereto that which they, in our opinion, have neglected to mention or have failed to explain adequately.

(*Ibid.*, trans. L. Nemoy, *Karaite Anthology*, p. 54)

What we know of David's philosophy agrees with Kirkisānī's comment. For example, wishing to define the unity of God, Al-Mukammis considers the various meanings of the word 'One'; in doing so he does not use Aristotle's classifications, but comes nearer to those of his Christian adversaries. Nevertheless, the plan of his discussion of the problem of God follows the scheme of the four Aristotelian questions (does the thing exist? what is the nature of the thing? what are its attributes? why they are attributed to it?). The influence of the *kalām* is felt not only in the conception of the divine unity expressed in David's affirmation that the divine attributes are not added to the essence, but also as regards other problems such as the perpetuity of retribution after death and the finality of man's creation.

In the present state of our knowledge, it is difficult to evaluate Al-Mukammis' influence on later Jewish thought; the Karaite philosopher Kirkisānī seems to have used him extensively, perhaps exclusively, in some chapters of his encyclopedic work; excerpts from chapters IX and X, translated into Hebrew, are quoted in the *Commentary on the Sefer Yeẓira* (*Book of Creation*) by Judah ben Barzillai of Barcelona, a twelfth-century author, and a few fourteenth-century writers have transmitted short citations. However, only a portion of the text has survived, and most of it is as yet in manuscript. We can recognize a reference only when David al-Mukammis is cited by name. He may perhaps have been the link between Christian and Jewish explanations of creation, for sometimes we find striking parallels between early Christian interpretations, for instance those of Saint Augustine, and medieval Jewish commentaries in the thirteenth and fourteenth centuries.

SAADIAH GAON

In presenting Saadiah ben Joseph, generally called Saadiah Gaon, it is usual to quote Abraham Ibn Ezra: 'Saadiah Gaon was the chief spokesman in all matters of learning', meaning that Saadiah first introduced the cultivation of all branches of Jewish knowledge, and this statement is so true that one cannot avoid citing it. Like his work, Saadiah's life was exceptional, and yet in some ways characteristic of his epoch. He was born in 882 in Fayyūm (in Upper Egypt) and we can only form suppositions about his education;

it is certain that men with knowledge of philosophy and religion were not lacking in Egypt, and Saadiah early engaged in a correspondence on scientific subjects with Isaac Israeli (the neoplatonic philosopher who will be discussed in the next chapter), who was then living at Khartoum.

Saadiah was by nature a 'fighter'. The events of his life, like a great part of his literary activity, can be explained by his aggressive attitude towards the enemies of rabbinical Judaism, as he conceived it. He considered himself the servant of the truth and in its service was prepared to meet all challenges. At the age of twenty-three, while still living in Egypt, he composed a treatise against Anan, founder of the Karaite sect. We do not know why he moved from Egypt to Palestine; he never returned, although he is known to have regretted this. Having left Egypt in June or July 915, Saadiah lived for some time in Palestine, and then at Baghdad and Aleppo. In 921, he joined issue, on behalf of the Babylonian Geonim, with Ben Meir, a Palestinian sage, on the subject of the calendar. In the biblical period, the Jewish festivals were fixed according to the observation of lunar and solar phases; later, although certain astronomical laws were known to the rabbis, up to the end of the fifth century the whole calendar was fixed according to observation, and the right to announce the new moon was the prerogative of the Palestinian Patriarchs. From the seventh century onward, the observation of the moon was given up and a complete and final system of calendation was introduced; the prerogative of promulgating the calendar attributed to themselves by the Babylonian Geonim was more or less contested by the Palestinians, who felt injured.

At the beginning of the tenth century, the decline of the two great Babylonian academies, Sura and Pumbadita, undermined by their dissensions with the Babylonian Exilarch and perhaps weakened by epidemics, gave Ben Meir, a Palestinian by birth and the head of a school in his native land, the impression that he might profit from the situation by retrieving for the Palestinians the privilege of determining the calendar. Perhaps relying on ancient traditions, he decided that the year 922 had two deficient months, so that Passover would differ by two days from the date fixed by the Babylonians. Saadiah was of the Babylonian party, and during the year 921 he sent several letters to Ben Meir, charging his reckoning with inexactitude and foreseeing the dangers of persevering in his decision. Returning to Baghdad, and finding that his attempts at dissuasion had received no response, Saadiah hurled himself wholeheartedly into the fray. After an official letter had been addressed to Ben Meir, the chiefs of the two Babylonian academies, together with the Exilarch and Saadiah, sent letters to all the communities setting out the dates of the year as they had calculated them, and putting them on their guard against a possible schism if the Passover were not observed by all Jews on the same date. It was Saadiah's stand that tipped the scale in favour of the Babylonians; this fact gives a good idea of the popularity and respect that he enjoyed. However, the conflict was not immediately resolved; for two years at least, the communities were divided and there was danger of a split within Judaism. Finally, Ben Meir had to give way. As a result, Saadiah became the target of his resentment, for he considered him, and rightly so, to have been the architect of his defeat.

Saadiah's activity during the crisis earned him an important place in the community. At this period the two academies of Sura and Pumbedita had deteriorated, as we have said, from their former flourishing condition, and the Geonim at Sura were often quite insignificant. In 928 a candidate was sought who would be truly capable of meeting the requirements of the position. It was the custom to appoint an individual chosen from one of five or six noble families claiming descent from David. The Exilarch David ben Zakkai found himself in a state of painful uncertainty, as Natan ha-Bavli relates, for he had the choice between Ẓemaḥ ben Shahin, of noble birth and some learning, and Saadiah, a foreigner, but extremely erudite. He finally chose a third person, Nissi Nahrawani, a greatly respected man, who refused the post because of his blindness. Asked for his opinion concerning possible candidates, Nahrawani is said to have recommended Ẓemaḥ: 'It is true', R. Nissi explained, 'that Saadiah is a great man, of extraordinary learning; but he is absolutely fearless and by reason of his great learning and wisdom, eloquence and piety, he does not consider anybody in the world' (H. Malter, *Saadiah Gaon*, p. 108). Notwithstanding this warning, the Exilarch appointed Saadiah, and soon had reason to regret his decision, for in less than two years the two men were engaged in a quarrel that continued for several years and led to the dismissal and then the reinstatement of Saadiah in the Gaonate. It seems that a struggle for power was the cause of the dissension. David ben Zakkai, the Exilarch, the head of a numerous and powerful faction, wanted the right of decision, an aspiration that had a historical foundation, for several centuries earlier the Exilarch had been the king and chief of all the Jews of Babylonia; the academies had gradually achieved independence, although the Exilarchs had never formally renounced their rights either over the academies or over the social and religious life of the communities. On the other hand the Gaonim, who wielded great spiritual influence, contested the Exilarch's hegemony over the Jews of Babylonia and other countries. The Exilarch and Saadiah both employed all the means at their disposal; that is, their influence at the court of the Caliphs and in the various communities; they did not spare each other. Saadiah's adversaries, including Aaron ben Sargado, who was to succeed him in the Gaonate of Sura, launched ignominious accusations. H. Malter writes: 'The document is full of the coarsest invectives, and some of its accusations, repeated again and again, are so vile and impudent that one shrinks from reproducing them' (*Saadiah Gaon*, p. 114). Saadiah's polemical pamphlets are more moderate in tone, but we know that his partisans, the powerful bankers Bnei Natira, were not over-scrupulous, and, like their adversaries, tried to buy decisions in favour of their faction when they judged this possible. The two sides held firmly to their positions and each man remained at his post for three years, neither having been able to obtain a ruling from the Caliph. But when a new personage acceded to the Caliphate, the Exilarch's party emerged victorious; Saadiah was deposed and for several years led a retired life. It was at this time that he composed his great book of theology, and his celebrity as theologian was perhaps due to his setback in the conflict with David ben Zakkai. Another juridical affair was to lead to the reconciliation that was in fact desired by the two adversaries and to an even greater degree by the whole Jewish community of Baghdad. It was celebrated with much ceremony and Saadiah was reinstated in the Sura Gaonate in 936 or 937. He died at the age of sixty, in 942. David ben Zakkai died before him, in 940.

Saadiah was an exceptionally prolific writer. He produced grammatical and lexicographical works; he translated almost the whole Bible into Arabic (twice: one translation is fairly literal, the other is rather a kind of paraphrase and commentary intended for cultivated readers); he composed a book of prayers and numerous liturgical poems; he introduced a scientific methodology and a new interpretation into the study of the Talmud, defined and codified numerous questions of *halakhah*, expounded important decisions in response to questions from communities of the Diaspora, and composed talmudic commentaries; he wrote many works on the calendar and on biblical and rabbinical chronology; he elaborated a rational theology to which many Jewish medieval thinkers later referred, and finally, he engaged in polemical strife against all enemies of rabbinical Judaism. These two activities, polemical and philosophical (the latter word being used in the special sense that I have defined), were closely linked. The doubt cast on rabbinical Judaism by other religions that proposed to supplant it and also by Jewish sects and various philosophies or scepticisms, demanded not a retreat behind the barriers of the *Torah*, but the elaboration of a system of rational thought capable of answering attacks, of vindicating the rightfulness of Judaism and demonstrating its absolute superiority.

Saadiah's rationalistic ideas, discernable in most of his works, are systematically expounded in two of them: *Tafsīr Kitāb al-Mabādī* (*Perush Sefer Yeẓira, Commentary on the Book of Creation*), several times translated into Hebrew and used in the eleventh and twelfth centuries, but later falling into oblivion; and *Al-Amānāt Wa-l-I'tiqādāt* (*Sefer Emunot we-De'ot, The Book of Doctrines and Beliefs*), which has to the present day remained one of the basic books of Jewish theology.

Saadiah's method, which is clearly polemic, is illustrated by his arguments in favour of the *ex-nihilo* creation of the world. He not only set out to prove that the creation of the world from nothing was as true according to reason as according to the *Torah*, but that all other theories were false. In the *Amānāt*, Saadiah cites twelve false theories and in the *Commentary on the Book of Creation* he gives eight (of which six are different from those noted in the *Amānāt*), making a total of eighteen mistaken theories of which he demonstrates the falseness. While some of these theories were in fact maintained at this period, most of them were drawn from doxographies and go back to philosophers like Thales of Miletus, Heraclitus, Anaximenes, and so on. These doxographies were in fashion until the sixth or seventh centuries, but by Saadiah's time, the most important works of Plato and Aristotle had been translated into Arabic. However, if Saadiah had read these translations, he hardly ever cites them. He aimed at more than the refutation of contemporary philosophy; he wished to demonstrate incontrovertibly that all the doctrines imagined in the course of history to explain the existence of our world are false and that none of them can contend against the truth of Judaism.

In his inquiry Saadiah often uses arguments drawn from the *kalām*, and the plan of the *Amānāt* immediately delimits his intellectual context. The first two chapters treat of the unity of God, as is generally done at the beginning of Mu'tazilite treatises, the next seven of the justice of God, the second Mu'tazilite principle. The tenth chapter is only a sort of appendix and is not an integral part of the work. We should remark, however, that one of the central ideas of the Mu'tazilites, atomism and creation renewed by God each instant, with its corollary, the negation of the laws of nature, was not adopted by the Gaon, who preferred a rather imprecise Aristotelian physics.

In the introduction to the *Amānāt*, Saadiah defines the theory of knowledge and what he calls 'belief' (*i'tiqād*):

> We affirm that this is an idea arising in the soul as to what an object of knowledge really is: when the idea is clarified by speculation, Reason comprehends it, accepts it, and makes it penetrate the soul and become absorbed into it; then man believes this idea which he has attained, and he preserves it in his soul for another time or other times, as is said, 'Wise men lay up knowledge' (Prov. 10.14), and as is further said, 'Receive, I pray thee, instructions from His mouth, and lay up His words in thy heart' (Job 22.22)
>
> (*The Book of Doctrines and Beliefs*, trans. A. Altmann, p. 34)

This conviction is sustained by three sources: (1) external reality apprehended by (2) reason, that is, the knowledge of good and evil, and (3) what reason necessarily deduces from the reality of things and the knowledge of good and evil.

> By the knowledge of sense perception we understand that which a man perceives by one of the five senses, i.e. sight, hearing, smell, taste, and touch. By the knowledge of Reason we understand that which is derived purely from the mind, such as the approval of truth and the disapproval of falsehood. By inferential knowledge we understand a proposition which a man cannot deny without being compelled to deny at the same time some proposition obtained from Reason or sense perception. Where there is no way of denying these propositions, the previous proposition must of necessity be accepted. E.g. we are compelled to admit that man possesses a soul, although we do not perceive it by our senses, so as not to deny its obvious functions. Similarly, we are compelled to admit that the soul is endowed with Reason, although we do not perceive it by our senses, so as not to deny its [Reason's] obvious function. (*Ibid.* p. 36)

To these three sources Saadiah adds a fourth: the true tradition, that of the *Torah* (which evidently includes the oral law, that is, the Talmud).

How can we be sure that this tradition is true? Its truth has been proven, says Saadiah, by signs and prodigies and especially by the miracle of the manna, the heavenly food that God bestowed on Israel in the desert.

Certainly, it is possible to create an illusion of miracle and simulate a prodigy. But the miracle of the manna could not have been counterfeited, for it continued for forty years, nor does the publicity that surrounded it allow the supposition of a carefully elaborated lie. Nor can one think of a natural phenomenon produced by Moses, for the philosophers would have known of it and would have used this technique for their own benefit. The true tradition, fourth source of knowledge, is thus founded on the historical experience of the Jewish people and the argument of Saadiah is so much the stronger because none of the other religions cast any doubt on the historical reality of the Exodus and the Jews' sojourn in the desert.

Now, the *Torah* itself enjoins us to attempt to understand its tradition, for two reasons: first, that traditionally transmitted knowledge should become firmly anchored in the intellect; secondly, that we may answer detractors of the Law.

All the various kinds of knowledge that scientific effort may uncover are in conformity with the true tradition. Saadiah was convinced that *Torah* and science spring from the same branch; they cannot contradict each other in any way, and, if there is an apparent contradiction, this is due to our faulty reasoning or to our failure to interpret the revealed text correctly. This optimism, this deep confidence in the harmony between faith and reason, is characteristic of Saadiah, and the whole book of the *Amānāt* is constructed on the basis of the identity of tradition and reason. Each chapter begins with an introduction to the problem, followed by an exposition of the biblical texts affirming the thesis, and the rational examination and refutation of antagonistic theses. I shall briefly discuss the creation of the world (first chapter of the *Amānāt*), and the unity of God (second chapter); divine revelation, treated in the third chapter and in the *Commentary on the Book of Creation*; and finally man's psychology and the explanation of the divine commandments.

The Creation of the world

In the chapter on creation, Saadiah first determines how this inquiry should be conducted. The senses can be of no help here; only rational proofs can be used; whatever the thesis advanced – eternity of the world, eternity of matter – and so on, one must try to establish it on rational proofs.

Now, Scripture teaches us that God created the world at a given moment of time; there are four proofs of this:

(1) The world being limited in space, if the force moving it were the world

itself, it would also be limited; since the world moves perpetually, a force other than that of the world must be the mover of the world.

(2) The world is made up of parts that are sometimes joined and sometimes separate: neither the separation nor the union are part of their essence; one must therefore admit that an external force joins or separates them in order to form bodies, small like plants, or large like the spheres; this force is God the Creator.

(3) The third proof is based on accidents: everything in this world is composed of necessary substance and of accidents (like the form of an object, its colour, its warmth, its movement); as no thing is without its accidents, which succeed each other in the same body and change continually, it must be God who produces these changes.

(4) The fourth proof depends on time, which is finite; for if the succession of instants were infinite, it could not be retraced in thought: only a succession with a temporal beginning could explain the existence of the world at the present time.

These proofs figure among those advanced by the Mutakallimūn. The world is composed of atoms disposed in such a way as to form the universe, and it only subsists by the continual creation of God: the only difference between the creation of the world and the moment at which we live is that the world, at its creation, was, after not having been, while at the instant at which we live the world is, after having been. The first and the fourth proofs are also found in the Christian critics of Aristotle. The second and third proofs are much less convincing in Saadiah, whose system does not admit atomism, but accepts Aristotelian physics. The text itself, often difficult to understand because of its concision and over-simplification, indicates that he used his sources without considering them deeply or criticizing them. He was profoundly convinced that only the infinite action of God is able to sustain and explain the constant alteration of the corporeal universe, the perpetual generation of a finite world in space and time.

The world and man, limited and imperfect, are evidence of an infinite and perfect being and lead us to the knowledge of the unique God. What is God, creator of the world? This is the question examined in the second chapter of the *Amānāt*, the unity of God. The introduction is instructive, for Saadiah describes all the objections to rational thought that were raised at the period.

I found that people rejected this whole inquiry, some because they could not see God; others on account of the profundity and extreme subtleness of His nature; still others claim that beyond the knowledge of God there is some other knowledge; others again go so far as to picture Him as a body; others, while not explicitly describing Him as a body, assign to Him quantity or quality or space or time, or similar things, and by looking for these qualities they do in fact assign to Him a body, since these attributes belong only to a body. The purpose of my introductory remarks is to remove their false ideas, to take a load from their minds, and to point out that the extreme subtleness which we have assigned to the nature of the Creator is, so to speak, its own warrant, and the fact that, in our reasoning, we find the notion of God to be more abstract than other knowledge shows that reasoning to be correct.

(Ibid. p. 78)

and a little further:

Our Lord (be He exalted and glorified) has informed us through the words of His prophets that He is One, Living, Powerful and Wise, and that nothing can be compared unto Him or unto His works. They established this by signs and miracles, and we accepted it immediately. Later, speculation led us to the same result. In regard to His Unity, it is said, 'Hear O Israel, the Lord our God, the Lord is One' (Deut. 6. 4); furthermore, 'See now that I, even I, am He, and that there is no god with Me' (Deut. 32. 39), and also, 'The Lord alone did lead him, and there was no strange god with Him' (Deut. 32. 12).

(Ibid. p. 80)

Thus God, Creator of the world, is One, but who is He? And when we say of Him that He is One, of what unity do we speak? What is His knowledge so that we may say that He is knowing? And what acts are attributed to Him so that we may say that He is acting? To these questions Rabbanite Jews answered with the biblical verses that often use not only adjectives like 'powerful', 'good' and 'merciful', 'jealous', in referring to God, but attribute bodily movements to Him: 'God ascends', 'God descends', and even members: 'God's arm', 'God's hand'. The *midrashim* also often present God in human form and we have already spoken of one of them, the *Shiur Qomah* (*Measure of the Divine Stature*), which attributes to Him measurements exceeding the limits of the human imagination. The Karaites often accused the Rabbanites of believing in divine anthropomorphism, and tenth-century Muslim authors made fun of the Rabbanite Jews who, contrary to the Karaites and to enlightened Muslims, believed that God had a body. Saadiah expresses himself vigorously against the notion of divine corporeality. One of the central points of his thought is the purification of the idea of God, and the demonstration of the divine incorporeality and transcendence.

All the things existing in this world are substances, that is to say, bodies, more or less dense, more or less light, but bodies. They can be described by answers corresponding to one or several of the ten questions propounded by Aristotle in the *Categories*: substance, quantity, quality, relation, place, time, position, possession, action, passion. Thus, to define a person, we say that this is a man (substance), measuring 1 metre 70 centimetres (quantity), white (quality), smaller than the average (relation), at Jerusalem (place), last year (time), standing (position), and so on. Everything that is to be found in our world can be defined according to these categories; even the soul and even, as we shall see, 'the divine Glory' are definable substances and in consequence more or less corporeal, for body and substance are, for Saadiah, one and the same thing. As for God, He cannot be defined by any of these categories; He transcends all of them, and there is nothing in common between bodies, finite, composite, subject to change, and God, immaterial

25

and immutable. His attributes, power, knowledge, mean first of all that God is not impotent, that He is not ignorant, but power and knowledge, as they are found in man, cannot describe Him, for in God the attributes are identical with the essence. In man, knowledge is acquired, and not only acquired at a certain age: it exists after not having been in existence; in old age it diminishes and disappears with death. God, on the contrary, is Knowing in all eternity. When we speak of God with the help of positive attributes, we are alluding to 'something else' of which we can only have a vague idea, and of which we know only that it cannot be compared with that which exists in this world. Can one, somehow, separate the attributes from the divine essence? More simply, when we say of God that he is 'living', 'knowing', 'omnipotent', we use three different words; does this mean that this distinction exists in God himself or does this simply mean that human thought expresses itself in sequences and not simultaneously? The question was important for the Muslims as well as for the Jews, for it was necessary to answer the Christians (or at least some of them) who identified certain attributes with one or another of the persons of the Trinity. For a Jew, as for a Muslim, this implies introducing an unacceptable multiplicity into God, so that all the Mutakallimūn, and with them Saadiah, affirm that the attributes, whatever they are, are identical with the divine essence (or quiddity), and none is outside His essence; in God there is only absolute unity.

If by the use of human reason we may arrive at a refined and exact knowledge of God, why were the prophets necessary? And how can we explain all the anthropomorphic expressions of the Scriptures and the Tradition? The first question was not rhetorical. At the beginning of the eleventh century a Muslim thinker and notorious heretic, Ibn Ar-Rawandi, was casting doubt on the necessity of prophecy. The second question also urgently required an answer. The Scriptures were being criticized in a book that is said to have been in vogue in the schools, the *Two Hundred Questions concerning the Scripture* by Hiwi al-Balkhi. Whatever the theological bases of his critique, and one can only offer suppositions on the subject, the fact remains that Hiwi drew attention to a number of contradictions in the Scriptures as well as in the conception of God as His actions are depicted in the biblical narrative. At the same time, the Karaites were attacking the talmudic and midrashic tradition precisely on the ground of its anthropomorphisms, and Saadiah wrote his *Commentary on The Book of the Creation* in order to show its non-anthropomorphic sense.

First of all, Saadiah thus had to demonstrate the necessity of prophecy, and then explain how, from the eternal and immaterial God, emanated the visible and audible messages that the Bible reports. Finally, the Gaon had to show how the various biblical passages can be interpreted according to this theory of prophecy, which conforms to reason:

For I have heard that there are people who contend that men do not need prophets and that their reason is sufficient to guide them aright according to their innate cognition of good and evil: I, therefore, subjected this view to the test of true reasoning and it showed me that if things were as they make out, God would know it better and would not have sent us prophets, for he does not do things which have no purpose.

(Amānāt III, 35, trans. A. Altmann, p. 103)

The first argument employed by Saadiah to justify revelation is that Omniscient God acted 'with a view to the good' and did nothing in vain. This argument is founded on the 'justice of God' (*'adl*) as it is conceived in the second of the Mu'tazilite theses. And it is only after having established the legitimacy of prophecy on the basis of the essence of God that Saadiah expounds the reasons why revelation is necessary to man, reasons to which he was to return in greater detail in his exposition on the commandments and the prohibitions.

– Revelation specifies the acts that allow one to put into effect in the best possible way the very general moral laws that reason imposes;

– It contributes other commandments which reason does not teach, and which are of undoubted usefulness;

– It permits immediate action, while reason, which in fact rests on the same principles, is not fully developed before a considerable length of time; furthermore, certain men never reach the level of rational knowledge because of their imperfection or their lack of inclination for study, or the doubts that assail them.

Revelation is therefore necessary, as much on the level of the divine essence as on that of human conduct. Nevertheless, the Bible often employs anthropomorphic terms, a usage that does not conform to reason, nor to Saadiah's description of the revealed Law. For reason teaches us that God is unique and incorporeal, and Tradition draws on the same sources as rational knowledge: namely the apprehension of the senses, the principle of reason, the necessary inferences, and it constitutes for believers the fourth source of knowledge. This tradition, the Bible, therefore cannot be contrary to reason; and a rational explanation should be given of the entire revealed text and especially of the prophetic visions.

The solution proposed by Saadiah is founded on two principles: first, supernatural apparitions are God's doing, and should be attributed to the divine omnipotence and not to man, and, secondly, God makes use of the 'second' air, the first of his creations, to manifest His presence in a way that men can perceive.

Supernatural apparitions, whether prophetic or magical in manifestation (such as the episode of the Witch of Endor) are due uniquely to a divine act. Saadiah does not consider it necessary to explain veridical dreams or witchcraft, the existence of which was commonly admitted by his contemporaries, for it would have been necessary to admit natural causes for these supranormal apprehensions. Neither does the Gaon admit the existence of an exceptional aptitude that may be designated as prophetic or favouring prophecy. To him, prophecy is a grace that God places in a human receptacle, which is then called 'prophet'. The prophet is as mortal as other men. He cannot live without eating or drinking, he leads a normal conjugal life, he cannot predict the future or perform miracles except in exceptional circumstances, for, if it were otherwise, one would have to suppose him the possessor of superhuman faculties. The prophet is only an instrument of the divine will: 'Since the prophets are in all ways men like ourselves, and, nevertheless, they do things which we are actually powerless to do, the signs accomplished prove the divine provenance of the prophetic words' (*Amānāt* III, p. 121).

For the same reason, it is not the angels who perform miracles, for men, ignorant of the capabilities and limitations of the angels, might attribute to them acts that belong to God alone. Thus, on the one hand, no creature has a specific nature permitting him, in any action at all, to equal the divine omnipotence; on the other hand, the fact that the receiving subject was less remarkable than he was often supposed to be, renders the prophetic word and the signs that accompany it more convincing. These miracles in their supernatural aspect stand out conspicuously against the well-ordered and predictable sequence of the natural laws that govern man and the world. The prophet receives the divine communication in the same way that he perceives things apprehended by the senses and the reason, by an act of apprehension in which the irrefutable evidence of the senses and the inner truths of reason are inextricably mingled. The conditions of rational truth, that is, sufficient knowledge of the object and diligent care in inquiry, are therefore applicable to prophetic apprehension.

How, in these circumstances, may one recognize a prophet? In the first place, by the intrinsic value of the Law that God has communicated to him. Then, by his miracles, which are the signs that God has given him as proof of his mission.

Miracles are of two kinds; they may transform the regular phenomena of nature, subduing the diverse elements and forming composite things in spite of the antagonistic character of these elements: preventing fire from burning or water from flowing are examples; they may also transform the original nature of beings: changing water to blood and a rod into a serpent. The miracle, proof of the divinity of the Word, is always preceded by an announcement to the prophet. However, a capital difficulty is present in the Scriptures themselves: if the accomplishment of miracles is of divine origin and proves the authenticity of the prophets, how were the sages and magicians of Pharaoh able to perform the same miracles as Moses? This, says Saadiah, was because they imitated the real miracles by ruse and enchantment, or, in modern language, they produced the illusion of these miracles by charlatanism and prestidigitation. In any case, they were able to simulate only the earlier miracles, and soon had to avow their impotence.

The announcement of a miracle and the miracle itself always coincide: thus, the prophet is always warned of a divine manifestation by the apparition of a pillar of cloud, or a pillar of fire, or a bright light. At the time of Moses the whole people could see the pillar of cloud.

God manifests himself to man pedagogically, going from the easier to the more difficult; this was his way with Adam, and with the revelation on Mount Sinai, and with Moses.

'When He wanted to make His voice heard by Moses, He was careful to treat his sight gently, taking into account its degree and strength.' Thus, He made a terrestrial fire appear to him in the bush, as it is said: 'He looked, and, behold, the bush burned with fire' [Exodus 3: 2]; when He was able to support this light, He made the light of the angel appear to him, as it is said: 'And the angel of the Lord appeared unto him' [although in fact the text mentions the angel before the bush]; when Moses could support [the light of the angel], He showed him the light called the *Shekhina* [Indwelling], as it said, 'God called unto him out of the midst of the bush'.

(*Tafsīr Kitāb al-Mabādī*, p. 39)

The apparition of God therefore signifies the apparition of the light called the 'Indwelling of God'.

The Bible speaks of God, unknowable and incorporeal, as manifesting Himself, but, in reality, He manifests His *Created Glory*. The glory may be compared, in a very inadequate fashion, to the air we know, the *First Air*; it impregnates all things and exists in all things, without however being affected by the defilements of bodies, nor divided by their divisions, nor touched by their imperfections. Thus, God is in relation with the created world by the intermediary of the first of created things, the Throne, which is an air in the air, a *Second Air*, finer and more subtle than the first one, the visible air.

The Holy Script calls the *Second Air*, which is finer, *Glory* . . . the people call it Indwelling . . . and the author of the *Book of Creation* called it the *Breath* of the living God . . .It is by this fine air, which is the second, that was carried the word of prophecy, as it is said 'The Spirit of the Lord God is upon me' [Isaiah 61: 1]. And it is by it that appear all the miracles visible to prophets, as it is said 'in a vision by the Spirit of God' [Ezekiel 11: 24] and it is evidently a created thing, for everything which is not God is a creature, as it is said 'there is none else beside Him' [Deuteronomy 4: 35].

It is through this second air, very fine, but created, which is in the world as life is in man, that was produced the created word heard by Moses in the visible air, and the Decalogue that our fathers heard in the visible air, and it was called 'the voice of the living God'.

(*Ibid.* p. 72)

This second air is both audible and visible and, relying on the verse 'And all the people saw the thunderings' (Exodus 22: 18), the Gaon links the graphic form of the letters of fire written on the black air to the movement that occurs when these letters are pronounced; he recalls the words: 'And the Lord spake unto you out of the midst of the fire: ye heard the voice of the words, but saw no similitude; only ye heard a voice' (Deuteronomy 4: 12); and also (Deuteronomy 5: 23) 'And it came to pass, when ye heard the voice out of the midst of the darkness, (for the mountain did burn with fire,) that ye came near to me, even all the heads of your tribes, and your elders.'

That sound can be visible we know from practical experience: 'when someone speaks on a cold day and the articulation of his sounds tears the air apart, it produces forms varying according to the line that the sounds follow in it, in a straight line or inflected' (*Tafsīr Kitāb al-Mabādī*, p. 11). When God wished to reveal himself to the people of Israel, 'He compressed the air which produced, as it were, *phonemes* and articulated sounds, perceptible and ordered sounds, analogous to human speech, which cuts up the air in sounds and words, so that the Israelites could hear the word of God' (*Commentary on Exodus*).

The Second Air, instrument of the divine Word, differs from the usual air; God models it according to His desire:

'[Sometimes] God wishes to speak to a prophet so that the person then near the prophet does not heard, thus Samuel alone heard the word of God and Elijah did not hear it although he was in the same place. The air prevented Elijah from hearing and carried the Word only to Samuel.'

(*Commentary on Leviticus cited in Kitāb Ma'ani al-Nafs*, p. 68)

The Second Air is also luminous, flamboyant, splendidly iridescent and colourful. In saying 'the throne of Glory and all the legion of the heights' the author of the *Book of Creation* had in mind the seven colours of the fire that Ezekiel saw:

'The first is a great cloud and fire infolding itself' [Exodus 1: 4]. The fire which condenses is feeble since there is a great quantity of air in it, because of the fineness [of the fire]; afterwards, in the interior, a bluish fire, as it is said: 'and out of the midst thereof, of the colour of blue' [Ezekiel 1: 4]. And the body of the four *Hayot* (Beasts) 'had the appearance of burning coals of fire' [Ezekiel 1: 13]. And it was surrounded by a radiance of yellow light, as it is said [in the same verse]: 'And the fire was bright and out of the fire went forth lightning.' And all over their bodies [there was] a black fire as if it were eyes, as it is said: 'And all their flesh and their backs and their hands and their wings, and the wheel were filled with eyes.' And on their heads was an arch of white fire, as it is said: 'And the likeness of the firmament upon the heads of the living creature was as the colour of the terrible crystal, stretched forth over their heads above' [Ezekiel 1: 22].

Above it was a throne of cristalline fire, less white than the vault, so that it could be distinguished from it, as it is said: 'And above the firmament that was over their heads was the likeness of a throne, as the appearance of a sapphire stone' [Ezekiel 1: 26]. And all this was created from the air after its humidity had been extracted, and was formed by the *sefiroth* and letters and from this resulted the mixture of these different kinds of fire.' (*Tafsīr Kitāb al-Mabādī*, p. 88)

The emission of light varies in intensity, and its brilliance is unbearable when its source is approached. This is demonstrated by the care that God takes in initiating his prophet to the advent of the apparition. But it seems that Saadiah conceived of a unique luminous creation, bearing different names according to its relation to the source and also to the events announced:

The names of the angels vary according to the events which they are sent by God to accomplish. When God sent them to Abraham [to announce] the good news, [they behaved] like men and were called 'men'. When he sent them to Sodom to destroy it, they were called 'messengers', . . . to Isaiah to burn with the ardent brand, 'seraphim'.

When Ezekiel saw them . . . they were called *Hayot* and those who were turned towards him were called *Ofanim* and the highest of them were called *Cherubim*.

(*Ibid.* p. 20)

The living God, immaterial, Eternal, Knowing, Omnipotent has revealed himself to man, whom He has created. How does Saadiah describe the recipient of revelation: man? We find some of his ideas in Book x of the *Doctrines and Beliefs*, or, more accurately, we have a glimpse of the ethics that a cultivated man like Saadiah could read in Arabic texts. This Book x seems to have been added as an afterthought in the arrangement of the *Amānāt* and, more than in the rest of the work, we find comments on everyday life.

Human conduct should be guided by the divine design. Now God has created a diversified world, in equilibrium between the contraries: existing beings are composed of four elements, not of only one. How can one construct a house entirely of bricks, or of wood, or of straw, or of nails? In order that a house should be stable and well-constructed, each of its materials must be utilized to the necessary extent.

In the same way, man should not devote himself to one particular virtue, whatever it is, but give a part of himself to each one. It is the cognitive faculty that determines this part, for it has to judge of the importance that the other two faculties have to assume: the appetitive, which comprises the senses and the corporeal pleasures, and the irascible, which gives rise to love and hate.

As long as equilibrium is maintained by reason, which should be regarded as paramount, man is on the moral road; if on the contrary, he lets himself be dominated by one of the passions, to the exclusion of the others, he is on an immoral road.

Thirteen things, loves and hates, may be chosen by man as the essential pivot of his conduct, and Saadiah enumerates them one after the other, illustrates them with biblical verses and demonstrates the disadvantages that each of them represents when it occupies the entire life of an individual:

First, isolation from the world, for – this is the reasoning of hermits – this world is no more than a vale of tears and no pleasure endures; it is therefore better to accustom oneself from the beginning to sadness and misfortune. It is indeed true, Saadiah answers, that human society, like man himself, most often produces sorrow; but these people forget that society is necessary to all men, for the satisfaction of spiritual as well as material needs, and if all men adopted their doctrine, this would mean the destruction of the human race and its reduction to the level of the beasts.

Secondly, gluttony carries with it its own dangers, which Saadiah enumerates with much medical terminology, although he concedes that food and wine are pleasures that give zest to sociability.

Thirdly, sexual voluptuousness justifies itself by the continuation of the human race, and the incomparable pleasure that it procures. The disadvantages, especially medical, are again numerous.

Fourthly, passionate attachment to another human being, i.e. homosexual or heterosexual love, is considered by some as the purpose of life:

They go even further in this matter, attributing the workings of this dominant passion to the influence of the stars. Thus they assert that, if two human beings were born in the ascendant of two stars facing each other, in full or in part, and both stand under the influence of one zodiacal sign, they will inevitably love and attract one another.

In fact, they carry their theory still further, attributing the consuming passion to the work of the Creator, magnified and exalted be He. They maintain, namely, that God has created the spirits of His creatures in the form of round spheres, which were thereupon divided by Him into halves, each half being put into a different person. Therefore does it come about that, when a soul finds the part complementing it, it becomes irresistibly drawn to it. From this point they proceed further yet, making a duty of man's surrendering himself to his passion. They assert, namely, that this is only a means of testing the servants of God, so that by being taught submissiveness to love, they might learn how to humble themselves before their Master and serve Him.

(*The Book of Beliefs and Opinions*, trans. S. Rosenblatt, p. 374)

Saadiah concludes his exposition of the chief disadvantages of this kind of attachment by affirming that it should exist only between husband and wife, for the greater good of procreation.

The fifth love is that of money.

The sixth is the longing for children, who bring joy to their parents' souls; they delight man in his old age and praise him after his death. It is true, says the Gaon, that this is very good, and without children a man has neither aim nor object; but to have too many children is an intolerable burden; it is not enough to bring them into the world; one must take care of them and nourish them properly, and this exhausts an over-prolific father and brings misfortune on his ravenous brood.

Follows, seventhly, the possession of goods, praiseworthy as long as it does not occupy a disproportionate place in a man's life, for otherwise it brings with it hardness of heart and envy, and the destruction of the possessor himself.

Eighth, longevity is a good thing, as long as it does not become of the first importance; some take a laudable but exaggerated care of their health, forgetting that hygiene preserves the body but does not give life, and those who take the greatest care of their body are not those who live longest.

Power and authority is the ninth, and vengeance the tenth of human tendencies.

The love of science, which comes eleventh, should also not be exclusive. The scholar who neglects all profitable work and lives at the expense of society risks losing his prestige. Besides, not to pay attention to nourishment or to the satisfaction of the other needs of the body does not make a man more apt in study, rather the contrary, as various biblical examples demonstrate.

The divine cult, fasting and prayer should not form an occupation that entirely absorbs one's life. The performance of God's commandments also forms part of the cult, and these commandments concern everyday life with its multiple material occupations. To fulfil all the tasks of existence, according to the divine will, is to worship God more perfectly than to pray to Him day and night in isolation.

As for rest, it offers pleasure only after work; without work, it is boredom and dissatisfaction.

Saadiah concludes this tenth book by a theory of mixtures of colours that bring pleasure to the eyes, and of music that suits different states of the soul.

Another text dealing with human psychology and defining the different faculties is the introduction to his translation and commentary on the Psalms:

Saadiah divides the revealed text into five genres. First there is the appeal, when God spoke to man and said to him 'Listen'. Then there is the 'question' which is not intended to teach us something that was not known before but to draw our attention to an impossible thing, as in Deuteronomy 30: 12–24, concerning the *Torah*: 'Who shall go up for us to heaven, and bring it unto us?' The third genre is the narrative, and this deals with the past, the present, or the future. The fourth is the commandment and the prohibition. This is the basis and the centre of the revealed text. The fifth is prayer and supplication. If God thus had to vary his discourse, it is because men are different; their natures and their sentiments are different; some of them are sensitive to threats and others to promises. At all events, the main purpose of revelation is the divine commandment, a commandment both positive and negative.

The aim of the commandments is to make man perfect and guide him in the way of salvation. The question then arises: Why did God create man as he is, that is to say free to obey and to disobey, and consequently free to be saved and not to be saved? Would it not have been more appropriate for divine justice to create man totally good? We know through our reason, affirms Saadiah at the beginning of Book III of the *Amānāt*, that he who attains good by free acts is twice as meritorious as he who has done nothing: God wished that man should deserve the highest reward. It was with the same intention that He ordained the commandments and the prohibitions. Saadiah divides these into two categories: those of which the necessity would have been shown to us by reason without the aid of revelation, and those which, without contradicting reason or being of lesser importance, are only taught by revelation. The prohibition of murder, adultery, theft and lying is considered as rational law, while the Sabbath and holidays, the dietary laws the existence of the priestly class are held to be made known by revelation. This in no way signifies that the latter commandments are inferior in importance to the rational laws. The Gaon stresses the fact that they permit the faithful to merit reward. And God always takes man's capacities into account.

The idea of pedagogy is important for Saadiah. One finds it again associated with divine justice in a passage of the *Introduction to Job*. This book was interpreted by the Aristotelians as an exposition of different philosophical conceptions of providence. Saadiah saw in it a description of divine goodness and justice, which in the final reckoning always acts for man's good. The misfortunes that man suffers in this world have three reasons: the instruction that God gives his creatures, the punishment of faults, and the suffering inflicted by love. One must not pass hasty judgement on the events that occur in the life of a man, for divine wisdom is not what creatures desire, and the actions that cause them to rejoice are not those which are veritably good. Experience teaches us these truths, and the successive stages through which man passes are far from being agreeable at their beginnings; it is against his will that man passes from one stage to another of his life, and when he is used to a way of existence he has much difficulty in passing to another which he does not know and which frightens him. Does not the child scream with terror when he leaves his mother's womb and is struck for the first time by cold air and light? And nevertheless, soon he will be happy with air, light, nourishment, knowledge and all the other pleasures. And when he is weaned, the child weeps and despairs because he is being deprived of his mother's milk and does not imagine that other foods will soon be sweeter to him and will suit him better.

It is still more difficult for man to leave this world, for he imagines that he is in danger when he passes from this world to the world of reward. Consequently man's veritable end cannot be judged by imaginary human criteria, God's wisdom being the only true measure of events.

The reward that God reserves for the faithful is the after-life, and this brings us to the soul and its destiny. For Saadiah the soul is a very fine and subtle substance. God only is above all corporeality and all definition; the soul, among created things, is of the greatest purity, greater even than that of the heavens. The idea that the soul is a very fine material substance is found in some of Aristotle's writings, but precisely those which were only fragmentarily preserved and did not form part of the medieval Aristotelian corpus. It is possible that Saadiah had encountered this notion in the doxographies. In the medieval Aristotle the soul is the form of the body, and for the Neoplatonists it is immaterial. According to the Gaon, the fine and subtle substance of the soul is separated from the body at the moment of death, nevertheless remaining more or less attached to it for three or four days after this separation; it will again be joined to the body in order to receive punishment or reward.

The traditional texts, when they deal with destiny in the world to come, often associate it with the Messianic era. Three terms are employed: life beyond the tomb (the next world), the resurrection of the dead and the Messianic age. These three terms have given rise to a number of different interpretations. Saadiah is satisfied to cite the traditional texts without giving his personal opinion. At all events, he remarks that the world to come differs from the resurrection of the dead, which will take place when the Messiah arrives, so that all the past generations may benefit from it. The theme that emerges clearly from all these passages is the 'justice' of God. This concept of divine justice, one of the foundations of the Mu'tazilite doctrine, is strongly emphasized by Saadiah, who thus answers the eternal question of the suffering of the just, propounded by Job: whether in this world or the next, God rewards good acts and punishes bad; the divine accounting is very exact, and no vain suffering is forgotten before God, not that of little children, nor that of the dumb beasts; to every one God will give the compensation that is due to him in the world to come. As for the end of the world, which according to tradition will be preceded by the coming of the Messiah and the resurrection of the dead, it seems that Saadiah, basing himself on Daniel (chapters 10–12), believed the end of the world to be near, and foresaw it within twenty or twenty-five years; an opinion shared by certain Karaites.

The link between God and man is the Law, which permits man to attain the supreme Good. Saadiah Gaon respects the literal sense of this Law, the *Torah*; the allegorical exegesis, sometimes necessary, should never be systematically employed. Each passage must be carefully examined.

As an example of Saadiah's exegesis, let us take the gift of speech to Balaam's ass (Numbers 22) and the account of the resurrection of Samuel by the Witch of Endor (1 Samuel 28), two biblical episodes hard to explain in rational terms.

For Saadiah, the she-ass could not have spoken to Balaam: the angel spoke in the proximity of the ass and Balaam imagined that his mount addressed him with words. Faced with this logical contradiction, an animal deprived of reasoning faculties to whom speech, that is, intelligence, is attributed, Saadiah interprets the text in such a way that both reason and the sense of the passage are safeguarded. A divine message was communicated to Balaam, who was misled by the nearness of the voice to the animal – a clear example of an error of the senses.

Rationalist exegesis, like that of Saadiah, was not unanimously accepted by the Jewish community; thus, in the twelfth century, a Spanish commentator, Ibn Balaam, asserted that Saadiah's explanation was contrary to the biblical text. Is it not written: 'And the Lord opened the mouth of the ass'? This means that in fact it was the ass who spoke, for omnipotent God had perfected the beast's vocal organs, and bestowed on it the necessary discernment and comprehension.

In fact, whenever possible, Saadiah preserves the literal sense of the biblical narrative. Thus, in the episode of the Witch of Endor, where Saul sees Samuel resuscitated in order to announce his approaching death, Saadiah admits that Samuel was indeed resurrected from the dead in order to inform Saul of his defeat and death: nevertheless, this was not the witch's doing; she had intended to deceive Saul as was her custom, but contrary to all her conjectures and to her great terror, God resuscitated Samuel.

The Geonim who succeeded Saadiah, *Hai Gaon, Samuel ben Ḥofni, Aaron ben Sargado*, were, like him, strongly influenced by the Mu'tazilite movement, although neoplatonic and even occasionally Aristotelian elements may be discerned in their texts. Like Saadiah, they are torn between two contrary demands, that of reason, which urged them to interpret the Bible allegorically, and that of fidelity to the literal text.

Thus, discussing the episode of the Witch of Endor, Samuel ben Ḥofni does not admit Saadiah's explanation, and gives an even more rationalist interpretation. God did not resurrect Samuel, the whole scene is no more than optical illusion and trickery and there is nothing in Samuel's prophecies that does not arise from the immediate conjuncture of events. The witch, quite simply, tricked Saul.

Following the same principles, Hai Gaon denies all efficacy to the use of the divine Names, and to superstitious practices in general. According to him, while it cannot be reasonably admitted that the enunciation of the Name of God, which in any case we no longer know with any accuracy, should be sufficient to alter the natural order of things, God can, in certain cases, elevate man above the human condition and thus allow him to see the world of the angels, a superhuman world.

This implies not only that the angels, made of the Second Air, are created by God when He wishes to communicate with man, according to Saadiah's conception, but that a hierarchy of existing beings is superimposed on the human world, and it seems, according to certain biblical commentaries by Aaron ben Sargado, that this was a generally accepted concept.

In reinstating the angelic world, a traditional world that Saadiah did not want to interpose between God and man, the Geonim perhaps made a concession to the common people, but may also, in some cases, have been influenced by Neoplatonism. The world of the angels, intermediaries between God and man, is alive, existing, efficacious. One can see it, one can obtain from it information with regard to the future. Hai Gaon does not deny that dreams may be true and he considers that recourse to intermediate angelical entities is lawful, while magic is not only not lawful, but, even more, inefficacious.

Two ideas derived from Saadiah's thought were to have a brilliant future in Jewish philosophical history.

The conception of the Second Air, luminous and audible creation, close to God and close to men, is found again among the Ashkenazi pietists of the twelfth and thirteenth centuries; it has often been preferred to the Aristotelian explanation, because it admirably safeguards the at least almost literal, if not totally literal, sense of the Scriptures.

The division of the divine commandments, that is, the very fact of distinguishing among God's commandments between those that are rationally justified and those that are not, was to have a great bearing on the history of Jewish thought, and, little by little, there was to be a tendency to assign greater value to the rational commandments, that is, to those common to all men gifted with reason, in contrast to those which are specifically biblical.

The Karaites

The Karaites represented a considerable danger to rabbinical Judaism during the Middle Ages; at a certain moment they even seemed to prevail over the Rabbanites, and their importance did not diminish until the beginning of the twelfth century. We know that the most important aspect of the Karaite doctrine was their rejection of the oral tradition, that is, the Talmud and the *midrashim*, which means that their quarrels with the Rabbanites were not only intellectual but more especially concerned with the performance of the divine commandments, the *halakhah*.

Karaite thought is relatively little known, for many of their texts have not yet been published, and some of the most important manuscripts are inaccessible. However, several points of their doctrine have been elucidated in scholarly studies and H. Ben-Shammai gives a masterly exposition of the religious and philosophical thought of the first Karaites, in a book and various articles that are soon to be published.

Very little is known of the founder of the sect, Anan, who wrote a book on the Commandments of the *Torah*. According to Japheth ben Ali, he is supposed to have declared, 'Search thoroughly in the Scriptures and do not rely on my opinion', and according to Kirkisānī, 'It is said about him that he believed in metempsychosis and composed a book about it; some of his followers also professed the same belief' (*Book of Lights*, trans. L. Nemoy, 'Account of the Jewish Sects', p. 386).

Of Benjamin ben Moses al-Nah'āwendi (*ca.* 830), who was the first exponent of the sect's thought, Kirkisānī says:

He asserted that the Creator created nothing but a single angel, and that it was this angel who created the entire world, sent out the prophets and commissioned the messengers, performed miracles and issued orders and prohibitions; and that it is he who causes everything in the world to happen, without [the interference of] the original Creator.

(*Ibid.*)

Daniel ben Moses al-Qumīsī is said to have been a pupil of Benjamin ben Moses al-Nah'āwendi. He lived during the ninth century; born in the north of Persia, he settled in Jerusalem (where he died), and perhaps founded there a spiritual centre that attracted later adherents of the Karaite school of thought. Only fragments remain of his biblical commentaries, together with citations in posterior Karaite texts. The fullest surviving passages belong to his commentary on the Twelve Minor Prophets. He also composed a *Book of the Commandments* and perhaps a treatise on the laws of inheritance. Kirkisānī says of him:

> First, he was opposed to speculation by means of pure reason, and he despised its devotees; this is to be found in more than one place in his writings. He did not have the same idea of the angels as the people of Israel have, that is to say, that they are living beings endowed with the gift of speech, who are being sent out on missions in the same way as the prophets. On the contrary, he asserted that this word of ours, 'angel, angels', denotes the bodies by means of which God does his doings, e.g., fire, clouds, winds, etc. (*Ibid.* pp. 390–1)

The corpus of Karaite doctrine was elaborated at Jerusalem, principally, during the tenth and eleventh centuries, and bears the strong imprint of the Arab milieu within which it was formed. H. Ben-Shammai draws attention to the fact that the Karaites used the Arabic script. Arabic texts composed by the Rabbanite Jews were generally written in Hebrew letters; the Karaites, on the contrary, tended to use Arabic characters even for the Pentateuch and books of prayers translated into Judeo-Arabic, and this is an unique phenomenon. On this subject Kirkisānī expresses a surprisingly modern opinion: the content of the words is important and not their language or their script. This idea is opposed to the Jewish consensus, which considers the Hebrew language and the Hebrew alphabet as the sacred language of humanity, an attitude that Kirkisānī himself expounds in another place.

The Mu'tazilite *kalām* was an integral part of Karaite thought, and its writings were not only read among the Karaites but transliterated into Judeo-Arabic. Certain Mu'tazilite ideas that were prominent during the eleventh century even became the 'true Jewish tradition' for medieval Karaites.

In the tenth century, however, Karaite thinkers were far from having achieved unanimity, and their positions regarding science and philosophy differed considerably. The anti-secular current was represented by *Solomon ben Jeroham* (mid tenth century, Jerusalem). Apart from a fierce polemic, in Hebrew, against Saadiah and the Rabbanites entitled *Milḥamot Adonai* (*The Wars of the Lord*), which he wrote while the Gaon was still alive, he was the author of numerous biblical commentaries in Arabic. His opposition to every object of study other than religion extended to Euclid, to Hebrew grammar, and to foreign languages, although he himself also wrote in Arabic.

JACOB AL-KIRKISĀNĪ AND JAPHETH BEN ALI HA-LEVI

Very different from Solomon ben Jeroham are Jacob al-Kirkisānī and Japheth ben Ali.

Jacob al-Kirkisānī (Abu Yusuf Yakub al-Qirqisānī) of Mesopotamia flourished in about 930–40, apparently in Iraq. He left a theoretical exposition of Karaite ideology that has remained the foundation of the doctrine. His great work, the *Kitāb al-Anwār wa'l-Marāqib* (*Book of Lights and Watch Towers*) devoted to the Law, is divided into thirteen chapters, the first four being historical and philosophical. Fragments of the introduction to his long *Commentary* on the non-legalistic parts of the Pentateuch and a short *Commentary on Genesis* also survive (in manuscript).

Japheth ben Ali ha-Levi (Abu Ali al-Hasan Ibn Ali al-Lāwi al-Bāsri), of Jerusalem, active during the second half of the tenth century, may to some extent be compared with Saadiah. Like Saadiah, he translated the Bible into Arabic and wrote commentaries on it. These commentaries, composed in Arabic, have nearly all remained in manuscript; however, long excerpts were translated into Hebrew in later Karaite works. He also composed a *Book of Precepts*.

Both authors, Kirkisānī, by his theological ideas, and Japheth ben Ali, by his biblical exegesis, exercised a great influence on all succeeding Karaite thought. Their basic religious conceptions are largely similar but they differ on the extent of the use of reason.

Both had to face their co-religionists' opposition to rational speculation. The titles of the first four chapters of the *Kitāb al-Anwār* immediately indicate the line of thought adopted:

(1) History of the Jewish sects (Christianity is included among these).

(2) The validity of rational investigation in theology and in jurisprudence.

(3) Refutation of the doctrines of various sects, including Christianity and Islam.

(4) Treatise on methods of interpreting the Law.

These chapters are a valuable source of information on the religious sects of the tenth century and their history, for the author's erudition extended not only to the rabbinical and Karaite Jewish texts, but also to Muslim and patristic writings. Among his informants Kirkisānī cites the 'bishop' Jašu' Sekha, with whom he had formed a bond of friendship.

According to Kirkisānī, rational speculation on religious matters is permissible; it is even a positive commandment, for it is the foundation of all religions and knowledge is acquired through it.

The true procedure should be this: laws should be made along the lines of research and speculation only; whatever is proved by research and speculation to be necessary and logical should be accepted as dogma, no matter who adheres to it, be it the Rabbanites, or Anan, or anyone else. Yea, if scholars engaged in research and speculation should arrive at some new doctrine which none (of the former authorities) had heretofore professed, its acceptance should be obligatory, inasmuch as it is (logically) correct and unassailable. There are other so-called Karaites, for example, those of Persia, especially those of (the city of) Tustar, who, notwithstanding their assertion that they are in favor of speculation, revile those who engage in rational speculation, i.e. in some of the secular sciences, especially dialectics and philosophy. What makes them averse to this (speculative method) is this: first, they are too lazy to learn all about this matter, and it is also too difficult (for their minds); therefore, they seek to be relieved from this fatiguing pursuit. Secondly, some of them erroneously think that rational speculation does harm to him who engages in it by leading him to heresy; in fact, they assert that they have seen some men who have been engaged in this pursuit and have become heretics. This opinion of theirs, however, is the very cause of (all heretical) doubts and suspicions, inasmuch as it makes the listener believe that rationalism is averse to religion and is directly opposed to it; if this is so, then religion is assailable (as something irrational), but this is utterly absurd. They certainly ought, therefore, if they would only try to be just, to refrain from accusing rationalism of being the cause of heresy for the mere reason that some men who have been engaged in speculation went astray (in their faith), since a great many scholars have been pursuing the same method (of thinking) and yet have not become heretics, on the contrary, it only strengthened their faith. Neither should they assert that renunciation of speculation is the cause of added strength of faith, inasmuch as there are a great many people who have never done any speculation by means of (pure) reason and have no idea of it, and yet they are dissenters and believers in all sorts of heresies. We shall show further on the absurdity of the views of these people, and we also shall prove that intellect is the foundation upon which every doctrine should be built, and that all knowledge should be derived by means of reason only.   (*Ibid.* pp. 320–1)

God manifests himself to man in two ways: by reason, which is given to every man normally constituted, and by revelation. But revelation is not unique, since Jews, Christians and Muslims each claim to have had a revelation of their own. Only reason, common to all men, allows one to determine the authenticity of a revelation. It is necessary therefore that the intellectual and rational process should precede and justify the acceptance of a prophecy, whatever it may be, for even in the Scriptures we see there are false prophets. Moreover, even before accepting the prophecy, one must be convinced that a good and wise God is at the origin of this prophecy; one must then, in the first place, prove, by means of reasoning, the existence of God. To reiterate, reason is the moral law that permits us to distinguish good from evil. It is because this moral law also applies to God that we can firmly establish the existence of a good and just God. It is also reason that allows the allegorical interpretation of ambiguous passages of the Bible, passages that might give rise to false opinions, that is, opinions rejected by reason or contrary to other biblical expressions of which the true sense is the literal one.

In the Scriptures, in effect, God addressed himself to men so as to make himself understood, like a pedagogue.

Scripture addresses mankind in a manner accessible to their understanding and about matters familiar to them from their own experience; this is what the Rabbanites mean when they say, 'The Law speaks with the tongue of men' (B. Běrakot 31b). Thus, when the Creator wished to describe Himself to the effect that nothing visible is hidden from Him, He described Himself as provided with eyes, because men are familiar with the sense of sight and know from their own experience that its seat is the member of the body which is the eye, not because He really is provided with bodily members. Likewise, when He wished to let them know that no sound is veiled from Him, He described Himself as provided with ears, because among men sounds are perceived by the sense of hearing. The same applies to all matters of this sort. This is similar to the reply of a certain scholar who was asked, 'How can the Creator address mankind, seeing that His speech is of a different species from men's speech, inasmuch as it is infinitely more sublime and exalted?' To this, the scholar replied that when God created His creatures and wished to address them with commandments, prohibitions, promises, threats, and narratives, He took into consideration the fact that their constitution could not bear to hear His natural speech because of its sublimity and exaltation and its dissimilarity from their own language, and He fashioned for them a speech akin to their own, near to their comprehension, acceptable to their understanding, and bearable to their faculties. This is comparable to our own procedure with animals and similar creatures, whose constitution is different from ours, whom we must govern and manage, to whom we must communicate our wishes, who do not know our speech, and whose sounds and utterances are not akin to ours. We therefore resort to signs, hints, and noises which make known our wishes, such as whistling, bleating, and various other sounds produced by movement of the vocal organs. Thus, we call *ǧurr* to an ass when we want him to start moving, and we call something else when we wish to make him stop. Likewise, we call *kiš* to some birds when we want to drive them away; to others we call *axx*. We say *axš* to a dog, while we whistle to other animals and use different sounds to signal other species of animals. This scholar's explanation is of great potency and is similar to our own view that God addresses mankind in a manner adapted to their minds and accessible to their understanding. It is for this reason, or one near it, that the children of Israel begged to be excused from listening to the Creator's address, when they said to Moses: *let not God speak with us, lest we die* (Exod. 20: 16).   (*Ibid.*, trans. L. Nemoy, *Karaite Anthology*, pp. 63–4)

Kirkisānī does not pursue the argument to the end; it is only much later that Aristotelian Jewish thinkers attempted to distinguish what, in the Bible, related to human psychology.

Rational speculation offers proof of a psychological process that exists in any case, for the need to know and to inquire exists in all men and no man is happy when he is called ignorant. Inquiry and reasoning form part of man insofar as he is distinguished from the animals. Like them, he has, certainly, a living soul, but he is different in that it is a 'speaking' soul, that is, a rational soul, thanks to his comprehension and discernment, which include language. Further, the different pieces of knowledge are parts of a whole and this, in itself, is proof of its necessity. Let us take a certain piece of knowledge acquired by rational investigation; it is proved by another piece of knowledge equally acquired by rational investigation, but this latter is proved by the intuitive knowledge that is thus shown to be the base of all logical reasoning.

The human soul, by its natural disposition, as it has been created by God, thinks and understands the true definitions of things and has the power to make a choice. It is the capacity of discerning and choosing the good rather than the bad, of perceiving past and future events and not only, like the animals, of obtaining what is necessary for physical survival, that is the 'image and resemblance of God'.

For Kirkisānī, the four sources of knowledge are:

(1) The perceptions of the senses;

(2) Things evident in themselves, like the fact that lying is bad and blameworthy;

(3) Demonstrative knowledge;

(4) Traditionally transmitted knowledge, which in fact depends on the three preceding sources.

Japheth ben Ali enumerates three sources of knowledge:

(1) Rational knowledge, which includes objects perceived by the senses and self-evident things;

(2) Revelation;

(3) The true tradition.

The first two sources, and most probably also the third, are divided into primary and secondary knowledge; the latter is demonstrated with the aid of speculation, argument and analogy.

The fundamental difference between Japheth ben Ali and Kirkisānī is that for Japheth revelation represents one of the sources of knowledge, while for Kirkisānī, revelation agrees with reason and perception, but does not constitute a separate source:

These, then, are the rational proofs built upon the knowledge based on sense perception; and it is for this reason that King David, in describing the Law and stating that it is allied with both reason and perception, says: *The Law of the Lord is perfect* (Ps. 19: 8–10); i.e., its perfection is due to its close connection with reason free from error. He says further: *The commandments of the Lord are upright, rejoicing the heart*, referring to the satisfaction felt by the human heart because of the truth of the premises and conclusions contained in His commandments; and further: *The precept of the Lord is pure, enlightening the eyes*, refers to the clarity and lucidity of the precept, caused by its freedom from ambiguities; and further: *The fear of the Lord is immaculate, enduring forever*, meaning that the word of the Law is firmly established in the face of disputes and attacks against it, and remains irrefutable. The full truth is then made evident by the combination and union of all five of these principles in the concluding words: *The judgments of the Lord are the truth, they are righteous all together*. (*Ibid.* pp. 57–8)

Another difference between Japheth ben Ali and Kirkisāni is their attitude to the limitations of human knowledge.

According to Yefet (comm. on Ps. CXXXI. 1), human knowledge is limited mainly in four areas: a) marvels of the creation; b) man's lot in this world; c) the success of wicked governments; d) the reasons for the revealed laws. The third of the four belongs to Yefet's tendency to actualize Scripture. With respect to the second and the fourth Yefet presupposes that he who deals with these matters is most probably liable to question God's wisdom and to reach conclusions which will influence his belief and behaviour. It is thus a moral–religious consideration which is involved in the limitation of human knowledge in these matters. To the first area Yefet devotes a lengthy discussion in his comm. on Prov. xxx. 1–6. Much of the knowledge of the scientists is unfounded, because they were unable to acquire it at first hand. Solomon knew these things by inspiration; therefore he was allowed to deal with them. But ordinary men should devote their time to the Torah, and not to the teachings of infidels and gentiles. Elsewhere Yefet explicitly mentions the target of his attack: the heritage of classical Greek philosophy and science. The whole body of human knowledge is thus classified by Yefet according to religious–moral criteria into two classes: the wisdom of this world and the wisdom of the world to come, i.e. the Torah. Yefet is not worried by the fact that his favouring and necessitating of rational speculation inevitably implies resorting to the achievements of philosophy and science. He is worried by the danger that preoccupation with philosophy may lead to heresy, and this worry causes him to adopt an 'anti-intellectualistic' position.

(H. Ben-Shammai, *The Doctrines*, pp. xvi–xvii)

For Kirkisānī certain verses of the Scriptures show that the study of science and philosophy is not prohibited. King Solomon studied science in the same way as did 'the doctors and philosophers'. There is no opposition between the doctrine of creation and the laws of science and philosophy; on the contrary, they prove each other. Science is an instrument for attaining the knowledge of the truths of the *Torah*. Like religious belief and revelation, the sciences are based on the use of reason, the foundation of which is the perception of the senses and the self-evident things.

We have mentioned there – by way of showing the validity of investigation into matters rational and disciplines philosophical, and proving that the Sages of our nation had engaged in such investigation – the biblical account of King Solomon as the most learned of the children of Adam, in that he discoursed upon all the various kinds of plants, from the largest, which is the cedar tree, down to the smallest, which is the hyssop, and upon all the various kinds of animals, including beasts, birds, fish, and insects. Consider now, what could he have discoursed about, as regards all these things, if not in the way of describing their natural properties and causes, their beneficial and harmful qualities, and similar matters? This in fact is what the Greek and other philosophers quote in his name and is now incorporated in their books. A similar thing is related in the biblical account concerning Daniel, Hananiah, Mishael, and Azariah; to wit, that they were skilled *in all matters of wisdom and understanding* (Dan. 1: 20), indicating that the king inquired of them about various matters of wisdom and that their knowledge of it was ten times greater than that of his advisers and court philosophers. This is an incontrovertible proof that they were scholars skilled in all branches of philosophy, since they were ten times more learned than the king's magicians.

(*Book of Lights*, trans. L. Nemoy, *Karaite Anthology*, pp. 55–6)

To the argument that science and philosophy can lead to heresy, Kirkisānī opposes a hierarchy of science and scholars. The highest, the subtlest degree, is reserved for the few who have a well-proportioned nature and a sound natural intellect, who look for truth without wanting to turn it to personal profit, and do not wish to do harm.

Thus, it is permissible to study magic, for example, in order to know how it differs from miracle, and to confound the magicians, but not for the purpose of using it. Similarly, man may study astronomy on condition that he does not do so for astrological ends, which are prohibited.

Certainly, many things cannot be understood by man and only God entirely understands them (for instance, the substance of the soul and its future destiny), but this does not necessarily prevent man from trying to understand them, within the limits of human possibility. Thus, according to Kirkisānī, the exploration of divine creation is limited by the nature and intellectual potential of the scholar, far more than by the subject of the study; it is not reserved for prophets, but for an intellectual élite of naturally gifted philosophers.

In the physics as in the cosmology of our two authors we can recognize the influence of philosophy, and probably more specifically that of Al-Kindī. Both Kirkisānī and Japheth ben Ali admit that the world is formed of four elements. For Japheth ben Ali, creation took place exactly as it is related in Genesis 1, taken literally. For Kirkisānī, the three first elements (earth, water and air) were created simultaneously, and composite bodies are born from their mixture. As for fire, two kinds exist: celestial (ether) and concrete fire.

Celestial fire arises in the following way:

Every moving body moves with it the body which is attached to it. The latter becomes hot by that movement. When the celestial sphere moves, it moves with it the air attached to it. This air, while moving with the sphere, becomes hot, and consequently becomes thinner and lighter. This [thinner and lighter air] is fire. This is why fire is the highest element. This [process] is also demonstrated by sense perception, for when two solid dry bodies are rubbed forcefully against each other fire is produced in between them. [The reason for] that is that the few particles of air which exist between the two solid bodies heat and change into fire.

(H. Ben-Shammai, 'Studies in Karaite Atomism', p. 5)

Since ether is born from the friction of two bodies and has no independent existence, it was not mentioned in Genesis. The void does not exist and all the interstices between the bodies are filled with air. Time is the duration of the celestial movement; nevertheless it is not absolutely bound to movement, for theoretically, even if the celestial bodies ceased to move, time would continue to be.

In the same way that time at its beginnings was not preceded by an anterior time, the universe is not in a certain place, but within the universe all bodies have a place and each body can be the place of another body.

The definition of the body is important and shows that Kirkisānī, and perhaps even more Japheth ben Ali, were aware of atomist theories. The three components of the world are body, accident, or substance, for everything is either a body or an accident or a substance. 'Substance' and 'accident' probably refer to the ten Aristotelian categories.

The body has length, width and depth, and is divisible. The accidents are indivisible and require a substance in which to inhere. The substances are generally bodies, except for the soul, the air and the angels, which are spiritual substances.

These definitions of the body are the basis of the Karaite refutation of the anthropomorphists, the Manichaeans and the Christians.

For Kirkisānī the Rabbanites are anthropomorphists:

They attribute to Him [human] likeness and corporeality, and describe Him with most shameful descriptions; [they assert] that He is composed of limbs and has a [definite] measure. They measure each limb of His in parasangs. This is to be found in a book entitled 'Shi'ūr qōmāh', meaning 'The measure of the stature', i.e., the stature of the Creator. This, as well as other tales and acts, etc., mentioned by them in the Talmud and their other writings, does not suit [even] one of the [earthly] creatures, much less the Creator. ('Account of the Jewish Sects', p. 337)

Now, God cannot be a body for two reasons:

(1) A body has three dimensions;
(2) A body cannot create another body.

He cannot be two, for each of two gods would be limited by the other; He cannot be three for 'a substance in three hypostases' would signify that one was applying to God Aristotelian definitions that only refer to the world of bodies; however, the Christians do not admit that God is a body with three dimensions. In reality, one cannot compare anything in this world to God; the divine acts are not analogous to human acts and His action is different from ours.

God is One, and commenting on the verse 'Hear O Israel, the Lord is thy God, the Lord is one', Kirkisānī shows how rational investigation agrees with the revealed text to give us an idea of the oneness as well as the unity of God.

This discussion about the meaning of the unity, the opinions about the oneness of the Creator and its significance, and an explanation of the passage which follows that verse is given in the fourth chapter:

We will first discuss the oneness and the meaning of the words of Scripture 'the Lord is one'. The learned have taught that the noun 'one' is used to signify the following six aspects:

(1) With respect to simplicity; e.g. the soul is simple, in contrast to the body which is composed and assembled.
(2) With respect to composition; e.g. soul and body constitute one composition.
(3) With respect to genus; e.g. man and ox with respect to animality.
(4) With respect to number; e.g. Khālid and Zayd, each of whom is counted as one.
(5) With respect to species; e.g. 'man' which is predicated of both Khālid and Zayd.
(6) In the sense that [that one] has no equal with it; e.g. you say [about someone] 'he is unique and no body equals him in his characteristic'.

[Opinions of various scholars about the predication of God as one:]

[a] God is one with respect to simplicity, i.e. He is one, not of any composite essence in any sense of the expression.

[b] He is one in His essence and His action, i.e. there is nothing similar to Him in His essence nor in His action. These two opinions are simultaneously true.

[c] It is admissible to say 'God is one' with respect to a number, not in a quantitative sense, rather in the sense that He is the first and that [His] creation does not resemble Him, but is second to Him as being after Him [in time]. [In other words, He is one because] He is eternal, without a second or a third [eternal being] except for the Eternal who is incessant, while the created has come to exist after it had not existed.

[d] He is one in a numerical sense, because He is the First and the One, and is therefore, by virtue of Himself, in no need for the existence of a second, while the second cannot do without the existence of the first. The reason for that is that the number one [as such] is separate, it is not attached [to the other numbers] while the numerical [noun] 'second' is attached to the first and [necessarily] indicates [its existence]. The same is true with regard to the following numbers, such as third and fourth etc. for this reason it may be said that God is one as any number.

[e] He is one in the sense that he has neither beginning nor end, while anything other than Him has a beginning and an end.

[f] God is one in that He is not an effect, but rather He is the cause of every effect. Any thing other than Him is an effect.

These are the opinions concerning the Oneness and the significance of the One in the words of the Scripture 'The Lord is one'.

(*Book of Lights*, trans. H. Ben-Shammai, 'Qirqisānī on the Oneness of God', pp. 107–9)

With the oneness of God is connected the polemic against the pre-existence of the Logos, and the eternity of the Word.

If one [of them] should ask, 'Since the Law is God's Word, how can that which is from God be incipient and created?' – the answer would run thus: [the concept of] a thing from a[nother] thing has several variations. One of them is a part of a whole – as we would say [for example], 'the hand is from the man', meaning that it is a part of him; this [variety of the concept] cannot be applied to God, since He is not subject to partition and division. Another variation is [exemplified by] the expression, 'the fruit is from the tree', meaning that it grew out of it; this, too, is inapplicable to God, since He is not subject to happenings and attributes applicable to [earthly] bodies. Another [variation] is [represented by] the saying, 'the ointment is from the sesame-seed', or 'the oil is from the olive', meaning that it had been expressed and obtained from it; again, God is exalted [far] above such an attribute. We say, further, 'justice is from the just', or 'action is from the agent', or 'truth is from the truthful', meaning that he has produced it and given it inception. When we say, therefore, that the Word is from God we mean that He has made it and caused it to be. (*Ibid.*, trans. L. Nemoy, 'Tenth Century Criticism', pp. 526–7)

One can only define God by negative attributes; the only positive attribute being eternity. The other adjectives used in referring to God – Living, Knowing, Powerful, are ways of expressing that He does not die, that He is not ignorant, etc.

In contrast to Kirkisānī, Japheth ben Ali makes only vague allusions to the negative attributes, and rather tends to employ terms like 'knowing by essence', or 'eternal by His essence', which reflect Mu'tazilite terminology.

For both, the problem of the attributes is associated with the revealed text, and Japheth writes:

... the Creator may not be described nor defined, and space does not contain Him. It is not permissible to say of Him that He is in the world or outside thereof, since this is one of the attributes of created things, which are contained in space and subject to accidents. This being so, there is no doubt that by saying, 'the Lord came down', [the verse] indicates a created, defined something and a local compression [of the air] on the top of the mountain.

(P. Birnbaum, *The Arabic Commentary*, p. xv, passage on Exodus 19: 20)

while Kirkisānī propounds the following exegetical principles:

Scripture as a whole is to be interpreted literally, except where literal interpretation may involve something objectionable or imply a contradiction. Only in the latter case, or in similar cases which demand that a passage be taken out of its plain meaning – e.g., where a preceding or a following passage requires it in order to avoid a contradiction – does it become necessary to take the text out of the literal sense. If it were permissible for us to take a given biblical passage out of its literal meaning without a valid reason for doing so, we would be justified in doing likewise with the whole of Scripture, and this would lead to the nullification of all the accounts therein, including all commandments, prohibitions, and so forth, which would be the acme of wickedness. Thus we are compelled to say that the verse, *And they saw the God of Israel* ... (Exod. 24: 10), must not be understood literally and does not signify seeing with one's eye, since it is contrary to reason to assume that the Creator may be perceived with man's senses.

(*Book of Lights*, trans. L. Nemoy, *Karaite Anthology*, p. 60)

Japheth takes up this theme at greater length at the beginning of his commentary on Daniel 11.

We are not justified in setting aside the literal meaning of the Word of God or of His prophets, save where that literal meaning is hindered or precluded as being contradicted by *the reason* or by *a clear text*. In such a case it is understood that the first text requires an explanation reconciling it with the reason or with the other text; the words having been used in some metaphorical or improper sense, as we have observed in a number of places in the Law and the Blessed Prophets. Ideas repudiated by *the reason*, are such as 'God descended', 'God ascended', etc.; precluded by the reason, because, if we take the verse literally, it follows from it that God must be a material substance, capable of inhabiting places and being in one place more than in another, moving and resting, all qualities of created and finite beings, and He must possess these attributes. Such texts must therefore be capable of being explained away, and the term indirectly interpreted may be either the *noun* or the *verb*. The first is done in cases like 'and God descended', 'and God ascended', where we affirm the action of the person of whom 'ascending' and 'descending' are attributes; only the person intended is the *Angel of* God, or the *Glory of* God or the *Apostle of* God, with the ellipse of a word. The second is done in cases like 'God was glad', or 'God was sorry', or 'God was jealous'; all of which are accidents

47

not to be predicated of the Immortal Creator. This phrase must contain a sense to be evolved in whatever way the words will allow. The language has employed in such cases metaphors and inaccurate expresions, because the application of the reason can point them out. Where one text is precluded by another, the one which admits of two or more interpretations must be explained away.

(*Commentary on the Book of Daniel*, p. 56)

The explication of the divine visions and the auditory revelations recounted in the Scriptures should be based on this fundamental principle: only created, therefore non-eternal beings and things, can be heard and seen.

If one [of them] should ask, 'But do you not believe that God addressed Moses from the thornbush?' – we would answer, indeed we do, in the sense that He created a Word and placed it in the bush; God was the speaker, although the Word was located in the bush, just as in the case of the Ten Commandments, the verses were God's Word, although they were located upon the two Tablets; the Word was God's, and not the thornbush's or the Tablets', even though it was placed in the bush and upon the Tablets. If he should retort. 'But it was the thornbush who said, "I am God"' – we would reply, 'Nay, God was the speaker of this, in the sense that He produced the Word within the bush by means of His omnipotence, not that He himself took up position in the bush, even as He created man within the belly of his mother without His setting foot in it himself, as Job expressed it [31 15], "Did not He that made me in the womb make him?"'.

(*Book of Lights*, trans. L. Nemoy, 'Tenth Century Criticism', p. 528)

That which was seen and heard by the Patriarchs and the prophets was thus the world of the angels, which was created by God.

We find in the Scriptures many places in which angels are mentioned, and in two different ways. Sometimes they appear sensibly and are seen by men when awake, like any other visible object; sometimes in dreams, and there too like other objects: instances of the first case occurred to Jacob, Moses, Balaam, Joshua, Gideon, Manoah, David, Nebuchadnezzar, Daniel; of the second to Abimelech (as some think), Jacob, and Balaam. Their voices too have been heard without their being seen, as by Hagar, Abraham, Samuel, David. These all occur in our Chronicles, and there is no ground for rejecting these texts. It is known that nothing but *body* can be perceived by the sense of the eye: and that an accident cannot exist by itself. An angel therefore must be a *body*. Now a body cannot bring itself into existence, but must have a Creator to create it; and it is a thing which admits of persistence.

(*Commentary on the Book of Daniel*, pp. 56–7)

Of these created beings, some are more terrible and frightening than others:

Observe, too, that in this chapter he says of one *like the similitude of a man*, and tells us that he came near him, and was not afraid, whereas he was terrified and alarmed by the *great angel*; such things are common in our books; and their powers are limited according as the Creator has given them. Observe that when Jacob wrestled with the angel, the angel was at the time unable to get rid of him (Gen. xxxii. 26). Though their forms be terrible, yet God has given the children of men power to behold them, save the great and mighty Glory which the blessed Apostle asked God to shew him, when He said 'thou canst not', etc. (Ex. xxxiii. 20).   (*Ibid.* p. 57)

The angelical beings were created by God for his Glory and to serve him as an instrument of communication with men; are they nobler than man in the order of the creation?

Mu'tazilites maintained that the angels are superior to man. Yefet expresses this opinion when he writes on Gen. 1.26 as follows: 'People are not in agreement as to the rank of the angels. Some say that they [the angels] are inferior to Adam, adducing the argument that Adam had qualities which angels lack, and that whatever is to be found in angels is likewise to be found in Adam, since he is the microcosm. Because, therefore, Adam surpasses the angels in eminence, he becomes the most important of created beings. We, however, say that the angels are higher in rank than he, for [the Psalmist] says, "Thou hast made him lower than the angels"' (Ps. 8.6).

(P. Birnbaum, *The Arabic Commentary*, p. xvi, passage on Genesis 1: 26)

In fact, there is a whole hierarchy of angels, and in the *Commentary* on Psalm 103 the Karaite exegete gives us a table of the angelical world, beginning from the bottom of the ladder.

The Angels (*malakhim*) are close to men in form and speech, and it is not always easy to distinguish them from men, as in the episode of Manoah and his wife (Judges 13: 6).

The Powerful (*giborei koah*) include the angels set over the nations, such as the tutelary angel of Israel and the angel who spoke to Daniel.

The Armies and the Servants are deployed close to the Glory. The Armies are like soldiers, who come and go, while the Servants remain constantly before the Glory, praising and exalting the Lord.

The Glory is the most eminent of all these divine creatures, and in his commentaries on Ezekiel 3: 13, Japheth relates the tribulations of the Glory: It was created by God on the sixth day and lived in the Garden of Eden until the day of the revelation on Mount Sinai. Afterwards, it moved with the Tabernacle and then resided in the Temple of Jerusalem. After the destruction of the Temple God restored the Glory to its primordial home, although He sometimes shows it to a prophet.

For Japheth as for Kirkisānī, the angels are simple, non-composite substances. Japheth writes that some angels are of air, live in the air and have no need of the heavy earth; they are like the winds that blow and they descend towards the earth with a swiftness that outruns the imagination.

The highest class of angels was created from fire, and their bodies are of fire, as it is said of the angel whom Moses saw in the bush:

'And the angel of the Lord appeared to him in a flame of fire out of the midst of a bush' [Exodus 3: 2], and in his description of the Glory Ezekiel says 'from the appearance of his loins even downward, I saw as it were the appearance of fire' [1: 27], *a flaming fire*, for their bodies flash and delight the sight . . . Those who descend on earth are the Angels and the Powerful, who are of air, while the Servants and the Armies remain on high for they are of flaming fire, and fire is more exalted and more sublime than air.

(*Commentary on the Psalms, MS cit.*, fol. 204v)

It is because the angels, in contrast to men, are simple, non-composite substances, that they remain in being. Probably in reply to Daniel al-Qumīsī, who thought that God creates an angel only with a view to the task with which He charges him and only for the duration of the task in question, Japheth affirms:

An angel therefore being created must be capable of persistence; and what is there to necessitate his annihilation? If any one hold that an angel is only created for the moment, for the sake of a message or something similar, and that, when that is finished, there is no reason why he should endure, – what, we ask, indicates that he is created at the moment, – or created merely for the message or purpose which renders him for the moment necessary? If you say: 'Then what has the angel to do besides delivering messages and similar tasks?' We answer: To praise and glorify his Creator. Is not the prophet too chosen to deliver a message? but nevertheless he is not created merely to speak. We find, too, in our accounts that angels *do* endure. Thus the Glory abode with the children of Israel nine hundred years; and Daniel says of Gabriel, *and the man Gabriel, whom I had seen in the Vision at the beginning*, and there had elapsed between the two occasions a year. Nor can we suppose the second Gabriel was merely like the first, who had been created a year before and then destroyed; for that would not entitle the second to be [called] the same as the first. Again, there are the words of this angel who is speaking to Daniel, who says: 'I have been some time in war, and am going to fight those who remain:' see also xii. 1. These verses point to their persistance: and after this discussion there may be a stop put to the assertions of those who maintain that they are created for a moment and annihilated. (*Commentary on the Book of Daniel*, p. 57)

While Japheth expounds the angelic hierarchies, often and at great length, in the course of his discussion of the biblical text, Kirkisānī is much more concise. He notes four characteristics of the angels:

(1) They live in the heavens, but are able to descend on earth to fulfil their mission, and to return to the sky.

(2) They do not die like men, but, like them, are intelligent and 'possess speech'.

(3) They do not need food or drink, since, instead of being composed of several elements, they are formed of one pure element only – air or fire.

(4) Contrary to men, they can accomplish miracles and change the nature of physical bodies.

This last point contradicts other passages in the same author, where the power of working miracles is attributed only to God.

The connection between the world of God and the angels on the one hand and the terrestrial world on the other is instituted by the intermediary of the prophets. As in Saadiah Gaon, the prophet is chosen by God for his moral and religious qualities, and is not distinguished from other men by any special faculties; prophecy itself however, according to Japheth, is manifested on six levels (or five according to another text).

(1) The first is the degree of Moses – 'mouth-to-mouth' – and no other prophet shares his rank;

(2) The Holy Spirit, or inspiration, common to Moses and to numerous prophets;

(3) The degree of Samuel, who heard God speak to him directly without the intervention of a 'vision' or of a 'dream'; this speech proceeded from a *Glory*, according to the verse 'And the Lord appeared again in Shilo' (1 Samuel 3: 21);

(4) The fourth degree is that of vision, the level of Aaron, Miriam, Ezekiel and most of the prophets;

(5) The degree of Daniel, who saw the angel directly and heard the words proceeding from him, according to the verse 'Yea, while I was speaking in prayer, even the man Gabriel . . .' (Daniel 9: 21); the apprehension thus did not present itself in a 'vision' or in a 'dream';

(6) The dream. The prophetic dream differs from other dreams, for in it one sees the Glory or the Angels, as Zechariah saw the angel of the Lord and heard the discourse proceeding from him. In the same way, Daniel saw the angel in his dream and heard the discourse that he addressed to him: 'I came near to one of them that stood by' (Daniel 7: 16) (*Commentary on Numbers, MS cit.,* fol. 77 r–v).

Of the six degrees of prophecy, the first and the third highest are auditive, the second highest is purely spiritual; the other three are both visual and auditive. This distinction between Voice and Glory is maintained even in the inferior degrees of prophecy. For all the personages seen by the prophets including Moses himself, are created beings: the most sublime of which is the Glory. It has the appearance of a man, rises to the heavens or descends on earth; the Voice of God, on the other hand, springs from God Himself; we do not know the nature of this voice, but it is certain that God sees, hears and makes His Voice heard, without the aid of organs. His voice is of the same nature as His 'Holiness'.

According to Kirkisānī, man cannot hear the veritable Voice of God, therefore God creates a 'Voice' adapted to human corporeal capabilities.

(1) The most eminent prophecy, that of Moses, comprises two different perceptions: Moses saw the Glory and heard the Voice. On the same level Moses was favoured with a face-to-face dialogue (he saw the most elevated Glory in his waking state) and with the mouth-to-mouth dialogue during which the Voice spoke to him as a man speaks to his companion.

(2) The second degree, the Holy Spirit, is spiritual inspiration; it is by means of the Holy Spirit that Moses composed the two last pericopes of Deuteronomy and eleven psalms. On the same level, we find David, the sons of Asaph and the Psalmists, the Solomon of the Song of Songs, of Ecclesiastes and the Proverbs.

How can one distinguish a true prophet from a false? Miracles are the only sign; however there are many and various reports about miracles, and it is difficult to determine their veracity, in the first place, because we learn of these miracles through tradition and not through direct perception.

Criticism of the tradition is thus one of the arguments used in polemics against the other religions which pride themselves on true prophets. Thus, on the miracles attributed to Muhammad in the *Hadith*, the Muslim tradition: 'The proof (of the veracity of a tradition about a miracle) does not consist of the multitude of its transmitters, but of the multitude of those from whom it was transmitted and those who witnessed the performance (of the miracle)' (H. Ben-Shammai, 'Attitude', p. 37).

The biblical miracles, on the contrary, have been authenticated by the entire people of Israel. Moreover, this tradition is not only a written but also an oral one since the entire Jewish people knows this tradition by heart in every generation. It is therefore impossible that additions or omissions could have been perpetrated.

Certain people, including the Rabbanites, admit the reality of sorcery, which is supposed to be able to effect prodigies, such as recalling a dead man to life, the transformation of one element into another, the inducing of love or of hatred, the infliction of diseases or the performance of cures without the aid of medicine, only by pronouncing certain words, and so on; but a person who adopts this opinion is no longer able to recognize a true prophet.

The authenticity of the divine mission is proved through miracles performed by the prophet that can only come from God. But if some other man, not sent by God, were able to produce the same phenomenon in some way or another, we could no longer be sure that he who claims to be a prophet does not succeed in producing a miracle in the same way as the other, who is neither prophet nor emissary of God. This would be the end of religion, of the prophet's mission and of the revealed Law. Some people, relying on the biblical narratives, attack prophecy itself, calling it a matter of magic and artifice. Their argument runs thus: assuming the veracity of accounts according to which the prophets performed prodigies and caused the metamorphosis of natural things, it is still possible that they succeeded in this through all sorts of artifices. We know of the existence of natural objects that perform operations contrary to the habitual course of things, like the setting of things in movement without contact between the mover and the moved; this is the case of the magnet that moves and attracts iron without touching it; or certain herbs which, thrown into the water, make fish leap on to the earth; or dragon's blood, which colours water to look like blood; or the stone placed under a woman in difficult labour, who thereupon gives birth; and many herbs and minerals used in the successful treatment of diseases and others that kill and cause to perish.

Given that these things exist in the world, where many people have seen and known them, although perhaps not everybody knows them, one can equally admit that there are other things in the world more subtle in their action and more difficult to find, not known even to those who know the first. They are hardly known except to those who are the most energetic in their search and who carry their ambition furthest, and especially those whom their ambition impels to claim for themselves the rank of leader, by the force of prophecy. One may admit that these claimants to prophecy, thanks to the energy and the care that they have devoted to research and investigation, have obtained information that others have not attained, and it is thus that they have succeeded in their operations.

To this Kirkisānī responds: it is impossible to accept that the prophet performs his prodigies thanks to his knowledge of the occult virtues of natural things like the magnet. In fact, while men are indeed not equal in theoretical knowledge and in the perception of the secrets of nature, many of them possess this knowledge, like the philosophers who know the plants and the minerals of multiple active virtue, and have composed books on the subject. We may say quite justifiably that they get all this from the prophets. The philosophers who possessed this knowledge were not a few isolated men, but were very numerous, Hippocrates, Aristotle, Galen, and many others, and they have recorded everything that they knew. If they had known and spoken of other things they would have recorded them also in their books. If they had had the means of proving that even one of the things accomplished by the prophets had succeeded thanks to an artifice or by the occult virtue of an element, they would not have failed to disclose it. If they have not done so, this proves that the miracle worked by the prophet was not performed either by means of artifice or by the occult virtue of an element. Besides, the philosophers have composed books on magical operations, artifices, prestidigitatory manipulations and automatons. Now in all this there is absolutely nothing that offers the least similarity with the acts, the prodigies or the miracles of the prophets. This shows that the actions and the signs of the prophets can only come from God. (Cf. G. Vajda, *Etudes sur Qirqisani*, pp. 89–91.)

The mechanism of the miracles is nevertheless not beyond understanding:

How was the serpent [in Paradise] transformed [into a rational being?]? The answer is that the accidents of serpent were taken away from it, and it was covered by the accidents of another being, like 'the stick which was turned into a serpent' [Exodus 8: 15]. In [that case too] the accidents of wood had been taken away from the stick, which was [then] covered by the accidents of animality. The same happened with the water turning into blood and the like.

(H. Ben-Shammai, 'Studies in Karaite Atomism', p. 5)

In conclusion, I would like to quote a short passage by Japheth ben Ali where the three leading preoccupations of Karaite thought at this epoch are brought together:

(1) The quest for rational knowledge;

(2) The certainty that this knowledge, given by God, is revealed in the Scriptures (and not in the Oral Law);

(3) The sentiment that the Karaites, contrary to other religions and to Rabbanite Jews, possessed the keys to the truth (a sentiment that all the

religions shared during the Middle Ages, each for itself), which is expressed in vigorous polemics.

Many shall run to and fro: i.e. the wise and the seekers of knowledge. This *running to and fro* may be of two kinds: (1) They shall run over the countries in search of knowledge, because scholars will be found in every region; the seekers of knowledge, therefore, will go to and fro to learn from them; this is expressed by Amos (viii. 12). This shall be at the beginning of their career; when they seek so ardently, God will make revelations to them. (2) They shall *run to and fro* in God's Word like those who seek treasures, and thereafter knowledge shall increase; knowledge of two things: (*a*) the *commandments*; (*b*) the *end*. God will not reveal the end until they know the commandments. They are the men that fear the LORD, who are *in possession of His secrets*, which cannot be had save by study and search and inquiry into the Word of God: compare the prayers *teach me, O LORD, the way of Thy statutes*; *open my eyes*. These and similar expressions shew the vanity of the profession of the *traditionalists* like *El-Fayyūmī* [Saadiah], who have destroyed Israel by their writings; who maintain that the Commandments of God cannot be known by study, because it leads to contradictions; so that we must follow the tradition of the successors of the prophets, viz. the authors of the Mishnah and Talmud, all of whose sayings are from God. So he has led men astray by his lying books, and vouches for the veracity of anyone who lies against God.   (*Commentary on the Book of Daniel*, p. 77)

YŪSUF AL-BAṢĪR

Yūsuf al-Baṣīr (Joseph ben Abraham ha-Kohen ha-Ro'eh al-Baṣīr) was blind, and was euphemistically called 'the seeing'. He lived in Jerusalem in the eleventh century and was one of the most important of Karaite thinkers and the one who paid most attention to the metaphysical foundations of religion. His great work, the *Muhtāwi* (*The Comprehensive Book*), although surviving in Arabic, is generally known in the Hebrew translation by Tobias ben Moses, called *Sefer ha-Neimot*. This book, in forty chapters, was summarized under the title *Al-Tāmiyiz* (*The Distinction*) in thirteen chapters, also translated by Tobias ben Moses under the title *Makhkimat Peti* (*Which gives Wisdom to the ignorant*). Of Yusuf al-Baṣīr's other works, it seems that only a unique manuscript of his book on the precepts has been preserved.

The *Muhtāwi* is quite simply a book of *kalām*, difficult to distinguish from Muslim *kalām* texts. Like them, it enunciates the five principles of the unification of God.

(1) The establishment of atoms and accidents. (2) The establishment of the Creator. (3) The establishment of the attributes of the Creator. (4) The rejection of the attributes [ascribed] to Him which are inadmissible with respect to Him. (5) The establishment of His unity; that there is no second with Him; and that His attributes are unique to Him.

(H. Ben-Shammai, 'Studies in Karaite Atomism', p. 33)

As in the *kalām*, the theoretical base of the argumentation on the divine unity is the distinction between the atom and the accident.

[All] generated [things] are divided into [two classes]: atoms of substance and accidents. Atoms of substance compose bodies and accidents abide in them.

The thin things [*daqqīm*] which you see [when looking] through the rays of sunlight are not like the atom [*hatīka*] which I have mentioned, for the atom is smaller. Those [thin things] are visible [to the eye] while the atom is not. However, God sees it, because He does not see with eyes. You should know, from now onwards, that when I mention in this book [the term] *daq* I mean that thing which is not divisible and not visible to the eye [i.e. atom of substance]. It is that [same] thing which I called above *hatīka*. [Consequently] when I mention [from now onwards] *hatīka*, I mean one particle of the accidents [*hā-afā'īm*] which do not occupy any space or place, but rather occur and abide on an atom of substance [*daq*]. (*Ibid.* p. 24)

The atoms of substance are invisible, the atoms of accident are visible and also audible, for Yūsuf al-Baṣīr, following in this the greater number of the Mu'tazilites, defines the voice as a succession of atoms. The problem is connected with divine speech, which certain writers considered as a spark, and Yūsuf al-Baṣīr affirms:

We omitted also the discussion of Divine Speech; although it is under dispute among the people. [We did so] for the following reasons: (a) The proof which demonstrates that God alone is eternal [at the same time] denies [the possibility of] the eternity of [His] speech. (b) The eternity [of God] denies that He be speech, since speech [generally] is instructive by virtue of its being a composite sequence [*bi-'l-muwāda'a*], of which the former parts inevitably precede the latter. A thing which is described in this way cannot be [other] than created. Therefore when God is said to be speaking, this does not constitute an Attribute which would be ultimately attributed to His Essence. Rather, this is related to Him by way of derivation from his creating [*fi'lihī*] the Speech, like 'doing good' or 'hitting'. (*Ibid.* p. 24)

We see that Yūsuf's problems, like their solution, are the fruit of thinking rooted in Mu'tazilism.

Jeshua ben Judah (Abul-Faraj Furqān Ibn Assad), Yūsuf al-Baṣīr's pupil, and like him a fervent Mu'tazilite, was also an exegete, and a prolific writer. Most of his works, like those of his master, were translated into Hebrew in the twelfth century by young scholars who came from Constantinople to study Arabic under his direction.

Karaite thinkers were still numerous during the Byzantine period. Their work has hardly been studied, but it seems that they were usually content to repeat their predecessors' ideas. Thus *Judah Hadassi* (*ca.* 1148), author of *Eshkol ha-Kofer* (*Cluster of camphire*: Song of Songs 1: 14), *Jacob ben Reuben*, author of *Sefer ha-Osher* (*The Book of Riches*), also of the twelfth century, and *Aaron ben Elijah of Nicomedia* (died in 1369), author of *Eẓ Hayyim* (*The Tree of Life*), tried to harmonize these ancient doctrines with more modern conceptions, availing themselves of certain texts by Maimonides. For Aaron ben Elijah, the *kalām* (and atomism) is a doctrine of Jewish origin, contrary to Greek philosophical thought. At all events, the great Karaite period had come to an end.

During the twelfth century, political events caused the spiritual centre of Karaism to move to Byzantium, where it survived until the sixteenth century. During the seventeenth and eighteenth centuries there were numerous Karaites in the Crimea and in Lithuania. A brief nineteenth-century renaissance occurred, thanks to the work of A. Firkovich, but the Karaite community was not revived in any great numbers, and only a few thousand adherents of the sect now remain, most of them living in Israel.

Chapter 3

THE NEOPLATONISTS

Medieval Neoplatonism, which was largely based on the writings of Plotinus and Proclus, dates from the ninth century. It provided the philosophical context for the thought of many cultivated Jews of the eleventh and twelfth centuries, and during the Arabic period it was more or less complemented by elements stemming from Islamic religious traditions and by some Aristotelian ideas.

Neoplatonism in a popular form often provided the intellectual structure of Jewish thinkers, even when they were not philosophers. Sometimes it was one of the constituent elements of an otherwise altogether religious thought, such as that of Hai Gaon or the ascetic theology of Bahya Ibn Paquda.

Similarly, in works devoted to the art of writing, the renowned poet Moses Ibn Ezra constructed his vision of the world in accordance with neoplatonic views. The Jewish thinkers, though not remarkable for the originality of their ideas, introduce us to the intellectual climate of their age, and it is possible that quotations from unknown authors occasionally occur in their works.

The foregoing remarks do not apply to Solomon Ibn Gabirol, who as a philosopher struck out a path of his own and had a considerable influence on Christian scholasticism.

The reconciliation of philosophy and revelation attempted in the Jewish neoplatonic texts is likewise of some interest. The science of astrology was equally an integral part of the vision of the world that can be gleaned from some of these writings.

ISAAC BEN SOLOMON ISRAELI

Isaac Israeli was the first writer after Philo to integrate philosophical ideas drawn directly from Greek sources into Jewish thought, and his thinking offers us an exposition of a Jewish neoplatonic philosophy. Saadiah, as we have seen, not only knew Isaac Israeli but exchanged several letters with him even before he left Egypt. Saadiah was then a young man and Israeli a doctor of repute. Israeli was born in Egypt in 850 and seems to have begun his career as an oculist. He emigrated to Tunisia and became doctor to al-Mahdi, founder of the Fatimid dynasty in North Africa. He lived to a great age, was never married, had no children, and died perhaps before 932 (but other indications suggest that he lived until 955). Israeli is supposed to have said: 'I have written four books which will cause my memory to survive longer than children would have caused it: the *Book on Fevers*, the *Book of Ailments and Drugs*, the *Book on Urines* and the *Book on the Elements*.' He was famous as a physician and the Imam al-Mahdi held him in high esteem; according to Abraham Ibn Ḥasdai, translator of the *Book on the Elements*; 'The Madhi raised him above all his scholars and all his people, and at his command he wrote all his books and composed his treatises. For this reason he composed them in Arabic, for it is one's duty to fulfil the command of the ruler.'[1]

Isaac Israeli's medical works were translated into Hebrew and Latin and were in use until the end of the Middle Ages. His reputation as a philosopher, on the other hand, was less general, and Maimonides held that he was 'only a doctor'. Maimonides' slightly contemptuous judgement may be explained chiefly by Israeli's association with the neoplatonic movement, while Maimonides was an Aristotelian. It is also true that Israeli was not an original philosopher.

He made use of two main groups of texts: the works of Al-Kindi, an Arab philosopher of the early ninth century who had access to numerous Greek philosophical works, some of which have since been lost, and the vanished treatise of a neoplatonic philosopher, which has been partially reconstituted by S. Stern. From Aristotelian thought Israeli borrowed the four sublunary elements and the quintessence of which the spheres are made.

Israeli's importance lies primarily in the fact that he was the first medieval Jewish 'philosopher', although his influence on later Jewish philosophers was limited. Latin authors used the *Book of Definitions* as well as the *Book on the Elements*, which were translated by Gerard of Cremona.

The following philosophical works by Isaac Israeli have survived:

– The *Kitāb al-Hudūd* (*Sefer ha-Gevulim*, the *Book of Definitions*), is perhaps the best-known of his works; only an incomplete copy of the original Arabic text was preserved in the Cairo Genizah;[2] this manuscript is written in Hebrew characters, but there are certain indications that it was transliterated from a manuscript written in Arabic characters. Moses Ibn Ezra, in his *Kitāb al-Ḥadīqa* (*The Book of the Garden*), composed in Arabic, frequently quotes the original text of the *Book of Definitions*. Other citations, or perhaps citations from a common source, are to be found in the Arabic work *Ghāyat al-Ḥakīm* (*The Aim of the Wise*). Two Latin translations, one of them abridged, date from the twelfth century, while Nissim ben Solomon's Hebrew translation is most probably prior to 1200. Another Hebrew translation, surviving only in fragmentary form, was made a little later.

---

[1] Abraham Ibn Ḥasdai's reference is to Saʿid of Toledo, who gives a biographical note on Isaac Israeli in his book on the *Categories of the Nations*; there are entries on Israeli in most medieval works on medicine.

[2] The Genizah was the place where during the Middle Ages books and documents that had outlived their usefulness were deposited. Documents of priceless worth were thus preserved, and unearthed, in the 'House of Ezra' in Cairo.

– The *Kitāb al-Jawāhir'* (*The Book of Substances*) has been found only recently, in Leningrad. The identified fragments were published in 1929, and more completely in 1956. This book also seems to have been written in Arabic characters, although the extant manuscripts are in Hebrew script.

– *Sefer ha-Ruaḥ Weha-Nefesh* (*The Book on Spirit and Soul*), preserved in Hebrew translation (except for a small fragment in Arabic), is perhaps part of a larger work. This is the only one of Isaac Israeli's works that refers to the Bible and it seems that it was intended for a Jewish public.

– *Kitāb al-Usṭuquṣṣāt* (*Sefer ha-Yesodot, The Book on the Elements*) exists in two Hebrew translations, of which one was made by Abraham Ibn Ḥasdai at the request of David Kimḥi and the second in a Hebrew closer to that of the tibbonids. The Latin translation is by Gerard of Cremona.

– *Shaʻar ha-Yesodot le-Aristo* (*Chapter on the Elements*), of which only one manuscript exists, at Mantua, is attributed to Israeli by two modern scholars who rely on internal criteria, although the manuscript itself contains an attribution to Aristotle.

From the first, Isaac Israeli situates himself in the tradition of Aristotle and the Alexandrians by defining the aim and means of the definition of things – that is, of the knowledge of them.

Isaac says: Many of those who read the books of the ancients and see their differences in defining things come to the conclusion that this must be due to differences in their opinions; this is not, however, so. As they endeavoured to investigate the definitions of things, they found that there are four inquiries without which one cannot reach the knowledge of these definitions. (1) The first is existence: when one inquires whether so-and-so exists; (2) the second is quiddity: when one inquires what so-and-so is; (3) the third is quality: when one inquires how so-and-so is; (4) the fourth is 'quarity': when one inquires why so-and-so is.

This can be explained as follows. (1) Existence inquires about the being of a thing, viz. if it has existence or not. The answer to this question must always be either 'yes' – if one admits the existence of the thing – or 'no' – if one denies it.

(2) Quiddity inquires about the nature and the essence of a thing, viz. what it is. and thus the answer to it is given by the definition of the thing, which declares its nature and substantiality.

(3) Quality inquires about the property and the inseparable commitments of a thing . . . For this reason, before replying, one must turn to the inquirer and say that a thing has many properties and concomitants; say therefore which of them you have in mind. When the inquirer explains his meaning, one can answer with either 'yes' or 'no', as we have explained above. On account of this the answer concerning existence and quality must always be 'yes' or 'no'.

(4) 'Quarity' inquires about the final cause of a thing, which is necessary for the generation or the being of the thing, why it is such.

(*Book of Definitions*, trans. S. M. Stern, in *Isaac Israeli*, pp. 10–12)

These philosophical questions show that the various definitions that have been given by the Ancients do not contradict each other but describe different aspects of what man knows about himself, the world and God.

Here the theme microcosm–macrocosm is introduced; it is found chiefly in the Alexandrian philosophers and Proclus, and it is present to a lesser or greater extent in all medieval philosophical writings.

Philosophy is man's knowledge of himself. This also is a description of great profundity and elevated intelligence, for the following reason. Man, if he acquires a true knowledge of himself, viz. of his own spirituality and corporeality, comprises the knowledge of everything, viz. of the spiritual and corporeal substance, as in man are joined substance and accident. Substance is twofold, spiritual and corporeal; spiritual, as for instance soul and intellect, corporeal; as for instance the long and broad and deep body. Accident is also twofold, spiritual and corporeal; spiritual, as for instance mildness, knowledge, and similar spiritual accidents which are predicated of the soul; corporeal, as for instance blackness, whiteness, yellowness, redness, thickness, variety, and the other corporeal accidents which are predicated of the body. This being so, it is clear that man, if he knows himself in both his spirituality and corporeality, comprises the knowledge of all, and knows both the spiritual and the corporeal substance, and also knows the first substance which is created from the power of the Creator without mediator, which is appropriated to serve as substratum for diversity; as well as the first generic accident, which is divided into quantity, quality, and relation, together with the remaining six compound accidents which derive from the composition of substance with the three accidents. If man comprises all these, he comprises the knowledge of everything and is worthy to be called a philosopher. (*Ibid.* p. 27)

Like the other medieval philosophies, Neoplatonism describes a hierarchical universe. Between the perfect God and the imperfect lower world are intercalated the more or less perfect essences that join the immaterial God to the world of matter. According to Isaac Israeli, the First Matter and the First Form arise from God and these engender the Intellect. From the Intellect emanates the world of souls, that is, the rational soul, the animal soul and the vegetative soul. Then follows the world of the spheres, then the sublunary world with the four elements and their compounds.

Our earth, a mixture of the four elements, earth, water, air and fire, is at the centre of the world, and does not move. The spheres, made of a more perfect substance, the quintessence, turn around the earth, and by their movements create the compounds, which are bodies.

The First Matter and the First Form are described by a citation from Pseudo-Aristotle.

Aristotle the philosopher and master of the wisdom of the Greeks said: The beginning of all roots is two simple substances: one of them is first matter, which receives form and is known to the philosophers as the root of roots. It is the first substance which subsists in itself and is the substratum of diversity. The other is substantial form, which is ready to impregnate matter. It is perfect wisdom, pure radiance, and clear splendour, by the conjunction of which with first matter the nature and form of intellect came into being, because it [intellect] is composed of them [matter and form].

(*The Chapter on the Elements*, trans. A. Altmann, in *Isaac Israeli*, p. 119)

The Neoplatonists

According to certain Neoplatonists, the First Form and Matter emanate from God, who produces them in a non-voluntary and non-temporal manner. Isaac Israeli, on the other hand, lays much emphasis on creation. God created the First Matter and the First Form; He brought them into existence *ex-nihilo*, a specifically divine mode of action.

This is proved by the hierarchical structure of the world, where we see the substance rising toward the perfection of God's Power, Will and Wisdom:

Having reached this point in our discourse, let us return to our promise to bring a proof for the statement that the first of created things are two simple substances, out of which is established the nature of the intellect. We say as follows: This is proved by the difference in the degrees of the substances, which are either simple or compound, spiritual or corporeal ... it is clear that the intellect is the most noble of all substances, of the highest degree and loftiest rank, and the one nearest to 'innovation' and 'making-anew' [creation from nothing] and most particularly affected by the action, without mediation, of the power and the will – as the perfect wisdom, pure knowledge, and true science is its form and the perfection of its substantiality. (*Book of Substances*, trans. S. M. Stern, in *Isaac Israeli*, pp. 85–6)

The Intellect emanates from the conjunction of the First Matter and the First Form and in some texts the term 'is created' is employed in this context.

The ancients also compared the soul to a splendour and said as follows: God created the intellect as a splendour; when its nature and essence were established, a radiance and brilliance went forth from its shade like the radiance which goes forth from the shade of the glass balls and the mirrors which are set in windows of baths and houses, when the ray of the sun falls on them; from this the nature of the rational soul comes into being. Its splendour and brilliance are less than the splendour and brilliance of intellect; the reason being that the degree of intellect is intermediate between the soul and its Creator, so that the soul acquired shadow and exhaustion, i.e. darkness, as the intellect intervened between it and the light of the Creator, the absolute brilliance, i.e. the perfect wisdom and the pure brilliance. On account of this it was affected by ignorance and is in need of instruction; while the intellect is not affected by ignorance, because it is near to the wisdom, the pure brilliance and the absolute light. When the nature of the intellectual soul was established, a radiance went forth from its shade, and the nature of the animal soul came into being. On account of this it became estimative and imaginative, and does not subsist in what it is, i.e. in itself. Between it and the pure light intervene the degrees of the intellect and of the intellectual soul. Likewise a splendour went forth from the animal soul, and the nature of the vegetative soul came into being. Its splendour was further dimmed, and its movement became restricted to the movement of growth only, and it was thus deprived of locomotion, owing to the intervening degrees and its distance from the splendour. Likewise, a splendour went forth from the vegetative soul, and the essence and the nature of the sphere came into being. It was coarse and fell under the sense of sight. As the nature of the sphere is movement, one part collided with the other, and fire came into being from its movement, and from fire air, from air water, from water earth. Out of these elements came-to-be the animals and the plants.

(*The Book of Spirit and Soul*, trans. S. M. Stern, in *Isaac Israeli*, pp. 110–11)

The mode of action of the Intellect and the souls differs from that of the spheres and the sublunary world. The first is a creation in the sense that nothing is lost of the essential light, and it is from the shadow of this light that the inferior beings are created. Beginning with the world of the spheres, the action of nature generates and corrupts, for the source of this action is diminished and changed by the action itself, which is exercised on bodies with opposite qualities.

Below the celestial sphere, all plants and animals are engendered from the four simple elements, fire, air, water and earth; one of them being predominant. Only the body of man is formed of the four elements joined in a harmonious equilibrium. Each being composed of elements receives a soul in accordance with his capacity.

In the world of Isaac Israeli, all beings are endowed with soul; the spiritual flow, the light that originates in the Intellect, penetrates the entire hierarchy of living beings to stop only at the mineral world. The further this light is from its source the more it darkens and thickens, but without disappearing altogether, and the ray of light traverses the entire material world and links it to the brilliant and perfect splendour of the Intellect.

... the reasons for the difference between the substances and for one taking precedence of another in their spirituality and degree. I say that this is for three reasons. Firstly, the quality of the emanation of the light which is created from the power and the will. Secondly, the quality of the reception of the light by one substance from the other. Thirdly, the difference existing between that which bestows and that which is bestowed, the bestowing and the reception of the bestowal. Regarding the quality of the emanation of the light from the power and the will, we have already made it clear that its beginning is different from its end, and the middle from both extremes, and this for the following reason: when its beginning emanated from the power and the will, it met no shade or darkness to make it dim and coarse – while its end met various imperfections and obscurities which made it dim and coarse; the middle partook of both extremes.

(*The Book of Substances*, trans. S. M. Stern, in *Isaac Israeli*, p. 88)

The rational soul is the noblest and most eminent degree of the soul, for it is at the horizon and the shadow of the Intellect. This is why man is able to distinguish between good and evil, between praiseworthy or vile objects, to pursue virtue and reject vice. Man can thus receive rewards or punishments, because he can differentiate between the acts that deserve one or the other.

The animal soul is inferior in clarity and eminence, for it comes into being from the shadow of the rational soul, and thus it is further removed from the light of the Intellect; it becomes clouded and is governed solely by the imagination; its knowledge is external, based on the perception of the senses; its characteristics are movement and locomotion. Thus animals make proof of audacity and of courage to achieve victory and power, but there is neither discernment nor knowledge in their conduct. In consequence, they receive neither reward nor punishment.

The vegetative soul is inferior to other souls since it arises from the shadow of the animal soul. It is very obscure and devoid of perception and of loco-motion. It is only capable of desire, of procreation, of nourishment, of grow-ing and diminishing, and of putting forth flowers and vegetables, odours and tastes, according to different countries and climates.

These three degrees of the soul are not absolutely separated, for certain animals are gifted with prudence and intelligence, like men, and certain plants have a delicious perfume. Among the plants Israeli mentions musk and amber, and among the animals, dogs, doves and other beasts and birds that have discernment and acquired knowledge approaching that of man. All this is due to the inclination of the souls towards each other. Sometimes, the rational soul inclines towards the animal soul and its actions incline to-wards those of the animal soul, which desires food, drink, and sexual pleasure. Similarly, the animal soul tends to conform its actions to those of the rational soul when the latter instructs and influences it. The rational soul has a ten-dency to come closer to the Intellect and to attain perfection; it then becomes clear and pure; it will seek good and true things like knowledge and under-standing, purity and sanctity, the service of God and closeness to Him – all this thanks to the influence of the superior substance:

One who is ruled by the rational soul will be intelligent, discriminating between things spiritual and corporeal, exceedingly humble, occupied with [the search for] truth and beautiful things, and shunning things which are blameworthy.

(*The Book on the Elements*, trans. A. Altmann, in *Isaac Israeli*, p. 138)

If this exceptional man studies and searches diligently, if he abandons animal appetites, he will attain the highest degree.

One whose rational soul has withdrawn itself [i.e. from the lower souls] and upon whom intellect causes its light and splendour to emanate becomes spiritual, god-like, and longing exceedingly for the ways of the angels, as far as lies within human power.

(*Ibid.* p. 139)

What role can prophecy play in this universe where, by its own nature, the rational soul aspires to rejoin its luminous source? Since man, of himself, elevates himself towards the Intellect, therefore towards God, what role can be played by revelation? Because humanity is divided into three kinds, according to the proportion of one of the three souls that dominate in each individual – the rational, the animal, the vegetative – only a small proportion of humankind is truly close to the light of the Intellect, and knows the will of the Creator.

For when the Creator, blessed be He, willed to create the world, make visible His wisdom, and cause its content to pass from potency to actuality, He created and formed the world out of nothing; He established it without any pattern; He set it up without there being any need on His part to do this for the purpose of either deriving benefit or avoiding harm. Our Creator is far exalted above this. He did it in His goodness and love, and seeing that His love was great and His wisdom was made visible, He desired to benefit His creatures and servants. Desiring this, He considered that it was not possible for men to obtain the benefits intended for them except by knowing the will of the Creator so as to do what He wanted them to do, and become worthy of receiving His reward and requital for serving Him. But it was again impossible to obtain [the knowledge of] the will of the Creator, blessed be He, except through messengers. (*Ibid.* p. 138)

These are the privileged persons, the prophets, whom God will take as intermediaries to bring the divine world to humanity:

For when the Creator wishes to reveal to the soul what He intends to innovate in this world, He makes the intellect the intermediary between Himself and the soul, even as the prophet is an intermediary between the Creator, blessed be He, and the rest of His creatures. (*Ibid.* p. 135)

The visions of the prophets are not the apprehension of external phenomena or of concrete beings seen and heard by the senses, but are spiritual images:

We mentioned that the forms with which intellect clarifies the spiritual forms are intermediate between corporeality and spirituality because they result from the imaginative representations of the corporeal forms, and are more subtle, spiritual, and luminous than the latter, which are found in our waking state and are full of darkness and shells. It is for this reason that the Ancients compared them to the forms in the higher world. (*Ibid.* p. 136)

The procession of revelation is comparable to the psychological process in dreams:

... there is agreement between all authors of books on religion and all who believe in prophecy that dreams are a part of prophecy.

After having explained and verified this, we should have made it clear that during sleep the *sensus communis* sees forms intermediate between spirituality and corporeality – i.e. forms in which intellect has clarified the spiritual forms – but knows them only in their corporeal aspects. For it is not within its power and ability to know more of them than their image and imaginary form on account of its proximity to the corporeal sense, i.e. that of sight. But once it knows their corporeal aspects, it transmits them to the imaginative faculty which resides in the anterior brain, and imagination receives them in a more subtle way since it is more subtle than the *sensus communis* and more remote from the corporeal sense, i.e. that of sight. Once the imaginative faculty has received them from the *sensus communis*, it transmits them to the memory and deposits them there. When the person awakes from his sleep, he claims these forms from the memory, and memory returns to him the remembrance of all their traces, impressions, and characteristics as received from imagination. Remembering them, one seeks to understand their spiritual meaning through the cogitative faculty, because the latter possesses the power to scrutinize, discern, and combine, and it discerns and distinguishes between the shells of a thing and its kernel. Having discerned and purified them, it returns them to the faculty of memory, and memory receives them and stores them away until such time as they are required. (*Ibid.* pp. 136–7)

During sleep, the forms received by the *sensus communis* are more exalted, first because they are farther from matter, then because they arise from the activity of the intellect, which gives an impetus to the rational activity of the imaginative faculty. If the forms of the intellect are intermediary between matter and Intellect, and not purely spiritual, this has a pedagogical purpose: they are more likely to make their impression on the *sensus communis*.

In this description the differences between the prophetic dreams, which include almost all the biblical visions, and other dreams are not explicitly stated. Both are of the same kind, and both use the same psychological mechanism, but the prophetic dream originates in God's desire to communicate with his creatures. However, on the human level, nothing permits the differentiation of the prophetic from the premonitory dream.

The dream requires interpretation and this can be done only by a person endowed with a rational soul of the highest degree.

When, therefore, the cogitative faculty of the person concerned is spiritual, pure, luminous, and hardly obscured by shells and darkness, intellect will cause its light and brilliance to emanate upon it and make known to it its own properties, forms, and spiritual messages; it will also enlighten it as to the properties and forms of the soul and its faculties, and as to the differences between its spiritual forms and corporeal ones. Then these forms will be completely purified of all shells adhering to them, and it [cogitation] will interpret those dreams without fault.

(*Ibid.* p. 137)

Thus, with Isaac Israeli, the ambiguous role played by the imagination first emerges. The imagination permits one to attain spiritual, abstract, and divine things, but it clothes them in a mantle of corporeality, of images, of which they must be divested. Since imagination is the 'medium' of dream and of prophecy, it is at the core of the revealed Book, which is also clad in image and corporeality so that it may be understood by all men whatever their level of comprehension. To be sure, the Divine Word provides keys to its interpretation, but only the philosopher is capable of recognizing and using them to decipher the whole Book, and fulfil God's design.

Some of His words therein are unambiguous, self-evident, in no need of elucidation and interpretation. Yet there are others which use corporeal expressions, and are doubtful and in need of elucidation and commentary. Not that the Creator, blessed be He, was incapable of stating everything He wished to say in His Book in unambiguous and self-evident terms. But He knew that His creatures vary in their intellect, understanding, thoughts, and decisions. For some are animal-like and foolish, who will never allow anything to enter their minds and to occupy their thoughts except what they have perceived with their senses and seen with their own eyes. Others are intelligent, of an inquiring mind, keep their eyes open to the truth of words, and distinguish between their spiritual and corporeal meaning. Still others are of an intermediate type, which includes a variety of shades too numerous to be counted. The Creator, blessed be He, put His message in spiritual, unambiguous words to serve as guide and true teacher to those endowed with intellect and understanding so as to enable them to reach an understanding of the meaning of those messages which are couched in corporeal and ambiguous terms.

(*Ibid.* p. 139)

Those capable of finding the pure sense will find it, for they have distanced themselves from matter and their spirit is unencumbered and luminous; they shall see the Light and the divine world. Those who are still incapable of seeing the Light will ask the sages to explain the Book to them, and, gradually, thanks to explications and discourses, they will understand and come nearer to the Source of purity, until they are so close to the Intellect that it will imprint its form on their soul. God thus gives the example: placing Himself within reach of the intelligence of His creatures, He institutes a divine pedagogy that the Intellect will imitate when it wishes to make future events known to men; this is also the road that the prophets will follow in their oral expositions of what their pupils cannot comprehend in the books. As the ray of light traverses the entire density of matter, so the superior beings, the Intellect and the philosophers, follow the divine footsteps in turning towards the inferior beings to help them climb the degrees of Light, each according to his own power and abilities.

A *Commentary on the Book of Creation*, written by *Dunash Ibn Tamim*, a pupil of Israeli, seems to supplement the passages that have been cited. Dunash Ibn Tamim associates his theory of prophecy with three terms of the *Sefer Yeẓirah: kol, ruah, dibbur*.

(1) *Kol*:

... this is a voice that God has created in the air and which He directs towards the ear of him who deserves to hear it. It is with this meaning that the Scripture says: '... When Moses was gone into the tabernacle ... to speak with Him, then he heard the voice of one speaking unto him. And the Lord called unto Moses [Numbers 7: 89 and Leviticus 1: 1].

This created voice is most probably that described by Saadiah Gaon in his *Commentary on the Book of Creation*, which Dunash Ibn Tamim knew and proposed to emend.

(2) *Ruah*:

Most of the prophets have prophesied by means of this ... All [these passages] and those that resemble them represent prophecy in dream. True dreams, without being prophetic, are of this kind.

This is also what Isaac Israeli says, and it is in fact the neoplatonist doctrine: supernatural visions are interior; they are closely related to dreams; and we may recall the talmudic adage (Bab. *Berakhot* 54b), 'dream is the sixtieth part of prophecy'.

(3) *Dibbur* is the speech

... by which Moses was distinguished, as it is said: 'And the Lord spoke unto Moses face to face ...' We shall say however that the soul of Moses was superior to that of all other men, it was subtle, light and united with the world of the rational soul even before it was separated from its body. In effect, when the souls separate from their bodies, being still alive, this separation is a union with the superior worlds, for, in this state, the soul becomes intellect and the intellect is united with the light, in a spiritual not a corporeal, union.

66

Forced by exegesis to give this third level of prophecy the name of *dibbur*, Dunash Ibn Tamim is careful to remark that 'this speech is not like human speech which is materialized by the organs of speech', nor is it 'a conventional discourse . . . which translates what is in the soul'. In fact we recognize, applied to Moses, the Plotinian ecstasy.

This ecstasy, regarded by Isaac Israeli as the final purpose of human existence, is not essentially different for Moses or for other men whose souls are purified and elevated. Only ecstasy permits one to justify the human soul's exile far from the pure and luminous world of the Intellect and imprisonment in a heavy and material body. It is by the union of soul and body that the truth of the sciences becomes evident, that man can distinguish good from evil, the praiseworthy from the despicable, and act according to truth, in justice and rectitude; he may then sanctify, supplicate and exalt his Creator, recognize His majesty, and obtain in the end the veritable recompense: union with the superior soul, illumination from the light of the Intellect, the beauty and the splendour of wisdom. Then he becomes again a spiritual being and joins the Light created without an intermediary, by the power of God. He becomes one of those who exalt and worship the Creator for ever and ever; this is paradise, the unsurpassed reward, the perfect beauty.

A case of a spiritual final cause is the union of soul and body to the end that the truths of the subject of science may become clear to man; that he may distinguish between good and evil, between what is laudable and what is not; that he may do what corresponds to truth, in justice and rectitude; that he may sanctify, praise, and exalt the Creator, and recognize His dominion; that he may avoid beastly and unclean actions in order thereby to obtain the reward of his Creator, blessed be He, which is the union with the upper soul, and the illumination by the light of intellect and by the beauty and splendour of wisdom. When attaining this rank, he becomes spiritual, and will be joined in union to the light which is created, without mediator, by the power of God, and will become one that exalts and praises the Creator for ever and in all eternity. This then will be his paradise and the goodness of his reward, and the bliss of his rest, his perfect rank and unsullied beauty.

(*The Book of Definitions*, trans. S. M. Stern, in *Isaac Israeli*, pp. 25–6)

If paradise is the eternal union with the light of the Intellect, hell is the prison of matter, where the soul heavy with sin cannot rejoin its source:

He who does not attach himself to the intellectual precepts which God has revealed to the elect among his creatures, his priests, and teachers, and perseveres in his own injustice, sinfulness, coarseness, and in the evil of his ways, will be rendered unclean by his impurities, and they will weigh him down and prevent him from ascending to the world of truth. He will not attain the light of intellect and the beauty of wisdom, but remain contained under the sphere, sorrowful, in pain without measure, revolving with the revolution of the sphere in the great fire and the torturing flame. This will be his hell and the fire of his torture which God has prepared for the wicked and sinners who rebel against the precepts of the intellect. (*Ibid.* p. 26)

The theme of the soul and of its destiny is one to which we shall return at greater length. However, first Solomon Ibn Gabirol must be presented.

SOLOMON BEN JUDAH IBN GABIROL

Ibn Gabirol was born in 1021/2, most probably at Malaga. As a child he lived at Saragossa and was well and carefully educated. His father died when he was still quite small, his mother in 1045. He himself died young, at about the age of 37 (between 1054 and 1058). Ibn Gabirol was a great poet, and his poetry gives us some information about himself and his life. He was, he says, small, ugly, and sickly; moreover, he was of a very disagreeable disposition and his arrogance caused him material harm, for, living entirely for philosophy and poetry, he depended for his subsistence on wealthy patrons. The most important of his influential friends was probably Yekutiel ben Isaac Ḥasan, whom he praises in numerous poems for his learning, wisdom, and generosity. But Yekutiel was a courtier, and various intrigues led to his assassination in 1039. As a result, Gabirol's financial situation deteriorated sharply, and he did not succeed in gaining the favour of any other Saragossa patron. It seems that he tried to settle in other towns, such as Granada, and later Valencia, where he died. His poems, religious and profane, won him wide celebrity in his own time, and today his verses still form part of the liturgy of the Oriental Jewish rite.

Ibn Gabirol's philosophy was expounded in a lengthy work written in Arabic. Only fragments of the original have been preserved, in a work by Moses Ibn Ezra, using a copy most probably different from that translated into Latin in the twelfth century by John of Spain (perhaps Abraham Ibn Daud, an Aristotelian philosopher will be discussed in the following chapter) and Dominicus Gundissalinus, under the title *Fons Vitae*. An English translation of the third book (*The Fountain of Life*) has been published by H. E. Wedeck.

In the Introduction I referred briefly to the history of this text, attributed by the scholastics to an Arab philosopher called Avicebron or Avencebrol. During the thirteenth century Shem Tov ben Joseph Falaquera made a Hebrew translation of portions of the *Fountain of Life* which he called, *Mekor Hayyim*, and these excerpts are preserved in an unique manuscript. S. Munk identified them with portions of the Latin work, published them and translated them into French, with the correct attribution.

Medieval Jewish authors were acquainted with Ibn Gabirol's philosophy, and in the fifteenth century he was still known to Isaac Abrabanel and his son Leo Hebraeus, who cite him under the name of Albenzubron.

The *Fountain of Life* contains no biblical citations nor in fact any allusion to revealed religion, except perhaps for some references to the *Sefer Yeẓirah*, the *Book of Creation*, and it is a good illustration of the non-confessional character of philosophy when the philosophy in question is a science and

68

not the application of this science to a revealed religion. And the *Fountain of Life* is indeed concerned with science: the science of matter and form.

Ibn Gabirol composed several allegorical exegeses on Genesis, but we do not know whether these are excerpts from an extensive commentary that has been lost. Also, in a long poem, still recited in Oriental synagogues, one finds philosophical allusions that agree with the neoplatonic basis of his system of thought.

Finally, a treatise on practical morality, preserved in the Arabic text, *Iṣlāḥ al-'akhlāq*, and translated into Hebrew by Judah Ibn Tibbon under the title *Tikkun Midot ha-Nefesh* (*The Improvement of Moral Qualities*), to a certain extent presents the psychological aspects of Gabirol's doctrine. Gabirol himself alludes to a work on the Will, but we know nothing more of this.

Solomon Ibn Gabirol's philosophical sources are not directly known, for he cites only Plato; but his 'doctrinal family' as J. Schlanger calls it, is quite clearly defined, He undoubtedly knew Isaac Israeli and most probably the texts used by him.

The idea of spiritual matter goes back to Plotinus and Proclus (according to the partial translation of the *Elements of Theology*), who affirm that matter is the basis of unity in the spiritual and material world. But Falaquera rightly mentions Empedocles in this connection (or, rather, the Pseudo-Empedocles and the *Book of the Five Substances*), for he maintains that matter and form are the first beings created, and are anterior to the Intellect. The idea that the Will penetrates down to the lowest degree on the scale of beings has a certain affinity with Ismaili writings.

The search for sources, in any case disappointing, can only serve as an introduction to the work itself, for Gabirol's thought is without doubt one of the most striking and original produced by a medieval Jew.

The *Fountain of Life* is written in the form of a dialogue, a literary procedure current in the Islamic period, evidently in imitation of Plato, but, in contrast to the presentation of the Platonic dialogues, neither master nor pupil possesses a vivid personality; the doctrine is expounded by the master, and the pupil only puts questions that give the master the opportunity to elucidate various points. In the quotations from the original, as in the Hebrew excerpts (*Mekor Hayyim*), the dialogue form is abandoned, but not to the detriment of the interest. It is probable that Jewish philosophers used a version different from, and perhaps shorter than, the one translated into Latin. I shall cite from these Hebrew extracts (with the help of the Latin text) since it is through these passages that the *Fountain of Life* was most probably known to Jewish thinkers.

The work is divided into five books: the first treats what must be initially established in order to situate universal matter and form, and to situate matter and form in compound substances; the second describes the spiritual substance that sustains the form of corporeality; the third shows the existence of simple substances; the fourth deals with the knowledge of matter and form in simple substances; the fifth studies universal matter in itself and universal form in itself.

One may say that the *Fountain of Life* analyses the profound movement of the mechanism of Creation, while in the *Kingly Crown* Ibn Gabirol gives a description of the three worlds that immediately present themselves to man's reflective thought: the divine world; the created universe; man. This poem opens with the praise of God:

> Mysterious are Thy works my soul well knows:
> Thine, Lord, is majesty, all pomp and power,
> Kingship whose splendour yet more splendid grows
> O'ertopping all in glory and wealth's dower.
> To thee celestial creatures, and the seed
> Of earth-sprung kind concede
> They all must perish, Thou alone remain,
> The secret of whose strength doth quite exceed
> Our thought as Thou transcendest our frail plane.

> (*The Kingly Crown*, trans. by R. Loewe)

And Ibn Gabirol goes on in a more philosophical manner:

Thine is the mystery of power, the secret and the foundation.

Thine is the name that is hidden from the wise, the strength that sustains the world over the chaos, the power to bring to light all that is hidden.

Thine is the mercy that rules over Thy creatures and the goodness preserved for those who fear Thee.

Thine are the secrets that no mind or thought can encompass, and the life over which decay has no rule, and the throne that is higher than all height, and the habitation that is hidden at the pinnacle of mystery.

Thine is the existence from the shadow of whose light every being was made to be, and we said 'Under His shadow we shall live'.

Thine are the two worlds between which Thou didst set a limit, the first for works and the second for requital.

Thine is the reward which Thou hast set aside for the righteous and hidden, and Thou sawest that it was good, and hast kept it hidden.

> (*The Kingly Crown*, trans. B. Lewis, pp. 27–8)

At the end of the first part of the poem we find, concentrated in several lines, the philosophical subjects treated in the *Fountain of Life*: God and His Wisdom, whose existence alone can be known to man; the first entity that can be known to man: will; matter (which is non-being, nothingness, since without form it does not exist) and form (which is being, light); and the conjunction of the two, which form all of creation.

Thou art wise; and wisdom, the fountain of life, flows from Thee, and every man is too brutish to know Thy wisdom.

Thou art wise, pre-existent to all pre-existence, and wisdom was with Thee as nurseling.

Thou art wise, and Thou didst not learn from any other than Thyself, nor acquire wisdom from another.

70

Thou art wise, and from Thy wisdom Thou didst send forth a predestined Will, and
    made it as an artisan and a craftsman,
To draw the stream of being from the nothingness as the light is drawn that comes
    from the eye,
To take from the source of light without a vessel, and to make all without a tool
    and cut and hew and cleanse and purify.
That Will called to the nothingness and it was cleft asunder, to existence and it was
    set up, to the universe and it was spread out.
It measured the heavens with a span, and its hand coupled the pavilion of the
    spheres,
And linked the curtains of all creatures with loops of potency; and its strength
    reaches as far as the last and lowest creature – 'the uttermost edge of the curtain
    in the coupling'.
                          (*Ibid.* pp. 32–3, slightly modified)

At the very beginning of the *Fountain of Life* Gabirol makes various statements, of the kind constantly found in neoplatonic treatises:

(1) Knowledge is the supreme aim of human life and its reason for
existing;

(2) The science of the soul, that is, the knowledge that man has of his soul,
opens up to him the knowledge of the world and of God, for man is a microcosm.

The knowing part being the best of man, that which man must seek is knowledge.
What he must especially seek to know is himself, in order to arrive at knowledge
of the other things that are not himself; for his essence comprehends all the things
and penetrates them, and all the things are subject to his power. As well as this,
he must seek to know the final cause for which he was created, so that he may
attain supreme felicity; for man's existence has a final cause for which he [was]
created, for everything is subject to the will of the one God.   (*Mekor Hayyim,* I, 1)

When one knows the art of demonstration [logic], what one should study first of
all, and what is the most useful study, is the essence of the soul, its faculties, its
accidents and everything that inheres in it and adheres to it, for the soul is the substratum of the sciences and it perceives all things by its faculties, which penetrate
everything. If you study the science of the soul, you will know its excellence, its
permanence and its subtlety in seizing everything, to the point where you shall be
astonished to see, at least in some way, its substance sustaining all things. You
will then realize that you yourself encompass everything that you know of things
that exist, and that the existing things that you know subsist in some way in yourself. In seeing yourself thus understanding (and penetrating) everything that you
know, you will see yourself comprehending the whole universe and understanding
it more quickly than the twinkling of an eye. But you could not do this if the soul
were not substance [both] subtle and strong, penetrating all things and being the
dwelling of all things.
                                                  (I, 4)

The first of these themes, that science is the ultimate aim of human life,
has profound philosophical resonances, and goes back to the very source of
all occidental philosophical thought; it is complemented by the second

theme, knowledge of oneself, which contains in embryo the knowledge of everything. The theme of the microcosm also returns at the beginning of the *Improvement of Moral Qualities*: 'If man's body is the reflection of the universe, his soul is the reflection of the Will.'

To the role of the divine Will Gabirol returns later at some length (the relation between God and His Will are in fact far from being clearly defined), but at the beginning of the book the author states that the divine Will has created the world, that it moves it and that nothing exists outside it. We thus see that, by knowing his own soul, man can know nature, that he has been created for this knowledge, and that the world was created by and depends on the divine Will. Some fine lines of the *Kingly Crown* express the bond that exists between the divine world and the soul.

> Who can contain Thy might, when from the abundance of Thy glory Thou didst create a pure radiance, hewn from the quarry of the Rock, and dug from the mine of Purity?
>
> And on it Thou didst set a spirit of wisdom, and Thou didst call it the Soul.
>
> Thou didst fashion its form from the flames of the Intelligence, and like a burning fire hast Thou wafted it.
>
> Thou didst send it into the body to serve it and to guard it, and it is as a fire within, and yet it does not burn it.
>
> From the fire of the spirit it was created, and went forth from nothingness to being, 'because the Lord descended upon it in fire'.
>
> Who can reach Thy wisdom, when Thou gavest the soul the power of knowledge which inheres in her?
>
> So that knowledge is her glory, and therefore decay has no rule over her, and she endures with the endurance of her foundation; this is her nature and her secret.
>
> (*The Kingly Crown*, pp. 49–50)

How can the soul acquire knowledge, and what knowledge does the author have in view? Gabirol takes up the theme of the prison of the soul, which is the world of nature. The soul belongs to the spiritual world, and, to return there, it must purify itself from the pollutions of this world by knowledge and the practice of pious exercises.

What exactly is meant by the word 'practice' is not further elaborated in the *Fountain of Life*, but one may form some notion of it from the treatise on morality, which is based on the idea of the golden mean. In the conduct of one's body and one's senses as in one's qualities and corresponding faults, one should cleave to the happy mean, and in support of the idea of qualities and faults contradicting each other, or corresponding with rather unrealistic neatness, Gabirol cites numerous biblical verses and passages from Arabic poets. It seems indeed that the 'practice' suggested by our author corresponds to a somewhat vague notion of moral conduct rather than to the precisely defined acts required by the rabbinical commandments.

To return to theoretical knowledge, the purpose of man's existence, Gabirol says that it means a knowledge of being:

There are only three things in being: matter and form, the first substance [God], and Will, which is the intermediary between the extremes. The reason that only these three things exist is that there cannot be an effect without a cause and there must be an intermediary between the two. The cause is the first substance; the effect is matter together with form; the intermediary between the two is the Will. Matter and form are like man's body and its shape, which is the composition of its members; Will is like the soul and the first substance is like the intellect. (*Mekor Hayyim* I, 3)

The rest of the book consists of an explication of these terms and of the entities that form the *Fountain of Life*: God, who is the first substance, His Will, Matter and Form. If man may apprehend them, this is because he finds himself the equivalent of these three beings: his intelligence corresponds to the first substance, his soul to the Will, his matter and his form to the First Matter and the First Form.

But can man really know God, that is, the Essence of the First Substance? He may know God's acts; but His very Essence, separated from the acts arising from it, is not within the sphere of human knowledge, for it is infinite and above all things:

The knowledge that is the purpose of man's existence is the knowledge of the universe as it is, and particularly the knowledge of the first substance, which carries it and sets it in movement. To know the veritable nature of substance, after setting aside the actions that emanate from it, is impossible; but it is possible to know its existence as it is described by the actions that emanate from it. If knowledge of the veritable nature of the substance is impossible this is because it is above all things and it is infinite.

(I, 5)

It also appears from the passage just quoted that the knowledge of which Gabirol speaks is that of being as it is, an understanding in the sense that to know a thing one must completely comprehend it. As Gabirol says in paragraph 4, concerning the soul: 'You shall see yourself comprehending the whole universe and understanding it.' This is evidently impossible as regards the infinite Being; thus God can only be known by His actions and by that which derives from Him; matter and form originate in God, and are therefore subject to our knowledge. The entire universe, spiritual as well as material, is composed of matter and form, and only of matter and form.

'These different kinds of matters and of forms, whatever their diversity, all come together in the idea of matter and form. In the perceptible things of nature, universal as much as specific, there is no other thing than matter and form' (I, 10). Matter and form are both one and multiple, similar and different. Since they are found at every degree of the hierarchy of beings, beings are first diversified by their forms, material and spiritual, while matter is one and universal. To the unity of matter corresponds the unity of form, and in another passage Gabirol declares unambiguously that what causes the diversity of beings is not form, for form is one and purely spiritual, but matter, which can be perfect and fine or coarse and heavy:

You should imagine the spiritual forms in the following manner: all of them are only one form and they do not differ in themselves; for they are all purely spiritual and their diversity arises only from the material basis that supports them. The closer matter is to perfection, the finer it is, and the form which is born by it is extremely simple and spiritual, and the converse. Take for example the light of the sun; this light in itself is one: if it meets a pure and fine air it penetrates it and one sees it quite other than one sees it in a dense and unclear air. It is the same with form. (IV, 2)

The properties, or the description, of these two principles that constitute the whole of reality are often and lengthily discussed by Gabirol, but not always in precisely the same way; thus in speaking of universal matter he declares that it is, that it is one, that it bears the diversity of things and that it subsists by itself.

If all things have only one universal matter, this necessarily has the following properties: that of being, that of subsisting by itself, that of having only one essence, that of bearing diversity and that of giving to all things its essence and its name. We accord it to the property of being, for non-being cannot be the matter of what is; that of subsisting by itself, for reasoning would go on *ad infinitum* if matter existed by something else; that of being one, for we require an unique matter for all things; that of bearing diversity, because diversity is reached through forms and the forms do not subsist by themselves; finally that of giving to all things its essence and its name, because, sustaining all things, it must be in all things and, being in all things, it must give to all things its essence and its name. (I, 6)

Nevertheless Gabirol declares elsewhere that this matter cannot subsist without form; universal matter cannot subsist by itself except potentially, not actively; and again, that universal matter and universal form cannot subsist without each other, even for a single instant.

The substance of matter, cannot be without form for a single instant, nor can the substance of form exist without matter. And in this there is a strong proof that the existence of each of them is of necessary existence only by the necessary existence of the other. Consider now the properties of unity, and you will find them attached to the form: it is unity that produces multiplicity and keeps it, it gives it its being, comprehends it and exists in all its parts, it is born by what is its substratum and it is more dignified than its substratum. In consequence, these properties are in form, because it is form which constitutes the essence of that within which it is, it gives it its being; comprehends it, retains it, is in all its parts, it is born in the matter which is its substratum, and it is superior to it, and matter is below it. (IV, 17)

Before going back to the source of matter and form and explaining how they are produced, one must descend towards the composite spiritual beings, which are called simple; for a being is called simple in relation to what is inferior to it, and composite in relation to what is superior; thus one can consider the entirety of existing things as if organized along a line that starts with universal matter and form; the further one goes away from this source, the more composite a being is in relation to that which precedes it, and simple in relation to that which follows it; even the Intellect, the first intelligible substance, is composed of matter and form. It may also be noted that however far one may be from the first source, the inferior is in a way the image of the superior.

Three Souls emanate from the Intellect: the rational Soul, the animal Soul and the vegetative Soul. These three souls are not only cosmic principles, but also the components of man, who unites in himself the image of all creation.

The Soul (for these three souls are in fact one single soul) gives its form to the beings of this world; but it does not thereby in any way diminish its own strength, for it is, contrary to corporeal substances, infinite, and close to the divine Will. The universal Soul, being very pure and infinite, totally penetrates the world, and in a way dwells in it. The Intellect being still purer, also pervades the world with its light, and more strongly than the Soul, for its light is finer. But the divine force, that is, the Will that is the source of the world, penetrates, encompasses and activates it more strongly still.

And when you observe that the essence of the simple substance has no end, when you consider its force, when you think of its faculty of penetrating into a thing that is before it and that is prepared to receive it, when you compare it with the corporeal substance, you will find that the corporeal substance is powerless to be everywhere and too feeble to penetrate things; and you will find that the simple substance, the substance of the universal soul, is diffused through the entire universe and that it sustains it in itself on account of its subtlety and simplicity: and you will find similarly that the substance of the universal intelligence is diffused through the entire universe and that it penetrates it. The cause of this is the subtlety of the two substances, their force and their light: and on account of this the substance of the intelligence is diffused into the interior of things and penetrates them. Therefore according to this view all the more ought the power of the holy God to penetrate all things, exist in all things and act in all things beyond time.

(*The Fountain of Life*, trans. H. E. Wedeck, pp. 34–40; cf. *Mekor Hayyim*, III, 14)

Contrary to the actions of sensible beings, the action of the simple substances in no way reduces their essential light, as the sun, irradiating the universe with its rays, is no less pure and luminous.

... the emanation or the issuance of the form from the simple spiritual substance and of its action in the corporeal matter, like the light of the sun, that is diffused in the air, penetrates it and yet does not appear visible on account of the subtlety of the air, until it meets a solid body, like the earth: then the light becomes sensible because it cannot penetrate the parts of this body and be diffused through them, but stops on the surface of the body, and its essence is concentrated so that its emanation becomes brighter. In a similar manner the lights of the simple substances penetrate and flow through each other without the perception of the senses, on account of the subtlety and the simplicity of these substances. But when the lights penetrate to the corporeal matter, then the light becomes visible and is revealed to the senses on account of the thickness of the corporeal matter.

(*Ibid.* pp. 40–1; cf. *Mekor Hayyim* III, 15)

First Matter and First Form are closest to the Will; from their combination is born the Intellect, then the Soul, and from the Soul, nature, the last of the simple substances, is born. Corporeal substance comes from nature.

Thus we have under the name of 'matter':

(1) First universal matter, which is entirely simple and absolutely without form, at least potentially, for according to some passages, it seems that the First Matter cannot subsist without form: it is the substratum of the intelligible world and the corporeal world, of everything that exists, except God;

(2) Universal corporeal matter, which emanates from nature; it acts as a substratum to the forms of corporeality and quantity; the celestial spheres and the sublunary beings are made of it.

(3) The matter common to the celestial spheres, which is eternal and is not subject to generation and corruption;

(4) The matter of this lower world, again called general natural matter, that of the elements (fire, air, water, earth), subject to generation and corruption;

(5) Natural particular matter, that of composite, material beings.

The second of these matters, universal corporeal matter, is the 'bearer' of nine of the ten Aristotelian categories and is universal form as it appears in our world; the tenth category, the substance, is universal matter as we see it in the corporeal world.

Let us consider this universal corporeal matter, starting point of human meditation, for it marks the frontier between the corporeal and the spiritual worlds. When Gabirol speaks of matter and of form, as I have pointed out, the source of diversity is sometimes matter and sometimes form; and often matter is the first emanation out of the essence of God while form is an emanation of the Will, while in other passages First Matter and First Form both emanate directly from the Will. In fact, matter and form meet at all levels, and what is simple in relation to the composite, is composite in relation to what is simpler than itself:

Which shows that the simple substances, which are superior to the composite, are composed of matter and form; as has been already mentioned, the inferior which issues from the superior is its image, for if the inferior issues from the superior, the order of the corporeal substances must be like the order of the spiritual substances; just as corporeal substance is ordered on three levels: the gross body, the subtle body and the matter and form that compose them, so also spiritual substance is ordered on three levels: the spiritual substance which corresponds to the corporeal substance, the spiritual substance which is more spiritual than the first, and the matter and the form that compose them. (IV, 3)

It may be added that the order of the composite substances enables one to perceive the order of the simple substances in the same way as a microcosm enables one to perceive the order of the macrocosm.

If you will imagine the structure of the whole, that is, the universal body and the spiritual substances that contain it, consider the formation of man and take it as an image. For the body of man corresponds to the universal body and the spiritual substances that move it correspond to the universal substances that move the universal body, and among these spiritual substances the inferior substance obeys the superior substance and is submissive to it, until the motion reaches the substance of the intelligence. You will then find that the intelligence orders and dominates these substances and you will find that all the substances that move the body of man follow the intelligence and obey it while it perceives them and judges them.

(Ibid. p. 131; cf. *Mekor Hayyim* III, 44)

If we are able to describe the whole of creation and its organization, this is because the inferior, in this case man, is the image of the superior; he is its image because the superior directs the inferior and flows into it; in man as in the universe, the surrounding substances are spiritual and more general, they are the matter of the inferior substances, commanding them and giving them movement and light; and thus, from level to level, one reaches the absolute unity, the Intellect.

You have revealed a great mystery to me and a profound principle by telling me that the inferior motion of the universal substances has its cause in the motion of the substances that are superior to them: and that for this reason the inferior substances are submissive to the superior substances and obey them, until the motion reaches the highest substance. We thus find that all substances are submissive to the highest substance, that they obey it, that they follow it and that they move at its command. And I consider that the order of the particular soul imitates the disposition of the universal world.   *(Ibid.* pp. 131–2; cf. *Mekor Hayyim* III, 44)

Let us return to corporeal matter, the substratum of the nine categories and the starting-point of human meditation. The source of the human soul is situated at a much higher point than this matter, for it arises directly from the Intellect. Why then must the soul begin its quest for knowledge from the body and its categories? In immersing itself in the corporeal world the soul has forgotten its celestial origin and it must purify itself through the knowledge of sensible things; it must recover the active knowledge which, because of its sojourn in this world, it possesses only in potentiality.

You ask me now: why is the soul deprived of impressions of knowledge, so that it must learn and remember? Know that the soul is created with the true knowledge, from which it follows that it possesses in itself a knowledge that is its own. But, when the soul is joined to the corporeal substance and is commingled with it, it is too far removed to be able to receive these impressions, for the darkness of substance envelope it to such an extent that its light is quenched, and its substance is coarsened; it becomes like a clear mirror whose light has been obscured and whose substance has been coarsened, because of its having been joined to a gross substance. It is for this purpose that the All High Creator has formed the substance, that is, the world, and disposed it in this beautiful regular order; and He has fixed the senses in the soul so that through them it can perceive the sensible forms and figures, and through these, remember the intelligible forms and figures and pass from potentiality to actuality.

... the soul in perceiving things is like a man who sees many things and only looks at some of them, and when he goes further away he preserves the impression he has of them in his imagination and in his thought ...

And the profit that the soul draws from its attachment to sensible things, is that it becomes clarified and purified; that which was hidden in it is manifested in acts and it reaches the knowledge of secondary substances and secondary accidents by that of the primary substances and primary accidents. (v, 65 and 66)

Knowledge of the world, that is, of matter and form, is not veritable knowledge, but only the road that leads to veritable knowledge, that of God, or rather that of the divine Will, for God Himself is unknowable. Knowledge as always in medieval theologies, is an ascent towards the divinity. This world and the world of the spheres, then the world of simple substances, are the aim and object of science, because they carry the traces of the divine Will. When Gabirol describes the relations of matter and form what he has in mind is the tracing of the divine Will; he compares the world to an open book where one may read the divine text when one wants and knows how to read it.

This science of the divine Will is twofold; on its highest level it is knowledge of the Will in itself when it is separated from matter and form, and is entirely divine and perfectly pure; but it is also knowledge of the Will as it is inscribed in matter and form, that is, knowledge of the material and spiritual world revealing the action of the Will.

The second way, the second manner of knowing the Will, is a preparation for the first and necessarily precedes it:

Strive constantly to understand the essence of universal matter and of universal form, each separately and without the other, and to understand the mode of diversity that form attains, in what way it is communicated and how it penetrates matter in the absolute sense and how it pervades all substances according to their different degrees; distinguish matter from form, form from Will and Will from movement, and distinguish in your intelligence all [these ideas] one from another, by a true distinction. When you shall have reached a sound knowledge of all this, your soul will be purified and your intelligence will become clear and will penetrate into the world of the Intellect, and your regard will embrace the universality of matter and form. And matter with all the forms that are in it shall be as a book placed before you; you will look at the signs traced thereon, you will contemplate its figures by means of your thought, and then you will hope to know what is beyond. The purpose of all this is to know the world of the Divinity, which is altogether great, while all that is here below, in comparison with Him, is extremely small. This sublime knowledge is reached by a double road: first by knowledge of the Will, which comprehends matter and form, secondly by the knowledge of that superior faculty when it is pure of all mixing of matter and form; but, to arrive at the knowledge of this faculty, which is entirely distinct from matter and from form, you must attach yourself to the faculty which is commingled with matter and form and by degrees ascend with this faculty, until you arrive at its origin and at its source. (v, 73)

The purpose of this long study, the final reward at the end of the difficult road, is the return of the soul to its Source, having the absolute certainty of having gone beyond the stage of death, for death and life only affect material substances; and when the soul has returned to the pure world of the Intellect, it has attached itself to the Will, which is higher by far than all the spiritual matter and form. The soul has thus reached the Source of Life: 'Deliverance from death and attachment to the source of life are the fruit that one gathers from this endeavour' (v, 73).

The concluding paragraph sums up the whole work. Man must first distance himself from all sensible things, concern himself only with the intelligible things and turn entirely towards God; God will then come to his aid. The desire for the good must come from man; it is man who must make the effort to detach himself from matter, and only then, when he shall thus have come closer to Him, will God help him to come to the end of the road and bring him close to Himself, in eternal life: 'He will favour you with His regard and He will be generous towards you, for He is the source of beneficence. May He be praised and exalted! Amen' (v, 74).

The quest for the intelligible, the spiritual ascent towards God, is, according to Ibn Gabirol, the hidden sense of the Scriptures. This is evident in the allegorical exegeses on Genesis 2: 8 that are quoted by Abraham Ibn Ezra as being Gabirol's words:

I shall reveal to you the mystery of the garden and the flowers and the tunics, and I have not found this mystery in any of the great, but only in Rabbi Solomon Ibn Gabirol, for he was profoundly versed in the knowledge of the soul; Eden is the superior world; the garden is full of angelic spirits which are its plants; the river is like a mother, that is, the universal matter of all bodies; the four branches of the river are the elements; man is the rational soul that gives names; Eve, as is shown by her name [*Hava*, from the root *haya*, to live], designates the animal soul, and the serpent the concupiscient soul, as is shown by the name *nahaš* (= serpent), which is of the same form as the verse [Genesis 44: 5] *ki naheš yenaheš* [which means, 'and whereby indeed he divineth']; the tree of knowledge is generation, which derives its force from the garden; and the vegetative is joined to the dust; and the seed of woman crushes the head [of the bodily appetite] that is lifted and the end of the animal is the beginning of the vegetative; the tunics of skin are the body; Adam was driven out of the garden to till the earth from which he was drawn, and this is the whole work of man; the tree of life is the knowledge of the upper world, and it is thus that it is written [Proverbs 3: 18]: [*Torah*] is a tree of life to them that lay hold upon her; and the cherubim are the angels, and the flaming sword symbolizes the sun.

(M. Friedlander, *Essays* (Hebrew Appendix), p. 40)

In the same commentary on Genesis, Ibn Ezra also cites Gabirol's interpretation of Jacob's ladder (Genesis 28: 12): 'Rabbi Solomon the Spaniard has said that the ladder is the symbol of the superior soul and that the angels of God signify the thoughts of wisdom (*hokhma*).'

Evidently, these two allegorical interpretations repeat themes and terms that occur in the *Fountain of Life*, the flow of matter from the superior towards the inferior world, the soul that enjoys felicity through knowledge of the superior world. Nevertheless, in this neoplatonic approach to biblical exegesis, we are struck by the lack of conceptions peculiar to Gabirol.

Another, very brief, exegesis, of Isaiah 43: 7 (also reported by Abraham Ibn Ezra) is even more cryptic. 'I have created him, I have formed him, I have made him. Rabbi Solomon, poet of finely rhythmical works, explained on this subject that it referred to the mystery of the universe, and in this he did not follow the sense of the chapter.'

Ibn Gabirol's last known exegesis, on Daniel 22: 30, is eschatological, and I shall return to it.

The last verses of the *Kingly Crown* show us the man Gabirol, not only as a philosopher but also as an extremely fervent believer, supplicating God to help him to accomplish on earth the mission of every man: to love and know his Creator.

Therefore let it be Thy will, O Lord our God and God of our fathers, sovereign of all the worlds, to have pity on me and be near to me.
To visit me with the visitation of Thy will, to bear to me the light of Thy countenance, to let me find Thy grace.
And so not recompense me according to my deeds, nor make me the reproach of the foolish,
In the midst of my days do not take me away, and do not hide Thy face from me.
Cleanse me of my sins, and do not cast me from Thy countenance,
Let me live with honour, and after that with honour take me.
And when Thou shalt take me out of this world, bring me in peace to the life of the world to come,
Summon me on high, and let me dwell among saints,
Number me among those who have a portion in eternal life.

And make me worthy to shine with the light of Thy countenance.

(*The Kingly Crown*, pp. 66-7)

Solomon Ibn Gabirol's influence on later Jewish philosophers was limited, for he did not treat the problem that in the thirteenth century became a matter of urgency, the relationship between philosophy and faith. We do not know if he himself profoundly felt this want of correlation between the God of philosophers and the God of Israel who revealed Himself to the Jewish people, a theme that was the principal matter of Judah Halevi's *Kuzari*, and, handled in quite another manner, the question that Maimonides set out to answer in the *Guide of the Perplexed*; but we find no trace of it in Ibn Gabirol.

Moreover, in the course of the next century the Aristotelian trend, where the process of emanation differs from that described by Gabirol, began to be widely accepted. All this explains why echoes of Gabirol's doctrine are only found in Neoplatonists like Moses Ibn Ezra, who held him in high esteem, or Joseph Ibn Zaddik, who will be discussed later. Abraham Ibn Ezra was also influenced by Gabirol, but did not explicitly cite him, except for the allegorical explications of which I have spoken. His ideas and terminology may still be found in the Spanish Kabbalah and especially in the philosopher and Kabbalist Isaac Ibn Latif. As I have said, Shem Tov ben Joseph Falaquera, the thirteenth-century translator into Hebrew of excerpts from the *Fountain of Life*, greatly admired Gabirol, and he often cites him in his commentary on the *Guide of the Perplexed*, entitled the *Guide to the Guide*. He is quoted by Ḥanokh al-Kostantini in the *Divine Visions*. However, many fourteenth-century Jewish philosophers have not yet been studied, and it is quite possible that he is cited by them. As already noted, Isaac and Judah Abrabanel knew of him. Like Ḥanokh, Abraham Ibn Daud, who wrote one of the first Aristotelian books and was perhaps one of the translators of the *Fountain of Life* into Latin, attacks him vigorously in several passages, accusing him of the following faults:

(1) Intending his book for all religious confessions and not for the people of Israel alone;

(2) Developing one single subject at exaggerated length;

(3) Lacking scientific method in employing unauthenticated premises and dissimulating this shortcoming behind a quantity of arguments each as unconvincing as the next;

(4) Inducing the Jewish people into error; but this last reproach, because of an incorrect translation of Ibn Daud's original Arabic, was turned into Hebrew and transmitted by scholars as 'he proffered great calumnies concerning the Jewish people'.

The philosopher Ibn Gabirol was evidently destined to misinterpretation.

BAḤYA IBN PAQUDA

The earliest appearance of an ascetic current in Judaism, inspired by a similar movement in Islam, belongs to the eleventh century. Baḥya ben Joseph Ibn Paquda, who lived in the second part of the eleventh century, most probably at Saragossa, is the author of one of the most celebrated books of pietism; his *Hidāya 'ilā Farā'iḍ al-Qulūb* (*Introduction to the Duties of the Hearts*), was the first work translated into Hebrew by Judah Ibn Tibbon, *ca.* 1160, as *Sefer Ḥovot ha-Levavot*. A second translation was made by Joseph Kimhi, at the same period, and other versions followed, in many languages. The book inspired generations of pietists and continues to be widely read. Ibn Tibbon's Hebrew translation has been constantly used and republished; that by Kimhi is still in manuscript.

The essential aim of the work is to call the attention of the faithful to the duties of the heart, those that concern the inner experience. These are often forgotten in favour of exterior practical duties and only the latter have given rise to an extensive halakhic literature. The book is divided into ten chapters, which, by progressive degrees, lead the faithful towards the veritable love of God: the Unity of God, the examination of Creation, the service of God.

The plan of the work is borrowed from the Arab mystics and their ascetic theology, but the first two chapters, that on the acceptance of the Unity of God, and that on the examination of created things, are neoplatonic in spirit and probably drawn from the *Ikhwān al-Ṣāfā* (*the Encyclopedia of the Sincere Brothers*) and, perhaps, from hermetic sources; the definition of reason is that of the Mu'tazilites.

In his introduction Baḥya affirms that knowledge, Science, is the supreme gift that God has made to man. It is divisible into three parts, physics, mathematics, and theology.

The book itself speaks only of theology, and here Baḥya gives a summary of Saadiah's distinctions:

The avenues which the Creator has opened for the knowledge of His law and religion are three. The first is a sound intellect; the second, the Book of His Law revealed to Moses, His prophet; the third, the traditions which we have received from our ancient sages, who received them from the Prophets. These avenues have already been discussed at adequate length by our great teacher, Saadiah.

The science of the Torah, moreover, falls into two parts: The first aims at the knowledge of practical duties and is the science of external conduct. The second deals with the duties of the heart, namely, its sentiments and thoughts, and is the science of the inward life.

The practical duties likewise fall into two divisions. The former consists of duties which reason would have enjoined, even if the Torah had not made them obligatory. The latter, of duties dependent for their sanction on the authority of Revelation, and of which reason neither approves nor disapproves.

(*Duties of the Hearts*, trans. M. Hyamson, p. 17)

The knowledge of practical duties is as important as the duties of the heart since

Man ... needs external means, by the aid of which he may resist his despicable instinct – the lust for animal enjoyments – and revitalize the marks of his noblest endowment – the intellect. These aids are the contents of the Torah, whereby God, through His messengers and prophets, taught His creatures the way to serve Him. Secondly, the intellect is a spiritual entity, originating in the higher, spiritual world. It is a stranger in this world of gross material bodies. Sensual lust in man is the product of natural forces and of a combination of his physical elements. Its foundation and root are in this world. Food gives it strength. Physical pleasures add to its vigour, while the intellect, because it is a stranger here, stands without support or ally, and all are against it. Hence it follows that it must become weak and that it needs an external means to repel the mighty power of lust and overcome it. The Torah is the remedy for such spiritual maladies and moral diseases. The Torah therefore prohibits many kinds of food, apparel, sexual relations, certain acquisitions and practices, all of which strengthen sensual lust; it also exhorts us to use those means which will resist lust and are its opposites. (*Ibid.* p. 195)

Throughout the journey leading the soul towards its union with the Divine Light, reason, taken in its kalāmic sense, assists and complements the revealed precepts. These various conceptual elements are, however, only the framework of Baḥya's resolutely ascetic thought.

The starting-point of the believer's itinerary is the profound comprehension of the idea that God is One; and here we should quote Baḥya's interpretation of the famous verse 'Hear O Israel . . .' In effect, Baḥya bases all belief on God as Creator of the world.

When we inquired as to what is the most necessary among the fundamental principles of our religion, we found that the wholehearted acceptance of the Unity of God – the root and foundation of Judaism – is the first of the gates of the Torah. By the acceptance of the Unity of God, the believer is distinguished from the infidel. It is the head and front of religious truth. Whoever has deviated from it will neither practise any duty properly nor retain any creed permanently. Hence, God's first words to us on Mount Sinai were (Exodus 20: 2) 'I am the Lord thy God . . . Thou shalt have no other gods before Me.' And later on, He exhorted us through His prophet (Deut. 6: 4) 'Hear, O Israel, The Lord our God, the Lord is One.' You should study this section (of the Shema) to its close, and you will observe how its contents proceed from topic to topic, comprising in all ten topics, that number corresponding to the Ten Commandments. First there is the command to believe in the Creator, when it says, 'Hear, O Israel, The Lord.' In using the word *Shema* (Hear), the text refers not to hearing with the ear, but to inward belief, as in the passages (Ex. 24: 7) 'We will do and we will hear'; (Deut. 6: 3) 'Hear therefore O Israel, and observe to do it.' Whenever the term 'hear' is used in this way, it is intended to express nothing else but believing and accepting.

Having thus been placed under the obligation of believing in the reality of the Creator's existence, we are enjoined to believe that He is our God, as indicated in the word *Elohenu* 'our God'.

(Ibid. p. 55)

As we shall see, it is not only the Aristotelian philosopher whom Judah Halevi opposes when he makes the Rabbi say in the *Kuzari* 'I believe in the God of Abraham, Isaac and Israel . . .', thus declaring his preference for particularism over universalism, but also a long Jewish universalist tradition of which Baḥya is a representative.

'QUESTIONES DE ANIMA'

The destiny of the soul brings us to a short treatise written in Arabic: *Kitāb Ma'ānī al-nafs* (*Questiones de Anima – A treatise about what is the soul*), which was probably composed between 1050 and 1150. The author is unknown. The work was at first attributed to Baḥya Ibn Paquda, author of the *Introduction to the Duties of the Hearts*, and a modern Hebrew translation by Isaac Broydé (Paris, 1896) still accepts him as author; but I. Goldziher, who published the original Arabic text in 1907, showed that this attribution was incorrect.

The philosophical elements utilized are of Platonic and neoplatonic, sometimes Aristotelian, origin. Saadiah, especially in his *Commentary on the Book of Creation*, is often cited with approval; Nissim ben Jacob of Kairouan (*ca.* 990–1062), a learned Talmudist of Mu'tazilite tendencies, is cited once; Ibn Janaḥ (a celebrated Spanish grammarian of the first half of the ninth century) is cited and refuted, also once. One of the characteristics of this treatise is the identification between the *true philosophers* and revealed religion, and throughout the book quotations from the Bible are used to support the philosophical exposition.

According to our author there are two sorts of substances: the spiritual substances and the corporeal substances; the first are good, luminous, divine; the second dark, crude, bad. All things come from God, but in a very different manner. From God emanates eternally a first intelligible entity, which the Greeks call the Active Intellect, and the *Torah* calls 'Glory', 'Indwelling', 'Name'. From this first entity necessarily derives a second, called universal soul and 'Glory of the God of Israel'; the third is 'Nature' or 'Angel'. These three first entities are eternal, luminous, totally spiritual. The fourth entity, contrary to the first three, is created in time and space, and not produced by emanation. This is matter, substratum of all bodies, which the author identifies with the 'Darkness' of Genesis 1: 2.

Then follow in ontological order the other simple bodies, each arising from that which precedes it: the celestial sphere, the celestial bodies, fire, air, water, earth. Only these seven simple bodies are created, the others being composites of various degrees. The two substances, corporeal and spiritual, are absolutely, or almost absolutely, opposed.

However, these two worlds, opposed as they may be, are joined in man. A spark of the Intellect, the human soul, is exiled in the human body, and the theme of the book is precisely a reflection on the drama of this separation and on the itinerary that may conduct the soul in its return to its dwelling-place and source, the Intellect.

The idea maintained by certain philosophers that the soul is the form of the body or is an accident of the body, and thus perishes with it is vigorously rejected by our author; as is also Avicenna's idea that the soul is created with the body, but does not perish, remaining eternally in existence. In truth, the soul is eternal 'a parte ante et a parte post'. When it is still within the sphere of the Intellect, the soul knows all things and nothing is hidden from it; but because of its descent into the body it forgets Wisdom and it is by again acquiring Wisdom that it will be enabled to liberate itself. The reason given by the writer for this exile is not very convincing: the soul must learn to appreciate celestial felicity at its true value.

The descent towards the corporeal substance is gradual; the soul must traverse the various spheres before joining the body, and each of the spheres and the elements leaves its imprint on the soul and invests it with shadow and darkness.

Not only the soul must clothe itself in corporeal forms; the angels, messengers of God, must also assume matter when they descend on earth to bring their message. This explains how the prophets were able to see the angels with their fleshly eyes, while seeing with the eyes of their souls that their interlocutors were angels.

The help that God gives the soul is not limited to the sending of messengers. There is also the *Torah*, which we know to be identical with Wisdom and to speak the language of men. However, the Word of God as it is addressed to the prophet differs from the essential Word, that is, the first emanation, the Intellect, which is also called, as I have said, 'Glory', 'Indwelling', 'Name', and 'Word'.

The mechanism of visions and auditory phenomena is that described by Saadiah, who is cited at length. The second air (see pp. 29–30) manifests itself in the various colours of fire, and the words are seen and heard by the prophets, and only by them. The idea of the divine pedagogy that one finds in Saadiah and, in another form, in Isaac Israeli is illustrated by the relations between man and the animals; when a man wishes to make an animal obey him, to come to him or to go away, to make it move or to feel it, he imitates the sounds of animal language or he uses an instrument, as the hunter plays on a flute when he wants to attract birds. God does the same with men. He speaks to the prophets according to their way of speech, and not in the essential language that He uses in His relations with the spiritual beings.

The *Torah* is thus an instrument of Wisdom; certainly, it is not only traditional; it is a great error to claim that the revealed Scripture has no authority in matters of philosophy and thus does not answer the essential need of the soul, which is to know. Revelation in its entirety is spiritual, but we do not know how to understand it. Nevertheless, if we apply all our forces to the analysis and study of revelation, we shall find a more complete wisdom in it than in rational thought. The rational soul, detached from the Intellect and invested with a body, must purify itself upon its descent on earth with the aid of this wisdom as well as of good deeds, in order to return to its source. But the human body does not only contain the rational soul. Since it is the most 'composite' body of all creation, it has also been endowed with the vegetative and animal souls. Before returning to the Intellect, the rational soul must accomplish its mission, which is to transform the two inferior souls, the vegetative and the animal, into its own substance in order to take them back with itself towards the celestial world. During its stay on earth, the soul must first recollect the knowledge that it forgot when it descended towards the world of the elements; secondly it must taste the sufferings of exile and aspire to the happiness of eternity and, finally, purify other souls.

The return of the soul to the celestial world is easy or difficult according to the degree of the purity of the soul in question: a pure soul will easily traverse the elements and the spheres; for a soul heavy with sin the road will be hard and sometimes even impossible. Our author describes at length the various and horrible afflictions that await the ignorant and wicked soul, the souls with the heaviest load of sins being obliged to dwell among the demons; on the other hand, the pure soul will dwell with the angels.

The Neoplatonists

JOSEPH BEN JACOB IBN ẒADDIK

Ibn Ẓaddik was one of the philosophers influenced by Isaac Israeli and Ibn Gabirol. We do not know the date of his birth, and we know very little of his life; he seems to have been a well-known poet, one of the circle of poets and philosophers that included Moses Ibn Ezra and Judah Halevi. From 1138 he exercized the functions of a *dayyan* (rabbinical judge) at Córdoba, and he died in 1149.

Written in Arabic, his work has only survived in an anonymous Hebrew translation called *Ha-Olam ha-Katan* (*The Microcosm*). Ibn Ẓaddik expounds familiar neoplatonic themes; the microcosm first, which gives its name to the book. Through knowledge of his own body, man understands the corporeal world, and through that of the soul he has access to the spiritual world.

Ibn Ẓaddik divides his work into four books:

– The first deals with the material world, matter and form, and the resemblance between the human body and the material world;

– The second treats the spiritual world and man as microcosm, souls and the intellect;

– The two last, in contrast to the two first, which are decidedly neoplatonic, discuss God and man from a point of view quite close to that of the *kalām*, although as regards the important doctrinal points the Neoplatonism of the beginning of the work is in no way contradicted. Book III speaks of God and His attributes, and Book IV of reward and punishment.

The non-denominational and nevertheless profoundly Jewish character of the *Microcosm* is evident in the following passage:

We have said that the way to the knowledge of the All is the knowledge by man of his soul, for in knowing his body he knows the corporeal world and in knowing his soul he knows the spiritual world; through this knowledge man attains the knowledge of his Creator, as it is said in Job 19: 26: yet in my flesh shall I see God. Do not imagine that this knowledge can be achieved without study or research; the absurdity of this idea is evident, for it is not for nothing that God has given man intellect and the faculty of reasoning, but precisely for this reason; secondly, the Creator, may He be blessed, is not the object either of sensation or of immediate comprehension and man can only know him by the intellect after study and research, as it is said of our father Abraham, that he inquired and thought and reflected and when he had understood the Holy One, blessed be He, He revealed Himself to him. We see very well that virtue, i.e. the knowledge of God attributed to Abraham, is considered in the Bible as the most eminent and the most important of all the gifts that God was to give to Israel: And they shall teach no more every man his neighbour, and every man his brother, saying, Know the Lord: for they shall all know me, from the least of them unto the greatest of them [Jeremiah 31: 34], and the reason for this knowledge is the prophecy according to the verse: And it shall come to pass afterward, that I will pour out my spirit upon all flesh; and your sons and your daughters shall prophesy [Joel 2: 28], and concerning this, the philosophers have said that only a man who is a prophet by nature in his generation, or a recognized philosopher, can serve the Cause of Causes. (Hebrew edition, p. 21)

This identification between prophecy and philosophy gives rise to problems, for philosophy includes a number of sciences hard to envisage as having been revealed to the Jewish people on Mount Sinai; Ibn Ẓaddik resolves the question by affirming that at the time of the giving of the *Torah* God had bestowed prophecy on the whole people, for such was His will; but since at the present time no one can attain philosophy, that is, prophecy, except by the intermediary of science, all must successively acquire the various degrees of science.

Science and the desire urging man towards God are common to all men; but the aptitude for science depends, according to Ibn Ẓaddik, essentially on climatic conditions. A temperate climate predisposes to science. It is known that the world is divided into seven climates, so that the fourth, that in the centre, is the best balanced. The idea of the excellence of the land of Israel and the fact that its inhabitants are predestined to the knowledge of God was to be expounded at some length by Judah Halevi.

Knowledge leads us to the divine attributes of action, but not at all to God's essence, for only His existence can be demonstrated and of His essence we can know nothing since one only knows through causes, and God has no cause. God is beyond space and time, and when we say that the Will of God has created the world, neither the statement that creation is taking place nor the statement that creation took place at a definite time correspond to the truth of the matter.

Speaking of creation, Ibn Ẓaddik uses a term and a theme current during the Middle Ages, that of 'secret'. Not all men can understand the secrets of philosophy; thus only an indication should be given, and the intelligent man will comprehend of his own accord.

Philosophy, however, is only the first part of the worship that we owe to God, the second being the performance of the commandments. But, how are we to explain that the Law of Moses is precisely the practice ordained by God, and not the Koran or the Gospels? Ibn Ẓaddik does not answer this question; he is satisfied, as was Saadiah, to attribute the gift of the Law to the divine Goodness. God has given the commandments so that man may accomplish the design of his creation: to serve God and free himself from matter, and thus attain the spiritual world. Like Saadiah, he divides the commandments into two kinds, those of which we know the reason and those of which we do not know the reason, for it is too secret and subtle for man's comprehension. Can one say that such or such a commandment is more important than another? From the point of view of the order given by God, there is no difference, and all the religious commandments should be accomplished with the same fervour and the same fidelity.

If reward and punishment are not meted out by God in this world, this is because they can in no way be corporeal. Each human being will receive what he deserves in the future world: the pure soul will rejoin its source and the sinful soul, heavy with transgression and the weight of matter, and thus unable to return to its natural place, will be drawn into the movement of the sphere and never achieve rest. Seen in this way, the paradise promised to small children and to animals in Saadiah Gaon's theology has no place in Ibn Zaddik's scheme of things and this author enumerates at length all the arguments (very close to the *kalām*) which absolutely exclude the possibility of any amends for sufferings endured by beings who could never have been philosophers.

During the twelfth century two currents of thought were added to those that have already been discussed. One of these was Ismailism, and some of its concepts have occupied a special position throughout the history of Jewish thinking, chiefly because of the work of Judah Halevi. The other was astrology; it will be discussed at some length when we return to Spain, where a brilliant group of poets and philosophers flourished in the twelfth century; I must, however, first speak briefly of Nethanel ben al-Fayyumi in whom these two currents, as yet not encountered in Judaism, are very much in evidence.

NETHANEL BEN AL-FAYYUMI

Nethanel most probably lived during the twelfth century in Yemen; he was perhaps the father of Jacob ben Nethanel ben al-Fayyumi, a scholar of San‘a, to whom Maimonides addressed his famous Letter intended for the Jews of Yemen.

The only work written by Nethanel is the *Bustān al-'Uqūl* (*The Garden of the Intellects*) which was published with an English translation by D. Levine (*The Garden of Wisdom* (New York, 1908)), after a unique manuscript preserved at Columbia University. A Hebrew translation was made in 1954, by J. Kafih. Even in Yemen the book was not widely known (only one Yemenite author cites it); and it was almost forgotten when D. Levine attracted scholarly attention to it.

The Ismaili theology that so strongly influenced the book was supposed to be esoteric, and although Ismaili missionaries were active in the greater part of the Islamic world, their ideas, for obvious reasons, were better known in the regions governed by Ismaili rulers. An outline of the doctrine may be useful.

The Shi‘ite schism is an outcome of the conflict over the succession of the prophet Muhammad. For the Shi‘ites, only the descendants of Ali, chosen by Muhammad himself, are legitimate successors, or Imams, and all the other Muslim sovereigns are usurpers. A whole theology was elaborated around the series of Imams.

The Imam is elevated above ordinary humanity, not only by superhuman qualities, or the dignity conferred on him by God, but by his descent from the line of Ali. Since the creation of Adam, a luminous and divine substance has been transmitted to one (or two) individuals in each generation, and, after Muhammad and Ali, it was transmitted to Ali's descendant in each generation, so that the Imam is purer than other men; he possesses divine spiritual forces; he is exempt from evil tendencies and holy forms inhere in his intelligence.

Many of the Shi'ites, whatever the series of Imams they admit, believe in a 'hidden' Imam, the last of the Imams, who will return to establish the reign of God. The 'Duodecimans' hold that the twelfth Imam, supposedly dead at the age of eight, has remained alive, invisible to men, in a hidden place, and will reappear at the end of days to purge the earth of all iniquity and establish the reign of justice and peace. The Ismailis, however, at their origin concluded the series of visible Imams with the seventh. They constructed a very special theology, strongly influenced by Neoplatonism. In Nethanel ben al-Fayyumi one finds not only the Ismaili ideas that were popularized by the famous *Ikhwān al-Ṣafā*, but also esoteric teachings that were divulged to the common people. One may assume that Nethanel had comparatively easy access to these esoteric writings when the official theology was Shi'ite, that is, during the period of the Fatimid Empire, which in Yemen lasted until 1174.

The *Bustān al-'Uqūl* is divided into seven chapters and the number seven is not accidental, for it plays an important role in Nethanel's theology.

The book begins with an invocation addressed to God, and the epithets used are immediately revealing, for God is called the Cause of the Cause of Causes:

Praised be God, yea the God of Israel, the First preceding every primeval thing; the Cause of the cause of causes; the Ancient who passeth not away; who is one, but not in the category of number, declared a Unity, Unequalled, Everlasting; who 'beareth not nor was He born'. [Koran, Sura CXII]

... the Absolute Unity, the One in eternity; who emanateth souls, originateth forms, createth and produceth the bodies. Great are His benevolence, honor and might. He is free from limitations, acting at will. His are the celestial sphere, wisdom and power, decreeing and disposing, laudation and eulogy, beneficence and munificence, dominion and perpetuity, majesty and grandeur, creation and empire, uniqueness, and omnipotence. He is the Living One who dieth not; the Eternal by virtue of His eternity; the Permanent because of His Permanence; the Divine Creator through His Supreme power, potent to do whatsoever He wishes. Nothing is like unto Him; He created all things out of nothing. Unto him we cannot apply definition, attribute spatiality or quality. He has no throne that would imply place nor a footstool that would imply sitting. He cannot be described as rising up or sitting down, as moving or as motionless, as bearing or as being born, as having characteristics or as in anywise defined. Before Him all the idols were humiliated, and all creatures bowed in adoration. He does not enter or go out, descend or ascend. He is far beyond the reach of the human intellect, transcending apprehension, conception, and even conjecture. His essence is indescribable and cannot be grasped by means of the attributes.

(*The Garden of Wisdom*, trans. D. Levine, p. 1)

Of God, one can know nothing and say nothing; and even the Cause of Causes, the First Created, identical with the intellect, cannot conceive Him who has created it outside time and space. The creative act cannot be called by the name 'cause', for the cause is bound to its effect, and God cannot be bound to the world. Nethanel reproaches Baḥya Ibn Paquda, author of the *Introduction to the Duties of the Hearts*, with having identified God with the Cause of causes, the First Created; 'The Universal Soul is caused by the Intellect, which is the Cause of the causes, and which the Creator, by his wish, his will and his commandments, has drawn from nothing' (*ibid.* 8).

These three terms, Wish, Will, and Commandment, it seems, designate the creative act, a mystery of which we know nothing, the non-being from which the Intellect burst forth. The veritable cult of the heart must recognize this impossibility of conceiving God, in any manner whatever, and even the epithets employed by the prophets were the result of necessity, and are not appropriate to God. Human thought can go as far as the first created being, the Intellect, which has some of the attributes commonly ascribed to God. It is the source of the world; it is intellection, intelligent and intellected, i.e. it is the act, the subject and the object of intellectual apprehension. This Intellect is absolutely perfect, and from the joy it experiences in seeing its own God-given perfection, emanates the Universal Soul. The Intellect is like the number One in the numerical series and the Universal Soul is like the number Two. In contradistinction to the creation of the One, which was outside time and space and which is the light of which it is said: 'Let there be light', the Universal Soul emanates in time and space. The Intellect is also called *Torah* and 'Wisdom', while the second to be created, the Universal Soul, is called the Garden of Eden. Nethanel recalls the talmudic sentence 'Seven things were created before the creation of the world: the *Torah*, the Garden of Eden, Gehenna, the Throne of Glory, Repentance, the Name of the Messiah King and the Place of the Temple' (Talmud Bab. *Pesahim* 54a). Other learned men have said that ten separate intellects emanate from the Intellect, basing this opinion on the sentence 'By ten "Words" the world was created', but Nethanel holds that they are seven, corresponding to the seven spheres; these spheres are formed of matter and form emanating from the Universal Soul, which emanates from the Intellect. In the same way as the Intellect, in cognizing its own essence, causes the Universal Soul to emanate, this in turn, wishing to emulate the Intellect, causes the celestial sphere to emanate. The Soul is thus, as it were, doubled: in its most eminent part it is close to the Intellect and receives its perfections; in its less eminent part, it transmits light and movement to what is below it, like the sun that irradiates the moon with its beams. And by the movement of the spheres the four elements merge and combine in such a way as to form all the beings of this lower world.

The mixture of the elements produces five orders, mineral, vegetable, animal, man and prophet; but although these five orders are well delimited, the highest degree of each of them is very close to the inferior degree of the immediately superior order.

Know, my brother – God strengthen both of us in His mercy! – that for every created thing the Creator set a goal which it reaches and where it halts. This goal is represented among the stones by the ruby, among the trees by the palm, among the animals by man, and among the jinns by the angels. But God Himself so far transcends comparison, similitude, representation, and the application of sacred numbers that he cannot be comprehended by the intellect be the thought ever so profound. In this sub-lunar world He created minerals, plants and animals. Of the non-liquefiable minerals He made a superior kind, the ruby; and of the liquefiable metals there is a superior kind, gold, which is very closely related to plants since it grows like them. Of the plants He made a noble species, the palm tree, which is very closely related to animals, since the male fertilizes the female which will otherwise not bear fruit; and when its top is lopped off the tree, animal-like, it dies. Similarly, God placed among animals a creature of the same class as man, the ape. In the horse also there is sagacity superior to that of other animals; and likewise the elephant accepts instruction more readily than other animals. All these are lower in degree than man. Since such is the case it necessarily follows that there must be in the genus man a class resembling the angels. This class consists of the prophets and their heirs, the latter being the imams, the administrators, the learned and the wise. Hence it is clear that the learned, the heirs of the prophets, are the noblest of human beings and in this world potentially angels, and that when God translates them to His Glorious Mansion they become angels in actuality. Consider, my brother, how splendid this arrangement is: the last member of each series is connected with the first of the succeeding series. It is the Praised God who creates, originates, forms and directs these series as He wishes and how he wishes, and He knows better than the learned.

(Ibid. pp. 50–1)

Here we find the saintly degree that is the Imam's attributed also to the prophets, the administrators, the learned and the wise.

The mixture of the elements is produced, as we have said, by the movement of the spheres, of which there are seven; an eighth sphere contains the twelve signs of the Zodiac. Nethanel is a fervent partisan of astrology, and the two figures, seven and twelve, as well as their total, nineteen, form the subject of long discussions.

Our author finds correspondences in man and the world to all the figures, but seven, twelve, and nineteen are particularly rich and full of significance in the domain of the Jewish religion (the nineteen benedictions of the prayer called *Shemone-esre*), and also among the Muslims, and here Nethanel gives an exegesis of the first verse of the Koran that again shows, if this were still necessary, that he knew Ismaili texts generally reserved to initiates.

According to our author, the Koran, like the Bible, is full of scientific and philosophical allusions that the wise may discover. Nethanel stresses the esoteric character of this science, which should be revealed only to men worthy of it; the people, the simple folk, must remain in ignorance.

Prophecy and the gift of revelation are expounded by Nethanel in a resolutely naturalistic manner. The divine influx which has its source in the Intellect, and which is darkened and obscured in proportion to its distance from it, gives rise to the world of nature; but God, in His wisdom, wanted to give human souls the means of deliverance from the prison of the world of generation and corruption. Thus He has given a revelation proceeding from the Universal Soul, expressed through the intermediary of a man whose spirit is absolutely pure and free from all the dross of this base world.

By this revelation, the prophet is able to foretell future events, work miracles, confound the wicked and reward the just, the aim of prophecy being to save man from the world of generation and corruption. To revolt against the prophet therefore signifies refusing the purification of the soul, remaining imprisoned in the material world. It seems at all events that, for Nethanel, the hidden sense, the veritable science, will not be truly attained before the end of time.

Prophecy assumes a decidedly 'political' role: the exterior duties that consist of the observance of the revealed Law are transmitted by the prophets, while the purely intellectual duties of the heart are common to all men and are linked to the interior illumination. Prophets have been sent to men at all times, for the divine influx is eternal; however, there can be no prophecy unless there are individuals capable of receiving this influx.

Thus, every nation has its prophet, who is sent especially to it and who speaks its own language. Nethanel's demonstration relies both on biblical verses and on the suras of the Koran. Should one see here a certain prudence prompted by the vigorous efforts then being made by Muslims to convert the Jews? Discussions, often public, were frequent, and it is evident that Jews had to be circumspect in order not to wound Muslim sensibility, but it also seems clear that, for Nethanel, Muhammad was not a false prophet, and his text does not represent an oratorical precaution only. In fact, not only in his constant citation from Islamic thought but also in the decidedly universalist tendency of his own writing, Nethanel adopts as his own an entirely naturalistic conception of revelation: God eternally causes His goodness and His perfections to emanate towards the Universal Soul, from which the divine influx emanates eternally towards the sages who are able to receive it and, since all the peoples have the right to be saved, each nation receives from its prophet the revelation appropriate to it, in the language that it speaks.

The only arguments in favour of the *Torah*, but according to Nethanel they are irrefutable, are that it was given to the people of Israel, that it is perfect, and that it cannot be abrogated, for God does not retract His word; therefore for the Jews until the coming of the Messiah the *Torah* has the force of law.

The Koran was sent, through Muhammad, to peoples who were then idolaters, and not to the Jews, who already had the revelation, that is, the means of attaining the supreme goal – liberation from the prison of matter, and salvation.

If revelations differ from people to people, this is because God, in His wisdom, knows the particular character of each of the nations, and, like a good doctor, who varies his prescriptions according to his patients, He gives each people the law that suits it.

This religious tolerance, so rare during the Middle Ages, except occasionally among philosophers, could not be advantageous to the Jewish people in its struggle against attempts at conversion; for if there is no intrinsic difference between the various religions, the decision to continue to remain Jewish in the face of persecution was undoubtedly not easily taken or kept. The same problem was to emerge again in Christian Spain, in the fifteenth century.

Astrology and Israel

The fate of the soul is not the only preoccupation of the two philosophers that I am going to discuss; astrology, and through it the history of mankind and especially the history of Israel, play an important part in their thinking.

This does not mean that relations between astrology and Jewish thought began to be manifested only at this period. The Talmud contains many sentences inspired by the popular astrology that was so much in vogue throughout the Hellenized Mediterranean basin. This popular astrology, still traceable in our daily lives, had hardly anything in common with the astrology codified by Ptolemy. Based on a scientific and precise astronomy that gave an account of celestial phenomena as far as they were observable with contemporary instruments, astrology was a science accepted by most cultivated men in Christian Europe, from the second to the seventeenth centuries. Undoubtedly, it was strongly opposed by the Church, but for religious reasons. On the scientific level it prevailed almost uncontested until and including Newton. Maimonides and Isaac Pulgar (fourteenth century) are among the extremely rare Jewish philosophers who cast doubt on the scientific foundations of astrology, following in this the Arab Aristotelians.

The difference between astronomy and astrology was as precisely defined during the Middle Ages as it is in our own time, even if the two terms are not always used in the texts.

Astronomy was the study of the movements of the celestial bodies and the inquiry into the laws that govern these movements. The movement of the celestial bodies causes the elements to mingle and compound bodies to exist on our earth; it regulates the tides and other physical phenomena.

Another influence, very special in character, joins the influence of the celestial bodies; this second factor, according to the astrologers, determines the fate of peoples and individuals. The laws that regulate these influences are known to us and have been transmitted from earliest antiquity. This pretension to scientific truth, based neither on observation nor on reasoning, is the chief reason for the rejection of astrology by the Aristotelian philosophers. As Maimonides was to say: a venerable lie is no better than a young one.

The astrological corpus is in fact very old, and, at least since the Greeks, was based on the system of astronomy of which Ptolemy has given the most complete account.

The basic astronomical and astrological texts, those written by Ptolemy, were translated into Arabic from the eighth century, Neoplatonism found itself in perfect accord with astrology. The harmony of the world implies that everything in this world has a celestial image and that to every astral configuration corresponds a sublunar being, whose vicissitudes may be known by observation of its astral prototype. Aristotelianism, on the other hand, does not accept the idea that the world here below is an image of the celestial world. The alliance of Neoplatonism and astrology was maintained throughout the Middle Ages, and Jewish Aristotelians adopted neoplatonic ideas and astrology as a combined whole into their thought.

Both astronomers and astrologers believed that the world was constituted of spheres, the earth being in the centre; each of the seven planets was set in a sphere. The eighth sphere, that of the fixed stars, was divided into the twelve sections known as the signs of the zodiac. To astronomers these signs of the zodiac represent purely intellectual divisions. To the astrologers, however, the signs of the zodiac are beings with a real existence.

Each planet and each sign of the zodiac has its character, its power and its particular attributes:

(1) It stands in a specific relation to the four elements, fire, air, water, earth; for instance, Scorpio is one of the three signs associated with water;

(2) It has the quality of either heat or cold, moisture or dryness; Scorpio, for instance, is cold and wet, and because of these qualities it is associated with death;

(3) It is either male or female; Scorpio, according to Ptolemy, is female;

(4) It is either nocturnal or diurnal; Scorpio, according to Ptolemy, is diurnal.

Since the characters of the planets and the signs of the zodiac are opposed to each other, a perpetual power struggle is waged between them. According to the moment and the place of birth (or conception) of every man and woman, the positions of the planets in relation to each other and to the signs of the zodiac will fix the limits of their respective influences and consequently the character and destiny of the individual.

The position of the planets, their interrelationships, and their relations with the signs of the zodiac, regulate not only the fate of individuals but also that of nations; this aspect of astrology, now forgotten, was of the greatest importance during the Middle Ages.

The introduction of astrology, both theoretical and practical, into Jewish life and communal thought was not achieved without opposition. There is proof of this in the letter addressed by Abraham bar Ḥiyya to Judah ben Barzillai of Barcelona, a celebrated rabbi and author of a *Commentary on the Book of Creation.*

This apologetic epistle recounts an event that took place in the community of Barcelona in about 1120:

One of Abraham bar Ḥiyya's favourite pupils was to be married on a Friday at the third hour, at the moment when the congregation left the synagogue. In everybody's opinion this was a particularly propitious hour to initiate a joyous act, for it is under the moon's influence; it was thus an hour as suitable from the planetary aspect as from the point of view of the astral body in the ascendant. However, the ceremony was delayed because of a funeral attended by the principal personalities of the community, so that the faithful found themselves reunited for the marriage only at the end of the fifth hour and at the beginning of the sixth, moments presided over by Mars. This meant that the hour was unsuitable, as regards the position both of the planets and of the astral body in the ascendant. Abraham bar Ḥiyya therefore advised his pupil to wait for the seventh hour, which was perfectly favourable; his arguments convinced the bridegroom as well as the rest of the assembly, except for Judah ben Barzillai, who declared that to wait an hour was equivalent to 'putting a question to the Chaldeans (magicians)' and that this was a great sin, and spoke so well that the young man, against his will, was married at the sixth hour.

Following this incident Abraham bar Ḥiyya wrote to Judah ben Barzillai, to justify both astrology and his personal position in this affair. One may, he said, compare astrological advice to preventive medicine; there can be no wrong in avoiding some kind of nourishment that might harm the body; in the same way there is no sin in choosing a favourable hour or avoiding an unfavourable one. When the rabbis of the Talmud put the faithful on their guard by saying 'you shall not put questions to the Chaldeans' they were not referring to the astrologers. The Chaldeans are idolatrous magicians and sorcerers, their counsels are thus bad and it is not licit to address oneself to them. But to propound a question to an astrologer is permitted, for astrology cannot be likened to magic, or idolatry, or sorcery. In the first place, many rabbis of the Talmud believed in astrology and practised it. Our father Abraham himself practised astrology, as we know from a famous talmudic anecdote (Bab. *Shabbat* 156b). Abraham had learned, by his knowledge of the stars, that he would have no descendants, contrary to the divine promise. God said to him, Leave your astrology, Israel does not depend on a star! The divine response does not mean that one may suspect Abraham of addiction to magic and not believing in God. Nor did God say to him, Leave your astrology, for it is false. Astrology is a science, its proofs are true and it is licit to study and apply it. What the rabbis affirm in this story is that astrology indeed allows us to know the decree of the stars, but that this decree is not absolute as regards the destiny of Israel. By their pious acts and by their prayers, the sages of Israel can abrogate this decree, but the wise men of other peoples do not have the same power.

There is thus a fundamental difference between the situation of Israel and

95

that of the other nations as far as the influence of the stars is concerned. The other nations are totally subject to astral influence and if God wished to spare a people doomed to destruction by the conjunction of the planets, He would have to act on the stars themselves and prevent their conjunction. In the case of Israel, such intervention is not necessary, for the chosen people is not absolutely and ineluctably subject to the influence of the astral bodies. The reason for this is clear: the whole world, including the stars, was created for the sake of Israel; how then can Israel be made to submit to the domination of these same stars?

The term 'Israel' remains to be defined, for to be subject to God alone, and free from the influence of the planets, it is not enough to be a descendant of Abraham; one must also be in a state of purity. When in a state of sin the Jewish people, like the other peoples, is subject to the decree of the stars. And who among us, asks Abraham bar Ḥiyya, can pride himself on always being just and pious and carrying out all the commandments? Astrology is thus very necessary, and in the same way as one should avoid food harmful to health, so one should abstain from undertaking a voyage or from marrying when the day and the hour are not favourable. Why tempt fate?

Judah ben Barzillai was opposed to astrology because he identified it with sorcery and idolatry. But, Abraham bar Ḥiyya argues, this identification is mistaken, as is proved by citing the rabbinical authorities, but especially by the fact that astrology itself, in its knowledge of the laws of the planets and their influence, explicitly recognizes that planets and stars are instruments in the hands of God. While one should reject all the other modes of divination and sorcery, for they are an active practice, an act forbidden by the *Torah* and partaking of idolatry, so one should regard astrology with favour, for it informs us about the world and its dangers.

This apologia perfectly depicts, it seems to me, the attitude of many medieval Jewish thinkers. In ordinary circumstances of life Israel, like other peoples, is subject to astral determination, and the usefulness of astrology appears evident to it, even if God maintains special relations with Israel that transcend the astral level.

The practical usage of astrology and the debates it led to are only one aspect of the question. I propose rather to show in what degree the fundamental ideas of astrology were adopted and utilized in Jewish philosophical systems during the Middle Ages.

Generally, astrology is only one element, more or less important and fertile in ideas, in the thought of Jewish philosophers, from the twelfth century onwards. Astrological arguments occurred chiefly in the following two topics of their discussions:

(1) The history of Israel and its place in universal history as it is fixed by the stars and their conjunctions. The era of the Messiah depends intimately on these planetary phenomena and was foretold by the different philosophers according to their own interpretations of these phenomena.

(2) Astrology suggests the reason for some of the divine commandments ordained for Israel. We remember that according to Saadiah certain commandments, without being contrary to reason, are not rationally necessary. Astrology provides an explanation for at least some of these commandments, integrating them into the universal order and giving them a new and positive dimension.

A final question perhaps emerges: was there a specifically Jewish astrology? The answer is quite decidedly no. As Jewish scholars participated in the progress of the various sciences, mathematics, astronomy, medicine, in an atmosphere which, whether Christian or Islamic, did not take confessional barriers into account, so they contributed to the progress of astrology. One excellent example is Māshā'allāh (Messahala), well-known astrologer of the eighth century.

Jewish astrologers adopted astrology without modifying any basic part of the system because of their religious ideas. Within the astrological tradition they chose what best suited their intentions and they sometimes made a personal application of the accepted principles; what was Jewish was the use of astrology in systems of Jewish philosophy and the use of astrological arguments concerning certain questions; astrology itself remained a universal science.

What was the attitude of the philosophers I have already considered towards astrology? Saadiah Gaon employed certain astrological notions in his *Commentary on the Book of Creation*, but, judging by his explication of Genesis 1: 16 (the creation of the sun, the moon and the stars), he does not seem to have been an earnest partisan of astrology. It was the same with the Mu'tazilites, Rabbanites or Karaites. Astrology quite simply did not form an integral part of their system of thought. It was altogether otherwise, as we have seen, with Nethanel ben al-Fayyumi, who constructed his thought on the astrological bases that form part of the doctrine of some Shi'ite sects.

As for the Neoplatonists of whom we have spoken, if Isaac Israeli, Joseph Ibn Zaddik, or the author of the *Kitāb ma'ānī al-nafs*, expressed any opinion on this subject, the texts have been lost.

On the other hand, Solomon Ibn Gabirol, in the *Kingly Crown*, gives a detailed description of the influence of the seven planets on this lower world and (according to Abraham Ibn Ezra's quotation concerning Daniel 11: 30) seems to have wished to link the coming of the Messiah with the great conjunction of Jupiter and Saturn.

However, the first really to introduce astrology into Jewish thought was Abraham bar Ḥiyya.

ABRAHAM BAR ḤIYYA

Abraham lived in the first half of the twelfth century and died after 1136. It is certain that he lived in Barcelona, but, apart from this fact, we can only form suppositions concerning his life. The appellation 'Savasorda' (a corruption of Sāḥib-al-Shurṭa) leads one to suppose that he occupied a post at the court of Alfonso I of Aragon and of the Counts of Barcelona; a fact that need not surprise us, for the Christian kings needed cultivated secretaries with a knowledge of Arabic in the administration of their territories and in their relations with the neighbouring Arab states. His rank might also be explained by his mathematical and astronomical aptitudes. He bore the title *Nasi* – 'Prince', the exact significance of which we do not know, but which seems to denote a judiciary function within the community. It is further supposed that he visited the South of France to assist in dividing the territories conquered by the Counts of Barcelona into fiefs, for he composed a treatise on land-surveying.

Abraham bar Ḥiyya is the first philosopher to have written in Hebrew; this is probably due to the fact that he wrote in Christian Spain.

Certainly, even in Christian Spain Arabic had not disappeared as a language of culture; Judah Halevi wrote the *Kuzari* in Arabic; however, in the twelfth century Arabic had already begun to give way to Latin in cultivated circles. For Jews living in a Christian environment, although some of them certainly knew Latin, the literary language was always Hebrew from the thirteenth century onwards, and people who knew Arabic became rarer and rarer in Europe.

The influence of the Christian milieu is strongly felt in Abraham bar Ḥiyya, perhaps because of the anti-Jewish polemic that began at that time. But relations with Christian scholars were not only polemical, for our author collaborated in the translation from Arabic into Latin of various scientific works, and Plato of Tivoli cites him as his co-worker up to 1136.

Apart from his mathematical works on land-surveying, Abraham bar Ḥiyya wrote two books on astronomy, where for the first time one finds Ptolemy's system expounded in Hebrew. His philosophical and religious thinking is presented in two books: *Megillat ha-Megalleh* (*Scroll of the Revealer*); and *Hegyon ha-Nefesh ha-Aẓuvah* (*The Meditation of the Sad Soul*).

The *Megillat ha-Megalleh* is an eschatological work, and the *Hegyon ha-Nefesh* is a book on morality, which is thought by some to have been designed to be read during the Ten Days of Penitence between the New Year and the Day of Atonement. In both these works the author expresses philosophical ideas, often of unknown source, that have not yet appeared in these pages.

In the first book of the *Hegyon ha-Nefesh*, Abraham bar Ḥiyya begins by affirming the validity of scientific knowledge, but in a rather ambiguous manner. On the one hand he declares that the science and the virtue that enable the soul to return to its celestial fatherland cannot be taught by philosophers, for they do not have the gift of the *Torah*; and even, he adds, if they could teach us this science, we would not have the right to learn it from them. On the other hand, after expounding a cosmology where Neoplatonism and Aristotelianism are mingled, he affirms that this is the opinion of the *Torah*. In fact, science in its entirety is the heritage of Israel, since the wise men of all nations have drawn it from the *Torah* – a theme very frequently found, as we have seen, in Jewish philosophy.

Abraham's *Meditation* begins with the creation of the world as it is narrated in Genesis. Before this creation, and in the unanimous opinion of Jewish and non-Jewish scholars, all creatures were nothing and non-being (*efes ubelima*). When God decided on the creation of the world, their existence in potentiality was matter, form and non-being. And when God wanted to actualize them He removed the non-being, and made Form inhere in Matter, and the body of the world came into existence; this is confirmed by the *Torah*:

Thus the hyle and the Form, which – according to the ancient philosophers – existed in potentiality until creation, are the *Tohu* and *Bohu*, mentioned in the Torah (Genesis 2). This was what the world consisted of until it emerged to actuality at the word of God, as the Bible states: 'The earth was *Tohu* and *Bohu*'.

(*Megillat ha-Megalleh*, in *Meditation*, trans. G. Wigoder, p. 132)

This creation was non-temporal:

'Time' is used here inexactly and according to human usage, but in fact, until things went from potentiality to actuality, there was no such thing as Time, because Time existed in potentiality when all beings existed in it, for Time has no substance and is only a measure signifying the duration of existing things. Without such things, there is no duration on which Time is dependent. (*Meditation*, p. 39)

The Matter and Form that partially existed before the creation of the world are not on the same level:

The hyle is too weak to be self-sustaining and to fill its own deficiencies, unless it is joined by the Form; while the Form cannot be perceived or sensed, unless it clothes the hyle which carries it. So each of them requires the other and is designed to enable it to exist or to be perceptible to worldly beings. Without the Form, the hyle could not exist, while the Form could not be perceived without the hyle. However, the Form is more important than the hyle, inasmuch as it only requires the hyle in order to be perceived, but it could exist on its own without being seen, whereas the hyle would not exist at all, were it not for the Form. This explains their association and relationship.

Each one of them, in turn, can be divided into two parts. The two parts of the hyle are (1) the pure, clean part; and (2) the dregs and sediment. The two parts of the Form are (1) the closed, sealed part, which is too holy to be linked with the hyle; and (2) the hollow, open section which can be attached to the hyle and be contained in it. The splendour of the self-subsistent Form, which is too pure to be linked with the hyle, spreads and shines on the hollow Form, enabling it to clothe the hyle with all forms, which the hyle is capable of receiving. These two principles, namely hyle and Form, were stored before God and existed in potentiality until such time as He saw fit to bring them out to actuality. (*Ibid*. p. 39)

All existing things arise from the conjunction between these different parts of Matter and Form:

They say that when [God's] Pure Thought decided to actualize them, He empowered the closed Form to come into existence and to be clothed with its splendour, without contact with the hyle. This Form, which is not connected with the hyle, is the Form of angels, seraphim, souls and all forms of the upper world. . . . These have said that this Form endured in one place with the shining light inside it. Its light spread over that Form that could combine with the hyle, strengthening it – through the Word of God – to become joined to the hyle. First this Form attaches itself to the pure, clean hyle and this is a strong attachment which does not change as long as they are joined. From this union the heavenly bodies were created. Subsequently, the Form attaches itself to the impure hyle, and from this union were created all kinds of terrestrial bodies, whose forms are mutable but do not change position, such as the four elements – earth, water, air and fire – and whatever is compounded of them as far as vegetation and plants. (*Ibid.* p. 40)

Thus the light of Form penetrates all beings, from the angels to the minerals. The ladder of being, for the sages, culminates in man, who possesses reason, and the *Torah* confirms this hierarchy.

(1) All living beings were created through the agency of something else, which received Divine permission to enable these living beings to pass into actual existence. Man, on the other hand, required no intermediary to assist in any aspect of the process of his creation . . .
. . . the creation of man incorporates all the actions which served in the creation of other living beings, and in addition, a soul was breathed into man, as it says (Genesis ii. 7) 'And He breathed into his nostrils the breath of life'. By this man is superior to every other creation in the subsolar world. This constitutes the second differentiation.
(3) The third difference is that God granted man dominion over other created beings, mentioned according to the order of their creation, beginning with the fish, which were created at the beginning of the fifth day; continuing with the fowl created at the end of the same day; and then the cattle and the creations of the sixth day. It concludes 'over all the earth', meaning over everything that exists on earth. In this way the Bible shows that man has dominion over all earthly creatures.

(*Ibid.* pp. 50–2)

Nevertheless, a fifth degree completes this hierarchy:

Just as God has distinguished man from all other living beings and granted him superiority over them, so He has distinguished one nation and sanctified it for His glory above all mankind. As the Bible says (Isaiah xliii. 7): 'Every one that is called by My name and whom I have created for My glory; I have formed Him, yea I have made Him'. As we have explained, it is man who exists after the processes of creating, forming and making, in that order. This verse shows that those men who were created, formed and made for His glory, are called by His name. To make this clear, I rearrange the verse to read 'Every one whom I have created and formed and made for My glory is called by My name'. (*Ibid.* p. 52)

The system of the world, however philosophical it may be, is ordained in view of the existence of Israel; its final purpose is not man in general, but the people of Israel; the history of Israel gives meaning to the history of the world, a theme that is further amplified by Judah Halevi.

Abraham bar Ḥiyya, however, still has some doubts, which Judah Halevi does not share, about the superiority of Israel in relation to the rest of humanity, and he concludes the chapter by writing:

Thus Israel's great superiority – on account of which it is called by the Divine name – is its acknowledgement of the Divine unity and the acceptance of the Torah. I do not say that such superiority is not available for the rest of mankind, for that would be wrong; we must believe that the gates of repentance are open for all who seek it; as it says (Isaiah lv. 7) 'Let him return unto the Lord and He will have mercy on him and to our God for He will abundantly pardon'. He has mercy on all who repent.

(Ibid. pp. 53–4)

The three other chapters of the *Meditation* are devoted to morality and penitence. In the *Scroll of the Revealer*, Abraham bar Ḥiyya returns to the same themes, but from a historical point of view.

In the *Meditation* he gives the four categories in which Form may exist:

(1) Self-subsistent Form which never combines with matter, such as all the previously-mentioned forms in the upper world.

(2) Form that is attached firmly and inseparably to matter; and its form cannot change under any circumstances – such as the form of the firmament and the stars.

(3) Form attached to matter temporarily, but moving from body to body and changing shape, namely the bodies of terrestrial beings. These two forms, which are joined to matter, have not the power to separate from matter and exist apart from it as they had done originally.

(4) There is one more part which can logically exist, and this is form which is attached to a body, but is eventually separated from it and returns to its pristine condition to exist on its own without matter.

(Ibid. p. 46)

The second category is not eternal; it has had a commencement and it will have an end; its history is bound to that of the soul. Man's soul, the fourth category, originates in the world of pure forms; after having dwelt in the body it must go back to the world of the angels, or more precisely towards one of the worlds of light, for according to Abraham bar Ḥiyya there are five of these, to which three levels of prophecy correspond, as he explains in the *Megillat ha-Megalleh*.

In the first chapter of Genesis, the word 'Light' is mentioned five times and the word 'Darkness' three times, in order to show us the five degrees of light or five worlds of light which are above the heavens and were created on the first day; these are the five degrees or five worlds according to the philosophers, and you may call them what you please.

The first degree is the resplendent light that appeared to the angels engaged in the divine service, to the prophets and to the most eminent of the children of Israel at the time of the Revelation on Mount Sinai. The philosophers call this light the luminous world, (*'olam hanurani*), and the Scriptures say on this subject: God said, Let there be light. (Genesis 1: 3)

The second degree is the Voice emanating from among the cherubim, which was heard by Moses; the angels hear it when they accomplish their missions, all the people of Israel heard it on Mount Sinai; the philosophers call it the upper world (*'olam ha-ribonut*; *'olam ha-ravrevanut*). Of it is said 'and there was light'. These two upper worlds are called by our Fathers 'Throne of Glory' and 'Holy Spirit'.

The third degree is the light of Wisdom, of Knowledge, of Intelligence and of the Law and it is the intellection transmitted to the angels and the seraphim; this intelligible light spreads and flows over the just among men and on this level are the angels, the *hashmalim* and all the celestial armies. The philosophers call this degree the World of Knowledge, and the Scriptures mention it in the expression 'And He saw', for vision comes neither by the view, nor by the heart, but by wisdom and science, as it is said: And God saw the light, that it was good (Genesis 1: 7), and here the meaning of 'God saw' is that God gave to wisdom the faculty to show what is good and to understand it.

The fourth degree is the soul, or the breath that God breathes into men, into sages and into those who are not wise, and the philosophers call this degree the world of the soul. The Scriptures say that God divided this light into two: And God divided the light from the darkness (Genesis 1: 7). The light alludes to the souls of the just over whom shines the light of science and the fear of God, and who by its action are bright and luminous, and the darkness is the souls of the wicked who are not touched by the light of the knowledge of God.

The fifth degree is that of the light that God has reserved for the just in the next world to come, and the philosophers call it the World of Creation, following the verse: God called the light Day, and the darkness He called Night. Day alludes to the paradise prepared for the just, and Night to the hell that awaits the wicked.

(*Megillat ha-Megalleh*, p. 22)

It is evident that the degrees of prophecy and the worlds described here correspond perfectly. The luminous world is that of the visual and auditory revelation reserved for Moses and the most eminent prophets. The world of the Voice is that of the spoken word, reserved for prophets belonging to the second degree. The world of knowledge is the internal, indistinct revelation that, according to Abraham bar Ḥiyya, the just among men, that is, Gentiles, may receive.

Our author makes this cosmology of light correspond to the destiny of Israel.

As the world only attained perfection after the creation of Adam, so human history will not be complete before Israel has accomplished its destiny and subjected to its rule all the peoples of the earth. The terrestrial history of Israel corresponds to a hierarchy of soul. There are, says Abraham bar Ḥiyya, three souls or three faculties of the soul (he does not seem to distinguish between these two formulations, the first being Platonic and the second Aristotelian).

The two inferior souls share the destiny of the plants and the animals and disappear with the death of each individual. The third soul, that which distinguishes man from other terrestrial beings, is the rational soul; this soul, endowed with intelligence, is eternal by its essence, for it is taken from the superior world, as it is said 'And [God] breathed into his nostrils the breath of life' (Genesis 2: 7). It is also rewarded and punished according to its merits. But this pure soul that God breathed into man at the moment of his creation was defiled by Adam's sin and immersed in the darkness of the two inferior souls. This is the reason why it exists only in one individual in each generation, instead of being found in all men. Since the deluge, the pure soul has begun to liberate itself from the prison of the inferior souls and has ascended one degree: instead of being sunk in the vegetative soul, it is imprisoned in the animal soul. But at the end of the third epoch of the world, that is, the third day of Creation, appeared Jacob, who announced the fourth day, and he begot a family of pious and just men worthy of receiving the soul of life and of forming a people worthy of receiving the gift of the *Torah*, and, in this way, able to conduct the world to a state of perfection; for the *Torah* and Israel were created for each other a long time before the creation of the world.

The idea of original sin as we see it in Abraham bar Ḥiyya already exists in embryo in the Talmud, but in him it may be due to Christian influence. As for the concept of a pure soul that is transmitted from generation to generation in a single individual, and also the notion of the fifth degree in the hierarchy of beings, these are Ismaili ideas, as S. Pines has shown, and have already been spoken of in connection with Nethanel ben al-Fayyumi.

Abraham bar Ḥiyya has noted that, according to the philosophers, there are four classes of souls, each with its destiny after death:

(1) The wise and just soul returns to the upper world and is eternally united with pure form;

(2) The wise and unjust soul is carried away into the heat of the sphere;

(3) The just but ignorant soul is reincarnated in one body and then in another until it has acquired knowledge and is able to ascend to the superior world. This doctrine of transmigration of souls was to have great importance in the Kabbalah.

(4) The unjust and ignorant soul will disappear, like the inferior souls.

But our author does not accept these philosophical conceptions and substitutes for them an exclusively religious hierarchy of reward and punishment.

If the history of the liberation of the soul corresponds to the history of the people of Israel, this is because the duration of the world, that is, 7000 years, is divisible by 7, corresponding to the 7 days of Creation. Moreover, each of the beings created during the 7 days of Creation symbolizes what will come to pass during the corresponding day of the advent of the Messiah. In each epoch, which symbolizes each of the days of creation, there are 7 generations that also symbolize these 7 days. God gave the *Torah* at the end of the third epoch and the advent of the gift of the *Torah* marks the beginning of the fourth; the seventh day, the seventh epoch, the seventh millennium, will be the Day of the Messiah.

J. Guttmann compares these ideas with those of Isidore of Seville, a Christian Spanish scholar of the seventh century and he points out that they do not seem Jewish in origin, but are probably taken directly from the Fathers of the Church. However, Abraham bar Ḥiyya does not copy Christian ideas as they stand; on the contrary, he adapts them to suit the history of Israel and transforms them into a grandiose view of the destiny of his people. In effect, in the *Megillat ha-Megalleh*, Abraham bar Ḥiyya's discussion is principally eschatological. The author wishes to calculate the date of the Messiah's coming; in the three first chapters of the book he bases his calculations on biblical verses; in the fourth exclusively on the Book of Daniel; and in the fifth he expounds astrological data that confirm the calculations of the preceding chapters.

ABRAHAM IBN EZRA

Ibn Ezra was born at Tudela in 1089. He was a poet, grammarian, biblical exegete, philosopher, astronomer, astrologer and physician. The first part of his life, until 1140, was spent in Spain, and during this period he was a friend of Joseph Ibn Ẓaddik, Abraham Ibn Daud, Moses Ibn Ezra and also of Judah Halevi, who accompanied him on one of his journeys to Africa.

According to legend, his peregrinations took him to Egypt, some say to Palestine, Baghdad, and even India. He composed most of his works between 1140 and 1146, and during these years he also undertook journeys to Lucca (1145), Mantua (1145–6) and Verona (1146–7). Afterwards he travelled in Provence, visiting Narbonne and Béziers, and later Dreux and Rouen. In France, he became friendly with Rabbenu Tam, Rashi's grandson, before going on to London. In 1161 he was again at Narbonne, and he died in 1164, in Rome, according to some sources; according to others, in Palestine. His son Isaac, probably the only one of his children to survive him, converted to Islam, like his teacher, Abu-l-Barakāt.

Ibn Ezra's works resemble his life, which was, as we have seen, rather adventurous and given to the unexpected. He wrote commentaries on the Bible, most of them in two versions, one short and one long. These commentaries enjoyed great renown. They are written in Hebrew, in an elegant style, interspersed with puns (Abraham Ibn Ezra never shrinks from a play on words, even at the expense of personalities whom he respects, such as Saadiah). These commentaries excited the curiosity of most medieval scholars because of their enigmatic aspect; Ibn Ezra alludes to 'secrets', which are philosophical or astrological doctrines, concluding with the phrase 'Let him who is able to understand, understand!' Numerous commentators felt themselves able to understand and wanted to prove this by writing a super-commentary on the 'secrets'. Such super-commentaries on Ibn Ezra's biblical exegeses abounded. The neoplatonic influence clearly marked in the Jewish philosophers of the thirteenth and fourteenth centuries was essentially expressed in terms and ideas drawn from Ibn Ezra. He is almost as frequently cited as Maimonides, although from the philosophical point of view his system does not provide a conceptual framework for later authors, but serves only to complement the Aristotelian schema.

Apart from his biblical commentaries, Abraham Ibn Ezra wrote numerous treatises, generally quite short, on grammar, astrology, and numbers.

He was certainly not the first to introduce philosophical considerations into the interpretation of the Scriptures; he forms part of a long line of allegorists that began before Philo. His commentaries covered not only certain passages but all the books of the Bible; and the great vogue that his works enjoyed introduced to the cultivated public a certain number of ideas that inspired personal reflection. He was not attacked by the orthodox as were the Maimonideans, since because of his ambiguity one could interpret his thought in a traditional sense without undue difficulty; further, he did not reveal the 'secrets', but only made allusion to them, and this discretion was much appreciated by the adversaries of philosophy.

It seems certain that Abraham Ibn Ezra's ideas were daring. But it is difficult to know how far he went, for his audacities are never clearly expressed, and he has been credited with a little more boldness than he really intended, especially on the question of biblical criticism. Spinoza's praise obviously does not predispose one in favour of the orthodoxy of our author's thinking.

Ibn Ezra's mode of expression being biblical commentary, a systematic exposition of his thought is probably a misrepresentation, even a sort of betrayal, for it would tend to codify ideas that perhaps only apply to the biblical passage that they directly explicate. Therefore it is not without hesitation that I shall expound these ideas outside their natural context. But a translation of a short extract of his commentary on Genesis 1 : 1 is sufficient to make us realize that, in the case of this author, fidelity to the arrangement of the text is impossible in the context of our work. Let me add that the interpretation cited here is based on a number of fourteenth-century commentaries on Ibn Ezra and particularly that by Joseph Tov Elem (the only one of these commentaries to have been printed in its entirety).

Here is a passage from the commentary on Genesis 1 : 1:

In the beginning God created (*bara'*) the heaven and the earth. Most of the commentators have said that *bara'* means to produce being out of nothing, according to Number 16 : 30: If the Lord makes a new thing; but they have forgotten the verse: And God created great whales [Genesis 1 : 21]; and a third verse: So God created man [Genesis 1 : 27] and again: I . . . create darkness [Isaiah 45 : 7]. Darkness is the opposite of light, which is 'being'. Grammatically, the word to create is twofold, it can be written *bara'*, as we have seen [= *bet, resh, alef*], or *barah* [*hay* instead of *alef* = *bet, resh, hay*] as in the verse: Neither did he eat bread with them [II Samuel 12 : 17]. The meaning of the verb is thus to cut, to decide, to set a precise limit, and let him who may understand, understand!

Ibn Ezra proves that the verb *bara'* has three meanings:

(1) To create something out of nothing as in Numbers 16 : 30;
(2) To create something out of something else as in Genesis 1 : 21, where the great whales were created with matter and form;

(3) To deprive an existing thing of being as in Isaiah 45: 7 where darkness, which is the absence of light, is created.

There is no reason to understand the first verse of Genesis in the first sense of the verb *bara'*. On the contrary the verb *bara'* with *aleph* as the third consonant here has the same meaning as the verb *barah* with *hay* as the third consonant and means 'to cut, to set a limit', as in II Samuel 12: 17.

Creation relates how God 'cut' the world of generation and corruption out of the four elements that constitute our world. Before the creation God existed and also the world of the intelligences, that of the eternal spheres and the four elements, each according to its nature: thus, water being lighter than earth covered it entirely. The emergence of the earth and the confining of the waters within determined limits, events contrary to the nature of the elements, are due to the creative will of God.

This creation was carried out in obedience to God's command, by the action of the circular movement of the spheres.

The divine decision is executed by the instrumentality of the separate intelligences; these bring the spheres into existence and transmit to them the divine commandments, and the spheres, that is, the fixed stars and the seven planets, govern this lower world, not by their own volition, but according to the order fixed by God. True religion lies in recognizing the place assigned to the stars in the natural order that God has willed. Idolatry consists of addressing oneself to the stars as if they had a power of decision; this is a procedure contrary to religion and totally inefficacious.

The 'decree of the stars' that governs natural laws is necessarily absolute and ineluctable in all that concerns the sublunar world of bodies. Not only bodies, but their movements and the relations between them are determined from all eternity. To wish to change the decree of the stars as regards material questions such as wealth or poverty is totally impossible. We shall see later that one can nevertheless avoid this decree, and, besides, the soul, which does not belong to this corporeal world, is not subjected to this absolute determinism.

Can we suppose that the intelligences that form the superior world, the spheres that are subordinate to them and the four elements that pre-existed at the time of creation, are co-eternal with God; Abraham Ibn Ezra often reiterates that they shall have no end. Did they have a beginning? If one can at all speak of a commencement in referring to them, this cannot be a commencement in time. They have an origin, for they have a cause: everything comes from God and as the sequence of the numbers draws its source from One, which provides the basis of the series without being part of it, so God is the source and foundation of the world of the angels and of this lower world.

In speaking of One, designated in the Bible by the Tetragram, Abraham Ibn Ezra uses terms that we already know: He exists by Himself and is self-sufficient; He is the foundation of all things, for He bestows existence on all that exists; although He is close only to the world of the separate intellects, one may say of Him that He is in everything, for His action can be recognized in everything; the One being the source of all numbers, all of them contain it, and without it they do not exist.

Now consider that One is the foundation (*yesod*) of all number, while itself no number; it subsists in itself, and has no need for what follows it. Every number too is composed of ones ... Hence it is written in the *Shi'ur Qomā* [*the Measure of the Divine Body*, which is an allegory of the macrocosm] 'Rabbi Yishmael said: Every one who knows the measure of the Creator (*yoẓer be-re'shit*) is sure to be a son of the world-to-come, and I and 'Aqiba vouch for this.' In this way the intelligent will be able to know the One in so far as the All is attached to it, whereas to know it in so far as its total good is concerned is beyond the power of a created being ... Being attached to the total good is like [the vision of] the face; and being attached to the created [things] is like [the vision of] the back. This is meant by 'And thou shalt see My back' [Exodus 33: 21].

(*Yesod Mora*, trans. A. Altmann, 'Moses Narboni's Epistle', p. 230)

But God is also the 'whole' of the Glory and the Angels, that is, the forms when outside of bodies are not only close to the 'One', but, in a certain way, are the 'One'. And these forms themselves contain the whole of the world since they are its source and archetype. The world in its entirety is therefore in God.

When trying to explain the relations between God, the world of the pure forms and this lower world, which is made in the resemblance of the world of forms, Abraham Ibn Ezra employs the image of the species, the genus and the individual; all the individuals in this lower world are part of a genus; thus each horse has the characteristics of his kind, the race of horses; but the genus 'horse', like the genus 'dog' or 'sheep' is contained or again defined within the species 'mammal', and the characteristics of the species can be recognized in each of the individuals of every one of the genera. It is the same in arithmetic: the one, source of the indefinite series of numbers, potentially contains them all and can be recognized in each of them. God is thus the world or rather contains the world in general and not in particular. He knows it because He knows Himself, more completely and more totally than if He knew it by innumerable individuals and accidents. God, certainly, knows all individuals, but in their generality, not in their particularity. Ibn Ezra uses a formula that is frequently found: 'The Whole [God] knows every part through the genera but not through the individual' (*Commentary on the Torah*, Genesis 18: 21). This formula could also be translated: 'Knowing the whole, He knows all its individual parts and ignores none of them.'

In the context of creation, man occupies a privileged place, because he is the only terrestrial being to have an immortal soul similar to that of the angels, and also because this soul can return to the world of the Unity from which it came. The spiritual itinerary that leads the soul to its source is evidently that of knowledge, and we know already that knowledge has a redemptory value.

Since man is a microcosm he may, through knowledge of himself, know the whole world. This does not prevent Abraham Ibn Ezra from declaring in another passage that it is impossible for man to know what is soul, whether substance or accident, if it dies on leaving the body, or why it has been joined to the body.

Revelation is given to aid and comfort man in his return to his immortal origins; but in no way can it replace the necessary intellectual effort.

The revelation between God and man is expressed in three ways:

– The first is God's revelation in the Scriptures and the giving of the laws that man must know and perform, and, in one of his commentaries, Abraham Ibn Ezra declares that all the commandments must necessarily be complemented by knowledge;

– The second is the intellectual knowledge that is given to all men; this signifies the moral principles and the rational principles of which Saadiah spoke.

– The third road that leads to God is prophecy.

In a certain sense, Ibn Ezra does not accept exterior revelation, only interior vision. Even in a spiritual vision, God does not speak to the prophet; it is an angel who appears. And perhaps the angel who speaks to the prophet is his own soul, which has become united to the pure forms. 'We call the angel by the name of God according to the verse: for my name is in him . . .' (*Commentary on the Torah*, Exodus 23: 21), i.e. he who speaks is man and he who listens is man and, if one knows the science of the soul, one will understand these things, for in all these visions, nothing is a body, nor does it resemble a body. This is a well-known neoplatonic theme, found particularly in Avicenna, declaring that the soul has two faces, that turned upwards being close to God and that bending downwards resembling this world.

As for Moses, it seems that according to Abraham Ibn Ezra his degree was not that of a man, even a prophet, but that of a pure form, very close to God, so that revelation came to him directly from God and without the intermediary of forms attached to God. This direct communication with God was also, says Ibn Ezra, the prerogative of all the people of Israel during the revelation on Mount Sinai.

In connection with the verse 'And Moses said unto the Lord: "See, Thou sayest unto me"' (Exodus 33: 12), Moses Narboni quotes Ibn Ezra:

That day, when Moses saw what he desired [to see], was to him what the day of the Giving of the Torah was to Israel. No man before and after him ever attained to his rank and his wisdom . . . Says Abraham the author: 'I have already explained that the glorious Name which is written one way and pronounced another denotes the essence [of God], and the essence is the glory . . . Since "All" is from "One" hence the mystery of the prayers and the praises, and the meaning of [the verse] "Thus will I magnify Myself, and sanctify Myself" (Ezekiel 38: 23); and, moreover, of [the verse] "in whom I will be glorified" (Isaiah 49: 3). The truly One has no image. He is like the universal aspect of all the images, for they proceed from

Him . . . Moses was able to know and to see with his intellect's eye the way in which the creatures are conjoined with the Creator, but it belongs to the way of the Glory that no created being is able to know it. This is meant by [the verse]: "man shall not see Me and live" (Exodus 33: 30); [that is, man shall not see Me] while the soul of man is still with the body, whereas after death the soul of the intelligent will attain to a level higher than is attainable during his lifetime. Moses turned into a universal. God, therefore, said: "I know thee by name" (Exodus 33: 17); for He alone knows the particulars and their parts in a universal way. The noblest on earth is man, . . . The noblest among men are the Israelites; . . . This is meant by [the verse]: "Let us make man in our image, after our likeness" (Genesis 1: 26).' He further said as follows: 'And the hand was like a shelter, just as one shelters [the eye] with the palm of his hand against the sun, lest the soul detach itself from his body. "And thou shalt see My back" (Exodus 33: 23), considering that He is all, and His glory filleth all, and from Him is all, and all is the image of All. And this is meant [by the verse]: "And the image of God doth he behold" (Numbers 12: 8).'

(Trans. A. Altmann, 'Moses Narboni's Epistle', pp. 266–70)

Nevertheless, during the revelation on Mount Sinai as well as at the time of the prophecies, visual and auditory phenomena were seen and heard. It seems that one must have recourse to miracles, in order to explain them.

Worldly events are regulated by natural laws and depend on the movements of the stars. When God intervenes in the course of these natural events, signs and miracles result. Abraham Ibn Ezra often affirms his belief in miracles, and refutes the philosophers who deny them. He argues that, since we do not know the natural laws in their entirety how can we know what exceeds nature? While the stars determine what happens in the world, they themselves receive their existence and laws from beings close to God, and these beings only carry out the divine will. God can therefore intervene in the succession of natural causes according to His will.

It is not only God who can accomplish miracles. The prophet, when he is perfect and has attached himself to the pure forms, understands the stars by their causes, and can act on them in certain specific circumstances though not with regard to his own fate or that of his family (we shall see however that he can influence his own destiny, if not positively, at least negatively); however, when the destiny of the people is at stake, he may act on the movement of the stars in the direction he desires, for when the purified man joins the celestial world he becomes more eminent and more powerful than the material stars.

In his super-commentary on Ibn Ezra's commentaries, Joseph Tov Elem expounds this theory by classifying the sages in three degrees:

– Those who can influence nature in the lower world by making use of its laws;

– Those who can influence the things of this world by using (for they know them) the celestial laws;

– Those who know the mysteries of the superior world and can perform in this world miracles that surpass the limits of the natural laws, celestial as well as terrestrial.

The third degree is that of the prophets. The first and second classes of sages are respectively savants in the natural sciences, and astrologers, who not only know the natural and celestial laws but also know how to use them.

Let us take the following instance: the astrologer knows what must happen according to the decree of the stars; he cannot change the decree but he can arm himself against it. Thus when horses are in full gallop on the open road, a blind man will be trampled down, a man with sight will jump aside in time. Like Abraham bar Ḥiyya, Ibn Ezra again uses the example of preventive medicine. It is better to be on guard against the inauspicious influences of the astral bodies, as one would abstain from unwholesome food.

It is known that each country and each people is ruled by a different star, and that each of these stars has a special character and particular laws.

Israel and the land of Israel are under the empire of the planet Saturn, which Abraham Ibn Ezra describes as follows:

Saturn is cold and dry; its nature is very pernicious; it denotes destruction, ruin, death, affliction, weeping, grief, complaint, and ancient things. In the human activity it has control of the mind, and its area covers the first zone, which is India. Its group of people embraces the Moors, the Jews, the natives of Barbary, the assembly of all the elders, the husbandmen, the cultivators, the tanners, the cleaners of lavatories, the servants, the outcasts, the thieves, the diggers of wells and ditches, and the undertakers who get the mortuary shrouds. Its metals of the earth include dark lead, iron-ore, black stones, all black marble, the magnet, and every heavy and dark stone. Its sections of land comprise the grottos, the wells, the prisons, every dim and uninhabitable place, and the cemetery-grounds. Among its wild animals there are the elephants, the camels, any big and ugly animal such as hogs, bears, monkeys, black dogs, and black cats. As its part of the birds it has every bird with a long neck such as the ostrich, the eagle, the vulture, every bird with a terrible voice, the raven, the owl, and every bird that looks black. Of the things that crawl on the ground it takes in the fleas, the lice, the flies, the mice, and any creeping thing within the earth which is destructive and mephitic. As for trees it has any tree with gall, the carob-tree, tragacanth known as balot, the medlar-tree, any tree which has thorns that hurt but which bears no fruit, lentils, and millet. Its medicinal species are the cactus, which is called aloe, myrobalan, albalileg, and almaleg, which are like prunes imported from India, in addition to any plant producing a deadly poison, any bitter thing such as absinth, and in general any black plant. Its nature is cold and dry; its savor is acrid, drawing together the tongue, and that which does not have an agreeable taste; its odor is fetid. Of the kinds of spices there are alcasat or cinamon, cassia fistula or barks of the tree, aromatic laurel, and almaha or gum. Its rainments are the cloak, the woolen clothing, the covers, and any heavy garment. To its part of the nature of man corresponds the mental faculty, paucity of words, astuteness, isolation from human beings, the power to dominate over them, to conquer, pillage, wrath, to be peremptory in one's word, concatenation of ideas, knowledge of secrets, worship of the Lord, the betrayal of fellow-men, contrariness, to be afraid, to tremble, in general to deceive consistently with little benefit and great harm, to plow and build up the land, to extract metals, to seek hidden treasures and to excavate, to meditate upon subjects of death and any thing which has lasted for years. Its occupation is any one which requires much work and which yields little reward, all menial tasks such as chopping stones, cleaning cisterns, and any sordid job. It denotes fathers, grandfathers, the deceased, tears, separation, wandering, poverty, indigence, humiliation, distant and bad roads in which lurks danger, and it does not meet with success in any undertaking.

(The Beginning of Wisdom, trans. F. Cantera, pp. 193-4)

A certain number of positive commandments have been given to us by God Himself in order to preserve us from the influences of Saturn and other malevolent planets and to allow us to receive the influence of the beneficent planets to the best advantage. The divine commandments are founded on three principles:

(1) Respecting the conditions that permit the reception of the good influences;

(2) Making a sacrifice to 'evil' when the evil is due to the nature of an astral body, and thus averting a greater evil;

(3) Attracting the power of the superior beings.

Sacrifices belong to the first group. God, who is perfect, has no need of sacrifices; if He has ordained them, it is nevertheless for a vital reason, the necessity of acting in accordance with the character of the star that rules over the Land of Israel. If the people does not conform to these celestial laws and ceases to offer the appropriate sacrifices, the Land of Israel will reject its inhabitants. Unions prohibited in the *Torah* will have the same unfortunate result. In Padan-Aram, which is Mesopotamia, Jacob could marry two sisters, and in Egypt Amram could marry his aunt without thereby transgressing the law of purity, but in the Land of Israel this kind of union is absolutely forbidden.

Certain sacrifices are linked to the second principle. The scapegoat that was sent into the desert on the Day of Atonement carried the sins of Israel, and was destined to appease the anger of Mars, who rules over goats and demons. This second principle is also one of the reasons for circumcision. According to the decree of the stars, every man of the people of Israel must shed his blood; in giving the planet Mars an acceptable substitute, the blood of circumcision, violent death is avoided.

The third principle is more complex and mysterious, for it quite plainly involves magic. To attract the powers of superior beings is a positive act, but magic is unambiguously forbidden in the Bible. The teraphim that Rachel stole from her father Laban were undoubtedly intended to attract the beneficent force of the stars, and are expressly prohibited. However, it seems that the cherubim in the Temple also had the function of attracting this benevolent force. Besides, Ibn Ezra affirms, Israel has no need to use forbidden magical means, for, if they are forbidden, this is because Israel has been granted the divine commandments and a direct communion with God, which are obviously much more efficacious.

We should note that these astrological explications of the commandments are not the only ones given by Ibn Ezra, for, according to him, each commandment has several reasons and motivations. If I have dwelt on this aspect of his interpretation at some length, this is because I wished to show the importance of astrology in Ibn Ezra's thought, an importance that has not been much commented on in histories of philosophy. Moreover, when Maimonidean philosophy had become preponderant in Jewish thinking, it was this astrological contribution that allowed thirteenth-, fourteenth-, and fifteenth-century philosophers to add a human and slightly mysterious dimension to the entirely scientific thought of Maimonides. But before I begin my discussion of Aristotelianism, I shall consider the thought of Judah Halevi, and Abu-l-Barakāt.

Chapter 4

JUDAH HALEVI AND
ABU-L-BARAKĀT

Judah Halevi

Judah Halevi was born in Tudela, before 1075. He received the Arabic and
Hebrew education of a child of a wealthy family, and was still a young man
when he travelled to Grenada, passing through Andalusia and Cordoba,
where he won a poetry contest. At this period he met Moses Ibn Ezra and
other great poets of Grenada, Seville and Saragossa. The situation of the
Jews deteriorated under the Almoravides, who conquered Andalusia after 1090,
and Halevi left Grenada. During the next twenty years he moved from town
to town in Christian Spain, meeting scholars, poets and nobles. He practised
medicine at Toledo and remained there until the murder of his benefactor,
Solomon Ibn Ferrizuel, courtier of Alfonso VI of Castile. Returning to
Muslim Spain, he went to Cordoba, Grenada and Almeria On very close
terms with Abraham Ibn Ezra, he visited North Africa with him.

Halevi's decision to go to the Land of Israel was the fruit of long meditations on the destiny of the Jewish people, and the *Kuzari* expounds the
reasons for this choice. It was at this time also that he wrote his poems of
love for Zion, which are among the most beautiful in all Hebrew literature.
In 1140 he arrived at Alexandria, where he was honourably received. Four
months later he sailed to the Holy Land, where after a few weeks he died.
We don't know if he ever saw the Jerusalem that he had celebrated in poetry
with so much faith and hope.

Judah Halevi wrote much poetry in Hebrew, on profane as well as religious themes. His philosophical work was composed in Arabic and translated into Hebrew by Judah Ibn Tibbon in 1167; and since then it has not
ceased to be read, commented-on, and quoted.

Since the twelfth century the work has been known under the name of
Kuzari (*the Khazar*), and in a letter by the author found in the Cairo Genizah
it was already given this title. The full Arabic name is *Kitāb al-Radd wa-'l-
Dalīl fī'l-dīn al-dhalīl* (*The Book of Refutation and Proof in Defence of the
Despised Faith*). In the same letter Judah Halevi declares that he wrote the
book in order to combat Karaism. The danger represented by this sect was
very real in twelfth-century Spain, when the Karaites were threatening to
prevail over the Rabbanites. In fact, Karaism is occasionally mentioned in

the text, but, to me at least, it does not seem to occupy an important place in the author's thought.

The title *Kuzari* expresses the contents. The work is an account of the conversion to rabbinical Judaism of the King of the Khazars. This is of course a literary fiction, but it is based on historical facts, for nomadic Jewish tribes related to the Huns formed an independent state between the seventh and tenth centuries. In the tenth century Ḥasdai Ibn Shaprut carried on a correspondence with the King of the Khazars, and Judah Halevi most probably had access to other documents as well, which have not reached us. The story of the conversion of the king of the nomadic tribe to a specific religion, in this case the Jewish, after examining various faiths represented by their respective wise men, is in itself quite close to certain historical facts, for the conversions to Christianity of Slavic nomadic peoples by emissaries from the Byzantine emperors are related in a very similar way. In addition, public debates between adherents of the different religions were current during the Middle Ages. In Book I of the *Kuzari* we find an exposition of the different doctrines: the philosophical, the Christian, the Muslim and finally the Jewish. The King of the Khazars undertakes the quest of the true religion in consequence of a dream:

A vision came to him repeatedly of an angel addressing him, saying, 'Your intention is pleasing to God, but your action is not pleasing.' Now he was exceedingly zealous in performing the worship of the Khazar faith, to such an extent that he personally used to officiate at the service of the temple and the offering of the sacrifices with an intention that was sincere and pure. Nevertheless, each time he exerted himself in these actions, the angel would come to him in the night and tell him, 'Your intention is pleasing but your action is not pleasing.'

(*Kuzari* I, I, trans. L. V. Berman)

The debate between the various religions is thus engaged on the level of the religious act. This act, religious, not intellectual or moral, is willed by God, who expresses His desire through the intermediary of an angel. Thus in the very first lines Judah Halevi considers certain points as evident:

(1) God positively demands certain acts from man;

(2) His will is communicated to man through the intermediary of a dream, which is 'true' and not deceitful;

(3) Pure intention is not enough; God demands acts.

The philosophical doctrine that I have cited in my introduction obviously could not satisfy the King of the Khazars. The God of the philosophers, perfect, knows only Himself; He alone is perfect, for all knowledge exterior to Himself would arise from a lack, a need. According to certain Aristotelian commentators, God also knows the laws of nature in so far as He is their cause, but He does not know individuals or the details of the imperfect world of bodies. How could this God demand such or another act from the King of the Khazars, since He did not even know of his existence?

The exposition of the philosopher continues with an explanation of what is meant by 'will of God'; this is a manner of speaking, of expressing something else, that is, the relations between God and the world. From God emanate necessarily and eternally a series of causes that produce the material universe; the Active Intellect, the last in the hierarchical order, presides over the destinies of this lower world, without on that account having a knowledge of individuals as individuals. Man is the product of a mixture of qualities; if the mixture is imperfect, he will be close to the beasts, if it is perfect, he will have, potentially, the intellect that he may, through good morals and the study of sciences, cause to become *in actu*. He will then be like the Active Intellect and will be blended with it. The human soul may survive only in so far as this soul has lost all individuality and has been transformed into knowledge, common to all men and to the Active Intellect.

Judah Halevi here expounds a certain current of Andalusian Aristotelian philosophy; his contemporary, the Muslim philosopher Ibn Bājja, affirmed the unity of the souls in their conjunction with the Active Intellect, that is, the conjunction of human intellects that have passed from potentiality into actuality with the eternal knowledge of the general laws of nature.

For the philosopher in the *Kuzari*, no one religion is superior to any other, for religion has nothing to do with knowledge that constitutes the final purpose of man's life; religion is the political law permitting the organization of human society in order that the perfect man, the philosopher, may live in it and attain his ultimate objective: conjunction with the Active Intellect.

To this the Khazar answers:

Your statement is persuasive but it does not fit my request, because I know myself to be pure of soul ... No doubt there are [courses of] action which are pleasing in themselves, not because of the thought behind them.　　　　(I, 2)

Then the Khazar said to himself, 'I will ask the Christians and the Muslims, for either one of their ways of acting is no doubt pleasing [to God]. But as for the Jews, their apparent lowliness, smallness [in number], and the hate of all for them is sufficient [reason to ignore them].'　　　　(I, 4)

The discourse of the Christian scholar is divided into two parts:

(1) He declares that he believes in eternal God, who created the world in six days, knows every man and is provident; in short, everything that is written in the *Torah*.

(2) The Christians are the legitimate heirs of Israel, for the divine essence was incarnated in Jesus, unique in his triple person: Father, Son and Holy Ghost.[1] Christianity has not abolished the laws revealed to the people of Israel; it continues to study them and it has brought them to perfection.

To this the King replies that logic does not allow one to accept such affirmations; between such unlikely doctrines and everyday experience there

---

[1] In most editions, for instance that of Vienna, where the text is accompanied by an excellent commentary, the text is cut by censorship; instead of 'Christians' we find 'Persians' and the whole passage on Jesus is missing.

must be a logical connection; but he does not see it, perhaps because these are new things that he has not known from childhood? At all events, the king decides to pursue his inquiries and addresses himself to a Muslim scholar, perhaps a Muʻtazilite, who affirms the absolute incorporeality of God and the prophecy addressed to Muhammad, seal of prophets. The proof of this prophecy is the Koran, living sign of the link between God and His prophet.

To this, the King responds:

> However, [even] if your book is a miracle, it is written in Arabic, then foreigners like me will not [be able to] distinguish its miraculous and wonderful nature. If it is recited to me, I won't [be able to] distinguish between it and anything else said in Arabic. (I, 6)

In other words, to admit something as hard to credit as the discourse of God to a being of flesh and blood, proofs more convincing, more certain, more public, than these are necessary. The King here echoes an ancient quarrel, going back, it seems, to the first centuries of the Christian era: pagan philosophers could not accept the Christian theory of incarnation and prophecy. Certainly, they admitted intermediaries between God and man, but these intermediaries could only be eminent beings, intellects or spheres.

The Muslim scholar, as before him the Christian, then speaks of signs and miracles, and these are the ones that God had wrought for the people of Israel, those that all men recognize, which have never been doubted. So the King sees himself obliged to interrogate a Jewish scholar. Questioned by the King, the Rabbi, the sage, says:

> I believe in the God of Abraham, Isaac, and Israel, who brought the children of Israel out of Egypt by means of signs and miracles, took care of them in the wilderness, and gave them the land of Canaan after crossing the sea and the Jordan by means of miracles. He sent Moses with his religious law and, subsequently, thousands of prophets supporting his religious law by means of promises to whoever observed it and threats to whoever transgressed it. We believe in what was published in the *Torah*, but the story is [very] long. (I, II)

The Rabbi thus proclaims his belief in a national God who intervenes in history to save a people whom He has chosen for Himself, and he confirms the King's apprehensions:

> I had decided not to ask a Jew because I knew of the destruction of their traditions and the deficiency of their opinions, since their downfall did not leave them [anything] praiseworthy. Now why didn't you say, O Jew, that you believe in the Creator of the world, its Orderer, and its Governor, He who created you and provided for you and similar descriptions, which are the proof of every adherent of a religion? Now, for their sake, truth and justice are sought in order to imitate the Creator in His wisdom and His justice. (I, 12)

In fact, asks the King, how can one not speak first of God who has created the earth and the heavens, God who is common to all men, instead of this God who is particular to one people?

We find here, in a striking epitome, the problem of universalism opposed to particularism, a problem still vital and perhaps even more so at the present day when more and more nationalisms are in the process of awakening. Should one seek what is common to all humanity, or should one cultivate the differences? Jews have been accused, and this is evidently one of the sources of antisemitism, of being different from other men and of taking pleasure in this difference; as the King of the Khazars says: you proclaim your belief in a national God because your despicable situation prevents you from seeing the world in its entirety, in its universal grandeur. The Rabbi is not abashed by this criticism. This universal God of whom the King speaks is the God of the intellect, of philosophy, and the proof that the intellect cannot really lead to God is that the philosophers are incapable of agreeing either on practical acts or on theories. No proof exists to confirm that one theory rather than another is true, these are only hypotheses, sometimes correct and sometimes false, and the disputes between philosophers are a striking illustration of this state of affairs. And the Rabbi proceeds to propose to the King another way that leads to God, more eminent than philosophy: that of the prophets. One cannot say that this is a critique of philosophy, it is rather the inclusion of philosophy in another system that transcends it. This is an extreme position. We have seen that the whole of philosophy was based on the axiom that rational thought is what makes man man; it differentiates him from the animals, it places him in contact with God, for it is the 'divine' part of his being. To superimpose another faculty over the intellect is thus to deprive philosophy of its whole *raison d'être*, and, in this sense, Judah Halevi indeed negates philosophy, or rather Aristotelian theology and its metaphysics, for to this metaphysics, founded on hypotheses and incapable of conducting to certitudes, he opposes mathematical science, the truth of which is universal and recognized by everyone. But let us return to the dialogue between the King and the Rabbi. The Rabbi is about to show the King why he began his discourse by the affirmation of his belief in the God of Israel. This is because the existence of the God of Israel and His participation in the history of the people is, precisely, 'proven'; it has been authenticated not only by the people of Israel, but also by the Egyptians, and nobody has ever evinced the least doubt on the subject. This is the certainty, the evident proof from which the search for God may start: the revelation of His link with Israel, the divine character of the people and its Law. The King then declares that if this is indeed so, then the people of Israel hold the exclusive revelation of God and no Gentile may participate in this revelation. The Rabbi responds that in fact this is the case; even converted to Judaism, a Gentile cannot be on the same level as an Israelite, that is, receive the prophecy. This is a serious affirmation, and if in the rabbinical tradition there is a tendency that agrees with Judah Halevi, other rabbis, more numerous, have affirmed the absolute equality of converts and Israelites by birth; but here, as on other points, the author chooses the most particularist interpretations.

The King, quite naturally, is not satisfied with this response, and it is in rather a chilly tone that he gives the Rabbi permission to continue his speech. The Rabbi recalls the hierarchy of created beings: minerals, plants, animals, men, and asks the King: Are there not beings higher than human beings, or does the scale of beings stop with them? The King thinks that sages are more eminent than other men; however, the Rabbi is not speaking of a difference of dignity within the same class, but of a difference like that of plants in relation to animals or animals to men; the King, of course, answers that he cannot see that among corporeal beings there can be any more eminent than man.

The sage then says:

I want a level which differentiates its possessors essentially, like the difference of plants from inanimate things and the difference of men from animals. However, differences of degree are infinite, because they are accidental. They are not really [different] levels.
The Khazar said: There is, then, no level above man among objects of sense perception.
The sage said: Well, if we find a man who enters fire in such a way that it does not cause him pain, delays eating and does not hunger, whose face is illuminated by a light which vision cannot bear, is not sick and does not grow old so that when he reaches his [proper] age he dies a death freely chosen like someone going to his mat to sleep on a certain day and hour, in addition to knowing the unseen with respect to past and future, isn't this a level which is essentially separate from the level of [ordinary] people?
The Khazar said: Rather, this level would be angelic if it exists. It [would] belong to the realm of the divine *Amr*. It is neither intellectual, psychic, or natural.

(I, 39–42)

The Arabic expression *Amr ilahi* (exact transcription *'Amr ilahī*) cannot be translated; it conveys the idea of 'word', but also 'thing'. The *Amr ilahi* is a central notion in Judah Halevi's thought, and I shall continue to use the Arabic term, in order to preserve the multiple meanings that this word assumes in the author's writing and his system.

To go on with the analysis of Book I. After having affirmed the existence of a class of prophets superior to ordinary mankind, the Rabbi explains to the King that all men agree on a certain number of verities based on the history of these prophets, who have transmitted the divine spark from generation to generation. Three facts, according to the Rabbi, prove the authenticity of the biblical narratives and chronology:

(1) Human languages have common and different aspects, which can only be explained by the history of the Tower of Babel and the confusion of tongues.

(2) Among all people the week has seven days, whereas it could have consisted of any arbitrary number.

(3) The decimal system, likewise, is universally in use.

The Khazar said: How is your belief not weakened by what is reported in the name of the inhabitants of India? They have historical remains and buildings which they affirm are a million years old?

The sage said: It would have injured my belief were a [soundly] established belief to exist or a book upon whose chronology a multitude had agreed unanimously. But that is not the case. Indeed, they are an abandoned people; they have nothing well founded. Thus they distress the adherents of the religions with speech like this, just as they distress them with their idols, talismans, and devices, saying that they help them. They scoff at those who say that they have a book from God. In addition, there are a few books which individuals have composed by means of which those weak in mind are deceived, like some books of the astrologers putting in dates which consist of tens of thousands of years, such as the *The Book of Nabatian Agriculture* in which Yanbushad, Sagrit, and Duani are named. It is claimed that they lived before Adam and that Yanbushad was the teacher of Adam and similar things.

The Khazar said: I concede that I attacked you by means of a calamitous multitude and a people who do not have an agreed upon doctrine. Thus your answer hits the mark. But what will you say about the philosophers since their stand with respect to investigation and accuracy is [of the highest]? They agreed generally on the eternity and the everlastingness of the world. This implies neither tens of thousands nor millions [of years], but what is infinite.

The sage said: The philosophers are excused because they are a group which had neither inherited knowledge nor a faith, because they are Greeks and the Greeks are of the sons of Japheth, who live in the north. However, the knowledge inherited from Adam, and it is the knowledge which is supported by the divine *Amr*, exists only among the descendants of Shem, who was the best part of Adam. Knowledge only came to Greece ever since they [the Greeks] began to have the upper hand, so that knowledge was transferred to them from Persia, and to Persia from the Chaldeans. Then the famous philosophers in that empire gushed forth, [but] neither before nor afterwards. Ever since dominion passed to the Romans [Arabic: *al-rūm*; possibly, the Byzantines] no famous philosopher has appeared among them.

The Khazar said: Does this imply that the knowledge of Aristotle [should] not be [considered as] true?

The sage said: Yes. He imposed a difficult task on his mind and thought since he had no tradition from someone he could trust. Thus, he considered the beginning of the world and its end. Conceiving the beginning was as difficult for his thinking as [conceiving of] eternity, but he made the reasoning which suggested eternity prevail by thought alone. However, he didn't think to ask about the date of those who existed previously or how men were related to one another. Had the Philosopher [lived] in a nation which inherited traditions and generally known [opinions] which could not be rejected, then he certainly would have employed analogies [Arabic: *qiyāsātihi*; possibly, syllogisms] and demonstration in making creation something firmly established despite its difficulty, just as he established [the doctrine of] eternity, which is more difficult to accept.

The Khazar said: Can [scientific] demonstration be tipped [in one direction over another]?

The sage said: And who can provide us with a demonstration in this question? God forbid that the religious law reaches something which rejects [the testimony] of the senses or demonstration! However, it does teach miracles and the breaking of customs by the creation of substances or the turning of one substance into another substance in order to prove the existence of the Creator and His power to do what He wishes when He wishes. The question of eternity and creation is profound and the proofs of the two arguments are equally balanced. In such a case, the tradition from Adam, Noah, and Moses, upon them be peace, [founded] on prophecy, which is more believable than reasoning, tops the balance in favour of creation. Even if the adherent of religion is forced into conceding and confirming the existence of eternal matter and many worlds before this world, there is nothing in that which rebuts his belief that this world is created from a specific time and its first individuals were Adam and Eve. (I, 60–7)

It is enough to replace 'Aristotle' by 'modern science' for this passage to assume a very modern tone. It contains historical testimonies that contradict the biblical tradition (and are rejected rather than refuted) as well as the affirmation of the relativity, but also the importance, of physical theories.

The central point is not history, or physics, whether Aristotelian or not, it is belief in 'the existence of the Creator and His Power to do what he wishes when He wishes'. After a critique of the philosophical concept of nature, which confers on nature the attributes of God, the Rabbi proceeds to explain the origin of the religion of Israel. The King supposes that it was first adopted by some individuals who formed a small community; in the course of time, this community waxed stronger; finally, with the help of the reigning king, a whole nation embraced the faith. This view is inspired by the King's awareness of the state of affairs in his own kingdom, since he is about to convert and to bring about the conversion of his subjects to Judaism. But the Rabbi does not agree. It is true that religions that are of human origin (he alludes to Christianity and Islam) are propagated in this way. But there is nothing gradual about the appearance in history of a divine faith, i.e. the religion of Judaism; it is characterized by its suddenness and its supernatural character.

The children of Israel were enslaved in Egypt, six hundred thousand men who were above twenty years to the age of fifty, tracing their genealogy to twelve tribal [chiefs]. No one separated himself from them and fled to another country and no foreigner intermingled with them. They awaited [the fulfilment] of a promise made to their ancestors, Abraham, Isaac, and Jacob, upon them be peace, that He would make them inherit the land of Canaan. Canaan at that time was in the hands of seven nations who were extremely great in number, power, and success. [On the other hand], the children of Israel were in utter humiliation and misery, with Pharoah slaying their children so that they would not become many. Then He sent Moses and Aaron, upon them be peace, despite their weakness, and they fought Pharoah, despite his strength, with signs and miracles and [other] matters contrary to the course of nature. He was not able to shield himself from both of them, nor orders [to do them] evil, nor could he protect himself from the ten plagues which took hold of the inhabitants of Egypt, in their waters, in their land, in their air, in their plants, in their animals, in their bodies, and in themselves, since the most previous of those who were in their houses and their most beloved, every first-born child, died in the twinkling of an eye in the middle of the night. No house was without a dead body, except for the houses of the children of Israel. And all these plagues came down upon them with knowledge, forewarning, and threat and they were lifted from them with knowledge and forewarning so that it might be believed that they were intended by a willing God who does what He wishes when He wishes. They were neither [caused] by nature, nor by astrology, nor by chance.

Then the children of Israel went out from the servitude of Pharoah by the command of God in the night at the time of the death of the children of Egypt and went towards the region of the Red Sea. Their guide was a pillar of cloud and [also] a pillar of fire went before them, leading them and governing them. Conducting them were two elders, men of God, Moses and Aaron, upon them be peace, who were over eighty years old at the time that prophecy came upon them. Up to that point, they had no religious commandments except a few inherited from those individuals descended from Adam and Noah. Moses did not abrogate them nor did he annul them, but he added to them.

Pharoah followed them, but they did not have recourse to weapons; the people did not know the art of fighting. Then the sea split and they crossed. Pharoah and his swarm were drowned and the sea cast the dead bodies out to the children of Israel so that they saw them personally. The story is very long and well known.

The Khazar said: This is the divine *Amr* in truth. One must accept the religious law connected with it because no doubt will enter the heart that this [miracle] could have been based on magic or tricks or imagination.

(I, 83–4)

These miracles are crowned by the giving of the Law on Mount Sinai:

The people prepared and readied themselves for the level of revelation and moreover, to listen to the address openly, all of them. That came about after three days of preparations of great trepidation, namely, lightning, thunder, earthquakes, and lights, surrounding that which is called the mountain of Sinai. That light remained for forty days on the mountain. The people would see it and they would see Moses entering into it and leaving it. And the people heard clearly the address of the Ten Commandments which are the foundations of the commandments and their roots.

(I, 87)

One should not conclude that God, having spoken, is corporeal, for, says the Rabbi:

And how shall we not strip [God] of corporeality when we strip many of His creations of it, such as the rational soul which is truly man? For indeed that which in Moses speaks to us, intellects, and governs is not his tongue, nor his heart, nor his brain; these are only instruments for Moses. [Actually], Moses is a rational soul which makes distinctions, is not a body, is not limited in place, nor is [any] place too limited for it; it is not too narrow for the forms of all created things to find their place in it. Thus we describe it with angelic, spiritual attributes. How much more so is this the case with the Creator of all!

However, we must not reject what has been transmitted about the scene [of Mount Sinai]. Furthermore, we should say we do not know how the concept became corporeal so that it became speech and beat on our ears, nor what [beings] He, exalted is He, created which did not exist [before], nor what existing beings He forced [to do His bidding], because His capacity is not limited, just as we say that He, exalted is He, created the two tablets and wrote them down in the manner of engraving, just as He created the heavens and the stars with His will alone.

(I, 68)

At this moment the dialogue takes a dramatic turn: the King recalls that grave episode which so deeply embarrassed the rabbis, the episode of the Golden Calf. How can one claim that the people of Israel is of a kind superior to the rest of humanity, that God chose to speak to it directly, and that the whole people was present at this supernatural scene on Mount Sinai, when, only a few days later, they fabricated a golden calf and descended to the lowest levels of idolatry?

The Rabbi makes a long reply, and its length is a proof of his discomfort. He surveys the whole history of the *Amr ilahi* and its relation with men. Adam, formed by the hands of God, was perfect:

Adam . . . received the soul in its perfection, the intellect in the highest degree possible for human nature, and the divine power after the intellect; I mean the level by means of which one may have contact with God and the spiritual beings and know truths without learning [them], but by means of the least thought. He was called the son of God by us and he and all of those descendants who are similar to him are [called] the sons of God.

He gave birth to many children, but not one of them was fit to be the representative of Adam except for Abel, because he was like him. When his brother Cain killed him because of jealousy over this rank, he was replaced with Seth who was like Adam, for he was the best part of him and his choice element. Others beside him were like peelings and dates of bad quality. The best part of Seth was Enosh. And in the same way the *Amr* attached itself to Noah by means of individuals who were choice elements similar to Adam, and they were called the sons of God. They had perfection by nature, moral qualities, longevity, sciences, and power. (I, 95)

[With the sons of Jacob] . . . is the beginning of the resting of the divine *Amr* on a group after only being found in separate individuals. Then God took charge of preserving them, raising them, and paying attention to them in Egypt, just as a tree which has good roots is taken care of until it produces a perfect fruit which is like the first fruit from which it was planted; I mean Abraham, Isaac, Jacob, and Joseph and his brothers. Then the fruit was produced in Moses, upon him be peace, and Aaron and Miriam, upon them be peace, [others] like Bezalel, Oholiab, the chiefs of the tribes, [others] like the seventy elders who were fit for sustained prophecy, [others] like Joshua, Caleb, Hur, and many besides them. At that time, they merited the appearance of light upon them and that lordly providence. (*Ibid.*)

The fault of the Golden Calf was not committed by these perfect individuals, that is, the greater part of the community of Israel, but by a small group of individuals, and even then, this fault can be excused:

Their sin consisted in making an image which they had been forbidden and, further, in that they related a divine *Amr* to a thing created by their hands and their free will without the command of God. Their excuse for that consists in the heedlessness which was widespread beforehand. But the ones who worshipped it were [only] about three thousand from a total of six hundred thousand. However, the excuse of the élite who helped in making it was that it was for a purpose – that the rebellious might be distinguished from the believer, so that the rebellious who worshipped the calf would be killed. For this they became subject to criticism because they made rebellion pass from [a state of] potentiality and internality to action.

Thus that sin did not constitute a departure from the general rule of submission to One who had brought them forth out of Egypt, but they disobeyed one of His commands. For indeed He, exalted is He, forbade images but they adopted an image. They should have been patient and not have produced for themselves a model, direction [of prayer], altar, and sacrifices. This came from the practical reasoning of the astrologers and the makers of talismans among them. They thought that their rational actions would be close to the actions of the truth. Their path in this (regard) was that of the fool whom we have mentioned [see below, p. 126] who took charge of the doctor's pharmacy so that the people, who used to benefit from it previously, were killed. In addition, the intention of the people was not to depart from submission [to God]. Rather, they were trying, they thought, to submit. Therefore, they went to Aaron. Aaron tried to reveal their real self, so he helped to make it and blame was attached to him since he realized their rebellion in actuality.

Now this story is shocking and shameful for us because of the removal of images which are objects of worship from most of the religious communities in our era. But at that time it was easy because all of the religious communities had images . . .

Despite this [apparent justification], punishment was meted out to those who worshipped the calf at once and they were slain. Their total amount was [only about three thousand from a total of six hundred thousand. Manna did not cease to come down for their food, the cloud to shade them, the pillar of fire to lead them, and prophecy was extant and increasing among them. Nothing was taken away from them by which they were distinguished, except the two tablets which Moses broke. Then he interceded for their restoration; they were restored to them; and that sin was forgiven them.

(I, 97)

One of the arguments that the Rabbi adduces in extenuation of the error of the Golden Calf is the idolatry that reigned at the time among all the peoples. The relation between the idolatrous cults and the biblical cult had indeed been perceived by Judah Halevi; the difference is not one of kind: since God Himself had prescribed the image of the two cherubim in the Temple, the intention was not that no created being should be represented; the difference lay in the fact that it was God Himself who did or did not desire such or another cult. The divine will is expressed in the written tradition, complemented by the oral *Torah*, and the sacrifices are precisely the illustration of the importance that each detail assumes:

Indeed, the description of the sacrifices, how they are to be offered, in what place, in what direction, how they are to be slaughtered, what is to be done with their blood and their limbs [depend] on different arts. All of them are clearly described by God so that the least thing may not be lacking from them. [If this were the case,] the whole would be corrupted. It is the same with natural things which come to be composed of minute relations, too minute for the imaginative powers [to grasp]. Were their relations to be disordered in the smallest way, then that thing coming into being would be corrupted. [If this happened], then that plant or animal or limb, for example, would be corrupted or deprived [of existence]. And similarly [Scripture] mentioned how the animal to be sacrificed should be dismembered and what should be done with each piece – what is for eating, what is for burning, who would eat, who would burn, who would sacrifice from among the groups of people which are responsible among them without leaving anyone out, what are the descriptions of the sacrificers so that there is no deficiency in them – even in their bodies and their clothes, especially the descendants of Aaron, who was permitted to enter into the place of the divine *Amr* where the divine presence was together with the Ark and the Torah. (I, 99)

The King of the Khazars is already convinced:

The Khazar said: You have supported my opinion with respect to what I believed and what I saw in my dream, that men will not arrive at the divine *Amr* except by means of a divine *Amr*; I mean by actions which God orders. (I, 98)

This could have been the end of the Book. It is certainly the central idea, and the development that follows only makes it more explicit.

Before the conversion to Judaism of the King of the Khazars, which is recounted at the beginning of Book II, the Rabbi answers two more questions:

(1) Why did God choose only one people and not all humanity?

(2) Are reward and punishment reserved for the soul only, after the death of the body?

From here on the dialogue begins to flounder and becomes a monologue, for the King of the Khazars contents himself with posing questions to the Rabbi that allow the latter to present his doctrine in detail, while the King listens to him like an attentive disciple to his master. I shall therefore leave my analysis of the *Kuzari* and expound the principal ideas.

For Judah Halevi, God revealed Himself in history, in choosing a people, a land, a language. This choice is the only real proof of the existence of God and is an integral part of the order of the world. In hierarchical system, the prophetic order, that of Adam and his sons, of Noah, then of the people of Israel as a whole, is superimposed on the mineral, vegetative, animal, and rational realms. The divine spark that is transmitted by spiritual lineage is directly in touch with 'divine *Amr*', that is, the *Amr ilahi*. Halevi uses this phrase in several meanings:

(1) The divine spark that is transmitted by heredity, a Shi'te concept; this divine germ offers the possibility of union with the *Amr ilahi* in its second sense, and perhaps it is one with it.

(2) The divine Word, the divine Action, the divine Will; this meaning seems to be borrowed from Ismaili theology, or from another theology going back in some way to the long recension of the *Theology* of Aristotle.

(3) *Amr ilahi* also has the sense of 'supernatural way of living', and S. Pines in this connection refers to Ibn Bājja, a Spanish Arab philosopher contemporary with Judah Halevi, whose philosophical doctrine is very similar to the philosopher's exposition in Book I of the *Kuzari*.

The mode of the divine action is two kinds:

(1) Natural; this is the emanation. The *Amr ilahi* is cause of the Intellect, which is cause of the Soul; then comes nature. But, one can begin from this lower world, as in the Rabbi's words:

I will summarize for you the essential points which will help you conceive shared Prime Matter, the elements, nature, the soul, the intellect, (and finally) divine science.

(v, 2)

This scheme of the universe corresponds exactly to that of Aristotle's *Theology* in its long recension.

(2) Each of the hierarchical levels of being can attain its own perfection and this, far from being withheld, is generously conceded to it:

For the divine *Amr* is, as it were, waiting for whoever is worthy to attach himself to it so that it may become a god to it, such as the prophets and the saints; just as the intellect waits for the one whose natural qualities have become perfected and his soul and his moral qualities have become temperate that it may dwell in him perfectly, like the philosophers; just as the soul waits for the one whose natural powers have become perfected and prepared for increased excellence so that it may well in it, like the animals; and just as nature waits for the mixture which is temperate in its qualities in order to dwell in it so that it may become a plant.

(II, 14)

If Judah Halevi had been content with this one hierarchy, his system would have been very similar to that of the Neoplatonists, who hypothesized intellectual illumination, but for our author God also acts in an immediate way, according to a second, non-intermediary mode. Moses presented himself to Pharoah, as the emissary not of the God of the Universe or of the Creator, but of the God present in history: 'I believe in the God of Abraham, Isaac and Israel . . .' (See p. 116.)

However, to progress from the union with the Intellect (that is, the degree of the philosophers) to that of the union with the *Amr* (that of the prophets) is not a gradual and natural process. There is a clear break in the hierarchy; by his own forces man can ascend to the level of the Intellect, and to do this he must follow the discursive way, that of philosophy. To be distinguished by the *Amr*, he must follow the supernatural way, that of the *Torah*. God has reserved this way for his chosen; in each generation since Adam there was a man pure and worthy of having the *Amr* repose on him, but at a certain stage it rested on the people of Israel as a whole, and only this people has been chosen by God.

To the choosing of the people of Israel corresponds the choosing of the Land of Israel, for it is for the sake of this Land that all the prophecies were given, and far from this Land prophecy cannot exist.

The sage said: Accepting the special quality of a [specific] land with respect to all lands is not difficult. You see places in which certain plants, minerals, and animals aside from others are produced. Their inhabitants are set apart by means of their [external] forms and their moral dispositions from others through the medium of their temperament. For the perfection and imperfection of the soul depend on its temperament.

The Khazar said: But I have not heard that those who inhabit Palestine are superior to the rest of mankind.

125

The sage said: Your mountain is the same. You say: on it a vineyard will flourish. [But] were grape [vines] not planted and it were not cultivated properly, it would not produce grapes. Now primary distinction belongs to people who are the best part and the choice element.

Second place in accomplishing that [belongs] to the land together with the works and the commandments which are connected with it. They are like cultivation with respect to the vineyard. However, this élite may not attach itself to a divine *Amr* in any place, as it is possible [so in Arabic – in the Hebrew translation 'impossible'] for the vineyard to flourish in another mountain.

The Khazar said: How can that be? For prophecy existed from the first man to Moses in other places, Abraham in Ur of the Chaldeans, Ezekiel and Daniel in Babylonia, and Jeremiah in Egypt.

The sage said: Everyone who prophesies only prophesies in it or because of it . . .

There [in the Land of Israel] no doubt are the places which deserve to be called the gates of heaven. Do you not see how Jacob did not attribute the visions which he saw to the purity of his soul, not to his faith and the firmness of his certitude, but he ascribed them to the place, as it is said: *And he feared and said, 'How full of awe is this place!'* [Genesis 28: 17] And before [Scripture] said: *And he lighted upon the place* [Genesis 28: 11]; he means 'the special place'.   (II, 10–14)

The central place occupied by the Land of Israel is not confirmed by the astrological treatises, and the problem was to be discussed at greater length by Judah ben Solomon ha-Cohen. Judah Halevi contents himself with affirming that the influence exercised by the heavenly bodies over the earth does indeed exist, but that their laws are not those of astrology.

Indeed, the things which are fitting to receive that divine influence are not within the capacity of flesh and blood, nor is it possible for them to determine their quantities and qualities. Even if they were to know their essences they would not know their [proper] times and places, their circumstances, and the way to prepare for them. For that, one would need a divine, perfect science explained completely by God. Upon whomever this *Amr* came down, and he conformed to its limitations and conditions with a pure intention, he is the believer. But whoever tried to dispose things to accept that influence through expertise, reasoning, and opinions based on what is found in astrological books, with respect to seeking to bring down spiritual powers and the making of talismans, is the rebel. He brings sacrifices and lights incense as a result of his reasoning and opinion, but he does not know the true [essence] of that which is necessary – how much, how, in which place, in which time, which men, how it ought to be handled, and many circumstances whose description would take too long.

He is like the ignoramus who entered the pharmacy of a physician who was well known for his helpful medicines. The physician was absent and men went to that pharmacy seeking help. Now that ignoramus dispensed to them [the contents of] those vials, but he didn't know how much ought to be dispensed of each medicine for each man. Thus, he killed people by means of those medicines which should have been useful for them. If it happened that someone gained benefit from one of those vials, people turned to it and said that that was a useful [medicine] until it was proven to be false, or they [came to] think that something else was useful by accident, [so that] they turned to it also.   (I, 79)

This parable is very characteristic of Judah Halevi's approach; every science, religious or not, which does not have its direct source in the *Amr ilahi* is a mistake; for the rules of the natural and supernatural world are not truly known except on high; man, by speculation, cannot reach a real comprehension of these laws, only an idea more or less false of their existence, and sometimes even a certain knowledge, but never the true knowledge and still less the use of it.

To the Jewish people, and the Land of Israel, corresponds a language superior to all the others: Hebrew.

But in its essence it is more noble [than the other languages] both traditionally and rationally. Traditionally, it is the language in which revelation was made to Adam and Eve and by means of it they spoke, as the derivation of Adam from *adamah* [earth] shows . . . Its superiority [may be shown] rationally by considering the people who utilized it insofar as they needed it for addressing one another, especially for prophecy, which was widespread among them, and the need for preaching, songs, and praises.

(ɪɪ, 68)

The commandments, given to the people in the sacred tongue, cannot be perfectly accomplished except in the Land of Israel; they are the 'mysterious' means that God uses for the survival of Israel.

The Khazar said: I have reflected about your situation and I have seen that God has a secret [means] of giving you permanence. Indeed, He has certainly made the sabbaths and the festivals become one of the strongest reasons for making permanent your esteem and splendour. The nations [of the world] would have divided you [among themselves], would have taken you as servants on account of your intelligence and your quickness, and they would certainly have made you soldiers also were it not for [the observance of these] times which you are so mindful of because they are from God, as well as for powerful reasons, such as *remembering the act of creation, remembering the exodus from Egypt, remembering the giving of the law.* All of them are divine commands whose observance is firmly held by you. Were it not for them, not one of you would put on a clean garment nor would you have an assembly in order to refresh the memory of your religious law, on account of the faintness of your concerns because of the sway of your contemptible [condition] over you. Were it not for them you would not have had any pleasure, even one day, during your whole lives. By means of them a sixth of life has been spent in the relaxation of body and soul which kings are unable to have. They are not tranquil on their day of rest because, if the smallest necessity calls them [forth] to exertion and movement on that day, they move and exert themselves. Thus, they are not in perfect tranquillity. Were it not for these [holidays], your property would go to others because it is liable to plunder. Thus your expenditure for them is profitable for you in this world and the next, because expenditure for them is for the essence of God.

(ɪɪɪ, 10)

The mode of action of the commandments can hardly be understood by men, but the mode of action of nature is also mysterious:

With each and every activity the divine *Amr* would be present because the works of the religious law are like natural beings, all of which are determined by God, exalted is He. Their determination is not in the power of a human being, in the same way you see that natural beings are determined, given their proper balance, and their temperaments are mutually proportioned from the four natural humours. By the least thing they are perfected, prepared, and the form comes to be present in them which they deserve, whether an animal or a plant. Each temperament receives the form which is proper to it and by the least thing it becomes corrupted. Do you not realize that the least accident of heat which is excessive or cold or movement will destroy the egg so that it will not receive the form of the chick? The heat of the hen perfects it for three weeks so that the form dwells in it perfectly. Now who is there who is able to delimit works so that the divine *Amr* dwells in them except it be God alone? . . .

The works of the religious law resemble those of nature. You do not know their movements and you think them to be in vain until you see the result. Then you recognize the jurisdiction of their governor and their mover and you concede (His existence), just as (would be the case) were you not to have heard of sexual intercourse and did not know it or its result. You saw yourself desirous of the vilest member of the woman, realizing that vileness is connected with approaching her and what lowness is involved in submission to the woman. Certainly you would be amazed and you would say, 'These movements are senseless and mad', until the time came when you saw your own like born from a woman. The matter would amaze you and you might imagine that you were one of the helpers in its creation and that the Creator desired through you to make this world flourish.

In the same way the works of the religious law are determined by God, He is exalted. You slaughter a sheep, for example, and become soiled by its blood and its skin, in cleaning its intestines, washing it, dividing it into pieces, sprinkling its blood, the preparation of firewood, lighting its fire, and trimming it. Were it not for the fact that this was the command of God, exalted is He, you would certainly disregard these practices. You would certainly think that they are something which keeps you far from God, exalted is He, not something which brings you near. [However], when it was complete in the proper way and you saw the heavenly fire or you found in yourself another spirit which you had not seen [before], or [you saw] true dreams or miracles, you knew that they were the result of what you did before and the mighty *Amr* with which you came into contact and reached it.

You would not care whether you died after you came into contact with it, for indeed death is only the extinction of your body alone. But the soul which reached that level does not descend from it and is not removed from it. Thus, it has become clear from this [argument] that there is no closeness to God, exalted is He, except by means of the commands of God, exalted is He, and there is no way to knowledge of the commands of God, except by the way of prophecy, not by individual reasoning, nor by individual intellection. There is no connection between us and those commands except by true tradition. Now those who transmitted those commandments to us were not single individuals, but a multitude consisting of scholars and persons of high degree and those who had contact with the prophets. Even were there no one else except the priests, the Levites, and the seventy elders who were the carriers of the *Torah*, who were not interrupted from [the time of] Moses, [it certainly would have been enough]. (III, 53)

The accomplishment of the commandments does not only bring with it the reward of eternal life. Certainly, every man, to whatever nation he belongs, receives from God, as an individual, the recompense of his good works.

However, the bond between the divine commandments and the result of their performance pertains to an order superior to nature.

But we are promised that we are to be attached to the divine *Amr* by prophecy and what comes close to it. The divine *Amr* attaches itself to us by means of [acts of] providence and minor and major miracles. Therefore the *Torah* never mentioned at all 'if you perform this religious law I will reward you after death with gardens and pleasures', but it says 'you will be a peculiar people to me and I will be a God who takes care of you'. One of you will enter my presence and go up to the heavens like those whose souls busy themselves among the angels and my angels will also be concerned with what is [going on] among you on earth. You will see them as separate individuals and armies protecting you and fighting for you. Your existence on earth will continue in the land which will help [you] to this level; it is the Holy Land. Its fertility and its drought, its good and its evil, depend on the divine *Amr* in accordance with your actions. The world will conduct its business according to the natural course [of events], except for you, because you will see, on account of the dwelling of the presence of God among you, the fertility of your land and the proper ordering of your rain – its times will not exceed that which is needed. By means of your victory over your enemies without preparation you [will] know that your affairs do not run according to a natural canon, but [rather] a volitional one, just as you will see, if you transgress, drought, dearth, uninhabited places, vicious animals, while the whole world is tranquil. Thus you will know accordingly that your affairs are governed by an *Amr* higher than the natural *Amr*.   (I, 109)

The passage just quoted answers the second question that the King of the Khazars asked before his conversion. The first: 'But isn't the guidance [of God] for everyone? That is appropriate to wisdom' (I, 120) received the following answer: 'Wouldn't it be better for animals to be rational?' (I, 103).

Divine will thus perfectly completes a natural and supernatural hierarchical system that constitutes the order of the world. To wish to explain it is to wish to become God.

Before the mystery of the Will, man can only bow down and render thanks.

Jewish history is miraculous; it is the expression of the divine in the natural chain of universal causality. How can one reconcile this miraculous history and the reality of history, that in which Judah Halevi lived? The historical reality was very different from this triumphant and glorious picture of the perfect people accomplishing a divine Law in a flourishing country, revealing by its power and beauty the sublime action of the *Amr ilahi*, perfecting the work of creation. The Jewish people is in exile; it is despised and humbled; it is not a people of saints, and the Hebrew language has become bastardized. What remains before our eyes of this almost divine people? – as the King of the Khazars does not fail to remark.

I see that you make us an object of shame because of our despised condition and poverty. Now because of them the best [individuals] of these [other] religious communities vaunt themselves. Don't they ask aid only from one who has said: 'He who slaps your right cheek, give him the left [cf. Matthew 5: 39]' and 'Whoever takes your garment give him your shirt [cf. *ibid.* 5: 40?' He and his companions and followers suffered hundreds of years of contempt, blows, and slayings to an extent which is well known. But these things are their ornaments. And the same is true of the master of the religious law of Islam and his companions until they conquered and gained victory. And the [former] are gloried in and their aid is sought, not the [latter day] kings whose glory has become great, whose territory has become wide, and access to them is difficult to achieve, and their vehicles strike fear. Now our relationship to God is closer than if we were to have victory in the world.

The Khazar said: That would be true were your submissiveness to be a matter of free choice, but it is a matter of necessity. If you were to achieve victory, you would slay [like the others].

The sage said: You have hit me in a vital part, O King of the Khazars. Yes, were most of us, as you say, to have cleaved to being despised out of submission to God and to his religious law, certainly, the divine *Amr* would not have neglected us so long. However, [only] a minority of us is of this opinion, but the majority does have a reward because it supports its low estate out of both necessity and free choice. For it could become, if it wanted, friend and equal to those who despise it, by means of a word which it might say without trouble. Something like this does not go to waste in the view of one who is wise and just. Thus, were we to support this exile and affliction for the sake of God properly, certainly we would be a glory of the age awaited with the coming of the Messiah. Thus we would bring close the time appointed for the hoped-for salvation. (I, 113–15)

In the memory of his past splendour, in the trace that the *Amr ilahi* has left in him, in the hope of the coming of the Messiah, the Jew finds the strength to remain faithful and not to pronounce the word that would make him Muslim or Christian and give him equality with other men, those who now reign over the world.

It is the man, the poet, not the philosopher, who brings the word to a conclusion:

Subsequently, it happened that the sage decided to leave the land of the Khazars in order to go to Jerusalem, may it be rebuilt and made firm. His leaving was hard to bear for the Khazar. He spoke to him about that, saying, 'What may be sought in Palestine today? The divine presence is absent from it and closeness to God may be achieved in every place by means of pure intention and fervent desire. Why should you undertake perils of sea, land, and the different nations?'

Then the sage said: As for the divine presence which appears eye to eye, it is that which is absent since it is revealed only to a prophet or to a multitude which is the object of divine pleasure in the special place. It is that which is to be awaited [on the basis of] His statement *For eye to eye they will see when God returns to Zion* [Isaiah 52: 8] and our statement in our prayer *and may our eyes see when you return to Zion*. As for the hidden, spiritual divine presence, it is with an Israelite who is honest, righteous in works, pure of heart, of sincere intention to the Lord of Israel.

Palestine is especially [distinguished] by the Lord of Israel and works are perfect only in it. For many of the commandments of the Israelite [nation] are not incumbent on those who do not dwell in Palestine. The intention is not sincere and the heart is not pure except in the places which are believed to be special for God. [This would be true even if that] were only [the product of] imagination and a [mental] representation; how much more so when that is the reality, as has been explained previously. Thus desire for it becomes intense and intention becomes sincere in it, especially for one who comes to it from afar, especially for one who has sinned in the past and wishes to be forgiven. There is no way to [accomplish] the sacrifices which were commanded by God for each sin, either *intentional* or *accidental*. Therefore one must have recourse to the statement of the sages, *exile atones for sin*, especially if one were to have to move to a place [Palestine, which is an object] of divine pleasure.

(v, 22–3)

Perhaps Judah Halevi reached Jerusalem after all, and the poem that will be cited to conclude this chapter renders his quest particularly poignant.

If only I could roam through those places where God was revealed to your prophets and heralds! Who will give me wings, so that I may wander far away? I would carry the pieces of my broken heart over your rugged mountains. [The hills of Bether (Song of Songs, 2: 17), in the vicinity of Jerusalem.] I would bow down, my face on your ground; I would love your stones; your dust would move me to pity. I would weep, as I stood by my ancestors' graves, I would grieve, in Hebron, over the choicest of burial places! [The burial cave of the Patriarchs (Genesis 23: 17).] I would walk in your forests and meadows, stop in Gilead, marvel at Mount Abarim; Mount Abarim and Mount Hor, where the two great luminaries [Moses and Aaron] rest, those who guided you and gave you light. The air of your land is the very life of the soul, the grains of your dust are flowing myrrh, your rivers are honey from the comb. It would delight my heart to walk naked and barefoot among the desolate ruins where your shrines once stood; where your Ark was hidden away, [According to Talmudic legend, King Josiah hid the holy Ark from the enemy] where your cherubim once dwelled in the inner-most chamber. I shall cut off my glorious hair and throw it away, I shall curse Time that has defiled your pure ones in the polluted lands [of exile].

Happy is he who waits and lives to see your light rising, your dawn breaking forth over him! He shall see your chosen people prospering, he shall rejoice in your joy when you regain the days of your youth.

(Ed. and trans. T. Carmi in *Hebrew Verse*, pp. 348–9)

Judah Halevi is the most particularist thinker we have encountered. Abu-l-Barakāt is one of the most universalist. It is difficult to class him. In a way he is part of the Aristotelian current of thought, for he used Aristotelian ideas. But he used them in a very non-Aristotelian way. We will therefore study him before entering the main current of Aristotelianism.

Abu-l-Barakāt: a philosophy outside the main current of thought

Hibat Allāh Ali Ibn Malkā Abu al-Barakāt (Nathanel) al Baghdādī al Balādī, whom I shall call Abu-l-Barakāt, lived at Baghdad in the second part of the eleventh century and the first half of the twelfth. A well-known doctor, he served at the court of the Caliph al-Mustanjid (1160–70) and survived to an advanced age. He enjoyed a considerable reputation during his lifetime, being called the 'Unique One of his Time'. In old age he converted to Islam, but it seems that in 1143 he was still Jewish, for he dictated a long commentary in Arabic on Ecclesiastes to his disciple Isaac, son of the celebrated Abraham Ibn Ezra, and Isaac wrote a poem in his honour as introduction to this work. Probably because of his conversion to Islam he is seldom cited in Jewish philosophy, although certain parallels with Abraham bar Ḥiyya and Ḥasdai Crescas may be significant. On the other hand, he was quite often quoted and used by Arabic philosophers, who seem to have forgotten his Jewish origins; in particular he strongly influenced the famous twelfth-century author Fakh-al-Dīn-Rāzi. We do not really know why Abu-l-Barakāt decided to convert; his biographers refer to different episodes – a gesture of hurt pride, fear of the personal consequences of the death of the Sultan Mahmud's wife while under his care, fear of execution on being taken prisoner; but these various reports mutually exclude each other.

Two philosophical works by Abu-l-Barakāt have reached us, the great commentary on Ecclesiastes, still almost entirely unpublished, and a book of philosophy in three volumes, which has been published. He perhaps also wrote a Hebrew and an Arabic grammar, and several works on medicine and pharmacy. Our knowledge of Abu-l-Barakāt's philosophy is wholly due to S. Pines' studies, and the brief account that follows is based on his work.

The title of the philosophical work, *Kitāb al-Mu'tabar*, which can be translated as *The Book of what has been established by personal reflection*, immediately indicates the method that Abu-l-Barakāt intended to employ; that of personal thought and reflection. This was a most unaccustomed procedure in the Middle Ages, for medieval philosophers usually appealed to the philosophical or religious 'authorities', without however abstaining from interpreting them in the sense demanded by their own conceptions.

In his introduction Abu-l-Barakāt traces the history of philosophical thought and explains the purpose of his book. The ancient philosophers expressed themselves only by word of mouth, and not in writing. Their teaching only reached those of their pupils who were capable of understanding it, and at the right moment in the course of their mental development. At that period scholars and their disciples were very numerous, and the sciences were transmitted from one generation to another, integrally and perfectly; nothing was lost, and knowledge did not reach those who had no aptitude for it.

Later, when the number of scholars had diminished, when lives were shorter and much scientific knowledge was lost because of the scarcity of disciples capable of transmitting this tradition, scholars began to compose books, so that the sciences might be stored up in them and transmitted by persons who had suitable aptitudes to their fellows, even at a different period or in remote places. And, in many writings, they used expressions shrouded in mystery and secret indications that only intelligent and subtle men could comprehend. This was a way of concealing the sciences from those who had no aptitude for them.

Then, as their number continued to diminish from one generation to the next, the scholars of later epochs set themselves to interpret these secret indications and to elucidate these obscure passages at length and in detail, with repetitions and amplifications, so that the number of books and of writings increased, and, apart from people who had aptitudes for the sciences, also many others, deprived of these aptitudes, concerned themselves with these works, and in the works the discourse of men of merit and talent was contaminated by that of the ignorant and the incapable.

Thus, when he wished to devote himself to the philosophical sciences, Abu-l-Barakāt, in spite of his diligence in reading the books of the Ancients, found in them only a meagre knowledge. Certainly his reflection and speculative thought are in accord on several points with the opinions of some of the Ancients, but, by virtue of scrutinizing the book of being, he came to conclusions that had never yet been formulated or, at least, had not been transmitted. Accordingly he consigned them to paper, and he concludes his introduction with the following sentences:

Nevertheless my notes became more and more numerous and they constituted such a considerable sum of scientific knowledge that ... having been implored again and by persons who deserved a favourable reply, I complied with their request and I composed this book treating of the philosophical sciences which have as their subject that which exists, that is physics and metaphysics.

I have called it *Kitāb al-Mu'tabar*, because I have put in it what I knew by my own intelligence, established by personal reflection verified and perfected by meditation; I have transcribed nothing that I have not understood and I have understood and accepted nothing without meditation and personal reflection.

In adopting such or other opinions and doctrines, I have not let myself be guided by the desire of finding myself in accord with the great names because of their grandeur or in disagreement with the small because of their insignificance. My purpose in everything was truth and as regards this the conformity of my opinions with those of others or their divergence was only an accident.

(Kitāb al-Mu'tabar I, pp. 2–4, trans. S. Pines)

All these considerations might lead one to suppose that our author's aim was only to reconstitute the perfect philosophy as it had existed in Antiquity; in fact, he depends far more on his personal intuitions, after having subjected current philosophical theories to a methodical questioning that recalls Descartes.

At that time the dominant philosophy was that of Avicenna, and Abu-l-Barakāt's book more or less follows the plan of the *Shifa'* (*Book of Healing*, the philosophical *summa* of Avicenna). He accepts several theses contained in it, rejects many others, even very important ones, and examines them all in the light of his personal reflection. This does not mean that Abu-l-Barakāt never uses other ancient or contemporary doctrines; he adopts a certain number of neoplatonic notions and others that belong to the *kalām*; but the fact remains that some ideas are strictly his own. They are not always logically arranged, sometimes only juxtaposed, and his philosophical system is not always coherent.

To understand Abu-l-Barakāt's thought, we must begin with his study of human psychology, since for our author man's conscience serves as criterion for a number of physical and metaphysical theses.

133

First, Abu-l-Barakāt stresses the fact that men believe that they have a soul and that this soul moves the body. As for knowing what the soul is, he declares, in this following Avicenna, that it is the same as 'selfhood', the sense of self, being. This knowledge of the 'I', the identity of man with his soul, is anterior to all knowledge and independent of the data provided by the senses, and, up to a certain point, of one's own body. This accounts for the fact that a man with an amputated limb does not have a lesser feeling of his own selfhood. Besides, this perception of self is not reserved for scholars; it is not acquired by a logical process; it is an immediate, *a priori*, knowledge, a firm and assured consciousness. The idea was Avicenna's, but he did not deduce all its consequences. If man perceives that he is one with his soul, the different activities of the soul cannot be anything else than this soul itself. However, traditional psychology divides the soul into different faculties.

Abu-l-Barakāt, after passing in review the arguments in favour of this division of the soul into multiple faculties, refutes them, opposing arguments drawn from the philosophical material of his time, as well as yet another argument, very different and in his view incontrovertible: when we see, hear, think, we are quite certain that we are a single being, admitting of no multiplicity:

> If it were the visual faculty which sees, that is to say a faculty which is other than myself, other than my soul and my selfhood, it would follow that he who sees is not I but somebody or something else. However, I have an awareness, a cognition and true knowledge of the fact that it is I that see, hear and act ... The fact is that the subject that sees, of whom, as far as all the categories of acts are concerned, I have knowledge and awareness, is myself; my soul is myselfhood and my being.
>
> (*Ibid.* II, p. 318)

This unity of the soul of which we are certain in our consciousness implies important consequences, in particular:

(1) It obliges us to find a theory of perception through the senses radically different from the two theories that have as yet been propounded.

(2) It leads Abu-l-Barakāt to a theory of consciousness and unconsciousness, or more precisely of attention and inattention, which has some very modern overtones.

(3) It denies the distinction between the soul and the intellect.

(1) Perception through the senses presents a problem that has not yet been solved, that of the relation between the world of the senses and the image that we have of it. In the case of visual perception – by what process does a landscape find itself reduced in our minds to a sort of photograph with all its details, even the most trifling, remaining present to us even after the disappearance of the object seen? In Abu-l-Barakāt's time two explanations of this phenomenon were known:

The first assumed that material images emanate from objects, representing them, and perception occurs when these images are engraved on the organ of sight. This material image, attached to the object and engraved in the pupil or in the animal spirits that are supposed to be in the eye, according to our author poses an insoluble problem. For how can the image of a great mountain be engraved in the pupil of a human eye? The difference in size is overwhelming!

The second theory holds that vision is due to a bundle of rays arising in the pupil. But, says Abu-l-Barakāt, if it is the rays that perceive, it is not man himself, but something else; however, we know perfectly well that it is man who perceives and that he perceives the object at the place where it is, whether near or far. In fact, man sees by the agency of the eye, but it is not the eye that sees. It is the same for the other senses; all are no more than instruments by which man, the soul of man, perceives the external world. But in this man there is no division; it is he himself who sees, feels, hears, and, at the same time, thinks or remembers.

As Abu-l-Barakāt says,

The original principle [from which these acts proceed] in one's individual self is ineluctably one, it is oneself. Whether one accomplishes these acts by oneself and directly, or whether one uses in [accomplishing] them intermediaries and instruments, one will not doubt that as far as one's perceived acts are concerned this is the original principle.

(*Ibid.* p. 319)

(2) The human soul, placed in a finite body, only apprehends a small part of the phenomena produced in the world; moreover, consciousness does not embrace all the movements or actions even of this soul. Thus, when the soul moves the body, it does not know what nerves it sets in motion or which muscles it dilates, and nevertheless the movement is made in such a way that it corresponds perfectly to the wish of the soul. This is because, according to Abu-l-Barakāt, there is a whole group of instinctive actions that do not belong to conscious thought and, by this very fact, are more intimately concerned with the soul than are the deliberate acts, for the relation of the soul and the body is a loving relationship like that of an animal for its young. Furthermore, the soul's attention is limited, which means that it cannot devote itself to or interest itself in too many things of different kinds. Thus, one cannot at the same time listen and look attentively; similarly, external perceptions deflect us from internal perceptions, so that, for instance, we have no awareness of the digestive process, which in any case is a part of the instinctive acts that are much more difficult to apprehend than are the deliberate ones. The limitation of the field of attention explains the phenomenon of forgetfulness and that of memory and remembrance, for it is only when man turns his attention towards what is within himself and wishes to remember something, that he succeeds in remembering it, by an act of the will; or else it may happen that a memory surfaces in the consciousness through an association of ideas: some particular thing evokes another that has some connection with it.

(3) What are these ideas, these forms, that can be stored in the memory? Medieval Aristotelian philosophy established an absolute distinction between the soul, which apprehends particular things, and the *sensibilia* and the intellect, which grasp what is general, intelligible.

Abu-l-Barakāt rejects this theory, which presumed superadded intellect, thinking and cogitating. It is man himself who feels, moves things; and in consequence there cannot be an essential difference between the sensible and the intelligible forms, for a distinction between the two would introduce a distinction between the soul and the intellect that our philosopher resolutely denies. For him, there are two sorts of things that can be apprehended, things that exist in external reality and the mental forms that exist in the mind. These are not the only ones that are general; thus existing forms like whiteness, redness, heat, exist in objects and nevertheless are general because the objects in which they subsist are very numerous. Even more, the idea that a person grasping general and intelligible forms does not also understand sensory and particular things, is false, and it is the contrary notion that is most probable; for it may happen that one grasps only the sensory and particular things and not the universal. But someone who grasps great and general ideas is necessarily capable of apprehending that which is less elevated, more obvious and more specific.

This last affirmation has important consequences in our author's theology, for it applies to God as well as to men.

For Abu-l-Barakāt it is not only the apperception of the self, but also the apperception of being and the apperception of time that are *a priori* ideas anterior to all knowledge.

What is intellectually cognised of the *esse* which is mentally conceived is an intellectual notion comprising both that which is perceived by the senses and that which is not. The mind has a representation of it, and the soul is aware of it for and by its own self, prior to its being aware of any other thing, as we have made clear in the *Science of the Soul*. The soul has a similar awareness of time by, and together with, its own self and existence prior to its being aware of any other thing of which it is aware and which it considers in its own mind.

(*Studies in Abu'l-Barakāt*, p. 289)

To understand Abu-l-Barakāt's originality in this domain, we must remember that for Aristotle and his commentators time is the measure of movement. It is measured by the movement of the celestial spheres, and the movement of the celestial spheres implies an unmoving mover, who is eternal, that is, outside time. The proof of the existence of the Prime Mover – a proof that we find, for instance, expounded by Maimonides in the first chapter of Book II of the *Guide of the Perplexed*, differentiates absolutely between everything within the sphere, which is body, movement, and time, and God, who is not subject to movement and is above time. Avicenna gives the following classification:

(1) Eternity, which is outside time and change;

(2) The relation between an eternal thing and a temporal thing, for instance the relation between the intellect and the spheres, or that of the soul and the body;

(3) Time, measured by movement, within which exist all corporeal beings.

For Abu-l-Barakāt there is only one time, which is similar for all beings, including God. To show what he means by the apperception of time without the existence of movement he takes as an example the sleepers in the cave (a story found in the Koran), who return to consciousness without realizing the passing of time. If these men had been awake, even in darkness and deprived of the possibility of perceiving any kind of movement, they would nevertheless have felt the passing of every hour. The problem of time is therefore not a problem of physics, but one that belongs to metaphysics. All beings, in movement and at rest, by the very fact that they are, exist in time. When you say to someone, May God protect your life! this means May God prolong your being rather than your time, for time belongs to an existing being in virtue of the *esse* (being) that subsists in him. There is therefore only one time, common to God and to all his creatures, since there is only one *esse*, whether it is necessary or contingent. Thus a being perceives time, his own being and his own existence by one and the same apperception.

Some of the things which are not perceived by the senses are more hidden for the intellect and more remote for us as regards the degree of knowledge involved than others; whereas others are better known to the intellect and more manifest for the mind in spite of their remoteness – as far as their quiddity and substance are concerned – from apprehension by the senses. Such are time and existence. As far as this is concerned existence from one point of view is more manifest than any other hidden thing. As regards the first assertion its being manifest is due to the fact that everyone who is aware of his own self is also aware of his own existence. Again, everyone who is aware of his own action is aware at the same time of his own self that is acting and of the latter's existence as well as of that which is produced by it and results from the action. Thus he who is aware of his own self is aware of existence, I mean the existence of his own self. And he who is aware of his own action, is aware of it and of the agent. And the existence of the latter is not doubted in this either by the élite of the people or by the common folk and is not hidden even from those whose faculty of mental representation is weak. Similarly every man or most men are in general aware of time; of to-day; of yesterday and of to-morrow, and, in general, of past and future, remote and near time, even if they have no knowledge of its substance and quiddity. And similarly they are aware of [the fact] that existence is, even if they are not aware of its quiddity. Now all that someone is aware of and knows is thereby apprehended by him; and everything that is apprehended by someone exists. And every existent either exists in external reality, or in the minds, or in both. However what is existent in the minds is also existent in external reality because of its existing in things that exist in external reality, namely the minds: for they exist in external reality. Thus existence is known by those who know in virtue of an *a priori* knowledge simultaneously with their knowing any existent or non-existent thing.

(*Ibid.* pp. 290-1)

Our philosopher uses the same arguments to attack and overthrow the Aristotelian theory of place. In opposition to Aristotle and his Arabic commentators, Abu-l-Barakāt asserts the existence of three-dimensional space and does not accept the impossibility of movement in the void. He affirms the infinitude of space, basing himself on the *a priori* knowledge of space, since man finds it impossible to conceive a limited space. According to Aristotle, space is the interior limit of the surrounding body; and for the world, which has nothing that contains it, the external surface of the last sphere marks the limit of space. Abu-l-Barakāt declares that if we imagine the totality of the spheres and we reach the last sphere, we cannot even then conceive a finite limit; there must be something afterwards, whether a body or the void; but the idea that there is no space after the last sphere is unthinkable to him.

On the question of the fall of bodies he similarly rejects Aristotle's opinion. For Aristotle, a body moves because it has a mover, and it continues to move because this mover continues to act. For example, an arrow thrown by the hand continues in its trajectory only because the air, set in motion by hand, propels this arrow; otherwise, it would stop moving. According to Abu-l-Barakāt, on the contrary, the cause of this movement is a violent inclination, a force, that. the hand flinging the arrow communicates to it. In this explanation he more or less follows Avicenna.

But concerning another problem in physics, the acceleration of the fall of heavy bodies, he is really innovatory. For he explains this acceleration by the fact that the principle of the natural inclination contained in heavy bodies furnishes them with successive inclinations. This is the earliest known text that implies a fundamental law of modern dynamics: a constant force engenders an accelerated movement.

The God of Abu-l-Barakāt could evidently not be an unmoving mover separated from the world. For him, God is known to us through the ordering of the world, establishing the chain of existing beings whose contingency demands a necessary being. His attributes are positive, contrary to Avicenna and later Maimonides, who admit only negative divine attributes. Through our knowledge, we can trace, know, or rather form a notion of, the Divine Wisdom; through our strength, an idea of the Divine Power; through our will, an idea of the Divine Will.

Accordingly the first originative principle is endowed with will, this being proven by the existence of wills in the things created by Him. He is endowed with knowledge, this being proven by the existence of knowledge in the things created by Him. He is bountiful, this being proven by His bountifulness with regard to the things created by Him. He is powerful, this being proven by His power over the things created by Him. He is endowed with various kinds of cognitions, this being proven by the knowledge existing in the things created by Him. Thus His essence is the first originative principle for the existence of the essences, His act for the acts and His attributes for the attributes. Accordingly He is the first originative principle, being endowed with [the quality] of being the universal originative principle with relation to all the other existents. (*Ibid.* p. 306)

138

As S. Pines says:

Abu'l-Barakat appears to posit a causal relation between the attributes of God and the corresponding attributes found in other existents.

These latter attributes derive from God either directly or through intermediaries, such as angels and spiritual beings, that are unknown to us. We know, however, that these intermediaries possess the attributes in question in a much greater measure than the existents known to us. In God every beauty, every excellency, every good, every nobility and whatever else is indicated by terms of praise exist in their ultimate perfection, in their *telos*, 'which in this case belongs to existence and to an existent, not to what is mentally represented and known. For the latter is not defined [in itself], being defined by existence. These are the positive attributes.'

(*Ibid.* p. 307)

Certainly God is wise in a necessary and perfect manner, as He necessarily exists and causes the other beings to exist. But there is a relation, an analogy, between this perfect Wisdom and our own, although the latter may be imperfect. 'These analogies or inferences and others justify Abu-l-Barakāt's following statement: "For man the ladder of the knowledge of his Lord is the knowledge of his own soul, for this latter knowledge is the first gate of the science of the world of the Divine."' (*ibid.* p. 314).

We may speak of God with the aid of attributes, for the essence of God includes will, power, and knowledge, as in a triangle the three angles are equal to two right angles. Without this equality, one cannot speak of a triangle, as one cannot speak of God if one denies Him these three attributes. And as in man the knowledge of general things necessarily includes that of particular beings, so God knows individuals, but perhaps not all of them; their number being infinite.

God, like man, directs His attention where He wishes.

He embraces in His knowledge those of them that He wills, as and where He wills. He directs His attention towards what He wills and turns away from what He wills. Accordingly He acts with regard to the things created by Him in virtue of His Will, which may not be turned back, His power, which does not fail, and His wisdom, which does not err.

(*Ibid.* p. 330)

And again:

He, may He be exalted, hears and sees, rewards and punishes, is angry and pleased, directs His attention towards things and turns away from things, as He wills and through what He wills; causes do not dominate Him. For it is He that has rule in and according to them. And He renews and changes according to the requirement of wisdom with reference to what He necessitates in accordance with motivating and deterrent factors known and cognised by Him in the whole world – no veil being interposed between the latter and His knowledge and scrutiny, and there being no obstacle to prevent them.

(*Ibid.* p. 332)

This God, so different from the Aristotelian God, who knows and is wise and powerful in a manner analogous to ours, could not have been under the necessity of causing the world to emanate. According to Abu-l-Barakāt things came into existence by a succession of acts of will, the first of the existing beings being created by the Divine Will, which is an attribute of the divine essence. This creation took place in time because God Himself is also in time. The God of Abu-l-Barakāt is a personal God, who speaks directly to men and who can be known.

Abu-l-Barakāt's thought is most probably closer to revealed religion than was the Aristotelianism of a later period. When Samuel ben Ali, Gaon of Baghdad, attacked Maimonides on the score of his eschatalogical conceptions, he cited Abu-l-Barakāt (and also Avicenna) with approval, as philosophers whose ideas were not contrary to orthodoxy.

However, as in Nethanel ben al-Fayyumi, the universalist tendency is very clear. Nethanel remained a Jew while Abu-l-Barakāt converted to Islam, and while the exposition of his ideas does not sufficiently explain this conversion, nothing in them is opposed to it.

Chapter 5

ARISTOTELIANISM

In Jewish theology, as in Islamic and Christian, Aristotelianism exacerbated the conflict between philosophy and revelation, a conflict that came to a head in the separation between reason and faith. Since the beginning of the medieval period, translations had brought the greater part of Aristotle's treatises to the knowledge of the Muslim, Jewish and Christian world, and they had been used by Arab and Jewish Neoplatonists. However, two vital characteristics distinguished these philosophers from the Aristotelians proper – first, the schema of the emanation of the superior beings, and, secondly, the definition of the human soul and its place of origin. 'Aristotelian' philosophy employed a greater number of truly Aristotelian notions, in a stricter sense, while admitting several neoplatonic notions. This medieval Aristotle is sometimes quite different from the Aristotle of Antiquity, for he reached the Arab philosophers already accompanied by commentaries written by Greek authors such as Alexander of Aphrodisias, Themistius, and others, and reached the Jewish philosophers accompanied by both Greek and Arabic commentaries. However, as we shall see, a number of ideas that we have encountered in previous periods were still in force throughout the later Middle Ages.

Abraham Ibn Daud is not altogether 'the first Aristotelian' in Jewish medieval thought. In 952, questions relating to physics were propounded by two Jewish savants, Ibn Abī Saʿīd Ibn ʿUthmān Ibn Saʿīd al-Mawṣilī and Bishr Ibn Samʿān Ibn ʿIrs Ibn ʿUthmān, to the Baghdad Christian philosopher Yaḥyā Ibn ʿAdī, and these letters have been preserved. Judging from the wording of the questions, it is clear that these Jewish thinkers were very well acquainted not only with Aristotle but with his commentators. However, the first book that one can designate as Aristotelian is that composed by Abraham Ibn Daud two centuries after these eastern precursors.

ABRAHAM IBN DAUD

Ibn Daud lived in Spain, between 1110 and 1180. Son of a scholarly family, the Albali, he received the careful education of the children of the aristocratic classes, which comprised both religious and profane studies, the latter including Arabic poetry, literature and philosophy.

Born at Cordoba, Ibn Daud fled before the Almohad conquest and took refuge in Toledo, which was Christian. He died there, a martyr to the Jewish faith, in unknown circumstances. It is possible that between 1160 and 1180 he collaborated in translations from Arabic into Latin. Translations were then often carried out through the intermediary of the vernacular. This meant that two persons worked together. The Arabic expert, a Jew or Christian who had lived in an Arabic environment, translated the text into a Spanish dialect, and a Christian scholar turned the Spanish into Latin. A certain number of translations are known to have been made with the collaboration of one 'Avendauth', or Ibn Daud, also called John of Spain, who may have been Abraham Ibn Daud. Among the texts perhaps thus translated is the *Fountain of Life* by Ibn Gabirol, of which Ibn Daud had a very poor opinion, as we have seen. The identification of Abraham Ibn Daud with Avendauth is somewhat doubtful, for the latter also worked directly from Arabic into Latin, and it is not very probable that Abraham Ibn Daud knew Latin, at least well enough to write in it. Like most of the philosophers, he was a physician and astronomer; he was also a historian, for he wrote a great work of history, of which the first part is the best known. It has been published under the title of *Sefer ha-Kabbalah*. His philosophical work, the *Exalted Faith*, was composed in 1160–1, like the *Sefer ha-Kabbalah*. The original Arabic text is not extant, but we have two Hebrew translations dating from the end of the fourteenth century. One was made by Samuel Ibn Motot in 1391, at the suggestion of Isaac Ibn Sheshet, and has not yet been printed; it is called *Emunah Nissa'a*, and is less readable than the translation by Solomon ben Lavi, which, under the title of *Emunah Ramah*, was published by S. Weil in 1852, together with a German translation. The Hebrew translations of the *Exalted Faith* are quite late, and the book had almost no influence on those medieval philosophers who did not know Arabic. It was further obscured by the *Guide of the Perplexed*, written some years afterwards and immediately translated into Hebrew, which introduced Jews to Aristotelian philosophy.

In his introduction Abraham Ibn Daud declares that he wrote his book in answer to questions on the subject of determinism and free will; however, this problem is discussed only at the end of the book, and rather succinctly. But, as he himself observes, the problem cannot be solved except in the context of a complete explication of the world. The book is divided into two parts. The first deals with physics, which he calls philosophy, and includes proofs of the existence of the Prime Mover. The second treats of revealed religion. In fact, the author declares, the two are the same thing, for the scientific truths are all to be found in the sacred books. The philosophical demonstration must always be perfected by showing that the biblical text includes or alludes to this philosophical demonstration. If certain verses contradict this demonstration, or contradict each other, they must be interpreted according to the guidance given by the intellect, for many verses were written with a view to the common people, and do not reveal their veritable sense. Abraham Ibn Daud was led to write this book by his profound conviction that religion and philosophy were in agreement, and that the cause of the non-recognition of this fundamental accord is ignorance of Aristotelian philosophy.

For I have observed that the confusion and blundering in this problem [free will and determination] and those that are akin to it have beset our scholars in this age because they have forsaken the inquiry into the principles of their Israelite faith and the quest for the concord and agreement which exists between the latter and the true philosophy . . . which philosophers themselves do rely upon . . . and because of this, they abandon the study of sciences; this was not the custom of the Sages of our People in the past . . . Indeed, in our times, it sometimes happens that one who investigates the sciences but slightly, lacks the strength to grasp two lamps with his two hands: with his right hand the lamp of his religion and with his left hand the lamp of his science. For when he lights the lamp of science, the lamp of religion goes out . . . When someone is just beginning his study of the sciences, he is perplexed about what he knows from the point of view of the traditional knowledge because he has not attained in science the degree where he could state the Truth in the questions which are not clear. Accordingly, this book will be very useful to him for it will acquaint him with many points of Science which we have built on the principles of religion.

(*Emunah Ramah*, pp. 2-4)

This passage is obviously reminiscent of the introduction to the *Guide of the Perplexed*; Abraham Ibn Daud, like Maimonides, composed his book because novices in philosophy did not see that science was in accord with religion and they felt obliged to choose between the two. It is possible that Maimonides knew Ibn Daud's work; in any case, it is clear that in twelfth-century Spain the problem was of considerable significance and that the questions our author proposes to answer were of great immediacy to many people. 'Science' was spreading rapidly, and it was necessary to justify religion in the face of this science, which had been rapidly adopted without being sufficiently studied. Abraham Ibn Daud did not provide a response that his contemporaries could accept as definitive; this was reserved for Maimonides; but he poses the same questions and outlines certain solutions. He was aware of the apparent contradiction between the scientific and the religious levels, as appears in the following passage, explaining why the biblical texts should be understood in a rational sense:

The first [reason] is that the *Torah* and philosophy are in flagrant contradiction when they attempt to describe the divine essence; for the philosophers, the incorporeal God is in no way capable of alteration; the *Torah*, on the contrary, narrates God's movements, His feelings . . . Given that philosophy and the *Torah* are in opposition on this subject, we are in the situation of a man with two masters, one great and the other not small; he cannot please the first without opposing the opinion of the second, and in consequence, if we find a method of making them agree, we shall be very happy with it . . .

The second imperious necessity arises from the *Torah* itself. If we reject the opinion of the philosophers as a whole, even if it is firmly based on demonstrations and is of an elevated level, if we cast doubt on their proofs, have scant respect for their eminence, and depend on what necessarily results from the revealed text, then we shall see that the texts themselves contradict one another and really agree only on the principle that we shall enunciate in this chapter [that is to say, the divine incorporeality].   (*Ibid.* p. 82)

In the first part of the book each chapter begins with an exposition of philosophical ideas, followed by biblical verses supporting this exposition; the juxtaposition of the two texts is not always convincing. As for the philosophical section, it is hardly more than yet another presentation of Avicenna. However, I shall summarize it in order to recall to the reader's mind some notions, perhaps forgotten, of medieval Aristotelianism.

The first chapter deals with substance and accident, as well as the various sorts of accidents, substance being what has no need of substratum and accident that which resides in a substratum. Accidents, defined by means of answers to nine questions, form nine categories: quantity, quality, relation, place, time, position, possession, action, passion.

Substance, first of the ten Aristotelian categories, is the subject of the second chapter. Everything found in this lower world is made of matter and form, natural or artificial. An example of matter is gold, a metal composed of the mixture of the four elements, fire, air, water and earth; these four elements transform themselves into each other, as one can see by bringing water to the boil and watching it lose its form of 'water' to assume that of 'air'. If air can be transformed into fire and water can become air, this proves that they have a common matter that serves as a substratum to these four forms. This is the First Matter, which God created at the beginning; it is the substratum and the foundation of the whole created world, a pure potentiality that can only exist by conjunction with the corporeal form that gives this *hylé* length, breadth, depth, that is, the spatial dimensions; then this First Matter, informed by the three dimensions, is ready to receive the forms of the four elements, fire, air, water and earth, and from the mixture of these four elements arises the compound that is capable of receiving a more elaborate form, that of the metals. If the mixture is finer and more evenly balanced, it will receive the form of the plants; if it is still finer and still more evenly balanced, that of the animals, and finally that of man. Substance is therefore defined by the form that inheres in a certain mixture of the four elements, for matter cannot be deprived of form.

Abraham Ibn Daud takes sides in what the Christian scholastics called 'the quarrel of the universals'. Do the forms 'dog' or 'horse' exist in themselves, detached from matter, pure forms that 'are' even if neither dog nor horse exist in this world (Plato) or are these forms the idea that we formulate intellectually, or rather that which arises from the entirety of the individuals existing in the world (Aristotle)? For Ibn Daud, it is evident that in the terrestrial world forms only exist in matter and have no separate existence. However, there are forms that subsist eternally and others that are subject to generation and corruption, that is, those of the plants and animals.

Only corporeal substance is discussed in this chapter, but there are also non-corporeal substances, like souls, which will be discussed later.

The first chapter describes the various kinds of movement. There are four. The first, voluntary and not subject to change, is explained later by our author, for whom the heavens are living beings endowed with reason. The second, not voluntary and not subject to change, is natural movement, that of the elements; for each of them is endowed with a movement natural to it that propels it towards its natural place. Left to itself, water descends towards the earth and rests on it; water that becomes cloud and rises in the air does not do this by a natural movement, but because the heat of the sun or the action of man forces it to rise.

The natural arrangement of the elements is circular. Earth is in the centre, then water, air and fire. In a compound body, each of the elements contributes its own natural qualities:

> Earth, dryness and cold;
> Water, moisture and cold;
> Air, moisture and heat;
> Fire, dryness and heat.

Each of the elements of a compound body tends to return to its natural place, so that every compound body, at one moment or another, is corrupted and decomposed into these four elements. The accidental qualities that one element contributes to another on combining with it, like the heat that fire communicates to water, are called movement for the same reason as movement from place to place is called movement, that is, the transporting of a body from one place to another.

In fact, what is performed in space is called 'movement'; this means not only spatial movement, but also movement which, being in a potential state, becomes active in a gradual, progressive manner. For instance, a black body that turns white passes through dark grey, then pale grey, and finally reaches white.

The third movement is that of plants, which change without willing this change.

The fourth movement is voluntary and subject to change. This is the movement of living beings – animals and men.

One can also divide movement into three kinds:

– Rectilinear movement, which is accidental or produced by force, like the movement of the stone pushed by the hand, or natural, like that of the elements returning to their places;

– Circular and perfect movement, which is 'natural', like that of the spheres in their place;

– 'Voluntary' movement, which can be rectilinear, or circular. The animal that sees food and approaches it moves of its own volition, that is, under the effect of a soul; but the animal is not free to make this movement, for it is imposed by the necessity of survival. Free will is discussed later, and we shall see that even for man its role is singularly restricted. Repose is the antithesis of movement, which means that every being capable of movement is also capable of not being in movement for a certain length of time.

The fourth chapter sets out to demonstrate that infinite length and breadth cannot exist. One of the axioms of Aristotelian philosophy is that the world is finite and that no body can be infinite. This statement is based on the impossibility of subtracting an infinite length from another infinite length.

The fifth chapter shows that movement cannot engender itself. A mover is necessary, and must be absolutely immobile; briefly resumed, the celebrated proof, by the Prime Mover, of the existence of God follows:

Since philosophers call movement not only a change of place but also a change of state, it can be produced in four of the ten categories: place, position, quantity, quality. To take the case of a stone thrown by the hand: the moving power forces the stone to rise, and the stone is forced to rise; if mover and moved could be one and the same thing, two contrary forces would be present, at the same time and place, which is impossible. If we take the case of qualitative movement, such as fire communicating its heat to water, we see that the fire is actively hot while the water is only potentially hot. The water cannot possibly be hot, simultaneously, both actively and potentially. Therefore there must be something outside the water that communicates heat to it, and this is fire.

In the case of the hand throwing the stone, the moving power is clearly visible; but when an animal moves the mover exists equally, even though it is not seen: it is the animal's soul. A hand throwing a stone is an illustration of one body moving another; that of the soul moving the body is an example of a non-corporeal substance as mover of a corporeal substance.

Since all things are moved by a moving power, which is moved by another moving power, we have a series in which the higher in the hierarchy moves that which is below it. Since one cannot have an infinite series of movers, one must reach the Prime Mover. If this Prime Mover were to move, another moving power would necessarily have to be above it; however, it has been said that it was the first; therefore, it must be not immobile, but beyond and outside the category movement–repose, that is, incorporeal: it must be God.

The sixth chapter is devoted to the soul. In the Aristotelian tradition, psychology, like the proof of the existence of God, is part of physics. For Abraham Ibn Daud the existence of the soul cannot be doubted, for we see evidence of it when we compare a stone to a man. He defines the soul as the 'perfection of the natural organic body'.

Is the soul substance or accident? Perhaps the soul is nothing more than the equilibrium of the humours, or else it is like the harmonious sound that is born with the passage of the fingers over the strings of the harp! In that case it would cease to exist when the parts of the body disintegrate. Ibn Daud offers two arguments proving that the soul is a substance and not an accident due to the combination of the parts of the body in a certain order:

(1) The human semen that produces the foetus is only a drop arising from the warmth of the body; one could, if absolutely forced to, accept that some of its parts harden into bones and that others remain liquid, like the blood; but one cannot comprehend or admit that this drop should be able to form hollow organs like the heart, the nerves and the veins, always in the same precise number; finally, that out of this drop should issue the body of a man with all its different and perfect parts. It must therefore be the soul, which does not spring from the semen but from a more elevated source, that gives human form to the foetus;

(2) The equilibrium of the humours is an extremely unstable affair, as one can see when one tries to keep water at a constant temperature;
however, living beings remain alive for decades, and some animals even for centuries. This proves therefore that the soul is a substance and not an accident in its relation to the body.

There are three kinds of soul:
  – The vegetative soul;
  – The animal soul;
  – The human soul.

The four elements are inert and have no soul; but their combination is more perfect than themselves, and closer to equilibrium. The bodies produced by this first mixing, still crude, are capable of growing through the absorption of food, the first of them being the plants – trees and grass. Thus, when the mixture is produced in this manner, it becomes a receptacle for the vegetative faculty, called the vegetative soul, because the plants are produced and nourished by means of it.

The vegetative soul has three activities:

(1) Nutrition through the nutritive faculty;
(2) Growth through the augmentative faculty;
(3) Generation, that is, production of a seed that resembles it – an act resulting in birth – through the generative faculty.

When the mixing of the elements is carried out in such a way as to be more finely balanced and closer to perfection, it becomes a receptacle for the animal soul, which has two further faculties:

(1) The faculty of action, through which the soul sets the body in movement;
(2) The faculty of perception, thanks to which the soul can perceive.

These two faculties belong to the same soul. As both derive from the same principle, their acts are linked to each other, so that when things are perceived, desire or aversion for these things accompanies perception and movement intervenes, leading to approach or withdrawal. Thus Will must be added to the faculty of action.

Will arises from need, a need to attain something or to free oneself from something, the first aspect causing one to obtain what is necessary to animal life (it is called concupiscent impulsion), the second causing one to reject what is not suitable to animal life and to flee from it (called the irascible impulsion). Fear represents a weakening of the irascible, and aversion a lessening of the concupiscent impulsion. These two impulsions command the faculty of action, the organ of which is the animal's body, for this faculty regulates the muscles.

Perception is external and internal. External perception is composed of the five senses: sight, hearing, smell, taste, touch; what Abraham Ibn Daud understands by internal perception, or *sensus communis* is memory and imagination. When an animal has suffered harm from a certain cause, and it meets again the thing that caused it harm, it recognizes its noxious character, which it would not do if it did not possess internal perception. In the same way, if it had experienced the usefulness of a certain thing, it would desire it again, without having to repeat the first experience. If the five senses did not depend on one principle, the cat would not know that the faintly yellow liquid that he sees is milk. With the aid of its senses alone and the experience that it has acquired, a sheep seeing a wolf approach for the first time cannot recognize its hostility, for hostility exists in the imagination while the senses do not perceive it.[1]

On the subject of the rational soul, the human soul, Abraham Ibn Daud does not expatiate, saying simply:

(1) That the upper limit of the animal soul is near to the human soul; the monkey quite closely resembles man;

(2) That the soul is at first in a state of potentiality, and then becomes active, which is not the case with vegetative and animal souls.

The seventh chapter is devoted to the human soul. The author demonstrates that the intellective faculty is neither a body nor a corporeal faculty, that life is linked to the body but the body is not indispensable to the survival of the soul; the human soul does not perish after becoming separated from the body, and does not incarnate itself in another body.

The rational faculty permits us to recognize in various individuals that which is common to all of them, that is, their human form, which is common to Simon and Reuben. It is by the rational faculty as well that man conceives the principles of reason. If the rational faculty were material, it would disintegrate together with the corporeal division, for each body is eventually decomposed into its elements, and the forms, like the principles of reason, would also be divided. However, we may confidently state that this is not the case, for both forms and principles are abstracted from matter, and are general. The rational faculty is therefore not a corporeal thing, although bound to matter in a certain manner, for it uses matter in order to apprehend

---

[1] In current psychology the reaction of a new-born lamb would be ascribed to instinct.

the world; but only the exterior world, for nothing is interposed between the soul and itself (I have expounded this theory of Avicenna's at some length in speaking of Abu-l-Barakāt). The soul does not reside in matter and is not a corporeal faculty. What then is it? What is its source? How is it linked to the body? Why is this rational faculty, this specifically human soul that is the ultimate point of worldly perfection, united with a heavy and imperfect body?

There are, says our author, three hypotheses on the subject of the origin of the human soul.

(1) That the soul exists of necessity, that is, eternally, *a parte ante*. For the Neoplatonists the human soul is a spark of the pure and exalted world, existing before the body; it is exiled in this gross corporeal world; and it is through knowledge that it can return to its source and recover its purity and perfection. To this theory Ibn Daud opposes the following argument: the totality of human souls must necessarily be one or multiple. If it were one for all men, it would be wise and ignorant, just and unjust; however, a simple and immaterial substance cannot be the receptacle of accidents, for, as we have seen, only corporeal substances are subject to accidents. And if human souls differed in their substance, then they would not be 'human soul', but a conglomeration of essentially different souls.

(2) That the existence of the soul is impossible, which is patently false.

(3) That the existence of the soul is contingent; this solution is advocated by our author, following Avicenna. It is based on the principle that everything that moves (and movement is change) is moved by a mover; the human soul, potential in each of us, can attain actuality, that is, receive its full flourishing and the perfection of its being, by the motion of the Active Intellect. This argument also proves the existence of the superior substances, always perfect and always active, for only an active being can make potentiality attain a state of actuality.

The Active Intellect gives their form to all living beings, from the lowest to the highest, each form being appropriate to the mixture of the elements, whether gross or subtle. Similarly, according to the degree of his knowledge and his intellectual activity, man can be intellect in potentiality, intellect in actuality, or acquired intellect.

It remains to be proved that the human intellect, when it is active, subsists after the death of the body. Ibn Daud's definition of the soul, very close to Aristotle (the soul, being the form of the body, is linked to it), does not necessarily involve the soul's survival after the dissolution of the body. However, with the help of two very different arguments, Ibn Daud shows that the soul can exist after the death of the body.

The first argument is based on the analogy existing between the body and the soul and paternity. The soul and the body are joined together in the same way as are a father and son; the life of one implies the life of the other but the death of one does not entail the death of the other.

The second argument is a demonstration by non-existence of the contrary;

one can argue against the survival of the soul by objecting that nobody, until now, has actually established that the soul outlives the body. But this proves nothing, for neither has it been incontrovertibly shown that the soul does *not* survive the body. To prove the impossibility of the survival of the soul one must prove that no soul, of all beings past, present, and future, has ever survived its body.

Since it is impossible to adduce such a proof, it is clear that every human soul is immortal in its individuality and this becomes even more evident in the course of the refutation of the idea of metempsychosis. If a soul belonging to a first body could be reincarnated in a second body, this second body would first possess its own soul, that which came into being at the same time as its individual mixture, and, in addition to it, have yet another soul, deriving from the first body. It would thus have two souls; however, two souls obviously cannot cohabit in one body. As for the idea that the soul of the first body should enter the second, this second body having come into being without a soul, this is equally impossible. At this point our author cites a great number of scriptural texts in support of his demonstration of the immortality of the soul.

In the eighth chapter, which deals with the souls of the spheres, it is demonstrated that the movement of the spheres is a voluntary movement, that is, a movement of which the source is the soul.

In medieval astronomy, the spheres have the appearance of concentric circles, being globes made of a material comparable to crystal; in some opinions, the stars are like diamonds set in this transparent matter, and each sphere carries in its movement the stars fixed in it. According to other authors, including Abraham Ibn Daud, only the last sphere, that of the fixed stars, carries these bodies unalterably fixed in itself, while the planets in their spheres move in circular motions that are not, as some declare, 'natural', i.e. not fixed by nature's law but voluntary. Natural movement is the movement of the stone that falls to the ground; it reaches its place through a rectilinear movement of which it is not conscious, and having reached its natural place, it does not move again, it is in repose. The planets, on the contrary, pursue their course without pause and without rest, passing places where they have already been, and never tiring. They, therefore, have no natural place like the elements, but move according to their will, not out of nature or necessity.

Another argument for these bodies having a soul is their eminence, for they are found at a degree immediately inferior to that of the separate Intellect. The separate Intellect bestows their forms on sublunary, terrestrial beings. However, among these beings, only the elements have no soul. Plants, animals, and men had souls. How can one then suppose that the celestial bodies, who rank much higher on the scale of being, have no souls? This soul is very different from that which we have the habit of observing, for it does not have the faculties of nutrition, reproduction or sensation. It is therefore evident, continues Abraham Ibn Daud, that the spheres have souls endowed with intelligence and will, and that this intelligence is very clearly superior to our own.

The theology that forms the subject of the beginning of the second part of the book is divided into six 'principles', and not 'chapters', as in the first part; for here Ibn Daud discusses 'faith' and not science. But what faith? We see at once at the beginning of the discussion of the first principle that it is not the faith of popular belief, which does not question and is accepted because of tradition, for the common people imagine that what is not matter does not exist and therefore do not believe in an immaterial God. When this common man has advanced a little in the knowledge of God, when he has 'awakened', he believes in the tradition of the sages; but there is still the danger that he will not know how to counteract doubts and difficulties. As for the faith of the élite, that is, the rabbis, it is founded on the actions of God, and it is to this form of faith that the *Torah* tends to lead the common people; however this true belief based on the divine acts does not provide proof that God is not matter: He might be a sphere or a star. The true sages among the élite (the philosophers) found their belief on the demonstration that God is the Prime Mover. At this point the author pauses, and completes his demonstration, proving that there is a First Mover by showing that this First Mover is unique and non-material. The other proof of the necessity of a unique and incorporeal God is by cause and effect, that is, by contingence: the existence of all beings is contingent and only a necessary being, God, can cause them to exist, producing them out of non-existence. Beings like the angels who are eternal, do not come into existence from a state of non-existence, but their existence is derived from another than themselves and, in the final analysis, from God.

The second theological principle is that of the unicity of God.

The third principle is that of the divine attributes, which, to be 'true', must be negative.

The fourth principle concerns the angels. Their existence is proved initially because the human soul is at first *in potentia* and then *in actu*; this passage from one state to the other is movement; all movement has a mover and the Active Intellect is the motive power of this movement. Another proof is that the course of the stars is only explicable through the existence of rational impelling souls. And finally, it can only be through intermediaries that the incorporeal and unique God produces this material, multiform and contradictory world. Multiplicity does not come directly from God, for only One can come from One, but it accompanies the First Being issued directly from God, which the philosophers call Intellect and the *Torah* Angel. It is imperfect in comparison with God, for it receives its existence from another than itself; 'duality' is thus at the very root of its being. From this first Intellect are born three beings: a second intellect (which is less perfect than the first, because it does not arise from God directly, but from a being already outside God), the soul of the sphere, and its matter. The soul of the sphere of the fixed stars and the matter of the sphere of the fixed stars emanates from the second intellect; thus, from intellect to intellect, we reach the last intellect, that which presides over this lower world, which gives forms to all sublunary beings, which makes our intellect pass from its potential state to that of actuality, and is the source of prophecy, the fifth principle of Ibn Daud's theology.

There are [says Abraham Ibn Daud] three kinds of prophecies and the first is the true dream ... There can be no doubt that the human soul, I mean the rational faculty which is drawn from the 'benedictions' of the Active Intellect ... receives from the Intellect the keys to the sciences, and this rational faculty may also receive from the Intellect, if it fortifies itself further and is even more prepared, the keys to the hidden events. Man is prevented from attaining the secret knowledge when he is awake because when he is in a waking state he is attentive to the perceptions of the [external] senses. When he sleeps and has ceased to concern himself with his senses, [other] impediments occur: the heaviness of the *pneuma* due to vapours provoked by food and drink, or else his heart rebels against a lack of food and drink; there is thus no difference between being hungry or being satisfied, being drunk or fasting; all these states are preoccupations and hindrances.

Another important obstacle is the imaginative faculty, which persists in presenting to the *sensus communis* its mirages and its chimeras, and which only detaches itself from the cares of the waking state in order to trouble man's sleep. Job says: When I say, My bed shall comfort me, my couch shall ease my complaint; Then thou scarest me with dreams, and terrifiest me through visions [Job 7: 13, 14].

Sometimes, this imaginative faculty becomes to some extent subject to the intellect. The rational soul is then ready to attract to itself the secrets of the eminent substances; nevertheless the imaginative faculty still strives to separate it from them, though not entirely, as usually happens – for the essential character of the imagination is, as we have said, to play with images and transform them into dreams – but [in another way], for it is [the imaginative faculty] which attempts to reach the future and to present it to the soul in the form of parables. Thus, one who has to undertake a voyage has the impression that he is flying, one who promises himself enjoyment sees [in dream] his marriage to a beautiful woman, and all the other examples that one finds in the treatises of oneiromancy. When the parables of the dream relate to a specific individual or concern a particular event, we shall not say that this is prophecy, or, at best, we shall say that this is a part of prophecy but of a very inferior kind. On the contrary, if the subject of [the dream] is an important event, of universal significance, which are to take place in the distant future, this is the prophetic dream [properly speaking].   (*Emunah Ramah*, pp. 70–1)

The second degree of prophecy is that of vision, when a torpor assails the prophet; he collapses, struck unconscious, and sees grand visions; then this state terminates and he recounts what he has seen.

The most eminent degree of prophecy is when the prophet sees a vision but himself remains perfectly awake and in a conscious state.

The degrees of the souls at this third level of prophecy differ considerably ... Divine providence on behalf of His creatures is already evident to all those who meditate, but since these are few in number, the perfect goodness of God makes it still more evident by making it repose on those men who are of perfect conduct and irreproachable morals, so that, as it were, they become intermediaries between God and His creatures. He elevates them to such a point that they have a power comparable to that of the eminent substances which incline towards them in prophecy. They have the power to change the course of the existence of beings and the usual modes of their nature. They can make a people triumph, and make [fate] turn against other peoples, bring death to those who spread falsehood, and resuscitate those who believe, as is related in our traditional writings. Reason has no argument that can refute or raise objections on these points. On the contrary, it furnishes verification and justification . . .

Only perfect and pure souls can attain such a level. This perfection and this purity are sometimes in a man from the beginning of his formation, and also moral perfection, but study is of great utility, as is the society of virtuous men . . .

When the soul is ready to receive prophecy, the latter flows out to it, for there is no avarice in God . . . and when he who strives to attain this supreme state has acquired all the perfect virtues, the spiritual forms flow over him . . . but the time should be propitious . . . and also the place is generally the Land of Israel . . . and the people elected for prophecy is Israel . . . but the Gentile may have prophetic dreams.

(*Ibid.* pp. 73–4)

Those rational human souls that have attained the level of the highest perfection are like the angels and do not differ from the veritable angels except in two aspects; they are at the moment souls of corporeal beings, which is not the case with the angels; the angels possess perfection by nature, men acquire it.

The eminent angelical substances love perfect human souls as a master can love an intelligent disciple who acquires sciences and excellent qualities from him. Such a master teaches numerous students desirous of acquiring knowledge, but some draw little profit [from this teaching], others find it of great utility; if among the latter there is one who lets nothing go to waste of what he is taught and reaches the highest point of perfection, his master holds him in high esteem and respect. And as the superior substances respect the human souls which derive their excellence from them, they prepare themselves for their visit and put on corporeal forms, since the human souls do belong to corporeal beings. The angels present themselves [to men] in bodily form and give the impression of being fatigued even to the point where the man says as did Abraham in Genesis [18: 4]: Let a little water, I pray you, be fetched, and wash your feet; or else, they have the appearance of very hungry persons: [18: 5] And I will fetch a morsel of bread, and comfort ye your hearts.

Thus, when a very learned man, endowed with physical force and all the other virtues, has a servant who works hard, but possesses none of these qualities, he will be good to him and will behave morally by not making him feel his own intellectual superiority or superior strength. On the contrary, the master will behave as if his servant could be compared to himself and as if he himself were at the same level of helplessness. In the same way, when the angelic substances concern themselves with human affairs they behave like men, and even sometimes as if they were weaker than a man, as in the combat between Jacob and the angel. (*Ibid.* pp. 84–5

According to these passages, prophecy is a natural phenomenon; even when Abraham Ibn Daud later restricts this definition of prophecy by adding conditions of place: the Land of Israel; of people: only Israel has the gift of prophecy and the prophetic visions that have been bestowed upon the Gentiles redound to the glory of Israel; of time: there must be a generation attentive to the divine Word. These limitations, which vividly recall Judah Halevi, confine prophecy to the biblical texts, but do not change the fundamental naturalistic definition.

On the basis of the whole system that he has expounded, Ibn Daud can now assert that the biblical text, being the fruit of prophecy, should not be interpreted as assigning to God a body or any corporeal attribute. To understand the anthropomorphic expressions of the Bible literally is a heresy, and our author regards with disfavour the attitude of certain Jewish anthropomorphists as compared with the views of Christians and Muslims, whom he praises for their allegorical interpretation of all the expressions where corporeality can apparently be attributed to God. The biblical verses can be perfectly well explained by the concept of the angelic hierarchy. The angel set over a people is higher in degree than the angel called *Panim* (face); lower again is *Aḥorim* (back parts), who is also called *Elohim* (Lord).

All this agrees perfectly with the revealed text and is not foreign to philosophy, but rather, it is a theory possible in philosophy, or even positively admitted ... The other, non-Jewish, religious communities have not wished to belittle God by attributing to Him these vile details unworthy of Him, thus, the Christians have translated the verses: God said, God descended, by: the Lord said, the Lord appeared; thus the Moslems have never claimed that God spoke to the prophets or appeared to them, but they affirm that it was a creature named Gabriel, the Holy Spirit, etc. .... while among our coreligionists certain have so little discernment that they are not satisfied with attributing to God change and movement, they go so far as to attribute to Him more transformations than to any of his creatures. Every time that one of the servants of God from wicked becomes righteous or from righteous becomes wicked, God, they say, changes according to the same number of wicked or good actions, and this number is almost infinite.

(*Ibid.* pp. 90–1)

The end of the book is devoted to morality and to the divine commandments; but before this Abraham Ibn Daud tackles the problem which he declared in his introduction to be the *raison d'être* of the whole book: the problem of free will. In fact, he assigns only one paragraph to the problem itself, and the chapter consists of a recapitulation of the entire book, and also of the various notions of the possible and the necessary. He finally treats of the various causes that are active in this world – divine, natural, accidental, and due to free will. Free will consists of the accomplishment of the commandments and the refusal of transgressions, for, if the possibility of choice did not exist, there would be no prophets, no reward and no punishment.

The three first causes of human events are illustrated with the aid of the verse I Samuel 26: 10: ' *David said furthermore, As the Lord liveth*, these are divine causes, *or his day shall come to die*, these are natural causes, *or he shall descend into battle, and perish*, these are accidental causes.' An example of the way in which free will, fourth cause of human events, intervenes in the unfolding of history is the account of the flight from Keilah. This was an episode in the struggle between David and Saul (1 Samuel 23). 'David, following the order of God, went to Keilah to deliver the town from the Philistines, then Saul, having learned that David was in Keilah proceeded there to make the notables give David up to him; David, having consulted the *Ephod*, learned of this, and, using his free will, fled in time.' It appears from this illustration that human events are determined by divine, natural and accidental causes, but that the wise man who hears the divine word can foresee these events and take some precautions. This idea, which is reminiscent of the conception of Abraham Ibn Ezra, defines free will as the moral liberty not only to accomplish the divine commandments, but also to purify one's soul and to come nearer to the noble beings, the Intellects, in order to learn from them the secrets of the future. Then, and only then, does God's providence watch over man in the sense that we have seen in the case of David. And a little later Abraham Ibn Daud quotes the talmudic sentence: 'All is in the hands of the Heavens, except the fear of the Heavens' (Bab. *Ketubot* 30a).

Our author thus expounds all these problems without finding a solution that convinced his contemporaries. It was left to Maimonides to achieve a more durable accord between Aristotelian philosophy and religion.

Chapter 6

MAIMONIDES

The whole history of Jewish medieval thought revolves about the personality of Maimonides; with him one period comes to an end and another begins; he is its term of reference as Thomas Aquinas is for scholasticism, and it is no accident but rather the mark of a profound affinity that the latter so often cites Rabbi Moses. Both followers of Aristotle, each constructed a *summa* of religion and philosophy, a summation constantly opposed, but still remaining a source of inspiration for the faithful of the two religions.

Moses ben Maimon (also called Rambam, acronym of Rabbi Moshe ben Maimon) was born in 1135 at Cordoba, where his father was a rabbinical judge. In 1148 Maimon and his family, fleeing the religious persecutions that accompanied the conquest of the town by the Almohads, wandered from place to place in Spain, and perhaps in Provence, and came to Fez in 1160. According to Arab sources the family converted to Islam, but, as Saadiah Ibn Danan, a fifteenth-century philosopher, remarked, rumours of this kind became attached to the names of many Jewish savants. It was during his sojourn in Morocco that Maimon, Moses' father, wrote his *Letter of Consolation* to Jews who had been forced to convert to Islam. According to this *Letter*, it was enough to say one's prayers, however briefly, and to perform good actions, in order to remain Jewish. Moses ben Maimon himself also wrote a *Letter* (*Iggeret ha-Shemad*), concerning forced conversion, where he recommends emigration from countries where Jews are obliged to transgress the divine law. Towards 1165 the whole family abandoned Fez and took refuge in Acre; for six months Maimon and his children lived in the Land of Israel and travelled in it; then they removed to Cairo and settled at Fostat. Maimonides rapidly acquired a high social status in Egypt, perhaps with the assistance of his family alliances with local notables. It seems that his vigorous action in the matter of ransoming captives helped to make him known among remote communities. From 1171 he was recognized as the 'chief of the Jews' of Fostat, and remained in this post for five years. Ousted from this function for about twenty years, he was then again appointed to it, and exercised it until his death.

The family of Maimonides was engaged in maritime commerce with India; the shipwreck and death of his brother David brought about their ruin. Although he continued to take some part in business affairs, Maimonides from then on earned his livelihood by practising and teaching medicine, an art he had acquired in North Africa. His reputation attained its zenith in 1185, when he was chosen as one of the official doctors of Al Fadil, Salāḥ-al-Din's (Saladin's) vizier. During this time he re-married, and his only son, Abraham, was born. These were years of fruitful and intensive work; while practising his profession and composing his medical books, Maimonides completed his two major works, the *Mishneh Torah* in 1180 and the *Guide of the Perplexed* in 1190, and maintained a flourishing correspondence with numerous communities in Egypt and the rest of the world. His death in December 1204 gave rise to manifestations of public grief in all the Jewish communities.

Maimonides' celebrity rests chiefly on his works as a jurist; it was as such that he was known to the Jews of the Diaspora, and to the present day many Oriental Jewish communities follow his juridical and religious prescriptions.

I shall not list the texts dealing with medicine or jurisprudence, but only those that are entirely or in part philosophical.

(1) Book I of the first part of the juridical code *Mishneh Torah*, also called *Yad ha-Ḥazakah* (*yad* = יד = 14, the number of the constituent books), which is entitled *Sefer ha-Madaʿ* (*Book of Knowledge*).

(2) In the *Commentary on the Mishnah*: the introduction to *Avot* (a treatise of the *Mishnah*, usually known as *Pirkei Avot*, the *Sentences of the Fathers*), called *Shemonah Perakim* (*Eight Chapters*), a brief summing-up of ideas on psychology and morality; and the introduction to *Perek Ḥelek* (*Sanhedrin* II).

(3) *Millot ha-Higgayon* (*Vocabulary of Logic*), a short treatise written in Maimonides' youth.

(4) Several *Letters*, which in fact are short dissertations on contemporary problems or were written in response to questions posed by various persons:

Iggeret ha-Shemad (or *Kiddush ha-Shem*) on forced conversion, or Sanctification of the Divine Name;
Al-Risāla al-yamaniyya = *Iggeret Teiman* (*Letter to Yemen*), on the emergence of a false prophet announcing the Messianic age;
Maqāla fi Teḥyat ha-metim = *Iggeret Teḥyat ha-metim* (*Letter on the Resurrection of the Dead*), in which Maimonides replies to the accusation that he does not believe in the Resurrection;
Iggeret le-Hakhmei Derom Tzarfat (*Letter to the Sages of Southern France*). It was the sages of Southern France and Provence who propounded the question of the legality and truth of astrology.

(5) *Dalālat al-Ḥāʾirīn* (*Moreh ha-nevukhim: The Guide of the Perplexed*) (The English quotations in the pages that follow are taken from *The Guide of the Perplexed*, translated with an introduction and notes by Shlomo Pines, and from *The Book of Knowledge*, translated by M. Hyamson.)

Except for *The Book of Knowledge* all these works were written in Arabic. They were almost immediately translated into Hebrew. *The Guide of the Perplexed* was translated by Samuel Ibn Tibbon in 1204; a second, more literary and less accurate, translation was made by Judah al-Ḥarizi some years later. This second translation was the basis for the Latin version that was used by the scholastics, especially St Thomas Aquinas.

Maimonides' works were not all addressed to the same public and cannot be studied on the same level; for this author, as for all medieval Arab and Jewish philosophers, men are not on the same level as regards their capacity to attain truth. In a parable contained in Book III of the *Guide*, Maimonides describes the various classes of men in their relationship to knowledge, that is, the search for God.

I shall begin the discourse in this chapter with a parable that I shall compose for you. I say then: The ruler is in his palace, and all his subjects are partly within the city and partly outside the city. Of those who are within the city, some have turned their backs upon the ruler's habitation, their faces being turned another way. Others seek to reach the ruler's habitation, turn towards it, and desire to enter it and to stand before him, but up to now they have not yet seen the wall of the habitation. Some of those who seek to reach it have come up to the habitation and walk around it searching for its gate. Some of them have entered the gate and walk about in the antechambers. Some of them have entered the inner court of the habitation and have come to be with the king, in one and the same place with him, namely, in the ruler's habitation. But their having come into the inner part of the habitation does not mean that they see the ruler or speak to him. For after their coming into the inner part of the habitation, it is indispensable that they should make another effort; then they will be in the presence of the ruler, see him from afar or from nearby, or hear the ruler's speech or speak to him.

Now I shall interpret to you this parable that I have invented. I say then: Those who are outside the city are all human individuals who have no doctrinal belief, neither one based on speculation nor one that accepts the authority of tradition: such individuals as the furthermost Turks found in the remote North, the Negroes found in the remote South, and those who resemble them from among them that are with us in these climes. The status of those is like that of irrational animals. To my mind they do not have the rank of men, but have among the beings a rank lower than the rank of man but higher than the rank of the apes. For they have the external shape and lineaments of a man and a faculty of discernment that is superior to that of the apes.

Those who are within the city, but have turned their backs upon the ruler's habitation, are people who have opinions and are engaged in speculation, but who have adopted incorrect opinions either because of some great error that befell them in the course of their speculation or because of their following the traditional authority of one who had fallen into error. Accordingly because of these opinions, the more these people walk, the greater is their distance from the ruler's habitation. And they are far worse than the first. They are those concerning whom necessity at certain times impels killing them and blotting out the traces of their opinions lest they should lead astray the ways of others.

Those who seek to reach the ruler's habitation and to enter it, but never see the ruler's habitation, are the multitude of the adherents of the Law, I refer to *the ignoramuses who observe the commandments.*

Those who have come up to the habitation and walk around it are the jurists who believe true opinions on the basis of traditional authority and study the law concerning the practices of divine service, but do not engage in speculation concerning the fundamental principles of religion and make no inquiry whatever regarding the rectification of belief.

Those who have plunged into speculation concerning the fundamental principles of religion, have entered the antechambers. People there indubitably have different ranks. He, however, who has achieved demonstration, to the extent that that is possible, of everything that may be demonstrated; and who has ascertained in divine matters, to the extent that that is possible, everything that may be ascertained; and who has come close to certainty in those matters in which one can only come close to it – has come to be with the ruler in the inner part of the habitation.

Know, my son, that as long as you are engaged in studying the mathematical sciences and the art of logic, you are one of those who walk around the house searching for its gate, as [the Sages], *may their memory be blessed*, have said resorting to a parable: *Ben Zoma is still outside*. If, however, you have understood the natural things, you have entered the habitation and are walking in the antechambers. If, however, you have achieved perfection in the natural things and have understood divine science, you have entered in the ruler's place *into the inner court* and are with him in one habitation. This is the rank of the men of science; they, however, are of different grades of perfection. (*Guide* III, 5, pp. 618–91)

The texts of the *Mishneh Torah* and the *Commentary on the Mishnah* are intended for simple men of faith, all Israel without distinction; for 'Those who seek to reach the ruler's habitation . . . the multitude of the adherents of the Law, I refer to *the ignoramuses* . . .'

The short treatises written in response to questions (or attacks) emanating from rabbis or heads of communities on specific questions (resurrection, conversion, the Messiah, astrology) were written for 'Those who have come up to the habitation . . . the jurists . . .' and also for '*the ignoramuses who observe the commandments*'.

The *Guide of the Perplexed* was addressed to a well-beloved pupil, Joseph ben Judah, of whom it is said in the dedicatory epistle:

I had a high opinion of you because of your strong desire for inquiry and because of what I had observed in your poems of your powerful longing for speculative matters. This was the case since your letters and compositions in rhymed prose came to me from Alexandria, before your grasp was put to the test. I said however: perhaps his longing is stronger than his grasp. When thereupon you read under my guidance texts dealing with the science of astronomy and prior to that texts dealing with mathematics, which is necessary as an introduction to astronomy, my joy in you increased because of the excellence of your mind and the quickness of your grasp. I saw that your longing for mathematics was great, and hence I let you train yourself in that science, knowing where you would end. When thereupon you read under my guidance texts dealing with the art of logic, my hopes fastened upon you, and I saw that you are one worthy to have the secrets of the prophetic books revealed to you so that you would consider in them that which perfect men ought to consider.

and again in the introduction: 'My speech in the present Treatise is directed, as I have mentioned, to one who has philosophized and has knowledge of the true sciences' (*Guide*, introd., p. 10).

But for the learned, those who 'have entered in the ruler's place', Maimonides wrote nothing. In other words, he wrote no book of philosophy directed at philosophers, at erudite men of his own kind, to whom he could have spoken without dissembling his thoughts. A letter to Samuel Ibn Tibbon probably contains the only evidence of our author's opinions as he would have formulated them for the benefit of philosophers genuinely capable of understanding them.

Samuel Ibn Tibbon proposes visiting Maimonides in order to submit to him the Hebrew translation of the *Guide*. He also asks him which scientific books Maimonides would recommend him to read.

Maimonides replies, first, that he would be very happy to see Samuel, but his many occupations would probably not permit him to devote time to joint study. He then continues (I quote some passages):

The writings [literally: words] of Aristotle's teacher Plato are in parables and hard to understand. One can dispense with them, for the writings of Aristotle suffice, and we need not occupy [our attention] with the writings of earlier [philosophers]. Aristotle's intellect [represents] the extreme of human intellect, if we except those who have received divine inspiration.

The works of Aristotle are the roots and foundations of all works on the sciences. But they cannot be understood except with the help of commentaries, those of Alexander of Aphrodisias, those of Themistius, and those of Averroes.

I tell you: as for works on logic, one should only study the writings of Abū Naṣr al-Fārābī. All his writings are faultlessly excellent. One ought to study and understand them. For he is a great man.

Though the works of Avicenna may give rise to objections and are not as [good] as those of Abū Naṣr [al-Fārābī], Abū Bakr al-Ṣā'igh [Ibn Bājja] was also a great philosopher, and all his writings are of a high standard.

(*Guide*, introd., pp. lix, xl)

As we see, he had some reservations on the subject of Avicenna. But reading any philosophers other than these, Jewish or Arab, is a waste of time.

Furthermore, Maimonides states his opinion (which has proved to be correct) that two works attributed to Aristotle, the *Book of the Apple* and the *Book of the Golden Palace*, are pseudepigraphs.

He advises against studying the commentaries on Aristotle of the Christian authors al-Ṭayyib, Yaḥyā Ibn 'Adī, and Yaḥyā al-Biṭrīq. To read them would be a sheer waste of time.

He also states that he has no use for Abū Bakr al-Rāzī's *Book of Divine Science* and for Isaac Israeli's *Book of Definitions* and *Book of Elements*. He regards both authors as mere physicians (and no philosophers). (*Guide*, introd., pp. lix, lx)

This letter and its judgements on other philosophers is of the greatest importance for our understanding of Maimonides. If we recall that the only philosophers cited in the *Guide of the Perplexed* are Greek and Arab, the ideological climate to which Maimonides declares his adherence becomes clearly defined: it is that of the philosophers who have unequivocally separated science from religion.

The Arab philosophers whom Maimonides admires or esteems are Al-Fārābī, Ibn Bājja, Averroes, and, up to a point, Avicenna. From this, to understand Maimonides as a philosopher as 'extremist' as Al-Fārābī and Averroes, expressing his opinions only under cover of obscurity in the works he destined for the general public, and with deliberate vagueness in the *Guide of the Perplexed,* is only one step, and it is not a recent one, for it was thus that his fourteenth-century commentators interpreted him – Moses of Narbonne and Joseph Ibn Caspi, to mention only the most important; and it was thus that he was seen by most Jewish philosophers up to and including the nineteenth century, and L. Strauss and S. Pines in the twentieth. Maimonides thus seems to form part of a long tradition of philosophical esoterism that, starting with Socrates, Aristotle and Plato, continued with Spinoza and terminated (in democratic countries, at least, for it is still alive under totalitarian regimes) with Voltaire, Rousseau and perhaps Kant.

In this esoteric tradition the truths that can be comprehended by only a few men capable of receiving them must be communicated from master to disciple; when these truths cannot be communicated orally they may be written only between the lines, so that those worthy of them may discover them, while others remain unaware.

There are two principal reasons for this necessity of concealing philosophical truths from the common run of men:

The first reason is political: on many points philosophy is in conflict with religion. Each of the formally constituted religions considered that it possessed the truth, an exclusive and necessarily intolerant truth. Only the philosophers' truth transcended the barriers and established a different demarcation, itself not lacking in a certain, different, kind of intolerance.[1] Those philosophers who regarded truth as independent and superior to the generally accepted religious laws were often persecuted by the partisans of the various faiths if they expressed their opinions too openly. It was thus that Averroes, it is related, was roughly handled by the populace in the mosque of Cordoba, and was forced to save his life by flight.

The second reason is founded on the philosophers' conviction that truth is not good for every man. This conviction is part of a whole pedagogical and political concept.

Man and society can be considered in two different ways:

– Man is naturally good; left to himself he recognizes good and evil and chooses the good; this was Saadiah's position; in this case the Revealed Law shows the right way and helps man to organize a society conforming to reason. The idea that the natural state is one of innocence, like that of Adam before the Fall, that contemporary society perverts this innocence and that primitive society was natural and reasonable, was maintained in Antiquity;

---

[1] As in a passage by Maimonides: 'Those . . . who have adopted incorrect opinions . . . They are those concerning whom necessity at certain times impels killing them and blotting out the traces of their opinions lest they should lead astray the ways of others' (*Guide,* III, 51, p. 619).

but it is hardly ever found among Jewish medieval philosophers. In the Renaissance it reappears with Abrabanel.

– Man is not really bad, properly speaking; but the individuals who make up the human race are so different that concord can prevail only with great difficulty. Contrary to other animals, men widely differ between themselves, and one man may be capable of killing his son in a fit of anger and another unable to squash a fly (cf. *Guide* II, 40). However, society is not simply a dimension added to the human race; man by his nature has need of society. Human civilization, the survival of man, is only possible when its laws allow harmony to reign among these various individuals, compensating for what is defective and moderating what is excessive. The laws that regulate society may be of divine origin, that is, determined by the prophets (for Maimonides, the only truly Divine Law was that promulgated by Moses), or it may be humanly conceived; but, at any rate, these laws are conventional in the sense that they purport to establish a certain 'convention' among men. Now, the great majority of men are only potentially rational, for very few of them are capable of being active intellect in actuality, that is, among other things, of studying the sciences. Among the common masses are included children who have not reached the age of reason, women, primitive populations, and all men who will never be philosophers. These simple people cannot, as we have seen, endure the radiance of truth. When we speak of 'political law' or of 'religion' we are then no longer in the domain of scientific truth, but in that of political convention. This is in no way a matter of falsehood, but of two totally different orders of reality, each as necessary as the other. In referring to this political law, the best of political laws, namely the *Torah* and the commandments arising from it, Maimonides says at the end of chapter 4 of the *Book of Knowledge*: 'They are the precious boon bestowed by God, to promote social well-being on earth, and enable men to obtain bliss in the life thereafter' (*Book of Knowledge*, p. 40a).

The philosophers, in distinguishing the good suitable for the people from that proper to the philosopher, were convinced that they were following the divine example, and safeguarding not so much their own lives and liberties as the civilization established by God and the happiness of each member of society.

Is it absolutely necessary to dissimulate the philosophic truths, and is the welfare of the people so totally opposed to that of the philosophers, or can one venture to think of the possibility of gradually educating the people towards the level of the philosopher?

For Averroes, in his *Decisive Treatise* on the harmony between religion and philosophy, there is no possibility of such a progress. He who reveals philosophical interpretations to the common people, and to those who are not apt to receive them, is an 'infidel', for he turns them away from the Divine Law, and corrupts them. In effect, the Divine Legislator tends the soul's health as the doctor looks after the body's well-being. Now, the Legislator has prescribed the commandments that must be respected, for on obedience to these practices depends the harmony of society in this world as much as beatitude in the after-life. In the same way, to be in good health men must observe their doctor's prescriptions without necessarily understanding them. Philosophical interpretations, when they are not understood, awaken doubt in the minds of simple people, and they neglect God's commandments, as they would disregard their doctor's recommendations if they doubted his competence. It is entirely forbidden to unveil philosophical doctrines to the people, both when they are true and, even more so, when they are false. It is because this principle has not been respected that sects have multiplied in Islam. Religious chiefs are duty-bound to forbid the reading of books on religious science, except by men of learning. The texts must be understood by the simple faithful in their literal sense alone.

In contrast to the Arab philosopher and judge, Maimonides contends in all his writings that the people must know and accept as authoritative the principles of the esoteric sense of the *Torah*: the divine unity and incorporeality. Not that one can 'teach' these matters to the vulgar folk:

The causes that prevent the commencement of instruction with divine science, the indication of things that ought to be indicated, and the presentation of this to the multitude, are five.

The first cause is the difficulty, subtlety, and obscurity of the matter in itself. Thus Scripture says: *That which was is far off and exceeding deep; who can find it out?* And it is said: *But wisdom, where shall it be found?* Now it is not fitting in teaching to begin with what is most difficult and obscure for the understanding. One of the parables generally known in our community is that likening knowledge to water. Now the Sages, peace be on them, explained several notions by means of this parable; one of them being that he who knows how to swim brings up pearls from the bottom of the sea, whereas he who does not know, drowns. For this reason, no one should expose himself to the risks of swimming except he who has been trained in learning to swim.

The second cause is the insufficiency of the minds of all men at their beginnings. For man is not granted his ultimate perfection at the outset; for perfection exists in him only potentially, and in his beginnings he lacks this act. Accordingly it is said: *And man is born a wild ass.* Nor is it necessarily obligatory in the case of every individual who is endowed with some thing in potency, that this thing should become actual. Sometimes it remains in its defective state either because of certain obstacles or because of paucity of training in what transforms that potentiality into actuality. Accordingly it is clearly said: *Not many are wise.* The Sages too, *may their memory be blessed*, have said: *I saw the people who have attained a high rank, and they were few.* For the obstacles to perfection are very many, and the objects that distract from it abound. When should he be able to achieve the perfect preparation and the leisure required for training so that what subsists in a particular individual in potency should be transformed into actuality?

· The third cause lies in the length of the preliminaries. For man has in his nature a desire to seek the ends; and he often finds preliminaries tedious and refuses to engage in them. Know, however, that if an end could be achieved without the preliminaries that precede it, the latter would not be preliminaries, but pure distractions and futilities.

... You know that these matters are mutually connected; there being nothing in what exists besides God, may He be exalted, and the totality of the things He has made. For this totality includes everything comprised in what exists except only Him. There is, moreover, no way to apprehend Him except it be through the things He has made; for they are indicative of His existence and of what ought to be believed about Him, I mean to say, of what should be affirmed and denied with regard to Him. It is therefore indispensable to consider all beings as they really are so that we may obtain for all the kinds of beings true and certain premises that would be useful to us in our researches pertaining to the divine science.

The fourth cause is to be found in the natural aptitudes. For it has been explained, or rather demonstrated, that the moral virtues are a preparation for the rational virtues, it being impossible to achieve true, rational acts – I mean perfect rationality – unless it be by a man thoroughly trained with respect to his morals and endowed with the qualities of tranquility and quiet.

The fifth cause is to be found in the fact that men are occupied with the necessities of the bodies, which are the first perfection; and more particularly if, in addition, they are occupied with taking care of a wife and of children; and even more especially if there is in them, superadded to that, a demand for the superfluities of life, which becomes an established habitus as a result of a bad conduct of life and bad customs.

(Guide I, 34, pp. 73–9)

And he continues in the next chapter:

Do not think that all that we have laid down in the preceding chapters regarding the greatness and the hidden nature of the matter, the difficulty of apprehending it, and its having to be withheld from the multitude, refers also to the denial of the corporeality of God and to the denial of His being subject to affections. It is not so. For just as it behooves to bring up children in the belief, and to proclaim to the multitude, that God, may He be magnified and honored, is one and that none but He ought to be worshipped, so it behooves that they should be made to accept on traditional authority the belief that God is not a body; and that there is absolutely no likeness in any respect whatever between Him and the things created by Him; that His existence has no likeness to theirs; nor His life to the life of those among them who are alive; nor again His knowledge to the knowledge of those among them who are endowed with knowledge. They should be made to accept the belief that the difference between Him and them is not merely a difference of more and less, but one concerning the species of existence. I mean to say that it should be established in everybody's mind that our knowledge or our power does not differ from His knowledge or His power in the latter being greater and stronger, the former less and weaker, or in other similar respects, inasmuch as the strong and the weak are necessarily alike with respect to their species, and one definition comprehends both of them. Similarly any relation can subsist only between two things belonging to one species. This likewise has been made clear in the natural sciences. Now everything that can be ascribed to God, may He be exalted, differs in every respect from our attributes, so that no definition can comprehend the one thing and the other. Similarly, as I shall make clear, the terms 'existence' can only be applied equivocally to His existence and to that of things other than He. This measure of knowledge will suffice for children and the multitude to establish in their minds that there is a perfect being, who is neither a body nor a force in a body, and that He is the deity, that no sort of deficiency and therefore no affection whatever can attain Him.

(Guide I, 35, pp. 79–80)

What would ensue if men did not profess these central notions of the divine unity and incorporeality, even without really understanding them, is designated by Maimonides as 'perdition'; that is to say, such men will have no part in the world to come:

Accordingly if we never in any way acquired an opinion through following traditional authority and were not correctly conducted toward something by means of parables, but were obliged to achieve a perfect representation by means of essential definitions and by pronouncing true only that which is meant to be pronounced true in virtue of a demonstration – which would be impossible except after the above-mentioned lengthy preliminary studies – this state of affairs would lead to all people dying without having known whether there is a deity for the world, or whether there is not, much less whether a proposition should be affirmed with regard to Him or a defect denied. Nobody would ever be saved from this perdition except *one of a city or two of a family*.   (*Guide* I, 34, p. 75)

Averroes in his *Decisive Treatise* has only political felicity in mind; to function well, the social body needs religious law, which establishes concord among men. These, whether ignorant or learned, have a well-defined place in society and only have to fulfil their assigned roles, without being troubled by doubts unfitting their state. Maimonides accepts this argument and adds a further one to it: survival in the world to come. This survival is linked to the possession of at least a minimum of true ideas – and it is, in part, to forestall the perdition of Israel that he wrote his 'popular' works.

In composing the *Mishneh Torah* Maimonides was undoubtedly convinced that he was contributing to the intellectual progress of Jewish and human society:

(1) In causing harmony to reign among men and in giving them peace, thanks to a unified jurisprudence;

(2) In allowing persons capable of displaying the necessary aptitude an initial taste of philosophy;

(3) In stating in an authoritative way the essential truths concerning God and the world of the intellects.

The *Mishneh Torah*: its purpose and its place in Maimonides' work

This is Maimonides' most popular work; in a clear and rational form it presents the entirety of the Oral Law – the *Mishnah* and the Talmud. The author declares that he composed the *Mishneh Torah* primarily as an *aide-mémoire* for his old age, to spare himself lengthy searches in the talmudic literature. If he attempted to introduce a systematic order in the dense forest of the Talmud and the *Responsa*, this was certainly for reasons of convenience, but, apart from this, he undoubtedly set a high value on reason and the clear and precise exposition of questions, wishing to give the Jewish people a legal code where the laws could be found assembled in a unified and rational manner.[1]

Further, he believed that the difficult political situation was causing a lowering of the level of halakhic as well as of philosophical study.

There is no opposition between Maimonides as philosopher and Maimonides as judge, and one of the most striking traits of his thought is precisely this consistency, which pervades his various works; those intended for the general public and those directed towards apprentice philosophers complement each other. According to the level aimed at, the same problem appears in a different shape and must be differently handled. Thus, in the *Mishneh Torah* and the other halakhic works, the exact manner of fulfilling certain commandments is studied and codified at considerable length. Each gesture necessary for their execution is very precisely fixed, for in order that the act may be easily performed by the simple faithful the frame of their conduct must be so clearly delimited that they will not be able to stray outside it. In the *Guide of the Perplexed*, on the other hand, which is intended for student-philosophers, who scrupulously carry out the commandments knowing their importance, the reasons accounting for them are revealed. It then becomes clear that the material aspect of the fulfilment of the commandments may be due to historical circumstances. Which, of course, in no way affects the binding nature of the law.

We read in Part III of the *Guide* (26, pp. 508–9):

The generalities of the *commandments* necessarily have a cause and have been given because of a certain utility; their details are that in regard to which it was said of the commandments that they were given merely for the sake of commanding something. For instance the killing of animals because of the necessity of having good food is manifestly useful, as we shall make clear. But the prescription that they should be killed through having the upper and not the lower part of their throat cut, and having their esophagus and windpipe severed at one particular place is, like other prescriptions of the same kind, imposed with a view *to purifying the people*. The same thing is made clear to you through their example: *Slaughtered by cutting their neck in front or in the back*. I have mentioned this example to you merely because one finds in their text, *may their memory be blessed: Slaughtered by cutting their neck in front or in the back*. However, if one studies the truth of the matter, one finds it to be as follows: As necessity occasions the eating of animals, the commandment was intended to bring about the easiest death in an easy manner. For beheading would only be possible with the help of a sword or something similar, whereas a throat can be cut with anything. In order that death should come about

---

[1] Maimonides was acting in conformity with the contemporary Islamic tendency to elaborate an official theology. In his youth he had seen the Almohads impose the opinions of their sect, and to an orderly man, a people united, even by force, was an impressive spectacle. Halakhic critique of the *Mishneh Torah*, especially that of Abraham ben David of Posquières, immediately pointed out that the very existence of a code endangers critical study. Not only does Maimonides not quote his sources (this is a further argument of the critics), but above all the student finds decisions already taken by another man, who is certainly very learned, but whose preoccupations are different from his own. It thus becomes unnecessary to search the multiplicity of the texts and to hope to chance on original ideas in the course of one's careful reading; it is useless to reflect; all is already written, ready to be put to use.

more easily, the condition was imposed that the knife should be sharp. The true reality of particulars of commandments is illustrated by the sacrifices. The offering of sacrifices has in itself a great and manifest utility, as I shall make clear. But no cause will ever be found for the fact that one particular sacrifice consists in a *lamb* and another in a *ram* and that the number of the victims should be one particular number. Accordingly, in my opinion, all those who occupy themselves with finding causes for something of these particulars are stricken with a prolonged madness in the course of which they do not put an end to an incongruity, but rather increase the number of incongruities. Those who imagine that a cause may be found for suchlike things are as far from truth as those who imagine that the generalities of a *commandment* are not designed with a view to some real utility.

The precept of offering sacrifices is in effect explained further on:

For a sudden transition from one opposite to another is impossible. And therefore man, according to his nature, is not capable of abandoning suddenly all to which he was accustomed. As therefore God sent *Moses our Master* to make out of us *a kingdom of priests and a holy nation* – through the knowledge of Him, may He be exalted, accordingly to what He has explained, saying: *Unto thee it was shown that thou mightest know, and so on*; *Know this day, and lay it to thy heart, and so on* – so that we should devote ourselves to His worship according to what He said: *And to serve Him with all your heart*, and: *And ye shall serve the Lord your God*, and: *And Him shall ye serve*; and as at that time the way of life generally accepted and customary in the whole world and the universal service upon which we were brought up consisted in offering various species of living beings in the temples in which images were set up, in worshipping the latter, and in burning incense before them – the pious ones and the ascetics being at that time, as we have explained, the people who were devoted to the service of the temples consecrated to the stars –: His wisdom, may He be exalted, and His gracious ruse, which is manifest in regard to all His creatures, did not require that He give us a Law prescribing the rejection, abandonment, and abolition of all these kinds of worship. For one could not then conceive the acceptance of [such a Law], considering the nature of man, which always likes that to which it is accustomed. At that time this would have been similar to the appearance of a prophet in these times who, calling upon the people to worship God, would say: 'God has given you a Law forbidding you to pray to Him, to fast, to call upon Him for help in misfortune. Your worship should consist solely in meditation without any works at all.' Therefore He, may He be exalted, suffered the above-mentioned kinds of worship to remain, but transferred them from created or imaginary and unreal things to His own name, may He be exalted, commanding us to practice them with regard to Him, may He be exalted.

I know that on thinking about this at first your soul will necessarily have a feeling of repugnance toward this notion and will feel aggrieved because of it; and you will ask me in your heart and say to me: How is it possible that none of the commandments, prohibitions, and great actions – which are very precisely set forth and prescribed for fixed seasons – should be intended for its own sake, but for the sake of something else, as if this were a ruse invented for our benefit by God in order to achieve His first intention? What was there to prevent Him, may He be exalted, from giving us a Law in accordance with His first intention and from procuring us the capacity to accept this? In this way there would have been no need for the things that you consider to be due to a second intention. Hear then the reply to your question that will put an end to this sickness in your heart and reveal to you the true reality of that to which I have drawn your attention. It is to the effect that the text of the *Torah* tells a quite similar story, namely, in its dictum: *God led them not by the way of the land of the Philistines, although it was near, and so on. But God led the people about, by the way of the wilderness of the Red Sea.* Just as God perplexed them in anticipation of what their bodies were naturally incapable of bearing – turning them away from the high road toward which they had been going, toward another road so that the first intention should be achieved – so did He in anticipation of what the soul is naturally incapable of receiving, prescribe the laws that we have mentioned so that the first intention should be achieved, namely, the apprehension of Him, may He be exalted, and the rejection of *idolatry*.

(*Guide* III, 32, pp. 526–7)

Maimonides, as a legal codifier and jurist, only imitated the divine proceeding, by guiding men on the road of knowledge through making 'opinions, moral qualities and political civil actions' clearer, simpler and more rational. For 'God does not change at all the nature of human individuals by means of miracles . . . It is because of this that there are commandments and prohibitions, rewards and punishments' (*Guide* III, 32, p. 529). Further, for Maimonides, as jurist, law *qua* law must be respected by all men, the ignorant as well as the philosophers. Whatever the motivation of the divine commandments, these commandments must be carried out to the letter. As for abrogating the Law of Moses in favour of another political law that would be less the outcome of historical circumstances, such a supposition cannot even be entertained, for Maimonides, elevating Moses above all prophets and legislators (in the seventh 'Principle', and at length in the *Guide*) declares the Law of Moses to be the only Divine Law.

It is therefore not surprising that Maimonides devoted long discussions to the laws of sacrifice and of Levitic purity. These laws are necessary, for they form part of the best of all possible laws, and the fact that they cannot be put into practice because of the destruction of the Temple does not in any way modify this essential fact.[1]

Through all Maimonides' halakhic works runs the motif of the intellectual perfectibility of man, and all the commandments in reality have one ultimate goal: to teach man to know God. In the last chapter of the *Guide*, he enumerates the 'perfections' as men have defined them:

(2) Wealth, the possession of material goods; this is a purely imaginary perfection;

(2) Beauty, strength and physical health; but on this point man is inferior to the animals;

(3) The perfection of moral qualities; most of the commandments of the *Torah* have no other aim than to make us attain this perfection, which in fact is only a preparation for the true perfection;

---

[1] It should be noted, besides, that Maimonides' juridical decisions are far from indulgent, and that he is one of the rare jurists to advocate the sentence of death for certain crimes, such as the lack of respect for a rabbi.

(4) . . . The fourth species is the true human perfection; it consists in the acquisition of the rational virtues – I refer to the conception of intelligibles, which teach true opinions concerning the divine things. This is in true reality the ultimate end; this is what gives the individual true perfection, a perfection belonging to him alone; and it gives him permanent perdurance; through it man is man.

(Guide III, 54, p. 635)

With this theme of intellectual perfectibility is associated that of survival in the world to come; the *Mishnah* says 'All Israel has a right to the world to come', and Maimonides has explained that only those who have accepted the thirteen principles, which he discusses in detail further on, may be considered as belonging to Israel. As for the world to come, this is the immortality of the soul.

The traditional texts contain three expressions used in connection with man's fate after death: the world to come, the Days of the Messiah, and the Resurrection of the Dead. These terms are sometimes interchangeable, and what they designate is not constant. Further, descriptions of corporeal delights can be found in the texts of the *Midrash*, side by side with conceptions of a purely abstract happiness beyond the tomb. Maimonides did not at any stage modify his position on this subject, which he repeats in greater detail but without any real additions in his last work – the *Letter on the Resurrection of the Dead*. This short work was composed in reply to the objections raised by Samuel ben Ali, the Gaon of Baghdad, who attacked Maimonides on the subject of his theories concerning the future world accusing him of not having mentioned the resurrection of the body or the individual survival of the human soul.

With frequently ferocious irony Maimonides again repeats what he has written elsewhere:

(1) The world to come is the immortality of the soul, which survives when it has attained perfection, that is, when it has become intellect, since to have a permanent existence after death it has to be detached from the body during life. Maimonides does not make it altogether clear if he is thinking of an individual survival of souls in the world of the intellects, as does Avicenna, or if, like Averroes, he believes that the human soul merges with the Active Intellect. Samuel ben Ali accuses him of not admitting the individual immortality of the soul, and cites Avicenna and Abu-l-Barakāt, as philosophers who did accept it. And, in effect, it seems that, if no Maimonidean text states his position without ambivalence, this was because he inclined towards the solution of non-individual survival, a conclusion that he could not postulate openly in writing.

(2) The Days of the Messiah: this to Maimonides meant the political independence of Israel and the return to the Land of Israel. The Messiah will be recognized without difficulty, for his coming will coincide with a new peace of history, a period totally differing from that of the Diaspora.

(3) Corporeal resurrection. This is not necessary from the scientific point of view, but neither is it theoretically impossible; if one believes in divine omnipotence, it is within the domain of the possible. It is evident that the Rambam did not attach capital importance to this resurrection, which, he asserts, would be followed by a second death of the body. But, respectful of tradition, he admitted the possibility of corporeal resurrection, recognizing the psychological importance of this for the people. This is undoubtedly the reason for its inclusion in the Thirteen Principles. For him, what is really important is the world to come, and not to be admitted to it is perdition.

In order to safeguard Israel from the perdition described in the religious tradition, Maimonides in his *Commentary on the Mishnah* codified the truths that the people should accept, and classified them in Thirteen Principles, which, versified in the fourteenth century, were introduced into the daily ritual of all communities except those of the Ashkenazic rite. These Principles include a certain number of articles of faith that were then far from having achieved unanimous adherence in the Jewish community; but Maimonides turned them into dogma, and the *sine qua non* of appertenance to the people of Israel.

When a man has accepted these principles and truly believes in them, he forms part of the community of Israel; and it is incumbent upon us to love him, to care for him and behave towards him as God has ordered us to do: to love and comfort him; if he sins because of his corporeal desires or his bad instincts, he will receive the punishment proportioned to his crime, and he may [afterwards] have the part [that belongs to him in the world to come], he is a sinner within the community of Israel. But if someone casts doubt on one of these principles, he has foresworn his faith, he is a renegade, a heretic, an unbeliever, he has rebelled against God and it is a duty to hate him and to cause him to perish.

(Introduction to the *Commentary on the Mishnah, Perek Ḥelek*, pp. 148–9)

These are the Principles:

(1) The existence of the Creator;
(2) His unity;
(3) The negation of His corporeality;
(4) Eternity, which Maimonides explains thus:

The Fourth Principle is God's precedence [or 'priority'], to wit, that this One who has just been described is He Who precedes [everything] absolutely. No other being has precedence with respect to Him. There are many verses attesting to this in Scriptures. The verse attesting to it [best] is: 'the God of eternity is a dwelling place' [Deuteronomy 33: 27].

(Trans. D. R. Blumenthal, *The Commentary of R. Ḥōṭer*, p. 91)

(5) God alone (to the exclusion of every inferior being – angel, star, etc.) should be served and praised; one must proclaim His glory only, and only His commandments should be observed.

(6) 'Prophecy', which is defined as follows:

The Sixth Principle is [the belief in] prophecy; to wit, it should be known that, within the species of humanity, there are individuals who have a greatly superior disposition and a great measure of perfection. And, if their souls are prepared so that they receive the form of the intellect, then that human intellect will unite with the Agent Intelligence which will cause a great emanation to flow to it. (*Ibid.* p. 114)

(7) Moses is superior to all the prophets who have preceded or will follow him.

(8) The *Torah* in its entirety, written or oral, was given to Moses by God, by the instrumentality of what is allegorically called his Word.

(9) The *Torah*, written and oral, coming from God, is absolutely unalterable; one cannot add to it or subtract from it.

(10) God knows the actions of men and has not abandoned the world.

(11) God rewards whose who observe the commandments of the *Torah* and punishes those who transgress them. The highest reward is the world to come, and the punishment most greatly to be feared is exclusion from it.

(12) The belief in the coming of the Messiah, which announces the national restoration of Israel.

(13) The Resurrection of the Dead. While all the other Principles are explained at some length, this one is simply noted, without any further detail.

These Thirteen Principles can be divided into three groups:

(1) The first five concern God, unique and incorporeal;

(2) The next four deal with prophecy and the Law;

(3) The last four deal with reward and punishment, the Days of the Messiah and the Resurrection of the Dead.

These Principles are presented in the *Book of Precepts* as well as in the *Mishneh Torah*. They are again discussed in the *Guide*. Two notable traits emerge in the first group:

(1) Inacceptance of the negation of the divine incorporeality, that is to say, understanding the verses of the Bible in their literal sense, that in which they are interpreted in many passages of the Talmud and the *Midrash*, implies exclusion from the community of Israel. This was an extreme position, for divine incorporeality was not admitted by all Jewish thinkers, whether philosophers or rabbis. In the thirteenth century Moses ben Ḥasdai Taku designated Saadiah, Baḥya Ibn Paquda, Maimonides and the Ashkenazi pietists as heretics because, in refusing to admit the divine corporeality, they refused an important part of the written and oral Law.

(2) The creation of the world *ex nihilo* is not mentioned, only the absolute eternity of God.

The second group of Principles describes the attributes of God,

As for the discussion concerning attributes and the way they should be negated with regard to Him; and as for the meaning of the attributes that may be ascribed to Him, as well as the discussion concerning His creation of that which He created, the character of His governance of the world, the 'how' of His providence with respect to what is other than He, the notion of His will, His apprehension, and His knowledge of all that He knows; and likewise as for the notion of prophecy and the 'how' of its various degrees, and the notion of His names, though they are many, being indicative of one and the same thing – it should be considered that all these are obscure matters. In fact, they are truly *the mysteries of the Torah* and the *secrets* constantly mentioned in the books of the prophets and in the dicta of the *Sages*.

(*Guide* I, 35, p. 80)

These are the mysteries that cannot be clearly explained to every man.

The third group has already been discussed above (p. 170).

Let us then return to the other groups. The first, the 'true' conception of God, must be explained as clearly as possible, while the second, the mysteries of the *Torah*, is only to be treated allusively and only for the benefit of the learned; this is the subject of the first four chapters of the *Mishneh Torah*: *The Book of Knowledge*.

The central idea of chapter I associates the divine unity and omnipotence with the divine incorporeality. That this conception of God implies the acceptance of the conception of the world defined by Aristotelian philosophy becomes clear in paragraph 5, where we read the proof of the existence of the First Mover through the eternal movement of the sphere.

This being is the God of the Universe, the Lord of all the Earth. And He it is, who controls the Sphere (of the Universe) with a power that is without end or limit; with a power that is never intermitted. For the Sphere is always revolving; and it is impossible for it to revolve without someone making it revolve. God, blessed be He, it is, who, without hand or body, causes it to revolve.

(*Book of Knowledge*, pp. 34a–34b)

The exposition continues by showing that this is indeed the veritable conception of God, the Law and the prophets, and that all the biblical expressions implying corporeality must be interpreted allegorically:

That the Holy One, blessed be He, is not a physical body, is explicitly set forth in the Pentateuch and in the Prophets, as it is said '(Know therefore) that the Lord, He is God in Heaven above, and upon the Earth beneath' (Deut. 4: 39); and a physical body is not in two places at one time. Furthermore, it is said, 'For Ye saw no manner of similitude' (Deut. 4: 15); and again it is said, 'To whom then will Ye liken me, or shall I be equal?' (Is. 40: 25). If He were a body, He would be like other bodies.

Since this is so, what is the meaning of the following expressions found in the Torah: 'Beneath his feet' (Ex. 24: 10); 'Written with the finger of God' (Ex. 31: 18); 'The hand of God' (Ex. 9: 3); 'The eyes of God' (Gen. 38: 7); 'The ears of God' (Num. 11: 1); and similar phrases? All these expressions are adapted to the mental capacity of the majority of mankind who have a clear perception of physical bodies only. The Torah speaks in the language of men. All these phrases are metaphorical.

(*Book of Knowledge*, p. 34b)

Then Maimonides outlines the theory of prophecy, an intelligible overflow towards the rational faculty, which the imagination of each prophet invests with images – a theory of which I have already spoken in connection with Abraham Ibn Daud. Finally, he affirms that Moses is – and will always be – the man who received a revelation from God superior to that vouchsafed to other prophets.

Chapter 2 describes the world of the ten immaterial Intellects, which the Bible calls angels.

Chapter 3 describes the spheres, beginning from our world and rising to the ninth sphere. The spheres are endowed with a soul; they know God, and without being as close to the knowledge of God as are the Intellects, they are superior to men, for their matter, delicate and subtle, is not subject to generation and corruption. The four elements that constitute our world are, contrary to the spheres, dead bodies, the movement of which is natural and subject to forces that they do not perceive or know.

Chapter 4 describes the four elements and their properties. These elements, which are matter, are not without form; although this form is not visible to the naked eye. Through the movement of the spheres the elements mix, and are ready to receive forms imparted by the Active Intellect: mineral, animal and finally human, that is, intellecting, form, the only one to subsist after the decay of the human mixture at the death of the body.

At the end of chapter 4 Maimonides himself explains what this introduction to the Law represents:

The topics connected with these five precepts, treated in the above four chapters, are what our wise men called *Pardes* (Paradise), as in the passage 'Four went into *Pardes*' [cf. Bab. Talmud *Hagiga* 14b, relating the entry into the Divine Garden of the Four Sages, Rabbi Aqiba, Ben Azai, Ben Zoma and Aḥer]. And although those four were great men of Israel and great sages, they did not all possess the capacity to know and grasp these subjects clearly. Therefore, I say that it is not proper to dally in *Pardes* till one has first filled oneself with bread and meat; by which I mean knowledge of what is permitted and what forbidden, and similar distinctions in other classes of precepts. Although these last subjects were called by the sages 'a small thing' (when they say 'A great thing, *Maaseh Mercabah*; a small thing, the discussion of Abaye and Rava'), still they should have the precedence. For the knowledge of these things gives primarily composure to the mind. They are the precious boon bestowed by God, to promote social well-being on earth, and enable men to obtain bliss in the life hereafter. Moreover, the knowledge of them is within the reach of all, young and old, men and women; those gifted with great intellectual capacity as well as those whose intelligence is limited.

(*Book of Knowledge*, pp. 39b–40a)

By the Story of the Chariot (*Maaseh Mercabah*) Maimonides alludes to the prophetic visions of Isaiah (chapter 6), Ezekiel (chapter 1), and Zechariah (chapter 3), describing the divine chariot, the divine throne and the angelic world. Elsewhere he also alludes to the Story of Creation (*Maaseh Bereshit*), by which he means the beginning of the Book of Genesis. From the talmudic period onwards these biblical passages were considered to conceal great mysteries. Maimonides interprets these terms as designating the two principal parts of science: the Story of the Chariot is metaphysics, the Story of Creation is physics, the Discussion of Abaye and of Rava is the Talmud, that is, the whole of the Law, written and oral.

Maimonides has here presented the essential verities of metaphysics. These verities should serve as an introduction to the study of the Law, written and oral, which is open to all, whatever their level of intelligence.

This exposition of the principles of metaphysics and physics begins with the most elevated – God – and concludes with the lowest on the scale of beings – the elements. But when we are not receiving them from on high, but are studying these principles, we must start from the lowest – physics – in order to rise towards the most difficult – metaphysics.

The really important subject is the Story of the Chariot, the knowledge of God, metaphysics. This does not alter the fact that the study of the commandments of the Law is indispensable before one engages in any scientific study, first because it is an introduction to science and then because it leads to happiness in this world and to eternal life. It is therefore indispensable for everybody, whatever his intellectual level. We are in the domain of political law, as Maimonides makes clear in the *Guide* (III, chapter 31, p. 524): 'Thus, all [the Commandments] are bound up with three things: opinions, moral qualities and political civil actions.'

When man has had his fill of bread and meat, and if he has a suitable disposition, he will be able to begin to study mathematics and physics and to read the *Guide of the Perplexed*.

The Guide of the Perplexed

The *Guide of the Perplexed* has given rise to a great number of interpretations; this is not at all surprising, for it is a deliberately ambiguous work. Its importance in Jewish thought will emerge more fully in the next chapter.

We have said that the composition of the *Mishneh Torah* displays clarity and system; both are traits characteristic of Maimonides. The scheme of the *Guide*, on the other hand, is at first disordered. Topics that are well ordered in Greek and Arab philosophical works are taken up several times in different contexts, with relatively little modification. The plan of the book itself is difficult to grasp. The first half of Book I, broadly speaking, deals with the expressions of the Bible and the Talmud that one cannot accept in their literal sense; the second half of this book describes the divine attributes, attacking the Mutakallimūn and, among them, Saadiah. Book II deals with philosophical doctrines, then with prophecy. Book III begins with an allegorical explanation of the Story of the Chariot, then discusses various questions: providence, the end of the world; it gives a psychological explanation of the Book of Job, then a historical account of religions and rites, and touches on religious precepts. This confusion is deliberately intended by Maimonides and he explicitly says so in his introduction:

If you wish to grasp the totality of what this Treatise contains, so that nothing of it will escape you, then you must connect its chapters one with another; and when reading a given chapter, your intention must be not only to understand the totality of the subject of that chapter, but also to grasp each word that occurs in it in the course of the speech, even if that word does not belong to the intention of the chapter. For the diction of this Treatise has not been chosen at haphazard, but with great exactness and exceeding precision, and with care to avoid failing to explain any obscure point. And nothing has been mentioned out of its place, save with a view to explaining some matter in its proper place.   (*Guide*, introd., p. 15)

The book begins with a dedicatory address to his pupil Joseph ben Judah. He relates how the latter, after having studied mathematics, astronomy and logic, seemed to him worthy to receive the principles of metaphysical knowledge, but Joseph ben Judah was obliged to leave him, so he composed this book for him and for those like him, even if they are far from numerous. This decision awakened an old project, that of writing a book on prophecy and a book on the talmudic homilies, the literal sense of which is very far removed from truth and even from reason; but he renounced this project for reasons he gives a little further on in this introduction: if the explanations given were in the form of allegory, in such a way as not to reveal the secrets, this would only replace one allegory with another, so that to 'an ignoramus among the multitude of Rabbanites' reading this book, this second allegory would be no more plausible than the first, for he would understand neither one nor the other; if, on the contrary, a 'perfect man', that is, a philosopher, were to read it, he might take the allegory in its literal sense and judge unfavourably of the author; or else, he might look for the esoteric sense and perhaps find it, or again he might be induced into error.

If the secrets were unveiled, that is, if the explanations were openly given, this would not be desirable for the vulgar reader.

It is therefore necessary to explain without really explaining, to introduce to this knowledge only those who are worthy of it, without misleading others. In deciding to write the *Guide*, Maimonides wished to achieve these two contrary aims, that is, to reveal the secrets and not reveal them. Let us return to the beginning of the introduction:

The first purpose of this Treatise is to explain the meanings of certain terms occurring in books of prophecy. Some of these terms are equivocal; hence the ignorant attribute to them only one or some of the meanings in which the term in question is used. Others are derivative terms; hence they attribute to them only the original meaning from which the other meaning is derived. Others are amphibolous terms, so that at times they are believed to be univocal and at other times equivocal. It is not the purpose of this Treatise to make its totality understandable to the vulgar or to beginners in speculation, nor to teach those who have not engaged in any study other than the science of the Law – I mean the legalistic study of the Law. For the purpose of this Treatise and of all those like it is the science of Law in its true sense. Or rather its purpose is to give indications to a religious man for whom the validity of our Law has become established in his soul and has become actual in his belief – such a man being perfect in his religion and character, and having studied the sciences of the philosophers and come to know what they signify. The human intellect having drawn him on and led him to dwell within its province, he must have felt distressed by the externals of the Law and by the meanings of the above-mentioned equivocal, derivative, or amphibolous terms, as he continued to understand them by himself or was made to understand them by others. Hence he would remain in a state of perplexity and confusion as to whether he should follow his intellect, renounce what he knew concerning the terms in question, and consequently consider that he has renounced the foundations of the Law. Or he should hold fast to his understanding of these terms and not let himself be drawn on together with his intellect, rather turning his back on it and moving away from it, while at the same time perceiving that he had brought loss to himself and harm to his religion. He would be left with those imaginary beliefs to which he owes his fear and difficulty and would not cease to suffer from heartache and great perplexity.

(*Guide*, introd., pp. 5–6)

The *Guide* will provide the basis of the method permitting us to unveil divine allegory:

Know that the key to the understanding of all that the prophets, peace be on them, have said, and to the knowledge of its truth, is an understanding of the parables, of their import, and of the meaning of the words occurring in them. You know what God, may He be exalted, has said: *And by the ministry of the prophets have I used similitudes* [Hosea 12: 10].

(*Guide*, introd., pp. 10–11)

The allegory that follows this remark is the example that Maimonides proposes to decipher and to imitate in the *Guide*:

The Sage has said: *A word fitly spoken is like apples of gold in settings (maskiyyoth) of silver* [Proverbs 25: 11]. Hear now an elucidation of the thought that he has set forth. The term *maskiyyoth* denotes filigree traceries; I mean to say traceries in which there are apertures with very small eyelets, like the handiwork of silversmiths. They are so called because a glance penetrates through them; for in the [Aramaic] *translation* of the Bible the Hebrew term *va-yashqeph* – meaning, he glanced – is translated *va-istekhe*. The Sage accordingly said that a saying uttered with a view to two meanings is like an apple of gold overlaid with silver filigree-work having very small holes. Now see how marvellously this dictum describes a well-constructed parable. For he says that in a saying that has two meanings – he means an external and an internal one – the external meaning ought to be as beautiful as silver, while its internal meaning ought to be more beautiful than the external one, the former being in comparison to the latter as gold is to silver. Its external meaning also ought to contain in it something that indicates to someone considering it what is to be found in its internal meaning, as happens in the case of an apple of gold overlaid with silver filigree-work having very small holes. When looked at from a distance or with imperfect attention, it is deemed to be an apple of silver; but when a keen-sighted observer looks at it with full attention, its interior becomes clear to him and he knows that it is of gold. The parables of the prophets, peace be on them, are similar. Their external meaning contains wisdom that is useful in many respects, among which is the welfare of human societies, as is shown by the external meaning of *Proverbs* and of similar sayings. Their internal meaning, on the other hand, contains wisdom that is useful for beliefs concerned with the truth as it is.

(*Guide*, introd., pp. 11–12)

The problem that the *Guide* sets out to resolve is that of the double character of the Law: sometimes, as in the example just cited, the exterior sense leads to the interior, and helps us to discover it. Sometimes the exterior sense prevents us from attaining 'the knowledge of the Law in its reality' and is contrary to reason. However, only those who have already studied the sciences can feel and be perplexed by the conflict between reason and the apparent sense of the Bible. The book is then not intended for the vulgar or for Talmudists, as were other books by Maimonides, but only for those who are already attracted by human reason and have had a taste of philosophy. In reality, there is no real opposition: the sciences are treated in a different way in revelation and in philosophical books; and here lies the reason for the confusion.

In the *Mishneh Torah* we have seen the identification that was to become traditional between physics, the Story of the Creation, and metaphysics, the Story of the Chariot. These subjects, physics and metaphysics, and especially metaphysics, are simultaneously glimpsed and withdrawn in the Law in order to conform to the divine design. It is not God's wish that the truths should be revealed to the vulgar, for the impact of truth would endanger the continuance of human society, which subsists thanks to the traditional Laws. God himself has spoken by allegory through the lips of the prophets. If physics may not be expounded, this is because it touches on metaphysics. Maimonides is most probably here alluding to the proof of the existence of God by the Prime Mover, a proof included by Aristotle in his physics; as for metaphysics, this is a subject that man cannot comprehend in its entirety, as I shall explain later.

You should not think that these great *secrets* are fully and completely known to anyone among us. They are not. But sometimes truth flashes out to us so that we think that it is day, and then matter and habit in their various forms conceal it so that we find ourselves again in an obscure night, almost as we were at first. We are like someone in a very dark night over whom lightning flashes time and time again. Among us there is one for whom the lightning flashes time and time again, so that he is always, as it were, in unceasing light. Thus night appears to him as day. That is the degree of the great one among the prophets, to whom it was said: *But as for thee, stand thou here by Me* [Deuteronomy 5: 31], and of whom it was said: *that the skin of his face sent forth beams, and so on* [Exodus 34: 29]. Among them there is one to whom the lightning flashes only once in the whole of his night; that is the rank of those of whom it is said: *they prophesied, but they did so no more* [Numbers 11: 25]. There are others between whose lightning flashes there are greater or shorter intervals. Thereafter comes he who does not attain a degree in which his darkness is illumined by any lightning flash. It is illumined, however, by a polished body or something of that kind, stones or something else that give light in the darkness of the night. And even this small light that shines over us is not always there, but flashes and is hidden again, as if it were the *flaming sword which turned every way* [Genesis 3: 24]. It is in accord with these states that the degrees of the perfect vary. As for those who never even once see a light but grope about in their night, of them it is said: *They know not, neither do they understand; They go about* in darkness [Psalm 82: 5]. The truth, in spite of the strength of its manifestation, is entirely hidden from them, as is said of them: *And now men see not the light which is bright in the skies* [Job 37: 21]. They are the vulgar among the people. There is then no occasion to mention them here in this Treatise.   (*Guide*, introd., pp. 7–8)

In describing the two meanings of the Bible – the exoteric and the esoteric – the duality that alone permits the reconciliation of science and revelation, Maimonides does not suppress the fact that esoteric meaning is more eminent than the other:

About this it has been said: *Our Rabbis say: A man who loses a sela or a pearl in his house can find the pearl by lighting a taper worth an issar. In the same way this parable in itself is worth nothing, but by means of it you can understand the words of the Torah.* This too is literally what they say. Now consider the explicit affirmation of [the Sages], *may their memory be blessed*, that the internal meaning of the *words of the Torah* is a *pearl* whereas the external meaning of all parables *is* worth *nothing*, and their comparison of the concealment of a subject by its parable's external meaning to a man who let drop a pearl in his house, which was dark and full of furniture. Now this pearl is there, but he does not see it and does not know where it is. It is as though it were no longer in his possession, as it is impossible for him to derive any benefit from it until, as has been mentioned, he lights a lamp – an act to which an understanding of the meaning of the parable corresponds.

(*Guide*, introd., p. 11)

Further on, in the introduction, Maimonides expounds the seven causes of textual obscurity.

The *Guide* being constructed, like the *Torah*, the prophetic books, and the *Aggadot* of the Talmud, in such a way as to reveal the internal sense and at the same time to dissimulate it, its obscurity belongs to the seventh type of the seven causes.

The difficulty of the book's plan, like the ambiguity of its writing, arises from the fifth of the causes of textual obscurity: the necessity of sometimes touching on a difficult question in order to explain a subject in itself easy to conceive, and also from:

The seventh cause. In speaking about very obscure matters it is necessary to conceal some parts and to disclose others. Sometimes in the case of certain dicta this necessity requires that the discussion proceed on the basis of a certain premise, whereas in another place necessity requires that the discussion proceed on the basis of another premise contradicting the first one. In such cases the vulgar must in no way be aware of the contradiction; the author accordingly uses some device to conceal it by all means.

(*Guide*, introd., p. 18)

So that Maimonides himself recommends that one should not study the book chapter by chapter, but rather problem by problem; not embark on it with preconceived ideas, but study everything that should first be studied; and not explain this book to others.

The first part of the introduction concludes thus (pp. 16–17):

God, may He be exalted, knows that I have never ceased to be exceedingly apprehensive about setting down those things that I wish to set down in this Treatise.

179

For they are concealed things; none of them has been set down in any book – written in the religious community in these times of *Exile* – the books composed in these times being in our hands. How then can I now innovate and set them down? However, I have relied on two premises, the one being [the Sages'] saying in a similar case, *It is time to do something for the Lord, and so on*; the second being their saying, *Let all thy acts be for the sake of Heaven*. Upon these two premises have I relied when setting down what I have composed in some of the chapters of this Treatise.

To sum up: I am the man who when the concern pressed him and his way was straitened and he could find no other device by which to teach a demonstrated truth other than by giving satisfaction to a single virtuous man while displeasing ten thousand ignoramuses – I am he who prefers to address that single man by himself, and I do not heed the blame of those many creatures. For I claim to liberate that virtuous one from that into which he has sunk, and I shall guide him in his perplexity until he becomes perfect and he finds rest.

I shall follow the first part of Maimonides' counsels and present certain problems without following the chapter-order of the *Guide*. Obviously I cannot examine in detail all the ideas discussed, which are often of profound interest; however, I shall at least attempt to define certain central themes in Maimonides' thought.

I shall treat in succession:

(1) God and his attributes;
(2) Divine providence and the world to come;
(3) The creation of the world;
(4) Prophecy;
(5) Human knowledge.

(1) GOD AND HIS ATTRIBUTES

The first seventy chapters of Book I are devoted to the interpretation of various biblical words, and especially those used regarding God. According to Maimonides, who is here in agreement with a neoplatonic current and certain Mu'tazilites, one can only assign negative attributes to God. There are five classes of attributes (cf. *Guide* I, 52):

An attribute predicated of any thing, of which thing it is accordingly said that it is such and such, must necessarily belong to one of the following five groups:

The first group is characterized by the thing having its definition predicated of it – as when it is predicated of man that he is a rational living being.

This means finding and defining the general species to which human belongs. This type of attribute cannot, obviously, be assigned to God, for He belongs to no species and He has no cause.

The second class is that where the thing has for attribute a part of its definition, as, for example, when one designates man by his quality of being animal, or by his reason. This is equally impossible in the case of God. If anything in God was inseparable from His essence without being His essence, His essence would be compound; however, God is One.

The attributes of quality (the third class), which are not part of the essence, like saying of a man that he is tall or short, also cannot be assigned to God, for He would then be what is left after the subtraction of changing accidents; such attributes are inapplicable to God:

Now when you consider all these attributes and what is akin to them, you will find that it is impossible to ascribe them to God. For He does not possess quantity so that there might pertain to Him a quality pertaining to quantity as such. Nor does He receive impressions and affections so that there might pertain to Him a quality belonging to the affections. Nor does He have dispositions so that there might be faculties and similar things pertaining to Him. Nor is He, may He be exalted, endowed with a soul, so that He might have a habitus pertaining to Him – such as clemency, modesty, and similar things – or have pertain to Him that which pertains to animate beings as such – for instance, health and illness. It is accordingly clear to you that no attribute that may be brought under the supreme genus of quality can subsist in Him, may He be exalted . . .

The fourth group of attributes is as follows. It is predicated of a thing that it has a relation to something other than itself. For instance, it is related to a time or to a place or to another individual, as for instance when you predicate of Zayd that he is the father of a certain individual or the partner of a certain individual or an inhabitant of a certain place or one who was at a certain time. Now this kind of attribute does not necessarily entail either multiplicity or change in the essence of the thing of which it is predicated. For the Zayd who is referred to may be the partner of Umar, the father of Bakr, the master of Khālid, a friend of Zayd, an inhabitant of such and such dwelling place, and one who was born in such and such a year. Those notions of relation are not the essence of the thing or something subsisting in its essence, as do the qualities. At first thought it seems that it is permissible to predicate of God, may He be exalted, attributes of this kind. However, when one knows true reality and achieves greater exactness in speculation, the fact that this is impossible becomes clear.

(*Guide* I, 52, pp. 116–17)

In fact, every relation implies something in common between the two terms; now, there cannot be any relation between an entirely separate being and another that depends on all other things. Even existence is not common to them, for existence does not designate the same thing when one speaks of God and when one speaks of a created being, for the existence of God is necessary and the existence of a created being is possible.

The attributes of action (the fifth class) are the only ones that can be predicated of God, for they imply no change in the divine essence. Here again, the need to speak 'the language of men', that is, to address the ignorant multitude and not the élite, has led to confusion:

The reasons that led those who believe in the existence of attributes belonging to the Creator to this belief are akin to those that led those who believe in the doctrine of His corporeality to that belief. For he who believes in this doctrine was not led to it by intellectual speculation; he merely followed the external sense of the texts of the Scriptures. This is also the case with regard to the attributes. For inasmuch as the books of the prophets and the revealed books existed, which predicated attributive qualifications of Him, may He be exalted, these were taken in their literal sense; and He was believed to possess attributes. The people in question have, as it were, divested God of corporeality but not of the modes of corporeality, namely, the accidents – I mean the aptitudes of the soul, all of which are qualities. For with regard to every attribute that the believer in attributes considers to be essential in respect to God, may He be exalted, you will find that the notion of it is that of a quality, even if these people do not state it clearly; for they in fact liken the attribute in question to what they meet with in the various states of all bodies endowed with an animal soul. Of all this it is said: *The Torah speaketh in the language of the sons of man.*   (*Guide* I, 53, pp. 120-1)

For Moses, as for men in general, to know God signifies to know nothing of His essence, but to know His acts.

Know that the master of those who know, *Moses our Master*, peace be on him, made two requests and received an answer to both of them. One request consisted in his asking Him, may He be exalted, to let him know His essence and true reality. The second request, which he put first, was that He should let him know His attributes. The answer to the two requests that He, may He be exalted, gave him consisted in His promising him to let him know all His attributes, making it known to him that they are His actions, and teaching him that His essence cannot be grasped as it really is. Yet He drew his attention to a subject of speculation through which he can apprehend to the furthest extent that is possible for man. For what has been apprehended by [Moses], peace be on him, has not been apprehended by anyone before him nor will it be apprehended by anyone after him.

His request regarding the knowledge of [God's] attributes is conveyed in his saying: *Show me now Thy ways, that I may know Thee, and so on* [Exodus 33: 13].
                                                        (*Guide* I, 54, p. 123)

And Maimonides cites with approval a talmudic anecdote (Bab. *Berakhot* 33b), where it is related that a believer lavished laudatory adjectives in his prayers. Rabbi Ḥanina pointed out to him that this language was as unsuitable as praising a king for possessing pieces of silver while he had a treasure-house of gold. In fact, says Maimonides, if we depended on our reason alone, we would not require any of these adjectives; we employ them because men need images in order to understand, and even then only because the *Torah* uses them. Because they are written in the *Torah*, we have the right to read them as a biblical text; but as for using them in our prayers, we can only do this on the authority of the men of the Great Synod, for they have assumed responsibility for this. Verbal prayer is in fact a concession to man's weakness. (There is no need to emphasize the audacity of Maimodes' judgement on the liturgical cult.)

'To know the actions of God'. This is the second stage of the knowledge of God; first in knowing His creation we learn what we must deny of God, and each of the branches of science teaches us something on this subject: arithmetic and geometry teach us that the unity of God is not like the unity to which one adds and which can be multiplied. Physics and astronomy teach us how God moves the world, that is, by the intermediary of the separate intellects; logic shows us how to reason correctly. But the knowledge of the sciences that leads to metaphysics also has a value in itself.

It is thus evident that the road leading towards God, that is to say, human perfection, the purpose for which man was created, is scientific knowledge: physics leads to metaphysics. But the preparatory studies – logic, mathematics – are long and wearisome, and few men are capable of going through the entire Aristotelian corpus; besides, tradition is there to teach us the minimum number of truths that one must believe to be a man, and as we have seen, this conviction was the reason for the composition of Maimonides' works of popularization.

To know the acts of God is to know the sciences. This is confirmed by the analysis of the unity in God of the cognizing subject, the cognized object and the intellectual cognition; or, in medieval terms, God is Intellect, Intellecting and Intelligible.

In chapter 68 of the first part of the *Guide* Maimonides grapples with this problem of divine and human thought. In God, he says, the cognition, the cognizing subject and the object cognized, come together for all eternity; if one does not understand this, one does not understand the unity of God, which is one of the fundamental principles of our religion. And here Maimonides, who had placed God at a great distance from the world and from man, who had made of Him a totally unknowable being, brings Him closer to man by comparing human thought and divine thought; for in explaining what is human thought we will come to understand the divine, and this, he says, is certain and demonstrated.

Before even understanding the process of cognition, man is potentially intelligent; that is, unlike the animals, there is something in him capable of becoming thought or intellect. When a man sees a tree, for example, a pine planted before his house, he sees the image of something that he recognizes as consisting of wood; this is a sensation followed by a judgement; but he has not yet 'thought' wood; for this, he has to extract the abstract form from matter, in order to formulate an intelligible notion. Here we are no longer on the level of the image, but on that of the abstract form divested of individual characteristics – that it is a pine, planted in front of the house. Of the ten Aristotelian categories that we have considered with Abraham Ibn Daud, one must retain only the first, the substance; and in this substance one must discard the matter and bear in mind only the form. At this moment, the thought of the form is the form itself, and the man cognizing this form is the same thing as the form; there is a real and absolute unity between these three things: the cognition, the object cognized and the subject cognizing. It is evidently not easy to conceptualize this thought from which all matter has been abstracted, and it is even more difficult for the modern than for the medieval reader.

Thus we have:

(1) A potential intellect;

(2) The cognition of an abstract form causing man to become actively intelligent;

(3) The cognized being, the abstract form, the object;

(4) The act of cognition;

(5) The knowledge that arises from the act of cognition and is afterwards preserved, which is called acquired intellect.

But, to transform his potential intellect into an active one, man requires the aid of the separate intellect, this purely immaterial entity that presides over earthly destinies. This does not change the fact that during the act of cognition, when the cognizing intellect, the cognizer and cognized are one, in spite of the infinite difference of degree, we are like God:

Now when it is demonstrated that God, may He be held precious and magnified, is an intellect in actu and that there is absolutely no potentiality in Him – as is clear and shall be demonstrated – so that He is not by way of sometimes apprehending and sometimes not apprehending but is always an intellect in actu, it follows necessarily that He and the thing apprehended are one thing, which is His essence. Moreover, the act of apprehension owing to which He is said to be an intellectually cognizing subject is in itself the intellect, which is His essence. Accordingly He is always the intellect as well as the intellectually cognizing subject and the intellectually cognized object. It is accordingly also clear that the numerical unity of the intellect, the intellectually cognizing subject, and the intellectually cognized object, does not hold good with reference to the Creator only, but also with reference to every intellect. Thus in us too, the intellectually cognizing subject, the intellect, and the intellectually cognized object, are one and the same thing wherever we have an intellect in actu. We, however, pass intellectually from potentiality to actuality only from time to time. And the separate intellect too, I mean the active intellect, sometimes gets an impediment that hinders its act – even if this impediment does not proceed from this intellect's essence, but is extraneous to it – being a certain motion happening to it by accident.

We do not intend at present to explain this, our intention being to affirm that that which pertains solely to Him, may He be exalted, and which is specific to Him is His being constantly an intellect in actu and that there is no impediment either proceeding from His essence or from another that might hinder His apprehending. Accordingly it follows necessarily because of this that He is always and constantly an intellectually cognizing subject, an intellect, and an intellectually cognized object. Thus His essence is the intellectually cognizing subject, the intellectually cognized object, and the intellect, as is also necessarily the case with regard to every intellect in actu.   (*Guide* I, 68, pp. 165–6)

According to Aristotle, God intellects Himself eternally; since He intellects only Himself, He is totally autarchic and there lies His superiority, for, intellecting nothing but Himself, He in no way depends on any other thing. *Qua* Prime Immobile Mover, He moves the world without being concerned with it, for He is self-sufficient. When Maimonides compares the intellecting activity of man to divine intellection, he juxtaposes two Aristotelian ideas that Aristotle himself did not juxtapose. Thus, the question arises: what is the object of the divine thought? Is it Himself uniquely, or is it an object other than Himself, as the chapter we have just cited indicates? According to Maimonides, God knows the world and its laws, not *ex post facto*, as we do who contemplate the world, but because He has established these laws, because He is the cause and the end of the world.

Such is the case with regard to that which exists taken as a whole in its relation to our knowledge and His knowledge, may He be exalted. For we know all that we know only through looking at the beings; therefore our knowledge does not grasp the future or the infinite. Our insights are renewed and multiplied according to the things from which we acquire the knowledge of them. He, may He be exalted, is not like that. I mean that His knowledge of things is not derived from them, so that there is multiplicity and renewal of knowledge. On the contrary, the things in question follow upon His knowledge, which preceded and established them as they are: either as the existence of what is separate from matter; or as the existence of a permanent individual endowed with matter; or as the existence of what is endowed with matter and has changing individuals, but follows on an incorruptible and immutable order. Hence, with regard to Him, may He be exalted, there is no multiplicity of insights and renewal and change of knowledge. For through knowing the true reality of His own immutable essence, He also knows the totality of what necessarily derives from all His acts.

(Guide III, 21, p. 485)

(2) DIVINE PROVIDENCE AND THE WORLD TO COME

Divine providence is intimately linked to the idea of divine knowledge. We have said that God knows the world and its laws because He is their cause; but does He know each individual in this world? Does He know that at this moment Shimeon is asleep? That Reuben is walking along the road, that he will take a false step and a passing vehicle will break his leg? For medieval philosophers the problem of God's knowledge of the individual was even more difficult to solve in view of the fact that in Aristotelian science everything that is particular arises from matter; only form, common to all individuals, is general, and it alone is intelligible. God, being pure intellect, evidently cannot understand material details, for there is nothing to 'understand', everything that is material being 'unintelligible'. When Judah Halevi says that the God of the philosophers does not know individual human beings, he is, philosophically speaking, correct, although in fact the philosophers have always attempted to mitigate a theory so sharply in contradiction to religious faith. Maimonides enumerates five opinions on providence:

(1) Everything in this world is the effect of chance (the opinion of the Greek atomists).

(2) Divine providence is assimilated to the laws of nature (this was Aristotle's opinion, opposed by Judah Halevi). In fact, Aristotle himself did not definitely state this view, but his commentator Alexander of Aphrodisias attributes it to him. Everything that is permanent or follows laws fixed from all eternity is said to arise from divine providence; this means the spheres and their movements and, depending on them, the terrestrial species, whose

preservation is ensured by the perpetual movement of the spheres. Certainly, in order that the species may be perpetuated, there must always be individuals constituting it; but which particular individual is of little importance.

To sum up, the basis of his opinion is as follows: Everything that, according to what he saw, subsisted continuously without any corruption or change of proceeding at all – as, for instance, the states of the spheres – or that observed a certain orderly course, only deviating from it in anomalous cases – as, for instance, the natural things – was said by him to subsist through governance; I mean to say that divine providence accompanied it. On the other hand, all that, according to what he saw, does not subsist continuously or adhere to a certain order – as, for instance, the circumstances of the individuals of every species of plants, animals, and man – are said by him to exist by chance and not through the governance of one who governs; he means thereby that they are not accompanied by divine providence, and he also holds that it is impossible that providence should accompany these circumstances. This is consequent upon his opinion concerning the eternity of the world and the impossibility of that which exists being in any respect different from what it is. (*Guide* III, 17, p. 466)

(3) The third opinion, that of the Asharites, professes that everything in the universe, the whole as well as the details, depends on will, therefore on the divine providence. All things, even the fall of a leaf, happen according to the decree of God. There are no laws of nature: God decides and acts in the world without being subject to what we call good and evil.

(4) The opinion of the Mu'tazilites (and of certain Geonim including Saadiah) admits laws which are fixed by the wisdom of God and to which He conforms; divine justice wishes each being to receive compensation in the world to come for the gratuitous sufferings inflicted on him in this world; not only men, but also animals, however lowly (Maimonides speaks of the louse and the flea) will have their reward in the world to come, for God knows all the acts of all the beings who are in the world.

The fifth opinion is our opinion, I mean the opinion of our Law. I shall let you know about it what has been literally stated in the books of our prophets and is believed by the multitude of our scholars; I shall also inform you of what is believed by some of our latter-day scholars; and I shall also let you know what I myself believe about this. I say then: It is a fundamental principle of the Law of *Moses our Master*, peace be on him, and of all those who follow it that man has an absolute ability to act; I mean to say that in virtue of his nature, his choice, and his will, he may do everything that it is within the capacity of man to do, and this without there being created for his benefit in any way any newly produced thing. Similarly all the species of animals move in virtue of their own will. And He has willed it so; I mean to say that it comes from His eternal volition in the eternity a parte ante that all animals should move in virtue of their will and that man should have the ability to do whatever he wills or chooses among the things concerning which he has the ability to act. This is a fundamental principle about which – praise be to God! – no disagreement has ever been heard within our religious community. It is likewise one of the fundamental principles of the Law of *Moses our Master* that it is in no way possible that He, may He be exalted, should be unjust, and that all the calamities that befall men and the good things that come to men, be it a single individual or a group, are all of them determined according to the deserts of the men concerned through equitable judgment in which there is no injustice whatever.

(Guide III, 17, p. 469)

In spite of these affirmations of principles, Maimonides' own explanation considerably resembles that of Aristotle.

As for my own belief with regard to this fundamental principle, I mean divine providence, it is as I shall set it forth to you. In this belief that I shall set forth, I am not relying upon the conclusion to which demonstration has led me, but upon what has clearly appeared as the intention of the book of God and of the books of our prophets. This opinion, which I believe, is less disgraceful than the preceding opinions and nearer than they to intellectual reasoning. For I for one believe that in his lowly world – I mean that which is beneath the sphere of the moon – divine providence watches only over the individuals belonging to the human species and that in this species alone all the circumstances of the individuals and the good and evil that befall them are consequent upon the deserts, just as it says: *For all His ways are judgment* [Deuteronomy 32: 4]. But regarding all the other animals and, all the more, the plants and other things, my opinion is that of Aristotle. For I do not by any means believe that this particular leaf has fallen because of a providence, watching over it; nor that this spider has devoured this fly because God has now decreed and willed something concerning individuals; nor that the spittle spat by Zayd has moved till it came down in one particular place upon a gnat and killed it by a divine decree and judgment; nor that when this fish snatched this worm from the face of the water, this happened in virtue of a divine volition concerning individuals. For all this is in my opinion due to pure chance, just as Aristotle holds. According to me, as I consider the matter, divine providence is consequent upon the divine overflow; and the species with which this intellectual overflow is united so that it became endowed with intellect and so that everything that is disclosed to a being endowed with the intellect was disclosed to it, is the one accompanied by divine providence, which appraises all its actions from the point of view of reward and punishment. If, as he states, the foundering of a ship and the drowning of those who were in it and the falling-down of a roof upon those who were in the house, are due to pure chance, the fact that the people in the ship went on board and that the people in the house were sitting in it is, according to our opinion, not due to chance, but to divine will in accordance with the deserts of those people as determined in His judgments, the rule of which cannot be attained by our intellects.

(Guide III, 17, pp. 471–2)

Divine providence is thus identified with the laws of nature as far as the spheres are concerned; as for the particular events and beings in our lower world, Maimonides believes, as does Aristotle, that providence only extends to species and not to individuals, except for the human species, or, at least, to those individuals of the human species who fulfil man's destiny, that is, those who receive the outflow of the Intellect, those who participate in this Intellect, that is, the philosophers, and then only when their thoughts are turned to God. In effect, the Intellect does not constantly illuminate us; it is like a flash of lightning that blazes and disappears, and providence, being linked to the Intellect, is manifested in proportion to the different degrees of connection with the Intellect. The light of the Intellect only illuminates one who has approached it, that is, one who knows God by His acts, who has studied the sciences; but this is not only a matter of intellectual knowledge; it has already been said several times that in the Middle Ages knowledge is also love of God, morality, abandonment of corporeal desires.

At the end of the third part, Maimonides again takes up the idea of providence and shows how his opinion in fact agrees with Aristotle's:

We have already explained in the chapters concerning providence that providence watches over everyone endowed with intellect proportionately to the measure of his intellect. Thus providence always watches over an individual endowed with perfect apprehension, whose intellect never ceases from being occupied with God. On the other hand, an individual endowed with perfect apprehension, whose thought sometimes for a certain time is emptied of God, is watched over by providence only during the time when he thinks of God; providence withdraws from him during the time when he is occupied with something else. However, its withdrawal then is not like its withdrawal from those who have never had intellectual cognition. But in his case that providence merely decreases because that man of perfect apprehension has, while being occupied, no intellect in actu; but that perfect man is at such times only apprehending potentially, though close to actuality. At such times he is like a skillful scribe at the time when he is not writing. On the other hand, he who has no intellectual cognition at all of God is like one who is in darkness and has never seen light, just as we have explained with regard to its dictum: *The wicked shall be put to silence in darkness* [I Samuel 2: 9].   (*Guide* III, 51, pp. 624–5)

Does this divine providence, which accompanies and is identified with the outpouring of the Intellect and with its actualization in man, also extend to material life and its corporeal accidents? The opinion of the commentators is far from unanimous, as we shall see, beginning with the Tibbonids. At any rate let us note that it is the intellect *in actu* that constitutes the immortality of the soul, and when Maimonides uses the verse 'the wicked shall be put to silence', he is probably alluding to life after death, since the death of the body leads the impious into the darkness and the wise to eternal light. Nevertheless, Maimonides also writes: 'All the stories figuring [in Scripture] concerning Abraham, Isaac and Jacob are an absolute proof of there being an individual Providence' (*Guide* III, 17, p. 472) and he quite definitely means events that took place and not the fate of the patriarchs' intellects.

(3) THE CREATION OF THE WORLD

The problem of the creation of the world is one of those that have caused a great deal of ink to flow, and opinions are always very divided. Maimonides' position is not easy to establish, for he has intentionally confused the issue.

In chapter 13 of the second part of the *Guide* (pp. 281ff) Maimonides cites three opinions regarding the creation or the eternity of the world:

(1) The first opinion, that of all those who accept the Law of Moses, is

that of creation *ex nihilo*; God, at a moment of His choosing, created the world as He wished it, from nothingness.

(2) God created the world from the first matter co-eternal with Himself, but caused by Him. This is Plato's opinion.

(3) God is the eternal cause of the world, which necessarily arises from Him, without change and in all eternity, as Aristotle holds.

Most of the early commentators have affirmed that Maimonides believed in the eternity of the world and have invoked the logic of the Maimonidean system, in support of their argument. In effect, the very foundation of Maimonides' thought is the divine incorporeality, demonstrated in Aristotelian physics, which is based on the eternity of the world:

As to this my method, it is as I shall describe to you in a general way now. Namely, I shall say: the world cannot but be either eternal or created in time. If it is created in time, it undoubtedly has a creator who created it in time. For it is a first intelligible that what has appeared at a certain moment in time has not created itself in time and that its creator is other than itself. Accordingly the creator who created the world in time is the deity. If, however, the world is eternal, it follows necessarily because of this and that proof that there is an existent other than all the bodies to be found in the world; an existent who is not a body and not a force in a body and who is one, permanent, and sempiternal; who has no cause and whose becoming subject to change is impossible. Accordingly he is a deity. Thus it has become manifest to you that the proofs for the existence and the oneness of the deity and of His not being a body ought to be procured from the starting point afforded by the supposition of the eternity of the world, for in this way the demonstration will be perfect, both if the world is eternal and if it is created in time. For this reason you will always find that whenever, in what I have written in the books of jurisprudence, I happen to mention the foundations and start upon establishing the existence of the deity, I establish it by discourses that adopt the way of the doctrine of the eternity of the world.

(*Guide* I, 71, pp. 181–2)

To which Shem Tov ben Joseph Falaquera, thirteenth-century commentator, objected:

How can one demonstrate such an important subject by means of a dubious thing, and so much more so if this thing is not true? For if the premises of the demonstration are not true, how can the conclusion be true, and how with such premises can one form a demonstration which is not doubtful?... Most certainly, this could not have escaped our master, who has disposed all his words wisely.

(*Moreh ha-Moreh*, p. 43)

Other passages by Maimonides in favour of the theory of the creation of the world hardly suffice to confute the hypothesis of the eternity of the world: if one admits that Maimonides believes in this eternity, one must also admit that he considers that this truth, if it were revealed, would destroy the foundations of religion, which is indispensable to human society as desired by God, and in consequence it must be concealed from the people. But philosophers would know how to recognize it thanks to the allusions in the *Guide* and especially thanks to the philosophical treatises of Aristotle and his commentators.

In speaking of the allegorical interpretation of the Bible, Maimonides remarks:

For the texts indicating that the world has been produced in time are not more numerous than those indicating that the deity is a body. Nor are the gates of figurative interpretation shut in our faces or impossible of access to us regarding the subject of the creation of the world in time. For we could interpret them as figurative, as we have done when denying His corporeality. Perhaps this would even be much easier to do: we should be very well able to give a figurative interpretation of those texts and to affirm as true the eternity of the world, just as we have given a figurative interpretation of those other texts and have denied that He, may He be exalted, is a body.

Two causes are responsible for our not doing this or believing it. One of them is as follows. That the deity is not a body has been demonstrated; from this it follows necessarily that everything that in its external meaning disagrees with this demonstration must be interpreted figuratively, for it is known that such texts are of necessity fit for figurative interpretation. However, the eternity of the world has not been demonstrated. Consequently in this case the texts ought not to be rejected and figuratively interpreted in order to make prevail an opinion whose contrary can be made to prevail by means of various sorts of arguments.

(*Guide* II, 25, pp. 327–8)

And he continues:

On the other hand, the belief in eternity the way Aristotle sees it – that is, the belief according to which the world exists in virtue of necessity, that no nature changes at all, and that the customary course of events cannot be modified with regard to anything – destroys the Law in its principle, necessarily gives the lie to every miracle, and reduces to inanity all the hopes and threats that the Law has held out, unless – by God! – one interprets the miracles figuratively also, as was done by the Islamic internalists; this, however, would result in some sort of crazy imaginings.

If, however, one believed in eternity according to the second opinion we have explained – which is the opinion of Plato – according to which the heavens too are subject to generation and corruption, this opinion would not destroy the foundations of the Law and would be followed not by the lie being given to miracles, but by their becoming admissible. It would also be possible to interpret figuratively the texts in accordance with this opinion. And many obscure passages can be found in the texts of the *Torah* and others with which this opinion could be connected or rather by means of which it could be proved. However, no necessity could impel us to do this unless this opinion were demonstrated. In view of the fact that it has not been demonstrated, we shall not favor this opinion, nor shall we at all heed that other opinion.

(*Guide* II, 25, pp. 328–9)

Thus, the texts can be interpreted according to Aristotle – which would be contrary to religion – but also according to Plato – which would not be contrary to it. The real problem is therefore not to bring revelation into agreement with one or the other of these opinions, but to know if the eternity of the world can be considered as scientifically demonstrated or whether this is one of the questions that human knowledge cannot resolve. Certain passages of the *Guide* seem to indicate that Maimonides held that we cannot either prove or invalidate the creation or the eternity of the world, and he adduces several significant arguments in support of this position:

Aristotle's physics are true in everything that concerns this lower world, but extremely dubious as far as celestial physics are concerned; in fact, even in his own time there was a strong awareness of the contradiction between the Aristotelian astronomical system, in which all the spheres revolved around an immobile centre – the earth – and the system of Ptolemy, which made the explanation of observed phenomena possible, but postulated excentric spheres and epicycles of which the numerous centres were not the fixed and motionless earth. Further, Maimonides speaks of attempts made in Spain to find a more adequate explanation of the solar system.

What was even more disturbing: it is not certain that celestial physics and the metaphysics of Aristotle are anything more than conjecture, and Maimonides casts doubt on the very possibility of knowing anything of the celestial world:

On the other hand, everything that Aristotle expounds with regard to the sphere of the moon and that which is above it is, except for certain things, something analogous to guessing and conjecturing. All the more does this apply to what he says about the order of the intellects and to some of the opinions regarding the divine that he believes; for the latter contain grave incongruities and perversities that manifestly and clearly appear as such to all the nations, that propagate evil, and that he cannot demonstrate.

(*Guide* II, 22, pp. 319–20)

A question of method also arises: our proofs for or against creation rest on what we apprehend of the world as it is now; however:

In the case of everything produced in time, which is generated after not having existed – even in those cases in which the matter of the thing was already existent and in the course of the production of the thing had merely put off one and put on another form – the nature of that particular thing after it has been produced in time, has attained its final state, and achieved stability, is different from its nature when it is being generated and is beginning to pass from potentiality to actuality. It is also different from the nature the thing had before it had moved so as to pass from potentiality to actuality.

(*Guide* II, 17, p. 294)

Another argument, this time theological, is often pleaded by our author and was to be frequently repeated after him:

Know that with a belief in the creation of the world in time, all the miracles become possible and the Law becomes possible, and all questions that may be asked on this subject, vanish. Thus it might be said: Why did God give prophetic revelation to this one and not to that? Why did God give this Law to this particular nation, and, why did He not legislate to the others? Why did He legislate at this particular time, and why did He not legislate before it or after? Why did He impose these commandments and these prohibitions? Why did He privilege the prophet with the miracles mentioned in relation to him and not with some others? What was God's aim in giving this Law? Why did He not, if such was His purpose, put the accomplishment of the commandments and the nontransgression of the prohibitions into our nature? If this were said, the answer to all these questions would be that it would be said: He wanted it this way; or His wisdom required it this way. And just as He brought the world into existence, having the form it has, when He wanted to, without our knowing His will with regard to this or in what respect there was wisdom in His particularizing the forms of the world and the time of its creation – in the same way we do not know His will or the exigency of His wisdom that caused all the matters, about which questions have been posed above, to be particularized. If, however, someone says that the world is as it is in virtue of necessity, it would be a necessary obligation to ask all those questions; and there would be no way out of them except through a recourse to unseemly answers in which there would be combined the giving the lie to, and the annulment of, all the external meanings of the Law with regard to which no intelligent man has any doubt that they are to be taken in their external meanings. It is then because of this that this opinion is shunned and that the lives of virtuous men have been and will be spent in investigating this question. For if creation in time were demonstrated – if only as Plato understands creation – all the overhasty claims made to us on this point by the philosophers would become void. In the same way, if the philosophers would succeed in demonstrating eternity as Aristotle understands it, the Law as a whole would become void, and a shift to other opinions would take place. I have thus explained to you that everything is bound up with this problem. Know this. (*Guide* II, 25, pp. 329–30)

(4) PROPHECY

The problem of miracle and its possibility is again taken up by Maimonides when he discusses prophecy. He enumerates three opinions concerning this phenomenon; the first one is Saadiah's:

The first opinion – that of the multitude of those among the Pagans who considered prophecy as true and also believed by some of the common people professing our Law – is that God, may He be exalted, chooses whom He wishes from among men, turns him into a prophet, and sends him with a mission. According to them it makes no difference whether this individual is a man of knowledge or ignorant, aged or young. However, they also posit as a condition his having a certain goodness and sound morality.

The second opinion is that of the philosophers. It affirms that prophecy is a certain perfection in the nature of man. This perfection is not achieved in any individual from among men except after a training that makes that which exists in the potentiality of the species pass into actuality, provided an obstacle due to temperament or to some external cause does not hinder this, as is the case with regard to every perfection whose existence is possible in a certain species. For the existence of that perfection in its extreme and ultimate form in every individual of that species is not possible. It must, however, exist necessarily in at least one particular individual; if, in order to be achieved, this perfection requires something that actualizes it, that something necessarily exists. According to this opinion it is not possible that an ignoramus should turn into a prophet; nor can a man not be a prophet on a certain evening and be a prophet on the following morning, as though he had made some find. Things are rather as follows: When, in the case of a superior individual who is perfect with respect to his rational and moral qualities, his imaginative faculty is in its most perfect state and when he has been prepared in the way that you will hear, he will necessarily become a prophet.

The third opinion is the opinion of our Law and the foundation of our doctrine. It is identical with the philosophic opinion except in one thing. For we believe that it may happen that one who is fit for prophecy and prepared for it should not become a prophet, namely, on account of the divine will. To my mind this is like all the miracles and takes the same course as they.   (*Guide* II, 32, pp. 360–1)

Maimonides' position is thus clear; only the philosophical definition is true, and conforms to that of Judaism, except on one point: All-powerful God can prevent a prophet from prophesying, a circumstance that appears to introduce a supernatural factor relating to prophecy. This is an explicit declaration of principle; but the example adduced in support of this principle is not very convincing. For while Maimonides, to begin with, states that God wrought a miracle in order to prevent Barukh ben Neriah from prophesying, a circumstance that appears to introduce a supernatural factor relating to prophecy, immediately afterwards he offers another, purely philosophical explanation of the biblical text, maintaining that Barukh was not sufficiently prepared. He goes on: 'However, we shall find many texts, some of them scriptural and some of them dicta of the *Sages*, all of which maintain this fundamental principle that God turns whom He wills, whenever He wills it, into a prophet – but only someone perfect and superior to the utmost degree' (*Guide* II, 32, p. 362).

Certain commentators – Moses Narboni, Joseph Caspi and Efodi, for instance – concluded from this that Maimonides quite simply wanted to let it be understood that he entirely accepted the opinion of the philosophers, since he leaves the 'numerous examples of this principle' to the reader's imagination, and also because the only instance cited with any precision, that of Barukh ben Neriah, is not conclusive. This interpretation depends on an understanding of the Maimonidean system taken as a whole: in this system it is unthinkable to attribute to God a 'supernatural' act that would prevent nature from spreading good, restrict the emanation of the Intellect, and restrain the overflowing of the spirit. Nevertheless, Abrabanel, wishing to clear Maimonides of the suspicion of heresy, looked for the 'numerous' scriptural and traditional texts where it is made clear that God decides the gift of prophecy; thus, he cites the case of the seventy elders who prophesied when the Spirit rested on them. But this verse is hardly conclusive, for, in enumerating the degree of prophecy, the author of the *Guide* uses this verse as an example of the lowest degree of prophecy, the divine succour, which is not yet prophecy properly speaking, and is not associated with the intellect.

Let us return to the definition of prophecy given by Maimonides: 'Know that the true reality and quiddity of prophecy consist in its being an overflow overflowing from God, may He be cherished and honored, through the intermediation of the Active Intellect, toward the rational faculty in the first place and thereafter toward the imaginative faculty' (*Guide* II, 36, p. 369).

The remote cause of prophecy is God, and the immediate cause is the Active Intellect. The receiver is the rational faculty, which in its turn overflows into the imaginative.

The rational faculty, which is accordingly the direct recipient of the divine overflow, must therefore be without any imperfection. Several conditions are necessary for this: the formation of the brain must be entirely perfect; the individual must have acquired knowledge and mastered all the degrees of physics and metaphysics; his morals must be good, his thought altogether occupied with God; he must be entirely detached from all sensual desire and all vain ambition. A man whose rational faculty fulfils all these conditions, undoubtedly receives the influx of the Active Intellect; he belongs to the class of men of knowledge. When the influx is superabundant, this man diffuses knowledge; otherwise, he is satisfied with perfecting himself.

When to this rational perfection is added the perfection of the imaginative faculty and those of the faculties of divination and intrepidity, then this man is a prophet.

Maimonides describes the imaginative faculty in the terms employed by Avicenna, which we have already encountered in Abraham Ibn Daud. 'You know, too, the actions of the imaginative faculty that are in its nature, such as retaining things perceived by the senses, combining these things, and imitating them' (*Guide* II, 36, p. 370). He thus includes in the imaginative faculty the two functions of preservation of images and of combination of forms.

The author of the *Guide* also defines the faculty of divination: 'You will find among people a man whose conjecturing and divination are very strong and habitually hit the mark, so that he hardly imagines that a thing comes to pass without its happening wholly or in part as he imagines it' (*Guide* II, 38, p. 376).

As for the faculty of boldness, this is a faculty of the soul that has a function similar to that of the expulsive among the physical faculties. This is one of the motor faculties, and through it one repels what is harmful and is enabled to face great dangers (cf. Moses before Pharoah). The three faculties, which should combine with the rational so that prophecy will ensue, are corporeal, and when the overflow of God reaches over these corporeal faculties only, we find men belonging to the classes of statesmen, legislators, diviners, and augurs.

Prophets, like legislators, are able to receive an influx abundant enough to suffice not only for their own perfecting, but also for allowing their contemporaries to benefit from this perfection.

According to this theory, all prophets are accomplished philosophers, but in reality only one prophet–philosopher exists for Maimonides, namely Moses.

This is evident from the arrangement of the chapters of the first part of the *Guide*: chapter 38 describes the prophet and shows that he is above all perfect in his rational faculty; chapters 39 and 40 present political considerations: only the Law of Moses is perfect, men need a law, for they are too different from each other to live in community without its help. And when Maimonides returns to prophecy and gives a classification of the biblical prophets, he concludes with these words:

... our principle states that all prophets hear speech only through the intermediary of an *angel*, the sole exception being *Moses our Master*, of whom it is said: *With him do I speak mouth to mouth*. Know then that this is in fact so, and that in these cases the intermediary is the imaginative faculty. For a prophet can hear only *in a dream of prophecy* that God has spoken to him. *Moses our Master*, on the other hand, heard Him *from above the ark-cover, from between the two cherubim*.

(*Guide* II, 45, p. 405)

These two 'cherubim' have been variously interpreted by the commentators, but they all agree in recognizing in the 'ark-cover' the Active Intellect, and in the two cherubim the human faculties, of which one is the rational. It is clear that if Moses was alone in not having prophesied through the intermediary of the imaginative faculty, he is thus also the only one who fills the role of prophet–philosopher that Maimonides outlines in chapter 38. Moses heard God speak directly (he was very close to the Active Intellect, as is shown by the image of the cherubim and the ark-cover), in a waking state, without experiencing any uneasiness, and whenever he wished to do so.

Having thus shown that Moses is the prophet–philosopher *par excellence*, Maimonides examines the other prophets, and we see that they are inferior.

These prophets prophesied through the intermediary of the imaginative faculty. This faculty has two functions: to preserve images and to recombine them. The material that it habitually uses is the product of the senses. During sleep, and sometimes also in a waking state, the senses cease to function and the imaginative faculty, freed from the continuous distraction of the perceptions, can give itself over to its own proper activities and reveal its true capabilities.

The process of perception is normally: the five senses $\longrightarrow$ the *sensus communis* $\longrightarrow$ the imaginative faculty; when the imaginative faculty is freed from the external world, cut off from the world of the senses, it turns towards itself and retrieves the images that it has stored while man is awake. 'This signifies that the imaginative faculty achieves so great a perfection of action that it sees the thing as if it were outside, and that the thing whose origin is due to it appears to have come to it by the way of external sensation' (*Guide* II, 36, p. 370).

In the case of visions, the imaginative faculty is under the influence of the rational faculty, and we have: the Intellect $\longrightarrow$ the imaginative faculty $\longrightarrow$ the *sensus communis* $\longrightarrow$ the five senses $\longrightarrow$ the *sensus communis* $\longrightarrow$ the imaginative faculty.

However, Maimonides does not describe the psychological process in detail. One can only infer from his words that he believed in a purely internal vision, like Avicenna, and not in an external phenomenon provoked by the senses themselves, like Al-Fārābī. This imaginative faculty is a corporeal faculty, exercised on images. It is not surprising that the fact of receiving entirely abstract ideas from the rational faculty provokes certain disturbances, since it is not in the nature of the imaginative faculty to conceive of anything other than forms clothed in matter:

The overflow in question comes to the rational faculty and overflows from it to the imaginative faculty so that the latter becomes perfect and performs its function. Prophetic revelation begins sometimes *with a vision of prophecy*. Thereupon the terror and the strong affection consequent upon the perfection of the action of the imaginative faculty become intensified and then prophetic revelation comes.

(*Guide* II, 41, p. 385)

From this definition of prophecy it appears that whenever one finds in the Scriptures the words 'God spoke', 'an angel spoke', it is this kind of vision that is meant, whatever the words and expressions used to express it.

There are eleven degrees of prophecy, and they are grouped on three principal levels:

(1) The two lowest degrees are those of the Holy Spirit: a divine inspiration, a divine succour, which are purely interior and which one can compare to that profound conviction that Abraham bar Ḥiyya calls the first degree of prophecy.

(2) The third to seventh degrees contain all the varieties of dream and vision, the hearing of God or the angels. These five degrees are characterized by the phantasmagoria of the imaginative faculty, which constructs images unrelated to reality, such as the representation of the divine word or the vision of God himself. All the prophecies of Isaiah, Ezekiel, Zechariah, were dreams.

(3) From the eighth to the eleventh degree the intellectual perception becomes increasingly refined; from parable, prophecy passes to the hearing of words without knowing their origin (ninth degree), these words are pronounced by an undefined personage (tenth degree), finally by an angel, which is the highest degree, for the prophet has recognized the very essence of prophecy: overflow of the Active Intellect into his rational faculty, through the intermediary of the imaginative faculty: this whole group of prophetic visions taker place in the state of *mar'a*: vision in the state of wakefulness:

One could also say that every *vision* in which you find the prophet hearing speech was in its beginning a *vision*, but ended in a state of submersion [in sleep] and became a *dream* . . . All speech that is heard, whatever the way may be in which it is heard, is heard only *in a dream* . . . On the other hand, in a *vision of prophecy* only parables or intellectual unifications are apprehended that give actual cognition of scientific matters similar to those, knowledge of which is obtained through speculation.

(*Guide* II, 45, pp. 402–3)

For Maimonides the intelligible vision is evidently superior to the imaginative. In fact, the four particular characteristics of Moses' prophecy are due syley to the non-intervention of the imaginative faculty:

(1) Moses prophesied in a state of wakefulness, for he had no need to free his imagination from the weight of sensory images;

(2) He experienced no uneasiness, for only the imaginative faculty is troubled by the divine influx;

(3) The prophetic state could be achieved at any moment, for Moses was not using this 'corporeal faculty which sometimes grows tired, is weakened, and is troubled, and at other times is in a healthy state' (*Guide* II, 36, p. 372);

(4) Moses' prophecy was without an intermediary, without requiring the imaginative faculty; Moses' intellect drew its knowledge directly from the Active Intellect.

For all other prophets the key and the explanation of their writings is the comprehension of the nature of the imaginative faculty and of what it imposes, and of what necessarily accompanies it – dreams, visions, images, metaphors.

Maimonides cites a verse from Numbers 12: 6 at least twelve times: 'I the Lord will make myself known unto him in a vision and will speak unto him in a dream.' The vision is the state during which God makes Himself known; in dream, He speaks with His voice or through an angel. There is no third way between these two kinds of revelation, dream and vision: the first kind is encumbered with images close to matter, while the other tends towards pure intelligibility.

The superiority of the vision that introduces intelligible notions similar to those of speculative thought is often stressed by our author. Only Moses is to be found at the highest level of prophecy, where philosopher and prophet meet.

We are like someone in a very dark night over whom lightning flashes time and time again. Among us there is one for whom the lightning flashes time and time again, so that he is always, as it were, in unceasing light. Thus night appears to him as day. That is the degree of the great one among the prophets, to whom it was said: *But as for thee, stand thou here by Me* [Deuteronomy 5: 28], and of whom it was said: *that the skin of his face sent forth beams*, and so on [Exodus 34: 29].

(*Guide* I, introd. p. 7)

There is one further point to consider concerning Maimonides' theory of visions: his explication of the revelation on Mount Sinai.

The Israelites had not attained any of the prophetic degrees, not even the level of the Divine Spirit. However, the text affirms that they heard God speaking to them. How can this text be brought into conformity with the theory of the interior visions? First of all, Maimonides affirms that Moses alone heard the divine words distinctly, while the other onlookers only perceived a terrifying noise, and they asked Moses to advance towards God; then they heard and saw voices and lights, which are the meteorological phenomena thunder and lightning. The scene on Sinai can be resolved into three acts:

(1) The hearing of a terrifying noise by all the people: this was a Voice created by God;

(2) Moses' hearing of the eight last commandments which were transmitted to the people;

(3) The sound of the horn, the thunder, the voice, which the Israelites heard and saw and which were meteorological phenomena.

The first act is evidently difficult to reconcile with philosophical views, but the *Aggadah* fortunately provides some texts which, interpreted, allow one to show that:

(1) The Voice of God caused only the first two commandments to be understood;

(2) This Voice was indistinct, it was no more than an inarticulate sound;

(3) These two first commandments do not belong to revelation, but to simple human speculation.

Thus, the physical voice created by God corresponded to the profound conviction that the Israelites had of the divine unity and existence.

The voice in question was audible, but its articulations were not distinguishable; in fact, it was only a great and terrible noise. Why did God create this spectacle witnessed by the Israelites? Maimonides replies to this question in another passage:

[Moses] told them similarly at the *Gathering at Mount Sinai*: Be not afraid; this great gathering that you have seen has taken place only in order that you acquire certitude through sight, so that if, in order to make publicly known the extent of your faith, *the Lord your God tried you out with a false prophet* who would call upon you to demolish what you have heard, you should remain firm and keep your feet from stumbling. For if I had come to you as a prophet, as you had thought, and I had said to you what had been said to me without your hearing it for yourselves, it would have been possible for you to fancy that what is told by another is true even if that other had come to you with something contradicting what has been made known to you; this is what could have happened if you had not heard it at this gathering. (*Guide* III, 24, p. 500)

The voice was therefore necessary because the Israelites had need of concrete demonstration that the *Torah* was the most excellent of laws. They were not sagacious enough to accept Moses' perfection and his Law as sufficiently convincing proof and they might have abandoned the good that God desired to give them as their portion. Therefore God created a sound that was perceptible by the senses and constituted a proof of Moses' mission. This phenomenon, which was and remained unique, corresponds to the unique eminence of Moses.

(5) HUMAN KNOWLEDGE

At the beginning of this chapter I wished to stress the homogeneity of Maimonides' thought; however, the attentive reader has probably observed a certain number of internal contradictions in the course of this discussion. In two recent studies S. Pines has treated these contradictions and proposes to resolve them by showing that another level of thought existed in Maimonides, superior to those I have expounded. These hypotheses concerning his 'epistemological' thought are based on a comparison with texts by Al-Fārābī and Ibn Bājja, and we know that Maimonides held them to be 'true' philosophers.

As said before, Maimonides wrote no book explicitly intended for philosophers; can one divine his intimate opinions in the *Guide*, a work designed for apprentice philosophers? If Maimonides did indeed express his personal opinion, it was only by allusion and by contradiction. We thus find ourselves on unstable ground where the dynamic of the thought relies on signs necessarily contradicted by other, more visible signs. A passage in the *Guide* (I, 31) seems to lend force to the notion that one must attribute considerable weight to Maimonides' prudence:

> The things about which there is this perplexity are very numerous in divine matters few in matters pertaining to natural science, and nonexistent in matters pertaining to mathematics.
> Alexander of Aphrodisias says that there are three causes of disagreement about things. One of them is love of domination and love of strife, both of which turn man aside from the apprehension of truth as it is. The second cause is the subtlety and the obscurity of the object of apprehension in itself and the difficulty of apprehending it. And the third cause is the ignorance of him who apprehends and his inability to grasp things that it is possible to apprehend. That is what Alexander mentioned. However, in our times there is a fourth cause that he did not mention because it did not exist among them. It is habit and upbringing. For man has in his nature a love of, and an inclination for, that to which he is habituated.

> (*Guide* I, 31, pp. 66–7)

This fourth cause of confusion is based on a passage in Aristotle (*Metaphysics* II, 3, 995a), and would suggest that in Maimonides' opinion 'our time', that is to say the period dominated by the revealed religions, is less propitious for the study of the truth than was the pagan epoch, that of Alexander of Aphrodisias.

Of the internal contradictions of the *Guide of the Perplexed*, two points appear to be fundamental and deserve more detailed examination:

(1) Metaphysics, or divine science, is the ultimate aim of human life. Although Maimonides gives no definitions of metaphysics, one may suppose that he alludes to it in the *Guide* (III, 51, p. 619):

> He, however, who has achieved demonstration to the extent that that is possible, of every thing that may be demonstrated; and who has ascertained in divine matters, to the extent that that is possible, everything that may be ascertained; and who has come close to certainty in those matters in which one can only come close to it – has come to be with the ruler in the inner part of the habitation.

This distinction between the things in metaphysics that one can know with certainty and those that one can only approach recalls Al-Fārābī's definition of metaphysics, which comprises the study of the principles of the particular sciences (or laws of nature) and that of God and the separate intellects, this last domain being of course the more important. However, in these two domains Maimonides considerably restricts the possible achievement of human knowledge.

Maimonides often reiterates that God cannot be known in His essence, and human ignorance regarding the essence of God and the intellects extends to the world of the spheres:

I have promised you a chapter in which I shall expound to you the grave doubts that would affect whoever thinks that man has acquired knowledge as to the arrangement of the motions of the sphere and as to their being natural things going on according to the law of necessity, things whose order and arrangement are clear. I shall now explain this to you. *(Guide* II, 23, p. 322)

And again:

I mean thereby that the deity alone fully knows the true reality, the nature, the substance, the form, the motions, and the causes of the heavens. But He has enabled man to have knowledge of what is beneath the heavens, for that is his world and his dwelling-place in which he has been placed and of which he himself is a part. This is the truth. For it is impossible for us to accede to the points starting from which conclusions may be drawn about the heavens; for the latter are too far away from us and too high in place and in rank. And even the general conclusion that may be drawn from them, namely, that they prove the existence of their Mover, is a matter the knowledge of which cannot be reached by human intellects.

(Guide II, 24, p. 331)

Maimonides' ideas on the limits of human knowledge may perhaps be summed up in this way:

(1) Man may truly know the laws of the sublunar world;

(2) He does not know the laws of the celestial world and can only make unverifiable hypotheses on the subject;

(3) He is totally ignorant of God and of the intellects and can only advance negative hypotheses about them.

(2) If we admit that for Maimonides nothing can be known of God, evidently His mode of intellection also cannot be known. Numerous passages support this hypothesis, and, in particular, that in which God, replying to Moses, denies him the possibility of knowing Him otherwise than by His attributes of action, which do not provide information concerning His essence.

Two causes of this ignorance may exist: either God is unknowable *per se*, and no one, whether man or intellect, is capable of conceiving His divinity (and several passages in the *Guide* support this possibility); or else man, because of matter, cannot apprehend God or the intellects. Thus Maimonides writes:

Matter is a strong veil preventing the apprehension of that which is separate from matter as it truly is. It does this even if it is the noblest and purest matter, I mean to say even if it is the matter of the heavenly spheres. All the more is this true for the dark and turbid matter that is ours. Hence whenever our intellect aspires to apprehend the deity or one of the intellects, there subsists this great veil interposed between the two. This is alluded to in all the books of the prophets; namely, that we are separated by a veil from God and that He is hidden from us by a heavy cloud, or by darkness or by a mist or by an enveloping cloud, and similar allusions to our incapacity to apprehend Him because of matter.   (*Guide* III, 9, pp. 436–7)

However, while Moses could know nothing of the divine essence and could only have known Him by His actions, since the only attributes predicated of God, even the attribute of His existence, are negative, Maimonides writes (I, 68, p. 165): 'It is accordingly also clear that the numerical unity of the intellect, the intellectually cognizing subject and the intellectually cognized object does not hold good with reference to the Creator only, but also with reference to every intellect.'

Another indication is offered by the beginning of chapter 68 of Book I of the *Guide* (p. 163):

You already know that the following dictum of the philosophers with reference to God, may He be exalted, is generally admitted: the dictum being that He is the intellect as well as the intellectually cognizing subject and the intellectually cognized object, and that those three notions form in Him, may He be exalted, one single notion in which there is no multiplicity.

This opinion, which is accepted by the philosophers, is not necessarily true for Maimonides: he by no means always admits the philosophers' propositions. If this opinion is not true, the similarity between the divine intellect and the human intellect would become no more than one of those hypotheses which are neither self-evident verities nor scientific demonstrations.

It seems that there is no way of resolving this contradiction between the positive affirmation of the identity of the divine and human intellections, and the far more numerous passages where Maimonides declares that there is no possibility of a positive knowledge of God and His intellects.

A solution could be that propounded by S. Pines:

It would thus seem that to Maimonides' mind the so-called Aristotelian philosophical doctrine would be divided into two strata: intellectually cognized notions whose truth is absolute, and which form a coherent system, namely terrestrial physics; a much more comprehensive and ambitious system, namely celestial physics and metaphysics which is concerned with the higher being. However the conceptions and propositions which make up this system cannot be cognized by the human intellect. They are in the best case merely probable. It is, however, possible, but there is no explicit Maimonidean warrant for this hypothesis, that they provide the philosophers with a system of beliefs, somewhat analogous, as far as the truth function is concerned, to the religious beliefs of lesser mortals. It is, however, significant that the thesis concerning the Deity set forth in *Guide* I, 68 is also propounded – as Maimonides quite correctly points out at the beginning of the chapter – in *Mishneh Torah* [II, 9]. In both works, the thesis in question forms a part of a theological system, which may be believed, but cannot be proved to be true. In passages in which this critical (in the Kantian sense) attitude is expounded,

Maimonides refers to his sources; he may also have had sources which he does not mention.   ('The Limitations of Human Knowledge', p. 94)

Since the only mode of existence that man can cognize is that of the objects of the senses, men can have no knowledge of immaterial beings and the only 'happiness', the ultimate aim of human existence, is political happiness. A passage of the *Guide* clearly supports this interpretation:

It is clear that the perfection of man that may truly be gloried in is the one acquired by him who has achieved, in a measure corresponding to his capacity, apprehension of Him, may He be exalted, and who knows His providence extending over His creatures as manifested in the act of bringing them into being and in their gover- nance as it is. The way of life of such an individual, after he has achieved this apprehension, will always have in view *loving-kindness*, *righteousness*, and *judgment*, through assimilation to His actions, may He be exalted, just as we have explained several times in this Treatise.   (*Guide* III, 54, p. 638)

If accepted, this interpretation would deny the permanence of the intellect after the death of the body for 'since man is incapable of intellecting abstract forms, his intellect cannot be transmuted into a perdurable substance; nothing in man escapes death' (Pines, 'Limitations', p. 88).

Other passages of the *Guide*, however, seem to demonstrate that Maimon- ides perceived as true the opinion accepted by the philosophers, that the intellect is the same in God and in us. If this is so, the numerous allusions to the world hereafter that we find in his popular writings do, in fact, correspond to his intimate opinion, as he expresses it in the *Guide* III, 51:

And there may be a human individual who, through his apprehension of the true realities and his joy in what he has apprehended, achieves a state in which he talks with people and is occupied with his bodily necessities while his intellect is wholly turned toward Him, may He be exalted, so that in his heart he is always in His presence, may He be exalted, while outwardly he is with people, in the sort of way described by the poetical parables that have been invented for these notions: *I sleep, but my heart waketh*; *it is the voice of my beloved that knocketh, and so on.* I do not say that this rank is that of all the prophets; but I do say that this is the rank of *Moses our Master* . . . This was also the rank of the *Patriarchs* . . . For in those four, I mean the Patriarchs and Moses our Master, union with God – I mean apprehen- sion of Him and love of Him – became manifest, as the texts testify . . . Withal they were occupied with governing people, increasing their fortune, and endeavouring to acquire property. Now this is to my mind a proof that they performed these actions with their limbs only, while their intellects were constantly in His presence, may He be exalted.

The philosophers have already explained that the bodily faculties impede in youth the attainment of most of the moral virtues, and all the more that of pure thought, which is achieved through the perfection of the intelligibles that lead to passionate love of Him, may He be exalted. For it is impossible that it should be achieved while the bodily humors are in effervescence. Yet in the measure in which the facul- ties of the body are weakened and the fire of the desires is quenched, the intellect is strengthened, its lights achieve a wider extension, its apprehension is purified, and it rejoices in what it apprehends. The result is that when a perfect man is stricken with years and approaches death, this apprehension increases very powerfully, joy over this apprehension and a great love for the object of apprehension become stronger, until the soul is separated from the body at that moment in this state of pleasure ... After having reached this condition of enduring permanence, that intellect remains in one and the same state, the impediment that sometimes screened him off having been removed. And he will remain permanently in that state of intense pleasure, which does not belong to the genus of bodily pleasures.

(*Guide* III, 51, pp. 623–8)

The traditional interpretation attributes to Maimonides the survival of the intellect, and it was the one agreed upon by most medieval commentators. Many questions arise concerning the quiddity of this intellect; they were generally resolved through Averroes' unambiguous confirmation of the possibility of conjunction with the Active Intellect. In consequence, the *Guide* has been read in the light of Averroes by most commentators from the thirteenth century until the present day, and it is in this tradition that Maimonides has been presented in this chapter. S. Pines, while remarking that the texts allow a choice between the possible interpretations, seems to prefer Maimonides' first interpretation. It is certainly the most interesting and the least in conformity with the traditional exegesis of the *Guide of the Perplexed*. Perhaps the veritable Maimonides, like the Al-Fārābī of the *Commentary on the Nicomachaean Ethics*, was a philosopher despairing of ever knowing anything but this corruptible world and looking for a reason to continue the struggle to understand and to hope?

Chapter 7

THE THIRTEENTH CENTURY

After Maimonides, Jewish philosophy took various directions. These I shall treat consecutively, although they were parallel in time and frequently in contact.

In the Islamic countries philosophers were not numerous. They drew on the Arabic philosophical literature, at the same time making use of the writings of Maimonides, although often in contexts very different from Maimonides' own. The most striking representative of this twofold tendency was Maimonides' son Abraham, who incorporated his father's philosophical definitions into an ascetic, mystical structure very akin to Sufism.

In Provence a school of Maimonidean exegesis arose with Samuel Ibn Tibbon, Hebrew translator of the *Guide of the Perplexed*, who considered it a sacred task to transmit the 'philosophical truths' contained in the *Guide*. In the course of the thirteenth century Samuel, his pupils and his family translated a large number of scientific works either composed by Arab authors or else transmitted and commented on by them, the most influential of them being *Averroes*. This great effort of translation was supplemented by the philosophical explication of various traditional texts, especially the biblical passages attributed to King Solomon, and the *aggadot* of the *Talmud*.

In Spain, and especially Toledo, a movement developed that saw in the 'Word' and the letters of the alphabet an esoteric science, based on the traditional texts and especially the *Sefer Yeẓirah* (*The Book of Creation*), and also on all the other aggadic and midrashic sources that deal with combinations of letters. This way of thinking was rendered illustrious by Judah ha-Cohen and Abraham Abulafia, among others. As far as the intelligible world is concerned, it is neoplatonic in tendency. It was extensively used in the Kabbalah.

In Italy, Maimonidean exegesis was transmitted by Jacob Anatoli, son-in-law of Samuel Ibn Tibbon, and Zerahiah Gracian. The influence of Judah ha-Cohen was also felt. Italian Jewish philosophy is distinguished by the importance accorded to the Latin scholastic texts, which are frequently cited in Hebrew translation. The Provençal movement, on the other hand, was far less overtly influenced by scholasticism.

In Islamic countries

In the Islamic environment Maimonides' thought made a strong and immediate impact. His halakhic works, the *Mishneh Torah* and the *Commentary on the Mishnah*, aroused impassioned reactions, some of them far from favourable. Maimonides was taken to task not so much for his use of philosophy as for 'the anti-religious character' of his thinking, and especially his position regarding life after death. The principal polemicist in the debate was Samuel ben Ali, to whom Maimonides himself replied in the Letter on the *Resurrection of the Dead*. The attacks against his halakhic decisions, emanating from rabbinical circles in Damascus, continued after his death, although little philosophical argumentation was deployed. However, in the course of the century, the halakhic decisions were accepted and Maimonidean concepts intended for the general public were adopted; for several centuries they constituted a veritable 'second Mosaic law'.

At the beginning, the *Guide of the Perplexed* exercised less influence among Jewish philosophers living in a Muslim environment than among those in the Christian world. This at least is the impression given by Joseph ben Judah, for whom the *Guide* was composed. Most probably he was *Joseph ben Judah of Ceuta*, who died in about 1226. Maimonides corresponded with him until the end of his life, and had a great affection for him. He has often been confused with his contemporary, Joseph ben Judah Ibn Aknin, and it is under the name of Ibn Aknin that his brief surviving work was published in its Hebrew version and also in an English translation. This is *Ma'amar bimehuyav ha-metsiut ve'eykhut sidur ha-devarim mimenu vehidush ha'olam* (*A Treatise as to* (1) *Necessary Existence* (2) *The Procedure of Things from the Necessary Existence and* (3) *The Creation of the World*). It is not known whether these three dissertations were written before or after Joseph of Ceuta's meeting with Maimonides. The latter is not cited, and the opinions attributed to the philosopher are those of Avicenna. Certainly, in the first dissertation, the necessity of God's existence is initially demonstrated by Avicenna's proof of contingency, but this demonstration, which is, as the author says, that of the philosophers, seems to him less convincing than that proposed by the theologians – the *mutakallimūn*, who affirm not only the existence of a necessary being, but the temporal creation of the world, which cannot be deduced by philosophical demonstration. In effect, only divine choice and will can explain the multiplicity evident in the world, for out of an absolutely One and Only God only unity can necessarily proceed; the multiplicity that exists in fact is therefore an act of will and not the consequence of a necessary cause.

The other Joseph ben Judah is closer to the author of the *Guide*, and draws on the same sources.

JOSEPH BEN JUDAH IBN AKNIN

Joseph ben Judah Ibn Aknin was more or less a contemporary of Maimonides, whom he met during the latter's sojourn in North Africa. Born at Barcelona in about 1150, he lived in Fez, concealing his Judaism, until about 1220. His numerous treatises deal chiefly with the *Mishnah* and the Talmud. Three of these works are philosophical, at least in part.

(1) *Sefer ha-Musar* (*Book of the Morality*), written in Hebrew, is a commentary on the *Pirkei Avot*, and is close to Maimonides' commentary.

(2) *Tibb-al-nufus* (*The Hygiene of Healthy Souls and the Therapy of Ailing Souls*), a book of psychology of which only the chapter on education has been published. According to Ibn Aknin, the study of the sciences – logic, mathematics, etc. – should be postponed until the age of thirty, so that the traditional education would be sufficiently strong and well-grounded to provide a defence against the danger that philosophical doubts might arise to shake religious certitudes.

(3) *Inkishāf al-asrār waṭuhūr al-anwār* (*The Divulgence of Mysteries and the Appearance of Lights*) is a commentary on the *Song of Songs*. In his introduction the author expounds the scheme of the emanation of the intellects from God, relying on a long quotation from Al-Fārābī, and concluding with the words: 'And between ourselves and Al-Fārābī there are no divergences except that Aristotle and his sectarians think that intellects have their source in God, by necessity, while we believe that it was by an act of will that God created creatures.'

The Lover of the Canticles is the last of these intellects, the Active Intellect, while the Beloved is the human soul urged by the Active Intellect to acquire intelligible knowledge and to abandon all that partakes of matter. The plan of the commentary does not lend itself to the exposition of systematic thought, and it does not appear indeed that Joseph ben Judah did anything more than accept contemporary Arab Aristotelianism. Each verse is expounded according to three different exegeses, superimposed but not in contradiction.

(1) The literal meaning, giving chiefly the grammatical explication, is based on the works of authors like Saadiah, Judah Ibn Balaam, etc., and also the Spanish grammarians.

(2) The rabbinical meaning consists of a collection of midrashic texts, and presents the historical and eschatological sense of the dialogue between the community of Israel and God.

(3) The allegorical meaning is the scientific (logical, psychological and philosophical) explication, for which the author declares his own entire responsibility. He claims that he is the first to give a philosophical explanation of the entire *Song of Songs*. In so doing he became the first of a long series of such commentators, but, unlike his successors, Moses Ibn Tibbon, Caspi, Gersonides, and although he mentions the *Guide of the Perplexed*, his commentary owes nothing to Maimonides. However, for him as for Maimonides,

the *Song of Songs* describes the human soul aspiring to unite itself with the Active Intellect and the love of the latter for the human soul. Can this allegorical meaning, which the author considers the most important, cause the faithful believer to reject the literal meaning?

Maimonides himself had foreseen this danger and had warned against it in the *Mishneh Torah*, declaring that 'he who uncovers the face of the *Torah* and interprets the commandments in a sense other than the literal is a heretic'.

As we have seen, Maimonides himself gave a number of explanations of the commandments. Nevertheless, he always declares that the commandments must be observed strictly according to the tradition, and that they should never be taken only in their spiritual sense.

Joseph ben Judah also denies that he wishes to reject the literal meaning of the biblical text and the commandments, as the Christians do. On the other hand, he does not want to restrict himself to the literal meaning, as do the Islamic anthropomorphists. It seems that he was not aware of an antagonism between science and revelation, convinced as he was that both have the same aims; he illustrates the text of the *Song of Songs* by citations and philosophical notions found especially in Al-Fārābī, but also in Avicenna, and by numerous poetical quotations from Jewish and Arab authors. However, on two points at least he is ill at ease: creation and the explanation of the commandments; and these were indeed the problems that were to preoccupy succeeding generations, but in a Maimonidean context.

In the present state of our information, it is difficult to assess the extent of Maimonides' influence in the East. His injunction to copy the *Guide* in Hebrew characters only was not strictly followed, for manuscripts in Arabic letters may be found, and Arab authors quote and comment on the *Guide* from the thirteenth century onward. A Persian Muslim, *Al-Tabrizi*, wrote a commentary on the twenty-five propositions on physics at the beginning of Book II of the *Guide*, and a remark in the introduction to this commentary seems to indicate that the author intended to prepare a commentary on the whole *Guide*. Written in Arabic, Al-Tabrizi's work was twice translated into Hebrew, and was used by Jewish philosophers, the foremost being Ḥasdai Crescas. Other thirteenth-century texts show that Maimonides was also known in Oriental Christian communities.

One eastern Jewish philosopher who is known to us is *Sa'd ben Manṣur Ibn Kammūna*, who lived in Baghdad and died there in 1284. Only three treatises by Ibn Kammūna have been printed. They display a decided philosophical tendency, and his exposition of prophecy is Maimonidean. It is not impossible that there were other philosophers but it is difficult to form even a moderately adequate idea of their work, for most of the texts, written in Arabic, have not been published. In the fourteenth century Joseph Ibn Caspi complained that the descendants of Maimonides knew nothing of philosophy.

He had gone to Egypt to study with Abraham, great-grandson of Maimonides, and returned home extremely disappointed. It is true that philosophy began to be abandoned in Maimonides' family with his own son Abraham.

ABRAHAM BEN MAIMONIDES AND HIS PIETIST CIRCLE

Abraham ben Moses Maimonides (1186–1237) was forced to defend his father against his oriental opponents, who attacked the halakhic works, as well as against the Provençals, who opposed the philosophy. It is certain that on many points he followed his father's views, and, especially, he firmly believed in the incorporeality of God, basing his defence of Maimonides on this fundamental thesis in his *Milḥamot Adonai* (*The Wars of the Lord*). He himself was not a philosopher, and quite clearly tended towards a religious and ascetic mysticism very like Sufism.

Around Abraham gathered a circle of pietists who stressed the fulfilment of the divine commandments in complete purity. This pietistic tendency had certainly already existed, but the fact that Abraham ben Maimonides participated in it greatly enhanced its importance.

Abraham ben Maimonides often quotes *Abraham he-Ḥasid* (the Pious), Abraham Ibn Abī r-Rabī'a, who was his contemporary, as well as his brother Joseph, one of the leading figures of the pietist movement. Joseph's work has survived only in fragmentary form, but he exercised considerable influence and his brother Abraham refers to him as 'our Master in the Path of the Lord'.

The asceticism displayed by Abraham ben Maimonides and his circle of believers is distinguished from Islamic Sufism on certain points, but remains akin to it: the Muslim texts were read by Jews. A text by Al-Ḥallāj written in Hebrew characters was found in the Cairo Genizah, and other medieval copies in Hebrew script of Al-Ḥallāj, Suhrawardi, and others, are evidence of the interest that Muslim ascetic thought aroused in Jewish circles.

Abraham ben Maimonides himself remarks: 'Do not regard as unseemly our comparison of that to the behaviour of the Sufis, for the latter imitate the prophets (of Israel) and walk in their footsteps, not the prophets in theirs' (*Kifāyat al-ābidin* II, p. 320, trans. P. Fenton in *The Treatise of the Pool*, p. 8).

Abraham exploited the power conferred on him by his position as head of the community in Egypt to transform pietism into a popular movement. With this end in view, he tried to impose on the congregations certain religious customs that had been abandoned centuries ago, and he did not oppose the adoption of other customs clearly borrowed from the Muslims. His principal work, *Kifāyat al-'ābidin* (*A comprehensive Guide for The Servants of God*) is a sort of compendium of moral theology, of which only fragments survive. It seems that the book was designed as a commentary on the phrase of Simon the Just (*Pirkei Avot* I, 2): 'The world rests on three things: the Torah, the divine cult and the charity of the pious.'

Of the four books of this treatise, the first three, it seems, dealt with the commandments concerned with external acts, which were to be accomplished 'in the fear of God'. Book IV returns to these commandments and indicates the mental attitude, the intention of the heart, that should preside at the fulfilment of the commandments 'for the love of God'. The three pillars of the world are interpreted not only as knowledge, the relations between man and God, and relations between men, but as the 'pious' mode of life that endows these virtues with their true importance, in this following Maimonides in the *Eight Chapters*: 'There is no greater virtue than piety, for it leads to prophecy.'

While the fear of God is linked to acts and to the fulfilment of the commandments, the love of God instils into this fulfilment a living fervour, an intensity, which can only be the result of correct opinions and of virtues imparted by the *Torah*. The esoteric meaning of the Scriptures is thus clearly bound to the moral and intellectual qualities of the pious, entirely directed towards the service of God. The purpose of human existence is knowledge and ecstatic vision. It does not seem, however, that Abraham believed in the possibility of a mystical union with the divinity, in this lower world; in any case, there is no mention of this in the parts of the work that have survived.

Simon the Just's phrase, understood in this light, refers not to 'this world' but to 'the world to come', eternal life, which can only be attained by the knowledge and fulfilment of the commandments in the love of God. Baḥya ben Joseph Ibn Paquda was the most illustrious representative of this form of ascetic piety in Judaism. In the case of Abraham himself the philosophical bases of his thinking seem to have been Maimonidean, but these philosophical foundations were to a great extent integrated into an entirely religious system.

Here, at the heart of the pietist movement, we find the concept of particular virtue redounding to the benefit of Israel, which we have already found in Nethanel al-Fayyumi, Abraham bar Ḥiyya and Judah Halevi:

The Torah was revealed through the Chosen Apostle who was the élite (*ṣafwa*) of the descendants of Abraham, His beloved, and the result of the purest lineage: Abraham, Isaac, Jacob, Levi, Qehat, 'Amram and then Moses, all of whom had been instruments of the Divine Word (*ḥuṣṣil bihim al-amr al-ilāhī*). So that through the Torah which was revealed to him, they may become prophets, and he that does not attain to prophecy shall draw nigh to its state through commendable deeds.

In Moses' days all Israel were set aside for the Path of proximity to God . . . indeed it was intended that they all become prophets as Scripture states 'And ye shall be unto me (a Kingdom of priests and a holy nation)'. (Ex. XIX: 6) Likewise we were promised (for the future) 'Ye shall be named the priests of the Lord' (Is. LXI: 6). They should have received all the precepts in the same way as they received the Ten Commandments at Sinai, were it not for their feebleness and incapacity to continue to receive in this manner, as Moses said 'Would that all the Lord's people were prophets' (Num. XI: 29).

(Anonymous pietist text, trans. P. Fenton in *The Treatise of the Pool*, pp. 9–10)

Abraham ben Maimonides states: 'Communion is of two sorts, intellectual ('*ilmī*) and traditional (*šar'ī*). The latter can be attained either in the world to come or in this world. The latter type of communion comes about in three ways, either through piety (*ṣalāḥ*), Saintship (*wilāya*) or Prophecy (*nubuwwa*)' (trans. P. Fenton in 'Some Judeo-Arabic Fragments', p. 57, note 42).

The way that leads to communion with God is not the knowledge of the external world and its laws; it is inner solitude and spiritual progress on a pattern known only to the initiated.

Also do the Sufis of Islam practice solitude in dark places and isolate themselves in them until the sensitive part of the soul becomes atrophied so that it is not even able to see the light. This, however, requires strong inner illumination wherewith the soul would be preoccupied so as not be pained over the external darkness.

Now this path is the last of the elevated paths and it is contiguous with the [mystic] reunion [with God], external solitude thereof being a journey, and the internal [solitude] being in its beginning a journey and at its end a reunion, 'and there are examples for all of them'.

Note: These elevated paths are associated with each other, as, for example, humility is associated with gentleness, and mercy with generosity, and contentedness with abstinence and so forth. Now the course that unites one [with God] consists of travelling through all of them and traversing the [various] stages of every path and reaching its end, or to traverse most of its stages until one approaches its end.

Second Note: These paths also have an order and some of them precede the others in order.

Third Note: What thou must know and grasp is that the useful course that leads to true union [with God] generally has it as its condition that it be [pursued] under the direction of a person who communes [with God].

(Trans. S. Rosenblatt, *The High Ways to Perfection of Abraham Maimonides*, II, pp. 419–23)

The difference in inspiration, if we compare Abraham with his father, is also revealed by the authors quoted. In the *Guide* Maimonides cites only Greek and Arabic writers (except for 'one of the Geonim', most probably Saadiah, whom he refutes). Abraham, on the contrary, refers only to Jewish authors, except, once, for Galen.

While his answers to questions of rabbinical law are always a model of exactness and brevity, in his long pietistic work Abraham often repeats himself and tends to digress. G. D. Cohen sees this as a literary procedure. The work is addressed to all the faithful, by no means only to the élite. Perhaps Abraham believed that the Day of the Messiah was approaching and that the Jewish people should purify their conduct in view of the Day of Deliverance. Cohen remarks that in his *Letter from the Yemen* Maimonides refers to a family tradition fixing the return of the gift of prophecy among the Jews in 1210 or 1216. It is possible that Abraham considered it his duty as head of the community to educate the people towards piety, which leads to prophecy.

One of Abraham ben Maimonides' sons, Obadyā, continued in the way traced by his father, as is demonstrated by his work *Al-Maqāla al-Ḥawḍiyya* (*The Treatise of the Pool*), which has recently been edited and translated by P. Fenton. This involvement of Maimonides' family in the pietist movement probably led to the attribution to Maimonides himself of a short treatise in two chapters written in Arabic and translated into Hebrew under the title *Perakim behaslaḥa* (*Chapters on Beatitude*). The influence of the *Quaestiones de anima* is felt, and Ibn Ṭufayl is cited (a Spanish Arab philosopher of the twelfth century, author of the well-known philosophical romance *Hayy Ibn Yaqzan*). It seems that of the pietist works only this little dissertation was translated into Hebrew, but it did not have much impact. This whole movement, in fact, is characterized by its restriction to the Arab world.

Another work, by *an unknown author*, has been preserved only in Arabic. It seems to have been written after the fourteenth century, and has been published by F. Rosenthal. Like Baḥya and Abraham ben Maimonides before him, the writer associates the various stages in the ascent towards God with a specific sentence (Bab. *Avodah Zarah* 20b and *Mishnah Sota* IX, 14), which presents a number of variants.

One should not indulge in such thoughts by day as might lead to uncleanliness by night. Hence R. Phinehas b. Jair said: Study leads to precision, precision leads to zeal, zeal leads to cleanliness, cleanliness leads to restraint, restraint leads to purity, purity leads to holiness, holiness leads to meekness, meekness leads to fear of sin, fear of sin leads to saintliness, saintliness leads to the [possession of the] holy spirit, the holy spirit leads to life eternal [lit. resurrection of the soul].

We don't find another Jewish philosopher in Islamic countries until the fifteenth century in Yemen. The true successors of Maimonides are to be found in the Christian world of the West, where a whole class of Jewish society embraced the 'philosophical faith'.

Provence

The Hebrew translation of the *Guide of the Perplexed* was a revelation to the cultivated Jews of Provence. Suddenly all the biblical passages that seemed to go counter to reason became clear and rational. The effect was dazzling. Maimonides was the renowned master of rabbinical science, he was recognized as the spiritual head of Judaism, and here, with the *Guide of the Perplexed*, he proved himself a fully-fledged philosopher, expounding the true science, that of Aristotle, and demonstrating that true Judaism was a religion that encouraged this science. In one generation, Maimonidean philosophy became a doctrine accepted by a large section of cultivated people.

The social position of the Jews in Provence and Catalonia lent itself admirably to this flowering of philosophy. In Spain in the eleventh and twelfth centuries philosophers usually belonged to the aristocracy; only wealthy families could allow their children the long period of education essential to the acquisition of the sciences. Twelfth- and thirteenth-century Provence and Catalonia provided the Jews, as well as the other inhabitants, with the material ease indispensable to the flourishing of culture, and, with the renewal of urban life, ensured a context for the encounter of ideas in the process of the elaboration of philosophical thought.

These three factors: the existence of towns, material ease, and relaxed social relations between the various religious communities, were conducive to the growth of a middle class nurtured on science and philosophy.

Until this time the philosophers had been an élite, and whatever their importance in the history of ideas, they represented only a tiny proportion of the community of the faithful. From about 1200 the position changed radically, especially in Provence. Philosophers were not only numerous in the Jewish community, they were also influential members of it. Philosophy was no longer a knowledge transmitted from master to pupil; it even became the subject of public sermons: in the face of the opposition voiced by certain of the faithful, Jacob Anatoli had to interrupt the series of philosophical homilies that he was giving in the synagogue on the Sabbath, but the mere fact that he had begun to pronounce them, with the consent of some members of the community, is a good indication of the public character of philosophical manifestations.

During the twelfth century both Christians and Provençal Jews living in the Christian milieu discovered the science that was transmitted from Spain, and also from southern Italy. While Spanish Jews read and wrote Arabic with perfect ease, the Jews of Provence usually did not know this language. The transmission of the sciences to these Jews in a Christian milieu was carried out by translators of Spanish origin, particularly the family of the Tibbonids. Almost all the authors whom I shall present in this section knew Arabic very well, and their translations, as well as the original works that they wrote in Hebrew, were intended for this cultivated audience, thus giving philosophy a 'sociological' dimension. Much more than the philosophy itself, it was this popular enthusiasm that was to provoke much heated debate and even quarrelling concerning philosophical studies.

The first of these translators was *Judah ben Saul Ibn Tibbon*. Like Maimonides, he was driven out of Spain by the Almohads' invasion; he settled at Lunel in about 1150. His first translation, in 1161, was of the *Introduction to the Duties of the Hearts by* Baḥya Ibn Paquda; then followed the *Kuzari* of Judah Halevi, the *Book of Doctrines and Beliefs* by Saadiah, Solomon Ibn Gabirol's book on psychology and two grammatical works. All these were by Jewish authors, and the translations were made at the request of members of the Lunel community. We may recall at this point that Maimonides' *Letter on Astrology* was written in answer to a question sent by persons living in Provence and the South of France.

Several generations of Tibbonids and their families and other later Provençal and Italian translators continued this enterprise, transmitting to the Jews almost the entire body of Greek science that had reached the Arabs through the great earlier translators from Greek into Arabic during the ninth to the eleventh centuries. This science was developed in Muslim scientific and philosophical works, and it was all this together that was translated into Hebrew, more or less at the same time that the Christian world in its turn received the same heritage. Jewish philosophical works are based principally on this Greco-Arabic philosophy, and the authorities constantly cited are Aristotle and Plato and their commentators, Alexander of Aphrodisias, Themistius, Al-Fārābī, Avicenna, Ibn Bājja, and, especially, Averroes, who occupied a predominant position in the structuring of Jewish thought.

Maimonides himself was transmitted to succeeding generations in the version of Samuel Ibn Tibbon. One particular result of this was that the concept of the possibility of union with the Active Intellect in this world, implicitly denied by Maimonides, except perhaps as regards Moses, was very commonly attributed to the *Guide*. Ibn Tibbon's translation of the *Guide* and of the *Letter on the Resurrection of the Dead* were accompanied by a *Lexicon* or *Glossary of Unusual Words to be found in the 'Guide'*. This established not only the terminology but also the meaning of the principal notions of traditional philosophy. A veritable 'school of thought', based on the *Guide of the Perplexed* and its official translator and commentator, Samuel Ibn Tibbon, flourished in Provence and Italy during the thirteenth century, providing the context for the work of Jacob Anatoli, brother-in-law of Samuel Ibn Tibbon, Moses ben Samuel his son, Moses ben Solomon of Salerno (author of an Italian–Hebrew philosophical glossary), Zerahiah Gracian and Hillel ben Samuel of Verona.

In addition to Maimonides and Averroes, the Provençal philosophers made abundant use of the biblical commentaries of Abraham Ibn Ezra. Transmitted by Ibn Ezra, neoplatonic ideas, accompanied by astrology, contributed towards softening and humanizing the thought of Averroes. During the thirteenth century astrology was universally accepted in Provence, although without as yet assuming the importance that we shall see ascribed to it at a later period.

The relations between Jewish philosophers and their Christian counterparts are much more difficult to define with any clarity. In the Islamic countries all children, whether Muslim, Jewish or Christian, were educated in Arabic, which was the general vernacular as well as the scholarly language. While educational institutions naturally differed according to the religion of teachers and pupils, Arabic culture, with the possible exception of law, and even there the separation was not entire, was common to all. In the Christian world conditions were different; the everyday language, Provençal, Castilian, Aragonese, or Italian, was only very rarely also the language of learning. Scientific works were written in Latin, and Latin was taught at Christian religious schools and universities, to which Jews were not admitted. Knowledge of Latin texts was therefore acquired by Jews privately. This attainment probably presented no major difficulty; the mother-tongue of such

Jewish scholars was one of the Romance languages, so that medieval Latin was certainly well within their reach, and learning the Latin alphabet was easy enough. Besides, there can be no doubt that oral exchanges of views took place between scholars of the two communities, exchanges that sometimes wore a polemical cast.

The intellectual atmosphere was more or less propitious to collaboration between scholars of different faiths; in Italy the social climate was always relaxed and barriers hardly existed between the exponents of various faiths. Groups of scholars, often collecting around a remarkable personality, were active in the pursuit of knowledge regardless of religious divisions. The most brilliant example is that of the court of Frederick II in South Italy and Sicily between 1225 and 1250. Frederick welcomed learned men of every nationality and every belief and I shall have occasion to speak of two of them, Jacob Anatoli (and his friend Michael Scott) and Judah ha-Cohen. At Toledo, in 1252–6, Alfonso X, author of the Alfonsine Tables, called on the abilities of several Jewish scholars, translators of Arabic into Spanish, such as 'Abraham', Isaac Ibn Sa'id and Judah ben Moses. Charles of Anjou, around 1279, seems to have commissioned the only known portrait of a Jewish medieval scholar (Paris, Bibl. nat. MS lat. 6912), that of his translator Faraj ben Salim (Moses ben Salem).[1] Robert of Anjou in Naples at the turn of the fourteenth century is another example: he employed Kalonymus ben Kalonymus and Shemariah of Crete. At Montpellier, then at Barcelona, around 1300, a group of Jewish and Christian doctors seems to have engaged in intense joint activity. Ermengard Blasius translated Jacob ben Makhir Ibn Tibbon's works on astronomy into Latin, with the aid of the author, and Estori ha-Parḥi, a relation of Jacob ben Makhir, translated a medical work by Ermengard Blasius into Hebrew. When Arnald of Villanova, closely related to Blasius and also a celebrated doctor, professor at the University of Montpellier, wrote his *Practica*, it was immediately translated into Hebrew.

Thus, one can understand what Jacob ben Makhir meant when he wrote to Solomon ben Adret during the dispute concerning philosophical studies:

We must demonstrate to the Gentiles our knowledge and our comprehension [of philosophy] so it cannot be said: They are devoid of all knowledge and all science. We must follow the ways of the Gentiles, of the most enlightened among them. They have translated scientific works into their various languages [according to two manuscripts: 'even if the propositions and the demonstrations run counter to their religion and their belief']. They respect the sciences and those who master them, and little do they care what belief they confess.

(*Minḥat Kenaot* (Pressburg, 1838), p. 85, trans. J. Schatzmiller)

This was at the beginning of the fourteenth century. In the thirteenth century, science, that is to say, Aristotelian science, reached Jewish scholars directly from the Arabic without passing through Latin intermediaries, and Jewish philosophers were conscious of possessing texts close to the original.

[1] See Bibliography, p. 433.

Nevertheless, at the very beginning of the thirteenth century, Samuel Ibn Tibbon was already writing: 'I have seen that the true sciences are widespread in the countries where I live [the Christian countries], far, far more than in the Muslim countries' (*Ma'amar Yikkawu ha-mayim*, p. 175). According to J. Sermoneta, Samuel Ibn Tibbon organized the introductions to his works on the model, traditional in Latin literature, of the *accessus ad auctores*.

However, knowledge of Latin was not very current, as can be seen from Moses Ibn Tibbon's introduction to his translation of the *Viaticum* of Al-Gezzar:

It is not because I believe myself expert in the two languages [Arabic and Hebrew] or in order to diminish the merit of a translator who preceded me that I decided to translate the excellent book of Al-Gezzar, it is simply because I have seen that the Latin translator [Constantine the African] has in some cases added [to it], and in others abridged it, as seemed good to him. Even less do I blame the man who translated the Latin into Hebrew; but, as he has preserved the Latin names of the diseases and the remedies, his translation can be of no use to those who are not familiar with the technical terms of the Latin language.

(Oxford, Bodleian Library, MS Poc. 353 (Cat. Neubauer 2111), fol. 1r)

It seems then that until the middle of the thirteenth century the Jews, with the possible exception of Samuel Ibn Tibbon and Jacob Anatoli, did not make great use of Christian texts; for them Latin Aristotelianism was still taking shape; it had not yet imposed itself as a way of thought independent of its sources and original in its development. From the second half of the thirteenth century Jewish Provençal philosophers began to be interested in Christian thought and its problematics. However, in Provence throughout the century, the two philosophies, Jewish and Christian, followed parallel but rarely converging roads.

Apart from the acquisition of the sciences, the Jewish philosophers, assumed the task of the philosophical explanation of the traditional texts, a procedure of which the foundations had been laid by Maimonides in the *Guide of the Perplexed*. The philosophical exegesis of the Bible confirmed the Jews in their conviction that philosophy leading to salvation was the profound sense of the divine revelation as of the rabbinical tradition. In its origins philosophy was Jewish; the Greeks gave back a heritage that had been lost during the persecutions and was restored in the guise of the literal text. The Law, the *Torah*, is divine, for, contrary to the human laws that only regulate political relationships, it rouses the attention of the intelligent man and directs him towards philosophy. The explication of the *aggadot* of the Talmud was added to that of the Bible. It seems in fact that Christian polemics played an important part in awakening a recognition of the necessity of rehabilitating the *aggadot*.

Let us recall that both Talmuds, the Babylonian and the Palestinian, are a commentary on the *Mishnah*, that is, the account of the discussions, chiefly juridical in nature, on the observance of the commandments of the Written and the Oral Law. The legalistic section of the Talmud (*halakhah*) is complemented by a non-legalistic part (*aggadah*), varying in length; it occupies much more space in the Babylonian than in the Palestinian Talmud. The *aggadah* consists of historical narratives, wisdom maxims, popular sayings, astrology, folk-lore, stories of miracles, etc. The rabbis gave free rein to their imagination, and the *aggadah* often defies what the medieval philosophers considered to be 'good sense' and 'wisdom'. Besides the talmudic *aggadot* there were also the *midrashim*, homilies on biblical verses, of ancient content and regarded as traditional texts. The crude anthropomorphism of some passages was particularly disturbing. Midrashic anthropomorphism was criticized by the Karaites and the Muslims, and Saadiah Gaon wrote a commentary on the *Book of Creation*, one of the purposes of which was to show that it should not be understood in the literal sense. Maimonides in the *Guide* demonstrated that a certain number of *aggadot* contained a philosophical meaning, deliberately concealed by the rabbis of the Talmud, for they could not expound truths that the general public was not capable of understanding, and from which conclusions dangerous to society might be drawn. The rabbis of the Talmud were philosophers and behaved as philosophers should: they revealed the truth only to those worthy of knowing it. Maimonides had formed the intention of systematically expounding (with the requisite caution) the *aggadot* of the Talmud; this great undertaking, which he abandoned, was to be pursued in Provence during the thirteenth century.

The acquisition of the sciences and the explanation of traditional texts were the two activities in which Jewish scholars engaged in Provence; the first of them, at the outset of the thirteenth century, was Samuel Ibn Tibbon.

SAMUEL BEN JUDAH IBN TIBBON

Samuel was perhaps born at Lunel, where he lived; but he also lived in Arles, Marseilles, Toledo, Barcelona and, it seems, spent a short time in Alexandria. The year of his birth is not known, but he is known to have died *ca.* 1232.

As a youth he rather disappointed his father, who found that he did not take enough interest in his studies, and wrote a particularly vivid and lively moral testament for his edification.

All Samuel's translations were made from Arabic. The first was almost certainly Galen's *Ars Parva*, with an Arabic commentary, which he finished in 1199; Aristotle's *Meteorologica* followed, with various notes most probably drawn from the commentaries of Alexander of Aphrodisias. After this he is said to have translated the *Alexander Romance*, again from the Arabic. This work, based on Greek texts and read in all languages during the Middle Ages, enjoyed four known Hebrew translations.

Of Maimonides' works he translated the *Guide of the Perplexed* (in 1204);

the *Letter on the Resurrection of the Dead*; and the introductions, that is, the philosophical parts, of the *Commentary on the Mishnah*. In 1213, he composed a *Glossary of Unusual Words to be found in the Guide*, which he finished on the boat on his return from Alexandria, 'near Carthagena', that is, one and a half days' journey from Tunis. As I have said, his translations and his *Glossary* established the basis of the 'traditional' exegesis of Maimonides. His correspondence with the Master, and the tone of esteem and affection discernable in Maimonides' replies, bestowed on Samuel the character of 'official' exegete and head of a school, to whom everybody deferred. His original works may be regarded as representing commentaries on ambiguous or difficult passages in Maimonides.

Apart from some allegorical explanations of biblical passages, scattered in various manuscripts, the following have been preserved: *Perush Kohelet* (*Commentary on Ecclesiastes*), not yet published; *Ma'amar Yikkawu ha-Mayim* (*Let the waters be gathered*), a treatise on Genesis 1:9; and a *Letter on Providence* addressed to Maimonides. The chief intention of *Let the waters be gathered* is to resolve a problem in physics. According to Aristotelian science, the four elements should be placed in their natural positions: earth, then water, then air, then fire. However in Genesis God says 'Let the waters under the heaven be gathered together unto one place, and let the dry land appear'; the natural order of the elements is thus disturbed, since the earth would now find itself contiguous to the air. By what power and in what manner was this natural order of things transformed so that man could live in it? Why did God transform a natural order that He had already created? According to the philosophers, or at least some of them, this was a false problem. The disposition of the elements was always such as we know it now, the earth was always in contact with the air and the water existed in the form of clouds, for it is this very disposition of the four elements and their transformation from one into the other that is the basis of the life of plants, animals and men. For these philosophers the question does not arise, for the belief that everything has to have a beginning is a simple effect of the imagination. Samuel Ibn Tibbon compares this attitude to that of the rabbis, who prohibit questions concerning the beginning or the end of the world.

For Samuel, there can be no doubt that the world was not created in time and *ex nihilo*, and, if Moses does not say so quite explicitly this is because the primary intention of the *Torah* is to be useful to the common people, that is, to provide a political law, and not to inform and awaken the wise. To be sure, the truth is, in a way, hidden in the *Torah*, but Moses, deliberately, presented to the ignorant people notions that suited the understanding that was theirs at that moment of history, and these notions were at some remove from the truth.

Contrary to Maimonides, Samuel Ibn Tibbon affirms the necessity of unveiling the philosophical allusions of the *Torah*, for Jews who understand them are few, with the result that they are less acquainted with the true sciences than are the Christians or the Muslims. It is clear that the dangers involved in the revelation of the secrets are of slight significance in the face of the necessity of introducing Jewish savants to knowledge. This knowledge, which had been suppressed since the age of the prophets and the sages, had, in effect, become the prerogative of other peoples, who mocked the ignorance of the Jews and declared that only the letter and not the spirit of the prophets' words had remained in their possession.

The progressive revelation of the verities is another reason for clearly stating the philosophical teachings. This progress of humanity towards more perfect knowledge explains why David and Solomon taught the work of creation more explicitly than Moses. Of course Moses knew it as well as they; but the people, for whom the *Torah* was intended, had no conception of an immaterial God, and Moses could not mention any being superior to the sky and the stars. In the story of Genesis, therefore, nothing is said of the separate intellects who are the necessary intermediaries between God, entirely incorporeal, and the spheres, already material. On the other hand, the four last verses of Psalm 104 (103), as well as two passages of the *aggadah* describe the angelic world and thus complement Moses' Genesis.

After long discussions showing that rabbinical opinion in the *aggadah* is more or less unanimous on the fundamental questions, Samuel asks himself what is in fact the difference between the opinions of the philosophers and those of the rabbis. They all agree in admitting that the separate intellects precede the world as cause, but the philosophers attribute to these separate intellects an existence co-eternal with God, and also accord eternity to the universe that arises from these intellects. The rabbis, who represent the religious tradition, affirm that the creation of the sublunary world took place in time, and that the separate intellects and matter existed before the world of the four elements.

This matter, pre-existing creation, is considered as eternal by Samuel Ibn Tibbon, as the reference to Abraham Ibn Ezra shows. As for the world of the intellects, an eternal world, it holds its existence from God. Everything therefore flows from God, true cause of the celestial world and the sublunary world, which He 'created' from eternal matter through the instrumentality of the separate intellects. What then does the word 'creation' mean for our author?

For him the third verse of Genesis, which mentions the light, precedes in the order of creation the two first verses, which refer to the earth and the heavens. Before creation, and before God said 'Let there be light!', the heavens already existed as we know them, and they underwent no change during the creative act. However, the sublunary world, that is, the four elements, were in their 'natural' order (*tohu va-bohu*) until God 'transformed' them, placed them in their present order, 'created' them. Light, that is the world of the intellects, had existed for all eternity. 'Creation', in this case, meant that light, or rather the divine emanation transmitted by the intellects, was strengthened, according to the divine wisdom, and that the spheres 'reinforced' their light, which is terrestrial, so that the relations between the elements were modified and life appeared and continues on the earth.

The action of light, striking the abyss, provoked the emergence of mountains and the hollowing of valleys where water gathered. This action of the stars on the elements continues, and maintains the waters in the seas and the oceans, allowing the earth to raise itself above the waters and the life of all the animals to be perpetuated; there is thus a continual creation in the sense that the emanation of God through the intellects and the spheres continues to be the cause of life on earth.

The fact nevertheless remains that 'something' changed, even if there was no change in God; when, on God's order, the light became stronger. It is clear that this very laborious solution that Samuel Ibn Tibbon drew from Avicenna could not satisfy the philosophers, for it nevertheless implied a change in God, either in His wisdom or in His emanation. It is equally clear that believers in creation *ex nihilo* were even less satisfied; and perhaps Samuel himself was not altogether happy with his solution.

In chapter 6 Samuel discusses prophetic visions. The vision of Isaiah 6 describes the whole of creation; each word represents one of the entities of the celestial and terrestrial worlds, and the interaction of these entities on each other. 'The Lord sitting upon a throne' – the divine existence, which is totally firm and assured, does not depend on any other. The 'Throne' is the world of the spheres and reveals to us the existence of the separate intellects; for the spheres, being limited by their corporeality, cannot by themselves be endowed with eternal movement; this movement is given to them by the separate intellects, which, being incorporeal, are eternal, and these incorporeal and eternal beings prove the existence of God. We thus find here, in a different form, the Aristotelian proof of the existence of God by the necessity of a Prime Mover.

Following the rabbinical tradition, Samuel declares that the visions of Isaiah 6 and Ezekiel 1 describe the same celestial and terrestrial beings, each in a different way; Isaiah wrote his vision beginning with the upper point, the ultimate stage of human perfection, while Ezekiel and Jacob began from our world, to rise step by step to the heavens. Isaiah, like Ezekiel and Jacob, wanted to show how man, ensnared in this world, may, by acquiring knowledge of the divine work, ascend to God, but they placed the beings that compose creation in a different order. The ladder of ascension where all men, prophets or philosophers, have their place, has a number of degrees, but the intellectual process that leads man to God always starts from the terrestrial world. Prophet and philosopher are not different in this aspect: both know God through his works, and they climb Jacob's ladder, the degrees of knowledge, the tree of life; the difference between them lies in another function: the prophets have a political role that the philosophers do not exercise; and here again one recognizes the influence of Averroes joined to that of Maimonides.

Another problem which seriously preoccupied Samuel Ibn Tibbon and which he discusses at length in the treatise *Let the waters be gathered* is that of providence. It had engaged his attention since he had translated the third book of the *Guide*. Chapters 17 and 18 give a definition of providence to which Samuel Ibn Tibbon entirely subscribes; however, chapter 51 seems to contradict the two earlier chapters; and it is not so much the problem itself that exercises our author as this contradiction in the text. Samuel Ibn Tibbon wrote to Maimonides on this subject, apparently in 1199 (but the date is not certain). The letter probably arrived after Maimonides' death for we know of no answer from him and evidently Samuel did not receive one.

Divine providence works in various ways, according to Samuel Ibn Tibbon, who here follows the Maimonides of the first chapters of the third book of the *Guide*.

A general providence covers all living beings; it affects the species and not the individual and is identified with the divine emanation that bestows existence. It comprehends the laws of the sublunary world, which are regulated by the movements of the spheres, and are necessary, since they rule the natural things, that is, bodies. This natural providence is attached to the world of generation and corruption, it is thus an 'imaginary' providence bound to the 'nothingness' that is the body. Man himself is part body and part soul; as long as his soul is not purified of every trace of matter, as long as his intellective faculty has not passed from potentiality to actuality, it cannot participate in the true providence, that which comes with the intellect, that which is true because it participates in eternity. There is an essential difference between the first and the last providences; both are necessary, but the second more than the first, for it belongs to the very essence of the soul.

Apart from these two sorts of providence, both natural on different planes of being, one may conceive of a miraculous providence. This is the one that Maimonides speaks of in chapter 51 of the third book of the *Guide*, or when he describes the protection accorded to the sages against all 'bodily ills, both the general one and those that concern one particular rather than another so that neither those that are consequent upon the nature of being, nor those that are due to the plotting of man would occur' (*Guide*, p. 626).

But, says Samuel, if God changes the laws of nature in favour of the sage who has attained the degree of the Active Intellect in order to save his body or his possessions from the corruption that is of the nature of material things, there are no laws of nature. Besides, what is the body and what are material possessions that God should abase Himself to preserve them? This is a religious, not a philosophical position. Samuel Ibn Tibbon concludes therefore that chapter 51 of Book III of the *Guide* was composed by Maimonides to satisfy the common people, so that the truth of providence should not be doubted.

The three books of Solomon, Ecclesiastes, Proverbs and the Song of Songs play a special role in Ibn Tibbon's exegesis. In his introduction to the *Commentary on Ecclesiastes*, Samuel relates that he had written to Maimonides to ask him to expound the three books of Solomon. The letter arrived, it seems, after Maimonides' death and it remained for the Tibbonids to accomplish this project.

These three books obviously lend themselves to philosophical exegesis, and complement each other; according to Samuel Ibn Tibbon, they expound the problem of the union of the human soul and the Active Intellect.

Solomon composed Ecclesiastes according to the views of the philosophers and of study by demonstration, and not according to his own belief. Thus one finds conflicting opinions on the persistence of the soul after the death of the body and its conjunction with the Active Intellect. Samuel Ibn Tibbon added to his *Commentary* a translation of three short treatises by Averroes on the hylic intellect. The Proverbs deal with matter, and show that ethics allows one to acquire a 'good' matter, which will not trouble the intellect by superfluous desires. The Song of Songs celebrates the union of the human intellect with its lover, the Active Intellect. The Book of Proverbs was further explicated in the work of Jacob Anatoli, Samuel's son-in-law, and the Song of Songs by his son Moses.

Among the erudite scholars attracted to the circle of the Tibbonids must be cited David Kimhi.

David ben Joseph Kimhi (1160?–1235?) is the very type of the average Provençal philosopher. He was also a remarkable exegete. David's father, Joseph Kimhi, was a celebrated grammarian, exegete, translator and polemicist, who emigrated to Narbonne from Spain during the Almohad persecutions. His son wrote, apart from works on grammar, a biblical commentary (on Genesis, the Prophetic Books, Psalms, Chronicles), the renown of which almost equals that of the commentaries of Rashi and Abraham Ibn Ezra. Very clear and readable, his exegesis tends to give a philosophical explanation of the text, without however neglecting homiletic explanations, which are quite distinct from the literal sense. Only two of his commentaries are philosophical, a commentary on the Story of Creation (Genesis) and another on the Story of the Chariot (the first chapter of Ezekiel), and both are more or less an amplification of passages of the *Guide of the Perplexed*.

The philosophical interests of David Kimhi were more varied than may appear at first sight, for it was he who urged Abraham Ibn Hasdai to translate Isaac Israeli's *Book of the Elements*. At all events, although he sometimes quotes the Jewish neoplatonists and Aristotle, his thinking faithfully follows Maimonides, and, on many points, Ibn Ezra.

THE DISPUTE CONCERNING PHILOSOPHICAL STUDIES

David Kimhi was not an original philosopher, but he played a considerable part in the dispute surrounding philosophical studies that continued throughout the thirteenth century. To begin with, the agitation against Maimonidean philosophy, launched by Meir ben Todros Abulafia of Toledo in about 1202, revolved about the resurrection of the dead, the subject of the controversy instigated by Samuel ben Ali during Maimonides' lifetime. Meir Abulafia declared:

(1) That the Bible and the Talmud teach corporeal resurrection;

(2) That this resurrection will take place in the hereafter, so that both soul and body will be found there;

(3) That retribution in the hereafter includes both body and soul;

(4) That death will be abolished in the hereafter.

In fact, the real danger that Maimonides' philosophy represented for religion had been recognized at the very beginning of the thirteenth century and admirably expounded by Nahmanides in his commentary on the biblical narrative of the appearance of the angels to Abraham under the oaks of Mamre (Genesis 18: 1).

And they did eat: (Gen. 18: 8) they appeared to be eating.

In the book Moreh Nebuchim it is said that this portion of Scripture consists of a general statement followed by a detailed description. Thus Scripture first says that the Eternal appeared to Abraham in the form of prophetic visions, and then explains in what manner this vision took place, namely, that he [Abraham] lifted up his eyes in the vision, *and lo, three men stood by him*, [Genesis 18: 2] *and he said, if now I have found favor in thy eyes.* [18: 8]. This is the account of what he said in the prophetic vision to one of them, namely, their chief.

Now if in the vision there appeared to Abraham only men partaking of food, how then does Scripture say, *And the Eternal appeared to him*, as G–d did not appear to him in vision or thought? Such is not found with respect to all the prophecies. And according to his [Maimonides'] words, Sarah did not knead cakes, nor did Abraham prepare a bullock, and, also, Sarah did not laugh. It was all a vision! If so, this dream came *through a multitude of business*, [Ecclesiastes 5: 3] like dreams of falsehood, for what is the purpose of showing him all this! Similarly did the author of the Moreh Nebuchim say in the case of the verse, *And a man wrestled with him*, [Genesis 32: 25] that it was all a prophetic vision. But if this be the case, I do not know why Jacob limped on his thigh when he awoke! And why did Jacob say, *For I have seen an angel face to face, and my life is preserved?* [32: 30]. The prophets did not fear that they might die on account of having experienced prophetic visions. Jacob, moreover, had already seen a greater and more distinguished vision than this since many times, in prophetic visions, he had also seen the Revered Divinity. [28: 13] Now according to this author's opinion, he will find it necessary for the sake of consistency to say similarly in the affair of Lot that the angels did not come to his house, nor did he bake for them *unleavened bread and they did eat.* [19: 3] Rather, it was all a vision! But if Lot could ascend to the height of a prophetic vision, how did the wicked and sinful people of Sodom become prophets? Who told them that men had come into Lot's house? And if all these [i.e. the actions of the inhabitants of Sodom], were part of prophetic visions, then it follows that the account related in the verses, *And the angels hastened Lot, saying: Arise take thy wife . . . And he said, Escape for thy life . . . See, I have accepted thee*, [19: 17–21] as well as the entire chapter is but a vision, and if so Lot could have remained in Sodom! But the author of the Moreh Nebuchim thinks that the events took place of themselves, but the conversations relating to all matters were in a vision! But such words contradict Scripture. It is forbidden to listen to them, all the more to believe in them!

(*Commentary on the Torah.* Trans. and ed. C. B. Chavel. New York, 1971)

Nahmanides objects to the philosophical exegesis of visions chiefly because it explains the prophetic vision as a product of the prophet's imagination; it is not, it seems to me, a reaction to the fact that one can interpret the biblical narratives in different senses, for these senses are not mutually exclusive.

Christian exegesis saw four senses in the Bible, all valid: the historical, the allegorical, the moral and the anagogic, that is, the most profoundly symbolic sense, alluding to the divine world. The Kabbalists, and Nahmanides among them, did not hesitate to make constant use of the anagogic sense; as for the historical and moral senses, they are always found in the *midrashim*, where the allegorical and anagogic senses are also not lacking. Certainly, Jewish philosophers had never claimed that only the allegorical sense of the Bible was true; on the contrary, they sometimes added a fifth sense to the other four – the astrological. Nahmanides does not criticize the philosophers' methods, for the idea that the Bible contained the whole truth, that it had 'seventy visages', was accepted by all Jews. The inadmissible was that the literal sense of prophetic visions should be cancelled to the benefit of the philosophical sense, thus reducing events that had already taken place, and formed the foundation of the very history of the Jewish people, to the narrative of a psychological experience.

Nahmanides' critique goes much further than that of Meir ben Todros Abulafia, but it was Abulafia's letters to Maimonides and afterwards to the 'Sages of Lunel' and the rabbis of the North of France that provoked the dispute among the communities. Perhaps this correspondence like other critiques would have remained on the level of the controversies frequent at the period, were it not for the zeal of Solomon ben Abraham of Montpellier, a celebrated Talmudist and moralist. He objected to the explication of the Story of the Creation and the Story of the Chariot, for this expounding of the mysteries is forbidden by the Talmud. This was a direct attack on David Kimhi, whose biblical commentaries were known to everybody. Solomon ben Abraham's opposition did not stop at the overt allegorization of the Bible and the Talmud, it extended to science in general, both physics and metaphysics, and to the very principle of bringing science and revelation into harmony. For some of Maimonides' opponents, even the rejection of anthropomorphism was already an offence to tradition. Jacob Anatoli gives a vivid account of the sort of encounter that could take place between philosophers and antiphilosophers:

On the basis of this worthless view, it happened to me, Jacob son of Abba Mari son of Shimon son of Anatoli, of blessed memory, that one of the rabbis of my generation sharply attacked me several times for my studying occasionally in the Arabic language a little of the mathematical science, before the great sage, my father-in-law, R. Samuel, may his soul endure, son of the sage Judah Ibn Tibbon, a righteous man of blessed memory. When the point came that my attacker had distressed me with his words and pressed me, I answered him in kind, for I would not allow him to think me [comparable to] a vagabond or a gambler while engaged in such study.

(*Malmad*, fol. 99a, trans. M. L. Gordon. 'The Rationalism of Jacob Anatoli', p. 296)

To this intellectual reproach was added another that does not seem to be well-founded: the philosophers were said to have become lax in their observance of the commandments. No exact facts were cited, and this is a facile argument, too often found in this kind of controversy to be uncritically accepted.

It must be admitted that some passages go rather far; for instance, the following, taken from the *Malmad ha-Talmidim*, where Anatoli stresses that the intellectual aim of the *Torah* transcends all practical commandments:

For he who has not accepted the [practical] Torah, but fulfills this [the apprehension of the Divine Unity] properly, it is as if he has fulfilled the Torah; since the entire Torah was given to draw man [to the apprehension of the Unity]. Therefore it is as if the entire Torah was spoken in one statement ['*Anoki . . .*' – the Unity principle]. On this basis did they [the rabbis of the Talmud] say, 'Whosoever denies idolatry is as one who affirms the Torah in its entirety'; that is to say, for this is the purpose of the entire Torah, and to this end were all the detailed [practices] of the Torah directed.

M. L. Gordon adds: 'Anatoli is quick to qualify this concession. He notes immediately that whoever arrives at an apprehension of the theoretical truths, which he terms *avot* (principles), will not deny the imperative nature of ceremonial performance, the *toledot* (corollaries), which preserve those conceptions' (fol. 22a. *Ibid.* p. 335).

This kind of declaration was certainly very shocking to non-philosophers. Solomon ben Abraham sent his pupil Jonah ben Abraham Gerondi to the north of France in order to obtain the support of the various communities for the proclamation of a ban against the *Guide of the Perplexed* and the *Book of Knowledge*. He obtained it, but the Maimonideans published a counter-ban and sent David Kimḥi to Aragon and Castille to get the support of the Spanish communities, while the anti-Maimonideans turned to Nahmanides. Maimonides' detractors in Provence and Catalonia were as impassioned as his disciples, and the quarrel engulfed a great number of communities in northern France, Provence and Spain, and reached Egypt, where Abraham Maimonides took up his father's defence. The dispute abated to a certain extent as the result of a circumstance which was serious in itself and was to have even more serious consequences. Certain Jews denounced the *Guide of the Perplexed* as heretical, and it was burned in public by the Franciscans. David Kimḥi, then ill in Avila, and extremely bitter, accused Solomon ben Abraham of being responsible for this denunciation, but this does not seem very probable. This was the beginning of a distressing series of events, involving the Inquisition and the burning of Hebrew books. In 1240 the Talmud was declared heretical in Paris, after a controversy in which the renowned Yehiel ben Joseph participated, and it was burned by the wagon-load. There was no direct connection between the two events; however, the leaders of the communities were forced to recognize that the quarrel had gone too far, and that it was high time to put a stop to it. Solomon ben Abraham's partisans also developed bad consciences, and some of them retracted. The danger represented to the Jewish community by the Church's intrusion in its internal affairs was only too clear to all, whether partisans or adversaries of philosophy.

However, the profound antagonism between philosophers and anti-philosophers continued to make itself felt throughout the thirteenth century on the level of polemics and controversy, and was experienced again in social affairs at the beginning of the fourteenth century, as we shall see with Levi ben Abraham.

The agitation against the philosophers did not prevent them from pursuing their efforts in the two directions that I have described: the intensive study and popularization of the sciences, and the allegorization of the revealed texts. We sometimes find references to the dispute, but they are infrequent and it seems that the polemic surrounding it in no way hindered the philosophical movement.

JACOB BEN ABBA MARI ANATOLI

Anatoli, Samuel Ibn Tibbon's son-in-law and pupil, continued his work of translation and exegesis of the traditional texts. Under his father-in-law's direction, Anatoli studied mathematics and began to make scientific translations from Arabic into Hebrew of works on logic and astronomy. In 1231 he became a physician at the court of Emperor Frederick II of Hohenstaufen at Naples. There he met the famous Christian scholar Michael Scott, who was translating Arabic works into Latin, and it is possible that Anatoli collaborated in these translations.

His only original work is the *Malmad ha-talmidim* (*Incentive to the pupils*), a series of philosophical sermons arranged according to the pericope for each week of the year.[1] However, almost every one of these sermons begins with a verse from Proverbs, and the sermon is rather a commentary on this verse than the exegesis of the pericope. In this sense, Anatoli continued the exegetic study of the Solomonic literature that Samuel Ibn Tibbon had begun and Moses Ibn Tibbon had concluded with a commentary on the Song of Songs.

---

[1] The five Books of the Pentateuch are read during the public service throughout the liturgic year. The passage read during the week is called the pericope. In Jewish medieval literature the Pentateuch is always cited according to the pericope and not by chapter and verse, which is a later division.

Anatoli's philosophy is neutral, and it is difficult to find an original idea in it. He limited himself to the moral concepts of Proverbs, of the struggle of the intellect against the evil instinct and matter, which aspire to draw it towards death and perdition.

The interesting aspect of Anatoli is his access to the Christian world and his relationship with Michael Scott. The terms he uses in speaking of Scott offer evidence of a real affection, and he quotes some twenty exegeses of biblical verses by Scott that hardly differ from those that he himself proposes; if Anatoli himself had not told us so, it would be impossible to guess that these explications are by a Christian scholar. Nor do other exegeses, by Emperor Frederick himself, strike a wrong note in this work of Jewish philosophy. It seems clear that Jacob Anatoli fully participated in the philosophical and interdenominational atmosphere that prevailed at the Emperor's court, venturing on the open declaration that science and even biblical exegesis may be true or false and that this does not depend on the religion of the man who enunciates them.

In the effort to actualize his form, a man achieves the purpose desired of him over all the other lower species . . . Now, in [the possession of] this Divine image, all the peoples are equal, for we do not say that only Israel possesses soul, as those foolish gentles do, who say that Israel possesses no soul; for this only reflects their arrogance and folly. In truth, they are all possessed of [the Divine] image, for such was the will of God . . . A member of any of the peoples who engages in the study appropriate for him is greater than any of the sons of our people, who does not engage in that [study] appropriate for him. As R. Meir said: 'Whence know we that even a non-Jew who engages in the Torah is like the High Priest? For it is said, "[Ye shall therefore keep My statutes and Mine ordinances,] which if *a man* [emphasis mine] do, he shall live by them" (Lev. 18: 5). "Priest", "Levite" or "Israelite" were not said, but "man". Thus we learn that even a non-Jew who engages in the Torah is like the High Priest' (*Baba Kamma*, 38a). Now, the Talmud understands this passage with reference to [the non-Jew's] seven commandments; the same applies to the study of any wisdom necessary for establishing the essence [that is, theoretical truth] of these [seven] mitsvot or the essence of the mitsvot of the Torah.

(Malmad (fol. 25b). Ibid. p. 329)

Jacob Anatoli is the only Jew known to have carried out experiments in alchemy. This science, so often encountered in Arab and Christian texts, is almost unrepresented in medieval Hebrew writings. In Latin texts the genesis of the art is often attributed to Jews, especially Jewish women. The almost total absence of unequivocally alchemic texts in the Jewish tradition until the period of the Renaissance, when some Latin and Arabic texts began to be translated into Hebrew, is thus the more surprising. Was this field of natural science so clearly linked to magical practices that all Jews believed it preferable to abstain from its exercise? Or was the practice of the art too dangerous to be risked by a frequently endangered minority? No Hebrew text offers any information on this subject. However, both Joseph Caspi and Gersonides take as an illustration of a natural event the fact that, to the ignorant, the transformation of gold into another element, that is, alchemy (they write the word in Hebrew characters), appears miraculous, and it seems that they speak from personal experience. The miraculous explanation of natural science (that is, alchemy) is also made fun of in a poem by Isaac Alhadib, an astronomer, native of Castille (d. 1429), who sought refuge in Sicily at the end of the fourteenth century. In this context, it is interesting to note that Michael Scott gives a formula for bleaching tin in his *Alchemy*, and he affirms that he often succeeded in this operation, which had been taught him by 'Rabbi Jacob the Jew', almost certainly Jacob Anatoli.

I shall return to the court of Frederick II, but first I must discuss a recently rediscovered author.

Isaac ben Yedaya lived in the south of France, most probably at Narbonne, between 1250 and 1280. M. Saperstein has reconstituted what remains of his work, which had been confounded with that of Yedayah ha-Penini. He seems to have written a *Commentary on the Aggadot of the Babylonian Talmud* and another on the *Midrash Rabbah*. As with Anatoli, his exegesis does not have a very well-defined character, and his philosophy consists chiefly of the description of the combat that the intellect must wage against the evil of the forces of matter. Misogyny is perhaps more marked in him than in most of his contemporaries. In the Aristotelian world, matter, always feminine, is the great obstacle to the realization of the ultimate aim of human life, accession to the intellect, totally form, totally pure. Woman is the constant symbol of matter, she is nothingness, void, imperfection.

The best matter, like the best of women, is that which remains in its place and is satisfied with the role of instrument that has devolved on it, without attempting to seduce form and drag it towards perdition. In the exegetic philosophical vocabulary that was used from the thirteenth century onward, following the example of the *Guide* and of Samuel Ibn Tibbon, woman, matter, nothingness, etc., are interchangeable terms.

In Isaac ben Yedaya's exegeses contemporary history is used to illuminate the ancient texts. This tendency became stronger in Moses Ibn Tibbon and later again in Joseph Caspi.

MOSES BEN SAMUEL IBN TIBBON

Moses Ibn Tibbon continued the work of translation that had become traditional in his family. His translations were made between 1244 and 1274, most of them at Montpellier where he lived, but he also spent some time at Naples, in 1244–5, with his uncle Jacob Anatoli.

He translated numerous commentaries by Averroes (*The Great Commentaries*, *The Middle Commentaries*, *The Short Commentaries*), and also Al-Fārābī's *Book of Principles*, Themistius' Commentary on Book *Lamba* of Aristotle's *Metaphysics*, the *Book of Intellectual Circles* by Al-Batalyōsi (Ibn al-Sid of Badajoz, d. 1127), and many books on mathematics, astronomy and medicine.

His original works are chiefly commentaries: first a commentary on the Song of Songs, which completed the grand project of expounding the works of Solomon formed by his father; a commentary on the 'secrets' of Ibn Ezra's *Commentary*, surviving only in fragmentary form, and commentaries on the talmudic *aggadot* called the *Sefer Pea* (*Pea* = 86; the work had eighty-six paragraphs; *pea* is also the angle of the field left by reapers for the benefit of the poor), and a *Ma'amar ha-Tanninim* (*Treatise about the Great Fish*). A commentary on the number of the commandments in Ibn Gabirol and Maimonides, called *Perush ha-Azharot*, is of hardly any philosophical interest, and the *Olam Katan*, the *Microcosm*, is perhaps not by him.

His philosophical opinions do not differ from those of his father except on some points: miracle, providence, and the creation of the world. This is not, as has been suggested, because he was returning to the religious tradition, but rather that on these matters he adopted Ibn Ezra's opinions. His interest in Neoplatonism is revealed not only in his commentary *On the Secrets* of Ibn Ezra's *Commentary*, but by his translation of the *Book of Intellectual Circles* by Al-Batalyōsi.

Thus, according to Moses Ibn Tibbon, apart from the providence dispensed to mankind by the laws of nature and that which accompanies the emanation of the intellect, there also exists a 'divine' providence. Man, arrived at perfection, becomes attached to the Active Intellect and can grasp the laws of the divine influence over the angels, the spheres and the stars. With this knowledge of the laws of the world and of events to come, the sage, and this is the working of providence, may arm himself and those close to him against inauspicious events and advance to meet fortunate ones. The place of astrology, as Ibn Ezra had defined it, is evident in this system; however, astrology is only part of the much greater and wider knowledge that the prophet or sage, conjoined to the Active Intellect, receives by divine grace. Nevertheless Moses Ibn Tibbon does not say outright if he believes in the possibility of positive action on the unfolding of events or on the astral laws, otherwise than by prayer, the fulfilment of the commandments and the sustained intention of the heart and the spirit always turned towards God.

Miracles are invariably the work of God. All nature is subject to laws and regulated by the movement of the stars, and miracles can obviously not be the result of a change in the laws of nature. For Maimonides, citing the *Midrash*, God, at the moment of the Creation, 'had made an alliance', 'had concluded a pact', with certain things, so that at a given moment of history they would abandon their constant nature and be changed into their contrary; in any case, this change can take place in a number of ways and proves the divine Will. Moses Ibn Tibbon also defines another kind of miracle; there are things of which the nature is not absolutely fixed, but which act very frequently in a certain way, which is then called a 'law'; for instance, a mouse is generally born of a mouse. Very rarely, a mouse is born from dust; this spontaneous generation, statistically very rare, is extra-ordinary, and is therefore a kind of perfectly natural miracle.

Moses Ibn Tibbon's originality is expressed especially in his exegetic talents; he excels in finding a rationally acceptable meaning for the most abstruse anecdotes, and in doing so he gives a particularly lively glimpse of medieval life. First of all, he places biblical poetry, like the talmudic *aggadah*, in a rhetorical classification drawn from Aristotle. These *aggadot* have to be explained for reasons stated in the introduction to the *Sefer Pea*:

I have realized that the Gentiles have invented stratagems against us and have scrutinized our own traditions; they laugh at us and at our Ancient Holy Ones who composed the Talmud, because of the *aggadot* that seem to defy the intelligence and are impossible in nature, and nevertheless most of them have a meaning for him who comprehends their content. This has happened because our coreligionists, wise in their own eyes, have understood them in their literal sense as they have done for numerous scriptural allegories and allusions, for they have not distinguished the things [regulated] by nature from those made in a miraculous manner; they have not understood [what separates] the impossible from the possible, what must necessarily be affirmed concerning the Creator and what must be absolutely denied [of Him]. They did not know that the ancient sages, in all nations, had the habit of speaking of the sciences by allegory, parable and symbol, using the narrative of events, genealogies and the history of their personages' lives, and sentences of morality and wisdom, and among their words there are many that have an exoteric sense and an esoteric sense.   (Oxford, Bodleian Library, MS Opp. 241, fol. 11r–v)

One cannot find an esoteric sense for all the *aggadot*; their strangeness, as well as the erotic character, at first sight shocking, of the Song of Solomon, demands a different explanation, which Moses gives in his introduction to the *Commentary on the Song of Solomon*, as also in that to the *Sefer Pea*.

The Song of Songs was written by Solomon (who was not a prophet but a wise man inspired by the Holy Spirit), and its hidden esoteric sense is the love of the human intellect for the Active Intellect. The poetic 'dress' is designed to attract the heart towards this love. Not that there is any relation between the letter of the text and its profound sense; but, in poetry, as one reads in Aristotle,[1] the more inflated the comparisons, the exaggerations and the impossibilities, the more efficacious the poetry. This is one of the modes of sophistry, and the vilest. No sage would use it if it were not the best way of curing the ills of hearts deprived of wisdom, of modifying wicked habits, cheering the melancholic and strengthening the irresolute. One should not ask here for truth or falsehood, only the necessity of awakening the imagination of the hearer, and, by means of images, leading him to love something or to hate it.

This appeal to the imagination, with the intention of moral edification,

---

[1] On this Arabic aphorism, attributed to Aristotle, cf. D. R. Blumenthal, *The Commentary of R. Hōter*, p. 50, n. 4.

explains the character of the talmudic *aggadot*. There are several kinds. Some are simple stories that the rabbis told for recreation between hours of study; sometimes, there are many and different exegeses of the same verse; only one of these is important and the wise man must find it; sometimes, there is discourse, intended to reinforce a true belief or destroy a false one strongly rooted in men's hearts, with the help of miraculous tales or hyperbolical examples.

Some of these *aggadot* have an esoteric sense, and for each one it is necessary to establish carefully the exoteric as well as the esoteric sense. The stranger the anecdote and the more it defies common sense, the more fervently will the stupid man feel that he recognizes the greatness of God, the more clearly will the wise man know that the esoteric sense is important and should be zealously sought. Moses Ibn Tibbon found many different explications for the *aggadot* – moral, medical, historical, geographical, arithmetical.

The thirteenth century is a century of translations and of encyclopedias. Translators, apart from the Tibbonid family, were numerous: Solomon ben Moses of Melgueil, Abraham Ibn Ḥasdai, Solomon ben Ajjub of Beziers, and others. The great encyclopedias produced at this period are also translations, such as the *Midrash ha-Ḥokhmah* of Judah ben Solomon ha-Cohen, which will be discussed later, and the *De'ot ha-Filosofim* of Shem Tov ben Joseph Falaquera.

Before dealing with the great encyclopedias, I should mention a little work of scientific popularization, the *Ruaḥ Ḥen* (*Spirit of Grace*). It has been attributed to Judah Ibn Tibbon, Samuel Ibn Tibbon or Jacob Anatoli. But all these attributions are very unlikely; it can be said however that the unknown author most probably belonged to a Provençal or perhaps Italian philosophical milieu. The date of composition may be established round about 1240. It was much read and much copied, for eighty manuscripts survive, the most recent dated 1824.

In his introduction the author says that he proposes to offer 'some words useful in the comprehension of the *Guide of the Perplexed*. I have gone to much trouble and I have found some [of these words] on the lips of writers and in the mouths of books'. We thus see that he used ideas orally articulated as well as written texts. The written sources have not all been identified. The author cites Maimonides, Averroes, Avicenna and certainly some neoplatonic texts.

The originality of the text can be seen in the arrangement of the chapters: chapters 1 to 6 cover the material of the *De Anima*; chapters 7 and 8 more or less the material of *Generation and Corruption*. Chapter 9 discusses matter and form and traces the road from the composition of the separate intellects to the divine non-composition, that is, the Unity of God. Chapters 10 and 11 are devoted to the ten Aristotelian categories; it is possible that the division of this material into two chapters is artificial, for in at least one manuscript it does not occur. These chapters conclude with the demonstration of the non-corporeality of God.

The *Spirit of Grace* thus does not follow the order of the Aristotelian corpus. It begins with a study of the soul and the sources of knowledge; then follows a study of the material objects of knowledge, and, in metaphysics, only the notions of logic that allow the affirmation of the divine unity and non-corporeality, or rather the denial of multiplicity and corporeality in God. This plan evokes a passage in the *Makāsid al-falāsifa* (*Tendencies of the Philosophers*), where al-Ghazāli remarks that there are only two starting-points for attaining knowledge of God: knowledge of the human soul and knowledge of the visible world. The idea is of course not new, but it was much more current among Neoplatonists than among Aristotelians.

This little treatise is important in the history of ideas for it shows the level of the average man. It most probably represents the minimum scientific knowledge that everybody should possess to be considered well-informed, not ignorant and unlettered, and capable of reading the *Guide of the Perplexed*. Even today, it remains one of the best introductions to Jewish medieval philosophy.

GERSHOM BEN SOLOMON OF ARLES

Gershom apparently wrote only one book, the *Sha'ar ha-Shamayim* (*The Gate of the Heavens*). Much read and pirated in the Middle Ages, the book was published in Venice in 1547, but in very incomplete form, and again several times afterwards, but never in a critical edition.

It is a sort of compendium drawn from the best sources of knowledge; the author presents it in these terms:

I, Gershom son of Solomon – I have written this book, I have called it 'The Gate of Heaven' and I have divided it according to the hierarchy of the beings, and made to precede it an exposition on the four elements. The first generated and corruptible being is constituted by the vapours and their different species. Then comes the mineral and its different species, then the vegetable species. Then I shall speak of the nature of animals not endowed with reason and finally of the nature of the species man, which is the ultimate composition. *The second part* [deals with] astronomy. I have written the essential part of it after the writings of Al-Farghani. I have joined to it some [elements borrowed] from the book of the Almagest and from other books. At the end, I have transcribed many things due to the wise Avicenna as well as some borrowed from the book of the wise Averroes and from the book *De Coelo et Mundo*. *The third part* [deals with] divine science and the soul. There I have innovated nothing but I have borrowed from the information on matters of divine science from the book of the soul composed by the Master, Light of the Exile, our Master, Moses b. Maimon. I copied all these as they stood, fearing to be mistaken and to betray his intention. At the end of this part I have added a treatise by the learned Averroes dealing with metaphysics.

(*Sha'ar ha-Shamayim*, p. 5)

The interest of the work lies in its sources, which are many and varied. Gershom used texts in Hebrew only, but he reports 'the spoken words' of both Jewish and Christian scholars. The written sources allow us to date the book in the second half of the thirteenth century, and I incline, following A. Neubauer and F. S. Bodenheimer, to fix this date between 1242 and 1275.[1]

The oral communications are difficult to ascribe and the problem of technical terms in languages other than Hebrew also arises: Latin, Arabic and Provençal words are very freely used. It is possible that some were copied by Gershom from the respective model. Others, particularly those in Provençal, seem to have been introduced by Gershom himself, or else adapted by him to the Provençal tongue that he spoke in everyday life.

The three parts are very unequal in length. The first takes up almost the entire book – sixty-nine pages out of the eighty of the usual edition. It is based on Aristotle and his commentators and deals with the four elements, meteorology, minerals, plants, the various kinds of animals, the human organs, sleep and waking.

The second part, on astronomy, is very incompletely represented in the published editions, as J. Lay has shown in a recent study. Apart from the *Elements of Astronomy* by *Al-Farghani* in Jacob Anatoli's translation, which the author cites in the introduction, he uses Averroes, Ptolemy (*Almagest* and *Mathematical Composition*), the *Introduction to Astronomy* by Geminus, 'Homer', certain as yet unidentified authors, and a treatise called *De Coelo et Mundo*, attributed in the Middle Ages to Avicenna, which is in fact a compilation of extracts from a commentary by Themistius on Aristotle made by Hunayn Ibn Isḥāq. This seems to have been translated into Hebrew by Solomon ben Moses of Melgueil towards the middle of the thirteenth century, perhaps from the Latin. Apart from the Greeks and Arabs, Gershom cites Maimonides and most probably the *Microcosm* of Joseph Ibn Ẓaddik. The problem is complicated by the fact that our author also uses secondary sources; thus Al-Fārābī is quoted according to the text of the *Guide of the Perplexed*.

The third part, the metaphysics, is divided into three chapters. The first, devoted to the soul and its faculties, has the *Eight Chapters* and the *Guide* of Maimonides as source, as well as the *Spirit of Grace*, the little encyclopedia mentioned earlier, and finally Al-Fārābī. The second chapter is based to a great extent on a compilation, attributed to Dominicus Gundissalinus, of texts by Avicenna, Solomon Ibn Gabirol and Costa ben Luca on the *De Anima*. The third chapter is quite simply a transcription of a short treatise by Averroes on the *Possibility of Conjunction with the Active Intellect*, translated by Samuel Ibn Tibbon. Here divine science comes to a halt for our

---

[1] Other scholars, and lately J. Lay, have preferred to date it not earlier than 1300, affirming that our author used a translation of Al-Fārābī revised by Yedaya ha-Penini, which I shall discuss only in the following chapter.

author; although he does indeed call union with the Active Intellect the 'Gate of Heaven'; and the book gives all the elements that permit everyone to reach it.

'This is no other than the House of God, and this is the Gate of Heaven.'

SHEM TOV BEN JOSEPH FALAQUERA

Falaquera has already been mentioned in connection with Solomon Ibn Gabirol; for his translation from the Arabic of excerpts from the *Fountain of Life* made possible the identification of Gabirol with the Latin author 'Avencebrol'.

Shem Tov ben Joseph Falaquera was born in northern Spain or Provence *ca.* 1225, and probably died *ca.* 1295. The Falaquera family was one of the richest and noblest of Tudela, but it seems that Shem Tov himself was quite poor and retiring; at all events he was not an important member of the community and intervened in public affairs only once, when he took the side of the philosophers during the anti-Maimonidean dispute. In his youth he was a poet and afterwards declared that he was renouncing poetry to devote himself to less frivolous pursuits; but this was perhaps only a figure of speech. His poetry is in contemporary taste, without further distinction. As a philosopher he was not original and did not wish to be. His numerous works often consist of excerpts from Arabic treatises, which he translated into Hebrew, rather than personal compositions. Thus, he translated and quoted a number of neoplatonic texts, including the *Book of the Five Substances* by Pseudo-Empedocles, especially in his two little encyclopedias, *Reshit Ḥokhmah* (*The Beginning of Knowledge*) and *Sefer ha-Mevakesh* (*The Book of the Seeker*).

He also wrote five works on ethics, a work on psychology, and another that describes the various degrees of intellectual perfection, *Sefer ha-Ma'alot* (*The Book of Degrees*). In his *Iggeret ha-Vikuaḥ* (*Letters on Discussion*), he tries to distinguish between the respective domains of science and religion. The *Moreh ha-Moreh* (*Guide to the Guide*) is an explication of a certain number of passages in the *Guide of the Perplexed*; it was used by all the later commentators.

Only quotations have survived from a biblical commentary, and an exegesis of the *aggadot* of the Talmud has not been preserved. Shem Tov's most important work, the *De'ot ha-Filosofim* (*The Opinions of the Philosophers*), and a work on ethics are still in manuscript, but shortly to be published. The introduction to the *Opinions* very clearly describes Falaquera's intellectual position: it is known and admitted everywhere and by everyone, by the revealed Law as well as by the sages, that the supreme and veritable happiness is to know the Creator and to reach Him by thought, to the extent that the human intellect is capable of this. Further, the true sages agree in saying that this knowledge comes to man through the apprehension of the divine acts and their intellectual representation, for what is separated from matter can only be the object of human apprehension through its actions.

Man is presented with two roads: the prophetic and the scientific. He who receives the influx of the intellect and is a prophet will attain the truth without study and search; to other men only the scientific way is open, that which Maimonides has described in the *Guide of the Perplexed*; it consists of examining, scrutinizing and understanding everything that exists, in its details and in its ensemble, for there is no proof of the existence of God other than this reality existing before our eyes; but to draw from this material reality the proof of the existence of an intelligible being we must represent it to ourselves intellectually, according to its nature and its form, and this can only be done by the reading of books composed by non-Jewish philosophers, for, if Jews have written philosophical works, these have been lost during the centuries of exile.

In this quest for true knowledge, all that has been truly demonstrated and is in accordance with religious faith should be admitted by the scholar, whatever the source of the demonstration. And, citing Aristotle, Palaquera reaffirms the universalism of science and philosophy; one should pay attention only to what is said and not to him who says it; truth remains truth whatever the lips that pronounce it, whatever the religion of him who enunciates it.

Education and habits of thought learnt in childhood play an important part; there are evident verities that man tends to reject, without even examining them, for they seem strange and unusual to him; if at first sight these ideas appear to him to be the contrary of the truth, this is because they are the contrary to what he has learnt. Falaquera cites Porphyrius in urging his readers to examine every new idea with care and without prejudice; one should neither adopt it nor reject it precipitately, but investigate, with application and patience, whether this new idea is true or not, or if it is partly true and partly dubious, as is the case with most ideas.

All the explanations of the world that have been enunciated or all those that may yet be formulated should be meticulously studied, and one should choose that which is better than the others, that which corresponds best to the material reality and to the intelligible things drawn from this reality, even if in this explanation of the world some things remain hidden.

Continuing his introduction, Shem Tov shows that the word philosopher – lover of wisdom – designates the two human perfections, that of morality and that of the intellect. A philosopher is by definition the virtuous man who attains knowledge of the truth. In Jewish tradition such a man is called *ḥasid*, pious, and, as the ignorant can be virtuous but not achieve intellectual perfection, the ignorant cannot be pious.

The purpose of the *Opinions of the Philosophers* is twofold. The first is to bring together in convenient form certain philosophical ideas permitting a choice between truth and error. One should not accept everything that the philosophers have said; like Maimonides, Falaquera repeats that physical science is supported by proof and that few things in it are doubtful, while in metaphysics many questions remain unresolved, for real proofs are rare in this domain. His second intention is to give a good Hebrew translation of philosophical doctrines. The Hebrew translations were too often inexact, and the Arabs as well as the Jews sometimes attributed to various philosophers opinions that were not theirs.

In his retrospective treatment of the development of philosophy, which attained its perfection with Aristotle, Falaquera follows Al-Fārābī, Averroes and Maimonides; to be sure, he objects to the status of 'divine' accorded to Aristotle, preferring the less categorical opinion of Alexander of Aphrodisias, but he is forced to admit that his *Opinions of the Philosophers* is, in fact, an exposition of Aristotle's ideas as Averroes presents them. More precisely, at least as regards physics, Falaquera gives a sort of résumé of the *Middle Commentaries* of Averroes, which he sometimes enriches with citations drawn from the *Short Commentaries* or the *Great Commentaries*. Falaquera, as he himself says, confines himself to reporting the words of the philosophers. This role of spokesman of philosophy that he claims in the introduction to his encyclopedia is fully deserved, and the publication of the text will certainly provide further proof of the erudition of this modest scholar.

The themes touched on in this introduction are the same as those found in Falaquera's other works. One of them is often encountered, and it is worth our while to pay some attention to it, for we find it variously expounded in nearly all the contemporary philosophers. This is the relation between scientific knowledge and prophetic knowledge. Relying on a long neoplatonic tradition, but also on Avicenna, in his introduction to the *Guide to the Guide* Falaquera declares that the prophet knows all things directly by the grace of God, and his knowledge is thus perfect and complete, without apprenticeship in the sciences; he does not need to climb the degrees of knowledge step by step; his knowledge does not differ from that of the philosopher; but, in contrast to the latter, he attains it by the way of intuition and not of demonstration. The philosopher can be more or less learned, more or less philosopher, the prophet is totally prophet and knowing. He is distinguished from the philosopher by another characteristic: divine providence attaches itself to him. In the second appendix to the *Guide to the Guide*, Falaquera returns to the problem of providence and answers the questions propounded by Samuel Ibn Tibbon: Should one believe that God changes the laws of nature in favour of the prophet, or intervenes in specific events of which the causes may be infinite in number? Falaquera first divides miracles into two categories:

– Miracles that change the order of nature, which God performs by the intermediary of his prophet; these miracles have nothing to do with individual providence;

– The miracles that God performs for the just to preserve them from the ills that may affect them. Not that He saves them from death, for this would be contrary to the laws of nature; but, more simply, the small, everyday miracles that save someone from drowning or from fire may be regarded as 'miracles' when the just are concerned, and 'accidents' in the case of ordinary people.

Certainly, this providence that we recognize in our everyday life is linked to the conjunction between the intellect of the sage and the Active Intellect, but, as Falaquera reiterates several times, this is not really a philosophical notion, for it does not necessarily follow that the sage is always saved from all ills because of his wisdom; it becomes rather an affair of statistics: it often happens that the sage is protected from a certain number of ills, which he avoids because of his wisdom. Although this is not a scientifically demonstrated truth, such daily miracles should be accepted by the faithful, and cannot be ascribed to hazard.

Another problem emerges that was to be discussed by Albalag: what should one believe when the philosophical truth differs from the religious truth? In Falaquera this is not yet a burning problem, but only the adjusting of a religious notion: personal providence is not intellectually proved but it does not contradict any scientific truth, and every believer must accept it. Falaquera does not give a philosophical explanation of providence, like that proposed by Moses Ibn Tibbon and developed in Moses Narboni. He simply states that the religious truth of providence is not defied by philosophy, but rather agrees with it, as various citations from Aristotle, Pythagoras and the Psalmist prove.

A refusal to adopt a rigid position, a juxtaposition of theories that do not always agree together, are characteristic of the expectant attitude of Falaquera. He did not look for any original solution; he proposed nothing new, as if all were settled and the philosophical tradition were unified and coherent. But in one case, concerning the specific problem of creation, Falaquera assumes a forceful attitude, for in his opinion this of all problems is the most important to the believer. In the letter he wrote in defence of Maimonides, Falaquera gives the two reasons that, he thinks, led to the writing of the *Guide*: the first one was Maimonides' desire to show that philosophic reasoning is not right where creation is concerned, the second was his refusal of anthropomorphism. For Falaquera, Maimonides affirms that the world was created, and the passages of the *Guide* are explained by him along these lines. As we have seen, Maimonides bases the explanation of miracles on creation, and creation is the basis of the acceptation of the divine revelation. In consequence, Falaquera refuses the proof of the existence of God by the Prime Mover, for this proof presupposes an eternal movement and the eternity of the world.

In the *Guide to the Guide* (pp. 74–8), he expounds a kind of historical study of the proofs of the existence of God that is remarkably modern and accurate. Maimonides, he says, has expounded the two proofs of God's existence:

– That of eternal movement;

– That of contingency (God is a necessary being, while all creation is only potentially existent and depends on God).

The first proof is contrary to the faith; as indeed Maimonides declared later that the only truly philosophical proof was that by the contingency of the world (*Guide to the Guide*, p. 77).

One may say that Falaquera expounds these problems with erudition and with an effort at attenuation; Albalag, on the contrary, emphasized all their asperities.

ISAAC ALBALAG

All that we know of Albalag the man is that he lived during the second half of the thirteenth century, but whether in Provence or Catalonia is uncertain.

With Albalag we are far from popularization, although it is true that he chose Al-Ghazālī's *Intentions of the Philosophers* as a basis for his one book. Al-Ghazālī expounded the doctrines of various philosophers, especially Avicenna, in order to be in a better position to refute them. Albalag represents himself as defender of the philosophers, declaring in his preface that he translated Al-Ghazālī's book for pedagogical reasons. It is a work easy to understand, he says, expounding philosophical theses in such a way that they accord with popular belief. Albalag's own *Sefer Tikkun ha-De'ot* (*Righting of Doctrines*) is designed to offer a commentary on Al-Ghazālī's text and lead the reader to comprehend these doctrines by way of demonstration.

The *Intentions of the Philosophers* in Albalag's Hebrew translation is as yet unpublished, but the *Tikkun ha-De'ot* can be separated from it without too much difficulty, since it practically forms an independent text, containing also an explanation of the Story of the Creation. The title immediately indicates that our author does not intend to accept everything that Al-Ghazālī says; in fact he criticizes him vigorously, and includes in this criticism Maimonides, Avicenna and Al-Fārābī, while for Averroes he has nothing but praise. Maimonides was no less mistaken in matters of philosophy than in matters of faith. These two terms, philosophy and faith, taken over from Averroes, are very characteristic of Albalag, for in his view philosophy and faith do not coincide. *Torah* and philosophy have different aims, and each is as necessary as the other:

Four beliefs are common foundations to all the revealed religions, and they are built on them. Philosophy also admits them and tries to establish them, with this difference that the revealed religion teaches them according to a method adapted to popular intelligence, that is, by way of tales, while philosophy teaches them by the demonstrative method which is suitable only to the élite. These are the four beliefs: the existence of reward and punishment; the soul's survival after the death of the body; the existence of a rewarding, punishing Lord who is God; the existence, finally, of a Providence which watches over men's ways to give to each according to his acts . . .

The *Torah* aims at the felicity of the simple people, their estrangement from evil and their instruction in truth, as far as their spirit is capable of it . . . On the other hand, philosophy does not purpose the instruction or the happiness of the vulgar, but only the felicity of the perfect, which depends on the knowledge of the whole of being according to its reality and of each thing such as it is.

(*Tikkun ha-De'ot*, pp. 2–3)

The necessity of 'concealing' from the simple people truths that would prove pernicious to them is here clearly emphasized. This attitude recalls Averroes' *Decisive Treatise*. The *Torah* conceals possibly harmful doctrine from the vulgar, and this method sometimes leads to the expounding of other ideas which our author does not explicitly call false, but 'which deviate from the truth'. Nevertheless, the *Torah* also, in a way, reveals the truth.

It is certain that if the expounding of the truth had some usefulness for the vulgar, or if this truth was not untimely for the realization of the aim [the material felicity] designed for them, the *Torah* would not have hidden it and would not have refused a benefit to those entitled to it. Besides, there is no true philosophical thesis which the *Torah* has not mentioned by some allusion of a nature to arouse the attention of the wise, while the ignorant do not notice it. Moreover, the *Torah* even alludes to the prophetic doctrines, which are above syllogistic reasoning and natural speculation. The mysteries of the *Torah* are thus of two kinds: philosophical doctrines and prophetic doctrines.

(*Ibid.* pp. 3–4)

Let us first see what Albalag means by philosophical doctrine. This is the doctrine obtained by demonstration and afterwards supported by the biblical text, which, however, supports the most contradictory theses:

It is not incumbent on the seeker after truth to establish it according to what he understands of the scriptural texts themselves, without first having recourse to rational demonstration. On the contrary, the truth is established first by means of rational demonstration, and afterwards one searches for corroborative authority in the Scriptures. This is the method that I apply whenever I corroborate a speculative thesis by the Scriptures and the Talmud. I consider the biblical text and, if I find that it supports the notion that has been established by demonstration, I interpret it in the light [of this notion]; [on the other hand] if the text does not admit any of these clearly established notions, I do not subject it to any exegesis, but I say that I do not comprehend it and that its intention eludes me; this is not a philosophical mystery, but one of those prophetic mysteries revealed only to those on whom God has bestowed a spirit of superior knowledge.

(*Ibid.* p. 37)

Philosophical truth is only truly understood by the philosophers, as prophetic truth is only understood by the prophets, but with a fundamental difference.

We know that the sages are capable of understanding the philosophical [doctrines] through their own reasoning, with the scriptural text as a starting-point, by means of their formerly acquired philosophical knowledge. They therefore have the right to meditate on this and to interpret the verses of the *Torah* according to this method. On the other hand, only the prophet is capable of knowing the prophetic doctrines, and one cannot receive them, directly or indirectly, except from him. In understanding them, the sage is in no way superior to the ignorant, for the prophetic doctrines are hidden things which only concern the prophets. In the same way, in fact, as the demonstrative doctrine cannot be understood except by a demonstrative faculty, the divine doctrine cannot be understood except by a divine faculty.

(*Ibid.* p. 4)

Must one then conclude that the prophetic verities are totally incomprehensible in our time because prophecy had disappeared? This is more or less what Albalag says.

The cognition of the prophetic doctrine will be knowledge (*yedi'ah*) as regards the prophet and belief (*'emunah*) as regards him to whom the doctrine is transmitted. And the more transmitters and receivers multiply, so doubt is intensified with regard to the doctrine transmitted, and belief in it is weakened, for it is possible that it may have undergone alteration in the course of time, whether through error or through deceit on the part of a master or a scribe. This is the reason why it must be made a condition that it must be taught by an upright master and studied by an irreproachable disciple. And this is also the reason why we experience doubts regarding this tradition, [that is] if it is authentical[ly traceable back] to Abraham, to such an extent that those who are worthy of receiving the prophetic doctrines and long for them, have despaired of them and have turned towards the philosophic doctrines that demonstration has placed beyond doubt. (*Ibid.* p. 4)

It is evident that Albalag does not admit the Kabbalists' claim to detain prophetic truth.

The method of the esoterists of our country is to scrutinize the Scriptures: when the majority of the texts seem to them to bear witness and to plead in favour of some doctrine – which truth, according to their knowledge has not been established by another method, traditional or demonstrative – they make of it an object of faith and transmit it in secret to other people as credulous as themselves, telling them that this is the truth received by oral transmission since our father Abraham, or that it was the prophet's intention and that they have understood it by their own abilities . . . If you are of those who wish to know the truth, be attentive to all opinions and choose among them that which is established by rational demonstration, or that of which you know, with certain knowledge, that it has been transmitted since the prophet, word for word, without alteration, whether of content or of form. Never admit in your belief any scriptural exegesis which is not confirmed by one of these two methods. And, if you are not one of those who have been judged worthy of acceding to this degree, it is preferable that you should content yourself with the literal sense, without asking for its reason, rather than accept in this regard some extravagant ratiocination which depends neither on philosophy nor on prophecy. For, as an adept of the esoteric sect of our country, you shall be neither philosopher, nor believer. (*Ibid.* p. 38)

But it may happen that the biblical text does not lend itself to interpretation by the philosopher; it may also happen that the biblical text contradicts a philosophical doctrine, or sets itself against it. In this case, there will be two truths, one 'knowledge', or 'science', the other 'belief', and these two truths may be opposed. Not, besides, that the biblical text proves anything at all in favour of a demonstrated doctrine, for, as we have seen, the text may support any doctrine, and, in consequence, 'knowledge' based on a text does not necessarily imply identity with belief based on the same text.

One should learn truth only from demonstration. Afterwards, one should consult the *Torah*, and, if its words may be interpreted in conformity with the demonstrated doctrine, we shall admit this in our belief both in virtue of demonstration and in virtue of faith. If no scriptural text can be found to support the demonstrated doctrine, we shall believe this in virtue of speculation alone. Finally, if a scriptural text is found to contradict this doctrine, we shall similarly believe the literal sense of the text in the manner of miracle, being aware that the doctrine of the scriptural text in question looks strange to us only because it is one of those divine doctrines reserved for the prophets to understand, and depending on a supernatural power.

It is in this way that you shall find my rational opinion contrary in many points to my faith, for I know by demonstration that such a thing is true by way of nature and I know at the same time by the words of the prophets that the contrary is true by way of miracle. Moreover, even if I confirm that a demonstrable doctrine is compatible with a scriptural text, I am not certain that this is the veritable intention of the text, and not another.

I do not claim to believe in the truth of the biblical exegeses that I have been able to give here nor to teach them as a belief that I transmit to you. Quite simply, I have shown you that speculative doctrines can be supported by the scriptural text, and that this provides them with a support, but this scriptural text could just as well, and perhaps better, support contrary doctrines. *(Ibid.* pp. 43–4)

Let us take as an illustration the eternity of the world, a philosophical truth, and the creation of the world, a truth of belief. Albalag does not doubt that the eternity of the world is proved by philosophy. Maimonides had written in the *Guide* that the text of Genesis could be expounded according to the thesis of the eternity of the world, and even somewhat more easily than according to that of its creation. Albalag interprets the first verse of Genesis as signifying the preservation of the existence of the world by God, supreme cause and Prime Mover; he also summons to his aid, and justifiably, the Kabbalistic doctrine that sees in Wisdom the archetype of the visible universe. It is by the instrument of Wisdom that God creates the world eternally, which is also proved in the continuation of the chapter of Genesis. Maimonides did not wish to reveal this philosophical truth to the general public; but our author does not hesitate to do so, and he explains why:

It is possible that, in his discretion, the Master did not think it useful to reveal what the *Torah* has concealed from the vulgar. In principle I should have done as he, but I have three reasons that he did not have to do the opposite.
(1) Maimonides wanted to maintain the literal sense of the *Torah* and demonstrate the falseness of the philosopher's doctrine with the help of speculation, something that absolutely cannot be done. As for myself, I recognize the literal sense of the *Torah* by the way of simple faith ('*al derekh 'emunah peshutah*), without proof, and the truth of the philosophers by the way of nature and human speculation.
(2) The present work is not of a religious (*torani*) character as his was. It is not intended for the common people, and, if an ignorant man accidentally starts to read it, having understood nothing from the beginning, he will grow tired of it,

will abandon the effort and will not even reach this point. Thus if he has understood all that precedes this, he has left the ranks of the vulgar and has raised himself to the level of those with whom one speaks of these questions. He will understand, from then on, that I only acquiesce in the doctrine of the philosophers because speculative research does not permit me to deny it and this is why I acquiesce in it by the way of human knowledge, not that of faith.

(3) In the period of the Master the theory of the eternity of the world was altogether alien to the minds of the common people, so much so that the simple believers imagined that if anyone accepted it he so to speak denied the whole of the *Torah*. In our time this question is widely known among them and is diffused in their circles to such an extent that most of them are not loath to accept the belief in the eternity of the world such as Epicurus professed it, that is, a universe eternal in itself and without cause. They think that it is this eternity that the philosophers demonstrate; while in fact the philosophers reject such a suggestion with horror. Thus the ignorant of our time find themselves denying both the *Torah* and philosophy.

(*Ibid.* p. 51)

And at the end of the commentary on the Story of Creation Albalag again emphasizes his affirmation of a double verity.

Surely my doctrine [= doctrinal position] is that of the latter [the philosophers] and faith in the *Torah* is my faith; the first by way of nature, the second by way of miracle. And, if you have understood all my words, you will know that my doctrine [founded in reason] is true and that my faith is equally so. May the Knower of truth teach me the truth for his Name's sake. (*Ibid.* p. 51)

This presentation of Albalag's ideas recalls the accusation levelled by the Sorbonne in 1277 against the Christian philosophers 'who claim that there are two contradictory truths'. Like Albalag, these were philosophers of the school of Averroes, and they included Siger of Brabant and Boetius of Dacia, who were writing in Paris round about 1270. Averroes himself had never maintained this doctrine, for he believed in one unique truth, the philosophical. The Koran does not purpose to establish the truth, but to institute a political system, and the people should believe in it, or else there is a risk of serious danger to human society as a whole. The philosopher is therefore absolutely forbidden to reveal to the people philosophical truths that might make them doubt religious notions, for the people cannot comprehend that there are two different levels that complement each other: that of the truth (philosophy) and that of politics (revealed religion). What should be totally condemned is the kind of bastard philosophy that seeks to harmonize religion and philosophy, that is, the *kalām*, and also Avicenna, who accepts kalamic notions while claiming to be a philosopher. In any case, Averroes does not deny that the prophets, and especially Muhammad, possessed truthful knowledge superior to that of the philosophers, but of the same kind, although this in no way affects the respective positions of religion and philosophy. Did Albalag agree with Averroes or with his Latin followers? The intellectual context of the Latin philosophers' writings was very different from that of the Jewish philosopher. Thirteenth-century universities, including that of Paris, taught the sciences – logic, mathematics, physics and metaphysics – and the Church was not very pleased when logicians and physicists interfered in theological questions, particularly since Christian theology maintained a certain number of doctrines that were not open to doubt. At all events, in their own domains, each of the 'arts' was studied at the universities. Among the Jews, on the contrary, there was no organized teaching of the sciences, no school, but only a transmission from master to pupil. Science was 'the Greek science' which came from outside and was not the affair of the community. The only organized study was that of the *Torah*, and the traditional teaching of *halakhah* and Talmud. On the other hand, Judaism has no dogmas and the interpretation of the revealed text lent itself to all kinds of ideas, at least in theory, for community pressure prohibited certain audacities. But neither in Judaism nor in Christianity could one ignore or criticize the revealed text; a philosophy such as Spinoza's is inconceivable during the Middle Ages; and for the Jewish thinker revelation had to be integrated in one way or another, that is, generally, it had to be allegorically explained; and we see Albalag introduce an explication of the Story of Genesis into a purely philosophical commentary. Christian philosophy was restricted to its own domain and stopped at the threshold of the theology accepted by the Church; it had to admit that theology was truth, even when natural reason, or philosophy, seemed to be opposed to it. Philosophy, servant of religion, confessed that it could not prove that the world was created in time. Albalag's position is very different. In the problem of creation, the revealed text cannot serve as criterion either of the eternity or of the creation of the world. The creation of the world, a truth of belief, is above the comprehension of the philosopher and is accessible only to the prophets; for, prophecy having been lost, the prophetic truth is inaccessible and only the philosophical way remains to man, the way that proves the eternity of the world and leads to knowledge, salvation and the survival of the soul.

Perhaps Albalag, like Averroes, thought that there was only one truth, the philosophical truth. Whether we accept this hypothesis or the one postulating his acceptance of two contradictory truths, Albalag's position remains clearly opposed to religious orthodoxy.

LEVI BEN ABRAHAM BEN HAYYIM OF VILLEFRANCHE DE CONFLENT

We now come to a personage who played an important part in the quarrel between partisans and adversaries of philosophy. At the beginning of this chapter we described the early stages of this dispute, which continued with greater or lesser acrimony on either side throughout the thirteenth century. At the end of the century and at the beginning of the fourteenth, until the expulsion of the Jews from Provence, the controversy degenerated into personal conflict, and the chosen target of the adversaries of philosophy was

Levi ben Abraham. By that time no one dared attack Maimonides, who had become, if one may use the term, 'sanctified'.

The complaints levied against Levi ben Abraham were 'sociological': philosophy was publicly taught, not as Greek philosophy, which would have been a lesser evil, but enveloped in the cloak of the Scriptures and the Talmud and claiming to be the true Judaism. The literal sense of the revealed text was no longer distinguished and the philosophical allegory became the principal meaning. Philosophy, its opponents maintained, should be taught only to those who are capable of distinguishing the true from the false.

In 1305 Solomon ben Adret wrote a letter from Barcelona to the Spanish communities of France and Germany.

For they say that Abraham and Sarah represent matter and form, and that the twelve tribes of Israel are the twelve constellations. Has a nation ever heard such an evil thing since the world was divided into territories? Or has such a thing ever been heard that men should reduce everything to chaos? The blasphemers of God further say that the holy vessels which were sanctified, the Urim and Thumim, are the instrument known as astrolabe, which men make for themselves ... A man who does such things reduces the entire Bible to useless allegories; indeed they trifle with and pervert all the commandments in order to make the yoke of their burden lighter unto themselves ... some of them say that all that is written from the section of Bereshit [Genesis] as far as the giving of the Law is nothing more than an allegory. May such men become a proverb and a by-word, and may they have no stay and no staff. Indeed they show that they have no faith in the plain meaning of the commandments ... They are more estranged than the Gentiles: for the latter fulfil some of the commandments, while they strongly desire to uproot all.

The chief reason of all this is that they are infatuated with alien sciences, Sidonian and Moabitish, and pay homage to the Greek books ... The children that are consecrated unto heaven from their birth and from their mother's womb are drawn away from the breasts and are taught the books and the language of Chaldeans, instead of rising early to study the Jewish faith in the house of their teachers. Now a boy born upon the knees of natural science, who sees Aristotle's sevenfold proofs concerning it, really believes in it, and denies the Chief Cause; if we refute him, he becomes all the more impious. They read the Law with their lips, but their heart is not sound inwardly, and they pervert it in seven ways ... They are ashamed when they speak and lecture; they speak with their mouths, but make hints with the finger that it is impossible to change nature, and they thereby declare to all that they do not believe in the creation of the universe, nor in any of the miracles recorded in the Torah.

Now when we saw that the generation had become corrupted and ready to treat religion lightly, we made a fence, and strengthened the wall round our flawless Torah. Had we not made a strong hedge round the vineyard of the Lord of hosts, we should have shared in the blame for their deeds. We have therefore interdicted in the most solemn manner, as ye see recorded with writing of truth in the book of the covenant which we made with God, anyone to teach or to learn these sciences, until the student and the teacher are twenty-five years old, and until they appreciate fully the delicacies of the Law, so that they will not depose it from its queenly rank; for he who espouses it in his youth will not turn away from it even when he grows old.   (Trans. F. Kobler in *Letters of Jews through the Ages*, pp. 256–7)

It must be admitted that some of these reproaches were well-founded.

Levi ben Abraham was probably born between 1240 and 1250. In 1276 he wrote *Bottei ha-nefesh we ha-lahashim* (*Chests of perfume and amulets*), a didactic poem that discussed all the sciences; the verses are so obscure that the author himself found it necessary to accompany them with a commentary. His great work, the *Livyat Ḥen* (*Ornament of Grace*) is an encyclopedia that must have been of impressive length, although only fragments have survived. The work was divided into six books. The first five discuss science and philosophy, the sixth faith. Only the forty chapters on astronomy, the last of them devoted to judiciary astrology,[1] a fragment of the metaphysics, and the sixth book, have been preserved.

The *Ornament of Grace*, in its definitive version, was finished in 1295, but one or two of the earlier versions, which were shorter, were circulating some time earlier, and in the astronomical section one finds the date of 1276.

The final version was very long, and we have no more than two thirds of the sixth book, the missing third having been preserved in a shorter redaction. Of Levi ben Abraham's thought we know only the part concerning religion. The relations between religion and philosophy are clearly described:

It has already been explained that our *Torah* is entirely philosophical [literally, intellectual, as opposed to practical, knowledge], that its commandments cannot be accomplished and its secrets known except through the theoretical sciences; it is thanks to these theoretical sciences that false beliefs are repulsed and the foundations of the [true] belief are strengthened for they are not all clearly explained in our books; very much on the contrary, certain verses contradict each other and numerous *midrashim* are opposed one to another. On what can we rely if not on the balances of the intellect? Science shall be the instrument of the examination of belief and through it we shall know the richness of the revealed text; we shall reject what is futile and deceitful and we shall not be like the fool who believes no matter what.

(Liviat Ḥen, Vatican, MS hebreo 192, fol. 115r)

For Levi ben Abraham 'science' is the Maimonidean–Averroist philosophy that was current at the period, and his erudition is truly remarkable. It is not very likely that he knew Arabic, but he cites almost all the authors whose texts existed in Hebrew. All the philosophical clichés are found applied to the biblical texts and the *aggadot*, and all the texts are allegorically explained. For each of them Levi proposes not only one philosophical explanation, but two or three or four, and one looks in vain for the literal sense of these texts; it has disappeared to make way for a multiplication of allegories and images. Certainly, at the beginning of every chapter, Levi reminds the reader that his interpretations do not diminish the literal sense in any way, but these two or three lines of orthodox declaration are followed by several pages of allegory. All those accusations formulated in the ban proclaimed in the synagogue of Barcelona on 31 July 1305 by a number of rabbis under the presidency of Solomon ben Adret, are strictly true: in the *Ornament of Grace* one

---

[1] Which has the function of drawing up individual horoscopes, taking into account the influences of the various astral bodies according to their configuration at the moment of birth.

finds the creation of the world allegorically explained, Sarah and Abraham designating matter and form, the twelve tribes of Israel representing the twelve signs of the zodiac; the four kings who fought the five kings and Abraham are respectively the four elements (and, in the long version, the four material faculties) and the five senses (and the faculties that can be saved from matter and brought into the service of God); the *Urim* and *Tumim* on the High Priest's pectoral are, among other things, a representation of the astrolabe. We shall return to the literal sense of the commandments later. Almost all these allegories were already to be found in the works of Levi's predecessors, especially Samuel and Moses Ibn Tibbon, but, and here Yedayah ha-Penini was right in his *Apologia*, they were only applied to the *aggadot* that were particularly disturbing to common sense, or else to the poetical parts of the Bible, Proverbs, Ecclesiastes and Job, or the Story of Genesis and the Story of the Chariot, where allegorization had been traditional since Maimonides. Levi ben Abraham makes no distinction between *Torah* and *aggadah*. His astonishing erudition permits him to link biblical verses and *aggadot* and the combination is treated allegorically without any distinction between the two. This amalgam is certainly one of the reasons for the scandal that he provoked. The lack of originality of his explications has led some scholars to think that his personal poverty made him an adversary easy to attack and that he was made to serve as a scapegoat for other, more powerful, philosophers, such as the Tibbonids. There is certainly some truth in this hypothesis. It is also possible that he had some association with Christians and such associations were not favourably regarded at the period by the Jewish community, which, sensing danger, was raising protective barricades. It seems to me, however, that other characteristics destined him to suffer the vindictiveness of the more orthodox rabbis: first of all, for Levi, Maimonides' philosophy, enriched by Averroes and Ibn Ezra, was quite simply true, and unquestionably so. His complicated exegeses clothe a philosophical thought that has the simplicity of a textbook.

This simplicity endows our author with the assurance and the arrogance of those who possess the truth. He himself is on the side of the intelligent, those who know, who are united with the Active Intellect and survive in the life after death. The others, the faithful, are the *vulgum pecus*, ignorant, attached to matter and to religion, fated to destruction. Averroes had written the same, but Levi constantly returns to the subject. This leitmotiv is associated with his horror of feminity (of all the medieval Jewish philosophers he is surely the most misogynist), which is matter, seduction, destruction but also religion. This negative aspect of religion is found again when he classes the commandments in two categories – those that are justified by reason and those that reason does not justify – a distinction that goes back to Saadiah. Those justified by reason have their source in theory, therefore in philosophy, the others, religious only, are no more than a preparation for the first; at the worst, since the whole world cannot be philosopher and philosophers are not philosophers from birth, these traditional commandments are 'the light that allows us to find the pearl'. But Levi ben Abraham makes no mystery of his conviction that these commandments, like politics and psychology, are only practical necessities, sadly accepted by the philosopher. Levi's philosophy is strident and aggressive; even after seven centuries it does not inspire sympathy. Let us add that his erudition is displayed with much prolixity, a fact that partly explains why his *Ornament of Grace* has not been published, and, generally speaking, little read. He is rarely cited, and only in the short version.

In a way Levi ben Abraham concludes the Tibbonid period, pursuing the ideas of Maimonides' immediate successors almost to a point of absurdity. In him this form of philosophy is resolved into a sterile allegorization, for everything is reduced to a comparatively simple play of philosophical notions; of the rich fabric of texts, biblical and aggadic, nothing remains except a web of already familiar ideas, the pattern of which offers nothing new. After a certain saturation point is reached, this philosophical net, cast into the sea of texts, only brings back the same fish.

His younger contemporary, Yedayah ha-Penini, who protested against the ban launched against philosophical studies, already belongs to another period, inspired by new ideas. Meanwhile, in Spain, the philosophers took a very different road.

Philosophers of Southern Spain

Originating in Southern Spain, several philosophers still belong to the Islamic cultural ambiance, and display mystical traits that bring them close to the Kabbalah.

In discussing the thought of Solomon Ibn Gabirol and Judah Halevi, I remarked that their ideas had a great influence on the Kabbalah. In the course of the first quarrel revolving around Maimonides' *Commentary on the Scriptures*, we encountered Nahmanides, one of the earliest representatives of the Kabbalist movement. Albalag also mentions the Kabbalists, either to laugh at their pretension to possess a knowledge that could be traced back to Abraham, or to acquiesce in their opinion concerning the creation of the world by the instrument of the divine wisdom. This is an appropriate point, therefore, to survey briefly this current of mystical thought, which so greatly exercised medieval Judaism.

The Hebrew word *kabbalah* means 'received tradition'. Until the thirteenth century the term designated the whole oral religious tradition – Talmud and *midrashim*, prayers, and also texts of a gnostic tendency emanating from circles of mystics during the talmudic and post-talmudic periods.

The two mystical currents of Ḥassidut and Kabbalah claimed to derive from an ancient and esoteric tradition. In Ashkenaz and more especially in the Rhineland, from the end of the eleventh century until the thirteenth, the ideas of the Ḥassidim (pietists) revolved around notions of the Glory, the Divine Throne and the Metatron, the angel highest in the celestial hierarchy. God is unknowable, and on this point the Ḥassidim were as opposed to anthropomorphism as was Maimonides. They knew Saadiah Gaon and his commentary on the *Sefer Yeẓirah*, and the commentaries on the same book by Shabbetai Donnolo (tenth century, southern Italy), and by Judah ben Barzillai. Although one finds echoes of neoplatonic ideas in these commentaries, Ashkenazi pietism was based rather on the heritage of the rabbinical tradition than that of philosophy. An ascetic mystical movement, it made a strong impression on the daily life of the communities, and its moral influence endured long after the initial, creative, mystical élan had been exhausted.

Between 1150 and 1200, in Provence, appeared the *Sefer ha-Bahir* and other texts originating both in the mysticism of the *Hekhaloth* (The divine palaces) and Ashkenazi Ḥassidut. Although based on the same texts as its northern contemporary, the strain that flourished in Provence and later in Northern Spain is very different from it, for its conceptual structure is neoplatonic. At first the Kabbalah was not opposed to philosophy; it accepted its fundamental notions as we have found them expressed in Abraham Ibn Ezra and Solomon Ibn Gabirol. During the thirteenth century, however, the philosophers took sides with Maimonides under the banner of Aristotle, and the Kabbalists distanced themselves from neoplatonic philosophy, developing a sefirotic conception of the divine world.

For the Kabbalists, the hidden God, unknowable and infinite, manifests something of His Unknowable Being in creation. The divine attributes, the *sefiroth*, are linked to the Unknowable, the *En-Sof* (Infinite), as the flame is joined to the coal; the *En Sof* could exist without the flame, but it is the flame that manifests the Unknowable. The word *sefiroth* no longer designates, as in the *Sefer Yeẓirah*, entities created by God; the *sefiroth* have become part of the divine *pleroma*.

The *sefiroth* are not the sign of the divine action, but the dynamic aspect of God himself.

The fixed and common names of the ten *sefiroth* are:

1. *Kether Elyon,* the 'supreme crown' of God;
2. *Ḥokhmah,* the 'wisdom' or primordial idea of God;
3. *Binah,* the 'intelligence' of God;
4. *Ḥesed,* the 'love' or mercy of God;
5. *Gevurah* or Din, the 'power' of God, chiefly manifested as the power of stern judgment and punishment;
6. *Rahamim,* the 'compassion' of God, to which falls the task of mediating between the two preceding Sefiroth; the name *Tifereth* 'beauty', is used only rarely.
7. *Netsah,* the 'lasting endurance' of God;
8. *Hod,* the 'majesty' of God;

| 9. *Yesod*, | the 'basis' or 'foundation' of all active forces in God; |
| 10. *Malkhuth*, | the 'kingdom' of God, usually described in the Zohar as the *Keneseth Israel*, the mystical archetype of Israel's community, or as the Shekhinah. |

(G. Scholem, Major Trends in Jewish Mysticism, p. 212)

All the *sefiroth* are linked to each other, and every event that concerns the terrestrial community of Israel has a repercussion in the world of the *sefiroth*, since its archetype is the last of these entities. God expresses Himself in the *sefiroth*; it is He who has given them appropriate names; they are the root of the existence of God as creator, but only as creator, for we know absolutely nothing of the hidden God, and some go so far as to say that nothing in the *Torah* alludes to *En-Sof.*

The *sefiroth* provide the key to a mystic 'topography' of the divine world and each of them is revealed in the multiple metamorphoses of the biblical and traditional texts. Far from being embarrassed by anthropomorphic texts, the Kabbalists interpret them as a network of symbols giving access to the divine world of the *sefiroth*. The study of the texts was then at the centre of the Kabbalah, and most of the Kabbalists were also very learned in *halakhah.*

In this context, the fulfilment of the divine commandments and prayer take on cosmic importance: God Himself depends on the harmony between the *sefiroth*. The religious life in its daily progress is exalted to the supreme degree, and every gesture, every thought of the faithful must be directed towards the restoration of harmony between the *sefiroth* and Israel, following the instructions given in the *halakhah.*

According to G. Scholem, the essential difference between philosophy and Kabbalah is the problem of evil. For the philosopher, evil is the deprivation of good; for the Kabbalists evil exists as a positive force. It is said to have developed gradually from a superabundance of *Din*, the *sefirah* of stern judgement, and this was made possible by the separation of *Din* from the *sefirah* called *Hesed*, love. An entire world of the 'evil *sefiroth*', 'the exterior tree', exists in the *Zohar.*

The *Zohar* (*Book of Splendour*), only appeared in the seventies of the thirteenth century. Preceding it, and existing from the beginning of the century, was the Gerona circle, with Ezra, Azriel, and especially Moses ben Naḥman (Nahmanides, *ca.* 1194–1270), whose great reputation together with his *Commentary on the Torah* conferred wide popularity on the movement. The *Zohar*, written in Aramaic and attributed to Simeon bar Yohai, a rabbi of the mishnaic period who lived in Palestine, gave the Kabbalah a pattern that has since been generally accepted.

However, throughout the thirteenth century the Kabbalah was still flexible and sometimes approached philosophy. When one finds the words *sefirah* and *kabbalah* in a text of this century they must be interpreted in the author's own sense. *Kabbalah* can signify the tradition, esoteric or not; and *sefirah* can quite as well be used in the sense of number as in that of one of the *sefiroth* of the divine *pleroma* of the Kabbalah. Similarly, it is sometimes not easy to know where to place certain authors such as Judah ben Solomon ha-Cohen, or Abraham Abulafia, whom Scholem considers a Kabbalist. The word *sefirah* does not occur in Judah ben Solomon ha-Cohen, only the word *kabbalah*. In Abulafia, on the contrary, both *kabbalah* and *sefirah* occur, as they do in Judah ben Nissim Ibn Malkah and also in Ibn Latif, but in none of these authors is God known as a *pleroma* of *sefiroth*, and the meaning that these authors give to the key words *sefirah* and *kabbalah* seems to me to weight the scales in favour of philosophy.

There are some essential differences between philosophy and Kabbalah. For a philosopher, for instance, God is the One from whom the separate intellects emanate, and not the One who expands the manifestation of His being into the *sefiroth*. Further, for a philosopher, prayer and human actions have a certain power over the individual himself, his psychology, his perfecting, his destiny, but not over the unfolding of the divine drama, contrary to the declarations of the Kabbalists.

Certain philosophers, however, considered themselves to have inherited an esoteric tradition and they were cited, taken up and amplified by the Kabbalists. The philosophical parts of Judah ha-Cohen's encyclopedia are found copied in numerous manuscripts together with translations of Averroes; but another part of his work, *The Explication of the Letters*, explains the Hebrew letters of the alphabet as manifesting the whole spiritual and material reality, and it was copied in kabbalistic circles until the eighteenth century. At the beginning of the fourteenth century Judah ben Nissim Ibn Malkah, who will soon be discussed, was cited by the celebrated Kabbalist Isaac of Acre, who in fact criticizes him.

JUDAH BEN SOLOMON HA-COHEN IBN MALKAH

Judah ha-Cohen was born at Toledo, *ca.* 1215, to a family of celebrated astrologists. Towards 1233 he began to correspond with the Emperor Frederick II's 'Philosopher' (Michael Scott?), and in 1245 he was at Frederick's court, in Lombardy. While living in Italy he translated his great encyclopedia, *Midrash ha-Ḥokhmah* (*Exposition of Science*) into Hebrew from Arabic.

In imitation of the world itself, as many medieval philosophers conceived it, the work is divided into three parts:

– Physical science, which describes the world of generation and corruption, constitutes the first part;

– The mathematical and astronomical sciences, which explain the world of the spheres, as treated in the second;

– Divine science, the object of which is the spiritual world, is expounded in three treatises, distributed at the end of the two other parts, and is identified with the *kabbalah*.

The first part begins with logic, preliminary instrument of the sciences. Aristotle's physics and metaphysics follow, and are succeeded by a first treatise on the divine science, which contains an explication of several verses of Genesis, Psalms and Proverbs.

The second part, mathematics and astronomy, is concluded by a second treatise on the divine science, giving an explanation of the letters of the Hebrew alphabet, and a third treatise comprising several of the talmudic *aggadot*, which in his opinion concern the Science of Unification, that is, theology.

The Aristotelian logic, physics and metaphysics that constitute the first part of the encyclopedia are essentially a résumé of Averroes' *Middle Commentaries* on these treatises. In contrast to the *Short Commentaries*, our author's text does not go into the detail of Aristotle's discussion, but presents the leading ideas, so that it is actually much clearer and more readable than that of the Arab philosopher. Apart from Averroes' commentaries Judah ben Solomon used Al-Farābī, Avicenna, and most probably other authors whom he does not always cite by name; but he also intercalates personal comments, usually based on a comparison between various texts by Aristotle treating the same subject and not agreeing, but also on other authors, especially Galen and Alpetragius (Nūr al-Dīn Abū Isḥāḳ al-Biṭrūdjī, a Spanish Arab astronomer, who lived about 1200), and once his own master, Meir Abulafia, who in his youth had opposed Maimonides on the subject of resurrection.

His discussion of the science of astronomy, preceded by Euclid's *Geometry* and Theodosius' and Menelaus' books on spherical figures, is divided into theory – the *Almagest*, complemented by Al-Biṭrūdjī's *Physics* – and practice – the Tetrabible. Astrology, as much as astronomy and geometry, is a science.

However, Judah ha-Cohen calls in question the whole of physics, and, naturally, Aristotelian metaphysics. The two kinds of knowledge that one can attain by reasoning differ profoundly in their methods.

> The kinds of demonstration adduced in physics are the opposite of those adduced in the mathematical sciences: in the latter, one goes from the anterior to the posterior, while in physics one goes from the posterior to the anterior, and as the things known by the mathematical sciences are also known by the physical sciences, the demonstrations of the mathematical sciences are absolute, while those of physics are not known completely, absolutely and in themselves, thus the demonstrations which are made in this physical science are called proofs.
>
> (C. Sirat, 'Judah b. Solomon', pp. 56–7)

This comparison between the proof offered by physics and the demonstration offered by mathematics is a sort of commentary on the first book of the *Physics*, where Aristotle describes the process of analysis in the natural sciences without referring to mathematics. This comparison is found in Averroes' *Short Commentaries*, and, more explicitly developed, in the *Middle Commentaries*, source of the *Midrash ha-Ḥokhmah*.

Here Judah adds:

Furthermore, all the things of which it is said that they are explained in this science [physics] are not properly explained, even by these demonstrations called proofs, but only some of them. The result is that the inferiority of physics is due to three faults arranged in order of gravity:

(1) The premises are not all based on primary evidence;
(2) There is no perfect demonstration, as in the case of mathematical demonstrations, but only proofs;
(3) A number of facts are not explained, even by the proofs.   (*Ibid.* p. 57)

In fact, Judah concludes, one should be able to adduce in physics proofs manifest to the senses, experimental demonstrations that one cannot question, like experiments carried out in the mathematical and astronomical sciences. In the absence of these demonstrations, one cannot choose between conflicting theories in physics, and the debates between physicists are only empty talk. The notion of experiment is very important to Judah, and when Aristotelian physics contradict experiment, represented here by Galen, Judah prefers Galen.

Throughout the eight books of the *Physics* he has noted affirmations which are not demonstrated and which philosophers often accept without remarking their non-scientific character.

For example, if it is proved that the principles are more than one in number and less than three, as we have said, it is not proved that they are three: form, matter, non-being.

And again:

The existence of the first matter also is not proved, nor that it is not subject to generation or to corruption.   (*Ibid.* p. 57)

Thus except in the case of the eternity of the world, Judah does not reject Aristotelian physics, but he casts doubt on the scientific bases on which it rests. Judah ha-Cohen distinguishes forty-eight principles on which the Aristotelian system is constructed. He says of them that some, which are self-evident and require no further demonstration, are accompanied by idle proofs and demonstrations, while others that are not self-evident nor demonstrated by another science are treated as if they were in fact self-evident. Our author's analysis tends to point out some of the logical and scientific incoherencies in Aristotle's physics, but this analysis is made from 'within'. He is very much aware that this system contradicts primary evidence, or experiment, or even the system itself, but he has nothing to propose in its place.

The limitation that can be observed in the knowledge achieved by human reasoning without the aid of revelation is strongly emphasized in Judah ha-Cohen; and he is convinced that revelation, the *kabbalah*, brings with it true and perfect knowledge. Where Maimonides despaired of attaining truth, Judah ha-Cohen declares that he has received it as his heritage through tradition, the *kabbalah*.

For Judah ben Solomon ha-Cohen this tradition is oral and can be traced back to Moses.

(1) It is not an opinion based on corporeal perception or cognition superior to man's natural cognition, but a knowledge that God Himself has transmitted to Moses, who transmitted it to Israel.

(2) The Kabbalah and prophecy are one and the same thing.

(3) This knowledge concerns the two superior worlds: the spiritual world and the 'essence' of the world of the spheres.

The relation between this *kabbalah* and the science of the spheres is very much underlined by Judah ha-Cohen:

He who wishes to know the divine wisdom must first know mathematical science [which also includes astronomy, astrology and music], and then the divine wisdom will repose in his heart in all its clarity, while he who has not first studied mathematical science . . . if he wants to study the divine wisdom, it will not be understood as it should be.
(*Ibid.* pp. 49–50, n. 22)

The Kabbalah, the divine science, is essentially different from the science of the inferior worlds; this latter, although it was the appanage of Israel, is no longer known except through the books of the Gentiles, which partly explains its imperfection.

The author, Judah ha-Cohen ben Solomon ha-Cohen of Toledo, says: when you reflect and preoccupy your thought with these sciences in order to acquire the knowledge of everything which exists from the beginning to the end, you will see in the end that you will know only a very few things concerning the two worlds perceived by the senses: the world of the spheres and that of generation and corruption. As for the spiritual world, even if you know by heart the thirteen books of Aristotle on divine science, you will not get from them more than the knowledge of the Prime Mover, Rock, One, Living, who is neither body nor force in a body, and that there is for each sphere a separate intellect; that is all that you will learn concerning this [spiritual] world, if you occupy your spirit with these treatises . . . The philosophers have endeavoured to know these three worlds, by opinion [conjecture] only, which is a knowledge rooted in corporeal perception as Aristotle has said, in his books *On demonstration* and *De Anima*. Also, it would be truly miraculous to be able, on the basis of corporeal perception, to know, understand and attain something that is not at all perceptible by the senses.   (*Ibid.*)

That the divine science has been revealed only to Israel is explained by the chosen people's closeness to the divine world: the two inferior worlds were given to the Gentiles, who prosper in them. In this world Israel is only a passing inhabitant (*ger vetoshav*). As Judah expounds the problem to a Christian opponent:

Do you not see that Adam before the Fall was naked in Paradise and after he sinned a garment was given to him and he was thrown out of Paradise? Would it not have been better if he had been naked, without garment and remaining in Paradise? And, if there are among the Gentiles more sciences and intellectual pleasures than there are in Israel, this is because they have inherited the two [inferior] worlds. You know, besides, that it is not the *midrash*, the interpretative study, the theory, which is the important thing, but the act; and of what use are your sciences to your learned men when one finds among them more vices and cunning than among the ignorant people? for they exploit their science to fabricate idols or [make philtres] of love, to make themselves appear important in the eyes of the great, or to make gold, [an operation] that they call the 'great work' and in which they will never succeed, for it is impossible. (C. Sirat, 'La *qabbale*', p. 193)

Thus, in the section devoted to the divine science, Judah does not quote any philosopher but only traditional texts, Rashi and Ibn Ezra. His reticence regarding Maimonides is due to the fact that he mingled philosophy with divine science, 'crowning a great king with a crown of clay'.

What Judah ha-Cohen means by divine wisdom is expounded fairly clearly in his commentary on the Story of the Creation, the Psalms and the Proverbs, and his explication of the Hebrew alphabet. As for the compilation of excerpts of the *aggadot*, it remains hermetically sealed to those who have not received this *kabbalah* and do not understand it of their own accord.

God, Himself, is absolutely unknowable and the further man advances in perfect knowledge, the better he understands how important it is to deny all attributes to God; it is only because of the beings emanating from God that one can use the words of the prayer describing God as great, strong and redoubtable.

The commentary on the Story of the Creation affirms the *ex-nihilo* creation of the two inferior worlds. Matter (created from nothingness) and form (the light that gives it life) are the first creations of God.

Light is form; matter is divided into superior, that of the heavens, and inferior, that of the earth. It is light, emanation of the Intellect 'that moves the ensemble of the existent created things and makes them emerge from nothingness to being'.

The words *beri'ah*, *yezirah*, *'asyah* (the three Hebrew words signifying creation) do not describe the same act: *beri'ah* designates the coming into existence of a thing out of nothingness, and at the beginning there was no matter nor form: here lies the difference with Aristotle: for him, nothingness is the opposite of form, and the First Matter, which is not subject to generation or corruption, is the receptacle of forms that succeed each other in it, as wax is always ready to receive the form of a seal. We, on the contrary, says Judah ha-Cohen, maintain that the nothingness is 'a real and absolute nothingness and that before creation there was no First Matter, but that the Lord, Blessed be He, created matter and form and it is from their union, as it suited them, that all that exists has been made'.

The intellect is thus at the second degree of superior beings; as for the human soul: 'This human form, it is as if it were in the third place in the order of the separate forms.'

This ontological scheme is clearly neoplatonic: the first two creations are matter and form and it would seem that matter in a certain way precedes form, which recalls Ibn Gabirol's idea, but Judah does not refer to Will.

After this come the nine intellects that govern the spheres: they are symbolized by the first nine letters of the alphabet, *alef* to *tet*: the nine simple digits. The world of the spheres is expressed in the nine decades *yod* to *zade* and the sublunary world by the nine hundreds, *qof* to final *zade*, for the finals are added to the twenty-two letters of the Hebrew alphabet to make twenty-seven.

Yod symbolizes the supreme sphere, which draws the entire celestial world in its daily movement; *kaf* is the sphere of the fixed stars; *lamed*, Saturn; *mem*, Jupiter; *nun*, Mars; *samekh*, Venus; *ayn*, the Sun; *pe*, Mercury; *zade*, the Moon.

The inferior world is represented by the following letters: *qof*, the primary matter of this lower world, different from that of the astral bodies; *resh*, the four qualities, heat, cold, humidity and dryness; *shin*, fire; *taw*, air; final *kaf*, water; final *mem*, earth; final *nun*, the metals; final *pe*, the plants; final *zade*, the animals.

Divine Science is the knowledge of the names of the separate intellects and the beings superior to them; it explains the relations that unite the different superior beings and the spheres, and those which unite the spheres to the beings of this lower world; it is the science of the disposition of the stars, this disposition depending on the names and functions of entities separated from matter. These relations, to a great extent, are arithmetical, and linked to the Hebrew characters.

The inferior world depends very closely on the world of the spheres. Everything that exists in this world has its correspondence in the celestial world: every part of the inhabited world, every historical event, the fate of each and every man.

All history is governed by the spheres. One particular planet presides over each day of the week: Saturn over Saturday, Jupiter over Sunday, etc. as well as over the months of the year: the periods dominated by various empires are regulated according to the revolutions of the planets; for instance, the period presided over by Mars was marked by the Babylonian exile and the destruction of the First Temple, and when Saturn is again dominant Israel will be delivered (fol. 300r ff).

These speculations were fostered by Jewish sources, which have already been discussed at length, but we must also compare them to Arabic texts, including that of Jābir Ibn Ḥayyān, which is analysed in a fine study by P. Kraus.[1] And, in fact, Judah ha-Cohen, like Judah ben Nissim, came from a Jewish milieu deeply rooted in Arab language and science.

ISAAC BEN ABRAHAM IBN LATIF

Isaac ben Abraham Ibn Latif seems to have lived at Toledo, between 1210 and 1280. In 1238 he finished the first and most important of his works; a

---

[1] *Jābir ibn Ḥayyān, contribution à l'histoire des idées scientifiques dans l'Islam* (Cairo, 1942).

shorter version, not bearing his name, composed *ca.* 1230, has been attributed to various authors, including Solomon Ibn Gabirol. This work, *Sha'ar ha-Shamayim* (*The Gate of Heaven*) is soon to be published; the introduction has already appeared. Several other works by Ibn Latif exist in print. These are a commentary on Ecclesiastes; *Ginzei ha-Melekh* (*The treasures of the King*); *Zurat ha-'Olam* (*The Form of the World*); *Zeror ha-Mor* (*Bouquet of Myrrh*), dedicated to the celebrated Talmudist Todros ha-Levi Abulafia; *Rav Pe'alim*, a collection of aphorisms; and philosophical *responsa*. A commentary on Job and another on the *Sefer Yezirah* seem to have been lost.

Isaac Ibn Latif wrote in Hebrew, but he had a remarkably wide knowledge of Arab philosophy. He does not use translations made by other hands, but it is clear that he knew the two Hebrew translations of the *Guide of the Perplexed*. The sources that he cites by name are Arabic or Greek in Arabic translation, but he also makes wide use of the Jewish neoplatonic philosophers, especially Ibn Gabirol, whom he does not quote by name, except as a poet, perhaps because he felt that his doctrine belonged to the 'secrets' that should not be revealed to the common people. I must point out, however, that the very marked resemblance between Ibn Latif and Ibn Gabirol does not prove beyond doubt that Ibn Gabirol was Ibn Latif's source, and in fact, we do not know much about the texts that Ibn Gabirol himself used. At all events, it is very likely that he exercised considerable influence over Ibn Latif.

Ibn Latif divides existing things into three hierarchized worlds: the world of the intellects, the world of the spheres, the world of generation and corruption. God is unknowable; He cannot be reached by the intelligence or defined in any human language, for God is infinite and every attribute is a limitation. God, through His will, has created the world. The divine Will, when it is conceived as active, is distinguished from the divine Essence. Will, at the same time God Himself and first emanation of God, is that which joins and unites universal matter and universal form. It is by the Will, which is also called the Word, that the world was created; it is also the source of all reality, the Source of Life; it is everything and everything is in it; nothing exists outside it. However, while one can say that the whole of reality is in God, God and reality are not identical.

God created the world by the Will. The whole first part of the *Gate of Heaven* is devoted to a critique of the eternity of the world based on Aristotle's; one of the arguments against the eternity of the world is the impossibility of joining the One to multiplicity, the infinite to the finite. If the world necessarily emanates from God, it too should be infinite in number and infinite in extent. This argument, adapted from Saadiah Gaon, who had borrowed it from the *kalām*, the ultimate source being John Philiponus, was taken up and amplified by Shemariah ben Elijah of Crete, and Crescas.

Ibn Latif's critique of Aristotelian science is as fundamental as that of Judah ha-Cohen, although it is vaguer. Maimonides wrote that everything that Aristotle said concerning the sublunary world, especially in his *Meteoro-logics*, was true beyond any doubt. Ibn Latif criticizes this assertion, for Aristotle's affirmations were pure conjecture and in no way scientifically demonstrated, and these conjectures are less plausible than others that one could make (*Zurat ha-'Olam*, p. 6). His critique of Ptolemy is equally radical: there is nothing to prove that the nature of the heavenly matter implies a circular movement. We do not even know if the sky is made of two sorts of matter, one shining – the stars; the other transparent – the spheres. We do not know the number of the stars, nor the number of the spheres, nor if their movement is natural or voluntary, regulated by a soul and an intellect. As for declaring that this movement is eternal, this is pure speculation.

Thus, the philosophers know almost nothing of the earth, the heavens, or God. In fact, intellectual knowledge employs logic founded on three modes: perception, syllogism and demonstration.

The mode of perception uses the perceptions of the senses, represents them to the soul and brings them as far as the spiritual *sensus communis*, which weighs them and compares them to images that are already known; in this way man learns the truth of the essence of things, as regards their coming into existence.

Syllogism is the second mode and it can be divided into three kinds: the first is that which deals with generation and corruption, that is, the relation between matter and form, and the transition from potentiality to actuality; the second only deals with what always exists in actuality, like the relation between the heavens and the earth, resembling the relation between the circle and the point, or the relation of the matter of the stars and the spheres to their form, a relation that is not subject to change or transformation; the third kind of syllogism if one follows the opinion of the philosophers, who are satisfied with a very vague analogy, is concerned with the relation between the spheres and the separate intellects. In reality, this kind of syllogism deals with the links that connect the whole of creation – the species and the intellectual and natural genres, and the hidden connection of the causes; it is in following this road that the initiate can attain a religious, marvellous, intellectual knowledge, hidden from the eyes of those who are learned in the 'foreign' science.

The demonstrative mode only applies to God; He is beyond time and place, no contingency tarnishes Him and no doubt, of any kind, obscures Him. He is pure truth (*ibid.* pp. 4–5).

The tradition, the *kabbalah*, teaches us about the creation of the world and the role of the divine Will, according to the modes of syllogism and demonstration, but this secret of the Will is not that of the combination of the letters, for the letters, their forms and their combinations belong to the realm of images, and the secret of the Will is entirely abstract, totally separated from material images. Those who wish to explain the secrets of the intelligible world by the letters of the alphabet are victims of their imagination, since it is difficult for man to think without the help of the images; but, when one rises towards what is separated from matter, the letters also disappear, and this is the sought-for aim: to achieve an intellection totally separate from matter, absolutely simple and pure, without any trace of image.

Ibn Latif sees in the Scriptures and the *midrashim* numerous signs of this eminently secret knowledge of God and His relations with the world. We are sure of the two ends of the chain: at one extremity God, total Unity, totally unknowable, is pure perfection and His existence is demonstrated absolutely; at the other extremity is the corporeal world that we perceive by the senses. Between God and the world of matter are the ten *sefiroth* and the secret of the creation of the world: the twenty-two paths of the *Sefer Yezirah*, the *Book of Creation*.

God is One above the One, Will, Aspect, which is also the Name of God, the sign showing the way towards what resembles the comprehension of the perfect and absolute Unity, the way of the demonstration of the One of whom we only know that He exists.

This first Aspect that reveals God is the ensemble of the Ten Words by means of which God created the world; Ten like the number of the letters of the three Names of God, symbol of the Ten Commandments; it is above One, first of the series of numbers, the first *sefirah*. This first *sefirah* is *esh*, Fire; the second is *ruah*, Air, and the third *mayim*, Water. We recognize the three terms of the *Sefer Yezirah*. Fire is intelligible matter and form, eternal in their unique aspect, Air is these two intelligible entities in their separated aspect, like two lines that converge towards a point. At this point in creation, all the entities were in potentiality, in intellect, and not active, that is, they did not exist 'outside'. With the third *sefirah*, the superior Waters, we see the appearance of the hidden substance which carries the form of corporeality and which cuts short the two lines that were stretching to infinity. This third dimension is that of space, and in relation to Fire it is as the light of the moon to that of the sun.

The fourth *sefirah* is *hylé*, First Matter, the light of the sun emanating from the spiritual light and it causes to appear, by its presence alone, the light of the stars and the planets.

The fifth *sefirah* is Form; it is designated by the name of the Sphere of the Intellect, and even the philosophers recognized its existence.

The sixth *sefirah* is the form of the ninth sphere, which encompasses all the other spheres, the four remaining *sefiroth* being the other forms of the spheres (*ibid.* pp. 29 and 34).

All the *sefiroth* are united, for diversity is contained in Unity, as the individual and the species are contained in the genus.

It is not beyond the capabilities of the human spirit to attain to some knowledge of these *sefiroth* and it may even succeed in arriving at the level of the Will, the Divine Name. For the human soul is like a spark of this Name that has been precipitated into matter, and can return to its source.

When all the sparks will have regained their intelligible fatherland, the corporeal world, it seems, will disappear.

Ibn Latif, who claims to be a follower of Maimonides, reveals with an abundance of symbols the secrets of an intelligible neoplatonic world. We can understand why scholars have not known whether to consider him a philosopher or a Kabbalist, for his philosophical system is arrayed in flowing symbolical terms; it is a *feu d'artifice* of comparisons and resemblances. We are far from the dryness of Averroist Aristotelianism.

JUDAH BEN NISSIM IBN MALKAH

Concerning Judah ben Nissim Ibn Malkah we possess only two dates, 1260, which he himself gives in his *Commentary on the Prayers*, and the fact that he is cited by Isaac of Acre in about 1300. He probably lived in Morocco. Only part of his work has been published, but it forms the subject of a comprehensive study by G. Vajda.

The principal work, *Uns al Gharīb* (*The Consolation of the Exiled*), a dialogue between a master and his disciple, followed by a Commentary on the *Sefer Yeẓirah*, is still in manuscript. G. Vajda has published an abridged Hebrew translation of it by an anonymous author, which includes a résumé of the Commentary on the *Sefer Yeẓirah*. Also written in Arabic, his Commentary on the *Pirkei Rabbi Eliezer* (a *midrash* attributed to R. Eliezer) is still in manuscript and the *Commentary on the Prayers* is in course of publication.

The *Consolation of the Exiled* is a dialogue on the soul, exiled in the corporeal world, which must die to this world in order to revive in the world of the intellect. The way is that of knowledge, not of God, who is unknowable, but of the forces that rule the world and manifest His existence. Judah ben Nissim's thought is firmly rooted in these two principles: God is unknowable, the world and its laws are determined and knowable.

The Intellect, the first emanation, is designated by the Tetragram; it is 'the most subtle of substances, the light of the world, the first knowable cause, perfect, without fault in itself and in its acts' (G. Vajda, *Judah b. Nissim*, p. 20). The human soul, which, as in Judah ha-Cohen and some Neoplatonists, is on the third degree of the hierarchy of the intellects, yearns for its Well-Beloved, the Intellect, and the Song of Songs depicts the mutual love of the Intellect and the human soul. The traditional texts, biblical as well as midrashic – *Pirkei Rabbi Eliezer, Sefer Yeẓirah, Sefer ha-Bahir* – and the liturgy, lead the initiate to comprehend the mutual relations between the worlds, give him the key of the universe and permit him to act on this world. The alphabet, with its twenty-seven letters, symbolizes the whole of creation. The simple letters from *alef* to *tet* represent the intellects, *yod* to *ayn* the spheres, and the last letters, starting with *kof*, the beings of this lower world. In Judah ben Nissim the system is complicated by the attribution of a male or female character to the superior entities, which form couples. Further, the author attempts to reconcile the figures and letters of the *Sefer Yeẓirah* with those of the principal system, an exegesis that contributes very little to the clarity of the whole, but offers some interesting elements. For instance, in his interpretation of *Tohu* and *Bohu*, these two principles are engraved in matter – *hylé*, which is *mayim* (water), the third *sefirah* of the *Sefer Yeẓirah*. *Tohu* is the male principle and *Bohu* the female, which has no manifested existence, but is eternal passivity.

Judah ben Nissim's exposition does not definitely state his position on the relation between God and Creation. Was Creation an emanation, as generally in the Neoplatonists, or was it *ex nihilo*, as Judah ha-Cohen energetically maintains? However, the structure of the world becomes clear in his texts with the introduction of Matter and Form, from which emanate the world of the Intellects, that of the spheres and finally this lower world, each of them subject to that immediately above it.

Two aspects of Judah ben Nissim are particularly interesting – his explanation of magic and his political ideas. A great part of his work is devoted to the stars and to their influence over the lower world. In these passages he justifies not only astrology but also sympathetic magic; the wise man, through his knowledge of astral and physical laws, can influence his own destiny and that of those near to him. Prayer is efficacious, and this efficacity depends on the strength of the intention. The soul, when it is pure, is an astral force, and when it longs for its original place with a pure intention, it prays to the astral forces and its prayers are answered. It can thus repel ills, but cannot abolish death. On the other hand, the prayers of a community are more efficacious than those of a single individual, even when this community does not include learned men, for collective prayer and invocations repeated with a pure intention set the astral forces and souls in motion. The power of the word is accompanied by the utilization of the sympathy between astral forces and terrestrial things. In sacrificing agreeable things to the astral force, the sage attracts it, puts it in 'a good mood', which evokes the same disposition in the sage's own soul and fills it with overflowing force. The great difference between the worshippers of the stars and the sage is that the latter knows that the stars are only intermediaries between God and man, and that their power is limited in time, but is nevertheless ineluctable.

The domination of a star, says the master, continues during several generations, so that the generations living in the middle of a period ruled by a certain star believe that the order depending on it is unalterable. They do not know that this domination, like every other thing in the world, has a fixed duration that it cannot exceed. It is thus that the ancient peoples who practised the cult appropriate to a certain star prospered in their time, and then disappeared, their time at an end. The properly qualified sage, who knows the star dominant in his time and in the place where he lives, is capable of regulating both useful and pernicious influences for the best. The latter, if not completely eliminated, will be greatly restricted, so much so that the common people will not even perceive them. If, at the end of the period of the star's domination, another sage appears who is capable of recognizing the situation, he will be able to do what is necessary and prepare his compatriots to take the change that is about to occur into account. But if the duration of the group involved has indeed reached its final point, nothing can prevent their ruin. As for the opposition between the 'talismans' and the Law, it is purely apparent; if carefully regarded, the religious writings express the same truths as the books of talismans and of philosophy.

Are there no miracles that may disturb the natural order and the astral determination? What the vulgar people call miracle, says Judah ben Nissim, is only an operation effected by the sage using the virtues of astral influence, which are added to the elemental qualities of things. An example of these virtues is attraction: the magnet attracts iron thanks to an actual quality, not an elemental one.

Up to this point, religious practices, divination, miracles, are the province of the sage; however, there is also vulgar magic, practised by the ignorant, especially women, where neither purity of soul, nor prayer, nor sacrifice, comes into play. According to our author, even in these base manifestations of spiritual life, vestiges of the astral forces can be found; sorcerers, although they do not know the causes, possess at least a certain routine procedure, acquired by contact with the wise.

Judah ben Nissim's political doctrine is remarkable; its principal ideas are as follows: there are several sorts of governments: the method of rule by a perfect philosopher is principally characterized by its subordination to astral determination. There is not only one determination, but several, each having a different range; the most general extends to the whole world, while the others only govern a lesser part of the universe, the least strong exercising authority only over the destiny of a single individual. The legislator who understands this state of things uses it to best advantage.

It may be that by the effect of the astral determination the philosopher meets in his generation many well-disposed individuals; if the contrary is the case he is sometimes forced to put recalcitrants to death, even if this is against the philosophical 'way'. Certain philosophers will do this out of concern for the good of the greatest number; others however, will prefer to flee from human society rather than have recourse to these extreme means. Two conditions must be fulfilled in order that the sage may accomplish his task.

First, he must explain to the common people, by discourse proportioned to the intelligence of his listeners, that it is necessary to respect God, whose wisdom is incompatible with ill-doing.

Secondly, he must secure for himself the assistance of a leader who venerates him as a disciple venerates his master; thanks to the power of this chief, the sage will be enabled to carry out his didactic work.

A much inferior type of regime is that of the 'naturalist' philosopher. Such a man (whose errors are refuted by the Scriptures as by Aristotle) sees no further than the movement of the sky whence comes the life of form and matter, and where the constituent elements of the 'mixtures' originate. He denies astral determination and attributes liberty to man. He does not believe in the survival of the soul. His government allows free rein to the satisfaction of so-called natural desires.

The Master in the dialogue of the *Consolation of the Exiled* considers the contemporary dominance of religions as the victory of ignorance – we would say of obscurantism; he recommends the sage to conform to the belief of the vulgar only through prudent calculation, without giving it his inner adherence; he admits at the most that the Law is a stage preparatory to attaining the truths of a superior order.

When he brings himself to speak of the Jewish law, Judah ben Nissim wraps himself in even more precautions than usual and cannot insist strongly enough on the absolute necessity of secrecy. What makes for the superiority of the Israelite religion, he says, is that it is orientated towards universal determination (he does not forget to repeat that this force must not be identified with God), while the other religions rely on partial forces that rule over one period only, or the nativity of a single individual.

Judah ben Nissim Ibn Malkah's philosophy had hardly any influence on later Jewish thought. During the fourteenth century he is cited only by Isaac of Acre and Samuel Ibn Motot, and in the fifteenth century by Johanan Alemanno. In fact, until the Renaissance the practice of magic was rejected, or ignored, by the Jewish Aristotelian philosophers, who in this instance followed in the traces of their Arab homologues.

Quite different was the fate of the work of Abraham Abulafia, Judah ben Nissim's contemporary. For Abraham ben Samuel Abulafia, the two basic texts were the *Guide of the Perplexed* and the *Sefer Yeẓirah*. Judah ha-Cohen and Judah ben Nissim conceived the world and God according to the neo-platonic schema, where the Intellect is the first emanation. For Abraham Abulafia, the Active Intellect is the last of the separate Intelligences, as in the Aristotelians and Maimonides. Judah ha-Cohen's principal research was directed towards the appreciation of the various sciences and their claim, real or imaginary, to understand the world and God. Judah ben Nissim, whose ontological schema agrees more or less with that of Judah ha-Cohen, was more particularly interested in the utilization, theoretical and practical, of the science of the letters. Abraham Abulafia declared categorically that this 'science of the letters' should not be used for ends other than accession to contemplation and prophecy.

ABRAHAM BEN SAMUEL ABULAFIA

Abulafia was born at Saragossa, in 1240 and spent his childhood at Tudela, in Navarre. In 1260, after his father's death, he left for Palestine, but got no further than Acre. He returned to Italy, travelling through Greece, and at Capua studied the *Guide of the Perplexed*, under the direction of Hillel of Verona who will be discussed presently. There he also studied the *Sefer Yezirah* with Barukh Togarmi, author of a commentary on this treatise, who was himself influenced by Isaac Ibn Latif. The 'tradition of the letters' was then quite lively in Italy. Judah ha-Cohen was quite well known, among others by Hillel of Verona, and he was often cited. The influence exercised by Judah ha-Cohen's theology on Abulafia's system might be evaluated with some precision if this theology were to be studied and published, but, as things stand at present, one can only suppose that it played an important role.

Returning to Barcelona in 1271, Abulafia left Spain again two years later and led an adventurous life in Italy, Sicily and Greece. In 1280 he was again at Capua and went on to Rome, in order to appear before Pope Nicholas III to ask him to improve the lot of the Jews.

Condemned to the scaffold, he escaped execution thanks to the death of the Pope and in the years that followed he continued his teaching, announcing the coming of the Messiah for 1290. Attacked on the ground of these Messianic revelations, he continued to write and to defend himself. We know nothing of him after 1291.

The list of Abulafia's works is long. There are over thirty, most still in manuscript. Their character evolves as the author progresses in the ways of philosophy, prophecy, and Messianism. A recent thesis, as yet unpublished, by M. Idel, allows us to form a better idea of the works and doctrine of this author, and I shall make use of it in the following pages.

A large part of Abulafia's writing is devoted to the description of the way that leads to prophecy. Prophecy itself is defined as the emanation of the Active Intellect, an emanation that originates in God and overflows into the intellect and imagination of the prophet. The Active Intellect is identified with Metatron, the Angel who possesses the key to the esoteric truths, Israel, the Word, Moses and even the *Sefirah Malkhut*, the kingdom of the adherents of the sefirotic Kabbalah.

The divine influence spreads over the human soul in two different ways. If this influx only reaches the intellect, the result is knowledge and science. If it spreads over the intellect and the imagination, it is called 'Word'; but this 'Word' is not corporeally heard by the prophet. Visual and auditory sensations are only the product of the prophet's imagination.

The 'Divine Word' is free of all corporeal attributes. Human imagination plays a preponderant role in Abulafia's system, but this importance is also ambivalent, for although it is a means of attaining prophecy, the author defines it in the negative terms usually found in Maimonides and his commentators: it is Satan, matter; and only the victory of the Intellect over the evil instinct (the imagination) can lead to eternal life.

Judah ha-Cohen said that the divine science, the science of the letters, contains and includes the two other sciences, physics and mathematics—

astronomy; but he wrote an encyclopedia based on the great scientific texts of his time. Abulafia declares that meditation on the letters, those of the Divine Name in particular, leads to mathematical, philosophical, scientific knowledge more easily than do the deductive methods of the natural experimental sciences, or philosophical logic.

In fact, the *Torah* is identical with God, the separate intellects and the Active Intellect. On the historical level, the Law, *Torah*, having been given to the human intellect and imagination, has a nature determined by these two human faculties. The esoteric sense of the *Torah* is the oral Law that is the combination of the Divine Names, and it was transmitted to Moses on Mount Sinai.

The mystic must understand the Law on three different planes:

– That of the commandments, an exoteric level that carries traces of the intellect and the imagination that received it;

– The philosophical level, where the relation between the human soul and the Active Intellect is described;

– An esoteric level, where the soul can mount towards the divine world and attempts to join the Intellect. This level precedes the comprehension of the Law as a tissue of Divine Names, the level of the prophet joined to the Intellect, where he can act on the world, a real possibility, which Abulafia firmly rejects. The aim of the combining of the divine Names is to attain prophecy, not to exploit magical powers.

Abulafia describes at length the techniques that allow one to reach the prophetic level, and it is evident that he is speaking of what he knows and that he has scaled the degrees of mystical knowledge. At this point we cite M. Idel:

Since the Merkava mysticism, through the evidences found in the Gaonic period and in Ashkenazi Hassidism, we find various techniques which use the Holy Names in order to change the level of consciousness; while the techniques before Abulafia use these names as a whole, in his technique we find combinations of the separate letters of the Names of God with the letters of the alphabets. There are three stages in Abulafia's techniques; the written combination, the utterance of these combinations and the intellectual combinations. Other elements of his technique are breathing and movements of the head according to the vowels. The breathing is composed of three elements; inspiration, expiration and obstruction; this threefold division reminds us of the Yoga system of breathing. There are some preliminary conditions to the process of 'remembering' the Name of God: an isolated room; white clothes; phylacteries and tallith; complete rejection of worldly thoughts.

The mystic has to visualize the letters of God's Name in order to attain the prophetic consciousness. The main difference between Abulafia's technique and Yoga, Hesychasm or Sufism is his concentration on a changing object; while these techniques try to still the mind, the aim of Abulafia's technique is the intensification of mental activity by the necessity to concentrate on a complex of actions.

There are three main uses of music in Abulafia's system: (a) the process of playing on the harp reminds him of the combination of the letters; the musical tones gladden the soul by their various combinations, while the combinations of letters gladden the intellect; (b) playing on the harp is an image of the prophetic experience; the well known image of the prophet as a lyre on which the Holy Spirit plays occurs twice in Abulafia's books; (c) music is an organic part of the technique; the mystic sings the consonants according to the vowels; in later manuals, like the book *Ladder of Ascension* by Juda Albotini, instrumental music also appears, apparently under the influence of Sufism.

The prophetic experience of Abulafia has two main characteristics: sensual aspects and imaginative visions. Throughout the experience, the mystic may see light at the beginning, and hear speech at the second stage. The first is attributed by Abulafia to the theosophic Kabbalists, while the second stage appears especially when using the 'path of names'. The speech is superior to the light because it is the origin of prophecy. Abulafia describes the process of prophecy as a conversation between the mystic and himself; he asks a question and answers it, changing the voice. Abulafia sees the form of a man, which is the projection of his own soul and its faculties: the intellect and the imagination. Another vision of Abulafia is the vision of the letters of the Holy Name, which also contains the faculties mentioned above. A peculiar vision of letters is that of the Urim and Thummim, which are also the intellect and imagination. The most interesting vision is that of the circle or the sphere, which reminds us of the mandalas described by C. Jung. This circle like the mandala, is a cosmogram and a psychogram because its movement alludes to the structure of the world and its processes, and the structure of the soul. The appearance of the Metatron is alluded to in the Book of Eternal Life and the Book of the Sign, where this angel is described as an old man.

Abulafia warns against the fire, which is an image of the demonic imagination which tries to burn the intellect; when the imagination is overcome the intellect cleaves to the Active Intellect and they become one; He speaks about a total fusion not only of the human intellect with the Active Intellect, but also with the Divine Intellect, God Himself. This fusion is attained when the knots of the soul are unknotted, and the soul knots itself to the intellectual world.

The main characteristic of Abulafia's mysticism is that it is a rational type of experience, because the intellect is the organ of the experience and the supreme object of the aspiration is an intellect, the Active Intellect or God, Abulafia's mysticism is a fusion between emissary prophecy and intellectual experience. He sees himself as one of the classical prophets and his books as worthy as the prophetic books. His experiences are eschatologic in character, because during the ecstasy the mystics feel the bliss of the next world in this world.

One of the most interesting features of Abulafia's mysticism is the fact that his visions are projections of the speculative concepts known before the experience. Lastly, there is no trace of asceticism in his system.

Describing the prophetic experience, Abulafia uses images which may be arranged according to this scheme: Kiss, Intercourse, Semen, Impregnation, Son and New Birth. These images are compounded of corporeal elements and their function is to describe the development of the prophetic process, which begins with the kiss, that is the cleaving of the soul to the Active Intellect, and ends with the birth of the son, the completely actualized intellect. This birth is also the new birth of man because he achieves immortality by this intellect; this is the Jewish counterpart of the motif of rebirth which occurs in the mystic literature. Remarkably enough, Abulafia's use of these images differs completely from the Kabbalistic use of intercourse as a symbol for theosophical processes; in Abulafia's view, the erotic imagery is only a means to exemplify the way in which prophecy reaches the soul, and there is no speculative or other meaning to the very act of intercourse. But, as during intercourse, the mystic experiences a feeling of intense delight, described as 'anointment'. This delight is, in Abulafia's eyes, the supreme aim of the prophet and is more important than the rational insight. The stress on the voluptuous aspects of the mystic experience reminds us of both Sufism and the Christian nuptial system.

('Abraham Abulafia's Works and Doctrine', pp. xiv–xviii)

We must note that this whole group of philosophers originating in Spain, who allied Neoplatonism to Aristotelianism while using a vocabulary close to that of the Kabbalah, is at present the subject of study by several scholars, and more substantial expositions will no doubt become possible in the course of a few years.

Moses ben Joseph ha-Levi of Seville should be mentioned for completeness' sake, before we leave Spain. He was a thirteenth-century philosopher of whom we know only his name and some fragments, admittedly quite long, of a work that has not survived in its entirety. He wrote in Arabic, and it was Judah Ibn Waqar, who will be discussed in the next chapter, who preserved his *Metaphysical Treatise* and two other fragments by incorporating them into his own work. The Hebrew translation of the *Treatise* has also been preserved, in three manuscripts, enabling H. A. Wolfson to reconstitute Averroes' lost treatise on the Prime Mover, which Moses ha-Levi cited in order to be able to refute it. Ha-Levi was particularly preoccupied with the problem of God and His relation with the Prime Mover; he accepts Al-Ghazālī's proposition intercalating another entity called the 'Word' between God and the Prime Mover. However, the surviving texts do not allow much more to be said about this author.

The Italian philosophers

The Italian philosophers have remained little-known until now. However, the research undertaken in Jerusalem by G. Sermoneta and his pupils has already yielded brilliant results, and the features characterizing Jewish thought in Italy have begun to emerge.

Jacob Anatoli, living in Naples, had brought the Maimonidean tradition to that city. His pupil *Moses ben Solomon of Salerno* (d. 1279) wrote a *Commentary on the Guide of the Perplexed*, which is still in manuscript. This commentary on the first two books of the *Guide* is an interesting example of the collaboration between Jewish and Christian philosophers. Moses of Salerno not only constantly refers to the Latin translation of the *Guide*, but gives the vulgar Latin equivalents of many Hebrew terms. Given the different contexts, the terms do not altogether correspond. Moses of Salerno consulted Nicholas of Giovinazo, a Dominican monk, on this subject, and quotes his comments on chapters 52 and 53 of Book I of the *Guide*, which discuss relation and correlation: to a scholastic, these terms evoke the relationships between the three Persons of the Trinity, where the categories of relation and correlation are defined with much more precision and distinct shades of meaning than in Arab and Jewish philosophy, so that the Hebrew translator and Maimonides himself are criticized for confusing philosophical notions.

Apart from a little treatise called *Ta'anot* (*Argumentations*), Moses of Salerno also composed a Hebrew–Italian philosophical glossary, based on Samuel Ibn Tibbon's *Glossary* of difficult words in the *Guide of the Perplexed*. In this *Glossary* problems are often posed in terms analogous to those used by Christian scholars. For Moses of Salerno, who in this is a good representative of Italian Jewish philosophy, Arab and Jewish philosophy agree with Christian Thought. But in this, he was in accord with a number of Christian Italian philosophers of the thirteenth century.

ZERAHIAH BEN SHEALTIEL GRACIAN OF BARCELONA

In Zerahiah, who considered himself an official commentator of Maimonides, the scholastic climate is less perceptible. Son of an old Barcelona family, he emigrated to Rome. All his works were composed between 1277 and 1291. He was a professor of Maimonidean philosophy, and was recognized as such by the Jewish community of Rome. He himself says that he found among his pupils an audience that accepted his ideas and his exegeses. Apart from books on medicine (Galen, Avicenna, Maimonides), Zerahiah translated, from Arabic only, Aristotle's *De Anima*, Themistius' *Commentary on the De Coelo*, Al-Fārābī's *Book on the Substance of the Soul*, the *Middle Commentaries* of Averroes on the *Physics*, the *Metaphysics* and the *Parva Naturalia* and finally the *Book of Causes* by Pseudo-Aristotle and fragments of the *Elements of Theology* (by Proclus), casting doubt on the attribution usually made to Aristotle.

It is possible that the eternal divine wisdom originating in God took on its very great importance for Zerahiah under the influence of these two latter neoplatonic texts, but one should also remember that he knew and used Judah ha-Cohen and perhaps other Spanish philosophical texts.

Zerahiah's compositions have not all been preserved; of his great work, a commentary on the *Guide of the Perplexed*, designed on two levels, for novices and for accomplished philosophers, there only remains the greater part of Book I, in two different versions. Letters to his relation Judah ben Solomon and his controversy with Hillel of Verona supplement this commentary on certain points. He also wrote commentaries on Proverbs and Job.

Basing himself on Moses Ibn Tibbon's distinction between statistical laws and rare phenomena, Zerahiah affirms the reality of certain extra-ordinary facts, like the existence of giants. To this philosophical proof he adds the reality of archeological finds: he himself saw at Rome a tooth of such great size that the head from which it came could only have been that of a giant; further, the existence of a complete gigantic skeleton was reported in a village near Rome, and the thickness of its skull was half a span. These statements in no way represent a return to the religious tradition. Following Averroes he carefully distinguishes philosophy from religion. He who mingles the two domains understands nothing of either. Maimonides can only be understood through the philosophical texts; a reading of them will illuminate the 'secrets' of the *Guide of the Perplexed.*

This tendency to interpret Maimonides in an Averroistic sense is also shown in his correspondence with Hillel of Verona. The latter, taking sides with Saadiah Gaon, understood Jacob's struggle with the angel as a real event; in the same way, he says, the gift of speech to Balaam's ass should be understood in the literal sense.

Zerahiah's answer is based on the *Guide*: all this happened in a vision, in the prophet's spirit, without anything taking place in exterior reality. These anecdotes, like many others, are allegories designed to teach us certain truths.

HILLEL BEN SAMUEL OF VERONA

The position of Zerahiah Gracian conforms to the Provençal Maimonidean doctrine and is supported by Spanish Arabic texts. On the other hand, Hillel ben Samuel of Verona, whom Zerahiah does not consider to be a true philosopher, had read and translated Christian texts. The sources of the Christian philosophers were often the Arabic authors used by Hillel (although Avicenna was preferred to Averroes by the authors that Hillel used) but the Arabic sources had already been reinterpreted by the scholastics, who often chose among these texts those that reflected a neoplatonic sense or contained notions borrowed from earlier Christian authors such as Chalcidius, Boetius, and others.

Hillel ben Samuel, physician and Talmudist, scion of a famous family of Talmudists, lived at Naples in 1254, and then at Capua. He translated from Latin a number of treatises on medicine by Hippocrates, Galen, and also by Bruno of Lungoburgo who wrote his *Chirurgia Magna* in 1254. Hillel played an important part in the counter-attack of the philosophers against the anti-philosophers during the resumption of the quarrel in 1289–90, and two letters that he had addressed on this subject to his friend Isaac ben Mordecai (Maestro Giao), have been preserved. It was most probably in part thanks to him that Solomon ben Abraham of Montpellier, instigator of the ban against the philosophers, was in his turn excommunicated by the rabbis of Babylonia, Israel and Italy. Although Hillel was an ardent defender of Maimonides, we have seen that he was eager to preserve the literal sense of the miracles and did not accept an allegorical interpretation. Similarly, in his principal work, concluded at Forlí in 1291, *Tagmulei ha-Nefesh* (*Retributions of the Soul*), he tends towards solutions more acceptable to religion than is the Averroistic solution; in fact, Zerahiah was right: Hillel was a poor enough philosopher, and the *Retributions of the Soul* is made up of bits and pieces. This book has recently been published in a critical edition, and I shall here make use of the analysis by the editor, G. Sermoneta, who thus describes the work:

In this section R. Hillel has combined three short tractates of different authorship concerning the soul, in particular concerning its intellectual part, which were popular and accepted in his time. The first consists of several fragments of the Latin version of Avicenna's book on the soul, *Liber Sextus Naturalium*, to which are added expanded sections from the *Liber de Anima* written by the Christian scholar and translator, Dominicus Gundisalinus (twelfth century in Toledo, Spain), who follows Avicenna on this question. Conscious of the fact that Avicenna's explanation could no longer satisfy the demands of contemporary readers and scholars, R. Hillel also appended to these writings a treatise by Averroes entitled *Three Articles on the Intellect*. This R. Hillel translated from the Latin version *Tractatus de Animae Beatitudine* into Hebrew, but also had before him the Hebrew version from the Arabic, translated by R. Shemu'el Ibn Tibbon. Finally, R. Hillel added to these texts the translation of the first chapter of the *Tractatus de Unitate Intellectus contra Averroistas* ('Article of the Unity of the Intellect against the Averroists'), written in 1270 by Thomas Aquinas. It had apparently reached R. Hillel very quickly and was the most recent commentary to appear, but R. Hillel does not mention the author's name. In contrast to the first two treatises, the third is presented as if it were Hillel's own new commentary whose aim is to bring the older and standard works up to date. R. Hillel reworked the material of the treatises he had read and translated, sometimes paraphrasing the texts or summarizing or deleting portions of them. He completely changed the order of the texts as if wishing to conceal his plagiarism. The tractate of Aquinas, in R. Hillel's opinion, proved the incorrectness of Averroes's conclusions regarding the end of the individual human soul at the time of the parting from the body; it showed that the individuality of the soul and the eternity of its intellectual part might be proved on the basis of Aristotelian psychology.   (*Hillel ben Samuel of Verona*; *Sefer Tagmulei ha-Nefesh*, pp. vi–vii)

In conformity with Thomas Aquinas, Hillel of Verona maintains the individual immortality of the soul. This allows him to reintegrate traditional notions of reward and punishment, a reward and punishment that are spiritual and not physical. The last part of the book contains three further small dissertations: (1) Knowledge and free will; (2) The question of death and the link with Adam's fall; (3) The Fall of the Angels; and these dissertations also are strongly flavoured with Christian theorism.

JUDAH BEN MOSES BEN DANIEL ROMANO

In the following generation a decidedly more profound philosopher appears: Judah ben Moses ben Daniel Romano.

Born *ca.* 1280, (d. *ca.* 1325) he was a pupil of Zerahiah Gracian and most probably succeeded him as a teacher of Maimonidean philosophy. For some time he was a translator at the court of Robert of Anjou, and his translations from Latin are numerous. Apart from the *Book of Causes* of the Pseudo-Aristotle and the *De Substantia Coeli* by Averroes, he translated a treatise on the *One and the Unity* by Dominicus Gundissalinus (whether compilation or translation is not known); several works by Aegidius of Rome (1247–1316), whom he calls the 'Friar Preacher'; and several others by Albertus Magnus (1193–1289); the 'Minor Friar'; Alexander of Hales (1170–1274); Angelo of Camerino (thirteenth century); and Thomas Aquinas. It is noticeable that these translations were made very soon after the appearance of the original works: Judah used Aegidius of Rome's treatises between 1315 and 1330. But this was also the case with other Italian Jewish philosophers, for Hillel of Verona translated the first part of Aquinas' *De Unitate Intellectus* about twenty years after it was written. In the literary field the situation was similar, for Emmanuel of Rome, to whom we shall return, produced a Hebrew imitation of Dante's *Inferno* and *Paradiso* contemporary with the publication of the work.

Apart from these translations, Judah Romano composed a Judeo–Italian glossary of the *Mishneh Torah*. His other works, all unpublished, include: a *Commentary on Genesis*; *Chapters on Prophecy* (sixty-six chapters); various exegeses on biblical passages; a commentary on the *Kiddush* and the *Kedushah* (sanctification of the Name of God); and *Ben Porat*, a commentary on the first four books of Maimonides' *Book of Knowledge*.

His original works are strongly coloured by the Latin scholasticism that he knew so well. In fact, when one reads him, one has the impression of reading a translation from Latin, even when this is not the case. Certainly, citations abound; but more than this, Judah, writing in Hebrew, seems to have thought in philosophical terms corresponding to Latin. This impression is particularly striking when one compares contemporary philosophical treatises written in Provence. This is not so much a matter of influence as rather of the Jewish philosopher's participation in an intellectual climate that he shared with the Christian philosophers of his time.

Concerning creation, he echoed Maimonides: there are no scientific proofs, either of creation or of eternity; we only have non-decisive arguments in favour of the one or the other hypothesis. From the philosophical point of view, the eternity of the world presents such difficulties that the hypothesis of creation is the only acceptable one. On this point scholastic opinion of his time was in agreement with Maimonides, interpreted in a certain way.

Union with the Intellect is evoked by Judah Romano in connection with Enoch; Adam was created pure and inclining towards the Intellect, but Eve caused man's potential tendency to materiality to become actual. It would not have been impossible for Adam to remain under the dominion of the Intellect, but he let himself be tempted and was expelled from paradise. Of the couple's first two children, the first was entirely material, and the second half material; only Enoch attained true intellection.

How far can man go in his search for the intellect? Like the Provençal philosophers, Judah Romano believed in the possibility of union with the Active Intellect. God cannot be known, either in His essence or in His existence. We do know the existence and the species of the separate Intellects, but not their essence nor the differences between them. The Active Intellect, on the other hand, can be known in its essence and in its existence, and, through this intellection, man can reach total conjunction with it.

For Judah Romano, this conjunction with the Active Intellect entails a conception of biblical exegesis *sui generis*: there is no connection between the content of the biblical verse and its explanation by the philosopher. First, the philosopher has to achieve the degree of abstract thought. This can be done by means of meditation on philosophical matters, including scholastic texts; this level of abstract and general thinking is the highest man can attain. The prophet as well as the philosopher reaches this level by studying all the particular sciences, which achieve a higher status when they become a part of the prophetic science of sciences, but they remain an essential part of prophecy, first because the prophet needs them in order to attain the degree of prophethood and secondly because the people receiving his prophecies understand them because of their profound accord with the sciences, known by natural knowledge.

When the philosopher exegete has reached the degree of intellect, of 'inspiration' (here G. Sermoneta invokes Dante), the explanations he gives of a biblical verse may be altogether different from the literal sense of this verse, for when this degree is reached there is no differentiation between truths. Every part of the true universal knowledge provides as valid an explanation of the verse as any other part. The symbols of the prophetic text are, like the particular sciences, a part of the universal science of sciences, and the interpreter will find as many truths in the verse as inspiration and association of ideas will bring him. And indeed Judah Romano gives fifteen different interpretations for one verse of the Psalms.

To Romano the prophet is a philosopher, a guide to intellectual knowledge, and not so much a lawgiver. This insistence on the ontological and cognitive aspect of prophecy is in agreement with Thomas Aquinas and the Christian scholastics, to whom Judah Romano was very close.

Immanuel ben Solomon of Rome (Emanuele Giudeo, *ca.* 1261–1328), was better known as a poet than as a philosopher; his compositions are celebrated and it is known that he imitated the Divine Comedy. He wrote poems on love, friendship, and wine, while in other poems, as in his philosophical commentaries, he exalted total detachment from matter and the superiority of the intellect.

He produced commentaries on almost all parts of the Bible, but only those on Proverbs, Psalms, Lamentations, Esther, Ruth and the Song of Songs have been published, sometimes only in part. A fragment of his *Commentary on Genesis* has recently appeared. He also wrote a work on logic, *Eben Bohan* (*The Touchstone*), of which only the introduction has been published. His explication of the alphabet does not seem to have survived except for the introductory poem included in the poetical compositions.

In his biblical commentaries, he first explains the literal and grammatical sense, then the intention of the text, that is, the philosophical meaning. These commentaries are, in fact, a kind of compilation, where one finds citations from Abraham Ibn Ezra, Maimonides, Jacob Anatoli, Judah ben Solomon ha-Cohen and Judah Romano. The theme of intellectual love, which was, as G. Sermoneta has rightly said, 'the philosophical faith', frequently appears in the work. The erudite illustration of this 'philosophical faith' seems to be the only purpose of these biblical exegeses, and one cannot help thinking of a stylistic exercise, brilliant in itself and appropriate to a literary, elegant society, where philosophical problems had become the subject of drawing-room discussion.

Chapter 8

THE FOURTEENTH CENTURY

The beginning of the fourteenth century is dominated by the great figure of Gersonides. Although drawing on the same sources as his contemporaries, his thought is in decided contrast to the comparatively homogeneous picture presented by the Jewish philosophy of the period. There was a great flourishing of philosophers, during the fourteenth century, in Provence, in Spain, and in the Byzantine Empire, and although some of them had original ideas, generally speaking the ingredients of their thinking did not change.

First, one sees a strong recrudescence of astrology, often accompanied by neoplatonic features. An astonishing number of commentaries on Ibn Ezra's commentary were composed: Judah Ibn Mosconi, writing in 1362, states that he knows of nearly thirty (of which only ten, he says, are of any interest). The first, by Abishai of Sagori, of whom we know nothing, seems to be dated 1170, only slightly later than Ibn Ezra; the second, by Moses Ibn Tibbon, is thirteenth-century, and all the rest fourteenth. M. Steinschneider gives a list of thirty-six authors of such commentaries, and there were at least twenty anonymous ones. A 'moral testament' recommending the study of Ibn Ezra was attributed to Maimonides, in spite of his strong opposition to astrology, this 'testament' was cited by Judah Ibn Mosconi (in the introduction to his commentary) and by Shem Tov ben Isaac Ibn Shaprut (also in his introduction).

While Maimonides and Averroes remained obligatory references and provided the basic structure of Jewish thought, the central problems discussed and the manner of approach reflected the proximity of scholastic philosophy. This can be seen in Yedayah ha-Penini's treatment of the problem of individual forms, at the very beginning of the century; in that of contingent futures in the twenties, and in that of non-Aristotelian (Parisian) physics at the end of the period.

During the second half of the fourteenth century translations of medical works from Latin into Hebrew were still more frequent than those of philosophical texts, but the first translations of logic begin to appear, and one feels that this was only the beginning of a great development.

At the end of the thirteenth century the Kabbalah was still in some respects an esoteric movement; in the fourteenth, it became popular, as had happened before with philosophy, and philosophers could no longer ignore the kabbalistic texts and theological constructions which claimed to be part of the tradition, and which the people, as well as many scholars, considered the true expression of Judaism.

YEDAYAH HA-PENINI

Yedayah ben Abraham Bedersi ha-Penini (En Bonet Profiat) (*ca.* 1270–1340) lived at the turn of the century. He or his family were natives of Beziers (Bedersi) but he lived in Perpignan and Montpellier. He was most probably a physician, for he indited some notes on a part of Avicenna's Canon, afterwards collected in a book that has remained in manuscript. As a boy he composed a poem in a thousand words that all began with the letter *mem*, and his father was so proud of this that he wrote an encomium, which figures in several manuscripts. Also well-known were a short treatise in defence of women and a book of moral sentences, called *Behinat Olam* (*Examination of the World*). This latter work had considerable and lasting success and there are many manuscript copies. In 1865 Renan enumerated forty-four printed editions of the Hebrew text, several translations (two in French, the first dated 1629; the English translation appeared in London in 1806) and more than ten commentaries. Yedayah was thus a *littérateur* of some renown when he wrote his *Ketav Hitnazlut* (*Letter of Apology*) in defence of the study of philosophy against its detractors. Addressed to Solomon ben Adret, probably before the decree expelling the Jews from France in 1306, it does not seem to have received a reply. Yedayah declares that he does not know the exegeses that Levi ben Abraham is accused of inventing:

You have been told that someone has explained Abraham as representing matter, Sarah as representing form and the tribes as representing the planets; but I can assure you that this is by no means the case. All that one does in the schools is to explain as allegories the aggadic passages of the Talmud, which cannot be taken literally, and in this we follow in the steps of our great master [Moses Maimonides] ... As for the crime of which we are accused, that instead of the Talmud we study foreign sciences, that is, the books of Aristotle and his commentators, we declare that the study of logic, physics and metaphysics is useful to fortify religion; thus these studies furnish us with proofs of the existence of God, of prophecy, of free will, of creation *ex nihilo*, and so on ... the rabbis in Spain, in Babylonia and in Andalusia, by their knowledge of Arabic, were able to make use of philosophical books; they were able to demonstrate the unity of God and to repel anthropomorphism.   (*Ketav ha-Hitnazlut*, fol. 114v)

After having surveyed the various Jewish philosophers since David al-Muqammis and Saadiah Gaon, Yedayah continues:

But the culminating point was reached by our great master Moses Maimonides, who knew philosophy through Aristotle and his commentators, mathematics through Euclid and his successors, astronomy through Ptolemy and his school, medicine through Hippocrates and Galen. He bases himself, in his theology, on the tradition, subjecting it to the examination of philosophy. It is he who has given the best explanation of prophecy and it is he who successfully combatted the anthropomorphic ideas current in his epoch. We have seen Letters coming from all parts of the world, attacking him, during the first dispute, especially because he denied the notion that attributed measure and body to God. The poet En Vidas [thirteenth-century] says in fact of his contemporaries in Spain that they know the Measure of the Creator, but they do not proclaim it for fear of being considered unbelievers. Nahmanides also says in his *Apologetic Letter* that Maimonides is he who has contributed most to the overthrow of anthropomorphic ideas. In fact, if this idea no longer exists among us, we owe this to the study of philosophy. We see by the letter addressed to us that you only forbid the study of natural philosophy and the subjects related to it, while you permit the study of medicine, because the Law is not opposed to it. Mathematics [and astronomy] are also not mentioned, probably because they are not harmful to the Faith . . . [but] in the branches of permitted studies there are as many dangers to the faith as in those that you prohibit. Astronomy, for instance, leads on to astrology, and can lead to idolatry, and as for medicine, if one turns to a man, it is because one does not have full confidence in God. Thus King Asa [II Chronicles 16: 12] was reproved by the prophet in that he did not interrogate God when he was ill, instead of consulting the doctors; this is why the rabbis approved King Hezekiah for hiding [placing in the Genizah] the books of medicine.

(Ibid. fol. 120v)

In conclusion Yedayah asks Solomon ben Adret to reconsider his decision regarding the excommunication:

(1) For the honour of Maimonides, whose works, whether of philosophy or of theology, will continue to be studied in spite of all the prohibitions; (2) For the honour of ben Adret himself, because his prohibition will be transgressed, in favour of Maimonides; (3) for the honour of Provence, which was and still is the seat of the Law, and especially for the honour of Montpellier, the great learned town.

It is certain that if the Prophet Joshua were to come to tell the Provençals of the present generation not to study the books of Maimonides, he would hardly succeed; for they have the firm intention of sacrificing their fortunes and even their lives to defend the books of Maimonides. The fathers would recommend their sons to do the same. Why then continue the struggle, since you have not succeeded up to the present, by any means? You have carried out your duty without profit; you should therefore abandon this position and rather make peace with the scholars of Provence. Then, there will be light for all the children of Israel in their dwellings.

(Ibid. fol. 125v)

It is clear that Yedayah believed that the dispute was with the Provençals in general but, also, he saw quite well that the accusations levelled against the 'bad' philosophers, Maimonides not being personally attacked, were in fact directed against the Master himself. And he was right in predicting that excommunication would not prevent philosophy from flourishing.

In another part of his letter he describes the way in which difficult passages from the Talmud and the *midrashim* were explained in the schools; and he himself wrote down some explanations of this kind. Only the part on the *aggadot* related to the Psalms has been published. According to citations in other works, it seems that Yedayah commented on the *aggadot* of almost the whole Talmud. These commentaries have not been preserved in their entirety;

however, substantial fragments occur in several manuscripts. They offer philosophical explanations of no great originality, repeating the well-known allegories of the human intellect and its relations with the Active Intellect. Providence is interpreted as being the natural law that God has determined for the world, and so on. Yedayah's method, however, considerably differs from that of his predecessors; far from trying to interpret each word or each expression of the text, he inquires into the general sense of the passage and analyses its philosophical signification. His interpretations display moderation and good sense; although he believes in astrology, he points out that daily preoccupation with this science hinders its fervent followers considerably on the practical level of taking decisions and in their professional activities, as also in the acquisition of learning. He repeats that philosophy is not destined for the people, and, ill understood, does them harm.

His purely philosophical writings concern the points being debated in his time by Jewish and Christian philosophers. It seems that his notes on Averroes' *Commentary on the Physics*, a commentary on the twenty-five propositions preceding Book II of the *Guide of the Perplexed*, some notes on logic and a *Treatise on the First Beings* have been lost. A unique manuscript (Paris, Bibliothèque nationale, MS héb. 984) contains five other treatises. The first two are devoted to the question of the intellect, and begin with a paraphrase of a short treatise by al-Fārābī that exists elsewhere in Hebrew translation; then follow the various opinions pronounced by philosophers concerning the hylic intellect. The next two treatises are an examination of the notion of opposition and of contrariness in movement, and refer to Averroes' *Great Commentary* on the *De Coelo* (I, 4). S. Pines' detailed analysis of these works cannot be summarised here, but I would like to note the points that seemed of particular interest to him:

(1) The fact that Yedayah had recourse to Aristotelian concepts of physics and logic in his discussion of mathematics or subjects related to mathematics.

(2) The distinction between space in the world situated under the sphere of the moon, in which the actual existence of a straight line is possible (which illustrates the first point) and space in the world of the spheres where the actual existence of a straight line is impossible.

(3) The nominalist idea that number, and what appertains to it, exists only in the soul or the intellect and not in the external world.

These three points to a certain extent follow the line of Aristotle and of Averroes' commentaries, although the details suggest that Yedayah had listened to discussions in Christian circles; the third point especially brings him closer to the nominalist notions that William of Occam investigated later. The last treatise indicates still more clearly our author's relations with scholasticism. In fact, his *Treatise on the Particular and Individual Forms* tackles a problem that had not been posed in Jewish philosophy, but had been discussed by Duns Scotus.

Every species, man, dog, horse, etc., has a form that distinguishes it from other species. However, within a given species the individuals differ. One dog is big, black, gentle and obedient, another is a little white mongrel, snarling and unruly; what accounts for the differences between these two individuals is not the form of the species but something particular: the *haecceitas*, which Duns Scotus does not identify with the individual form. However, the distinctions that he established between the *haecceitas* and the individual form tended to become effaced after him. Yedayah, after a detailed discussion, affirms the existence of individual forms, which places him in contradiction to the whole Judeo–Arabic philosophical current, since form, by definition, is general; his affirmation can only be explained by the strong influence of the Scotist school. However, Yedayah never cites Duns Scotus, but only the Arabic and Jewish philosophers. In fact, even when the Jewish philosophers of Northern Spain and Provence in the fourteenth century were aware of philosophical theories emanating from the Christian milieu, they did not cite their sources, and it is only by comparing ideas current in both circles that one can recognize common notions and influences.

NISSIM BEN MOSES OF MARSEILLE

Nissim ben Moses has left a commentary on the *Torah* called *Sefer ha-Nissim* (*Book of Miracles*). It is also called *Ma'assei Nissim* (*Miraculous Works*) and *Ikkarei ha Dat* (*The Principles of Religion*). This last title is a good description of the commentary, probably written between 1315 and 1325 or even 1330, which echoes all the problems presenting themselves to a Jewish philosopher. He does not fail to specify that his book is not made for the ignorant or for young men of less than forty, and he indignantly rejects the accusation that the philosophers do not strictly observe all the commandments; if there are any such, they are not true philosophers.

The book has been preserved in several manuscripts, and I shall cite that in Paris (héb. 720). The commentary is preceded by a general introduction in which the principles of biblical exegesis are elucidated. Science and *Torah* both come from God but they do not have the same function in the economy of Creation:

Your great principle should be the following: try whenever you can to adjust the texts to what the intellect positively indicates, even if the explanation be far-fetched; if you cannot [make them agree with reason] place [these verses] in the class of the promises that no religion can do without. In fact, religion is a general law which is given to the few, the philosophers, and to the common people, the ignorant, and also to women and children. However, the law applies to all without distinction.

(Fol. 31r)

The separate roles of philosophy and faith are very clearly delimited: knowledge leads to supreme felicity, which is union with the Intellect; religion, which includes ethics and politics, is designed to correct the faults of the human composition, to perfect corporeal nature and institute harmony between individuals in society. From philosophy comes light for the spirit, from faith, health of the human body and peace in human society. The philosopher attains knowledge and does not occupy himself with the continuance of material life; the prophet has no part of philosophical truth and his only role is to make the communities aware of dangers that may menace them, dangers which he recognizes thanks to his knowledge of the astral laws. For, although the celestial bodies taken as a whole are appointed to bring good to the world, there are circumstances when this good is accompanied by sundry ills, which are due to matter, or else to the fact that little ills are often concomitant with a great good. True wisdom therefore consists in modelling one's conduct according to the nature and the disposition of the skies.

Divine providence may be defined as the care that God has taken to give men righteous commandments to keep them in the straight path of nature, and to give them prophets who warn them of coming ills, so that they may arm themselves against them. There is no essential difference between the prophet and the sage who knows the astrological laws, for both must concentrate, and acquire a preliminary knowledge of the peoples or the individuals whom they wish to protect; both must be near to God and far from futile thoughts. For both, it is the imaginative faculty that brings them knowledge of the future; and their degree of perfection will depend on their nature, their virtues, their conduct and their lesser or greater concentration. When it is said: 'The LORD . . . heareth the prayer of the righteous' (Proverbs 15: 29), what is meant is this knowledge that is received by the pious, and not any change in the nature of things.

Nissim ben Moses quite openly admits that certain objects of certain rites possess a special power in the acquisition or preparation of divination and prophecy; thus the sacrifice of animals, or the concentration of the gaze on talismans or stones such as those on the pectoral of the High Priest, have particular virtue in awakening the imagination and helping it to reach the future.

Miracles are also in part the fruit of the prophet's ability to attain knowledge of the laws of the world. The *Torah* and the prophets, and also the tradition of our sages, tell us of miracles and prodigies, things marvellous and strange, which are impossible, and go outside the domain of scientific demonstrations. These miracles are of two kinds:

(1) Those of which it is told that they were performed through the intermediary of a prophet or some other privileged individual;
(2) Those that are narrated without mention of a prophet.

In the first category may be included events occurring only in the presence of God and the prophet, and also events involving other persons. The events involving only God and the prophets took place either in a prophetic vision or in a waking state. The very strong sensations experienced by the prophet are due to the action of the imaginative faculty and the internal senses; they have no correlative in the external world and are not based on external sensations; an example is Abraham's vision in Genesis 15. Some of Moses' miracles, such as the transformation of the rod into a serpent and the leprosy that covered his hand (Exodus 4), were most probably of the same kind.

Miracles that took place in the presence of other persons as well as the prophet can be further divided into two kinds:

(1) The announcement of future events; and here the prophet's superiority over the diviner is manifested, for the events predicted by the prophets always materialize.

(2) Efficacious action.

These two kinds correspond to Ibn Ezra's definitions: 'When the part knows the Whole, it attaches itself to the Whole and causes prodigies and miracles to exist.' For in both cases the knowledge of secrets that God has concealed in His works and His creatures is indispensable, but, in the second kind, one must also know the appropriate actions that are indispensable to the miraculous operation: thus, when Moses sweetened the waters of Marah (Exodus 15: 23f), the piece of wood that he threw into the water was the instrument indispensable to the sweetening of the water.

The strict dichotomy that Nissim ben Moses posits between science, that is, philosophy, and prophecy, leads him to address a serious problem – that of the value of the biblical text. One must remove from the text everything that is the fruit of the prophet's imagination. Our author does not however deny the existence of prophet-philosophers:

Although the purpose of the prophetic vision is the announcement of future events, it may happen that intellectual notions that the prophet had intellected while in a waking state mingle with it. In effect, the habits and manner of being of the prophet are present in his imaginative faculty and colour the prophetic vision. The prophet who has devoted his spirit to the intelligibles will thus have imaginative perceptions that are coloured by his intellectual preoccupations, and Isaiah will say: For mine eyes have seen the King, the Lord of hosts.

(*Ibid.* fol. 36r)

Here, Nissim radically separates the *Torah*, or Pentateuch, from the other revealed texts. In fact, the Law of Moses, the *Torah*, is essentially different from the prophecy of the other prophets because the imaginative faculty, the very essence of prophecy for all other prophets, is missing in the prophecy of Moses. If the Law given by Moses were to be allegorically interpreted, like some prophetic passages, then the Jews would not fulfil the commandments in their corporeal sense, and this is exactly what the Christians propose.

Our philosopher's arguments are based on the excellence of Moses' Law, a perfect Law that therefore cannot and will not be abrogated. However, only true philosophers feel the perfection of the Mosaic Law strongly enough, and a more demagogic method was required to impose it, and to make it benefit those whose unaided intelligence is not sufficient to make them appreciate this great good and sacrifice their instincts to it. Since coercion cannot be used always with every one ('one cannot place a watchman in every house') Moses had to use threats and promises to force the ignorant to accept the Law. His use of fear and material promises proves his great political intelligence; in this matter he used the same method as the French kings who, always, at the beginning of their reigns, punish some important Prince, for no reason at all, their aim being to instil fear and respect in their subjects. This is an allusion to the trial and execution of Angerrand of Marigny by Louis X, le Hutin, in 1315.

Like all religious and political leaders, Moses used non-intellectual notions; one of them being that the 'Law came from Heaven' literally.

Nissim then summarizes the principles of faith that Maimonides had listed, and confronts them with philosophy. Eight doctrines are proved by the intellect: these are (1) the existence of God and (2) His unity, (3) that He is neither body nor force within a body, (4) that one must serve only Him, (5) that He knows men's actions and nothing is hidden from Him, (6) that prophecy exists, (7) that the divine commandments are unchangeable and eternal, (8) that the Messiah will come. Three doctrines are founded in faith only: (1) the resurrection of the dead, (2) temporal creation, (3) the difference between the prophecy of Moses and that of the other prophets. Two doctrines are a compound of the two first classes: (1) that there is divine reward and punishment, and (2) that the *Torah* is of divine origin.

Each of the first eight doctrines is demonstrated by philosophical reasoning, and is part of the religious law. Let us cite only one of Nissim's arguments: the coming of the Messiah is proved by a quotation from Aristotle, according to which, in things that persist in being, the possible will necessarily be accomplished. Now, the people of Israel are a people that persist in being and do not die out, as history has proven to this day. The political sovereignty and the liberty of Israel belong to the domain of the possible, therefore they will necessarily achieve it at some moment.

From this our author comes to the three doctrines of faith:

(1) The resurrection of the dead has nothing to do with the intellect, and it is clearly destined for the common people, for they need material promises in order to remain in the straight path. The Christians, says Nissim, reprove us for admitting the resurrection of the dead. Nevertheless, this is very necessary for fortifying the hearts of the faithful, while the incarnation of Jesus is not necessary.

(2) Temporal creation is also not proved by philosophy; but its religious usefulness is evident. Belief in the temporal creation of the world is necessary to us, declares Nissim, for if there is no temporal creation, there is no possibility of miracles (as Maimonides proved), and the gift of the *Torah* from heaven, as it is generally conceived, that is, Moses' hearing the commandments and transmitting them to the people, according to the verse 'Go say to them' (Deuteronomy 5: 30), is a miracle, since God does not 'speak'.

Now, without this simplified belief in the divine provenance of the *Torah*, all the people, or most of them, would hold the words of the *Torah* in contempt, would not carry out its commandments, would not fear its prohibitions, and would destroy its principles and its foundations, for few are the wise who receive truth because it is truth, who do good because it is good and maintain themselves in their rectitude because it is rectitude. Without belief in the creation of the world one cannot show how the *Torah* was revealed by God in a visible fashion, and the people would not accept a Law of which they did not have the provenance through their senses.

(3) The difference between Moses and the other prophets. Without this the Jewish religion could not subsist, for the words of the prophets other than Moses are allegories and their visions are prophetic visions. As we have already said, if Moses' prophecy was similar to theirs, all the commandments of the *Torah* would have to be understood allegorically. However, the fact that Moses prophesied in a waking state and without intervention of the imaginative faculty, and that this whole prophecy is linked to the intellect, contrary to the prophecies of other prophets, cannot be scientifically demonstrated: it is a truth of faith.

The two doctrines that are proved by philosophy and are part of the faith are reward and punishment and the divine origin of the religious Law.

(1) Reward and punishment are proved by philosophy when they are understood in their intellectual sense, that is, when they concern the soul, its survival after death, its power over the body and its knowledge of future events. Reward and punishment are matters of faith when one interprets the biblical and talmudic promises in their literal and corporeal sense.

(2) The divine origin of the *Torah* is similarly true from the scientific point of view, since Moses in fact gave the only 'divine' law that prepares the intellect for philosophy. But if one understands this divine origin as a voice corporeally come from the heavens, then it is a principle of faith.

Many more of Nissim's ideas deserve comment. However, one point should be mentioned. Posterior authors have made abundant use of Nissim but never by name. The reader will notice this on coming to my discussion of Moses of Narbonne. Gersonides also read him, and perhaps found one of his most original ideas in the *Book of Miracles*, that of knowledge defined as apprehension of the individual and not as a generalization abstracted from multiple sense data.

To cite Nissim:

We must represent to ourselves everything that we know and everything that can be known by anybody as being the object of divine knowledge but in a much more perfect manner, for our knowledge is imperfect and that of God is not. We must therefore not say that God does not know those things that we know. We must represent God's knowledge to ourselves as not being drawn from existing things, as ours is, but as being the intellection of itself and through this the intellection of all existing things, for these draw their existence from the truth of His existence. Divine knowledge has no imperfection, for it does not resemble the knowledge of the universals. For the universals are abstracted from existing things and are posterior to them; because of this, they are a part of the category of potential knowledge, and potential knowledge is inferior to knowledge in actuality. Divine knowledge resembles rather, to some extent, the way in which we know individuals, for this is an actual knowledge. It is dissimilar to it in that our knowledge of individuals is renewed and augmented according to the multiplication of individuals and is drawn from them, while the divine knowledge is always in actuality.

(Ibid. fol. 32r)

GERSONIDES

Gersonides Levi ben Gershom (Leon of Bagnols) (1288 – 20 April 1344) lived at Bagnols-sur-Cèze, in Languedoc, Avignon and Orange, and does not seem ever to have left the south of France. He is often considered the greatest Jewish philosopher after Maimonides. Like Maimonides, he was a philosopher, Talmudist and accomplished man of science. His works, written concurrently and mutually illuminating each other, are numerous. Of his scientific compositions the most important is a *Treatise of Astronomy* in 136 chapters, which is part of his book of philosophy; however, because of its length and specialized character it is not included in the manuscript copies or the printed editions of the *Milḥamot Adonai* (*Wars of the Lord*). The Hebrew text and a Latin translation are extant, both still in manuscript.

In this treatise Levi attacks several of the fundamental principles of Ptolemy's astronomy and suggests other solutions. Contrary to the usual practice in the Middle Ages, he prefers to depend on his own astronomical observations; he mentions ten eclipses of the sun and moon and nearly a hundred other astronomical events that he himself observed. In addition to these very technical discussions one finds in this treatise the method of constructing and using the instrument called *Baculus Jacob* (Jacob's Rod), which allows one to measure the angular distance between two stars or two planets. This instrument, perfected over the centuries, was used in navigation for several centuries.

Certain details suggest that Gersonides' astronomical research was commissioned by Christians. In his introduction to the astronomical tables of the treatise he himself declares that they were composed 'at the request of many great and noble Christian personages'. Moreover, the chapters on trigonometry and the *Baculus Jacob* were translated into Latin in 1342 by the Augustine monk Peter of Alexandria and dedicated to Pope Clement VI at Avignon. Not long after Gersonides' death, another treatise was translated into Latin by the same monk with the help of Solomon, one of the author's brothers. Finally, Levi mentions 'a distinguished clerk who studies this science [astronomy] with us'.

Three poems, a confession and a parody for the Purim festival, together with two *responsa* (one on a liturgical problem, the other on a question of rabbinical law) and a lost commentary on the talmudic treatise *Berakhot*, constitute Gersonides' 'rabbinical' work.

In his biblical commentaries, composed between 1325 and 1338, Gersonides uses different methods according to the books; *Job* and *Ecclesiastes* present a philological commentary, an explanation of each part of the book and a résumé of the existing theses. The commentary on the *Song of Songs* describes the stages of the ascension of the human soul towards intellectual perfection, thus recalling Moses Ibn Tibbon, although Gersonides declares that he only knows the commentary included in the *Midrash*. In the *Commentaries on Esther* and *Ruth* the literal explication is followed by a list of moral theological and juridical 'lessons' (*to'alyot*, literally 'useful things') that one can deduce from the text. The *Commentary on The Torah*, which was one of the first Hebrew books to be printed, is addressed to a cultivated public, and, apart from the sense of the words and the explanation of each pericope, it strives to define the moral, philosophical, theological and juridical 'lessons' contained in them.

Gersonides followed the same procedures in the commentaries *On the Early Prophets, Daniel, Ezra with Nehemiah and Chronicles and Proverbs*. The 'lessons' have been published in two separate volumes.

Unlike the biblical commentaries, which have all been published, the philosophical commentaries on Averroes' *Short Commentaries* and *Middle Commentaries* are still all in manuscript. Composed between 1319 and 1324, they cover the greater part of the Aristotelian corpus. Purely philosophical, these commentaries do not discuss questions of religion, and in the excursus, where he expresses his personal thought, Gersonides refers the reader to the *Wars of the Lord*.

The *Milḥamot Adonai* (*Wars of the Lord*) a work in six books that took twelve years to write and was finished in January 1329, is the best known and most important philosophical work of Levi ben Gershom. Twice published, it still awaits a critical edition. Only Books III and IV have been translated into English, and I shall cite the other parts of the book on the basis of the Riva di Trento edition of 1560, recently reprinted.

In the introduction Gersonides gives a list of the problems to be treated, namely:

(1) Whether a rational soul that has only partly attained perfection has an afterlife and, if so, whether men may achieve different degrees of immortality.

(2) When a man knows the future, in a dream, by divination or by prophecy, whether this knowledge comes to him by virtue of his essence or by accident, that is, without an active cause; if there is an active cause, one should know what it is and how this knowledge comes to man from this cause.

(3) Whether God knows existing things and, if He does know them, in what manner He knows them.

(4) Whether there is a divine providence for existing beings; what it is in particular for humanity and its individuals.

(5) In what way the movers of the spheres set these celestial spheres in motion, what the number of these movers is and how this movement is produced.

(6) Whether the world is eternal or created in time; how it was created if it came into existence.

Two religious questions are added to the sixth book, an examination of miracles and the criteria by which one may recognize the prophet.

The author stresses the fact that he has written a scientific work: the proofs that he will adduce come from the mathematical sciences, or from physics, or from philosophy.

Let not the reader think that when, in this book, the truth of a problem was proved it was because the *Torah* moved us to find it true. [On the contrary] it was because of its being true in itself. The Rabbi, the Guide, has already declared that it is appropriate that we believe in what speculation proved as true. If the *Torah*, understood as what appear to be the literal meaning of its words, contradicts it, we should interpret these words in such a way that they do not contradict speculation.

(Fol. 2b)

The *Torah* is not a political law that constrains us to believe false things; therefore, the truth necessarily agrees with the *Torah*, and in the *Torah*'s words we must discover the meaning that agrees with demonstrated truth.

After these preliminary remarks Gersonides discourses at length on the necessity of studying these problems in the order that he has established for his book. We must recall that the *Guide of the Perplexed* was composed in such a way as to incite the reader to search for a meaning that the author had deliberately and carefully concealed. Levi ben Gershom's intention is altogether different; considering it to be his duty to offer the reader the fruit of his own patient research, he composed his book in the order in which it should be read. There are seven reasons for this that are inherent in the subject itself (e.g., the knowledge of certain things naturally precedes others; general things precede the particular), others are due to the author or the reader or both together. The book that he presents has matured over a long period; each of the subjects is in the place where it should be if the reader does not wish to succumb to confusion; nor should the book be commented on, and Gersonides adjures the reader to follow his advice, and again gives the titles of the six parts.

This notification should not be taken lightly; the dynamics of Gersonides' thought is linked to the order of the questions treated, and I shall analyse the book as the author wished, trying to show why he wished it. I shall not engage with the labyrinth of the longest section – the exposition and refutation of the doctrines that do not accord with our author's. It must be noted, however, that the method that he follows – exposition of different points of view, refutation, then exposition of correct theses and their demonstrations – is new in Jewish philosophy. It was of course Aristotle's method, but, closer in time and space, it was also the mode of exposition of the Christian scholastics. We have only to open a volume of St Thomas Aquinas' *Summa Theologica* to find the same order: exposition of the question, citation of the difficulties and discussion of them, solutions. Besides, Gersonides' exposition and discussion of the various theories is centred on Aristotle's interpretation. Whole pages are devoted to harmonizing the contradictory passages in the work of the 'Philosopher'. On many points Gersonides contents himself with referring to the demonstration given by Aristotle in one or another of these treatises. The fact is that the books of the *Wars of the Lord* were written at the same time as the commentaries on Averroes, and, in a way, it is a collection of difficult questions; however, it is certainly a very systematic work.

Book I treats of the immortality of the soul, that is, the definition of the human soul and of the intellect. Let us recall that the Maimonideans, although rejecting any analogy between God and man, accepted that in both of them the intelligent, the intelligible and the act of intellection could be defined in a way that was, if not identical, at least relatively comparable. Human intellect connects man to an eternal order, which is not subject to generation and corruption; conjunction with the Active Intellect, perhaps impossible while man is still bound to the body, becomes possible after death. Averroes thought that conjunction with the Active Intellect was possible in this world and devoted several treatises to the problem of the hylic intelligence and the possibility of conjunction. These treatises were translated into Hebrew several times, and nourished the belief of Jewish philosophers in the union of the human intellect with the Active Intellect.

According to Averroes, as Gersonides represents him, the human soul, being subject to generation and corruption, cannot become eternal. Within it, what participates in eternity is the Active Intellect itself, immersed in matter and reduced to potentiality until the discovery of the intelligibles and the reunion with the Intellect. While it remains in a state of potentiality, not in essence but by its attachment to man, the intellect is generated and corruptible; only through becoming active is its eternal character restored to it. At all events the Intellect in itself is universal, and survival cannot be individual.

It is this problem, here stated in rough outline, that Gersonides first discusses. In fact, his philosophy can only have human knowledge as a point of departure, for this alone can furnish the primary evidence serving as a basis for the understanding of the world. He therefore tries to define the soul and the intellect in relation to the soul. The human soul is the ultimate stage of the souls that succeed each other hierarchically in matter, each serving as substratum to that above it. Thus, by the intermediary of matter, forms necessarily succeed each other, each one being 'potentially' the succeeding form, which is more complex and purer than itself. One can say that matter is the support of the hylic intellect by the intermediary of the reasonable soul. This reasonable soul, nevertheless, is one of the divisions of the imaginative soul, itself a part of the sensitive soul, which, since it is the support of the other souls, is thus the support of the potential intellect. If these souls carry the possibility of the intellect, they only do so through the presence of a superior soul, which attracts them towards a certain perfection, and, from this point of view, the imaginative soul in an animal is different from what it is in a man.

Aristotle had proved that the reception of the intelligibles is not mingled with the support. The form borne by the hylic intelligence is thus necessary to its existence but is in no way sufficient for the reception of intelligibles. Like all the other forms that matter can receive, the reasonable soul, which carries the potential intellect, is generated and corruptible. Can, then, the reception of the intelligibles confer on it immortality?

For Averroes, when the human hylic intellect becomes actual, thanks to the intellection of intelligibles, and is united with the Active Intellect, it becomes eternal. Therefore, before considering the conjunction with the Active Intellect, one has to know what the Active Intellect is. Here Gersonides declares that he will not list the opinions of his predecessors, for nothing pertinent seems to have been written on the subject.

First, Gersonides sets out to prove that the human hylic intellect is made actual by the Active Intellect because the latter intellects the law and order of all the creatures of this lower world. The way in which the Active Intellect comprehends sublunary things resembles that of an artisan building a ship: the conception of a ship is a unity, and the various operations necessary to its construction are disposed according to this first conception, which sees the materials and their building together, not as details added to each other, but as parts of a single thing that is present in its unity even before the construction has begun, and in accordance with which everything is ordered. It is only because it is not capable of conceiving the law of the world in its oneness, for it needs the senses in order to attain the intelligible, that the hylic intellect adds the intelligibles one to another, and understands one fragment of order after another. If the Active Intellect knows all the forms of the lower world according to their order, their organization, their law, this is because it is also the giver of forms, the 'creator' of all existing beings. In effect, the celestial bodies spread their warmth over matter through the intermediary of the rays of the sun, and this natural warmth, necessary to every living creature, prepares generation. However, the cause of the design which, using this matter, determines the generation of the organs of a living creature is a divine force, an intellect, the Active Intellect.

The Active Intellect acts according to two modes: in the immediate mode it thinks itself, and in the mediate mode it acts with the aid of an instrument, in the same way as the intellects of the sphere think themselves and move the spheres. The instrument that the Active Intellect uses is the natural warmth, to which it gives a soul, according to an order and a law which it knows in themselves and of which it knows the purpose. However, the knowledge of the Active Intellect is not limited to this sublunary world; in fact, all the spheres contribute to the formation of the mixture of the elements that will be able to receive form, and all their intellects participate in the emanation of the Active Intellect. Arising from the ensemble of the intellects, the Active Intellect, knowing itself, finds in itself the knowledge of the other intellects and the ordering of the celestial bodies.

What is the nature of the knowledge of the Active Intellect, which is to be communicated to the hylic intellect? This is the first problem that Gersonides poses. The second point will be the demonstration that this knowledge, eternal in the Active Intellect, is generated in man, and is nevertheless both immortal and individual once it is constituted. We remember that for Maimonides as for Al-Fārābī knowledge was a grasp of the object itself, which leads to an identification between the intellecting subject and the intellected object. When the subject intellects a material and perishable object, it becomes perishable like the object. On the other hand, when the subject intellects an eternal object it becomes thereby eternal.

Gersonides opposed to these notions a different theory:

The acquired intellect is a perfection which is given by the Active Intellect to the [human] potential intellect and this perfection is of two kinds:

(1) *Siyyur* [i.e. intelligible representation] does not have any connection with anything outside the mind; it is the knowledge of the order [of the universe] which is in the soul of the Active Intellect.

(Fol. 14v)

This knowledge, which has no connection with the material world, contrary to common opinion, includes also the accidents.

Knowledge is that of the things that subsist by themselves outside the [human] intellect and it is the order found in the soul of the Active Intellect. Universality befalls it because of its connection with the particulars which are the object of perception and which exist outside the soul, and in the same way as the order which is found in the soul of the artisan is also found in a certain manner in all the things that are instrumental [to his purpose] and whose existence derives from him, so this order will be found in each of the individuals whose existence comes from this order . . . The definition [of a being] will therefore be this same order that exists in the soul of the Active Intellect, which is the source of the generation of this species, and this order is already found in some manner in each of the individuals of this species . . . and in this manner there will also be a knowledge of accidents and not only of substances, contrary to what follows from the argument of those who say that the universal forms exist outside the soul; since they have grasped that it is not possible that the accidents should subsist separately and in themselves, they have therefore not been able to say of the accidents taken in their universality that they exist outside the soul, so that they are obliged to deny that there is a knowledge of accidents. If one accepts the theory that we propose on the subject of the Active Intellect, then the accidents are also ordered according to an order which exists outside the [human] intellect, that is, they exist in the soul of the Active Intellect.

(Fol. 9v)

(2) *Imut* or *a'amata* [i.e. the existence of the *siyyur* in the particulars perceived by the senses], has some connection with the things that exist outside the soul,

for example when we say: every animal has perception; but this connection applies to the *a'amata* only by accident, because it is composed of intellect and perception.

If things are as we say, the perfection which is achieved by the [human] intellect is only *siyyur* and it is not in connection with any of the particulars as they exist outside the mind; for example in a sweet yellow form, only the yellowness is apprehended by the sense of vision and not the sweetness which is associated with it.

(Fol. 14v)

Everything intellected by man is either *siyyur* or *imut*; it has been proven that neither of these is general [universal] but rather pertaining to a particular, which may be any particular whatsoever; in consequence to say that the intelligibles are general [universal] is an error.

(Fol. 12v)

Nevertheless, this knowledge is one and the same in mankind. Not only the celestial bodies, which are unique and not subject to corruption, but all existing things are known by every human intellect in the same way.

This happens to all that exists, for this knowledge comes from a being separated from matter: the Active Intellect. It is from it that our knowledge derives and it is from it that the truth reaches us. Sensation is thus not the efficient cause of our knowledge, it is only the occasional cause.

The world as Gersonides sees it begins to emerge: the Active Intellect is the source of two orders of reality that are superimposed: the intelligible order, a sort of blue print where the plan of the universe is unified according to a perfect finality and unity; and the material order in which forms of this lower world are joined to matter. Because of this materiality, some deviations from the intelligible order occur.

Siyyur is the knowledge of the intelligible order and *imut* is the knowledge of this same order perceived in its material existence.

There are, however, differences between men; the degrees of intellectual perfection are numerous, for the intelligible order of the universe, present in the Active Intellect, cannot be conceived by man in its totality; he only knows parts of it, which though they can be added to one another are not unified. Each of us conceives different parts of this total plan, for each of us has known different things and has formed his knowledge using one or several different fragments of this unique conception. This is why knowledge differs in each one of us, and the perfection acquired in this life will be the one that we will have in the world to come.

Book II is devoted to dream, divination and prophecy, that is, to the knowledge of the future.

The first important point is that this knowledge of the future that men have, thanks to dream, divination and prophecy, is not a haphazard knowledge. Experience teaches us that events announced in dreams nearly always come to pass, with all their details. From this state of fact two consequences derive:

– These events, in order to be known in advance, must be determined and ordered, they must form part of an organized whole;

– A being exists who has present knowledge of these events and communicates it to us; this being can only be the Active Intellect, for it acts without corporeal intermediary.

What are these future events of which we have said that they are determined and ordered, and how are they so determined?

The knowledge of future is not concerned with a future of which the advent is necessary, at least not generally; it is concerned with contingent future events occurring to individuals of the human species; these accidents may concern a man or things relating to a man, as in the story of Samuel and the she-asses of Kish, Saul's father (I Samuel 9). Among these contingent future events, some are related to human beings, like the announcement of the birth of a son, or of his actions; others are accidental, or depend on free human choice or on nature; and thus derive from determined things. Knowledge of the future through means employed in divination comprises all these events; thus the diviner predicts which of two adversaries will win a combat, or if it will rain tomorrow; thus Samuel predicted to Saul that he would meet three men who would give him two loaves of bread and that he would accept them (I Samuel 10: 3–4). The first point, that events to be known must be determined and organized, seems to contradict the facts based on experience: divination and prophecy concern events due to chance and to coincidences. In fact, if one of the alternatives of the possible is determined and ordered, since one knows it in advance, there is no more 'possible' and everything becomes necessary. Similarly, free choice will be no more than a word, since no event is then contingent and everything that happens is necessary, while what is 'possible' is precisely that which depends on free human choice. No animal or plant performs a contingent action; all their movements are determined by nature. Thus an animal moves towards its food when it sees it; it does not make a personal decision to move; but man renders this movement contingent when he hinders the animal from moving towards its food or removes the food and so prevents the animal's movement. We thus reach a contradictory proposition: we may have a preliminary knowledge of events due to chance, therefore without a predetermined cause. When Averroes reached this point he declared that in fact there can be no preliminary knowledge of events due to chance. However, our experience shows us that on the contrary it is precisely these events that are announced by dream and by divination.

I myself have had the proof of this many times, in premonitory dreams, not to speak of what I have been told on this subject. Now, it is a poor method to reject the testimony of experience to justify some theory; it is better to inquire how indeed one can have a preliminary knowledge of events due to chance.   (Fol. 17r)

That accidental events are subjected to a certain order is proved by the existence of men of whom it is said that they were born under a lucky star; all success is theirs, while others, on the contrary, accumulate misfortunes; however, since misfortunes and successes are accidental, they could on principle be more or less evenly distributed.

Another argument: man being the most eminent of creatures, the celestial substances take extreme care of him, to the point that his actions and his thought come to him from the celestial bodies. Thus the astrologers know thoughts and their predictions are often correct. When they are false this is due to our remoteness from the stars and our inadequate science.

Since what is accident for man is for the stars order and determination, we shall say that these events are in fact ordered and determined.

There are nevertheless acts that are not foreseen in the order of the astral conjunctions, and these are the acts that are freely chosen by man, but they are few in number. In fact, almost all the thoughts, almost all the movements of men are determined by the stars: men are the noblest of creatures and the order of the stars is designed for the good, thus, contrary to animals, men profit most from the beneficent influence of the stars. It rarely happens that men oppose this order and, in fact, the great majority of events that we call accidental are determined and knowable.

We say that it is clear beyond any doubt that these things are defined and ordered, from which respect there is foreknowledge of their generation and from which respect the senses reveal to us that they [the particulars] are defined from the heavenly bodies. However, the respect in which they are contingent, undefined, and not ordered is the intellect and the choice found in us. [This is] because our intellect and choice move us to what is different from what was defined [to happen to us] by the heavenly bodies. Indeed this is the case because human events are ordered from the heavenly bodies, and the heavenly bodies govern the generation of what is below the sphere of the moon when one opposite dominates at one time and another at another time. This [may happen] because of the changing situation of the stars. For example when the sun is in the north the natural [elements] air and fire dominate simple and complex bodies there but when [the sun] is in the south the natural [elements] water and earth dominate simple and complex bodies in the north. Or [it may happen] because the stars undergo change. For example, [because of] Mars the natural element fire dominates and [because of] the moon the natural element water dominates. From the mixture of these opposites which are subject to generation, individual human beings are marked by them [i.e., by the heavenly bodies' determination of the elements in either of the two ways noted above] with virtue and prudence. [Thus] the heavenly bodies necessitate that in a certain situation man is ordered with respect to a given attribute, whereas in the opposite situation he is ordered with respect to an opposite [attribute]. Similarly, this is the case with all of the events which are ordered by [the heavenly bodies].

Also it necessarily follows that differences are necessitated by the different stars in that some men are ordered with respect to a given attribute and others of them [are ordered] with respect to its opposite, so that some of them [are ordered] with respect to a certain event while others [are ordered] with respect to its opposite. Consequently it happens as a result of this that when wicked men perceive evils, God, may He be blessed, governs this, because He set in us a finite intellect to enable us to bring about what is different from what has been determined by the heavenly bodies [to take place], to prepare for something else to happen insofar as [this is] possible.

(Trans., N. M. Samuelson, *Gersonides on God's Knowledge*, pp. 295-7, note 602)

Thus the Active Intellect that intellects the order of this world also bestows knowledge of future events. Following Averroes, Gersonides does not admit the possibility of a theoretical science given in a dream.

It is not impossible that the first intelligibles should be given in dream, with their causes, if the imaginative forms necessary to the acquisition of the intelligible are present; however, this will seldom happen because these imaginative forms necessary to the acquisition of the intelligible are generally due to an effort, which can only be made in a waking state, since in sleep man has not the free choice of images. So that the obtaining of this [intelligible] knowledge does not arrive in dreams, except in some accidental way; similarly for the second intelligibles – for one infers the second intelligibles from the first by an effort, through using the first intelligibles, which lead to an apprehension of the second intelligibles that one wants to know. It is not impossible that when in sleep the first intelligibles are present in the intellect, they give birth to the second intelligibles, but again, this is very rare. (Fol. 18r)

Thus, a person who throughout the day is preoccupied with scientific thoughts and problems may also be preoccupied with them in dream, and sometimes the process of discovery takes place of itself, as if by accident. When the prophets expound notions of physics or of metaphysics (the Story of Creation or the Story of the Chariot) one may suppose that they had studied these problems at length and in a waking state, or else that they had not mentioned the preliminary notions, either forgetting them or deliberately preferring to conceal them.

But most of the prophets did not have revelations on intelligible subjects; thus Abraham did not know the number of the stars for it was not known in his time. Ezekiel thought he heard the voice of the celestial spheres, which was imagined to exist in his time.

The Active Intellect is always ready to transmit knowledge of the order of the stars at a certain instant, under a given aspect, to whoever among men is capable of receiving them.

If the prophet can receive intimations concerning a person other than himself, this is because the purpose of these intimations is the safeguarding and the good of the greatest possible number of human beings.

The concentration and the reflection on one precise person or subject that are required for such communication, is mentioned by Gersonides when explicating Joshua 5: 13:

When Joshua was by Jericho . . . he lifted up his eyes and looked, and, behold there was a man . . . Joshua was not yet before Jericho for the taking of the town is narrated only in the next chapter. But Joshua was concentrating all his thoughts on Jericho in order to provoke a prophetic revelation about it.

(*Commentary on the Bible* (Venice, 1617), fol. 244r)

This concentration is very painful, especially during old age, when man's faculties decline or are troubled by distress and anguish. The stimulants may then be the sensory perception of the person concerned (thus Jacob wanted to touch Menasseh and Ephraim), or contact with something that partakes of him (thus Isaac asking for a dish prepared by Esau's hands), or else music (Elisha demanded a musician). This intense concentration isolates the prophet from the rest of mankind and makes him perform bizarre acts, for it cuts him off from daily reality, thus earning for prophets the name of 'madman'.

Why are some revelations clear and others not? This depends on two kinds of causes:

– The rank of the prophet, that is, the degree that he has attained in the acquisition of the intellect;

– His preparation for revelation by concentration on a given subject.

The more perfect a person's intellect, and the greater ease with which he can separate it [from his other faculties] the more perfect will he be in prophecy. The varying degrees of these qualities account for the different degrees of prophecy. Men receive these prognostications about different subjects in accord with their natures: the more a man directs his thought to a subject, the more will he receive prognostications about it. This is common to both the diviner and the prophet. Thus, it is found that some diviners predict certain kinds of events exclusively, such as those who direct their thoughts – either naturally or by custom – to the matching of men and women, as is common among female diviners. He who directs his thoughts exclusively to the success of the intellect will single out those matters conducive to the success of the intellect and those matters which direct one to it.
(Trans. M. M. Kellner, 'Maimonides and Gersonides on Mosaic Prophecy', p. 71)

If the two essential conditions (the perfection of the intellect and the ability to concentrate) are fulfilled, the prophet receives from the entire astral system information that concerns *inter alia* a certain people or a certain individual; therefore the information is clear and exact. If the conditions are only partially fulfilled, the prophet will receive a revelation by means of symbols and parables; this information will apply to many individuals, for it will be vague, like a distant contour.

To these differences between the perceptions is added that of the greater or lesser perfection of the imagination. An imagination well prepared to receive the influx will copy perfectly what the intellect has perceived; a deficient imagination will transmit it less precisely, and in the form of a parable.

This information generally arrives during sleep. It may happen however that a man may attain prophetic knowledge in a waking state, and this for three different reasons:

– This man's intellect is perfect;

– His faculty of concentration is very intense and the other faculties accept the yoke of the intellect without difficulty;

– His sensory faculties are imperfect; such are the blind.

Moses' prophecy is distinct from that of other prophets in four ways: he prophesied in the waking state; his knowledge was purely intellectual; he had distinct and unambiguous knowledge of individuals; he had complete knowledge. The three first characteristics are borrowed from Maimonides,

the fourth refers to knowledge of the complete astral order. These characteristics are the result of Moses' eminence in the two qualities necessary for
prophetic knowledge: perfection of the intellect and power of concentration.

We know that the prophets were accomplished philosophers. However,
we know also from observation that knowledge of the future comes to simple
and uneducated people.

How, then, is prophecy different from divination?

– Prophecy can be learnt (we read in the Bible that there were schools of
prophets) and can be taught;

– The prophet must first of all be a perfect scholar;

– All prophetic forecasts are true (when they predict events that are regarded as fortunate);

– Prophets watch over the good moral order of the peoples.

Accordingly, dream and prophecy are not of the same kind: since the soul
is one, there are two faculties different in kind that receive the two varieties
of revelation:

– The intellect receives prophecy;

– The imaginative faculty receives dream and divination.

One single entity is the source of these several kinds of knowledge: the
Active Intellect. In the first case, the Active Intellect transmits directly to the
human intellect the clear and distinct knowledge of individuals, this knowledge being part of the overflow it – the Active Intellect – receives from the
intelligible order of the stars. In the second case the Active Intellect uses the
soul of the spheres, as an intermediary leading to divinatory, partial, imperfect knowledge, ignorant of the possibility that divine providence has
provided for man: free will.

Nevertheless, certain psychological dispositions are common to dream and to
prophecy: these are the desire of obtaining knowledge, the choice of a subject
of meditation, and the importance of reflection during the waking state preceding sleep. Peculiar to dreams is the necessity of a perfect imaginative faculty.

Book III is devoted to God's knowledge of the singular and contingent
things of the sublunary world. Gersonides begins by enumerating the arguments of the Philosopher showing that God does not know individuals, and
those of the *Torah* scholars who affirm, on the contrary, that God knows
everything that happens in this world. Two chapters deal with an exposition
and refutation of Maimonides, who had attributed to divine knowledge five
characteristics absolutely different from those of our human knowledge:

(1) That it is One, at the same time embracing a multitude of objects of
different species;

(2) That it has as its objects, *inter alia*, things that do not exist;

(3) That it encompasses that which is infinite;

(4) The divine foreknowledge does not determine which of two possible
mutually exclusive events shall come to pass;

(5) That this knowledge does not undergo change when events occur.

Gersonides holds that these characteristics of the divine knowledge, attributed by Maimonides to the 'sectarians of the Law' (in the *Guide* III, 20), expressed his personal opinion. Gersonides himself has a very different position; in his own words:

We say that it seems that God, may He be blessed, knows these particulars from (the following) aspects.

[The first] of these [aspects] is that since it is clear that God, may He be blessed, is the cause of everything, substances and accidents, that is subject to generation and corruption in this lower world, and [it also is clear] that the Active Intellect and the heavenly bodies are His instruments – this is because all of these things emanate from the overflow which overflows upon them from God, may He be blessed – it being clear in the case of an instrument *qua* instrument that it cannot move to do that for which it is an instrument except by means of the knowledge of the craftsman, it therefore clearly is apparent from this that God, may He be blessed, knows all of these particulars.

[The second] of these [aspects] is that since it is the case necessarily that God, may He be blessed, knows His essence at a level [which is equal to the level] of His existence, and [since] His essence is such that all existents emanate from Him by degrees, it [therefore] necessarily follows that God, may He be blessed, knows of all existents which emanate from Him. The reason for this is that if He did not know them, His knowledge of His own essence would be deficient. This is because He would not know what could possibly emanate from Him in accordance with that existence which He possesses. This being so, and it [further] being clear that every substance and accident which is subject to generation emanates from Him, [therefore] it is clear that He knows every substance and accident which is subject to generation which emanate [from Him]. Therefore, it clearly follows necessarily from this that God, may He be blessed, knows all of these particulars.

[The third] of these [aspects] is that it is clear from what was stated above that the Active Intellect in some way knows these things subject to generation in this lower world. This being so, and it [further] being [the case] that God, may He be blessed, is the cause, the form, and the end of all other separate intelligences, as is explained in the *Metaphysics*, it necessarily follows that cognitions of all other intelligences are found in God. This is because those cognitions proceed materially from the cognition of God, may He be blessed. Similarly it is necessarily the case that an architect of a house should know the form of the bricks and the beams which these workmen know who are engaged in those arts which aid the art of architecture. But he who is engaged in the primary art will have more perfect knowledge of them with respect to their being part of [the total plan of] the house, as was mentioned above. This being so, it is clear beyond any doubt that these cognitions which the Active Intellect has of these things [are possessed] by God, may He be blessed, in a more perfect manner. This also shows that God, may He be blessed, knows particulars.

(Trans., N. M. Samuelson, *Gersonides on God's Knowledge*, pp. 227–31)

Thus, it is proved that God has knowledge of particulars. Not only does He know particulars, He knows also the future contingents, for they are known insofar as they are ordered and defined:

We say that it already was made clear above that these contingents are defined and ordered in one respect and are contingents in another respect. This being so, it is clear that the respect in which He knows them is the respect in which they are ordered and defined. Similarly, [this] is the case with the Active Intellect, according to what was explained, because [only] in this respect is it possible that they should be known. The respect in which He does not know them is the respect in which they are not ordered, which is the respect in which they are contingents. This is because in this respect it is impossible that they should be known. However, from this [latter] respect He knows that they are contingents which possibly will not be actualized with regard to the choice which God, may He be blessed, gave to man in order to perfect what was lacking in the governance of the heavenly bodies, as was explained in the preceding treatise. But He does not know which of the two possible alternatives will be actualized from the point of view that they are contingents. The reason for this is that if this were so, there could be no contingency in this world at all.

(Ibid. pp. 231–4)

In other words, God is a sociologist who knows that a certain proportion of the population of a certain country will commit suicide during the coming year. He also knows the reasons for their suicide and the proportions of these reasons, but He does not know which individuals will commit suicide. This definition of science is also that of the quanta physicists.

His lack of knowledge, may He be blessed, of which of two possible alternatives *qua* possible will be actualized, is not a deficiency in Him. This is because perfect knowledge of a thing consists in knowing the nature of the thing. Were [the thing] to be conceived to be other than it is, this would be error and not knowledge. This being so, [it is clear that] He knows all these things in the most perfect way possible. This is because He knows them with respect to their being ordered in a clear and definite way. In addition He knows those respects in which they are contingent with regard to choice, according to their contingency.

(Ibid. pp. 235–8)

Chapter 4 continues with arguments in support of Gersonides' thesis, and chapter 5 expounds further arguments against the notion attributed to Maimonides.

It is proper that we should explain that this view which was concluded from Philosophic Thought is also the view of our Torah. We say that the basic tenet of the Torah and the axis upon which it revolves is that in this world there exist contingents. Therefore the Torah can command [us] to do certain actions and to refrain from doing certain [other] actions. [At the same time] the basic tenet of the words of the prophets in general, peace be unto them, is that God, may He be blessed, made known to the prophets, peace be unto them, these contingents prior to their coming to be. As [Scripture] says, 'Surely the Lord God does nothing without revealing His secret to His servants the prophets. But it does not follow necessarily from their testifying to a certain evil that it will be actualized. As [Joel] said, peace be unto him. 'For the Lord is gracious . . . and repents of evil.' Thus a combination of these two tenets is possible only if it is posited that these contingents are ordered in one respect, namely the respect in which knowledge of them occurs, and that they are not ordered in another respect, namely the respect in which they are contingent. [Furthermore] since God, may He be blessed, knows all of these things with respect to their being ordered, and He knows that they are contingent, it is clear that the view of our Torah is [in agreement with] what was concluded from Philosophic Thought concerning the knowledge of God, may He be blessed.

(Ibid. pp. 293–4)

God thus does not know concrete individuals of flesh and blood. He knows those individuals inasmuch as they are part of the universal order.

Furthermore, it clearly is the view of the Torah that God, may He be blessed, knows these things universally [and] not particularly. [This view] is clear from what [Scripture] says, [viz.] 'He who fashions the hearts of them as one, and comprehends all of their deeds,' i.e., He fashions the heart and thoughts of mankind as one by making these orderings which the heavenly bodies possess from which generally they are ordered. In this way, [God] comprehends all of their deeds, i.e., in unity. [But it is] not the [case] that His knowledge is connected with the particularity of a particular. Thus it is clear that He understands all of their deeds generally.

(*Ibid.* pp. 296–8)

God does not know Abraham, Isaac and Jacob as concrete individuals, but He knows the history of Israel, a collectivity whose destiny is determined by the stars, and, as we shall see in Book IV, He thus watches over His people.

It is easy to point out, as Crescas would, that there is nothing left in common between the God of Gersonides and the biblical God. According to Crescas' interpretation of Gersonides, Jacob's descent into Egypt is an act of free will, therefore not known to God. From this act flows the entire history of Israel, which God likewise does not know. To be sure, Gersonides had written in his biblical commentaries that Jacob's descent into Egypt was not a free but a necessary act, therefore known to God. This does not alter the fact that Gersonides' theory of the divine knowledge radically destroys the whole of history as told in the Bible, and that all his biblical exegesis cannot mitigate the fundamental impossibility of harmonizing the two conceptions of God: God knowing the world in its order and law, mathematically and harmoniously disposed in accordance with its eternal being; or, God knowing man in his body and soul, from the mess of potage, that Esau exchanged for his birthright to the coat of many colours for which Joseph was sold into Egypt.

The two conceptions of divine knowledge evidently imply the same opposition between the different conceptions of providence.

Book IV defines divine providence, and inquires whether it extends to individual human beings or only to the human species, as is the case with other species.

Three theses are proposed: that of Aristotle, who denies that divine providence is exercised over individuals; that of most believers in the *Torah*, who affirm that this providence extends to every human individual; and that of 'great Jewish thinkers', who declared that divine providence watches over certain human individuals but not over all of them. Discussions of these opinions, says our author, basing himself on the *Guide* (III, chapters 22ff), are presented in the Book of Job, and his commentary on this book treats the arguments for and against at length. The chapter we are dealing with here is comparatively succinct.

Aristotle's opinion is refuted in the following terms:

We maintain that the refutation of the Philosopher's premise that Divine Providence extends to man only in regard to the nature of the species [and] not in regard to the individual nature has been made clear in what has preceded in the treatise concerning the final cause of foreknowledge which is received through magic, dreams and prophecy; I mean that there it was explained that the individuals having the potential of receiving this foreknowledge receive this foreknowledge in order that they may be saved from many of the misfortunes which are about to come upon them, especially individuals whose minds have enabled them to achieve this fore-knowledge by means of prophecy since this foreknowledge is received by them more perfectly than by other people, as has been explained in what has preceded. Since this is the case, it is clear that this Providence [extends] to prophets by virtue of the individual nature which possesses this form of wisdom and perfection for the sake of which they are guided by this manner of Providence. Therefore it is clear that Divine Providence extends to some people by virtue of their individual nature. The Philosopher has conceded this point according to Ibn Rushd's under-standing of him in his summary of *De Sensu et Sensibile*.

(Trans. J. D. Bleich, *Providence*, p. 57)

The thesis of those who affirm that providence extends to all individuals is refuted by speculation, experience and the *Torah*. By speculation, for the author recalls that divine knowledge is limited by human free choice; God cannot therefore reward or punish man for acts that He does not know.

On the other hand, evil only comes from God by accident; matter or hazard are responsible for it. Here I must cite Gersonides, for he attacks the fundamental problem of the origin of evil, and resolves it by an explicitly stated dualism:

Also, the benefits ordained for many by the human form are more noble than the benefits ordained for the donkey by the form 'donkey'. That which is found [to be the case] concerning this in regard to material forms is clearly also found to be so in regard to non-material forms. This is so because that which is found to be true regarding this with reference to the material forms is [so] due to the non-material forms through which these things are ordered in this [sublunar] world Since this is the case, and it is clear that God is the most perfect of all forms to the extent that there is no relation between the perfection of other forms and His per-fection, it is [therefore] clear that it is proper that only benefits in the greatest degree of good and value possible be received from God by that for which He is the form and perfection, namely, existence in its totality.

In general, the misfortunes which occur are to be attributed in their totality to the material cause or to accident. This is so because the principle of misfortune is necessarily in the recipient himself or external [to him]. Now the misfortunes which originate in the recipient himself are either due to the combination of the humors or due to the propensities and natural tendencies of the soul. Those related to the combination of the humors are clearly attributable to matter because the cause of [these misfortunes] is that the passive powers do not obey the active powers as has been explained in Book Four of the *Meteorologica*. This will also become sufficiently clear with regard to the misfortunes which occur due to the propensities and natural tendencies of the soul. [These misfortunes] do not proceed from the intellect because the nature of the intellect is to lead man in the proper way with regard to each and every human matter. As for the misfortunes which originate externally, they necessarily originate either in the combination of the humors, the will, or in something else. Regarding those [misfortunes] which originate in the humors or the will, as is the case with regard to wars and similar things, it is clear from what has preceded that they are to be attributed to matter because the wicked choice by means of which a man is aroused to harm another does not proceed from the intellect. Similarly, the unbalanced combination of the humors which is at times the cause of harming another is not itself ordained by the form since the form endeavors to establish the most perfect balance of the humors so long as nothing prevents it from doing so. With regard to those things which do not have their origin in the balance of the humors or in the will, such as the devastation of countries, earthquakes and fire which falls from heaven and things similar to these, it is clear that misfortune accrues from them only through chance, e.g. the fire in falling may by chance fall on a man and kill him or the earth may turn over on those living [at the site of an earthquake] because they happened to be there. It has also already been explained that the misfortune which occurs as a result of these matters is accidental because [the cause] from which these occurrences are derived is intended for good and for the protection of all sublunary existent things, not for evil. This is so because there are present here [in the sublunar world] contrary elements and it is the nature of contrary elements to destroy one another and as a result of this that which is composed of them is destroyed. This necessitates that there be present here [in the sublunar world] causes to produce them and to preserve their existence and the existence of that which comes to be from them. Since this cannot be accomplished unless at times one of the contrary [elements] becomes dominant over the other and at times the other [contrary element] becomes dominant and [since] this [takes place] according to a regular cycle and with constant order as has been explained in the *Physics*, this necessitates that at times fire, at times air, at times water and at times earth [become dominant] according to the relationship between the agent and that which is acted upon. Through this, this lowly sublunar existence is preserved, since its preservation consists of the equilibrium existing between the elements of which it is composed, and the cause of this equilibrium is this activity received by the elements from the heavenly bodies. Since this is the case, it is clear that misfortune which occurs as a result of the dominance of one of these elements over the other is accidental, since the dominance is in itself intended for good and preservation as [has been explained in what] has preceded. Similarly, it is clear that misfortunes which befall individual human beings through the constellations of heavenly bodies are also not intrinsically [evil] nor are they intended primarily [as evil] because the purpose of those arrangements is the attaining of good. However, some misfortunes may occur through them by chance as we have mentioned in the second chapter of this book. God has placed an intellect in man to protect him in so far as possible from these misfortunes. Therefore, it may be said that, in a sense, these evils which befall individuals through the heavenly bodies are attributable to matter, because if man would follow his intellect, as is proper, he would be protected from them, as has been explained in the Third Treatise of this book. In general, since God is, in a beneficial manner, the source, the purpose and form of existent things, as is explained in the *Metaphysics*, it is therefore false that His essence might be a source of misfortune to existent beings. Therefore, those who have succeeded in philosophical speculation have agreed that evil enters existent beings by virtue of the corporeal substance, which is the recipient, since it is impossible that it enter by virtue of the agent, which is the form.

Indeed [the belief] that the principle of good is different from the principle of misfortune is a very ancient opinion, as if the nature of the truth forced philosophical investigators to believe this. Therefore, some ancient philosophers posited love and strife as principles, some posited the one and the many, some posited the finite and the infinite and some posited union and separation. Many recent religionists posited God and evil spirits, I mean *Shedim* [as being the source of benefit and misfortune].

(Ibid. pp. 59–61)

Providence as our author conceives it is described in chapter 6:

... the Providence which we have posited is compatible with our admission that God's knowledge does not extend to particular things *qua* particulars. That is, the Providence which accrues to the righteous by virtue of foreknowledge regarding benefits and misfortunes which are imminent can be perfected even though the One from Whom this foreknowledge emanates does not perceive the individual who receives the emanation [and] even though the particular details which are the [subject of] foreknowledge are not known to the One from Whom [it] emanates *qua* particulars. We have already explained this in the Second Treatise of this work. There we have explained that foreknowledge with regard to particulars is received from the Active Intellect by the recipient of the emanation by virtue of [his] sentient existence. The Providence which brings fear [to people] in order to preserve [them] from misfortunes and in order to instill in them other animate instincts [to prompt them] to strive for things which bring benefit and to draw away from things which bring misfortune is also a weak form of foreknowledge, as we have explained in what has preceded, but its [nature] is the same as that of perfect foreknowledge with regard to this matter. This is self-evident; I mean that just as God does not prevent the receiving of perfect foreknowledge with regard to particulars so also does He not prevent that foreknowledge be received from Him which is not perfect with regard to particular things since the lack of perfection which is found in this foreknowledge is due to the recipient. [The recipient] perceives that this particular thing is about to come to him in this manner [rather than] it being the emanation which is concerned with particulars.

(Ibid. p. 72)

Continuing this chapter, Gersonides demonstrates that the suffering undergone by the just can be very well explained by his theory, as well as the providential aid that sometimes seems to be granted to evil-doers. As for the chastisements that God has imposed on the peoples who are hostile to Israel, they are miraculous events and do not enter into the concept of providence as it is here expounded. This matter is discussed in relation to miracle, at the end of Book VI.

Book V of the *Wars of the Lord* is the heart of the work, and its importance cannot be overestimated. Gersonides' thought is that of an astronomer and his philosophy is not comprehensible, it seems to me, except in the framework of a conception where the stars occupy the central place. The author himself notes this at the end of the fifth book (fol. 48r), in presenting a résumé of the three parts that compose it: the science of the stars is the fruit and purpose of all the sciences, and its degree is decidedly superior to theirs.

The first part is the fruit and the final issue of the mathematical sciences, for it includes true physics, gives the exact dimensions of the stars, and describes their movements. This part, let us remember, used to be copied out separately. Very extensive, comprising 136 chapters, its scientific value cannot now be judged objectively, but it was very much appreciated by contemporaries; it was translated into Latin and sought after by Kepler.

The second part is the fruit and final issue of the physical sciences; because the celestial bodies are like the form and entelechy of the other physical beings, to understand them is thus to understand the form and entelechy of the other existents.

The third part is the fruit of 'general' science, that is, metaphysics and its aim; divine science comprises a number of subjects that one must search to elucidate; but they all converge towards what man, in the measure of his possibilities, can attain in the knowledge of God and the intellects, movers of the spheres.

We remember that according to Maimonides, who in this follows Al-Fārābī, it is extremely improbable that man may achieve any true idea of God and of the intellects. Nor do we have certain knowledge as regards astronomical theories and celestial physics.

Gersonides asserts that he has produced a theory of the heavens and the movement that is very close to the reality; he is convinced that he has understood the relations that unite the heavens and the earth, and he is sure of having fully attained what man can achieve with regard to the knowledge of the movers of the heavens. This assurance flows from his astronomical theories, which are based on observations that in his opinion, are not open to doubt. Thus, the astronomical section forms an integral part of the book, for without it, Gersonides' assurance would only be overweening presumption.

Gersonides' astronomical theories cannot be described here; nevertheless a few words have to be said about them for on certain points they deviate in a significant way from those of his predecessors. The earth is still held to be at the centre of the universe. The planets move within solid spheres. All their movements can be analysed into a certain number of circular and uniform movements in such a way that each planet will have as many spheres as it has distinct movements. Between these spheres, continuity and transmission of movement are assured by a fluid body, incapable of opposing resistance to the deformations that the celestial movements enforce on it, a body 'that does not conserve its shape', the first body, which Gersonides defines at greater length when he speaks of creation.

One of the basic principles of astronomy was that the simpler movement, like the simpler body, was hierarchically superior to the more complex; Gersonides refutes this principle by pointing out that the four simple elements are inferior to composed matter. Similarly, movement was only conceived from outside to inside, that is, the movement of the external, simpler spheres, was transmitted to the interior spheres, closer to the earth. This also

Gersonides rejected: movement can be transmitted from inside to outside, and it is precisely the fact: in the complex of spheres belonging to a planet, the movement is transmitted by the interior sphere of the planet to the exterior one and not vice-versa. The statement that movement is transmitted from the centre towards the exterior upset all the accepted relationships between the moving intellects that preside over the movement of the spheres, for this movement is produced by a mover, a separate intellect; to the Aristotelians and the Neoplatonists the order of transmission of the movement also indicated the hierarchical order between the movers; among the moving intellects, the noblest moved the most elevated sphere, that of diurnal movement, the humblest was that which gave movement to the lunar sphere, and sometimes the soul of the terrestrial world. It was accepted by Maimonides, for example, that the intellects are hierarchically disposed, each being the cause of the one immediately inferior to it. Gersonides does not accept the emanation of one intellect by another, as we shall see, and the Active Intellect, the giver of forms to this lower world, the 'last' Intellect for non-Gersonidean philosophers, would be ranked as the most eminent of all the Intellects.

Let us give a resumé, chapter by chapter, of the second part of Book v of the *Wars of the Lord*. It begins by giving the reasons for the arrangement of the spheres described in the first part. Gersonides starts from the affirmation that the order that is fixed in things subject to generation arises from the celestial bodies. In fact, this order is perpetuated in its changing: terrestrial things change into each other at different points of time, but this changing and these transformations are regularly ordered. The cause of the perpetuity of the sublunary order is the stable and unchangeable nature of the celestial bodies. The cause of the changes is the movement of these celestial bodies, constantly renewed and constantly like itself. Given the eminence of the celestial bodies, it had seemed that this bond of cause and effect between the celestial bodies and the lower world was of secondary intention. For Gersonides, this was not so.

Let us compare, he says, the sublunary beings and the celestial bodies. The matter that carries the form of these celestial bodies is simple and *in actu*; it is therefore not matter in the sense that we understand the term on earth. The terrestrial beings are endowed with organs because they are composed of contrary elements and they must look for what completes their existence and preserves it. We see that words do not have the same sense when they are applied to celestial or terrestrial bodies respectively. When one says that the star is the organ of the sphere, the word 'organ' is a homonym. Spheres and stars are made of one and the same matter – quintessence – which is always *in actu*. The differentiation between the non-luminous parts and the luminous – the stars – is thus not due to an imperfection in the celestial bodies but corresponds to the very purpose of their movements: to impart many and diverse effects to the sublunary world. It is because they represent the law and order of the world that the movements of the spheres and stars have for objective a perfect terrestrial order, and not because this movement is necessary to their existence. Not only is it possible that the superior exists for the sake of the inferior, but we see that it is so. God acts on what is below Him and emanates His influence over it. Similarly the Active Intellect acts and emanates over terrestrial things, and this emanation exists for the sake of these material things and for their benefit.

Since the spheres are in movement for the sake of terrestrial creatures, it is more appropriate to their eminence that their movements should be numerous so that their influences may be numerous and varied; one should not, therefore, attribute to the most eminent of the spheres one sole simple movement; furthermore, given that it is the astral body which, by its light, influences terrestrial things, which are multiple, to suppose a diurnal sphere deprived of stars and carrying the world in one simple movement is altogether senseless.

The sphere of the fixed stars with its numerous luminaries is thus superior to the five spheres that each hold only one astral body.

Gersonides then propounds the question of the mechanism of the celestial bodies' influence on the lower world.

Thus, one cannot say of the sun that it warms the earth because it is hot; in fact, only the four terrestrial elements are endowed with the qualities of heat and cold, dryness and wetness. Nevertheless, the closer the sun is to the earth the hotter is the latter. There is, says our author, an affinity between the sun and the element of fire, as there is an affinity between the moon and the element of water. It is because of this affinity that the light of the sun, through a divine force that is in it, makes the fire to move and heats the air that is mingled with the fire. Similarly, each of the stars, by its movement and the affinity that it has with a terrestrial quality, influences the change and transformation of sublunary things.

Six principles preside over sky–earth relationships:

(1) Each of the astral bodies exercises a different influence, which is specific to it: the sun has a great effect on the generation of warmth and dryness whereas the moon has an effect on the generation of coldness and moisture.

(2) The planets have a different action according to their position in relation to the fixed stars, so that these fixed stars have a part in what happens on earth; winds and rain are an example of this.

(3) The longer a planet remains in a certain position in relation to the sphere of the fixed stars, the longer the influence of these fixed stars, influenced by the presence of the planet, will dominate.

(4) The actions of the planets will vary according to whether the planet inclines towards the north or the south, and its action will be the strongest possible when it is in its exaltation in the middle of the sky.

(5) The more luminous the rays of light of an astral body, the stronger its action.

(6) The closer the astral body is to the earth, the more strongly its influence will make itself felt.

If all the stars unite in common movements and if each of them has its own particular movement, this is because the terrestrial things are subject to a general order and to particular orders. Each of the movements of the stars and the ensemble of their movements forms part of a disposition of the world where everything is necessary and willed. The spheres and their astral bodies are not independent entities; they move within a vaster plan willed by God, in which they participate.

In the third part of the fifth book, our author explains what he means by 'movers of the spheres' and what is the relation between these movers and God. The inquiry must begin with the beings endowed with a soul on our earth, for, being closer, they are better known to us. Now, terrestrial beings are too perfect to have been born of hazard; the perfection that we see here below can only arise from an agent who deliberately willed it as it is; it cannot be the effect of an accident.

The demonstration given by Gersonides of the existence of the separate intellects that move the spheres is too intricate to be reproduced here. Let us only say that his demonstration that the natural agent of the spheres is a separate being, organizing itself and knowing its own action, uses notions of physics like the principle of inertia, which Galileo and Descartes were later to formulate more completely, and that it refutes at length the hypothesis of the seminal generation of the spheres.

These separate beings moving the spheres know what is produced by their movement, in the same way as the stonecutter knows perfectly well the stones that will serve to construct a house, because he is the cause of them and he knows them in knowing himself, but of the total plan of the building he has only the feeling that his work takes place in a greater whole. Should one conclude from this that the movers of the spheres do not know God and the other intellects? They know their cause, which is not an intellect superior to them (since the intellects are not hierarchically ordered) but the First Intellect, God himself. They know Him as every caused being recognizes its own cause in itself and this knowledge is far from being perfect, whereas the knowledge of the effects that flow from its own being is perfect. Thus the knowledge that the mover of a sphere can have of the order and the law of the world is partial; moreover, it is incomplete, for the bond that encloses all the parts in order to unite them in a coherent whole is lacking. From this description of the intellects that are movers of the spheres, it appears (1) that God cannot be the mover of a sphere (according to Averroes He was the mover of the outermost sphere); and (2) that the Active Intellect, giver of forms in this lower world, likewise cannot be the mover of a sphere. It is emanated from all the movers of the spheres and, from them, emanates the existents; the movers of the spheres prepare matter by means of the rays of the stars, and bestows form by the intermediary of the Active Intellect.

The world of the intellects, therefore, appears thus: there are forty-eight intellects, movers of the spheres (forty-eight separate movements in the skies, thus the same number of orbs); above them is God, Intellect totally detached from matter, obviously non-mover, ordering everything; between God and the intellects, movers of the spheres, is the Active Intellect, non-mover, who unites all the threads of all the intellects and of their spheres, and disposes terrestrial things.

God, the First Cause, cognizes Himself, and, in cognizing Himself, cognizes all beings in the most perfect form that may be, since it is cognized from the aspect of unity. This intellection, which unites with the intelligible and the intelligent, is, says Gersonides, first of all 'Joy'.

In one of his biblical commentaries (1 Chronicles 16), Gersonides gives a list of the principles of the *Torah*, and among them cites first one divine attribute: Joy. The fact that joy is given by Gersonides as the first of the divine attributes, linked to knowledge, recalls the reflections of his contemporary Shemariah ben Elijah of Crete and anticipates those of Crescas. The other attributes follow: Life, Substantiality, Existence, Unity, Action, the Good, Purpose, Beneficence, Generosity, Overflowing, Duration and Eternity, Justice and Righteousness. In Book I of the *Wars of the Lord*, but as if incidentally, Gersonides had given a shorter list: Essence, Eternity, Unity, Substantiality, Beneficence, Power and Will. All these attributes are homonymous, *per prius et posterius*, that is, they do not have the same meaning for God and for man but they are applied to the two in the relation sustained between them by cause and effect, and in any case, they are only a way of expressing that God is Form in the highest degree, the Form of Forms.

In Book VI Gersonides solves the problem of the creation of the world. This intensely difficult question can only be answered, he says, if one states it in adequate terms, which means (1) that one one must know the totality of this 'creation' of which one wishes to speak; (2) that one must know something of the First Cause. This is a difficult task, but not impossible, for, according to our author, the essential is to choose carefully and well the points that will serve in our demonstration. We have only a feeble knowledge of the substance of the First Cause, and it is therefore difficult to affirm in regard to it the possibility or impossibility of temporal creation. As to the world of generation and corruption, it can prove nothing at all.

The only proper objects of investigation are those things which have continuous existence, for they are the ones that may be thought of as not being subject to generation. These are the heavenly bodies and their movers, time, motion and the part of the earth that is visible above the water. If it can be proved that these things came into being, it will be clear without any doubt that the world as a whole is generated.

What are the properties of generated things?

The first particular character of what is generated, says Gersonides at the beginning of chapter 5, is to be the product of a final cause; both when they are generated in nature and when they are the fruit of art, generated beings are produced with some end in view. Now, when a thing is produced in a certain manner with some end in view, we know immediately that it has been produced by an agent. Things not produced by an agent, whether this be nature or free will, have no final cause; thus one does not ask what is the final cause of the equality of the three angles of a right-angled triangle, and in mathematics one does not look for the active or final cause. Nevertheless, when one draws a triangle for any purpose, then one asks oneself why it is so and not otherwise. If one rejects the possibility of phenomena that resemble the effects of a final cause and in reality are the effect of hazard, for this possibility is rarely present, the hypothesis of eternal creation remains. This is the opinion of Averroes and that of most Jewish philosophers after Maimonides. In their view, the movement of the celestial bodies is the effect of a final cause – the separate intellects; since these have no temporal beginning, and since the movement of the spheres is the most perfect that there is, this movement will be constantly renewed according to their final cause. In fact there will be a movement regulated in terms of a final cause but without temporal beginning. This would be so, Gersonides answers, only if the existence of cause were necessarily linked to that of the effect; everything that is the effect of a final cause, and does not necessarily and perpetually arise from it, has a temporal origin; thus a house is the work of a mason but its existence does not constantly depend on his; it was thus necessarily produced at a given moment. If one can know in this way that a being was generated and produced by a final cause, to prove that it was generated in time one also has to show that cause and effect are not necessarily related. This is a weak point in Gersonides' demonstration, which he palliates with historical considerations.

The two other properties he recognizes in generated beings also do not permit one to differentiate between what is generated in time and what is eternally generated:

(1) What comes into being can be the substratum of accidents that are not part of, or do not follow from, their definitions. For example, a piece of wood can be a chair or a box; non-generated beings cannot possess a character that is not a part of their essence and their nature.

(2) Only generated things can serve as a means to an end, but the ungenerated being does not have a final cause.

It follows that the celestial spheres are generated:

(1) Because they are not the effect of hazard and have a cause. Gersonides has shown in the second part of Book v that the disposition of the spheres and the heavenly bodies, their distance from the earth, and all the details of the organization of the skies were combined in order to maintain equilibrium in the sublunary world.

(2) They do not eternally emanate from their cause.

Here Gersonides points out the many absurd conclusions implied by such a conception and, *inter alia*, affirms that an eternal creation means in fact a constantly renewed creation where the instant of creation and that of corruption coincide.

(3) The celestial bodies have many non-necessary and non-essential characters, for although they are made of a unique body, simple, homogeneous and without contraries, they are nevertheless diversified: each sphere has a particular intellect, a size and a movement specific to it, one or several stars, in short, individual characteristics that do not accord with an identity of nature.

(4) The numerous movements of the celestial bodies are not a necessity of their own nature; they are destined to perfect something else – the sublunary world.

The diversity of the celestial bodies and of their movements again shows that they were created by an act of will and choice. It is in no way due to nature, for nature always produces the same effect; while free will produces very different ones. Moreover, voluntary movement precedes natural movement, as Aristotle proved in the *Physics*.

The next part of Gersonides' demonstration sets out to show that time and movement had a beginning.

The basic argument is that time belongs to the category of quantity and therefore cannot be infinite; Aristotle had proved that the infinite could not be *in actu*, excepting time from his demonstration. Gersonides systematically uses the Aristotelian system against Aristotle himself and his disciples, believers in the infinite duration of the world.

In support of temporal creation, Gersonides adds arguments founded in history:

(1) The progress of the sciences, which is far from being complete, and has not reached an equal level in the different branches of knowledge, which would have been the case in a world of infinite duration, since the desire to know is part of human nature.

(2) Divine law, the *Torah*, is only now spreading among men; however, since the preceding laws were very imperfect, this perfect law would long ago have been accepted by humanity if creation had existed since eternity.

(3) Languages are not natural but conventional, therefore appearing at a given moment of history, a moment that can only be close to the creation of humanity.

Having shown that the world was generated – and also that it would not perish – our author now proposes a new solution to the problem that all his predecessors could not resolve, namely, was the world created *ex nihilo* or from a primary matter? His solution is this: the first body from which the world was created is something that is nothing: a non-generated body absolutely deprived of form and thus 'non-being'. Since only form confers being, this first body, which does not keep to 'any shape', is totally neutral and is pure potentiality.

It is this fluid body that is found between the various spheres and allows them to move without getting in each other's way, for it is incapable of opposing any resistance: a neutral body, without life, absolute opposite of God, who is Form in the perfect state, a body of which the eternity is not a positive quality since it is an empty eternity, placed just above nothingness. This first body, the existence of which between the spheres is known through the senses, was endowed by God's will with a fixed geometrical shape and the power to maintain it as the matter of the spheres, and in the sublunary world it has the shape of the elements and consequently the ability to receive all other shapes.

I shall leave aside the answers to Aristotle's nine objections and conclude this long analysis of the *Wars of the Lord* by noting that the book concludes with a philosophical exegesis of the story of Genesis and a justification of miracles.

Like Maimonides before him, Gersonides links the problem of the temporal creation of time and that of miracles. Creation and miracle are the generation of one thing from another that does not contain it directly and potentially. At all events, only the adventicity of the world makes possible the adventicity of miracles and especially the gift of the *Torah*.

Miracles cannot be produced except in substances or accidents of the sublunary world, and in the presence of a prophet. The author of the miracle is the Active Intellect, which plays on the natural laws: it can thus violate a rule of nature and substitute another for it; it can also precipitate the succession of causes as the alchemist does, a comparison that we shall also find in Joseph Caspi.

Some miracles as they are literally narrated in the Scriptures are quite simply impossible, for instance, the sun standing still at Gideon.

Gersonides' main point is that the miracle could not have involved the actual stopping of the sun. This is true, he says, for a number of reasons. First, it is impossible that a miracle occur with respect to the heavenly bodies. This is so because, as we have already explained, the Active Intellect is the cause of these wonders, as explained above, and it is not possible that the Active Intellect could work upon the heavenly bodies, since it is an effect of them. Second, miracles are performed only as an act of divine goodness and grace; any unnatural alteration in the configuration of the heavenly bodies can only cause great harm to befall the sublunar world. This latter claim follows from Gersonides' acceptance of astrology and his belief that the heavenly bodies which determine the future are so ordered as to maximize to the greatest extent possible the good of those whose futures are so determined. Any change in their interrelationship can thus only cause more harm than good.

Third, the Torah testifies to the fact that the miracles of Moses were greater than the miracles of all the other prophets (Deut. 34: 10). If Joshua's demonstration were such as to have effected a change in the law [*nomos*] governing the movements of the heavenly bodies then this demonstration would be immeasurably greater than the demonstrations of Moses, our Teacher; this is very clear. This is clear, Gersonides maintains, since none of Moses' miracles affected the heavenly bodies.

Gersonides advances a fourth argument in defense of his interpretation of the miracle at Gideon: This stopping of the sun – if it occurred – would have no particular advantage for Israel or others. This is so because the Israelites believed in prophecy at that time, and we have not found that any of the other nations tried to turn to God, blessed be He, on account of this demonstration.

(M. M. Kellner, 'Gersonides and his cultured despisers', pp. 274–5)

The two last parts of the book, the exegesis of Genesis and the explanation of the miracles, are designated by Gersonides as 'religious' (*toriim*), while he declares the rest of the work to be philosophical.

Gersonides' thought is undoubtedly a very original and systematic one. He developed a far-reaching view of God, the world and man, incorporating his personal ideas on astronomy as part of his overall system. Using ideas borrowed from predecessors and contemporaries, he quotes only his adversaries by name, leaving the authors with whom he agrees in anonymity. This proceeding does not help us to identify his sources. They are however essentially the traditional Arab–Jewish Aristotelian writings, and the predominant role assigned to the Active Intellect seems to be based on a passage of Al-Fārābī. Gersonides' description of God's positive attributes resembles that of Duns Scotus, and even more so that of Thomas Aquinas; his discussion of the 'now', the moment that divides the past and the future, is not far from the *Questiones* on physics attributed to Siger of Brabant, nor, again, from Thomas Aquinas. Some other aspects of his thought indicate that Gersonides was conversant with the discussions and the problems that occupied Christian philosophical circles. His system is certainly not the more or less faithful copy of a scholastic model, but it belongs to an intellectual climate where scholasticism was no stranger. The question has also been raised whether his affirmation of human liberty was made in response to Abner of Burgos, and it is difficult to believe that he was not aware of this celebrated affair, even if he does not explicitly speak of it.

ABNER OF BURGOS AND THE QUESTION OF FREE WILL AND PROVIDENCE

The question of free will became one of the central problems in Jewish thought at the beginning of the fourteenth century with the appearance on the scene of Abner of Burgos. Towards 1320, this Jewish doctor and philosopher, already quite old, experienced a revelation of the truth of the Christian religion. Converted under the name of Alfonso of Valladolid, he became an ardent propagandist of the Catholic faith and attacked his former co-religionists in numerous works, in Hebrew, Latin and Castillian. The best-known of his writings, *Mostrador de Justicia*, has been preserved only in Castillian; other treatises exist in Hebrew.

In these works of Christian propaganda intended for Jews, Abner exerted himself to prove the superiority of the Catholic religion, and, at the same time, to justify his own conversion; however, for the first time in Christian Europe the public debate between Jews and Christians was in fact placed on the philosophical level.

In these debates, instigated by the Christians, rather than the Jews, the point at issue had until then chiefly been the interpretation of biblical texts. The Christians set out to show that the Bible supported their claim to be the true Israel, and that only stubbornness and obduracy prevented the Jews from recognizing this verity. There was no lack of philosophical discussion, however, between individuals, Jews and Christians, and we have seen indications of this for, instance, in Nissim of Marseilles. But now, Abner, a philosopher, an ardent devotee of astrology and learned in the Kabbalah, was using all the arguments that his erudition, which was wide, furnished him, in order to attack his former co-religionists on their own territory.

Moses of Narbonne gives this account of the beginning of the debate:

There was a scholar, an older contemporary of mine, one of the singular men of his time, who composed a treatise on Determinism, in which he stated that 'the possible' does not exist, but only 'the inevitable', since everything is predestined . . . Now this man, called Abner, possessed great knowledge, so that I do not believe that he was himself in error, but that his intent was to mislead others. For he had come upon hard times, and he realized that he could expect no assistance, only opposition, from his correligionists, who, being strangers to philosophy themselves, hated those who cultivated it – so he turned apostate . . . For he was not one of those pious men whose faith remains unimpaired even by extreme material want . . . Later, when he saw that what he had done was wrong even according to philosophy – for even a philosopher should not discard the Torah in which he was nurtured – he tried to absolve himself of guilt by preaching an all-embracing determinism, claiming that everything was preordained.

(Moses Narboni, *Treatise on Free Will*, trans. I. Baer in *A History of the Jews In Christian Spain*, vol. I, p. 332)

Abner's opinions were based on an absolute determinism. Human actions in his view flow necessarily from causes, as do the processes of nature. Man chooses between alternatives, but this choice is not free, for it depends on necessary laws. In fact, if human choice were free, God could not know human decision until the last moment, because it would be unforeseeable, even for man, until the last moment. He would thus not be omniscient. From the philosophical point of view, providence and free will are only one aspect of a more general problem: can one say that all events are the results of necessary causes, even if man does not always conceive the causes that produce them? Or must one admit that certain events are truly contingent, that is, not determined, until the moment they occur, as are accidental events according to Aristotle, or acts arising from human liberty? While asserting absolute determinism, Abner still maintained that the commandments and prohibitions of God keep all their force and that the reward and punishment that accompany them are the necessary consequences of human acts, even if these acts are necessary.

If this determinism justified Abner's conversion, it is evidently opposed to Judaism; for why should one go to such trouble to fulfil the divine commandments if the much easier way, their abandonment, is already anticipated in the order of the universe?

This problem of free will is part of the philosophical problem of contingent futures, the question of divine justice remaining in the background; its importance in Jewish thought in the fourteenth century was due not only to Abner's attacks but also to the increased importance of astrology, and to the fact that contingent futures were at the time the object of a quarrel in the Christian universities.

The problem was discussed from the point of view of logic: does the contingent future objectively exist as such for God as for us? or is contingency only an illusion caused by ignorance? As L. Baudry points out:

Some thinkers, exclusively philosophers or philosophers before being theologians, first affirm contingence, free to explain afterwards or to leave to others the task of explaining that God can have a certain knowledge of contingence, and so also even men, to the extent that God reveals it to them. The others, theologians before philosophers, first affirm that God knows everything with an infallible knowledge, only to strive afterwards to show that this does not mean that everything happens by necessity. These will reproach the first with denying the divine prescience and the truth of the prophets. The first will reproach the second with expelling from the universe both contingence and free will.

(*La Querelle des futurs contingents*, pp. 14–15)

The Jewish philosophers are on the side of the philosophers. Abner of Burgos – Alfonso of Valladolid – is, on the contrary, on the side of the theologians.

The problem of man's free will was always present in Judaism. Jewish thinkers had generally accepted that man is free to choose between good and evil. Saadiah linked this problem to divine justice. If man was not free, God would not be just in punishing his bad acts and rewarding the good ones, since the bad like the good would only be a carrying-out of His will. Besides, for Saadiah, man has the feeling that he can act or refrain from acting, be silent or speak, and that nobody can prevent him from doing what he wishes,

Judah Halevi also admits the free human will, and, like Saadiah, he does not think that God's knowledge of human decision is contrary to free will; but we already find in him the Aristotelian distinction between natural, accidental and willed events, and though the first two kinds are not totally determined, only the third is free, and this is because free decision is only an intermediary cause caused by the First Cause.

At the end of the twelfth century Abraham Ibn Daud in his introduction to the *Emunah Ramah* declared that the purpose of the treatise was the discussion of free will, and he affirmed its existence, defining it, in terms more moral than philosophical, as a choice between good and evil.

Concerning divine knowledge of contingent futures, he distinguishes between: (1) what we call contingent because of ignorance – for example whether the King of Babylon is alive or dead, for people in Spain cannot know if this fact is true or false; and (2) contingent that God has made contingent which means that it can become a thing or its contrary; God knows it as contingent but does not know which of the two alternatives will be realized (*Emunah Ramah*, p. 96). Al-Fārābī had already mentioned this thesis and rejected it; and perhaps Abraham Ibn Daud found his source there.

In the *Mishneh Torah* Maimonides also states his position with reference to good and evil and divine justice, but in the *Guide* he examined the question in connection with divine omniscience and declares that the problem cannot be resolved by a human being, for our instruments of thought are not adequate to understand divine knowledge. The possible contingent remains contingent and nevertheless God knows it from all eternity.

The link between astrology and the necessity or the contingence of possibles is clearly expressed by Al-Ghazālī in presenting Avicenna's doctrine. According to him:

As God knows the kind and the species, so He knows the contingent [things] that are generated, although we do not know them, because as long as the contingent is contingent, it is impossible to know of its realization or non-realization; in fact, all that one knows of it is its attribute of contingency, which means that it will be or it will not be. If we know that Zaid must ineluctably arrive tomorrow, his arrival has become necessary; to say that it is contingent is without sense. Thus, as long as one knows of the contingent only its contingency, one cannot conceive of knowing if it will take place or not.

However, we have already said that what is possible in itself is necessary through a cause. If therefore the existence of its cause is known, its existence is necessary [and] not possible; if it is the non-existence of its cause that is known, it is its non-existence that is necessary [and] not possible. Thus, regarded from the point of view of the cause, possibles are necessary . . . If we could consider all the causes of a determined thing and we know that [they] exist, we shall affirm the existence of this thing as we have affirmed Zaid's arrival . . . The First Being knows the events which are generated by their causes, because the motivations and the causes go back to the Being whose Existence is Necessary. But everything that happens [after not having been] and everything that is contingent is [in the final analysis] necessary, for its cause is necessary, and impossible if its cause does not exist. But its cause is equally necessary [and the causal series continues in the same way] until [it] arrives at the essence of the One Whose Existence is Necessary. And since God knows the hierarchy of the causes, He necessarily knows the effects.

The astrologer investigates some of the causes of existence of an event but his regard has not encompassed the totality of these; so, indubitably, his judgement concerning the realization of this event rests on a conjuncture, for sometimes an obstacle will rise up before the partial cause that he has been able to discover. His prognostic does not take into account all the causes [of the predicted event]; even more his prognostic is valid only with the reservation that contrary causes do not intervene. If the astrologer is informed of the greater part of the causes, his conjecture is strengthened; if his information covers all of them, he has achieved knowledge.

(Paris, Bibliothèque nationale, MS héb. 908, fol. 78v. Albalag's translation)

Albalag, who had already criticized this position in the part of his work dealing with logic (pp. 23–5) comments here:

Of a contingent whose near and remote causes follow each other in an essential way and conform to a certain order in their working, so that it is impossible that any obstacle comes to thwart any of them, I affirm that this contingent is for the knowing subject as determined as is the necessary. However, as regards the other contingent, neither their realization nor its moment can be known with certainty before they are [in fact] realized.

You think perhaps that I am denying that God knows the contingents before their realization. Far from me such a thought. What I reject is that God knows them in the way that Al-Ghazālī thinks. There can be no doubt, in fact, that divine knowledge as the latter admits it is of the same kind as human knowledge, the difference only being one of degree. This appears clearly from his words and from the comparison that he proposes with astrology.

For popular instruction Al-Ghazālī's belief is altogether acceptable; but it is not applicable according to the opinion of those who seek to know the tenet on which depends the life of the world [to come]. If we closely examine Al-Ghazālī's words, we confirm that they imply the suppression of man's free will and the determination of his acts, as well as the total elimination of the nature of the contingent. Such opinions do not only constitute the negation of philosophy, but serious heresy as regards the revealed Law. Other [= several] Ancients have already striven to refute them either from the point of the faith, or from the point of view of philosophy, so well that they have left me nothing to do. (*Sefer Tikkun ha-De'ot*, pp. 76–7)

Not only does Abner of Burgos – Alfonso of Valladolid – affirm absolute determinism, he also gives a definition of will that justifies in advance the forced baptisms and all the tortures that the Inquisition reserved for the *conversos*.

In his *Minḥat Kenaot* (*Offering of Jealousy*) written in reply to a polemical letter from Isaac Pulgar, he affirms that Will is the immediate cause of the act itself; that this will is due to an irrevocable decree or is dependent on another cause changes nothing. One may argue that a will of which one knows that it is fixed in advance is no longer a will; in effect, what one calls consent, or perfect will, from which acts arise, is an attitude that is born in the soul on the basis of multiple causes that are all due by linkage of causes to the movements of the spheres. If it leads to action, the will is perfect even if it is due to an exterior constraint . . . The man who is obliged to will something under torture is no less willing and consenting and freely choosing. So much the more is he freely willing when the constraint is not recognized as constraint and its causes are not recognized as causes.

Answers to these affirmations were provided by three philosophers whose thought will now be presented: Moses of Narbonne (who is dealt with in more detail on pp. 332–41), Isaac Pulgar and Joseph Caspi.

I have already quoted Narboni's *Treatise on Free Will*, where he speaks of Abner. Narboni first briefly summarizes the theories that he intends to refute:

(1) All things are fixed and determined in advance;

(2) Effort and zeal are, however, indispensable for they are the intermediary causes necessary for the necessary things to come into existence.

The term 'will' only applies to the necessary things; one cannot 'want' a thing that does not take place. Nevertheless, the first point was hidden from the people lest effort and zeal should disappear.

Narboni first refutes the second point: if all things are fixed and determined in advance, neither effort nor zeal are necessary, for, if a man is to become rich, he will become so, whether he works towards this goal or not. If we accept Abner's thesis, 'effort', 'zeal', 'will' are terms deprived of meaning.

The first point, that all things are fixed and determined in advance, is false, first from the logical point of view, as Aristotle showed, and then from the point of view of our own experience. Contingency is introduced into the order of nature on two levels, that of accident and that of free will.

Not all the things that can come into existence do actually come into existence; the cause does not necessarily arise from what precedes it in the chain of causes, and what comes into existence is not necessarily caused by the First Cause, for among the intermediary causes there are some that are not necessary but accidental. Thus the non-necessary exists on the level of generated and corruptible things.

On the level of the human intellect, free will has been given to man, as experience proves to us; to be sure, God knows all things, but reckoning from Himself, not from the things that happen.

Narboni's position is that of Maimonides:

For we know all that we know through looking at the existent beings; therefore our knowledge does not grasp the future or the infinite ... with regard to Him, there is no multiplicity of insights and renewal and change of knowledge. For through knowing the true reality of His own immutable essence, He knows the totality of what necessarily derives from all His acts ... everything is revealed to His knowledge, which is His essence, and it is impossible for us to know in any way this kind of apprehension.

(*Guide of the Perplexed*, III, 21, trans. S. Pines, p. 485)

Joseph Caspi, in arguing for human free choice, does not accept that we cannot know anything about the divine knowledge of contingent futures.

First of all, we affirm that God knows contingent futures: in fact, it is known regarding the contingent future that contraries are not divided according to truth or falsehood, so long as they are contingent; and it is as such that they are intelligible to us today, and also by nature, and this is demonstrated by logic. This is why the philosophers have striven to say how God knows the future before it has happened. How can He know which of the two terms of the alternative will take place, so that he often reveals this secret to His servants the prophets, and this knowledge does not necessarily insure the realization of this one alternative?

This is what Rabbi Akiva the perfect Sage said, one of those who have entered into the garden of theoretical sciences: 'All is foreseen and liberty is given to man

(*Pirkei Avot* III, 17).' Let us take an example: God revealed to Jeremiah that Jerusalem would be destroyed by Nebuchadnezzar if Zedekiah did not surrender to Nebuchadnezzar; if he surrendered to him, the town would not be destroyed; He also revealed to him that Zedekiah would freely choose to rebel against Nebuchadnezzar. It is as if He had said to him; Know that Zedekiah the accursed will choose the evil way. Our sages are practised in conjecture and supposition; they foresee that a man accursed in his actions and in all that he touches will take a bad decision tomorrow or the day after tomorrow, whether in an affair of marriage or in some other affair concerning common things – business or a journey. Now, if we are seldom mistaken in our anticipations, how much more certainly can God, who presides over intellectual prediction as over established knowledge, direct His knowledge towards the decision that we shall take in one or other specific situation. There can be no doubt that the prophets likewise are altogether excellent in supposition and prevision, as Maimonides says in the *Guide of the Perplexed*.

Thus, what is extraordinary in the fact that Moses foresaw that after his death the people would arise and betray God with false divinities? This was a thing very easy to divine, as he had already declared: 'Behold, while I am yet alive with you this day, ye have been rebellious against the Lord [Deuteronomy 31: 27]'; all the more reason that God should know the contingent futures and know today what our choice will be tomorrow or the day after tomorrow, this absolutely free choice which is fixed in our hearts.   (*Tam ha-Kesef*, pp. 20-1)

To sum up, God knows all the contingent things with a probable knowledge, to a perfect degree.

Caspi refers to Maimonides, and it is a fact that the *Guide* does mention the prophets' faculty of divination, but there is no hint that this sort of knowledge could be attributed to God. In this connection, S. Pines quotes a phrase from Durandus of Saint-Purçain (d. 1322) which very much resembles Caspi's theory of divine conjectural knowledge, and it is not very probable that this is mere coincidence.

Nunc autem Deus non solum cognoscit causam contingentem in se et absolute, quia sic in ea vel per eam non cognosceretur infallibiliter aliquis effectus nisi tantum coniectura probabili (ut bene dicunt alii) sed cognoscit omnia quae eam determinare possunt et quae determinabunt, insuper cognoscit omnia quae eam impedire possunt et quae impedient vel non impedient, ergo Deus in causa contingente sic cognita potest certitudinaliter cognoscere effectum futurum contingentem.

God not only knows the contingent cause in itself and in an absolute sense – for if it was so an effect of the cause would not be known without possibility of error in it or through it unless it be by means of a probable conjecture (as some say) – but He knows all things which can and will determine the cause and, in addition, He knows all things which can hinder it and which will or will not hinder it. Hence, in a contingent cause which is known in this way, God can know with certitude the future contingent effect.

(Comm. Sent. bk. 1, dist. 38, qu. 3, p. 89c; quoted in G. Leff, *Bradwardine and the Pelagians* (Cambridge, 1957), p. 183, note 1)

The Fourteenth Century

ISAAC PULGAR

Pulgar was Abner's chief opponent; he was also the first to answer his attacks, and perhaps indeed provoked them. We know practically nothing of him except that he was intimately acquainted with Abner before his conversion. In his book *Ezer ha-dat* (*The Support of the Faith*) he cites other works by himself that have not, it seems, been preserved; these include commentaries on Genesis, Ecclesiastes and Psalms, a book on ethics, and a treatise against astrology. In a note contained at the end of a copy of Albalag's introduction to Al-Ghazālī's *Intentions of the Philosophers* he declares that he finished this translation, which Albalag was unable to terminate, and that he inserted a gloss in the commentary.

The praise that he bestows on Albalag is an indication of a certain affinity between his thought and that of his predecessor, an affinity that is also found in their treatment of philosophical questions.

I shall quote I. Baer's masterly analysis of the arguments of the two adversaries, Abner of Burgos and Isaac Pulgar.

A short time after his conversion Abner sent Policar a tract that he had written, explaining his messianic doctrine. Policar replied in a Hebrew pamphlet, dubbed by Abner 'The Epistle of Blasphemies' (*Iggereth ha-Harafoth*), which contained the personal attacks upon the apostate quoted earlier. Policar's main purpose, however, was to oppose to Abner's Christian faith his own rationalist credo. Taking as his authority the political theory of Aristotle, he seeks to prove that

law and convention are absolutely necessary for orderly human behavior ... Because we are endowed with a rational soul, we are obliged to accept those tenets whose truth had been logically established. However, the human being, in his youth – and, indeed, in the case of most people, throughout life – has neither the leisure nor the disposition to learn these tenets through the study of their sources, namely, the exact sciences. Therefore, the founder of the divinely revealed faith found it necessary to incorporate into it all those fundamental truths without which the human being cannot achieve perfection and to make them part of Tradition, so that a man would not remain throughout his entire lifetime, until he dies, ignorant of them.

Only the Torah of Moses fulfils these conditions, both in its ideology and in its law. The people of Israel were distinguished from all other nations and consecrated to keep this Torah. Those who observe the commandments of the Torah, suppressing their base instincts, merit eternal life. Following this brief exposition of the fundamentals of his rationalist doctrine Policar set forth his belief in the Messiah who is destined to redeem his people. 'No thinker would believe that our faith is contingent upon the coming of the Messiah ... Yet we must believe that his coming is presaged in the Torah.' Policar then cites biblical verses to show that the order of nature will not change in the Messianic Age, and that contrary to Christian belief the Messiah has not yet come and the messianic prophecies were not fulfilled in the days of the Second Temple.

Isaac Policar circulated the *Epistle of Blasphemies* throughout Spain. Abner replied to it with a tract which he called, 'Refutation of the Blasphemer' (*Teshuboth la-Meharef*).

In the body of the work Maestre Alfonso advances, against the position of the religious rationalists, two telling arguments which had already been used by the cabalists of the preceding century in their war against rationalism. He writes:

Your statement in the first chapter that, 'because we are endowed with a rational soul, we are obliged to accept those tenets whose truth has been logically established, and since the [average] human being has neither the leisure nor the disposition to learn these tenets through the study of their sources, namely, the exact sciences, the founder of the faith found it necessary to incorporate into it all those fundamental truths without which the human being cannot achieve perfection and to make them part of Tradition, so that a man would not remain throughout his entire lifetime, until he die, ignorant of them', is full of serious error. Precisely because man possesses a rational soul he does not have to accept any traditional belief; for that which one learns from tradition, whatever the reason for it, can be called knowledge only in a homonymous sense, and in accepting it he is not functioning as an active thinker. Yet according to you it is for the exercise of that function that man needs those tenets, as you put it: 'Because we are endowed with a rational soul etc. . . . a man should not remain throughout life ignorant of them.' Furthermore, the human being, as a rational being, should know all the sciences in the world, for a knowledge of *all* of them is necessary for his achievement of perfection as a rational being, not merely a knowledge of a few of them, as you specify when you say, '*those* without which the human being cannot achieve perfection'. Now, if the perfection of the human being cannot, because he is a rational being, be achieved by his derivation of even all existing knowledge and creed from tradition, how can it be achieved by his acquisition of only a part thereof, two or three doctrines perhaps, from the same source?

The fact is that a human being is ready to accept authoritative tradition not in his capacity as a rational being, as you claim, but as a master of some specialized branch of knowledge which takes some or all of its basic premises from the established traditions of a higher and more comprehensive science. The specialized lore, whose premises are the tenets you mentioned, is the Torah, which you extol. But a man acquires his knowledge of its basic tenets not because he is a generally rational being, but as one versed specifically in the Torah . . . From your statement, 'so that a man would not remain throughout his entire lifetime, until he die, ignorant of them', it appears that you regard these tenets not as premises on which the Torah is based but as the Torah itself or as parts of the Torah, and that one's purpose in learning them is not the performance of any commandment (*mitzva*) but merely the attainment of knowledge as an end in itself . . . But this does not accord with the teachings of the Torah or the Prophets or the Sages. For if those tenets were part of the Torah itself, then Scripture would not have imparted them in veiled references but in clear and explicit statements, like the other commandments; for it is written, 'It is not hidden from you nor is it far away . . . but the thing is very near to you' (Deut. 30. 11–14). Certainly they would not have been stated in metaphors which, if taken literally, indicate the opposite of their real meaning, for example, 'the mouth of God', 'the hand of God', 'the eyes of God', 'the feet of God', and like phrases which, in their literal meaning, imply the corporeality of God; or expressions such as 'God regretted',

'He was grieved at heart', 'God savored the pleasing odor', and others like them, which, taken literally, would imply that God undergoes change and assumes accidents; or references to God in the plural (*i.e.*, *Elohim*, and adjectives and verbs in grammatical agreement with it), which, in the literal sense, deny the unity of God. Then there is the verse 'In the beginning God created' and others of similar meaning which literally aver *creatio ex nihilo*, a tenet denied by some philosophers, and the biblical accounts of the miracles, likewise discredited by the same philosophers, and you say that 'the perfection of man is unattainable without a knowledge of those philosophies'.

Likewise, your statement – which you base on the words of Maimonides (*Guide of the Perplexed*, III, 54) – that the verse, 'Therein shall man glory, understanding and knowing Me' (Jer. 9: 23), means that a man must know and understand the philosophic theories which explain the existence of God, His unity and all His other attributes, is nonsense. The same verse explains forthwith what is meant by 'understanding and knowing Me' when it continues, 'that I am the Lord who practices kindness, justice and righteousness on earth', meaning that man must know and understand that the Holy One, blessed be He, exercises His Providence over the earth and practices in it kindness, justice and righteousness . . . From this standpoint the study of the various branches of knowledge has as its purpose the performance of the commandments, and the love enjoined by the Torah is one which is 'not hidden from you nor is it far away'. It is not a love which is contingent upon the comprehension of the secret of all creation, which is very far away and beyond the capacity of the human being to grasp. The other view appears to suffer from a contradiction, for most of those who pursue that knowledge are free-thinkers who make light of the Torah and of the commandments to a greater extent than other people.

(I. Baer, *A History of the Jews*, vol. I, pp. 335–9)

In *Ezer ha-dat*, his principal work, Isaac Pulgar seeks to answer Alfonso of Valladolid, and to justify Jewish rationalism and its interpretation of religion. The book is divided into five parts, preceded by an introduction, where five kinds of opponents of the true religion are described. These are the ignorant, the credulous and the sceptics, the astrologers and those who believe in absolute determinism, the Kabbalists and all those who believe in miraculous tales, and the non-believers who do not believe in the next world or in reward and punishment.

In the first part Pulgar expounds the excellence of the Jewish religion. Using the traditional definition of theoretical reason, the specific characteristic of man and the purpose of his creation – that is, philosophy – and that of practical reason, which allows him to subsist in this world within a just society, Pulgar defines the *Torah* as that which helps man to develop on three levels:

(1) On the moral level, by teaching him virtue;
(2) On that of his social instinct, by giving him just and equitable laws;
(3) On that of his intellect, since it provides man with the minimum of true knowledge necessary for the survival of his soul.

The third level is the bridge between theoretical science and political necessity, between truth, philosophy, and ethical and social needs.

One chapter is devoted to the king–statesman of a virtuous people. He is perfect in his body, with a natural sound understanding of things and discourses: he must have a retentive memory, an intuitive knowledge of hidden things, fluent speech and the faculty of persuasion, the ability and the willingness to teach, love of truth and the hatred of falsehood. He is remote from all bodily pleasures; he is proud of his pure soul and disdainful of all mundane possessions and envies. He will naturally love justice, and hate wrong; he will have a strong, decisive character and all his decisions will arise from his 'human' side, that is, his intellect.

These are the qualities Al-Fārābī demanded from the King of the Virtuous City, the statesman 'who almost passes beyond the human virtues to what is a higher class than man; the ancients name this man divine' (Al-Fārābī, *Fusul al-madanī*, ed. and trans. D. M. Dunlop (Cambridge, 1961), par. 11, p. 32).

Such a man by his nature would prefer to be solitary, but his kindness of heart moves him to rule a people who, through his rule, will attain such perfection that it will need neither judge nor doctor. And at the end of his life, he will write down the laws that will become their true and sacred Law (*Torah*).

This divine man, says Pulgar, was Moses, and he finds all these qualities in Moses' character and history.

He documents each virtue by means of biblical quotations, concluding that:

We are obliged to believe that all these eminent qualities were in Moses because his soul was withdrawn, detached from its matter and despising it. [The soul of Moses] changed the laws of nature and performed the well-known miracles in the same way as the separate forms change matter at their will. Moses prophesied whenever he wished to do so . . . and all this because he was always conjoined to the spiritual [beings] and had become divine, perfect.   (*Ezer ha-dat*, p. 15)

After a chapter describing the true life, which is the death of the body and all bodily pleasures, our author explains the utility of miracles: The true motive of belief in a prophet is not his causing of prodigies and supernatural events; only the ignorant believe because of a miracle. The Israelites were not like the virtuous people ruled by the virtuous King, and therefore

Moses was obliged to make audible a voice from the heavens that spoke [to the Israelites], as it is said: That the people may hear when I speak with thee, and believe forever [Exodus 19: 9]. He also had to promise all kinds of bodily pleasures in recompense for the accomplishment of the commandments . . . If Moses had thought that their intellects were perfect, he would have explained to them that in fulfilling the commandments which are for the good of man, and avoiding the things prohibited, which are bad for him, they would be granted eternal life, which is the world to come, and this was a better reason to believe in God and in Moses, His servant.

                                                                 (*Ibid.* pp. 19–20)

Nature and its laws are the best arguments for believing in God and the history of Israel does not disprove the Law of Moses because it is a 'natural' consequence of the Law itself; this Law developed in the Israelites the love of peace and religion, the contempt for bodily pleasures and for envy, greed and hatred. So that when the people of Israel were attacked by envious and hating nations, they could only pray God to save them. However, perhaps as a precaution, we find at the end of this 'natural' explanation of the Diaspora: 'It is because of our faults and our offences that we are expelled from our Land, and God, in His compassion, will pardon them and take us back to our Land' (*Ibid.* p. 22).

The end of this first part discusses the prophecies about the Messiah – which speak of the future and not the past – a justification of the Talmud, and a rehabilitation of the *Aggadah* and its educational role. All this is in answer to the attacks of Abner of Burgos.

The second part recounts a dialogue between a youth who is a philosopher, and a old man representing religion. I will summarize only the arguments of the philosopher, since the 'religious' arguments are the classical ones. The commandments, says the philosopher, were given to men for their own sake; God does not benefit by them and does not need them. The reward of fulfilling the commandments is the good brought about by the very act of accomplishment, and nothing else.

There follows a condemnation of the belief in the magical power of letters and other miraculous traditions, which, says Pulgar, are no more than a meaningless rigmarole. Here the philosopher explains the essential differences between religion and science: the philosopher and the prophet both attain divine science but the philosopher, using his intellect, understands the causality, the middle term that ties the known to the unknown, the visible fabric of the world to the invisible intellects. The prophet does not understand what is happening to him because the divine overflow is received only by his imaginative faculty – the degree Maimonides granted to statesmen and diviners is here elevated to the degree of the prophets, as it was to be in the *Tractatus theologico-politicus* of Spinoza.

For our youthful philosopher 'the Sage is superior to the prophet'. Indeed, the prophet described here is inferior to the sage since he receives the divine overflow only in a bodily faculty, the imaginative; and this conception does not fit the Moses described in the first part, who is the perfect philosopher as well as a prophet. Since the prophets do not understand their vision intellectually, they cannot teach what they know. We cannot learn anything from the prophets' experiences. Here we see the influence of Albalag.

The judge chosen to decide between philosophy and religion is 'the King of Israel, who, because of his great science, is the Prince of the people of God'.

His judgement reconciles the two sides. The divine overflowing is one but comes to us in two ways:

319

The first is the way of the perfect theoretical science, the second is God's perfect religion; we need the first to imprint in the soul the beginnings of the intelligibles which are part of the existing beings and also of the Separate Forms; we need the second to guide our actions in the right path, to direct our activity towards good and beautiful works. (*Ibid.* p. 41)

Science and religion are necessary to man.

A philosopher without religion is like a man standing in the desert without any society: he will not be able to live and subsist alone, without help. A religious man without science, who studies the *Torah* for its own sake only, is like a beast without a herdsman. He will not know where his pasture is. Thus they [*Torah* and philosophy] must be narrowly conjoined and tied together. (*Ibid.* pp. 43–4)

The real danger is represented by those who, having learnt a little logic, apply to religion the principles of science; the *Torah* has its own way of thinking and one should not try to alter its nature. Once again we have an echo of Albalag.

And the 'King of Israel' affirms that the eternity of the world is compatible with a divine Will constantly *in actu* and concludes with the perfect concord between Jewish religion and philosophy.

The third part is directed against Abner and the astrologers and begins with a description of the popular astrologer who impresses the vulgar with his display of books and astronomical instruments. Pulgar repeats Maimonides' argument against astrology in detail; the qualities attributed to the planets are not supported by any demonstrable fact; we know the physical influence of the sun and the moon, the rest is empty talk. More serious is the problem of the prophecy of future events and God's knowledge of contingent future events.

His solution calls on a universal harmony that reminds one of Leibniz' pre-established harmony:

We know already that the external sphere that encompasses all is like a single man and all the beings that it contains are like its members; God's general will is to the whole world what the soul is to the body, it comes anew simultaneously with the will of man who is like a part or a member of God. You see that the nerve moves the finger at its own will and nevertheless one also says that man moves his finger at his will. The two wills are simultaneous and concordant. It is because of this that the sage said that all is revealed and liberty has been given to men to act according to their wish and their will [*Pirkei Avot* III, 17] . . .

Certainly, I am far from believing that it is by my own zeal and my own will alone that I obtain anything, whatever it may be, but, as I have told you, my will is linked to that of my Creator and both unite at the same instant so that my will is part of His, and thus I am drawn by Him; when He wishes and desires to act, then I too wish it. In all this, we are concerned only with voluntary acts and not natural or accidental events, for as regards these I have no liberty. As for what you have said, that my will is determined without my being aware of it, that all my acts are necessarily fixed and decided in advance without my thought, my reflection or my counsel taking a real part in their production, this is contrary to all our visible experience and destroys the nature of [the contingent] as it has been placed in it.

(Ezer ha-dat, pp. 57–8)

And on p. 71, he writes:

I have revealed to you the existence of the absolute nature of contingency which is that of everything coming into being before it comes about. I mean, before God wills it, realizing one of the alternatives; in consequence it could be said truly and justly, that it is impossible for anyone to encompass and to know which of the alternatives will be realized, as long as it is contingent, meaning as long as it is non-existent; and when the Creator knows it, [the realization] will be necessary and unavoidable because His knowledge which is His Will is the compelling [factor], but this necessity does not produce a change in His knowledge or in His essence.

Here S. Pines mentions Peter Aureoli, for whom God's knowledge gives the thing existence *in actu*.

A little earlier Pulgar writes:

God knows the future things freely chosen by man since He chooses them at the same time as man, but He does not communicate to the prophets His eternal knowledge of this will; what He communicates is a probable knowledge of the world, which permits the prophet to judge for himself of the greater or lesser possibility of an event being realized.

Thanks to the Active Intellect which overflows into the imaginative faculty of the prophet or the seer, or thanks to the light which this intellect makes to shine over it, the prophet or seer sees and attains the different degrees of the existing things; he encompasses with his intellect and knows the existence of the causes of the things that are susceptible of happening, or, on the basis of these causes, to come into existence when these causes approach each other and the active [power] is strengthened in order to act or the passive [one] is ready to be acted, and also when the impediments and the obstacles disperse and disappear . . . When [the prophet] apprehends this, he announces it; however, because of the nature of contingency that exists eternally in everything, as I have explained, this prophecy and this aptitude to know will not make necessary or obligatory the existence of a thing as long as the moment that the necessary and obligatory will of God has willed has not yet arrived. It is sometimes possible that this moment changes and that the realization does not occur as we see in connection with the episode of Jacob: God had promised him, and Jacob had prophesied concerning himself, supreme good and success, and nevertheless, he was very afraid of Esau, thus doubting the realization of the divine promise: 'For I fear him, lest he will come and smite me' [Genesis 32: 11] and our sages have said, perhaps [Jacob's] fault is the cause of this ? . . .

When a man who is not a prophet seeks to learn and to know some one thing of those that, according to him, will soon happen, he explores in his spirit, weighs in his thought and reflects in his intellect on the causes that render the thing necessary, those that exist and those that don't exist, those that are strong and those that are feeble, those that are far and those that are near, he also reflects about far and near obstacles and hindrances. If he sees a thing strong in action and of matter ready to receive this action, and that the active factor is approaching; if he sees that the hindrances are remote or weak, then in his spirit he sets out to judge, to affirm and to decide concerning this thing that it will be realized in the future. However, sometimes this judgement shall not be correct for an impediment will appear that he did not foresee and will create an obstacle, or else a feeble [hindrance] will become stronger or even the active factor will be weakened or change purpose. Thus people are in the habit of saying: I shall do this or that, God willing. This is what happens to the prophet or the seer for the light which flows from God, may He be blessed! over his imaginative faculty, as I have said, shows him and teaches him the causes of the future things and the next effect [the consequence] that will arise from these causes, with all the conditions that I have mentioned concerning the thinker who reflects, while the prophet announces the thing in question and foresees that it will happen, except that, sometimes, what happened to the thinker who reflected happens [here as well] and the thing does not conform to the prediction; this always because of the nature of the possible. What is the difference between these two kinds of apprehension? In the two cases:

(1) The thinker will attain the visible and exterior things and the prophet will attain the hidden and veiled things, and thus it is said: The secret things belong to the Lord our God: but those things which are revealed belong unto us ... [Deuteronomy 29: 29].

(2) The thinker will attain some of the causes and not all, and some of the obstacles and not all, while the prophet will attain all the causes and all the impediments for nothing shall be hidden from him, so that his prediction will be correct in most cases. (*Ezer ha-dat*, pp. 55–7)

This is the 'probable' knowledge that Caspi attributes to God, but in a perfect way.

The fourth part of the book deals with the inanity of magical beliefs and the absurdity of miraculous tales, and the fifth part contains a dialogue between a dead man and a living on the soul and its immortality.

This brief summary does not do justice to a work in which touches of contemporary interest, lively descriptions and reflections full of good sense abound; moreover, the style is remarkable, and poetical passages enliven the prose. Unfortunately the work has not been translated into any occidental language, and the analysis by the editor of the first Hebrew publication is inadequate.

Pulgar found it easy to refute Abner since he rejected astrology *en bloc*. The matter was much more difficult for other Jewish philosophers, for to all of them except Pulgar astrology was an integral part of science. The importance ascribed to astrology varied considerably among the individual philosophers. It is not really very significant in Joseph Caspi, although he wrote two commentaries on Ibn Ezra.

JOSEPH CASPI (EN BONAFOUX DE L'ARGENTIÈRE)

Joseph ben Abba Mari ben Joseph ben Jacob Caspi is a philosopher of remarkable temperament and biography. Contrary to other philosophers, who furnish hardly any details about themselves, Caspi often brings himself on to the scene, and his thought is in the likeness of his personality: brilliant ideas against the background of a comparatively unoriginal system. He was born in 1279 at l'Argentière or Largentière (Languedoc); hence the name Caspi (or Kaspi), 'silvery', and his Provençal name En Bonafous (or Bonafoux) de l'Argentière; the word *kesef* (silver) occurs in almost all the titles of his works.

Joseph Caspi was wealthy, if only according to rather modest criteria, and he loved to travel. He lived at Tarascon and visited Arles, Aragon, Catalonia, Majorca, Egypt and perhaps Fez, always with the purpose of broadening his knowledge. He had three children; the older son, Abba Mari, married and settled in Barcelona, a daughter lived in Perpignan and a younger son, Solomon, was twelve years old in the autumn of 1332 and lived at Tarascon; his father addressed to him a moralizing epistle from Valencia, which provides us with the last dated reference to the life of Joseph Caspi.

Our author himself drew up a list of his works entitled *Kevutsat Kesef* (*The Collection of Silver*) in two different versions that do not agree. Making use of both, E. Renan arrived at a total of thirty works, which have not all been preserved. Moreover, a certain number of these works have more than one name, the author himself having endowed them with different titles. Thus, the *Sefer ha-Sod* (*Book of the Secret*) which we shall cite here and which was criticized by Kalonymus ben Kalonymus under that name, is also called *Tirat Kesef* (*The Tower of Silver*) and has been published under the name of *Tam ha-Kesef* (*End of Silver*). We must also point out that most of the works were revised by the author himself, so that the manuscript copies of a work may differ to a considerable degree. In consequence, and although quite a large number of the texts have been published, a complete variorum edition is needed before the serious study that this philosopher fully deserves can be undertaken.

Caspi's writings are chiefly commentaries, on the Bible, the *Guide of the Perplexed* and the *Mysteries* of Ibn Ezra's *Commentaries*, but he also composed works of Hebrew grammar. His Arabic was not extensive and he had to have recourse to those more proficient in the language when he wanted to understand certain texts; he knew Latin, and he cited the Vulgate and terms used in logic, but in the present state of research it is difficult to determine whether his knowledge enabled him to read scholastic texts with ease.

One can gain an idea of the subjects that seemed important to Caspi from the moral testament that he addressed to his son Solomon, in which he outlined a programme of study:

To-day thou art twelve years of age. For another two years be a diligent student of the Scriptures and Talmud. When thou art fourteen, fix regular hours for continuing thy previous studies, and give also a good part of thy time to mathematics; first Ibn Ezra's Arithmetic, then Euclid, and the Astronomical treatise of Al-Fergani and [Abraham b. Ḥiyya]. Besides, appoint set times for reading moral books, which will introduce thee to all good qualities – viz. the Books of Proverbs and Ecclesiastes, the Mishnaic tractate *Fathers*, with the Commentary of Maimonides

and his preface thereto, and the same author's Introductory chapters to the Code.
Also read Aristotle's *Ethics*, of which I have made a digest. There is also available
among us the Collection of the *Maxims of the Philosophers*.

This course should occupy thee for two years. Then, when thou art sixteen
appoint times for the Scriptures, for the writings of Alfasi, Moses of Coucy, and
the Code of the perfect teacher (Maimonides). Also give much time to Logic. With
the help of God I will make a compendium on this subject, sufficient for thy needs,
as I did with the *Ethics*.

In this way thou shouldst pass another two years, by which time thou wilt be
eighteen years old. Then review all thy former work, and study natural science.
By that date, being twenty years of age, 'build thy house'. Do not intermit the
reading of moral books, but also take up theology, i.e., the *Metaphysics* of Aristotle
and his disciples, as well as the *Guide* of Maimonides.

(Trans. I. Abrahams, Hebrew Ethical Wills, pp. 144–5)

And Caspi adds:

Jews despise or neglect the *Guide* nowadays, though the purpose of that treatise is
to demonstrate the existence and unity of God. The Christians honor the work,
study and translate it, while even greater attention is paid to it by the Mohammedans
in Fez and other countries, where they have established Colleges for the study of
the *Guide* under Jewish scholars!

(Trans. I. Abrahams, Hebrew Ethical Wills, p. 153)

The historical reality of the study of the *Guide* by the scholastics and some
Arab thinkers does not really prove that there were official courses on
Maimonides at Fez and in other Arab countries, but, as we have already re-
marked, the first commentary on the *Guide* was by an Arab, Al-Tabrizi.

We see that Yedayah ha-Penini, writing to Solomon ben Adret that the
decisions of the Spanish rabbis would not be respected in Provence, was
right. If Solomon ben Joseph Caspi followed his father's advice he began to
study physics at the age of eighteen, and not at twenty-five. As for the inter-
diction on revealing the mysteries of philosophy to the profane, our author
openly laughs at it:

I declare today before God that I have committed no sin in this, and for several
reasons: firstly because I have revealed nothing except to those who have arrived
at the degree [of intellectual development] mentioned by Maimonides [in his introduction to the *Guide of the Perplexed*]. Then because what I revealed is perhaps
not at all the real thing, for God knows that in this or in any other of the secrets
of the Law, I have never received any tradition either by the intermediary of writers
[possessors of the tradition] or by the intermediary of works [written by them]; and
even, by the Living God, I do not remember ever having posed a question on this
subject to anyone whatever. Thirdly, He who permitted the *Guide* to explain a small
part of these mysteries, as Maimonides does in the Introduction to his works and
in the preliminary Observation of the Third Book, will allow us also to explain a
small part, for the little has no predetermined measure. Finally, I have done no
more than transcribe the words of philosophers such as Aristotle and his like, who
in their books have discussed these subjects, I mean the explication of the three

worlds that is called the Story of the Chariot. Their books are known among all men although, in truth, they are hidden from our people because of our sins.

(Menorath Kesef in *Asarah Keley Keset,* vol. II, p. 77)

As for the study of the ritual laws, Joseph Caspi does not attach much importance to this. Solomon ben Joseph Caspi was enjoined to study the Scriptures and the talmudic commentaries of Alfasi, the *Book of Command-ments* of Moses of Coucy and the *Mishneh Torah* of Maimonides. His father's opinion of the niceties of the ritual law is illustrated by the following anecdote:

I will confess to thee, my son! that though in my youth I learned a great portion of the Talmud, I did not acquire (for my sins!) a knowledge of all the *posekim.* [scholars in the Law, decision-pronouncers]. Now that I am old and grey, I have often to consult rabbis younger than myself. Why should I be ashamed of this? Can one man be skilled in every craft? If, for instance, I want a gold cup, I go to the goldsmith, and I feel no shame; and so with other products, I turn, in case of need, to those whom God has gifted with the requisite skill.

Once I made a great feast at which all kinds of delicacies were served. I had the table prepared, I invited my friends to eat and drink with me, for it was a family party. Then the luckless handmaid put a milk spoon into the meat pot. I did not know the ritual law, how one ought to estimate the lawfully permissible proportion of intermixture. Perturbed in mind, as well as famished in body, I went to one of the rabbis, held high in popular repute. He was (for my sins!), at table with his wife and family, eating, and drinking wine. I waited at his door until the shades of evening fell, and my soul was near to leave me. He then told me the law, and I returned home where my guests and the poor were awaiting me. I related all that had happened, for I was not ashamed to admit myself unskilled in that particular craft. In this I lack skill, but I have skill in another craft. Is not the faculty of expounding the existence and unity of God as important as familiarity with the rule concerning a small milk spoon?

(Ibid. pp. 151–2)

Let us note that the mere fact of referring to the ritual law as a 'craft', that is, to bring it down to the level of a practical *métier* in contrasting it with science and philosophy, was already extremely impertinent in the eyes of the Talmudists.

In the study programme devised for his son we do not find a reference to Hebrew grammar, most probably because Joseph Caspi considered that Solomon, at twelve, had mastered its difficulties and could advance further. In fact, Joseph Caspi despised the grammarians who had not gone beyond the stage of grammar. Not that he was unaware of its importance: he devoted several treatises to the Hebrew language and grammar (which have not yet been studied), and he sees in Hebrew the very root of the knowledge of the revealed book:

Once a bishop honoured in our country, who was versed in the Holy Scriptures, asked me: Why do you demand that kings, popes and bishops respect and render homage to your Scrolls of the Torah when they enter a city as we do with the Cross? . . . It is true that we must hold in veneration the *Torah* of Moses and, after it, the other writings written by the prophets, but we possess them in our own tongue and our own writing and, if our kings and our great men wish to be met with these books, we can do this with the volumes that we have. What superiority and sanctity have the Hebrew language and writing over the Latin language and writing since the meaning intended in them remains the same?

My answer was: My lord, certainly our books are superior and more saintly than yours because these books were first made in our tongue and in our writing. And this is for two causes: (One): the writing our books are written in is the Script of God and it is in this tongue [Hebrew] that they were given. If a king gives us a letter of freedom and if he writes it with his own hand and in our own tongue it will be more precious to us than anything else. The copy of the letter, called *vidimus*, is a truthful testimony that he has signed it. But if we take the *vidimus* to the court of the king, it will not be as precious and reliable as the letter itself; and even more, if it is changed to another language and another writing which is not this king's own language and writing. Our books are written in the language of the King . . . (Two): The meaning intended by the metaphors has been changed and has so deteriorated in a number of passages that they cannot be understood even by the One who has made them, God. The Book of Moses translated into another language and written in another writing is not at all the Book given to us by God . . .

Now I shall give several examples of the imperfection of a translation of the Holy Scriptures. The Christian translator renders the first verse of Genesis by the following words: *In principio creavit Deus caelos et terram* [Caspi thus transcribes the Latin in Hebrew characters]. These five words seem to correspond exactly to the five Hebrew words, which are: *Bereshit bara' Elohim et ha-shamayim ve-et ha-arez* [he does not count *et* and *ve-et* as separate words]; but this is not so. The word *bereshit* means in Hebrew the eternity of time and of cause, and this word was expressly chosen by God for the common people to understand in one sense and intelligent individuals to understand in another; but all must recognize in it a creation *ex nihilo*. *In principio* does not have this double sense in the language of the Christians; this word implies the sense of eternity in relation to time or to creation, but not the two meanings at once . . . *Deus* is a general name for God, while in Hebrew different names are used.

(Shulhan Kesef. Turin, MS ebreo A vi 34/7, fols. 165r–166r)

The great importance accorded to logic ('Also, give much time to Logic!' says Caspi to his son) is illustrated by the exegesis given to the biblical text:

At the beginning of *Tirath Kesef* Caspi says 'Our holy Torah is divided into two sublime categories. One includes stories and narratives and that is "categorical statement" (*omer gozer*). The second includes commandments and warnings from the Torah and in general what is not categorical statement. Of the second there are the following types: commandments in general and statutes and norms and precepts. But of the first [category] the names of the types are not explained in the words of David or Solomon even though it is undoubtedly divided into many types, as anyone who understands language knows. However, these words concerning the term for the general category must suffice and that is the term "word" (*imrah* – statement); as David said, "I have laid up thy word (*imrathkha*) in my heart" [Psalm 119: 11]. For most, if not all, of the deepest mysteries and the secrets of the Torah are included in this category.' Perhaps the most crucial difference between the two types of statement is that truth and falsity apply only to the categorical statement and not to the non-categorical statement. As Caspi said in his *Gevi'a Kesef*, [referring to the testing of Abraham at Mt Moriah] '. . . and the second benefit is that it is correct both for God and for us to command one thing and after a period of time to command its opposite as occurred in this case. Both are correct in their proper time, "and a word in season how good it is" [Proverbs 15: 23]. There is no deceit here for neither truth nor falsehood can be derived from the non-categorical statement'. Thus the statement 'Abraham went to Mt Moriah' is a categorical statement and is either true or false. The statement 'Thou shalt not kill' is a command and is neither true nor false ... The commandments of the tongue and of action are found only in the non-categorical statements, while the commandments of the heart are found in both categorical and non-categorical statements. The *Book of Genesis* is the supreme example of a book which is entirely composed of categorical statement. Caspi says that in it are 'all of the "commandments of the heart" which later in the Torah are found in a non-categorical way like "I [am the Lord your God]" ... and "Hear O Israel" and "thou shalt love [the Lord thy God]" ... All of these are found in this Book [Genesis] by way of narrative and story.'

(B. Mesch, *Studies in Joseph Ibn Caspi*, pp. 87–8)

The biblical narratives talk of real people, who have personalities, habits, ways of living differing from ours and differing from each other. To understand these biblical personages one must replace them in their geographical and historical context, and not make stereotyped images of them; the biblical narratives should be interpreted in their literal sense and one should not laboriously look for an allegorical sense as if 'Eliezer, Abraham's slave [Genesis 24] was Moses our master, and, in the story of the mandrakes [Genesis 30: 24] that Leah and Rachel were Rabbi Yohanan and Rabbi Akiba and that Reuben facing his father [Genesis 42: 37] was Aristotle' (*Mishné Kesef*, p. 31).

The events recounted in the Bible quite simply took place and the text must be accepted as it is, without correction or edulcoration.

The scene on Mount Sinai took place in reality, as it is told in the Bible. It was not a prophetic vision, as Maimonides thinks.

We read in the *Guide of the Perplexed* 'And cause a barber's razor to pass upon thy head and upon thy beard.' [Ezekiel 5: 1]. – All of it was in a vision of prophecy in which he saw that he carried out the actions he was ordered to carry out. God is too exalted than that He should turn His prophets into a laughing-stock and a mockery for fools by ordering them to carry out crazy actions. (II, 46, p. 405)

This passage surprises me very much, says Caspi.

For one may ask Maimonides the question whether he thinks that Adam before the Fall was drunk and mad when he walked about naked with his arse in the air? In general, there can be no doubt that there are no rules or criteria permitting us to affirm of acts that the prophets performed to bring the faith to a people fed [not on true ideas but] on conventional conceptions, that they were mad, for this is a judgement that one could pronounce only if these acts were destined for the few, for the élite who admit the intelligibles. However, these acts come from God, who is the source of intellect and its root, and there can be no doubt that the *nazir* [holy man] consecrated to God, appears mad in the eyes of most people, and nevertheless the *Torah*, which is wisdom, says: The consecration of God is upon his head [Numbers 6: 7]. It is not necessary to enlarge on this subject for it is well

327

known that the prophets, because of their words as well as their acts, were generally considered mad and lunatic by their contemporaries, as Hosea says [9: 7]: The prophet is a fool, the spiritual man is mad. However, their words and their acts were not the doings of madmen from the point of view of the intellect but only from the point of view of their contemporaries, who harboured generally accepted ideas.

(Mishné Kesef, p. 23)

This relativity of judgement pronounced on the conduct of biblical personages leads Caspi to situate the history of the Jewish people within a complex of customs and habits, which explains many facts and expressions of language. Thus for him miracle, that is divine action that upsets the natural order of things, did exist, but what one calls 'miracle' is usually no more than a rare event and more or less 'miraculous' in proportion to its rarity; thus the transformation of copper into verdigris is usual, but its transformation into gold is not. It is not impossible, as some think, but excessively rare, although still conforming to the laws of nature. The miracle will therefore appear more or less miraculous in relation to the spectators and the extent of their knowledge. Similarly, benediction and malediction will be more or less efficacious according to the personality of those for whom they are meant. We should interpret the prophetic text in the light of these same distinctions and not seek to explain every word of every biblical verse: the Bible is not a book of philosophy. If Ezekiel in his prophecy gives the exact year, the month, and day, while Isaiah does not, the reason is quite simply that they were of different character and education.

Caspi's explications of the text in terms of daily life and habits are numerous, and often quite subtle. Here is an example based on what he observed in the course of his voyages.

His voyages opened his eyes to many different ways of life. It is true that his sojourn in the Orient disappointed him.

Twenty years ago . . . I crossed to Egypt where I visited the College of that renowned and perfect sage Maimonides: I found there the fourth and fifth generations of his holy seed, all of them righteous but none of them devoted to science. In all the Orient, there were no scholars. (Trans. I. Abrahams, *Hebrew Ethical Wills*, p. 130)

However, thanks to his sojourn in Egypt he was able to understand a great many details of the biblical narrative; for example, three verbs are used in the Bible to express taking one's shoes off:

The people of our country cannot understand when God says to Moses: Put off thy shoes [= *shal*; Exodus 3: 5] and [in Ruth 4: 7] concerning Boaz, A man plucked off his shoe [= *shalaf*], and, regarding the levirate [Deuteronomy 25: 9], [she] shall loose his shoe [= *halats*]. In fact, in these countries [Egypt] people are in the habit of wearing leather sandals which are not attached to the foot, and when one wishes to remove them, it is enough to move the foot about a little to make the sandal fall off by itself; the verb *shal* has the same sense in Deuteronomy 19: 5: The head slippeth from the helve . . . On the other hand, when one pulls off the shoe with the hand one will use the verb *shalaf* as in the expression: Draw the dagger out [cf. Judges 3: 22]. But if the shoe is attached and tied to the foot with straps, one will use the word *halats* as in Leviticus 14: 40: They take away the stones, and also in the ceremony of the levirate, as our sages have explained.

(Mishné Kesef, pp. 19–20)

The 'natural' explanation of the Bible leads Joseph Caspi on to a 'natural' exegesis of prophecy and miracles. Repeating Averroes' definitions, our philosopher affirms that the prophets' function is not to teach philosophy but to foresee the future.

It is in this light that Caspi foresees the return of the people of Israel to the land of Israel. The Jews were expelled from their land because they had abandoned the *Torah*, thus becoming stupid. Therefore, as Maimonides said, they no longer knew how to make war and conquer other countries and when they were attacked they were content to pray to God, instead of defending themselves. There is no need to link Israel's return to its land with some constellation or astrological cycle, it is enough to remember that peoples are sometimes victorious and sometimes vanquished. History is made up of victories and reverses and the incessant wars between Christians and Muslims in the land of Israel show this very well. Israel was captive in Egypt and Moses arose and obtained deliverance from Pharoah. At the time of the second Exile it was Cyrus who proclaimed in all his states the return of the Jews to Jerusalem. Similarly, in a different form, a man will arise, perhaps the Sultan of Egypt, or the King of France, and he will let the Jews return to the Land of Israel. For Joseph Caspi the whole of history is a proof that the Jews would one day return to the Land of Israel.

Joseph Caspi is not an author inviting indifference, and it is not surprising that his defenders and detracters, throughout the centuries, have been rather vehement. From the start of his philosophical activity he corresponded with the scholars of Salon, in Provence – Moses of Beaucaire and Sen Astruc of Noves. One of their pupils, *Kalonymus ben Kalonymus ben Meir*, collected their objections and his own to the *Book of the Secret* (cited under the name of *Tam ha-Kesef*).

Kalonymus rightly accuses Caspi of boasting that all his explanations were original; he also reproaches him with unveiling 'the secrets' without shame, a reproach also fully justified. But chiefly he criticizes his disrespectful attitude to the biblical text; the expressions he uses concerning biblical personages are shocking, and, in fact, as we have seen, Caspi was inclined to impertinence.

More seriously, Kalonymus remarks that the 'natural', historical and 'sociological' explanations are not scientifically founded for there is nothing to prove that the customs and habits of the peoples of the East have not changed since the biblical period.

Kalonymus was himself learned in philosophy. Born at Arles in 1287, he was a prolific translator, rendering at least twenty-nine works of mathematics, astronomy and astrology, medicine and philosophy, from Arabic. His first translation is dated 1306 and the last dated mention of him is in 1328, when he was forty-one years old. It seems that all his translations from Arabic were made before 1317. After this date he most probably entered the service of Robert, King of Naples, who was in Avignon in 1319, going on to Naples and Rome and meeting Emmanuel of Rome, who spoke of him most flatteringly. For King Robert he translated into Latin the *Incoherence of the Incoherence*, Averroes' reply to Al-Ghazālī's treatise: *The Incoherence of the Philosophers*. This translation was completed on 18 April 1328, and the colophon likens Robert of Naples to a new Solomon. Like his master, Moses of Beaucaire, also a well-known translator, Kalonymus wrote no philosophical works, except for the letter addressed to Joseph Caspi.

Among translators of philosophical works we should also mention *Todros Todrosi* who made numerous translations of Al-Fārābī, Avicenna and Averroes, and *Samuel ben Judah ben Meshullam ben Isaac of Marseille*, also called Miles of Marseille, Miles Bongodas or Barbevaire (1294–after 1340). Like Kalonymus ben Kalonymus he studied with Sen Astruc of Noves; he translated, among other works, texts of political philosophy, Averroes' *Middle Commentary* on the *Nicomachaean Ethics*, and the *Short Commentary* on Plato's *Republic*. In September 1321 he concluded the first revision of these two translations at Beaucaire while he was in prison in the fort of Rodorta and still hoped (in vain) to obtain Al-Fārābī's commentary on the *Ethics* from Christian scholars. His only original composition, a *Commentary on the Almagest*, has survived only in citations.

SHEMARIAH BEN ELIJAH THE CRETAN

King Robert of Anjou was patron of yet another Jewish philosopher. Shemariah ben Elijah the Cretan, ben Jacob ben David ben Eli Romanos, or more simply Shemariah ben Elijah of Crete or Shemariah of Negroponte, addressed an *Epistle on the Creation of the World* to Robert of Anjou in 1328, and also dedicated to him a long commentary on the Song of Songs, comparing him, in his turn, to King Solomon. According to a poem by Moses ben Samuel of Roquemaure, who later converted and took the name of Jean of Avignon, Shemariah proclaimed himself prophet and Messiah in 1352 and announced the Day of Deliverance for 1358. He was the author of numerous biblical and talmudic commentaries, of which only a small part has been preserved. The short *Commentary* on the Song of Songs and the *Epistle on the Creation* have been published.

Shemariah constructed a rather remarkable philosophical mysticism. A theme to which he often returns is that of the union, the conjunction, between the human soul and the Active Intellect. Since the Active Intellect is strongly attached to the other intellects, the result is that there is a real identity between the First Cause and the human soul. From this union between the intellect on the highest level and the soul, there ensues for the soul the purest joy, that procured by cognition of the existents associated with the cognition of the *Torah*. The joy of the philosophers, like that of the 'Talmudists' who only occupy themselves with religion, is incomplete. Each of these two joys is incomplete without the other, but conjoined, they are the state of the perfect happiness to which the human soul aspires and which the religious intellectual soul will attain. The human soul is capable of enjoying the supreme pleasure that accompanies the contemplation of the intelligibles and the 'reasons' of the *Torah*; while God rejoices in the intellectual activity of the learned soul. In Shemariah's words:

God knows my thoughts and the commentaries that I have engendered in this book [the *Sefer ha-Mora* (*Book of Fear*)] and in my other books. He speaks them in my name. Not only do I affirm that God knows them and speaks them in my name, but I add that He praises them and takes joy and pleasure in them for they were made in His Service and His Glory.

('*Mikhtav al Hiddush ha-'olam*', p. 207)

The proximity of God and the soul, their selective affinity, makes it difficult to explain the exile of the human soul in this world of bodies. This is not a punishment or the consequence of the Fall, Shemariah assures us. The human soul was sent on earth to serve as a representative of the divine. Without the presence of the human soul, and thus of God, the world of bodies, celestial as well as terrestrial, would collapse, for God is Life and without Him nothing exists. But this divine mission is not fulfilled by all the souls, and some are lost in the desert of the body and cannot return to their source. Others, however, gladden God, attach themselves to Him and bring Him joy. One of the thoughts that God glorifies in Shemariah is to have irrefutably proved the creation of the world in time, which is the very base and root of the *Torah*.

The argument in favour of creation in time *ex nihilo* is expounded in the *Epistle on the Creation* and in the *Book of Fear*, but the emphasis is differently distributed in the two works. The first was most probably destined for King Robert and a Christian public. We do not know if Shemariah translated it into Latin. The second is clearly designed for Jewish readers and the argument against the negators of creation – Plato, the Pantheists and the Dualists – joins that directed against Aristotle and his followers.

In the *Epistle*, Shemariah enumerates several arguments, but two of them are of particular interest, and Shemariah discusses them at length:

(1) If one declares that it is impossible for God to create the world by an act of will, it is absurd to say that this impossibility becomes not only possible but necessary without God willing this to happen.

(2) If God has not created the world *ex nihilo*, it is evident that a part of divinity was transformed into what is now the world. To this, the philosophers respond that to ask why does the world exist and how, has no more sense than to ask concerning God, why does He exist and why in this manner?

To place the two questions on the same level, Shemariah argues, is particularly erroneous, for obviously the notion of existence has not the same meaning in speaking of God as in speaking of the world: to say that God exists is the same as saying that God does not exist, because His existence does not enter into the categories of being. God, in fact, is neither body nor force within a body, He has neither quantity nor limit.

It is absolutely impossible to compare in any way the finite and the infinite, God and the world; a necessary relation is inconceivable; only the free will of God can explain, or at least render possible, a bond between the two.

The claim that a unique Intellect emanates from God does not resolve the problem but only pushes it further away, for in any case one reaches an impossibility: that from the infinite necessarily arises the finite.

The size of the corporeal world also does not affect the problem; however big it may be, the world will always be corporeal, that is, finite, facing an infinite God, from Whom it cannot arise unless God, by His free will, thus decides.

It is possible that the importance accorded by Shemariah to divine infinity was due to his knowledge of the thought of Scotus. One of Duns Scotus' pupils, Francis of Meyronnes, also frequented the court of Robert of Anjou. Perhaps Shemariah had also heard of the theories of Henry of Gand. The Jewish sources that our author used, in particular Isaac Ibn Latif, do not seem sufficient to explain his resolutely anti-Aristotelian thought, although, in contrast to Judah ha-Cohen before him and Crescas after him, he accepts Aristotelian physics without discussion.

MOSES BEN JOSHUA NARBONI

Moses ben Joshua ben Mar David of Narbonne, called Maitre Vidal Belsom, whom we shall sometimes designate Moses Narboni, as did later philosophers, was born at Perpignan at the end of the thirteenth or the beginning of the fourteenth century to a family originally from Narbonne. At the age of thirteen he began to study Maimonides. His schooling, directed by his father and private teachers, comprised the Scriptures, the rabbinical literature, philosophy and medicine. He exercised the profession of doctor and composed a book of medicine, *Oraḥ Ḥayyim* (*The Road of Life*), in which he gives prescriptions of his own invention and speaks of cures that he had effected. He also refers to his master, Abraham Caslari, calling him a plagiarist. He left Perpignan in 1344 and lived in several Spanish towns: Cervera (whence he was forced to flee from anti-Jewish persecution in 1349 with the whole community, abandoning his possessions, and his books), Barcelona, Toledo and Burgos, where in 1355 he began his *Commentary on the Guide of the Perplexed* and discussed a difficult point of this work with Joseph Ibn Waqar. He finished this *Commentary* at Soria in 1362, dying shortly afterwards.

His works are numerous.

A. Commentaries:

(1) On the writings of Maimonides: the *Vocabulary of Logic* at the start of his career, and the *Guide of the Perplexed* at the end of his life; the latter work has been published, rather inadequately, but new editions are announced.

(2) Commentaries on the commentaries and treatises of Averroes, concerning the intellect: on the *Treatise of the Intellect* by Alexander of Aphrodisias; on *The Possibility of Conjunction with the Active Intellect*; on *The Perfection of the Soul* (*Shlemut ha-Nefesh*), which has recently been published; on the *Middle Commentary* of Averroes on the *Physics*; on the short dissertations on the *Physics* and the *Treatise on the substance of the sphere*; also on the beginning of Averroes' commentary on the *Organum*.

It seems that his commentaries on Averroes' Commentaries on the *De Caelo* and the *Metaphysics* have not been preserved.

(3) A commentary on Al-Ghazālī's *Opinions of the Philosophers* and Ibn Ṭufayl's *Hayy Ibn Yaqzan*.

(4) A commentary on Lamentations, in which he expresses his surprise that his predecessors neglected to comment on this book which, he says, is part of the same series as Proverbs and the Song of Songs.

B. In three short works he expresses his ideas in an organized form:

(1) *Iggeret Shiur Qoma* (*Epistle on the Measure of the Divine Stature*)
(2) *Ma'amar ha-Behira* (*Treatise on Free Will*)
(3) *Pirkei Moshe* (*The Chapters of Moses*)

These three works have been published. The first has been translated into English; the second and the third into French.

Moses' erudition was encyclopedic, and to cite his sources would be to cite almost all the Arab and Jewish philosophers. He probably also knew Latin, for we read in a note inserted in his *Commentary* on Averroes' *Dissertation on the Physics* (Vatican, MS Urb. 41, fol. 123r); 'This treatise in a way forms part of his work on the matter of the sphere and we see that the most ancient of the Romans called these treatises, taken together, by the name of *Substantia Orbis* (in Latin, transcribed in Hebrew characters), on the matter of the spheres.'

Moses of Narbonne was a subtle commentator, and his explications are always profound and intelligent. However, it is chiefly his three original dissertations that reveal his personal thinking. His ideas of course recur in the commentaries, which are among the best of medieval philosophical commentaries; but the literary form is of little assistance in distinguishing explication of the text from the commentator's own opinion; while in the three treatises Narboni speaks in the first person and gives in condensed form the ideas dispersed throughout his very extensive exegeses.

The problem of God's knowledge of the world and of our knowledge of the world and of God was, as we have seen with Gersonides, among those that especially preoccupied philosophers, both Jewish and Christian, in the first half of the fourteenth century. To these problems Narboni devotes his commentary on the *Shiur Qoma* (*Measure of the Divine Stature*), the anthropomorphic *midrash* which had been attacked by the Karaites and which Saadiah Gaon had already attempted to explain rationally. Moses of Narbonne's work is in fact a meditation on God, Measure of all existing things. It is based on Abraham Ibn Ezra's commentary on Exodus, and, with the aid of biblical and rabbinical passages, studies two kinds of knowledge: God's knowledge of his creatures, called knowledge of the Face; and His creatures' knowledge of God, called Knowledge of the Back (an allusion to Exodus 33: 23).

The philosophers have explained that there exists nothing but two things: God and His creatures [*Guide of the Perplexed* I, 34, p. 71]; and that all existents other than God exist through Him; [that] He is the truly existent Who knoweth all; [that] His knowledge and He are identical, and [that] in Him, blessed be He, intellect, intelligent, and intelligible are one and the same thing.

(A. Altmann, 'Iggeret Shiur Qoma', p. 271)

Knowledge and the gift of existence are intimately mingled; in fact, of the forces engaged in matter, those that are placed lowest in the hierarchy have a conceptual knowledge of the highest; the highest not only perceive the lowest but also give them existence; in this sense God is all the existents.

The philosophers said that God, blessed be He, is one, and that He is the most glorious of existents, and that in this sense He is the latter's principle. Rabbi Moses [ben Maimon] of blessed memory therefore explained [the verse] 'And thou shalt stand upon the rock' (Exodus 33: 21): 'Rely upon, and be firm in considering, God, may He be exalted, as the first principle. This is the entryway through which you shall come to Him' (*Guide*, I, 16). He means to say that the ultimate knowledge we may have concerning God, may He be exalted, consists in our knowing in which way He is the first principle. For thereby we know as much of the truth concerning Him as is in our nature to know: that is, [by knowing] that He is the first principle insofar as He is [the unity of] intellect, intelligent, and intelligible, which is perceived in a variety of ways, while He thinks the forms in the most glorious existence possible. (*Ibid.* p. 276)

It is evident that one cannot speak in this context of creation in time; for if the world is in a certain way the divine thought, even if in a mode very remote from its mode of existence in God, the world can have no beginning or end. This is not only a statement of position concerning the eternity of the world, but is one of the foundations of Narboni's whole philosophical system.

God is the cause of the world in a way infinitely more profound than if He had created it in time, for He continually gives it existence, and from all eternity; the flow of forms comes from Him and it is these forces that constitute the world.

'All that is called by My name and which I have created for My glory, I have formed it, yea I have made it' (Isaiah 43: 7).

Since 'all' is the whole, and the whole is that outside which there is nothing, [it follows that] what is truly 'all' is that outside which there is nothing at all. This [latter] is meant by the word 'all' which occurs in the verse quoted. And since knowledge, knower, and known are one, it says that 'all' – that is, all existents – are called by His name: that is, subsist in His essence. It then explains the manner in which they necessarily exist in themselves, apart from their existence in Him, and their ultimate purpose by saying: 'and which I have created for My glory', that is, [for] the *kabod*; 'I have formed it', that is, the supernal body [the celestial spheres]; 'yea, I have made it', that is, the lower [body] (= the sublunar world). By His 'glory' His essence is meant, which is His will and His wisdom, all denoting one and the same thing. For His essence is also called His 'glory', as in [Moses'] saying: 'Show me, I pray Thee, Thy glory' (Exodus 33: 18). From this verse it is apparent that all existents subsist in the glorious Name.
(*Ibid.* p. 265)

One can pose the question of the source of matter. If God is the source of forms, where does matter come from? For our author, matter has no existence; even the primary matter, which is eternal, is eternal because it is provided with the form of corporeality, that which gives the three dimensions of space. Form can exist: (1) alone and detached; (2) with a body without being in this body, or (3) in a body, like the inferior forms; but matter is nothing without form. Non-informed matter does not exist. There is nothing in the world except form, matter, and nothingness.

... all existents have different [levels of] existence. The philosophers reflected this [view in their] saying that the [existents'] first existence is their material existence [as found] in the throne of glory, the heavens and the highest heavens, and the sublunar bodies in themselves. The material existence they possess qua material represents their most inferior existence. Then their existence is elevated in as much as matter is made an object of vision, and the process of elevation starts when they are impressed as it were in the crystal lens of the eye. For they are [then] abstracted from matter in a way that a mountain of an altitude of a thousand parasangs will be contained in the pupil of the eye. At the next level they will be abstracted from sense perception: they will be visualized by man and found by him [to exist] in his soul (in his *sensus communis*), even though they are no longer within range of the [visual] sense. At a still further stage 'the soul speaks to the angel', and they will be elevated by being impressed in the imagination. [Imagination] will take them apart and combine some parts with others, this being its function, while they still remain particular and individual [existents]. They achieve, however, a still more noble [level of] existence when intellect abstracts them and through definitions and concepts takes hold of them as separate forms and universal images. Then their [level of] existence attained by the mind will, for example, be the one attained by the definition of man: that he is a rational animal. For there can be no doubt that the imaginative form which is [still] material has now become intellect and is counted among the intelligible forms. Rabbi Moses [ben Maimon] alluded to this when he said that the intellect when thinking the form of a certain tree and abstracting it [from matter ... is identical with the object of its thinking]. You will be able to understand that this [level of] existence – that is, the intellect *in habitu* – possessed by the existents is still characterized by [a measure of] inferiority in that the forms thereof are impressed in the intellect by way of definitions, and bear the marks of plurality on account of their relatedness to the [imaginative] forms and on account of being multiple in number themselves. When, however, there connects with these intelligibles a force called 'agent intellect' ... and thinks itself, it conceives the universal forms in [total] abstraction, unrelated to the imaginative forms and definitions and what appertains to them, in a knowledge which is universal, unified, and simple. For this is how the agent intellect acts, notwithstanding the fact that it is the cause of those forms; that is, its conceiving [them] is the cause of the lower forms' existence (the latter are, however, not the cause of its [i.e. the agent intellect's] thinking, while they are indeed the cause of man's acquired intellect). Herein lies the difference between the agent intellect and the human intellect so long as the latter has not yet become angelic. The existence of the existents in the agent intellect differs, therefore, from their existence in the intellect of man as regards the universality and simple unity of each form, and as regards its abstraction from the plurality which affects it ... on account of their matter, and as regards the fact that the intellect of man is caused by the existents in the way mentioned: namely, that they are objects of vision first, then impressed in the imagination, and then invested in the intellect, which is at first but like a tablet ready to be inscribed. The lower existents are caused by *Keneset Yisra'el* [the agent intellect]; that is, the concept formed of them by the latter is the cause of their being, and comprises them, for which reason the followers of the Torah called the agent intellect by that name. You should further know that just as the existents are raised up from their material [level of] existence to [that in] the agent intellect, so their existence – that is, their essence – continues to be elevated in [these] ten separate intelligences as regards [the degree of] their simplicity and unity. The superiority of one angel over another consists precisely in this: that is, in the varying degrees of the existents' simplicity and unity in the respective angels. Each [angel] conceives, furthermore, a sphere, and this conception is, in some respect, the cause of the existence of the sphere. In this way one particular intellect is the cause of one particular sphere – that is in so far as it moves it – but God, blessed be He, is the cause of all.

(Ibid. pp. 271–4)

In the *Pirkei Moshe,* Narboni reveals the five 'mysteries of the *Guide of the Perplexed*'. It is difficult to believe that our philosopher really thought that he was continuing in Maimonides' way, for at the end of the third chapter, he writes: 'Maimonides did not go in this way and did not want it.' But this 'revelation' may not be merely a literary fiction, for Narboni tends rather to harmonize than to show the differences between his masters, Maimonides, Averroes and Ibn Ezra. However, we have here a glimpse of the personal opinions of Narboni, and a list of the problems he was particularly interested in.

The first is the eternity of the world and the political necessity of not revealing this to the vulgar.

Who is among you that feareth the Lord, that obeyeth the voice of his servant, that walketh in darkness and hath no light? Let him trust in the name of the Lord and stay upon his God [Isaiah 50: 10].

Those who know the verities are few indeed; true belief and perfect knowledge are only attained by some élite beings; in consequence it suited the divine wisdom that all His people, Israel, should resemble the perfect, so that they would possess the privilege of the secrets that the wise men of the nations do not know, so that they will all survive for ever in the islands of happiness, the true paradise of the soul. Thus the perfect and glorious Law has explained and transmitted the true doctrines to the common order of our people, some of which are not known to the best of the sages of the Gentiles and others are accessible to them only after long and complex study.

Thus in the verse with which we began, the prophet gives counsel to the vulgar among our people, to those who have not studied science and whom the light of wisdom has not illuminated: *Who is among you that feareth God*, for fear is in itself different from knowledge and its purpose is that [the simple man] *obeyeth the voice . . .* [for he] *walketh in darkness and hath no light*, for his way is not lit by the light of science, he does not know the true doctrines through speculative demonstration, his hope is therefore to confide in God and to believe the true ideas transmitted by a tradition going back to the Torah; in other words, *Let him . . . rely upon his God*. The prophet himself promises the people that knowledge will come to them when the Messiah comes, according to the divine will. *The light of the moon shall be as the light of the sun, and the light of the sun shall be sevenfold as the light of the seven days* [Isaiah 30: 26]; this is an allusion to the light of the seven days of the inauguration of the Temple, for the light and the emanation, at that moment, were as strong as they could be; this verse also designates allusively the emanation which is symbolized by the light of the sun; this is to teach us that the emanation of existence is comparable to the light of the sun or to that of the Active Intellect on the man cognizing; through this, one understands the meaning of *Let there be light!* God emanates existence and maintains existence, thus the emanation of existence and the perpetuation of existence are called 'light'. However, the vulgar people are convinced that the doctrine that the sages are agreed upon [that is, the eternity of the world] is contrary to the traditional teaching and to the prophetic teachings, that it violates the law and the divine will. In consequence, since God wishes the continuation of the existence [of human civilization] – and it is impossible to revolt against this will, for that would be to rebel against God Himself – and since this civilization is founded [on principles] universally admitted and, among them, the creation of the world, belief in creation is absolutely necessary. Thus Maimonides constructed a wall around the *Torah*, out of fear that the whole *Torah* would crumble and, with it, the aim that God set himself in the religious laws, that is, human society, since in fact this society cannot exist without retribution and punishment in the next world, which are not admissible if one does not admit creation. This is why Maimonides wrote the parable of the child [and built a wall] surrounding the *Torah*, so that the *Torah* can continue to play the part for which God destined it.

(*Pirkei Moshe* I, pp. 302–3)

This last sentence is an allusion to *Guide* II, 17, where Maimonides asserts the possibility of the world being created in time and says: 'For it is a great wall that I have built around the Law' (p. 298).

The second chapter treats of the conjunction of man's intellect with the Active Intellect, a possibility of which Narboni, following Averroes, does admit the existence, for to him the chain that links the forms together is intellection, and it is the cause of existence. The conjunction with the Active Intellect occurs when the imaginative forms that lead to the threshold of comprehension disappear.

337

Know that imaginative forms themselves change to intelligibles and do not remain [as imaginative forms] at all. Thus you will be able to see that imaginative forms are in [the category of] the first force [i.e., possible existents], changing completely and becoming intelligible theoretical forms; and that imaginative forms are subjects of intelligible forms as sensible forms are [subjects] of sensory forms . . . Nor is the [faculty of] imagination [suited to be the recipient of intelligibles], inasmuch as it is the subject of imaginative forms and they do not remain [constant] to their nature, since they become intelligibles and as such are not in it [in their subject, the imaginative faculty]. In this manner it will also become clear that it is the agent intellect which is the true recipient of intelligible forms, which [forms] are foreign to its true nature.

(Trans. A. Ivry, Treatise on the Perfection of the Soul, pp. 284–5)

The Active Intellect, of which the human hylic intellect is part, is also conjoined with man.

Inasmuch as, 'Lo, in the end of days the mount of the Lord's house shall be established on the top of the mountains', and with the perfection of the theoretical intelligible forms, the disposition which occurs with imaginative forms will be destroyed, and the disposition which occurs with theoretical intelligible forms will be generated. The theoretical intelligibles will then be destroyed, for the agent intellect will abstract from them the multiplicity which occurs with them; and then the hylic intellect will be conjoined perceptually with the agent intellect, which exists eternally by itself. (Ibid. p. 287)

And Narboni confirms in *Pirkei Moshe*: 'One of the Divine secrets . . . is that God, may He be blessed, is in the heavens and the agent is in man' (*ibid.* p. 294).

When man has attained the level of the Active Intellect and is conjoined with it, he has power over the forms of material things, and can thus accomplish miracles.

Our Sages have designated God by the name of Intellect: He is the First Intellect and his intellection of the existents is the cause of their existence; the intellect being, in this way, the cause of the existents and the prophet greatly resembling the Active Intellect [the tenth intellect], the soul of the prophet tends to completely encompass all the existing beings and their secrets; thus, when it is necessary, the prophets produce [intelligible] representations of existing beings so that they concord with the aim that they propose to themselves; sometimes, these representations differ from what these beings are in reality, and, according to the predominance of the Intellect over the imagination, the force of miracles differs among the prophets. The intelligible being is thus transformed according to the representation that the prophet imposes on its essence. The *Name* designates the essence and what makes a being remain in existence; on the other hand the will is called 'word', the will of the representation of this essence is called Word [pronunciation] of the Name of God . . .

Doctrines are only maintained by acts; similarly the intelligible representations [of the prophets] are not maintained unless a certain act is accomplished, which sustains the representation and makes it accord with the reality that is outside. Thus all the prophets carried out a certain action at the moment of the miracles:

the waters were only sweetened when the rod was thrown into them. However, the essential and particular cause of [the material act] was known to the prophets alone ...

In the same way, each doctrine requires a certain act which maintains it; thus the perfect *Torah*, which for every true opinion knows the action particular to it and by which it maintains itself, has provided for us the holy commandments.

For instance, circumcision, for it shows the unity of God; however, the knowledge of this important principle is not maintained in him who is not circumcised and Aristotle himself did not know the divine unity in the way that the vulgar among our people know it ...

This is what God taught Moses, the most perfect of all created beings, and, by his intermediary, He has enjoined on us all the commandments, some positive, some negative; [the aim of all of them] being either to maintain a true belief or to make persist the existence [of the civilization] which is willed by God.

(Pirkei Moshe 2, pp. 303–4)

This rehabilitation of corporeal precepts is accompanied by considerations linking the commandments to astrology and to something that rather resembles magic; it fits perfectly into a system affirming the correspondences between the upper and lower worlds, the macrocosm and the microcosm. However, while a certain form of magical thinking is present, it is undeniably bound up with intellectual and moral considerations and not with practice. This is the subject of chapter 3:

You also know that the aim of the religious laws is the continuation of existence; thus it even more benefits the perfect *Torah* to have as its final purpose the continuation of human existence and its implantation in the chosen land which has been given to it. You also know that the Sages have attributed each climate to an angelical prince, this for all the climates. The true Sages have said that the Temple of this lower world is made in the image of the Temple above. Thus the *Torah* has ordained the things that have an analogy with the Temple above and declared contemptible those that it holds in disgust. It was the custom to cut up lions, wolves and bears for their sacrifices, but Melchisedek, king of Salem, loved the golden mean and only accepted sheep and doves, as it is said: God requireth that which is past [Ecclesiastes 3: 15], and Every abomination to the Lord, which he hated, have they done unto their gods [Deuteronomy 12: 31], for God is jealous and the Lord revengeth [Nahum 1: 2], and it is not because of our actions that you have led us into this land but because of the wickedness of these peoples. The *Torah* thus recommended all the things that the justice of the God of Israel had chosen. For God is just, and it rejected the things that God held in horror, for God did not wish one to serve the other gods, the sun the moon and the army of the sky. [He hates] him who makes sacrifice to other gods, for it is to our God alone that one must sacrifice, and the meaning of the verse: And the Lord smelled a sweet savour [Genesis 8: 21] is given by another verse: Offer unto God thanksgiving; and pay thy vows unto the most High: And call upon me in the day of trouble: I will deliver thee, and thou shalt glorify [Psalms 50: 14–15]. As for the wicked, God says to him: What hast thou to do to declare my statutes, or that thou shouldest take my covenant in the mouth [Psalms 50: 16].

Jeremiah [44: 21–3] and all the prophets bitterly lament the reason of their exile from the Land of Israel; The incense that ye burned in the cities of Judah ... so that the Lord could no longer bear ... therefore is your land a desolation ... And similar verses are numerous. This is also the meaning of the talmudic anecdote [*Baba Kama* 82b, Sota 49b]: [the informer] shows the Greeks the allusion to this subject in Greek science: as long as [the Jews] shall carry out the sacrifices [that please God] you shall not conquer the land [of Israel]. Thus, [the Greeks] did the opposite of what God wished [that is, offered a pig in sacrifice]; the land of Israel was conquered and remained in their power from four hundred years to four hundred years. This is the mystery of the perpetual sacrifices and of the day of Atonement which is particularly consecrated to these sacrifices according to the true *Torah* and in this there is nothing that contradicts the Kabbalists, for they retained by tradition the true doctrines attesting that the *mizvah* is nourishment and aromatic [spices], that it contains four forces and that the fourth force comes from the divine grace.

(*Pirkei Moshe* 3, pp. 304–5)

The source of this particular sentence has not been found, and in general Narboni's quotations from Kabbalistic writings do not agree with texts that have been preserved. It is certain that for him Kabbalah and astrology were very close. In another passage he says, even more explicitly, that the sacrifice of the scapegoat on the day of Atonement should appease the soul of the planet Mars. Other practices are either forbidden by the *Torah* because they offend the Princes of the Planets, or ordained because they suit these Princes:

There can be no doubt that the sexual relations forbidden by the *Torah* are particularly favourable to the selective production of a great number of excellent children, but the *Torah* has forbidden them precisely because of this secret, knowing that the God of the country held them in horror; now, the *Torah* abominates that which God hates, so that the existence of Israel may continue; and because the question of the sacrifices is a great secret and cannot be transmitted except to the privileged, the sacrificial cult was transmitted to the Priests. It is thus perfectly clear that the spirituality we have in mind should be clad in this same smoke and that thus would the land of Israel and its inhabitants subsist. Maimonides did not follow this way and did not accept it.

(*Ibid.*)

In chapter 4, Narboni makes it clear that astrology is confined to the observation of divine commandments coming to our aid in combatting evil influences.

For every man who is born, something necessarily causes all the accidents and the hazards [of his life], and the man versed in the sciences of the prediction of the future knows them in advance; similarly the people, as a whole, came into existence when the stars were under a certain disposition, and, according to this horoscope, a certain number of events must mark its existence. Abraham was a great prophet and versed in astrology, according to the verse: And he brought him forth abroad [Genesis 15: 5], which says: Go out, away from your astrology.

Thus Abraham knew all the events that would happen to his people even before it was established in its first engendering. He saw that our fate was to be constantly slain and that much blood would be spilt among our people and he did all that was in his power to avoid this misfortune a little, causing it to be that no man among us would not have his blood spilt during the first eight days of his life [a reference to circumcision].

(*Pirkei Moshe* 4, pp. 305–6)

The last problem discussed in the *Pirkei Moshe* is that of providence, and Narboni declares that he agrees with the opinion of Moses Ibn Tibbon: divine providence is in proportion to what man attains of the Active Intellect.

Almost at the end of his life, in 1361, Moses of Narbonne wrote the short treatise on free will that was quoted earlier; thus, in 1360, thirty years at least after the publication of the theses of Abner, the problem posed by him was still important enough to elicit the composition of an epistle.

Moses of Narbonne, who was a profound thinker, is a good representative of Jewish fourteenth-century philosophy. We remember that Isaac Pulgar declared that Jewish thinkers were divided between philosophy, which he approved, and astrology and Kabbalah, which he condemned. This classification in fact more or less corresponds to the texts, although the divisions between the different classes are less clear-cut; philosophers are also astrologers and sometimes Kabbalists, Kabbalists are generally also astrologers. Only Pulgar seems to be a pure philosopher; his contemporaries are less exclusive.

Joseph ben Abraham Ibn Waqar sought to bring these three doctrines into agreement with each other. Scion of a celebrated family of physicians in the service of the Castillian court, he enjoyed great renown, and had as a pupil, among others, Solomon Franco, who answered Abraham Ibn al-Tabib's objections in his name. He was already an old man in 1362 when Moses Narboni visited him. His great work, written in Arabic, *Al-Maqāla al-jami'a bayna l-falsafa waš-šari'a* (*Discourse of conciliation between philosophy and religion*) has survived in only one manuscript, and has not yet been published. G. Vajda has devoted a remarkable essay to it.

Ibn Waqar believed that by using dialectics he would be able to establish fundamental agreement between the three rival schools, that is, philosophy, astrology, and Kabbalah. Astrology provides sound information concerning events in the sublunary world; natural philosophy is valid when its teachings concern the structure of the world, which is the intermediary between the celestial bodies and the separate intelligences. Kabbalah reveals in symbolic expression the amount of knowledge available to man concerning the divine world. Each thus contributes to our knowledge and complements the other. But Ibn Waqar's reconciliation was very complex and no philosopher, astrologer or Kabbalist was able to agree with him.

There is also at least one text of purely astrological thought. *Solomon ben Abraham Paniel*, author of *Or eynayim* (*Light of the Eyes*) gives, in three parts, a total explication of the world and of religion according to the planets and the stars. The first part explains all the divine commandments and their relation with one or another planet. The second part presents the process of Genesis, each day symbolizing a thousand years. The third part tells the history of the Patriarchs, from the same aspect. This short book, printed at Cremona in 1557, concludes with a table of contents and useful explanations for the reader who is pressed for time. It has the advantage of being systematic and of assembling all the information that other authors veil in a spirit of decency or propriety.

The picture that I have tried to present in this chapter is very incomplete. All the great philosophers of the fourteenth century are present, certainly, but a large number of philosophical texts that have not yet been studied are left in obscurity. This period was perhaps the most flourishing of all Jewish medieval philosophy. Nevertheless the texts have not been published or even adequately listed. There are several reasons for this. At the end of the fifteenth and during the sixteenth century, when Hebrew books began to be printed, the prevailing state of people's spirits was profoundly affected by the danger of annihilation that the Jewish communities of Spain, and to a lesser extent Provence, had experienced. Fourteenth-century works, while remaining within the context of the Jewish tradition, are not apologies for Judaism. Moreover, they are firmly anchored in Aristotelianism. Even if Aristotelianism provided the mental structure of the European man until the eighteenth century it was becoming clear that it could no longer satisfy either scientific experiment or metaphysical aspiration.

During the nineteenth century, when Jewish philosophy was studied as a humanistic discipline and a cultural phenomenon, scholars gave preference to the greatest thinkers, those who are cited throughout Jewish history. This is not the case with the philosophers of the fourteenth century. To be sure, medieval manuscripts occupied an important place in scholarly affections, and these texts are mentioned in historical works and in bibliographical reviews, but they were not studied from the point of view of the history of ideas. At first sight, admittedly, this philosophical literature seems not particularly original, but this is only an impression arising from a rapid reading and I am inclined to think that more careful work will dissipate it.

One of the striking characteristics of the intellectual atmosphere of this epoch is the participation of Jewish scholars of all origins: Provençal, Byzantine, Italian. Books, ideas and persons travelled much, whether forced to do so or not, and a fusion of ideas took place throughout the Mediterranean world under Christian control. The Karaites, such as Aaron ben Eli of Nicomedia, also took part in this philosophical flowering, and read the same authorities as their rabbinical colleagues. On the other hand, we do not find the 'continental' Jews of Germany or Bohemia represented, nor Jews living in Islamic countries, the first because they perpetuated the traditions of the talmudic schools, the second for reasons that perhaps reflect the intellectual stagnation of the surrounding milieu.

Commentaries were written on the *Torah*, such as the *Sefer Megalleh Amukkot* (*The Revealer of Hidden Things*) by *Solomon ben Ḥanokh al-Kostantini* who allies astrology with Averroes, and the *Sefer Ma'ayan Ganim* (*Source of Gardens*) of a philosophical tendency close to that of the

Tibbonides; also the *Zafenath Paneach* (*Revealer of Secrets*; this title follows the traditional exegesis of Genesis 41: 45) by *Eleazar Ashkenazi ben Nathan Ha-Bavli*, who wrote between 1364 and 1375, perhaps in Crete, and gives decidedly intellectualist allegories.

There were also commentaries on other parts of the Bible, such as the *Ma'amar Gan Eden* (*Treatise of Paradise*) by *Hayyim ben Israel of Toledo* (which is actually a commentary on the biblical commentary of Abraham Ibn Ezra); or the visions of Isaiah, Ezekiel and Zechariah as well as the *Mareot Elohim* (*Divine Visions*) by *Hanokh ben Solomon al-Kostantini*, where one can recognize, against a background of Averroism, features drawn from Gabirol and some knowledge of Christian scholasticism. Let us also note commentaries on Job, such as that by *Abba Mari ben Eligdor* (En Astruc of Noves); on subjects of religious science, such as prophecy, by *Judah ben Benjamin Ibn Roqques*, or the *Arba 'ah Kinyanim* (*The Four Possessions*) by *Judah ben Solomon Campanton*, pupil of Yom Tov ben Abraham Ishbili (Ritba); the works of *Moses Cohen Ibn Crispin of Toledo*; or even long treatises discussing in succession all the problems of philosophy and faith, like the *Even Sapir* (*The Sapphire*) by *Elhanan ben Moses Kalkish*, or the *Matok la-Nafesh* (*Sweetness for the Soul*) of *Moses ben Isaac Ibn Waqar*.

I should also mention exegeses on the allegories of the Talmud and the *Aggadot* such as the *Mikhlol Yofi* (*The Fullness of Beauty*) by *Samuel Sarsa* (*fl.* 1360–70) and the *Midrashei ha-Torah* of *En Solomon Astruc of Barcelona* (*fl.* after 1359). The *Yesodot ha-Maskil* (*The Principles of the Intelligent Man*), by *David ben Yom Tov Ibn Bilia* (*fl.* 1338, in Portugal), poses the problem of principles, which was to assume great importance in the fifteenth century.

I have not yet mentioned *Judah ben Isaac Cohen* (second half of the fourteenth century) who wrote an excursus on Al-Ghazālī's *Opinions of the Philosophers*; nor have I mentioned *Judah Ibn Mosconi* who wrote so many interesting works, or several others whom one can consider rather Kabbalist than philosopher, such as Samuel Ibn Motot and *Nehemiah Kalomiti*. The latter regarded the eschatological texts of the Kabbalah and a neoplatonic text translated from Arabic as 'profound secrets'.

In addition to textual commentaries, encyclopedias were also composed, such as that of *Abraham Avigdor* (*Bonet*) *ben Meshullam ben Solomon* (b. 1351), who chiefly used Al-Ghazālī's *Opinions of the Philosophers*, or the *Ahavat Ta'anugim* (*Love of* [*Intellectual*] *Pleasures*) composed in 1354 by *Moses ben Judah Nagah* (*fl.* 1335).

It was also a period of commentaries on logic: on the treatises of Al-Fārābī, Al-Ghazālī and Averroes, but also on the *Tractatus* of Peter of Spain (who became Pope as John XXI). These commentaries mark the beginning of a 'scholastic' logic among the Jews of Spain and Provence. The *Tractatus* was translated into Hebrew five times during the fourteenth century, and commented on as early as 1320 in Provence, by Hizkia ben Halafta, who also cites several Christian scholars.

There was also *Elijah ben Eliezer ha-Yerushalmi*, who wrote a book of logic as a dialogue between a master and his pupil, a commentary on some parts of the *Guide of the Perplexed*, and also other commentaries.

While Christian logic spread, translations of medical works from Latin to Hebrew were also very numerous, especially in Provence, where important treatises were translated shortly after they appeared. Arnald of Villanova *Regimen Sanitatis* was translated in Avignon in 1327 by Isaac ben Joseph ha-Levi, called Crescas Vidal of Caslar, as well as other treatises by the same author; Abraham Avigdor translated Bernard Albert's *Introduction to the Art*, and so on. It would be tedious to enumerate all the medical works translated from Latin between 1310 and 1320. The frequency of these translations seems to indicate that in general Latin was not well known; it is also possible that it was easier for a Jewish doctor to get a book from a co-religionist than from a Christian colleague. One must also remember that in the Middle Ages reading and writing did not always go together. Very many people were able to read, but not to write, and it is possible that Jewish doctors could read Latin but not copy a manuscript that interested them, while they could easily do so in Hebrew. Thus, the influence of the Christian intellectual milieu made itself felt more or less according to the authors, but it was rarely altogether absent.

In the introduction to this chapter I mentioned the very numerous commentaries on Ibn Ezra's *Commentary*. Among the more important of these is that by *Joseph Bonfils ben Eliezer ben Joseph the Spaniard*, a work called *Sophnath Paneah* (*The Revealer of Secrets*), and the *Mekor Hayyim* (*The Fountain of Life*), by Samuel Sarsa, both of which have the great advantage of having been published. Of the commentary of *Samuel Ibn Motot* (*fl.* 1370) and the introduction to the commentary of Judah Ibn Mosconi, only extracts have so far been published. All the other commentaries are still in manuscript, although they certainly merit scholarly attention. They include the commentary by *Shem Tov ben Isaac Ibn Shaprut of Tudela* and that of *Solomon Franco* (*fl.* 1360), pupil of Joseph Ibn Waqar, which was a source of inspiration to his contemporaries.

Whatever the interest of these texts, an interest that cannot yet be evaluated, philosophy, astrology and Kabbalah remain the three great doctrines of reference for Jewish philosophers of the fourteenth century.

Chapter 9

THE FIFTEENTH CENTURY

Spanish Jews between Judaism and Christianity

For Spanish Jewry the fifteenth century began in 1391 and ended with the Expulsion, in 1492.

Beginning in 1345, the Black Death decimated European Jewry together with the rest of the population; moreover it provoked popular riots against the Jews, suspected of having brought about the epidemic. The full impact of these events was only felt towards the end of the century, but in the latter half of the period a certain mounting apprehension begins to be sensed; one encounters in the texts reports of discussions with Christians, and polemical arguments proliferate, especially concerning the advent of the Messiah. Christian missionary activity began early in the thirteenth century, but it was as yet sporadic. It became more insistent from the middle of the fourteenth century, in Spain as well as in Provence. The sermons that Jews were forced to hear, sometimes under police protection, often dealt with the coming of the Messiah. According to the Christians, Isaiah 53 clearly announces the coming of Jesus, and it is no accident that many Jewish interpretations of this chapter were written at this time; those of Moses Cohen Ibn Crispin of Tordesillas, in 1375; that of En Solomon Astruc of Barcelona and of Isaac Eli the Spaniard (after 1359), and that of Shem Tov ben Isaac Ibn Shaprut (in 1385, at Tarazona).

The work of *David of Rocca Martino* seems to me to belong to the same period; this author, whose dates are uncertain, wrote a small treatise called *Zekhut Adam* (*Adam's Justification*), demonstrating that the expulsion from paradise as well as all the chastisements proceeding from the Fall are not punishments but natural processes contained within the laws of nature. Presented in syllogistic form, David of Rocca Martino's arguments are an answer to polemical debate, and his thought is aggressively rationalistic.

Thus, despite the tensions and uneasiness engendered by a certain number of conversions to Christianity, Jewish philosophical activity did not falter during the second half of the fourteenth century; indeed, it was intensified, as we have seen in the previous chapter.

A brutal end came to an already precarious equilibrium. In the early summer of 1391, anti-Jewish riots ravaged the communities of Andalusia and Castille, Navarre and the Balearic Islands, but spared the kingdom of

Aragon. Very many Jews were killed; many others converted to Catholicism to escape death or slavery. Synagogues were transformed into churches, and nothing remained of formerly prosperous Jewish centres except ruined buildings and a greatly diminished group of the faithful, those who had found refuge with Christian friends or had fled in time. A vivid impression was made on people's minds not only by the massacres but also by the wave of conversions, which, starting in 1391, continued throughout the fifteenth century until the final Expulsion in 1492, at which time the new Christians, later called Marranos, outnumbered the Jews. Aristotelian philosophy was accused of having troubled the minds of the people, causing the leaders of the communities, wealthy and generally acquainted with philosophical ideas, to be among the first to convert instead of providing an example of heroic conduct. This accusation, which has been taken up again by contemporary scholars such as I. Baer, is presented in the work of Shem Tov.

Shem Tov Ibn Shem Tov (*ca.* 1380–1441), who was rather unoriginal as a Kabbalist, wrote his *Sefer ha-Emunot* (*Book of Beliefs*) to demonstrate the noxiousness of Jewish philosophy, far more pernicious than Greek as such, for it was dissimulated under the names of venerated men such as Abraham Ibn Ezra, Gersonides, Albalag and, especially, Maimonides. Shem Tov does not deny the importance of science, but he rejects its application to matters of faith; but this was the way of thinking of Maimonides and his successors, who do not admit that, where God is concerned, only the science given directly by Him to Israel is valid. Saadiah and Abraham bar Ḥiyya clearly understood this and preserved the literal meaning of the biblical text on such points as individual providence, reward and punishment, the creation of the world, the miracles, the resurrection of the dead, and so on.

How, asked Shem Tov, could one remain firm in the face of ordeals and confront persecution if one had been taught that there is no punishment for the wicked and no reward for the just? that only the intellect survives, an intellect acquired through knowledge of logic, mathematics, natural sciences and metaphysics, and that this knowledge is accessible only to philosophers? that the divine commandments are no more than a preparation for the acquisition of this knowledge? that the stories of the *Torah* are intended for the simple people, for if philosophical truth were known to all, the political order would be imperilled? and so on.

These are valid arguments, and we have met them all in the works of Jewish philosophers after Maimonides. However, in lieu of this dangerous philosophy, Shem Tov can only propose a return to the literal text or to the Kabbalah, which the rationalists could not accept. Moreover, apart from emphasizing the risk of conversion, he does not prove that this philosophy is false, as Ḥasdai Crescas would attempt to do.

It is true that eminent philosophers were to be found among the converts, such as *Solomon Ha-Levi of Burgos* who took the name of Pablo de Santa Maria, becoming a Christian theologian, possessed by a fervent desire to convert his co-religionists. The arguments on both sides, of those who had remained Jews and of converts to Christianity, are drawn from the same texts and utilize the same logic. On both sides people were tormented by doubt.

After his conversion Pablo de Santa Maria wrote a letter to Joseph Orabuena, chief rabbi of the kingdom of Naverre, in which he remarked that he had come to the conclusion that Jesus had fulfilled Jewish Messianic prophecies. The letter circulated among the Jews; it had perhaps been written with this purpose in mind.

Joshua Lorki, another celebrated scholar, author of a manual of therapeutics in Arabic that was translated into Hebrew, took it upon himself to champion Judaism and replied to his former friend.

JOSHUA LORKI

After having declared his astonishment and spoken of his anxiety at hearing of Solomon ha-Levi's abjuration of his faith, Joshua Lorki enumerates the reasons that might have caused this apostasy and this attack against his former co-religionists: perhaps a longing for worldly honours, or for wealth and the pleasures associated with it – refined dishes and beautiful women? Or perhaps philosophical motivations had led him to judge religious considerations as frivolous and consequently to assign greater importance to physical and intellectual satisfactions? Perhaps the misfortunes afflicting his people had made him despair of divine aid and brought him to think that God would not again remember his people Israel? All these, according to Lorki, are not very probable reasons, and a fourth motivation seems to have led to the conversion of Solomon ha-Levi of Burgos – the fact that he had experienced revelations concerning the foundations of the prophecies and their meanings. Besides, he remarks, Solomon of Burgos is very learned in the Latin tongue, and he, Lorki, has seen in his friend's house books of Christian theology explaining the roots of the Catholic faith; moreover, he has seen a letter addressed to Joseph Orabuena in which Solomon of Burgos says that he believes that Jesus is the Messiah awaited by the Jews. For Joshua Lorki, it was not ambition, nor contempt for religion engendered by philosophy, nor the obvious contradiction between contemporary Jewish suffering and the divine promise of election and providence, that caused his friend to convert to Christianity, but rather a genuinely religious reason: the belief in Jesus who had come to fulfil the biblical prophecies.

Joshua Lorki continues by expounding eight objections to admitting that Jesus is the Messiah; in conclusion he remarks that if the claims of the Christians are true; if Jesus were indeed the Messiah predicted by the prophets; if he were born from the word of God, without intercourse between man and woman; if his resurrection, as well as the other miracles had, in fact occurred, he, Lorki, could only remain silent, for the mind may hesitate concerning all these matters; these are things that it lies in God's power to accomplish, by working miracles and changing the course of nature.

All these miracles took place in this lower world, during Jesus' terrestrial life; one can therefore explain them in a way similar to that employed by Moses of Narbonne in speaking of other miracles, which belong to the spheres of the possible. It is the same with the subtleties of the Trinity that the theologians have adopted, as well as the doctrine of consubstantiality, for one can argue that these were ancient opinions that were already known, and that certain persons had already accepted in the time of the prophets; besides, he, Joshua Lorki, has found them in Aristotle, in a passage speaking of the eternity of the world.

All these opinions, inadmissible to those who participate in Abraham's covenant, may nevertheless be accepted by those who incline to lend faith to them. This argument rests on a psychological difference arising from education; Jewish scholars admitted that Christian theologians had their own habits of thought, which inclined them to admit distinctions that a Jew could not accept.

Of the three Christian dogmas: Jesus as the Messiah, the Trinity and the Incarnation, the Incarnation was the most obnoxious to Jews. Lorki asks:

How can one believe that a Messiah of flesh and blood, who eats and drinks, who lives and dies, is the true God, cause of causes, whose emanation of power moves the spheres, and of whose overflowing existence are formed the separate Intellects who are not body nor power in a body and whose dwelling is not among mortals? How can their existence be continuous and perpetual if He is corporeal? That [terrestrial] matter should persist eternally *in actu* is one of those impossible things of which the sages said that the impossible has a stable nature. In truth the intellect cannot conceive this opinion, and no doubt on this subject can arise in the mind.

(Ketav Divrei Hakhamim, p. 45)

However, Joshua Lorki now poses an even more fundamental question. If a man professes a certain religion, is it for him a religious duty to examine, to prove deeply and to seek to know the foundations of his law and of his religion, to know whether it is true, or whether another religion has more truth in it; or is he not obliged to do so? Let us now consider the consequences of these two suppositions: If we admit that it is his duty to compare by reason the dogmas of his law and belief with those of other religions, until he thinks he has found the truth (and it is most probably this way of thinking to which Solomon of Burgos conformed when he meditated, probed, searched, until he had found the truth, in his opinion, and acted in consequence) – if it were so, the result would be that no religious man would remain attached to his faith; he would be in perpetual doubt and perplexity; it would also follow that each man would have to make a decision concerning the validity of his religion; he would no longer accept as truth the law of the prophet, of the legislator; he would rely exclusively on the inspirations of reason; no faith, in the true meaning of the word, would remain. Solomon of Burgos himself has adopted a difficult position; while, after reflection, he has accepted the law of the Christians, he still has to judge between it and that of the Muslims, and yet other beliefs; for the intellect acknowledges that one can find yet other faiths and that it is possible that none of these laws are divine, and that there is another that has this character, and thus the quest will never come to an end.

Let us now examine the other side of the question. If it is not fitting, and it is in no way the duty of a religious man to reason about his religion, the consequences will be that he who practices a religion, whichever it be, will be saved by his belief; one religion will not be better than another, unless God acts contrary to justice, and punishes unjustly. If a man attached to one religion should not meditate on the foundations of his faith, and compare it to another, he is forced to believe in the religion in which he is born, whether it is true or false, and if he worships God in the manner that his religion prescribes, he will therefore be happy and saved by it; if it were not so, the ways of God would be unjust, for how could God punish a man who has taken the wrong road if he was obliged to do so? It would follow from this opinion that Solomon acted ill in denying his faith, for he should not have done this, being attached to one religion.

Finally, Joshua Lorki asks the following question: Let us consider the various nations: the Christians who live at the extreme end of England have not heard about the Israelites or the Muslims; those who are attached to the religion of Muhammad dwell in a land too far away to know the Israelites and the Christians; all the men of these different religions are born and have grown up in their faith, and have never heard about any other religion than their own; they are happy in the practice of their religion, they do not even think that any other may exist, and their faith is for them not only a tradition but a reasoned doctrine; they adore God in the purity of their hearts.

Evidently one of these religions is false, and a lie bequeathed by their fathers. How may those who belong to a different religion tell them that God will punish them if they do not convert to the true faith that they have never known? And in truth, according to reason, it is a strange thing that God should condemn to eternal punishment innumerable thousands of innocent mortals, who do not and cannot know their error (*Ketav Divrei Hakhamim*, pp. 19–28).

This last problem raised by Joshua Lorki, although formulated under the pressure of Christian missionary activity, is purely philosophical, and has a rather modern sound: should religion be measured by the yardstick of reason? Since a choice is given in matters of religion and one can be Jew, Christian or Muslim, is it every man's duty to examine the faith in which he is born, according to scientific criteria, and to reject it if he decides that another faith is more in conformity with a philosophical ideal? What then are the criteria for judging one particular religion as the best?

This is to state the problem in terms according to Arab–Jewish Aristotelian philosophy, where the criterion of truth is human reason and religion is a political law that accords with reason; the source of truth is not revelation. Besides, Lorki observes, since one specific revelation is not universally recognized, it would be unjust on the part of God to exclude a great part of the human race. One can see how, by taking reason as a criterion of religion, one may come to place all religions on the same level. Because of its universality, philosophy was not therefore particularly advantageous to the preservation of religious identity, whose absolute necessity appears to be doubtful. On the other hand, no philosophical argument can turn the scale in favour of one or other religion.

As D. L. Lasker has remarked, for both Jewish and Christian polemicists and philosophers philosophy was only the servant of theology, or of other less spiritual tendencies. Joshua Lorki demonstrated this himself when he converted to Christianity. It was as a Christian under the name of Geronimo de Santa Fé that he took part in the Disputation of Tortosa in 1413–14.

One of the instructive aftermaths of the events of 1391 was the notion of the bankruptcy of reason, in religious life as well as in practical existence. This accounts for the importance that was henceforth assigned to faith, and the affirmation of its superiority over reason.

If it is true that the spiritual climate, strongly influenced by Aristotelian philosophy, was not a good preparation for martyrdom to the faith, nevertheless on the individual level philosophers, like other men, were capable of resisting pressure. We do not know how many preferred death to conversion, but we do know of some who remained Jewish. Moreover, they remained faithful to Maimonidean philosophy.

Such was *Ephraim ben Israel al-Naqawa*. This celebrated rabbi took refuge in North Africa after the massacres of 1391. He is revered not only at Tlemcen, where his tomb is found, but throughout Algeria and Morocco. For many generations his grave has been a site of pilgrimage, and legend attributes many miracles to him. This is not surprising; did he not arrive at Tlemcen riding a lion and using an enormous serpent as a rein? This personage, metamorphosed by popular belief into a wonder-working saint, was a convinced Maimonidean who hardly believed in miracles at all. In the book *Sha'ar Kevod Elohim* (*The Gate of the Glory of God*), he replies to Nahmanides' objections to Maimonides' theories on supernatural vision. With the help of philological and psychological arguments drawn from his own experience, he proved that Maimonides was correct in believing that the prophetical visions of Abraham and Jacob occurred in dreams, and that the biblical text should not be taken in its literal sense. Fervent rationalism shines forth on every page.

Despite persecutions and assaults, Jewish and even Aristotelian Jewish philosophy was far from extinct in the fifteenth century. Thus in 1405, Meir Alguadez, Chief Rabbi of Castile, translated Aristotle's *Ethics* from Latin into

Hebrew, aided in this by Solomon Benveniste Ibn Lavi (della Cavalleria), who, like his son Judah, remained among the most ardent defenders of Judaism.

With the Expulsion of the Jews from Spain, philosophy was to flourish throughout the Mediterranean basin, and it took new root in Italy. Moreover, while defending itself with varying success against polemical attacks, Jewish philosophy was increasingly interested in the Christian thought that it was called upon to confront. In Spain as in Italy there were numerous translators from Latin to Hebrew. Not only works on medicine and logic were translated, but also works on metaphysics: Elijah ben Joseph Habillo translated the works of Thomas Aquinas, three treatises by William of Occam and perhaps a treatise by Vincent of Beauvais. Azariah ben Joseph ben Abba Mari (Bonafoux Astruc, of Perpignan) translated Boetius' *Consolation of Philosophy*; Abraham Shalom translated Marsilius of Inghem.

As the century progressed these translations became less and less necessary, for Jews were reading Latin and the great majority of the learned men who will now be introduced spoke this language perfectly.

Joshua Lorki wrote to Solomon ha-Levi at the time of his conversion that he had seen in his house 'treasures of Christian books . . . for you are versed in their tongue more than any of the learned men of our days'. This was true of most Jewish men of erudition, and public controversies like the Disputation of Tortosa were conducted in Latin. In Spain this knowledge of Latin among Jews had defensive connotations, but the phenomenon was general throughout the Christian countries of the Mediterranean. In Italy, where the atmosphere was much more relaxed, both Christians and Jews participated in the Renaissance, as we shall see a little later, and the languages of this Renaissance were Latin, Greek and often Hebrew.

One of the major themes of Spanish Jewish philosophy after 1391 was that of the commandments given by God, commandments that must be accomplished literally through bodily actions, which are enjoined by and in accordance with reason.

Let us recall that Maimonides did not accept Saadiah's distinction between 'rational' and 'revealed' commandments. For him, all the commandments had a 'reason', sometimes known and sometimes not. However, while the general reason of each commandment should be looked for, one should not speculate about the practical details, such as the number of animals that should be sacrificed in the Temple. The reasons for the commandments are divided into two great classes:

(1) The good of human society;

(2) The good of the soul, prepared by and to a great extent depending on the good of the body, which is achieved through the physical accomplishment of the commandments. To this is added the acquisition of true opinions, which prepare the soul for the acquisition of the intelligibles, conducting it to supreme felicity.

These explanations of the divine commandments are comparatively negative and in any case very austere. They were complemented by the much more positive reasons given in the commentaries of Abraham Ibn Ezra.

Moses of Narbonne and other Jewish philosophers of the fourteenth century thought that the physical accomplishment of the divine commandments had an immediately efficacious virtue: these acts contribute to the functioning of the celestial and terrestrial world, which is regulated by a pre-established harmony favouring the survival of Israel. These ideas were reinforced by the vogue of astrology and the popularity of Neoplatonism.

Judah Halevi's thought, centring on Israel, its people, its land, its law, again became a theme of meditation and study in the fifteenth century.

The centrality of Israel, whose acts and thoughts participate in the cosmic drama, was also proclaimed by the Kabbalah, and these convergences enhanced the great importance attributed by Jews to the divine commandments carried out in the flesh.

The reasons for the commandments and the liaison between their corporal observance and the survival of the soul is one of the major themes of the century, and we shall frequently encounter it. The physical act of the accomplishment of the commandments also tends to be interpreted as a sacrament embodying its own salvationary virtue.

These tendencies are still very discreetly voiced in a theological treatise in fifteen chapters entitled *Ya'ir Nativ* (*He who lights the Way*), by *Judah ben Samuel Ibn Abbas* (most probably the brother of Moses ben Samuel Ibn Abbas, who together with Joseph Albo took part in the Disputation of Tortosa). Ibn Abbas recapitulates the problem: profoundly Maimonidean, he classes the divine commandments in two groups: those that are designed to perfect the body and those that are designed to bring perfection to the soul.

Some people cease to fulfil the commandments on the pretext that they are intended to teach us the virtues, and once virtue is acquired, need no longer be observed. These, says Judah Ibn Abbas, are ignorant people or else false scholars, and he declares that he has never met a truly learned man who is a heretic.

Here the problem was still formulated in Maimonidean terms. With Efodi this was no longer the case.

ISAAC BEN MOSES LEVI

Isaac ben Moses Levi, called Maestro Profiat Duran and often designated by the acronym Efodi, lived at the end of the fourteenth century and the beginning of the fifteenth. Born in Catalonia, he suffered the persecutions of 1391, and converted to Christianity. Deciding to go to Palestine in order to regain the free practice of Judaism, he was about to leave with his pupil and friend David Bonet Bonjorn, when David informed him that he intended to remain faithful to Christianity. Efodi renounced his plans, and lived as a Christian at Perpignan, under the name of Honoratus de Bonafide, astrologer, in the service of John I of Aragon, without however giving up his literary activity in Hebrew. During this period he wrote his anti-Christian polemical works and exchanged an erudite correspondence with his pupils Meir Crescas and Shealtiel Gracian, while continuing to dedicate his scientific productions to high-ranking Christian personages. In 1403, when he composed his grammar, Efodi had again become a Jew. No more is known of him after that date.

Efodi's work is encyclopedic, comprising medicine, grammar, philosophy, arithmetic, astronomy and astrology, and various controversies. His polemical works show his profound knowledge of Christian culture; in *Kelimat ha-Goyim* (*Opprobrium of the Gentiles*), most probably dedicated to Ḥasdai Crescas and composed in 1397, Efodi points out the errors in the translation of Jewish texts in the New Testament and in the Church Fathers; he also made use of the arguments of internal Christian criticism.

Al-tehi ka-Avotekha (*Do not be as your fathers*) is a satirical letter written between 1391 and 1397, addressed to his former friend David Bonet Bonjorn. Under the name of *Alteca Boteca* this humorous *chef d'oeuvre* attacking Christianity was disseminated by Christians, who did not grasp its satirical intention. However, after the appearance of an illuminating commentary by Joseph ben Shem Tov, in about 1450, the book became an object of great aversion to the Inquisition; it was placed on the Index and remained on this list of forbidden books until the nineteenth century.

Here is an excerpt from the beginning of the work:

Now, my brother, I became aware of thy good intentions, and that all thou dost is for the sake of the Lord. Faith is for thee a girdle round the loins, and Reason with all her lies is unable to entice thee and divert thy paths. Therefore I made up my mind to show thee clearly the ways of the faith which thou hast chosen as thy compass in the light of the Messiah.

Be not like unto thy fathers, who believed in one God from whose unity they removed any plurality. They have erred indeed, when they said, 'Hear Israel, the Lord is One!', when they understood this unity in the purest sense without inclusion of species, kind or number. *Not so thou!* Thou shalt believe that one can become three and that three united make one. Lips will never tell it, ears never take it in.

Be not like unto thy fathers, who conceived by deep meditations the eternal Ruler beyond change and body, as expressed in the words 'I change not', and who explained in this sense even those passages which, when interpreted unskilfully, perplex simple souls. *Not so thou!* Heaven forbid that thou shouldst deny His corporeal embodiment, but believe rather that one of His three persons became flesh, when He wanted to shed blood for the atonement of mankind. Offer Him thanks that He suffered death in order to redeem thee... For this was surely the only way which could be found by the wisdom of the Almighty! Believe that He became flesh in the womb of a virgin, of an 'Almah' as the Hebrew word reads; it occurs also in the passage 'the way of the man with a young woman'. This miracle was able to encourage the faint-hearted Ahaz, although he had lived five hundred years earlier...

Be not like unto thy fathers, who by close scrutiny tried to find a deep philosophical meaning in the account of creation, and who had much to disclose about the first human couple, about the four rivers, the tree of knowledge, the serpent, and the coats of skin which the Lord made them for clothing. *Not so thou!* Conceive all this literally! Add, however, yet an inner punishment to Adam's misfortune, increase through it the burden of his bitter fate that he has to carry on his back. He will never get rid of it, and is entirely in the grip of Satan, until the Redeemer comes and purifies him by his death. Now that sin is abolished, although it is not mentioned in our holy Scripture, while the other curses, the punishments of hell, remain for ever ... Stick to the mystery of hereditary sin which the head of the Apostles proclaimed, he whose name is identical with that of thy teacher. Thy reward will grow immensely like thy faith.

Be not like unto thy fathers, who were continuously engaged in sciences of all kinds, in mathematics, metaphysics and logic, and tried to penetrate to the foundations of truth. *Not so thou!* Far be it from thee to recognize the first fundamental rule of reasoning in logic. For this would entice thee to deny thy faith by saying: God is Father; the Son, too, is God truly: the Son is therefore the Father. Brother, stick to this belief! It will lead thee to eternal life, and God will be with thee ... Alas, thy fathers ate the bread of affliction, suffered thirst and hunger; thou, however, hast saved thy soul, thou eatest and becomest satisfied, thou rejoicest in the Lord and praisest the Holy One of Israel ...

But above all believe sincerely in the almighty Redeemer. He is the root ... of thy faith ... But do not believe in the metaphysical principle that affirmation and negation cannot exist at the same time, further that transformation of an accident into essence is impossible, and also that the being of a thing consists in its essence, but that the being of an accident depends on the object which carries it. For the body of the Messiah who sits on the throne in heaven does not move while that on the altar moves in every direction. The wafer is, before the utterance of the priest, nothing else than bread, but by this utterance the essence of the bread becomes an accidental quality or disappears entirely, and the previous accidental qualities become independent and enter the stomach of the priest who eats the wafer. None of the believers denies this ... In general, brother, do not accept the principle, 'What is impossible in itself remains impossible', but, on the contrary, accept faithfully all those impossibilities, for the almighty Messiah dominates all things, near or far, possible or impossible.

(Trans. F. Kobler, *Letters of Jews through the Ages*, vol. I, pp. 277–9)

Efodi did not expound his ideas systematically; they are dispersed in his various writings. His *Commentary on the Guide of the Perplexed* is rather literal; he continually attempts to refute the exegeses that make Maimonides appear a philosopher disdainful of the *Torah*, and he also stresses the danger of certain Maimonidean positions. In his astrological conceptions Efodi is very close to Abraham Ibn Ezra; he annotated passages of the latter's commentaries in response to the questions of his pupil Meir Crescas, and he developed these same ideas in a letter of condolence addressed to En Joseph Abram on the occasion of the death of his father Abraham Isaac Halevi in Gerona, October 1393.

Two other letters, commenting on II Samuel 14 and 16–17, are more historical than philosophical in character. On the other hand, his commentary on Abraham Ibn Ezra's *Book of the Name* treats entirely of mystical arithmetic, and his answer to Ibn Ezra's commentary on Exodus 25 is essentially grammatical.

In the introduction to his grammar, *Ma'aseh Efod* (*Making of the Ephod*, an allusion to Exodus 28: 15 and to the name Efodi) we find a summary of his opinions.

The *Torah* is perfect; it alone leads to eternal, supreme felicity; to safeguard it, to observe its commandments, is the only way that leads to God; and since the role of humanity is to serve God and accomplish His commandments, only Israel really fulfils human destiny.

The *Torah* is perfect, for it leads to eternal felicity; but it also leads to terrestrial felicity.

So far, all the Jewish sages might be in agreement; but opinions differ as to the manner of observing the *Torah*. Here Efodi draws up an inventory of the different opinions current in his time:

Some say that only the accomplishment of the *miẓvot*, the commandments, is important; these commandments have virtues which we do not know but which are efficacious; some go so far as to say that intention is not indispensable to the efficacity of these *miẓvot*, as a medical treatment cures a sick man whether he has faith or not in the efficacity of the remedy.

Others affirm, and Efodi agrees with them, that the *Torah* has two parts. The first part is knowledge and leads to eternal felicity, the second is act, the performance of the commandments, and brings about terrestrial happiness. But the two parts of the *Torah* are intimately linked. The acquisition of knowledge, apart from the eternal felicity it brings, will also bestow a little terrestrial happiness; and he who fulfils the commandments will receive, in addition to earthly happiness, something of the joy that awaits the learned in the next world.

In fact, the two parts of the *Torah* cannot really be separated; only knowledge allows one to really carry out the commandments, even if this fulfilment is not the ultimate aim of the acquisition of knowledge, but only its necessary accompaniment.

The Talmudists reject the physical and metaphysical sciences because they are Greek in origin; some of them are even opposed to the study of the Bible. For them only the Talmud is the voice of the *Torah*. Efodi concedes that the Talmud sharpens the intelligence.

As for the philosophers, they want to reconcile two contraries, Aristotelian philosophy and the *Torah*, holding that the latter leads to the acquisition of the moral virtues that precede the acquisition of the sciences of logic, physics and metaphysics. But, says Efodi, not only is the *Torah* a preliminary course, but true knowledge derives from the Jews: science and Judaism are intimately bound together and Maimonides never placed philosophy above the *Torah*.

Religious acts aim to attract the emanation of God Himself, saintly beings

and pure angels. The perfect worship is the accomplishment of the commandments in the Land of Israel, for these commandments are dictated by the
angels who preside over the Land of Israel (literally 'The Gods of the Land');
however, it is imperative to fulfil them wherever one may be, because of the
needs of the human body.

While the Kabbalah is not 'proved', one must admit that the *Torah* and
the prophets are much more in accordance with its doctrines than with those
of the philosophers, and if what is told of the Kabbalists – that they change
the nature of created things by miracles – is true, this would even more
definitely confirm their claims to possess the truth. However, since the
Kabbalists are far from agreeing among themselves, the danger of error is
greater here than elsewhere.

Efodi concludes thus: one must return to the study of the *Torah*, the only
sure way to supreme felicity. For, if it is true that the entire *Torah* is composed of divine names, the study of biblical texts, like prayer, participates in
the efficacy of the names of God.

The different books of the Bible all have this virtue, to a lesser or greater
degree, provided that one studies them in Hebrew.

When the Temple existed and God was worshipped there, the divine emanation, the divine presence and providence dwelt among the people of Israel;
when the Temple was destroyed, this was because the study of the Bible was
neglected. At present the Holy Book, its reading and study, fulfil the task of
the Temple; it is the Book that attracts divine providence and ensures the
continuation of Israel's existence.

The symbolism of the cosmos and the Temple is found in the Bible; the
world of the intellect, the world of the armies of the God of Israel, is the
Holy of Holies and the Ark of the Covenant; it is also the Pentateuch. The
celestial world is the Table of Offerings and the Lamp; it is also the Books
of the Prophets. The world of bodies is the Temple precinct, open to everyone, the altar of sacrifice; it is also the poetical books and the Wisdom
literature.

The two Temples, that of Jerusalem and of the *Torah*, have as their final
purpose the bringing of man to a purely intelligible eternal felicity. Therefore, Israel has taken the greatest care to preserve exactly each of the *Torah*'s
words, to pronounce it correctly, for fear that its virtue should be lost or
enfeebled, as one notes carefully the ingredients of a medicine without
changing anything in it; however, not only does the *Torah*, contrary to
medicine, preserve the body by its physical virtue, but its virtue of wisdom
leads man to conjunction with the divine.

Certainly, Efodi admits, we do not have any philosophical proofs for this,
but the natural virtues and qualities of existing things are also not known
through demonstration and reasoning; it is sensory experience that instructed
us in them; and the philosophers with all their seekings are not capable of
reproducing the form of the smallest of plants.

Moreover, we see that it is because the Jews have studied the Bible for 1200 years that God has preserved their existence among the dangers and persecutions of the Diaspora, where every other people would have disappeared. Contemporary history is an illustration of this: the Jews of France and Spain neglected the study of the *Torah*, consecrating only one hour a week to it, that of the reading of the weekly pericope. This is the cause of their exile and persecutions. The Jews of Aragon, on the other hand, were saved because they prayed day and night and constantly recited the Psalms. Do we not see, says Efodi, that the Christians and even the Muslims have begun to recite the Psalms? While the Jews, instead of doing likewise, lose themselves in the subtleties of talmudic learning! Efodi proposes that one third of the time of study should be devoted to the Bible, the second third to the *Mishnah*, the final third to the *gemarah*. As for profane sciences, one should study everything that does not contradict the foundations of the *Torah*.

Efodi's ideas reflect a conjunction of all the currents of neoplatonic, astrological and magical thought that tend to rehabilitate the *Torah* in its positive aspects. The *Torah* is no longer a stage in the conquest of knowledge, it is the purpose of human existence, in flesh and in spirit. This is a major theme in Jewish philosophy of the fifteenth century.

The pre-eminence of the *Torah* is again expounded in a short work written in 1378 by *Abraham ben Judah Leon of Candie* in Crescas' house at Barcelona. His *Arba'ah Turim* (*Four Rows*) has been preserved in a unique copy thanks to Shabbetai ben Levi, who says that he transcribed it from the author's manuscript.

This book, which cites the philosophers as well as the *Sefer ha-Bahir*,[1] deals in succession with the existence of God, with providence and its degrees, with the importance of the *Torah*, and with the purpose of the *miẓvot*. The *Torah* and the commandments play the principal role. With this work we reach Ḥasdai Crescas, the last of the great medieval philosophers, who already introduces a new era.

ḤASDAI CRESCAS

Crescas died in 1412 at Saragossa. In 1367, in Barcelona, he was already well known for his communal activities and he was among the representatives of the Jewish community who negotiated the renewal of the privileges of the Jews of Aragon in 1383. From 1387 Crescas enjoyed the favour of John II of Aragon and exercised the function of rabbi at Saragossa. During the anti-Jewish riots of 1391 his only son was killed in Barcelona; Crescas himself was saved thanks to the presence of the royal court at Saragossa. The rest of his life was devoted to the reconstruction of the communities that had

[1] See above, p. 248.

been destroyed, from the material as well as from the spiritual point of view. His philosophical activity was an integral part of this great outburst of compassion and reflected his profound conviction of the mortal danger incurred by the Jews as individuals and as a religious community.

To combat the abundant literature aiming at the conversion of the Jews, Crescas wrote at least two polemical works in Catalan. Only one of these has survived, the *Refutation of Christian Dogmas* (1397–8) in the Hebrew translation of Joseph ben Shem Tov (*Biṭṭul 'Iqqarrey ha-Noṣrim*), made in 1451.

The *Or Adonai* (*The Light of God*) was written in Hebrew, in 1410. In the introduction Crescas explains that the book is only the first part of a vaster project that was to include a section on the *halakhah* to be called *Ner Miẓvah* (*The Lamp of the Divine Commandment*). This second part was never written but the project throws light on the author's motivation. His aim was to replace the work of Maimonides, from both the philosophical and halakhic points of view. Crescas of course renders homage to the immense erudition of his illustrious predecessor, but the service of God takes precedence over respect for the Master.

According to Crescas, the very foundation of Maimonidean thought is false. The way that leads to God is not the knowledge of the intelligibles but the fear and love of God. God, in His goodness, has chosen the House of Jacob as the dwelling-place of His glory, so that Israel will love Him and fear Him, follow Him and join itself to Him, and this is the ultimate purpose of human existence. All the relationships between thought and act must be reconsidered. It is the accomplishment of the *miẓvot* that leads to perfection; this accomplishment is impossible without knowledge of the *miẓvot*; thus knowledge receives its importance from the fact that it leads to the accomplishment of the divine commandments.

So that this knowledge may play the part imposed on it, three conditions are indispensable: that each commandment should be precisely defined; that it should be easily understood; that it should be accomplished and preserved in the memory. However, the *Mishneh Torah* does not fulfil these conditions: Maimonides does not cite his sources nor the reason for his decision, so that when in another work one encounters a decision that runs contrary to his, one is plunged into uncertainty. This reproach is already found in Abraham ben David of Posquières, but Crescas adds a more philosophical argument: Maimonides did not make clear the causes of the *miẓvot* and their general laws. He expounded a certain number of commandments, a necessarily finite number, instead of seeking their principles and the causes, principles and causes that would permit one to understand and resolve an infinite number of particular problems; he therefore did not give a real knowledge of the commandments.

The work that Crescas did not write, the *Lamp of the Divine Commandment*, was to have answered these conditions of precision, clarity and knowledge by the four Aristotelian causes, which one does not find in the halakhic writings of Maimonides. Further, according to Crescas, Maimonides unduly mingled beliefs and commandments; to place the belief in God as the first of the positive commandments is absurd, for the knowledge of the divine existence is a necessary presupposition: what would be the significance of a commandment if one did not believe in the existence of Him who ordained this commandment? Besides, belief does not depend on will or on choice; one cannot therefore impose it or argue for it.

For Crescas the cause of all Maimonides' errors and those of his successors is Aristotelian science. The traditional science that had been lost through Israel's tribulations had been replaced by this false science.

The whole of Book I of *Or Adonai* is devoted to a criticism of Aristotelian science, and this refutation forms part of new physical conceptions of the world that Crescas calls 'roots', for they are necessary to the conception of the divine Law.

The first part of the book expounds and refutes the twenty-five propositions in physics that Maimonides had placed at the beginning of the second book of the *Guide of the Perplexed*. These twenty-five chapters are followed by seven others expounding and refuting in detail the proofs of the existence of God given by Maimonides. The second part returns to some of these subjects in a different order and adds arguments to the demonstrations already given in the first part. The third part is entirely devoted to proofs of the divine existence and its unity, subjects already touched on in the two earlier parts.

Book II gives, in six parts, the bases or foundations of the *Torah*, describing God, His attributes and His relation with the world.

Book III enumerates and explains the other beliefs that necessarily accompany the *Torah*.

Book IV discusses some ideas or speculations that can or cannot be accepted.

A. *Infinity, space and vacuum*

One of the definitions of infinity according to Aristotle is: a kind of extension or magnitude which, although it might be finite, is infinite. Extension can only be corporeal; however, corporeal extension cannot be infinite and a body cannot extend to infinity, for this body may be either an element of the sublunary world, endowed with rectilinear motion, which cannot go on infinitely, or else the quintessence, which is endowed with circular motion, and no infinite can have a circular motion.

In fact, the finite, being a magnitude, (1) must be contained within boundaries; (2) must have gravity or levity; (3) must have a spherical shape; (4) must revolve round a centre; and (5) must be surrounded by external perceptible objects. These five characteristics, Crescas objects, are those of finite bodies, and the infinite is only conceived in this context in relation to the finite. The infinite, if it exists, will not be contained by boundaries; it will be devoid of both lightness and weight; it will have neither form nor figure; if it is endowed with circular motion, it will not move around a centre and although it moves voluntarily, it will not need exterior objects to draw it into movement. Similarly, it may be simple or composite. In fact, it must not be described by any of the terms used to describe a finite object.

Another of Aristotle's propositions that was generally accepted in the Middle Ages is the definition of place:

(1) It is the limit that surrounds the body;

(2) This limit is equal to it, neither greater nor smaller than the thing surrounded;

(3) This limit is not part of the body itself but something separate from it.

These characteristics can easily be applied to the places of the elements within the sublunary sphere: earth is surrounded by water, water by air, air by fire, fire by the lunar sphere and so on; the spheres fit perfectly into each other and each of them is the place of the one that is within it. The internal surface of the outermost sphere, that most remote from the centre of the world, was generally considered as place of this sphere and 'the place' of the world. However, 'place' could not have the same meaning here, since there is no surrounding limit for this outermost sphere.

Crescas maintains that body and space must be separated. What is called vacuum when it contains no body is called place when it contains a body.

If space can be empty of body, then the definition of the place of the world as being its external limit no longer applies and one can conceive of an infinite space. Space is no longer a relation between bodies; it pre-exists bodies, it is pure extension, having three dimensions. The possibility of an infinite number of worlds is not rejected. Concerning our world Crescas does not affirm that it is infinite, but that this finite corporeal world is within an infinite vacuum, as is implied in the citation of a passage from the Talmud (Babylonian Talmud, *Avodah Zarah* 40b):

Accordingly, since the Blessed One is the form of the entire universe, having created, individuated and determined it, He is figuratively called Place, as in their oft-repeated expressions, 'Blessed be the Place'; 'We cause thee to swear not in thy sense, but in our sense and in the sense of the Place'; 'He is the Place of the world'. This last metaphor is remarkably apt, for as the dimensions of the void permeate through those of the body and its fullness, so His glory, blessed be He, is present in all the parts of the world and the fullness thereof, as it is said, '[Holy, holy, holy is the Lord of Hosts], the whole earth is full of his glory', the meaning of which may be stated as follows: Though God is holy and separated by a threefold holiness, alluding thereby to His separation from three worlds, still the whole earth is full of His glory, which is an allusion to the element of impregnation, which is one of the elements of Glory.

(Proposition I, part II, trans. H. A. Wolfson in *Crescas' Critique of Aristotle*, p. 201)

B. *Motion*

Motion is common to all the elements, including the matter of the spheres. What distinguishes the quintessence from the terrestrial elements is their internal structure and their tendency to move in a certain direction. Like Gersonides, Crescas considers the movement of the spheres to be 'natural', and not 'voluntary'. As for the movements of the elements, it is not due to their tendency to return to a natural place, for there is no natural place for each element. All the elements are invested with a downward movement, more or less determined by their weight. As for the elements that rise upward, like fire, their movement is due to a pressure exercised over them by other, heavier bodies that are below them.

C. *Time*

For Aristotle, time is 'the number of motion according to the prior and the posterior'. Years and months are the measure of the motion of the spheres: without the motion of the spheres, there is no time. Time was also considered as the measure of rest when understood as a privation of motion. Consequently, eternal beings, God and the Intellects, could not have the attribute of time, for this would imply corporeality and mobility. For Crescas 'time is the duration of motion or of rest between two instants'. Like Abu-l-Barakāt before him, who defined time as the measure of being, Crescas dissociates time and motion. God and the Intellects could thus again receive the attribute of time, for 'it seems therefore that the existence of time is only in the soul': 'the Intelligences, though immovable, may still have existence in time, inasmuch as it can be demonstrated that time existed prior to their creation on the ground that time does not require the actual existence of motion, but only the supposition of the measure of motion or rest' (Proposition xv, *ibid.* p. 291).

This does not mean that God has a beginning and an end: He is infinite in time, from the beginning as of the end; but past and future exist for Him. God is no longer an unmoving Mover who remains outside all the happenings of the world.

D. *The infinity of causal series*

Its possibility is also affirmed by Crescas:

Examination of the third proposition, which reads: 'The existence of an infinite number of causes and effects is impossible.'

I say that the argument framed here by Altabrizi, which has been discussed by us in the third chapter of the first part, and of which there is a suggestion in the eighth book of the *Physics* and in the *Metaphysics*, is not altogether sufficient, considering the particular view espoused by the Master. For the Master, as has been shown, does not preclude the possibility of an infinite number except in the case of things which have order and gradation either in position or in nature. According to this, it will be possible for one Intelligence to be the cause of an infinite number of other Intelligences. On general principles, it must be admitted that the emanation of an infinite number of effects from one single cause would not be impossible, if it were only possible for a single cause to be the source of emanation of more than one effect. And so, inasmuch as it is evident that there can be an infinite number of effects, despite their all being dependent upon a common cause, it must follow that the assumption of a common cause for more than one effect would not make it impossible for those effects to be infinite in number. This being the case, assuming now a series of causes and effects wherein the first is the cause of the second and the second of the third and so on for ever, would that I knew why, by the mere assumption of a common cause for the series as a whole, the number of causes and effects within that series could not be infinite?

(Proposition III, *ibid.* p. 225)

If the infinity of a numerical series does exist then one cannot accept the proof of the existence of God by the First Mover, for this proof is based on the affirmation that a series of causes cannot be infinite and necessarily terminates in a First Cause.

Infinity of space, infinity of time, infinity of causal series, because God is infinite – this is Crescas' central intuition. The essence of the infinite God cannot be attained by the human mind; this is evident both from the philosophical point of view and from that of revelation. Rejecting Aristotelian physics, Crescas also rejects the science of the divine that is based on it. There are no 'proofs' of the existence of the divine. Crescas expresses surprise that Maimonides should have interpreted Moses' demand of God, 'I beseech thee, show me thy glory' (Exodus 33: 18), as a demand for knowledge of the divine essence, for this would ascribe extraordinary ignorance to the prince of prophets. The most insignificant student of philosophy knows perfectly well that the divine essence, which is infinite, is totally unknowable. We know God's existence because He is the cause of the world that we apprehend.

Crescas repeats several times that God is the cause of all creation, for it is He who gives it existence. To affirm this, one does not need to accept a limited series of causes. God is, totally, the cause of the world, for without Him there is no world; whether there is an infinite or a finite series of causes and effects does not affect the evidence that the world has a cause. All things are effects, the existence of which is possible from the point of view of their essence; they must have a cause that makes them turn from nothingness towards existence, and this cause is God.

If God is unknowable in His essence, this does not signify that we know nothing of Him. Like Gersonides, Crescas affirms the existence of positive attributes of which we know something. Between God and His creatures there is no possible comparison but one can conceive something of God as one can have an idea of the infinite on the basis of the finite.

At this point Crescas discusses the meaning of the word 'existence' when it is applied to God and to His creation. This problem, already discussed at length by Gersonides, had been resolved by admitting, in contradiction to Maimonides for whom existence in man and existence in God were absolutely unrelated, that the attribute 'existence' is predicated in God *per prius* and in man *per posterius*. There is thus no relation, properly speaking, but an analogy between the use of the term in connection with God and in connection with His creatures, as with the question of substance and accidents.

Crescas goes beyond Gersonides in the affirmation that one cannot use the word existence in the same sense concerning God and concerning other creatures, for he adds to the argument the essential difference between the infinite and the finite.

In God the attributes are infinite and in man they are finite. And nevertheless, as one can have an idea of the infinite through the finite, we believe that we know of God that He exists because of the existence of the things that exist in this lower world.

Crescas does not admit the objection made to the positive attributes – that they would introduce the notion of multiplicity in God – for this would be as if one conceived of God as depending on something other than Himself. The attributes are 'one' in the infinity of the good; nor does God depend on some other being which would join His attributes, like essence and existence in man; He is cause of His own unity.

The two aspects of the One God, unity of essence and unity of action, are expressed in the 'Hear O Israel, the eternal God thy God is One.'

That God should be, in His infinity, cause of our world only, or cause of an infinity of worlds, does not in any way affect His unity, which is a unity different from that which we know in created beings.

Among the attributes of God that we find in the Bible, there is one that Crescas examines more attentively: joy. What is joy? According to Aristotle and his disciples joy is intellection, and the more exalted and glorious the thing intellected the greater is the joy. God therefore rejoices in the contemplation of His own essence, the only and unique object worthy of His contemplation.

For Crescas this definition of joy is false for two reasons:

First, joy is the sentiment that one experiences when one has wanted something and obtains it; these are 'sentiments' and not at all 'intellections'. God is pure intellect for the Aristotelians, and evidently He cannot 'undergo' joy or pain. Secondly, the joy of intellection is provoked in man when he passes from ignorance to knowledge; the possession of knowledge is a much lesser joy than that of the acquisition of this knowledge.

God's joy thus cannot be the contemplation of His essence. It is joy of giving, joy of the good that is lavished. According to Crescas, it is absolutely proved that God is the true active agent of all the creatures, that He makes them act by His will and intention, that He makes them persist in being by the emanation of His Good. God loves to spread Good and Perfection; the joy that He feels is that of this constant gift of being that spreads throughout creation, in the most perfect manner possible.

The joy that God experiences in an infinite and essential way is thus giving; it is also love and desire; God loved and desired the Patriarchs, and God loves and desires the love of Israel. It is with the love of God, a love entirely separated from matter, as he emphasizes in the last chapter, that Crescas concludes the first book of his work.

Book II enumerates the fundamental doctrines of the *Torah* and first of all the principle that God is Knowing. The divine knowledge is defined by three characteristics:

(1) God knows infinity;
(2) God knows what is not yet;
(3) God knows possible things and this knowledge does not prevent them from being possible.

Here Crescas' adversary is Gersonides, whose doctrine becomes the object of a vehement critique. According to Gersonides, God on the one hand knows things because He is their cause, but He does not know free human decision except as possible, and thus does not know its outcome; on the other hand, He only knows particular things in their place in the general order and as part of a whole, and not as they exist materially in this world. To Crescas this is an absurd and impious doctrine: absurd because it attributes to God ignorance of the creatures that He brought into being, impious because it is contrary to the biblical text, which is the account of direct relations between God, the Patriarchs and Israel.

To accept Gersonides' ideas would mean that nothing of the literal text of the Bible would remain intact, for God would not have known the Patriarchs, would not have spoken to them, would not have made them promises. Further, since free human decision is an important factor in the biblical stories, one would reach the point of denying God all knowledge of the history of the people of Israel, and, in fact, all knowledge of what happens on earth.

In reality, Crescas concludes, divine and human knowledge cannot be compared; one cannot define the infinite on the basis of the finite. It is not because our intelligence stops at a certain limit that we should attribute ignorance to God; one must maintain that God knows the possible inasmuch as it is possible, at the same time knowing what will necessarily take place, and this knowledge does not change the nature of the possible. It is because God knows the individuals of this lower world that He can exercise His providence in their favour.

Divine providence, the second fundamental doctrine, acts with or without intermediary; only Moses enjoyed divine providence without intermediary. The intermediaries between God and men may be angels, that is, the separate intellects, or prophets, or sages, or the celestial bodies. The prophets are the object of providence by the intermediary of the angels and serve as intermediaries for the providence of the sages; the sages serve as intermediaries for the providence of the people of Israel. As for the other peoples, they are abandoned to the domination of the astral bodies.

Providence itself is of three kinds:

(1) Natural providence, equal for all men;

(2) The providence special to Israel, equal for all its people;

(3) Personal providence, which is in proportion to the deserts of every man in Israel.

This last providence can be perfectly proportioned to a man's merits, and this is the spiritual reward or punishment that is decreed and ordained by God's eternal will; it is also sometimes imperfectly proportioned; this is corporeal reward or punishment. And in fact there is hardly any convincing solution to the problem of the sufferings of the just, says Crescas, except that of ordeal by love, for sufferings supported in the love of God make the soul acquire a special quality, a particular virtue, which brings it nearer to God.

The special providence of the People of Israel is first of all the *Torah*. But Crescas insists on three points which, he says, throw light on the action of providence; and here, as in many other cases, we see the influence of Judah Halevi.

(1) Certain places, that is, Jerusalem, that are particularly suited to receive divine providence;

(2) Certain times that are particularly propitious;

(3) Circumcision redeems original sin.

This is a passage that calls for more detailed analysis, for we here recognize certain Christian ideas which, adapted to Judaism, were used to combat the Christian pretension that baptism and not circumcision was the real sign of God's covenant. There was, says Crescas, an original sin (the idea is talmudic and one also finds it in the Kabbalah) that defiled mankind from birth. Abraham, Israel's ancestor, was in every way Adam's opposite; and he gave rise to a new race destined to perpetuate itself. This persistence of being does not mean the corporeal eternity of the race of Abraham, but implies true eternity, that of the world to come. Cleansing from original sin and access to the spiritual life are provided by circumcision. Circumcision is the sacrament that leads to salvation; like baptism, it washes away original sin; it makes the Jew enter into the divine alliance. However, in itself it is only an initiation rite leading the Jew to the threshold of the commandments that he must accomplish in order to approach the divine presence. This covenant of circumcision was confirmed by the sacrifice of Isaac; in Isaac, the lamb of sacrifice, the entire people of Israel consolidated the covenant; it is through this sacrifice that Israel escapes the decrees of the stars, the laws of nature, and accedes to the favour of truly divine providence. The sacrifices offered in the Temple recall this perpetual sacrifice of Isaac, which is perpetuated in the accomplishment of the commandments and in the first and most important of them: circumcision.

The third fundamental doctrine is that God is Omnipotent. Divine power does not signify that God can abolish the first intelligibles, for what the intellect conceives as impossible, for instance, that a thing should be true and false at the same time and from the same point of view, cannot be an object of the divine power. But divine power is infinite in strength and in time. Aristotle's great mistake had been to affirm that since the world is finite, the cause that moves it, although infinite in time, is limited in strength; he thus bound with a necessary bond the cause, God, and the caused, the world, and attributed to the cause a statement that is only applicable to the caused. Divine power is infinite; if it had caused a finite world, this is by will and choice; it is not only infinite in power but infinite in act; the divine Omnipotence, whose infinite force in act is proved by reason, is revealed in the biblical miracles when substances are created or destroyed, such as Moses' rod, which changed into a serpent.

God has given the *Torah*. One cannot conceive the existence of the divine law, which is a commandment proceeding from Him who orders – God – to those who receive the order – the whole people – without some kind of relation or tie between the two; this link is prophecy.

Prophecy is defined as 'an emanation which flows over the human intellect; this spiritual emanation brings a teaching and has its source in God. With or without intermediary, it teaches man, in any domain, a thing or things that he does not know and whose premises he does not know, in order to guide him or to guide other men' (*Or Adonai* II, 4, fol. 41a).

For Crescas, prophecy is first of all that which guides men and teaches them the divine will; it can teach intelligible and sensible notions even when the premises of these notions, indispensable to the scholar who reasons by deduction, are not present to the mind of the prophet.

Crescas emphasizes the difference between prophetic perception and dream:

In defining prophecy as an emanation which emanates from God, we have distinguished it from dream and from divination. The proof of this is that the prophet has not the slightest doubt concerning his prophecy; it is because of the divine origin of prophecy that we have received the order to listen to the prophet and to follow him, and that, according to the tradition, the prophet who pays no heed to his own words is liable to be executed. (*Or Adonai* II, 4, fol. 44a)

However, there is nothing that the prophet represents to himself in the prophetic dream that he cannot naturally represent to himself in the non-prophetic dream; this is self-evident. Thus, if there were no indication proving to the prophet that the dream is of divine origin, then the prophet alone would be judge (of the origin of the dream) and this is not possible.

We must then admit that the sign is the intensity of the perception at the moment of the representation; the sensible perception is superior to the imaginative perception, for, thanks to the sensible perception, the subject knows, being awake, that his perception is not only in the imagination, that he is not dreaming. In the same way, the perception of the prophetic imagination, although it be a dream, is superior to the imaginary non-prophetic imagination. (*Ibid.* fol. 44b)

The second idea that Crescas develops is a comparison between Moses and Balaam and the miraculous status of these two personages, according to the Tradition. Our author severely criticizes those scholars who depart from the traditional explanation. Nevertheless his own conception also deviates from rabbinical exegeses; in fact, he considers that Moses' perfection does not surpass the limits of natural laws, for perfection has no potential limits, although in action it is limited.

However, when Crescas, in Book III, returns to the difference between Moses and the other prophets, he cites the same factors as Maimonides: prophecy without intermediary, in a waking state, without fear and face to face, and at any time.

Free will is also one of the fundamental doctrines of divine Law. Crescas repeats arguments that I have already expounded. He affirms that things are possible from the point of view of their essence; but everything, including that which depends on free will, is totally necessary insofar as it is caused, as necessarily as the production of a chemical reaction when its causes are present.

Nevertheless, in Crescas' opinion, this ineluctable causality should not be revealed to people, for it might serve as an excuse for the wicked, who, when doing evil, would forget that punishment is necessarily caused by crime.

We see therefore that Crescas is very close to Abner of Burgos. Although he constantly uses the words 'will' and 'free will', he empties them of their sense, for, if all human acts are made necessary by their causes, man is called 'will-ing' when the cause is interiorized and not perceived by him, and 'non-will-ing' only when an external cause is perceived as forcing him, against his interior assent, into a certain action. Crescas thus goes very far in the direction of reducing human liberty, in order to safeguard divine knowledge; like Abner, he is on the side of the theologians against the philosophers.

But he is well aware of the difficulties. He attempts to palliate them, first by saying that this truth should not be published, since it could lead to a disastrous fatalism, and secondly in his analysis of the notions of pleasure and will; referring to the joy experienced by God, Crescas says that this joy cannot be an act of contemplation, a static pleasure; joy is for God the gift of Good. For man, joy, pleasure, and thus even reward, is also to do good, to perform the commandments of God; this joy accompanies the fulfilment as effect accompanies cause, but only when the soul acquiesces, wills, without exterior obligation felt as constraint.

Beliefs, and especially true beliefs, are received in the soul as obligation and not will, since they impose themselves from without, and their reality constrains the soul to accept them. Thus neither reward nor punishment follow beliefs; and it is impossible to accept that reward and punishment should be linked to the knowledge of intelligibles. What sense would reward have when a man admits, as reality forces him to admit, that the sum of the angles of a triangle is equal to 180°? Crescas does not deduce from this that knowledge counts for nothing in the survival of the soul; but he denies that the intelligibles, becoming the substance of the soul, should be what is called 'the survival of the soul'. What brings about reward, joy, is the effort towards knowledge, the desire to know, the will to understand.

The purpose of the *Torah* is to lead to the acquisition of the perfection of morals, the perfection of beliefs, material happiness and the happiness of the soul. The happiness of the soul is the most important of these and this is the final purpose of the divine Law.

However, the eternal felicity of the soul is the love and fear of God; love and fear of God are the ultimate stage, not only of the *Torah* but also of true philosophy.

Three principles are to be accepted on this matter:

(1) The human soul, which is the form of man, is a spiritual substance which is disposed for intellection but is not, by itself, intelligent *in actu*.

(2) The perfect, in virtue of its perfection, loves the Good and the Perfection, and desires them. The love and pleasure generated by the object in the will are in proportion to the perfection of this object.

(3) The love and pleasure that the will experiences differ from intellection.

Will is defined as the concordance and the relation between the appetitive faculty and the imagination, that is, consent by the latter to what's willed by the former, the pleasure caused by the object being in proportion to this concordance and this relation.

Intellection on the other hand is representation and verification, and both are produced by the intellective faculty. Given that the intellective faculty is other than the appetitive and the imaginative, it is thus proved that the love and pleasure suscitated by the object of desire are other than intellection.

From love proceeds conjunction, communion with God since, even in the case of natural things, the love and the harmony that dominate in their structure cause their perfection and their unity to such a degree that an ancient philosopher (Empedocles) saw in love and concord the principle of generation, that of corruption being hatred and discord. All the more reason that harmony and love should be factors of communion and unity in the spiritual domain.

In the same way, the greater the love between God and man, the closer, stronger and greater their communion. The aim of the *Torah* is that of the whole of creation: Love.

Book III expounds true beliefs: the creation of the world, the survival of the soul after death, reward and punishment, the resurrection of the dead, the eternity of the *Torah*, the difference between the prophecy of Moses and that of the other prophets, the miraculous properties of the High Priest's breastplate in the Temple of Jerusalem, the coming of the Messiah. Crescas does not deny that these eight 'roots', however important, are not absolutely necessary, for the absence of one or another of them would not involve the disappearance of the divine Law. Certainly, the world was created in time, but, in fact, whether God created the world in time or eternally is of little importance, as long as He willed its creation.

What is important, is the manner of being of this one God, His attributes, His relations with the world and man, for these are the bases of the *Torah* and the *Torah* is the only way that leads man to his eternal salvation, bringing man to God.

After having examined, at the end of Book III, the beliefs that depend on particular commandments of the Law of Moses: prayer, the blessing of the people by the priests, repentance, the Day of Atonement and the festivals, Crescas devotes Book IV to the examination of various traditional and philosophical opinions that are probable or credible according to reason.

(1) Some rabbinical texts hold that the present world is doomed to destruction. The Aristotelians maintain that since the world has no beginning, it cannot have an end. The movement of the heavens is perfect and has no contrary and therefore no cause of corruption; besides, their perfect and eternal movement is caused by an eternal intellect that is not subject to change; after having expounded arguments for and against, Crescas concludes that it is probable that the world will persist to eternity; however, he does not altogether dismiss the other hypothesis, that of the end of the world.

(2) There is disagreement on whether there is one single world or several. There too, contrary to Aristotle, Crescas tends to believe that there are numerous worlds; for why should the infinite goodness of God be limited to a single world?

(3) Are the celestial spheres beings endowed with reason? Crescas does not seem to accept that the stars are intelligent beings; he rather tends to believe that their movement is natural; but tradition insists that they are intelligent beings.

(4) Do the stars have an influence over the conduct of human affairs? The answer is yes, and Crescas refutes various objections.

(5) Do amulets and incantations have an influence over human actions? Yes, says Crescas; in fact, they are linked to the stars and serve as intermediaries to the astral influx.

(6) The existence of demons is proved for our author by biblical and traditional texts, as by everyday experience and universal consensus. Let us note that as with the preceding point, Crescas starts with the perceived reality of things and then looks for the philosophical explanation.

Crescas continues by refuting the theory of the transmission of souls; he declares that the child who has been circumcised and can say 'Amen' has a right to the world to come; he affirms the existence of hell and discusses its site and that of paradise; he refuses to identify the Story of the Creation with physics, and the Story of the Chariot with metaphysics. He denies the unity of the intellecting, the intellect and the intelligible; he remarks that the philosophers' dispute as to whether God or the first emanation is the First Mover is not of the slightest interest; and he concludes his book by stating that it is not impossible that the angels, and even men, should have an idea of the essential attributes of God.

Crescas was not the first Jewish philosopher who undertook to overthrow Aristotelian philosophy; Abu-l-Barakāt, in the East, had done so before him; but it seems that this resemblance was due to a parallel thought-process and not in any way to a direct influence. Other anti-Aristotelian philosophers, like Judah ha-Cohen and Shemariah ben Elijah of Crete, cast doubt on certain aspects of the Aristotelian theses but not the system as a whole (as did Abu-l-Barakāt). Crescas was also not the only philosopher of his time to reconsider the entire physical system on which Aristotelian science rested. S. Pines, in his article on Scholasticism, has discussed the resemblances between Crescas' theories and the theories of 'Parisian physics' as well as other theories of the school of Duns Scotus.

Crescas certainly drew on the scholastics, but he borrowed from them the ideas and conceptual tools that he needed for the elaboration of his personal theories, those that were in accord with the Jewish tradition as he understood it. Another influence is very perceptible in Crescas' work, that of the Kabbalah. Not only does his idea of the infinite evidently evoke the *En-Sof* of the Kabbalists, but other, less important, points of resemblance can be traced. Here too, Crescas did not adopt the system of the Kabbalah, but borrowed ideas suiting his personal thought.

Crescas' philosophy did not meet with much success. His rejection of all the commonly accepted notions, and especially of Maimonides, aroused astonishment and indignation. Many scholars, who in fact admired Crescas, rallied to the support of the 'Second Moses' (who was whitewashed of all his philosophical audacities), and the period saw more Maimonideans than partisans of Crescas. They made great use of a little book called *Mesharet Moshe* (*Moses' Servant*), written before 1273 but attributed to Kalonymus ben Kalonymus: in six chapters he answers in advance Crescas' attacks on Maimonides. To give one example: we remember the interpretation of Exodus 23 and Crescas' expression of his surprise that Maimonides should have attributed to Moses a demand to know the divine essence, an absurd demand that a mere novice in philosophy would not dare to formulate. Our author gives two reasons for this exegesis. One is exoteric: Maimonides uses the pedagogical method, which consists of proposing provocative questions inciting the pupil to display his critical sense. The other is esoteric: Moses, having reached the level of the Active Intellect and joined with it, posed the question of the knowledge of the divine essence by the separate intellects, and God answered: 'For neither man nor intellect may know Me.'

A further consequence of the religious and political situation at the beginning of the fifteenth century was the need experienced by Jewish thinkers to define themselves as clearly as possible in relation to their own tradition. The question of the principles of Judaism assumed considerable importance and became even more prominent at the time of the Disputation of Tortosa, as we shall see with Joseph Albo.

There are no dogmas, properly speaking, in Judaism. The Jewish tradition, the Bible and the Talmud are a whole, where for a long time no differentiation was made and which had to be accepted in its entirety, belief in each of the commandments being implied. However, when faced with other religions Judaism found itself obliged to clarify and systematize the principles of the faith. The first to do this were the Karaites, with Judah Hadassi (*ca.* 1150), who, most probably following older sources, enumerated ten principles but does not use the Hebrew word '*iqqar*. *Elijah ben Moses Bashyatchi*, a Karaite scholar living in Constantinople (*ca.* 1420–90), does use the word when quoting these principles in his '*Adderet Eliyahu* (*The glory of Elijah*): (1) all physical creation has been created; (2) it has been created by a creator who is eternal; (3) the Creator has no likeness and is unique in all respects; (4) he sent the prophet Moses; (5) he sent, along with Moses, His Law, which is perfect; (6) it is the duty of the believer to know the language of the Law (Hebrew) and its interpretation; (7) God inspired also the other true prophets after Moses; (8) God will resurrect all mankind, on the Day of Judgement; (9) God requites each person according to his ways and the fruits of his deeds; (10) God has not forsaken the people of the Diaspora; rather they are suffering the Lord's just punishment and they must hope every day for His salvation at the hands of the Messiah, the descendant of King David (trans. L. Nemoy, *Karaite Anthology*, p. 250).

Of the Rabbanites, Maimonides was the first to make a list of principles, thirteen in number, which I have discussed at some length. This list gave rise to much discussion. Some refused the very notion that there could be dogmas in Judaism, others did not agree with the principles or with their number. Nahmanides spoke of three fundamental principles: divine creation, that is, the non-eternity of matter, divine omniscience, and providence. Abba Mari ben Moses of Montpellier, in his *Minḥat Kenaot* (a collection of antiphilosophical epistles) also lists three. The first is metaphysical; the existence of God as well as His unity and His incorporeality; the second is Mosaic: the creation *ex nihilo*, with the consequence that God can change the laws of nature according to His will; the third is ethical: particular providence, for God knows human acts in all their details.

Another Provençal rabbi, David ben Samuel d'Estella (*ca.* 1320) gives seven principles and Shemariah ben Elijah of Crete has five. David ben Yom Tov Ibn Bilia accepts the Thirteen Principles of Maimonides and adds to them thirteen more, in the *Yesodot ha-Maskil* (*Principles of the Intelligent Man*).

However, the problem remained marginal until the end of the fourteenth century; in the fifteenth, it became urgent. Let us note that among these principles the coming of the Messiah is always a minor theme; one of the polemical arguments of Christianity was precisely the advent of the Messiah, Jesus. The Jews therefore were not inclined to assign too great an importance to this topic.

SIMEON BEN ZEMAḤ DURAN

Duran (1361–1444) was born in Majorca and after the 1391 massacres left Spain for Algiers, where he was appointed Chief Rabbi in 1408. He was a physician, knew Arabic and Latin, and, like all young men of good family, had enjoyed an encyclopedic education.

He is especially known for his rabbinical decisions, which usually had the force of law in North Africa. Of his philosophical works, it seems that his glosses on Gersonides' biblical commentary, which were followed by four discourses refuting Crescas' theories, have been lost. We still have two major works.

Ohev Mishpat (*Lover of Justice*) deals with providence. It is divided into two parts; the first is a kind of introduction to the book of Job, also discussing the principles of Judaism; the second is a commentary on Job.

Magen Avot (*Shield of the Fathers*) is in four parts; the first three, each discussing one of the principles of Judaism, were published at Leghorn in 1785 and recently in Jerusalem in a reprint edition; the fourth is a commentary on the *Pirkei Avot*.

His polemic directed against Christians and Muslims, called *Keshet u-Magen* (*The Arrow and the Shield*) is the fourth chapter of the second part of the preceding book, but was printed separately.

Duran displays great erudition in his philosophical writings, and he cites Greek, Arab and Jewish philosophers in profusion. However, the thrust of his thought is essentially religious. The search for truth is possible only with divine aid, that is, revelation.

While it is true that God created man capable of understanding alone and without a teacher, two conditions are indispensable for the acquisition of knowledge; zeal and study, and divine succour.

The philosophers often erred because they were without this divine help. The Jews, who have the good fortune to have received the revelation and therefore the truth, do not need philosophy, except perhaps in order to argue against unbelievers.

This principle granted, the various philosophical and Kabbalistic opinions that our author approves are evidently not very interesting in themselves; they were chosen because they seemed to him capable of convincing the infidels, Jews and non-Jews, of the truth of verities that surpass human reason.

This does not mean that Duran was an adversary of reason. He classes the philosophical subjects treated in the texts in three kinds:

(1) Those which are demonstrated at all points by correctly directed reasoning and which no man can refuse to admit, unless he is totally ignorant of the laws of logic, or else out of bad faith; for instance, the existence of God and His unity.

(2) Those that human reason cannot demonstrate apodictically, such as the creation of the world; for demonstration is performed on the basis of premises and causes, and, in the case of the creation of the world, the causes and premises are God Himself, Whose essence we cannot know. The ways of knowledge on this subject are therefore irrevocably closed to all but God Himself.

(3) Subjects where intellect affirms one thing and sensible experience refutes it; thus, according to philosophy, God is not concerned with his creatures, while experience shows us divine providence in all things.

Concerning these three kinds of problem, the *Torah* makes affirmations, and does not demonstrate with the help of arguments, for it is not a book of philosophy, and the proof offered by the *Torah* is the *Torah* itself, sufficient here as elsewhere; in the third type, however, it is easier to make mistakes than in the others; and indeed we find in the Bible a whole book devoted to the problem of divine providence. These considerations are an introduction to the Book of Job, which, says our author, in this following a long tradition, presents the different arguments for and against particular providence. The Book of Job is thus considered as *Torah* and Duran does not differentiate between the books of the Bible; they are all of equal importance and all present the 'true' revelation.

He also does not discriminate between the divine commandments; all of them have the same importance and none of them can be abandoned with impunity. To abandon any one of the ideas of the *Torah*, if this abandoning is the result of conscious knowledge, is to abandon the entire *Torah*. In a certain sense one can say that the principles of Jewish law are as numerous as the number of letters of the Bible or the number of the words of all the verses or the number of the commandments. It is thus not surprising that Simon Duran attacked Maimonides on the score of the Thirteen Principles of the faith, and it is in this light that one must understand the Three Principles that he himself defined, which serve as a basis for his *Shield of the Fathers*. These three principles are the existence of God, revelation, and reward and punishment.

For Maimonides the Thirteen Principles represented the minimum of intelligible notions to be intellected by every human being in order to be truly a man, with a right to the world to come. In the case of the non-philosophical, these intelligible notions should be received by tradition. For Duran, the right to the next world, which he describes only in traditional terms and not as the more or less individual conjunction with the Active Intellect, does not depend on the acquisition of the intelligible notions but on the purity of the soul, which is sustained, since the soul is initially pure, by the accomplishment of the commandments, that is, all the divine commandments. The 'principles' thus correspond to a very different need, that of grouping all the revealed beliefs around the three essential themes of the Jewish religion, and of showing where philosophy is in accord with religion and where it is contrary to it and therefore false. In J. Guttmann's felicitous phrase, he wanted to fix the limits of the rationalization of the Jewish religion, and decide how far a Jew's scientific investigation could go if he wished to remain a Jew. Philosophy, when it is true, is essentially human. Duran takes his arguments wherever he finds them; J. Guttmann remarks that Duran's theory of the divine attributes is a brief formulation of the Thomist theory. As for the Three Principles, Guttmann finds their source in Averroes' *Decisive Treatise on the Harmony of Religion and Philosophy*; however, while the Three Principles are literally the same, they do not have the same sense in the two authors. For Averroes,

> This [latter] error is that which occurs about matters, knowledge of which is provided by all the different methods of indication, so that knowledge of the matter in question is in this way possible for everyone. Examples are acknowledgement of God, Blessed and Exalted, of the prophetic missions, and of happiness and misery in the next life; for these three principles are attainable by the three classes of indication, by which everyone without exception can come to assent to what he is obliged to know: I mean the rhetorical, dialectical and demonstrative indications.
>
> (*On the Harmony of Religion and Philosophy*, trans. G. Hourani, p. 58)

Immediately afterwards Averroes shows that the interpretation of the revealed text permits one to give extremely different definitions of these three principles, which may be contrary to the literal sense.

Duran, however, conceives his principles as chapter headings introducing the entire traditional divine Law. Joseph Albo conceived these principles in the same way, perhaps receiving them from Simon Duran (or did Duran find them in Albo?). At all events, it was Albo who made these principles popular.

JOSEPH ALBO

Albo, one of Crescas' disciples, finished writing the *Book of Principles* at Soria in 1425. He died in 1444.

The *Sefer ha-Ikkarim* (*Book of Principles*) can only be understood in the context of the great public Disputation that was taking place in Spain at this period. These public debates were designed as illustration and manifest demonstration of the errors of the Jews. The first, opposing the apostate Nicholas Donin and the well-known French scholar Yehiel ben Joseph, was held in Paris in 1240 and terminated in the burning of the Talmud.

The Disputation of Barcelona in 1263 witnessed the confrontation of Nahmanides on the Jewish side and on the Christian side Pablo Christiani, a converted Jew. In 1413–14 the last of these great public controversies was held at Tortosa. It was inaugurated with great pomp by the Pope himself,

Benedict XIII, on 7 February 1413 and concluded on 13 November 1414. Among the Jewish delegates summoned to appear and defend their religion was Joseph Albo of Daroca. The Christian faith was represented by Geronimo de Santa Fé, converted in 1412, who died in 1419. We have already encountered him at the beginning of this chapter under the name of Joshua Lorki, defending the Jewish religion against his former master Solomon ha-Levi of Burgos, who had converted and taken the name of Pablo de Santa Maria, later becoming Bishop of Burgos.

Geronimo's knowledge of Jewish sources was remarkable and his attacks against his former co-religionists were therefore particularly incisive. He wrote two polemical books in Latin, and it was perhaps he who had the idea of calling together the Disputation.

It was in the course of this controversy that Joseph Albo took the decision to elucidate the problem of the principles, concerning which Jewish scholars had not yet succeeded in formulating a commonly-accepted opinion. He wanted to integrate the Law of Moses within the framework of the political laws of human society, and to show its place in the economy of mankind.

The *Book of Principles* is composed of an introduction followed by four books. In fact, Book I contains Albo's chief ideas; the three other books, written at the request of the author's friends, only explicate the Three Principles, adding a number of often interesting features or definitions. The subject of the book and the respective place occupied by faith and reason are stated at the beginning:

Human happiness depends upon theoretical knowledge and practical conduct, as the Philosopher explains in the book *On the Soul*. But it is not possible by the human intellect alone to arrive at a proper knowledge of the true and the good, because human reason is not capable of comprehending things as they are in reality, as will be explained later. There must therefore be something higher than the human intellect by means of which the good can be defined and the true comprehended in a manner leaving no doubt at all. This can be done only by means of divine guidance. It is incumbent therefore upon every person, out of all laws to know that one divine law which gives this guidance. This is impossible unless we know the basic principles without which a divine law cannot exist. Accordingly the purpose of this work is to explain what are the essential principles of a divine law, and for this reason it is called *The Book of Principles*.

(*Sefer ha-Ikkarim*, trans. I. Husik, vol. I, pp. 1–2)

In his introduction, Albo first compares the Law to other sciences; only one who knows the principles of medicine can be a physician. Since all men accept and are subject to laws, they should therefore have a knowledge of the principles of these laws; if a real knowledge of them is not always attainable they should at least have one sufficiently close to reality. However, scholars are far from being in agreement: Maimonides enumerates thirteen principles of the Law, others (probably David Yom Tov Ibn Bilia) twenty-six, others (Crescas) six, and none of them has explained precisely in what way these principles characterize the divine law and if it is possible to have several divine laws.

The inquiry can only be undertaken within the context of a study of all human laws. It is in this context that one must define what the divine law is, and since all agree in attributing this status to the Law of Moses, one must know the principles that make this Law divine; and also the principles that are specific to it and make it this particular divine Law.

The general principles are three in number. They state that God exists, that law comes from God, that reward and punishment exist. It is evident that these three principles are necessary to the divine Law, for if one suppresses one of them, one suppresses the divine Law itself, which can only be authenticated by the existence of a legislator: this is God, who is the source of the Law and who rewards men corporeally in this world and spiritually in the world to come. Otherwise, what would be the difference between divine Law, and law enacted by men?

Following the whole philosophical Arab–Jewish tradition, Albo in fact defines religion (*dat*) as a political law. It can be of three kinds: natural, conventional and divine.

– Natural law is equal for all men, at all times and in all places. Its purpose is to repress evil and to promote good, so that human society may subsist and that all may be protected from the wicked and the criminal.

– Conventional law was promulgated by one or several sages in conformity with a certain period or place, and also the nature of the inhabitants of the country. Some of these conventional laws were decreed in accordance with human reason and without divine help. Conventional law has the role of eliminating what is ethically ugly and encouraging ethical good, this ethical good and evil being generally accepted in human society; thus, while having the same aims as natural law, it is superior to it because it is concerned with the ethical conduct of its subjects.

– Divine Law was given by God through the intermediary of a prophet, Adam, Noah, Abraham or Moses; its aim is to guide men towards the true happiness, which is the happiness of the soul and its immortality.

Thus the superiority of the conventional law over the natural law lies in the fact that it is concerned not only with causing order to prevail, but with making men acquire good ethics. Divine Law has all the advantages of the other laws, but it also directs men towards the true God, and the immortality of the soul.

To this basic superiority, Albo adds some others. For instance, only divine Law truly discerns good from evil, independent of time and place; it alone precisely defines the acts that should be accomplished at each moment of life and in each circumstance, while the teachings of conventional laws are very general (we have here an echo of Saadiah Gaon).

Is divine Law one or several? A genuine divine Law can be recognized by two criteria:

(1) The content of this Law, where the Three Principles must necessarily figure (as well as the roots attached to them, which will be discussed below) and where nothing may be contrary to the principles or the roots.

(2) The messenger or the law-giver who transmitted this Law.

One must be absolutely sure of the prophets and prophecy and prove in a direct manner that the law-giver has received a prophetic message and was sent by God to give mankind a law. This certainty must be essential, that is, it must be based on the causes of the thing in question as well as on its essential properties. And the performance of miracles by a person claiming to be a prophet does not necessarily prove that he is a messenger sent by God to give a law.

And so we shall find that all the miracles which Moses performed before the revelation of the Torah on Sinai, merely proved that he was a worthy instrument for the performance of miracles, but not for the transmission of a law. This is all that the Israelites believed about him. And they followed his directions because they believed that God heard his prayer and granted his requests . . . This is the meaning of the expression used in the narrative of the division of the Red Sea, 'And they believed in the Lord, and in His servant Moses.' [Exodus 14: 31]. They believed that he was the servant of God, that God performed miracles through him, and that He granted all his requests. We find in the case of other good men too that God performed miracles through them, though they were not prophets . . .

Seeing therefore that miracles are not a direct proof of prophecy, the people doubted whether Moses was a prophet, despite the miracles he performed, which were numerous and of a remarkable character in changing the laws of nature. It is only after the revelation on Sinai that the people said to Moses, 'We have seen this day that God doth speak with man, and he liveth.' [Deuteronomy 5: 21]. This shows that until that time they were still in doubt about the reality of prophecy, though they believed that Moses was the servant of God, and that miracles were performed by him, as we read, 'And they believed in the Lord and in His servant Moses.' [Exodus 14: 31].

This is the reason why at the time of the revelation on Sinai, God said to Moses, 'Lo, I come unto thee in a thick cloud, that the people may hear when I speak with thee, and may also believe thee forever.' [Exodus 19: 9]. The meaning is, I desire to prove to them directly the reality of prophecy, and also that you were sent by Me to give them the Torah. I will make them experience the prophetic spirit themselves. This will convince them that prophecy is a reality. And they will hear Me speaking to you, and indicating a desire to give them a law through you. This constituted a direct proof of prophecy and of the authentic character of the messenger, and there could no longer be any doubt or the least suspicion of fraud after that sublime experience; for through it were verified the two elements essential to prove the reality of revelation. The reality of prophecy was proved, because they were all prophets at that time, and heard the voice of God speaking the ten commandments. The second element was proved when they heard the voice saying to Moses, 'Go say to them: Return ye to your tents. But as for thee, stand thou here by Me, and I will speak unto thee all the commandments, and the statutes, and the ordinances, which thou shalt teach them, that they may do them in the land . . .' [Deuteronomy 5: 27]. In this they had a direct proof that Moses was a divine messenger through whom a perpetual law was to be given.

(Ibid. pp. 156–9)

If we examine the pretensions of the two great religions to be divine, we see that the Catholic religion contradicts divine unity. However, divine unity is an essential attribute of the very existence of God, therefore the Catholic religion cannot be divine. As for the Muslim belief, the messenger who transmitted it does not correspond to the criteria that are expected of such a personage. In fact, only Moses corresponds to the definition of 'messenger'.

Besides, if one considers the Law from the point of view of Him who gives it, God, Who does not change and therefore cannot change His Law, divine Law can but be unique. Nevertheless, this divine Law was given to guide men, and men are very different, even if they all belong to the same species – mankind. One can thus understand that the divine Law should be adapted to different kinds of temperaments in human societies, which have different climates, diverse traditions, and changing manners.

In the divine Law the three fundamental principles (and the roots attached to them) cannot be other, for these are the things that depend on Him who gives the Law – God, and God is immutable.

There have been divine laws other than the *Torah*, and they correspond to the preceding definitions; thus the Law given by God to the sons of Noah agrees with the Mosaic Law in its general principles, that is to say, from the point of view of Him who gave it, but it differs as regards the specific principles. In fact, the Law of the sons of Noah, which is addressed to all mankind, coexists in time with the Law of Moses, which is addressed to Israel only, and differs from it in that it is destined for peoples living everywhere except in the Land of Israel, whose culture and heredity are also different. It offers all the peoples felicity, felicity lesser than that of Israel, but felicity nevertheless.

The fact that two divine Laws designed for different peoples coexist in time does not give rise to difficulties. But what about other divine religions which preceded the *Torah* and which were abrogated by the Law of Moses, for instance the religion of Abraham? May it not be admitted that another divine Law might come to abrogate the *Torah*? This was an urgent question, and Albo devoted a large part of Book III to it.

One must first declare that the three great principles on which every divine Law rests, existence of God, God as giver of this Law, reward and punishment, cannot change in any way, any more than God Himself can be subject to change. The question only arises for a certain number of commandments specific to the Law of Moses, which a new prophet could conceivably change. If one affirms that a prophet sent by God cannot change a divine Law that has been faithfully transmitted, without adulteration, by a tradition which goes back to the people's ancestors, one would then ask oneself why the Israelites accepted the Law of Moses and abandoned that of Noah, which nevertheless also answered these criteria.

On the other hand, to affirm that every prophet can abrogate a divine Law would remove all permanence and value from it.

Albo himself thinks that one cannot abandon a traditional belief that has come down in an uninterrupted chain of transmission since the prophet himself, unless one is absolutely certain that the principles, general as well as particular, of the proposed new Law are true, and one is totally convinced that God wishes to abolish the words of the first prophet.

To achieve certainty on this subject, one must proceed to a very searching verification of the authenticity of the second prophet. The proof cannot be produced by miracles. We have seen this in the case of Moses. The Israelites did not believe in Moses the legislator because he performed miracles but first of all because the second prophet, Moses, was greater than the first, Noah; and secondly because the authenticity of his mission was as well demonstrated as that of his predecessor.

If Moses came to bring a new Law, may not another prophet, greater yet than Moses, do the same? In this Albo answers that the Bible, in advance, refutes the possibility that a greater prophet than Moses may appear (cf. Deuteronomy 34: 10). A new prophet, besides, would have to prove his mission in as striking a manner as Moses did on Mount Sinai, when all Israel heard the divine voice proclaim the Ten Commandments and order Moses to promulgate the Law that would be communicated to him.

An event of this nature is not beyond the bounds of the possible, and depends on divine will; one cannot affirm that it will happen, or that it will not happen, but as long as it has not happened, the revelation on Mount Sinai remains the solid foundation on which the divine Law, the *Torah*, rests, destined for Israel, and no Jew can listen to a prophet who might attempt to abolish an iota of this divine Law, so manifestly given by God.

The general principles of the divine Law are three, according to Albo, and no more than three. The acceptance of these principles is in effect the sign determining that a Jew belongs to the community of believers. If one held that Maimonides' Thirteen Principles were those that every Jew must consider true, this would mean classing among unbelievers, for instance, all those for whom the coming of the Messiah is not a fundamental dogma of Judaism.

Here Albo clearly dissociates the Law and the rationalization of faith. According to the sages, every Israelite must believe that everything that is written in the *Torah* is absolute truth; the problem of the principles only arises when a Jew has accepted this *Torah* and tries to understand it with his reason, and then to interpret it. He may make mistakes; he may refuse a principle, or he may deny a miracle that is described in the biblical text. These Jews, far from being unbelievers, are wise and pious men who err; they should realize their errors and do penitence.

The three general principles thus determine the legal status of the Jew in relation to God and the community of Israel; if he accepts them, he is a believer and will have his part in the world to come. Acceptance of the principles nevertheless involves the acceptance of what is connected with them:

Thus one who believes in the first principle, the existence of God, must also believe that God is one and incorporeal in any sense, and other such corollaries as follow from or are dependent upon the first principle. Similarly one who believes in divine revelation, which is the second principle, must believe in the reality of prophecy, and in the genuineness of the divine representative's mission. Likewise one who believes in the third principle, reward and punishment, must believe in God's knowledge and providence, and in retribution, spiritual and corporeal. To deny any of the secondary principles which are derived from the fundamental principles or based upon them, is tantamount to a denial of the fundamental principle itself.

(*Sefer ha-Ikkarim*, trans. I. Husik, vol. I, p. 121)

The 'secondary principles' or 'roots' are not identical with the commandments given in the *Torah*, the *miẓvot*, for he who violates a biblical commandment receives adequate punishment, but is not on that account considered to be an unbeliever.

There are eight 'roots':

– Four of them are attached to the first principle, which is divine existence: the unity of God, His incorporeality, His independence of time, and the negation of every fault or lack in Him.

– From the second principle, the divinity of the *Torah*, arise three 'roots', divine knowledge, prophecy, and the authenticity of the Messenger's mission.

– From the third principle arise reward and punishment; or, more exactly, divine providence precedes it.

The superiority of Moses and the immutability of the law we regard as neither fundamental nor derivative principles, because they are not essential to divine law. They are merely like branches issuing from the belief in the authenticity of the prophet's mission. If they are principles at all, primary or secondary, they are peculiar to the law of Moses, and not common to all divine law. Thus, belief in the Messiah and in the resurrection of the dead are dogmas peculiar to Christianity which cannot be conceived without them. But the law of Moses can be conceived as existing without the belief in the superiority of Moses and the immutability of the law. It is better to say therefore that they are like branches issuing from the belief in the authenticity of the lawgiver's mission, and not independent principles. Similarly, resurrection and the Messiah are like branches issuing from the dogma of reward and punishment, and not independent principles, primary or secondary, common to all divine law or peculiar to the law of Moses. (*Ibid.* vol. I, pp. 158-9)

The denial of the importance of the Messiah's coming responds very definitely to the Christian affirmation that the Messiah has already come. It is related that during the Disputation of Tortosa, Geronimo de Sante Fé set out to prove with the aid of a passage from the Babylonian Talmud (*Sanhedrin* 97b) that the Messiah had already come; Joseph Albo answered him: 'Even if it were proved to me that the Messiah had already come, I would not consider myself a worse Jew for all that (*Posito Messiam probari iam venisse non putarem deterior esse judaeus*).'

Albo's sources have been analysed by J. Guttmann. The division into divine, conventional and natural law, which one already finds in Moses Ibn

Waqar, first appears in Thomas Aquinas (together with other less important ideas), and the three fundamental principles were probably drawn from Simeon ben Zemaḥ Duran or perhaps directly from Averroes. At the end of the fifteenth century Jacob Ibn Ḥabib was already reproaching Albo with not having cited his sources. This accusation, which was well founded, is not of great importance in the case of a work like this, more apologetic than philosophical and perfectly performing the task for which it was conceived, namely, to show that the Law of Moses was the only one that corresponds to the definition of divine Law, and therefore to establish its particularism in the larger context of the universal laws, that tie man to God.

Albo's *Ikkarim* enjoyed a prolonged success in Jewish circles. Some Christian theologians, including Hugo Grotius and Richard Simon, held the work in high esteem; a Latin translation of the two anti-Christian chapters (III, 25–6) ,with a refutation by G. Genebrard, appeared in Paris in 1566.

Aristotelian philosophy took on renewed strength towards the middle of the century, and in 1450 and a little later several very fine copies were made of the *Guide of the Perplexed* and of a number of philosophical works composed during the fourteenth century. In this renaissance the sons of Shem Tov Ibn Shem Tov played a far from negligible part.

JOSEPH BEN SHEM TOV IBN SHEM TOV

Joseph ben Shem Tov (1400–60) served at the court of John II of Castile, then at that of Henry IV of Castile. His political position led him to participate in philosophical and religious debates with Christian scholars. It seems that he fell into disgrace in 1456, or thereabouts, and afterwards wandered from town to town, preaching on Saturdays and writing down his sermons. He died a martyr to his faith.

Between 1440 and 1460 he engaged in intensive philosophical activity, composing a long commentary on the *Nicomachaean Ethics*, two commentaries, one long and one short, on Averroes' *Possibility of Conjunction with the Active Intellect*, and another commentary on Averroes' *Paraphrase* of Alexander of Aphrodisias' *Treatise on the Intellect*, with appendixes discussing the same problem.

He also commented on the Lamentations of Jeremiah. His homiletic activities induced him to write a treatise on the art of preaching (preserved in two manuscripts). In the course of his polemical activity he translated into Hebrew and commented on Crescas' *Biṭṭul 'Iqqarrey ha-Noṣrim (Refutation of the Christian Dogmas)*. Two of his other works were also published, *Kevod Elohim (The Glory of God)* in 1556, and the commentary on the satirical epistle *Alteca Boteca*, the very commentary that opened the eyes of the Inquisition to the satirical double meanings of Profiat Duran's work, and led to its being placed on the Index.

The *Glory of God* is designed as a new attempt at a synthesis between religion and philosophy. Using a translation from the Latin version of the *Nicomachaean Ethics*, Joseph ben Shem Tov states that the views of Aristotle, as expressed in the first and tenth books of this work, can be reconciled with the teachings of the *Torah*. Some later Jewish scholars had doubts in regard to this point and, in consequence, were in a state of perplexity (an evident allusion to the *Guide of the Perplexed*), but these doubts were not justified.

The supreme good and the way that leads to it are the subjects of the book, which presents Aristotle's texts translated from Latin and accompanied by the exegeses that the author was able to collect on the subject, or by his personal commentaries. The aim of this work is thus a return to Aristotle, in his original purity, thanks to the Latin texts. The first question that should be asked concerns the relation of Jews to philosophy: is philosophy useful, permissible or prohibited to a Jew in the attainment of perfection?

A Jew should accomplish the divine commandments and he will thus attain perfection. The principles that govern the universe, and the philosophy that underlines the gift of these commandments must be accepted by every Israelite, but he does not necessarily have to know them with a profound and demonstrated knowledge, as the goldsmith, to carry out his work perfectly, has no need to know how the metal that he is using is formed under the earth; or, again, the astrologer can draw up excellent horoscopes without on that account knowing the nature of the celestial bodies, or whether they are perishable. The Talmud, and the Bible before it, tell us what act to perform, and what is the best act to accomplish.

Philosophy has two fields of investigation.

The first field is the true knowledge that one can draw from the existents. This science, divided into mathematics, natural and divine, is the necessary activity of the intellect and its perfection; the world of the existents, object of this science, being the work of God, knowledge of the existents leads to knowledge of God and to attachment to God, which are, undoubtedly, infinitely laudable and extremely useful. Intellectual perfection is also the road that leads to another perfection: that bestowed by the *Torah*. The Law given by God is thus seen to be acquired through intellectual research; in the hierarchy of forms the intellective form is superior to the animal soul and the latter becomes better and more perfect in the former; similarly, when the intellectual form is received in the man who is traditionally religious, it functions even more successfully. The religious man, who has attained perfection as a man, is more perfect in religious and divine perfection, for he unites in himself the two perfections, and he is superior to him who has only acquired one of these two perfections.

The second field of investigation is that where the Greeks ventured to contradict the revealed religions, and in these texts one cannot speak of science, for everything that is contrary to the *Torah* is not knowledge but illusion.

Nevertheless, adds Joseph ben Shem Tov, one cannot deny that some of our contemporaries considered intellectual perfection as the supreme good, and that they entrenched themselves behind this perfection and despised the *Torah*, while the Jews who did not know philosophy, like the Jews of France, were capable of dying for the *Torah*.

This in no way means that the study of the sciences should be abandoned. Nevertheless, Joseph ben Shem Tov approves of those who insist that the sciences and philosophy should only be taught after a certain age, when religious truth has formed the spirit, and man is capable of discriminating between truth and falsehood, of repelling doubts and resolving difficulties. Science should not be prohibited, our author repeats; on the contrary, as long as one recognizes its limits it is useful to religion.

However, one must know that the human spirit cannot discover the reasons for the divine commandments, for the divine cannot be born in a natural thing nor aim at a natural end. To understand the truth of the commandments one must have a guide to whom God Himself has revealed His purpose. The natural qualities of things exist and one cannot deny their existence; thus the magnet attracts the iron and this power is not linked to heat or to cold, or to dryness or humidity, which are the qualities of the four elements; this power of attraction is not natural, but supernatural and we witness it without understanding it. It is the same regarding the divine commandments, the reason for which we do not know, although it exists.

We see, then, that although he supported Aristotelian philosophy, Joseph ben Shem Tov Ibn Shem Tov could not set aside his concern for the survival of the Jewish people, and the accomplishment of the commandments, which is the condition for it, and the extremely difficult political situation weighed heavily on his philosophical thought. This distress is less marked in his younger brother.

Isaac ben Shem Tov Ibn Shem Tov left only purely philosophical works, in which he does not consider the relation between faith and reason. Some of his writings have disappeared: a composition entitled *Eẓ ha-Da'at* (*The Tree of Knowledge*), treatises on the creation of the world and on metaphysics, commentaries on Averroes' *Possibility of the Conjunction*, Al-Ghazālī's *Intentions of the Philosophers* (most probably the part dealing with physics), and perhaps on the *Hayy Ibn Yaqzan* of Ibn Ṭufayl. Other works have been preserved (in manuscript): four commentaries on Averroes' *Middle Commentary* on Aristotle's *Physics*, a commentary on Averroes' *Great Commentary* on the *De Anima*, and one on *Generation and Corruption*. The first two commentaries on the *Physics* and the two last commentaries were finished before 1471. The commentary on *Metaphysics* in Al-Ghazālī's *Intentions of the Philosophers* was completed in 1489. Of the commentary on the *Guide of the Perplexed* it seems that only Book I has been preserved.

It is very probable that these commentaries were the outcome of his teaching of philosophy over a period of some decades.

The second part of the fifteenth century also gave rise to several philosophers of some eminence. Let us first mention *Shem Tov ben Joseph ben Shem Tov*, son of Joseph and nephew of Isaac. This last-known scion of the family wrote a commentary on the *Guide of the Perplexed* which can be found in the classic editions. Another of his books, *Derashot ha-Torah* (*Sermons on the Torah*) appeared in Salonica in 1525. Great defender of Maimonides and of Aristotelian philosophy, he makes fun of Crescas and ridicules him.

Three other philosophers are important, although they are of unequal philosophical interest: Abraham Bibago, Isaac Arama and Abraham Shalom.

ABRAHAM BEN SHEM TOV BIBAGO

Abraham Bibago lived at Huesca, in Aragon. We know that in 1446 he had a wife and children. In 1470 he was head of a religious school at Saragossa. He died before 1489.

His education was not restricted to Hebrew texts, and he knew Arabic and Latin, comparing works in the different languages, and using the Gospels, Eusebius and Thomas Aquinas. Of his numerous writings many have disappeared, including the medical and astronomical works and some of the philosophical treatises.

The texts in existence are *Eẓ ha-Hayyim* (*The Tree of Life*) which deals with the creation of the world, letters to Moses Arondi, who lived at Huesca, most probably written after Bilbago had left the town; commentaries on Averroes' *Middle Commentaries* on the *Posterior Analytics* and on the *Metaphysics*, and some philosophical notes. A sermon on the first pericope of Genesis, and his principal work, *Derekh Emunah* (*The Way of Faith*), were printed in 1522.

Abraham Bibago's philosophy has recently been studied by A. Nuriel; his work has revealed the originality and the interest of Bibago, and it provides the basis for this discussion.

God is the existent in the absolute sense, and He gives existence to all existing things. This conception is that of Averroes, and also of Moses of Narbonne, and, like them, Bibago affirms that the plurality of existing things arises from the divine unity and that God moves the ultimate sphere directly without the need of a supplementary intellect as posited by Avicenna.

God has infinite attributes that are identical with His essence and do not involve multiplicity; they differ from human attributes as genus differs from species; they are positive, but man can only know them in a negative way; since the intellect, the intellectually cognizing subject and the intellectually cognized object are one in man, to know the divine attributes would mean that we might identify ourselves with God, which is absurd. To this is added the fact that for man to know means to apprehend the causes of existing things; however, God has no cause. Our knowledge of the divine attributes can thus only be negative. Here Bibago seems to be in agreement with

Maimonides, but the resemblance is only in the verbal expression. For Maimonides the only way leading to the knowledge of God is the multiplication of negation, while for Bibago God's attributes are negative if considered in relation to their own infinity. For God limits His Infinity by creating the finite world. The attributes of action[1] represent the limitation of the creation of God in as far as His infinity is confined to the boundaries of the finite creation.

This double relation between the infinite and the finite can only be known by man in a negative way, for he can only reach the meeting-point between the finite and the infinite and cannot penetrate further into divine knowledge.

God, knowing Himself, thereby knows all creation, but in a perfect way, and Bibago goes as far as to say that God knows all the actions and all the thoughts of men.

Among the attributes identical with the divine essence is Will, and only Will can explain the limitation that the infinite divine action undergoes in restricting itself within the limits of the finite. This divine Will maintains the world in existence, and it is found in all things, from the ripening grain of corn to the chicken emerging from the egg. Divine Will, however, does not destroy the laws of nature but is identified with them. The form of existing things is present in matter through the divine Will. If God, by His will, is present in the existence of existing material things and is that which gives them life, He is also the Form and Soul of the intelligible existing things, the separate intellects; He is the soul of the world of the angels, it is He who sets the sphere in motion and maintains its movement. He is the soul of the world and its measure; as the particular souls are superior to the bodies that they move, but do not on that account take less care of the corporeal details of the bodies that they move. God, although He is infinite, by His will moves the world and cares for it, confers on it being and maintains it in existence.

We find various divisions of the world in our author, and they are generally in conformity with the tripartite division of the Aristotelians; to the three worlds correspond the different names of God: the Name of seventy-two letters to the world of generation and corruption, the Name of forty-two letters to the world of the spheres, the Name of twelve letters to the world of separate intellects, and to God who is above all creation, the supreme Existing Being, the Tetragram.

However, in another place, Bibago speaks of a world where there is a gradual passage between absolute actuality, God, and absolute potentiality, matter.

The creation of the world is its emergence out of God; it seems that the world was in God in its perfect mode before creation, and Bibago appears to conceive creation as the emergence of the world, through the divine will, to a less perfect existence, outside God.

Since Maimonides, miracle had been associated with creation. Bibago

---

[1] See above, pp. 180ff.

undertakes to make the miracles fit into the schema of the four Aristotelian causes, that is, to understand them within a philosophical framework.

The material cause of a miracle is the object that is transformed; thus with the Nile water that turned to blood (one of the plagues of Egypt), the liquid was the material cause. But this object must in itself have the possibility of change. This eliminates the likelihood that the substance of the celestial bodies and the world of the angels might be perceived by men as being the object of miraculous manifestations. When in Joshua 10: 12 the sun stands still over Gibeon, the matter of the miracle was not the substance of the sun but its movement; it is thus possible that the movement of the sun should have been arrested, for movement can be slow or quick; but the matter of the miracle was not the substance of the sphere of the sun for this is not susceptible to change.

To explain the formal cause of miracle Bibago takes as an example the case of the rod that changed into a serpent; the formal cause being neither the rod nor the serpent but the substance of change of one form into another, for the causes of the change from rod to serpent were not naturally present in these forms.

To regard the prophet, as Ibn Ezra does, or the Active Intellect, as Gersonides, or else the astral influx as the immediate cause of a miracle is not acceptable, for the action of these agents is natural and irrevocably fixed, while miraculous action is voluntary and free. Here Bibago defines four kinds of phenomenon that one tends to confound:

(1) The prodigy (*pele*) is the change that occurs in the law of nature, and it reinforces the truth of the miracle, the sign, the proof.

(2) The miracle itself (*nes*) brings about the salvation of a man, of a community or of a people, by the instrument of divine providence.

(3) The sign (*'ot*) is a general thing that represents an exception to the laws of nature, while its particular signification is not immediately evident.

(4) The proof (*mofet*) is a sign of which the particular signification is clearly expressed.

All these supernatural phenomena have God as their causal agent; however, for the miracle (*nes*) the Prince of the World, the Active Intellect, is the intermediary agent; for the sign and the proof the prophet is the intermediary causal agent; while the prodigy is the direct act of God.

The final cause of miracles must be more exalted than the other causes, matter, form and agent; this is the true faith.

We thus see the appearance of the term 'faith' in a clearly Aristotelian system, and faith plays a large part in Bibago's work, a fact that differentiates him profoundly from philosophers who may seem close to him, like Moses of Narbonne.

Supreme felicity and the ultimate aim of man's existence is the imitation of God. Since man participates in two worlds, that of the intellect and that of matter, subject to generation and corruption, he must achieve full development and perfection in the two worlds. To wish that man should conjoin himself to the intellect alone is to wish that he should not be man; 'to go in the divine way' means perfection in bodily acts as in intellect.

This rehabilitation of act in Bibago's thought is supplemented by the rehabilitation of non-intellectual faith. Following Averroes, our author considers that the acquisition of the intelligibles is a disposition that disappears when it has reached its goal, making way for another disposition that is not subject to generation and corruption but is of the same kind as the world of the intellects. This second disposition, which according to Averroes cannot be acquired except by acquiring the intelligible notions, can then be actualized by the action of the Active Intellect. According to Bibago, at this second stage the soul is attracted by the Intellect (an attraction described by Ibn Ṭufayl in his *Hayy Ibn Yaqzan*) and this is the degree of prophecy. In using Ibn Ṭufayl's passage, Bibago gives this stage of the conjunction with the Intellect a mystical colouring that is not at all Averroistic. The conjunction with the Active Intellect is no longer, properly speaking, a natural and automatic phenomenon, for divine will should be added to human knowledge. Moreover, the conjunction with the Intellect is not identification; rather our author says, man preserves his individuality and the degrees of the conjunction with the Active Intellect are the degrees of prophecy. On the level of conjunction with the Intellect, sage and prophet are the same.

Bibago adds two specific characteristics to prophecy:

(1) The knowledge of things that the human intellect, left to its own forces, cannot attain;

(2) The foreseeing of future things.

The prophecy that has been described is that which is desired by man, for which he prepares himself and which he attains, if God so wishes; but there is another sort of prophecy: that which God places in the mouth of a man when He wishes to address Himself to the people. In this case, the prophet only transmits the divine word; he is the instrument of divine providence.

The eminence of the prophecy depends on the prophet, and, like Maimonides, Bibago links the perfection of the *Torah* with the perfection of Moses. Moses did not commit any fault, for his perfection is the ultimate degree of human perfection, and it is a guarantee that no more perfect law will come to abrogate that which he gave to the people of Israel.

In the same way as Bibago adds to the intellectual Maimonidean prophecy that given by God to a non-philosophical man, he also adds to the two kinds of providence defined by Maimonides, natural providence and that linked to the conjunction with the intellect, a third type of providence; that which takes special care of Israel.

Should one see in this a concession to popular mentality or to the misfortunes of the time? This does not seem to be the case, for the faith and the ontological status of the people of Israel, far from being added on as an afterthought, form an integral part of Bibago's system.

To understand the place occupied by the people of Israel in the economy of the human world, one must first see what our author means by 'faith'.

Mankind can only attain perfection if it achieves plenitude for the two parts of which it is composed: the body and the soul; these two perfections are equally necessary, and one cannot ignore this fact and pretend that man belongs only to the spiritual world. Divine providence therefore gave the *Torah* and the faith, which offer, without hardship and without difficulty (in contrast to science), the truths necessary to salvation.

Further, while the true faith guides the body and the spirit, the science of the intelligibles is restricted to the only part of man that is close to it, the intellect. Knowledge is not inferior to faith; it is more limited, but it also belongs to the superior world.

The ultimate aim of faith as of knowledge is the eternity of the soul, and this eternity is purely intelligible. The learned man and the believer will both attain conjunction with the intelligible and eternal world, and the difference between them is the road they respectively adopt.

Logicians use demonstration to prove a truth; the demonstration itself, truth once established, is no longer necessary to the logician. It is the same for the intelligible truths; whether one takes the road of knowledge or that of faith, the object is to reach the stage of truth. The two definitions of the faith are based on Thomas Aquinas, for whom the object of faith is not only what is above reason, but also what is known by the reason which faith knows in a different, more perfect, manner.

Bibago's own definition of faith is the following: intellectual acquisition conceived according to the truth on the basis of premises received from tradition. This faith is only acquired freely and voluntarily, for one cannot receive divine reward for the acquisition of knowledge that necessarily imposes itself on the reason. Faith is indissolubly linked to will and choice: thus the belief in the creation of the world, which cannot be proved, is faith. From this it follows that faith cannot be acquired by perception or by axiomatic intelligible data, or by experience, or by demonstrations based on natural premises, for these are the logically necessary foundation of knowledge, and knowledge imposes itself on man; he does not choose it. That the domain of faith is more restricted for the scholar than for the simple believer is obvious, for the scholar scientifically acquires a large part of the knowledge that the simple believer acquires by faith, but both are equal when they come to problems that human reason cannot resolve without divine assistance.

This brings us back to divine providence and to the part played by Israel in human economy.

Divine providence takes greater care of the people of Israel than of any other people because the people of Israel are 'intellect *in actu*', thanks to the perfect *Torah*. Particular providence takes more special care of the individual in proportion to the intellect that he has acquired, and the same applies to the people of Israel. Now, one could ask: are people, other than Israel, an intermediary species between mankind and the individual? In that case, it would be enough to belong to the people of Israel to enjoy particular providence. Bibago absolutely rejects this distinction between the peoples, which was made by Judah Halevi. There is only mankind and the individual.

If an individual is the particular object of divine providence, this is not because he is part of the people of Israel, but because he is an individual identifying himself with the essence of Israel, which has received the truths of the *Torah* and, because of its beliefs in these verities, is intellect *in actu*. The definition of a Jew is thus that of a man believing in a true faith, who has knowledge (literally of things) as a man and supplementary knowledge as believer in a true faith.

As a man, he has attained the knowledge that every man should acquire, since he is intellect, intelligent and intelligible, and he will thus resemble the world of the intelligibles. As a Jew, he must acquire the perfection of faith, study the *Torah* and believe what he should believe as a Jew. This second perfection is more particular than the first, but the individual form to which these two perfections contribute is that of the Jew and of the believing Israelite.

I will not follow Bibago in his very scholastic arguments demonstrating that the people of Israel, according to the definition given above, is on the level of substance, assuring it eternity, while the other peoples are on the level of accident. We may remark that Bibago's philosophy opens out onto historical perspectives. Israel plays the role of the intellect in mankind, in relation to the other faculties, which hate it and fight against it; thus Israel has been exiled three times, the first time in Egypt, which means the senses, the second in Babylon, which symbolizes the imagination, and a third time in Christianity, which symbolizes practical wisdom (*tevuna*); this wisdom is so eminent that its difference from the intellect is hardly discernible; this is why the exile will be prolonged until the imagination and the sophism that dominate at present finally disappear.

ISAAC BEN MOSES ARAMA

Isaac Arama (*ca.* 1420–94) was a rabbi in various communities of Aragon, then at Calatayud, where he wrote most of his works. His sermons were often the basis of his later compositions. He also participated in the public debates against Christian scholars. After the expulsion of 1492 he removed to Naples (where he met Isaac Abrabanel), and died there.

The best known of his works is *Akedat Yizhak* (*The Sacrifice of Isaac*), a collection of philosophical sermons and of allegorical commentaries that follow the order of the pericopes of the *Torah*. It is divided into 105 chapters (or porticos), each forming a sermon in 2 parts. In the first part the author examines a philosophical idea in the light of biblical and rabbinical texts; in the second, the scriptural commentary dominates, and the textual difficulties are resolved with the help of the philosophical idea expounded at the beginning. First printed in Salonica in 1522, the *Sacrifice of Isaac* has frequently been republished (at least twelve times). Apart from another polemical work, dealing with the relations between religion and philosophy, Isaac Arama wrote commentaries on the Song of Songs, Ruth, Lamentations, Ecclesiastes, Esther and Proverbs, the last being dedicated to the memory of his son-in-law. He may also have written a commentary on Aristotle's *Ethics*, which he often cites, but this is not certain.

In contrast to Abraham Shalom, who will be discussed shortly, Isaac Arama does not hesitate to criticize Maimonides. For him, the superiority of religious truth over human reason is never in doubt; our intellects receive the data of the senses, which are far from providing exact information about the world; similarly, our rational knowledge is limited and certain domains are entirely closed to it. Philosophers are incapable of answering difficult questions, such as how the diversity of creatures issued from the divine unity, if the world is eternal or created in time, if the celestial spheres have a soul or not, why some of them move from west to east and others in the opposite direction, and so on. It should not be supposed that one day these questions will be resolved by man; they cannot be, for they are beyond the realm of human reason, as Maimonides admitted concerning creation.

Philosophy makes one know the God of nature; it cannot teach man the mystery of the Last Day and of the supreme felicity. The Patriarch Abraham began by knowing God according to reason, and, like the philosophers, he only believed in what he could know. Thus, when he made his act of faith, 'He believed in the Lord; and he counted it to him for righteousness' (Genesis 15: 6), for to make an act of faith is a spiritual degree superior to that of rational knowledge. But Abraham had not yet reached perfect belief, simple belief, which is satisfied with the received tradition, asks no questions and imposes no conditions, for Abraham asks God: 'Lord God, whereby shall I know that I shall inherit it?' (Genesis 15: 8), and God says to him: 'Go before me and be thou perfect [*tamin* = simple, perfect]' (Genesis 17: 1).

Arama inveighs against the scholars of his time who wish to base faith on the intellect and on human reason, and prove religion by demonstration. There are decided contradictions between faith and reason and one cannot harmonize the two as Maimonides tried to do. This does not mean that the biblical text must be taken only in its literal sense. While faith is superior to reason, it does not contradict it but surpasses it, and some verses should be interpreted allegorically. In fact, this is what the rabbis of the Talmud constantly did, but the allegorization should not make one lose sight of the literal sense. Arama objects to the excessive allegorization of the biblical text practised by the philosophers. However, he takes fewer precautions with the *aggadot* and gives a philosophical interpretation of a large number of talmudic narratives that offend reason, with the evident apologetic intention of endowing the talmudical rabbis with a philosophical status that the Christian polemicists denied them.

Arama proposes six principles of faith: creation; divine omnipotence, that is, miracles; prophecy and the revelation of the *Torah*; providence; penitence; and the immortality of the soul.

These principles are not designed to define philosophical religion or divine religion in general, but the religion of Israel, in its difference from philosophy and from the other revealed religions. The principles complement philosophy, as faith is added to reason and contains it. The existence of God, His unity and His incorporeality are included in the *Torah*, but in spite of that, they are not principles.

One of the points that Arama stresses is divine omnipotence; God can suspend the laws of nature and perform miracles. In fact, there are two laws of nature: 'natural' nature, which obeys the laws of causality and bears witness to the First Cause; and supernatural nature, the visible or hidden miracles of which (the influence of Nahmanides is seen here) penetrate everyday life and bear witness to the biblical God, omnipotent and exercising His will.

If philosophers like Moses of Narbonne and Gersonides denied this supernatural nature, this was because they placed man below the level of the celestial spheres; but these spheres are only dead bodies, and man, thinking being, is the beginning and end of creation, and its master. In fact, according to Arama, man, when he is 'the image of God', has power over natural nature, for he has received from God the key of cosmic harmony, and he knows that 'the macrocosm and the microcosm are two cords that vibrate together with one sound'.

Human error, the lack of harmony in man, leads to cosmic disorder:

For there is a strong relation and a very powerful link between the actions performed by the classes of men, from the best to the worst, and the existing things, in general and in particular, to the point that one may believe that by the ordering and the rectitude of their actions in general the nature of existing things is maintained and is fortified. And when these actions become vile and degenerate, this nature is also debased and humiliated. This marvellous thing is due to the fact that the human edifice is like the edifice of the entire world: one is called microcosm and the other macrocosm, because of the relation that there is between the two, in general and in particular.

It is necessary therefore that there should be between the two a great correspondence which resembles that created by musicians between two instruments of music altogether alike and tuned to the same note, for when a string vibrates in one of them, the voice of the second instrument is awakened because of the relation between the two ... The construction of the universe is like the first of the instruments and it has an order and structure fixed in all its celestial and terrestrial parts, and, thanks to them, life in the world is maintained in its wholeness.

Facing this order and this structure, and similar to them, are the strings of the second instrument, the microcosm, which vibrates in unison with the first. And when the second instrument is well tuned and its strings are disposed as they should be, in relation with the mystery of existence, its nature, its general and particular plan, then when one makes them vibrate, their sound awakens the harmony of the universe and causes to vibrate the strings of the macrocosm and the two instruments vibrate in unison, that which acts and that which is acted on, so that the existence of everything that exists and its mode of being should be perfect, in the most complete manner that there may be.

(The Philosophy of Isaac Arama, pp. 130–1)

The power that Arama ascribes, to God as to man, of using the laws of 'supernatural' nature and of performing miracles, does not prevent our author from giving a rational explanation of most of the biblical miracles. Supernatural law perfects nature, and does not destroy it. Man also is free to do good or evil, and the divine omniscience is not affected by this. Nevertheless, this does not mean that God justifies man by free grace, for such a grace would deny the power that man has over his own destiny, and therefore his free will.

The path that Arama strives to follow between philosophy and faith is narrow and difficult, for our author does not sacrifice one or the other. This is clearly seen in his treatment of the Law of Moses: it is the natural law of the philosophers, it is identical with the moral and intellectual virtues, but it is also the way that leads towards other virtues unknown to philosophers, and it alone bestows true felicity, that which is the supreme human good – a life turned towards God: through the accomplishment of religious acts that make the soul climb the degrees of the fear of God, of faith, of love, of the cult, and assure it survival in the next world.

From the purely philosophical point of view Arama is hardly original; however, his sermons had a great influence on later generations and were held in esteem by Christian theologians. This is easily comprehensible: Arama gave an image of God, the world and of Israel, that was entirely human and also faithful to Israel's specificity.

ABRAHAM BEN ISAAC SHALOM

Abraham Shalom lived in Catalonia during the fifteenth century and died in 1492. He translated the *Philosophia Pauperum* attributed to Albertus Magnus and Marsilius of Inghem's *Questions* concerning Aristotle's *Organon* from Latin into Hebrew.

Abraham Shalom's *Neveh Shalom* (*Dwelling of Peace*) is divided into thirteen books, a clear allusion to Maimonides' Thirteen Principles. Each book consists of chapters, varying in number, which are in fact homilies examining various philosophical problems: the creation of the world; the existence of God; His unity and His incorporeality; the other divine attributes – knowledge of particulars and divine providence; the intellect and its survival after death; the *Torah* and its eminence, various divine commandments, sacrifice and prayers; and so on. Apart from the fact that the work is not systematic, the author often returns to the same subjects for further discussion. In his introduction he explains that his work has two aims:

(1) To demonstrate to Jews influenced by 'Greek' ideas that the *aggadot* of the Talmud contain profound wisdom, when they are correctly interpreted.

(2) To survey the philosophical opinions of his predecessors in order to decide which are consistent with the *Torah* and which are not.

In practice, Abraham Shalom also gives an exegesis of numerous biblical verses, and the *aggadot* that he explicates are all taken from the first tractate of the Talmud, *Berakhot*.

In his philosophical interpretations, Abraham Shalom begins by presenting the views of Maimonides, Gersonides and Crescas, and although he avows a high degree of esteem for the two latter, he generally adopts the ideas of Maimonides, which he defends against his two opponents. Thus, he accepts the proof of the existence of God founded on the eternity of movement, although he affirms that God has created the world by His will, *ex nihilo*. Nevertheless, in this following Maimonides, he admits that creation by will on the basis of a pre-existing matter is not inconceivable, and can be brought into agreement with religion.

However, it is sometimes difficult to reconcile Maimonides with orthodox religious ideas, such as those regarding providence and its relation to the intellect. Abraham Shalom agrees with the Jewish tradition and Crescas that divine providence is especially attached to Israel and that this providence differs from that which is concerned with mankind as a whole. In this case Abraham Shalom almost displays bad faith, for he does not say that Maimonides is wrong, but he interprets the word *sekhel*, 'intellect', as meaning 'knowledge, actions, or the two together'.

Even in the passages discussing the principles of Judaism his thought is not very coherent and he sometimes gives a list of four dogmas, once of five and sometimes uses the term 'principle' in a looser sense.

In fact, H. Davidson is most probably right when he says that Abraham Shalom, whose philosophical culture is displayed on every page of his lengthy work, was not really interested in philosophical questions. Profoundly convinced of the doctrines of the Jewish religion on the one hand and the truth of the Maimonidean positions on the other, he endeavoured to communicate his certitudes in the philosophical style of the period.

ISAAC ABRABANEL

With Isaac Abrabanel we leave Spain and almost the Middle Ages. I shall still speak briefly of Jewish fifteenth-century philosophers in Yemen, in North Africa, Greece and Turkey, and especially in Italy, where Jewish scholars often found asylum and participated in the great movement of the Renaissance. But 1492, the date of the Expulsion of the Jews from Spain, marked the end of an epoch.

It has been said of Isaac Abrabanel that he is the last of the medieval Jewish philosophers of Spain and the first of the humanists. This judgement is exemplified by his life as well as by his works, for, if he was a man of the Renaissance, he was also a medieval philosopher who again took up all the themes that I have already presented.

Born in Lisbon in 1437 of a family of merchants and courtiers, he received a careful education, which included the sciences as well as Jewish subjects, classical texts and Christian theology. At the age of twenty-five he had already composed a treatise on providence and prophecy, and was giving public lessons on Deuteronomy in the synagogue.

Like his father Judah he was the treasurer of Alfonso V of Portugal, and was head of a flourishing business. Accused of conspiracy by Joan II, who come to power in 1481, he fled in 1483 and a year later entered the service of Ferdinand and Isabella of Castile.

In 1492, he attempted unsuccessfully to obtain the revocation of the Edict of Expulsion. On 31 May of that year he sailed for Naples, where in 1493 he entered on functions similar to those he had performed in Castile, at the court of Ferrante I, King of Naples. He remained at this court until 1495 and then, settling at Venice in 1503, he participated in diplomatic negotiations between the Venetian Senate and the kingdom of Portugal. Most of his works were committed to writing during the sixteen years of his sojourn in Italy, where he died in 1509.

His works, both philosophical and exegetical, are abundant.

(1) Commentaries on the whole of the Pentateuch, on the early Prophets – Joshua, Judges, Samuel and Kings – and the later Prophets – Isaiah, Jeremiah and Ezekiel – and the twelve minor prophets.

(2) Commentaries on the *Haggadah* and *Pirkei Avot*.

(3) Three works of messianic tendency, including a commentary on Daniel.

(4) A commentary on the *Guide of the Perplexed*, as well as answers to questions on the subject of the *Guide* and a short treatise on the composition of this book.

(5) Various works discussing philosophical or theological questions:

– A youthful work, *Ateret Zekenim* (*The Crown of the Ancients*), which deals with prophecy and providence;

– *Shamayim Hadashim* (*New Skies*), on the creation of the world;

– *Mifalot Elohim* (*The Works of God*), also on the creation of the world;

– *Rosh Amanah* (*The Principle of Faith*), on the principles or dogmas of the Jewish religion;

– A short work on the *Form of the Elements: Tsurat ha-yesodot*;

Two other works, announced by Abrabanel in a letter to Saul Ha-Cohen of Candia in 1507, one on divine justice and the other on prophecy, have not been preserved and were perhaps not finished.

All Abrabanel's works were printed, most of them in the sixteenth century.

Abrabanel maintained an intense and ambivalent attitude towards Maimonides; he does not write a page without citing him with immoderate respect, and without criticizing him with acerbity. His three principal subjects of meditation were the creation of the world, prophecy and the principles of Judaism. On these three points he is often in accord with the letter of Maimonides' text, and in disagreement with Maimonides' thought; he is then obliged to rehabilitate the literal text whenever this is possible or to refute it word by word and phrase by phrase. His philosophical writing may be considered as an extremely precise commentary on the work of Maimonides (his original ideas are to be found in his biblical commentaries) and he most probably considered his commentary on the *Guide of the Perplexed* as his chief work.

For Abrabanel, the creation of the world *ex nihilo* is the only hypothesis that religion accepts, even if it cannot be philosophically demonstrated. Opposing Gersonides, he affirms that a pre-existing and unformed matter cannot be admitted because of the correlation necessary between matter and form; arguing against Crescas, he remarks that the idea of a necessary will on the part of God destroys the very concept of will. As regards the question of the exact moment when the act of creation is supposed to have taken place, he tries to resolve it by the idea that God creates innumerable worlds and destroys them after a certain time.

Prophecy is what Maimonides describes in the first opinion he gives on the subject, that attributed to the simple and the ignorant: God chooses whom he wishes among men in order to make him His prophet, provided that he be of pure morals and pious heart. Prophecy is a divine knowledge that God causes to descend on the prophet, an essential and detailed knowledge, through or without an intermediary; if the intellect receives this knowledge, the prophet's words will be clear and explicit; if it is the imagination, they will be expressed in images and allegories. As for the difference between the sage and the prophet, one finds it in the different influx that each receives. The prophet receives an influx incomparably more abundant and more eminent. Thus, superabundance of divine emanation also allows one to distinguish the prophetic from the premonitory dream. The prophetic images impose themselves on the imagination by their power and intensity.

A supernatural phenomenon that corrects the natural failings of the prophet, his imagination and his intellect, prophecy can only reside in a man whose soul is constantly turned towards God. This can only happen in a free nation living in its land, the Land of Israel, and never when the Jew, overwhelmed by calamities, is dependent on the good will of gentile kings. In his book, *The Principle of Faith*, Abrabanel sets out to defend Maimonides' Thirteen Principles, and this he does in the first twenty-two chapters.

However, in the two last chapters, he declares that since the Law of Moses is a supernatural law, no principle is more important than another; everything is equally important and must be accepted by the believer. Why did Maimonides choose to single out these Thirteen Principles? It was, declares Abrabanel, because he wished to make it easier for the vulgar to understand the principles; besides, are not these Thirteen Principles part of the *Mishneh Torah*, which is not destined for philosophers but for the simple faithful?

While Abrabanel as a philosopher is not remarkable for originality but rather for depth and erudition, he holds particularly interesting opinions concerning politics and history.

For Maimonides, the prophet–philosopher promulgated a law that in the case of the *Torah* was the only divine Law, because Moses was closest to the Active Intellect and attained the highest degree of the human spirit.

For Abrabanel prophecy is a supernatural phenomenon and the Law a divine Law that is very much connected with the natural phenomena and the events of the human history in which we live.

There are therefore two histories: human and natural, and divine and supernatural, and at the meeting-place of the two is biblical history, where God's intervention took place.

The Messiah is not the conquering king who will re-establish the independence of the Jewish people and restore it to its land by means of its military virtues, as he was for Maimonides, but a man inspired by God, whose miracles will be manifested in a context of war, revolution, and the end of the world.

So far there is nothing here that had not been said, more or less, in the trend of thought that began with Judah Halevi. But Abrabanel adds another theme, deriving from Seneca, which considers the whole of human civilization as we see it something 'artificial' and 'superfluous'.

Human history, 'natural' history, in fact is not so at all; it is 'artificial', for true 'nature' is miraculous in essence. The life of Israel in the desert, where everything depended on the divine generosity, is analogous to the 'natural' life, that of Adam before the Fall. Adam's sin overthrew the whole order of nature; civilization, with its cities and governments, is a rebellion against God; the only 'natural' life is that of free and equal men, leading a rural existence. The different languages and the different nations are also the outcome of man's rebellion. When Abrabanel discusses the best form of government possible in our civilization, it is in the context of this false life, and the question is rather of the least bad government, for all are fundamentally bad; only the Messianic reign will re-establish 'natural' human life.

But our author was a statesman, and he could not help being interested in the government of men as it existed at his time. Discussing two biblical passages (Deuteronomy 17: 14 and 1 Samuel 8: 6), he refutes the philosophical arguments that would make monarchy the best possible government; these arguments were based on the principle of hierarchy, essential principle of all medieval thought: the king is to the nation what the heart is to the body and the First Cause to the universe. Only monarchy, it was said, assures the three conditions of the good functioning of society; unit, continuity and absolute power. According to our author, society can be maintained and subsist with other governments as well. Unity can be achieved through the unanimous will of several persons far better than by the irresponsible will of one man; continuity may result from the government of successive leaders, if they know that they must give an account of themselves. As for absolute power, Abrabanel sees no necessity for this. Besides, collective government is that advocated by the *Torah*. After various theoretical arguments, Abrabanel comes to actual experience. Government by elected judges, as it is seen in the Italian cities, Venice, Florence, Genoa, and so on, is greatly superior to monarchy; and we know that Abrabanel had experienced both kinds of rule. Nevertheless, he remained respectful towards established power; in a monarchical state, absolute obedience is owed to the king.

For Israel the true guide is God, who preserves it with His particular providence; a king is thus not necessary to it, and experience has shown that the kings were disastrous and the judges, on the contrary, always faithful; its best government therefore is that of an élite of judges letting themselves be guided by the will of God. The Messiah will not be a king in the proper sense of the word, but a judge and a prophet. Abrabanel interprets the passage in Deuteronomy (17: 14), following Abraham Ibn Ezra, as a simple concession, a permission given by God to Israel to elect a king. The expression, like the idea, recalls a postil by Nicholas of Lyre, belonging to an anti-monarchical current fairly widespread in Christian tradition, while the monarchical idea was generally preferred in the Jewish. Other details of temporal (human) government and spiritual (that of God) are borrowed from other Christian authors. Thus, while he remains very medieval in his philosophical and religious conceptions, in his political ideas Abrabanel is clearly a man of the Renaissance.

The last philosophers in North Africa, Provence and Turkey

While the Spanish philosophers strove to perpetuate their tradition by preserving both Judaism and what remained of medieval philosophy, the Jews living around the Mediterranean also tried, with considerable difficulty, to keep their philosophical culture alive.

This soon descended to a scholastic level, where logic predominated. The domain of philosophy was considerably reduced, almost of its own accord. Metaphysics, the noblest science, no longer inspired the confidence and respect that it had enjoyed during the thirteenth and fourteenth centuries; it was no longer believed that it was possible to attain the total truth through the acquisition of philosophy. The sciences had become detached from the

philosophical corpus and medicine, in particular, was taught after comparatively restricted preliminary studies.

Logic, instrument of the sciences, remained an honoured discipline throughout the fifteenth century. In North Africa, at Oran, *Samuel ben Saadiah Ibn
Danan*, born in Granada, wrote a commentary on Maimonides' *Logical
Vocabulary. Moses ben Shem Tov Ibn Habib*, who was born in Lisbon and
lived in the South of Italy, also wrote a commentary on the same work.

Provence, hardly at all represented on the philosophical level in the second
half of the fourteenth century, saw a passing revival thanks to the teaching
of *Salomon ben Menahem Prat Maimon*. Nothing seems to have been preserved of his works, but his pupils committed to writing certain commentaries
based on his teaching. They include:

– Jacob ben Hayyim, the earliest, also called Comprat Vidal Ferussol, who
gave to his commentary on the *Kuzari* the name *Beit Yaakov* (*The House of
Jacob*), and finished it in 1422, at the age of seventeen.

– Nethanel ben Nehemiah Caspi (Bonsenior Macif of Largentière) concluded his commentary in 1424. He also wrote a commentary on the *Ruah
Hen* (*Spirit of Grace*) and on the *Eight Chapters* of Maimonides, as well, it
seems, as notes on the *Torah*.

– Solomon ben Judah (Solomon Vivas of Lunel) also composed a commentary on the *Kuzari*, when he was thirteen years old.

All these commentaries resemble each other and are evidently academic
exercises giving a good idea of the level of Prat Maimon's teaching in Provence in the 1420s. The choice of texts: the *Eight Chapters* (ethics), the
Spirit of Grace (a little introduction to the natural sciences), the *Kuzari* (the
divine knowledge exalting Israel above the other nations), is still valid for
beginners in Jewish philosophy.

Abraham Farissol (*ca.* 1452–1528), born at Avignon, lived in the north of
Italy and especially at Ferrara. He was the most celebrated scribe of the
Renaissance. His own works include philosophical commentaries on Job,
Ecclesiastes and *Pirkei Avot*, and also a polemical book directed against the
Christians, *Magen Avraham* (*The Shield of Abraham*). Farissol often returns
to the same philosophical problems; the question of God's ability to know
particulars; His providence extending to every individual being; and the
destiny of the soul in the world to come. It is striking to find how far a man
so well launched in the erudite circles of the Renaissance remained a man
of the Middle Ages.

In Turkey we find a higher level of philosophical teaching. *Mordecai ben
Eliezer Comtino* (1420 – before 1483) was a teacher of influential personality.
Apart from works on mathematics and astronomy he wrote commentaries
on Maimonides' *Vocabulary of Logic*, on several books by Abraham Ibn
Ezra, on Aristotle's *Metaphysics*, and the Pentateuch. He was especially
known for his tolerance and his humanism; he taught Rabbanites and
Karaites without distinction and considered that his duty lay in propagating

an indispensable general culture without which the religious texts could not be understood.

One must admit that all these philosophers waged a difficult battle; medieval philosophy no longer satisfied contemporary demands, and the spiritual void was to be filled in the sixteenth century by the Kabbalah.

A new philosophy arose in Italy, that of the Renaissance, but before discussing it, I must mention developments in Yemen.

Jewish thought in Yemen

The fourteenth and fifteenth centuries saw a sort of renaissance of philosophical thought in Yemen; more precisely, one may say that this period was one of great intellectual activity and that philosophy was cultivated like other domains of Jewish thought. The philosophical tradition had been known in Yemen since the twelfth century when Nethanel ben al-Fayyumi wrote his *Bustān al-'Uqūl*. Yemenite philosophy is essentially Maimonidean; the Andalusian philosopher was truly the undisputed authority, from the point of view of the *halakhah* as well as that of science. In the biblical commentary *Nūr al-Ẓalām* (*The Light Lighting the Darkness*) written in 1329 by *Nethanel ben Isaiah*, the Maimonidean citations (except for the very long ones) show that the text was known by heart as was the Bible.

However, Maimonides was interpreted not in the light of Averroes, who was unknown in the Eastern tradition, but in the light of midrashic texts and the writings of Eastern Arab authors, in particular Neoplatonists, who were sometimes copied in Arabic characters.

One interesting characteristic of this Yemenite milieu was the use of Arabic as the language of culture, for biblical and halakhic commentaries, philosophy and even poetry. This partly explains why we do not know this literature well. The great Jewish authors who wrote in Arabic were translated into Hebrew in the twelfth and thirteenth centuries, and afterwards, except for a few exceptions, the learned tongue was Hebrew. Even now, the original works in Arabic are less easily accessible to students of Jewish tradition than works in Hebrew. The Yemenite tradition was rediscovered by the West at the end of the nineteenth century and manuscripts emanating from Yemen have contributed an abundant harvest of texts believed lost, in particular in the area of the *Midrash*. Several contemporary scholars have already given us some notion of the richness of Yemenite Jewish philosophy.

In the 1320s, a controversy arose among the learned men of Yemen concerning the allegorical exegesis of the Bible. An unknown author of Sa'dah composed an allegorical biblical commentary called *Kitāb al-Ḥāqā'iq* (*The Book of Truths*). The audacity of his allegories offended the sages of San'a, including Nethanel ben Isaiah, who has already been mentioned. The citizens of Sa'dah took up the defence of their colleague, and composed a defence of biblical allegory in ten points.

Their arguments were based on the antiquity of the allegorical method, which one already finds in the *Midrash*, and on citations from Maimonides, reinforced by the authority of Al-Ghazālī. The adversaries of the allegorical method did in fact admit it, but only for certain parts of the Bible, the Story of Genesis and the Story of the Chariot, while its supporters extended it to the entire biblical text.

Notwithstanding this controversy, the trend of Yemenite philosophy was to harmonize and not, as was often the case in Europe, to oppose philosophy and religion (the absence of Averroes' influence is significant in this context).

A particularly remarkable example of this harmonizing thought is contained in the work of a fifteenth-century scholar who is now quite well known, thanks to D. R. Blumenthal, who has edited two of his major compositions.

HOTER BEN SOLOMON

Hoter, also called Mansour Ibn Suleiman al-Dhamārī, wrote a long series of works. The following have been preserved:
- A commentary on the *Torah, Sirāj al-'Ukūl*;
- A super-commentary on Maimonides' commentary on the *Mishnah*;
- Two collections of *Questions and Answers*, in two versions, one containing seventy questions and answers and the other one hundred. Of these, twenty-eight are direct questions dealing with various philosophical issues and seventy-two deal with the harmonization of Hoter's philosophy with various biblical, rabbinic and Maimonidean texts.
- The *Commentary on Maimonides' Thirteen Principles*.

Other works that the author himself mentions do not seem to have been preserved. The only date available is that given by Hoter in the first version of the *Questions and Answers*, that of 1423.

Hoter's Jewish sources include, apart from the traditional literature, numerous *midrashim*, the *Midrash Haggadol*, which took its final form about 1350 and the *Midrash al-Ṣiyānī* (1422), and also the mystical *midrashim* that Maimonides did not consider as part of the tradition; the works of Saadiah Gaon; the poems of Judah Halevi and of Abraham Ibn Ezra; and also works composed by Yemenite scholars such as the *Nur-al-Zalam* (cited earlier), the works of Zechariah ha-Rofe (about 1430) and probably others, anonymously cited. The Arabic sources are also diverse and include philosophy and literature. In his commentary on the *Torah* he cites Muhammad twice and follows his name with the formula 'may God bless him and give him peace'.

Hoter's philosophy is based on three currents of thought: Maimonides, Neoplatonism, represented by the *Encyclopedia of the Sincere Brothers* (*Ikhwān al-Ṣāfā*), and Aristotelianism, with Al-Ghazālī and Avicenna. His cosmology unites Aristotelian and neoplatonic features, and its complexity is due to this synthesis of discordant elements. D. Blumenthal sums up:

From God, there emanated, *ex-nihilo* and from His free Will, the [Universal] Intellect. In it, are all the ideas and, from it, went forth the command 'Be', and the universe came into being as follows: The Ten Intelligences emanated from the Intellect, the last of them being the Agent Intelligence. From it, emanated the Universal Soul. From it, there proceeded three emanations each of which continued into reality: the First Prime Matter, Nature, and the particular souls. The Universal Soul in-formed the First Prime Matter directly with various species-forms to generate the various kinds of celestial matter. It also gave those bodies souls particular to them (and they received particular intellects directly from the Intelligences). From the lunar sphere (the last in the sequence), the Second Prime Matter emanated. It was in-formed by Nature – i.e., the four qualities of dryness, wetness, hotness, and coldness – to generate the four elements. The four elements were further combined and in-formed by Nature to generate the compounded beings. The living compounded beings received particular souls directly from the Universal Soul and the rational beings (men) received particular intellects directly from the Agent Intelligence.

(D. R. Blumenthal, *The Commentary of R. Ḥōṭer ben Shelōmō*, pp. 21–2)

Given this alliance between Neoplatonism and Aristotelianism, the problem of the existence of ideas will not be a simple one; according to our author, the ideas that give form to matter indeed have an extra-mental existence, but those produced by intellectual analysis have only a mental existence.

The problem of perception is resolved in the context of a meditation on a passage of the *Guide of the Perplexed* (I, 73, p. 209): 'The action of the intellect is not like the action of the imagination but its opposite . . .'

R. Ḥōṭer's theory of perception, then, is: (1) In every object, there is a 'trace of the intellect' (also called 'the idea of the object' and the 'form' of the object). (2) This 'trace' is perceived by the innermost vision of the soul but not alone, for the intellect (which contains within it all forms) must represent the 'trace' in corporeal form to the soul. (3) The intellect does so represent the 'trace' (or 'idea' or 'form') to the rational soul. (This process is called 'corporealization' or 'rationalization'.) (4) Meanwhile, the senses have perceived the physical form of the object, have passed that perception on to the imaginative faculty of the soul which, in turn, has abstracted that perception and passed it on to the rational soul. (5) The rational soul, then, proceeds to coordinate the two perceptions now within it – the one from the intellect and the one from the senses – imagination. This it does by corporealizing the former even further into 'natural characteristics'. (6) These 'natural characteristics' are identified with the abstracted results of the senses-imagination ('re-enter the soul in another shape'). (7) This whole process is set in motion when the rational soul, which is incomplete by essence and only acquires perfection, 'wishes to know from', '[seeks] perfection from', or 'unites with' the intellect which, being complete in itself, would not otherwise be jarred into action.

(*Ibid.* p. 29)

Hoter also says that reality has four levels of inwardness: writing, the word, the idea and the talking of the soul to itself.

The rational soul is one of the forms of the intellect; it perceives *in actu* according to the process that has been described above, and it has no knowledge except in potentiality. The intellect on the contrary is always *in actu*. The rational soul, by the re-acquisition of the perfection that was its own before it was exiled to this world, can rejoin the world of the Intellects and come closer to the Active Intellect. The soul is then clad in resplendent light; it becomes virtuous, knowing, pure and refined, no dissatisfaction comes to mar its joy and it is conjoined in the Intellect.

It is remarkable that Hoter ben Solomon, who did not know Averroes, should have arrived at the concept of the conjunction with the Intellect that in European Jewish philosophy was unequivocally associated with Averroes. For Hoter, Moses attained intimacy with the Universal Soul: when Moses' rational soul attained perfection and the link with the Active Intellect was consolidated, then his soul was joined to the Universal Soul and his intellect was conjoined with the Active Intellect, and it was then that the supernatural perfections and brilliant lights that are called the *Torah* emanated over him.

This difference between the rational soul and the intellect is perpetuated after death. Human intellect seems to identify itself with the Intellect. Perfect rational souls become angels and join the world of the souls of the spheres, and finally the Universal Soul. For Hoter ben Solomon it seems indeed that the Garden of Eden was the Universal Soul, which is a world of continuity, of existence without end, of pleasure, of divine presence. The souls of men without any knowledge rejoin the world of animal souls. The souls of men who have had knowledge and have used it for evil ends shall be punished eternally.

Our author's philosophical mysticism sometimes recalls that of Shemariah of Crete, whose works were in fact known and copied in Yemen.

Jewish philosophers in Italy of the Quattrocento

While in Spain Jewish thinkers were on the defensive, and built barriers around the *Torah*, Italian scholars were open to the new ways of thought that were loosening the rigid institutions of the Middle Ages and creating the modern world.

Two features are particularly important in this context. First, the fact that these Jewish thinkers can no longer be understood in the limited context of Jewish philosophy; they are part of the Renaissance of the Quattrocento, for profound resemblances, literary sources and personal relations united them effectively with Christian scholars and Christian society in general.

Secondly, one can no longer describe them like the medieval philosophers. Up to this moment, the ideas rather than the men were important. Often we know nothing of the authors whose works we have analysed, but their systems of thought survived, and this was the essential. It is very different with the authors of the Renaissance; they are rarely systematic, and ideas that at first sight appear contradictory may coexist in their works. Their conceptual instruments are medieval and one looks in vain for a new idea in the works of these fifteenth- and sixteenth-century writers. What is essentially new is their way of using the words and ideas inherited from the Middle Ages. The dislocation of the medieval Aristotelian world was at first felt as a loss of equilibrium on which nothing further could be built. Former notions could not be accepted as they stood, and the earth was beginning to turn, although not yet around the sun. The need of the absolute, in this world falling into tatters, was often manifested by an intense and aggressive religiosity. The era of the Reformation was approaching, of the wars of religion, of witches. For the Jews, it was also to be the epoch of the Kabbalah of Safed, which left explicit traces on Jewish culture, the epoch of the *Shulhan Arukh* of Joseph Caro, which determined the practice of the commandments in a rigid system from which the *halakhah* has not yet freed itself. This was to be the time of Shabbetai Zevi, who threw the Jewish world into confusion and whose adventure ended in disaster.

We are far from the ordered world of the Middle Ages and from the harmonious system of the celestial spheres animated by an eternal movement. Was the thought of the Renaissance philosophical? In any case, it was a philosophy very different from the medieval, although it preserved a number of its characteristics.

Several circles of Jewish thinkers existed in fifteenth-century Italy. First, those whom we may call the traditionalists: such as Judah ben Yehiel Messer Leon and his son David; then the Neoplatonists, who were predominantly Kabbalists, like Johanan Alemanno, but also philosophers like Judah Abrabanel, also called Leo Hebraeus; and, more isolated, Elijah Delmedigo, follower of Averroes.

All these Jewish thinkers read Latin and Italian, and most of them wrote in these two languages. In 1409 the Faculty of Arts (philosophy, astronomy, medicine) of the University of Padua opened its doors to Jews, and, in a letter to David ben Judah Messer Leon on the subject of the sciences, written in 1490 in Italy, Jacob ben David Provençal complained bitterly that young Jews were studying the sciences under Christian masters, for these, being supported by the kings or the municipalities, demanded only a nominal fee.

Judah ben Yehiel Messer Leon (d. 1498) is a good example of a philosopher who is still a scholastic but already belongs to the Renaissance. His numerous works include commentaries on Aristotle, which have not all survived, studies on logic, and especially a commentary on the *Vetus Logica*, that is, the *Isagogus* of Porphyrius and the beginning of Aristotle's *Logic* (this is the only one of Messer Leon's works to have been published), a biblical commentary, a commentary on the *Guide of the Perplexed*, poetry, letters, and so on. His Jewish traditional culture was comprehensive, as was also his knowledge of philosophical texts in Hebrew. He was also well versed in Latin literature and he corrected the Hebrew translation of Aristotle's *Logic* on the basis of the Latin translation. He also composed a work on medicine in Latin, and he cites contemporary Christian logicians.

His son, *David ben Judah Messer Leon*, was born *ca.* 1460 at Venice and afterwards lived at Bologna, Padua and Naples; he left Italy for Salonica in 1508 and died in Albania *ca.* 1530.

Of his numerous grammatical, philosophical, poetical and musical compositions little remains. Only one work, *Tehilah le David* (*Praise to David*), was printed, at Constantinople by the author's grandson; other works are still in manuscript: *Magen David* (*The Shield of David*); a commentary on the *Guide of the Perplexed*; another on Lamentations; an *In Praise of Women*, and various compositions, *responsa* and letters. I shall discuss later a question on the study of the sciences that Jacob Provençal answered in 1490.

David Messer Leon's philosophy is close to that of contemporary Spanish philosophers; like them, he affirms that the existence of God is not demonstrable by philosophy, but must be conceived as an act of faith, supported by tradition. The philosophical method only supplements this fundamental intention.

The three worlds, that here below, that of the spheres and that of the intellects, are hierarchically disposed in order of spirituality and are placed below God, who is the fourth world.

The ten Kabbalistic *sefiroth* are seen by David Messer Leon as the content of the divine thought. God is thus at the same time the supreme world in the chain of existing things and the creator of the world; He is outside the world but, also, He is in the world as creator, First Mover and universal and particular providence.

From the two superior worlds, the divine world and the world of the intellects, issue respectively the souls of the people of Israel and those of other men. The *Torah* is therefore the way that leads to eternal life; it is also truth, the only divine law and the only tradition that transmits divine revelation. In his discussion of divine law, David Messer Leon tries to reconcile philosophy and Kabbalah; the exterior aspect of the *Torah* is the revelation on Mount Sinai, the hidden aspect is the divine Wisdom, which God took as a model in the work of Creation. It is through study of the exterior *Torah* and of the Talmud that one can, under the veil of the parables and the images, have glimpses of the hidden *Torah*; in this study, philosophy is a necessary intellectual tool; it sharpens the intellect and makes it pass from potentiality to actuality. However, it is faith that conducts the believer to the spiritual level where he will be able to conceive the divine Law.

It can be seen that David Messer Leon used the medieval Jewish and Arab philosophers, but also Thomas Aquinas and the Kabbalah. Philosophy is only one of the components of his thought.

Jewish philosophers in Italy

ELIJAH BEN MOSES ABBA DELMEDIGO

Elijah Delmedigo (*ca.* 1460–93) was one of the most influential of the erudite Jews of the Renaissance. He gave public lessons in philosophy at Padua and perhaps other Italian towns. Among his Christian pupils the best known is Pico della Mirandola. His works, in Hebrew and Latin, were essentially super-commentaries or reflections on Averroes' *Commentaries* on the Aristotelian corpus. His Latin translations are also from the works of Averroes and his philosophy of religion was strongly influenced by the Arab philosopher.

Apart from his scientific works, his letters are of interest, for Elijah Delmedigo, like all men of the Renaissance, carried on an erudite correspondence with his humanist colleagues and pupils.

His *Behinat ha-Dat* (*Examination of Religion*), written at Candia in 1490, is especially important, for it returns to the theme of the double truth of which I have spoken in discussing Albalag. Further, the fact that this work was found in Spinoza's library gives it a place in the history of modern philosophy. In this short treatise Elijah treats the problem of the relations between philosophy and religion, basing himself on Averroes' *Decisive Treatise*. Science is a true knowledge, demonstrated by the method of demonstration; the *Torah* is a religious law and the principles underlying it are different and properly speaking religious. The philosopher who believes in the *Torah*, like the simple believer, has to accept a number of religious principles that cannot be demonstrated by philosophy: the existence of prophecy, of reward and punishment, and the possibility of miracles. The other principles of the *Torah* may or may not be subjected to scientific examination, but they do not contradict scientific truth. Philosophers should ask themselves questions and study the *Torah*; but the simple believer should not do this; and the philosopher is very wrong in troubling the simple man by making him doubt his faith. For instance, anthropomorphism: to think that God has a body, as do most people, is in no way to contradict the *Torah*; and if it is contrary to philosophy, this is not of the slightest importance to the simple believer, who need know nothing of the philosophical domain, for this would only disturb him. Averroes said the same thing; but in Jewish philosophy since Maimonides the principle of the divine incorporeality was considered as the basis of the true opinions that all Israel, simple believer or philosopher, must accept. For Elijah, apart from the principles that he mentioned earlier, the two truths, faith and philosophy, do not coincide, not even on the level of the definition of God. In fact, the aim of the *Torah* is political: to guide men towards the truth, each according to his capabilities. But since not all men can attain intellectual good, the most important purpose is to organize a 'good' society, where the philosopher may, without impediment, achieve the true 'good'. For this, it is necessary that all should accomplish the *Torah*, the best of political laws; to trouble the people with intellectual explications is the greatest error possible.

Elijah also violently attacked the Kabbalists, who claimed that their tradition went back to Simeon bar Yoḥai, while in fact the *Zohar* had only appeared 300 years before, as well as the philosophers who deprived the biblical texts of their literal sense, explaining them by philosophical notions. The biblical text should be understood in its literal sense, except when, from the internal point of view, there is a contradiction between the verses – in such a case the exegesis must remain within the limits of the revealed text; one should not explicate the Bible by another system of thought, whatever this may be.

In the Talmud and the tradition, everything that concerns the commandments and their fulfilment must be accepted without discussion. As for the rest, in particular the *aggadot*, it is possible not to admit them. The prophets and the sages did not constantly transmit only the divine word. Everything that they said as men must be subjected to rational examination.

Should the commandments, which must be applied without discussion, also be explained? Have they a 'sense'? Elijah affirms that all the commandments have a reason that is not metaphysical; that is, the directed thought of a man performing a commandment certainly does not affect the cosmic equilibrium, as the Kabbalists claimed; but the *miẓvot* have a political or moral reason that man sometimes discovers and understands, and sometimes not.

The *Torah*, the purpose of which is essentially political, has its own truth; philosophy its own as well, and one should not attempt to harmonize them.

In the *Question on the Efficiency of the Universe*, Delmedigo states:

> If anything will be said [in this treatise] contrary to the Law [Torah], this will not be surprising since I want to speak of the ideas of the philosophers according to their foundations [of the ideas], for the approach of the Law, in which faith is placed, is different from the philosophic approach.
>
> (Trans. D. Geffen, 'Insights into the Life and Thought of Elijah Delmedigo', p. 82)

In the introduction to the *Treatises on the Intellect*, he writes:

> I do not think that the words of the Torah are explained through the method of philosophy nor does the former [Torah] need the latter [philosophy]. No one thinks this way, according to my point of view, except for the man who is neither an adherent of Torah nor a philosopher ... Moreover no one should think me in error because in my philosophic works I deal with the philosophers according to their methodology.
>
> (*Ibid.* p. 82)

We see that the great dream of the medieval philosophers to accord science and religion has been abandoned. Elijah Delmedigo, convinced disciple of Averroes, is nevertheless far from Averroes; for the Arab philosopher science and religion, although different, were ordered in the same, unique, hierarchical system. Albalag spoke of two truths, but he tried to merge one (religious truth) in the other (philosophical truth). For the Jewish philosopher of the fifteenth century, it was clear that there were two different disciplines, two methodologies, two independent visions of the world, each drawing man in its own direction.

In his attachment to Averroes, Elijah Delmedigo placed himself in a school of thought with its main centre at Padua. Neoplatonism was cultivated more at Florence, and its most illustrious Jewish representative was the son of Isaac Abrabanel, Judah ben Isaac Abrabanel, also known as Leo Hebraeus (*ca.* 1460 – after 1523). Judah, elder son of Isaac Abrabanel, was born at Lisbon and received a scientific and philosophical education. In 1483 he was physician at Lisbon and shortly afterwards he followed his father in his flight. In 1492, so that his own small son, Isaac, then one year old, should avoid baptism, he sent him with his nurse to Portugal, but King John II laid hands on the infant and had him baptized. It is not known what happened afterwards to the child, and perhaps he was able to return to his family and to Judaism, but this tragedy weighed heavily on Leo Hebraeus' life. After the Expulsion Judah Abrabanel continued his career as physician at Naples, then at Genoa, and later again at Naples. He may have visited Florence and met Marsilio Ficini and Pico della Mirandola. At all events, he read Ficini's works.

Apart from numerous poems, Leo Hebraeus wrote *Dialoghi d'Amore* (*Dialogues of Love*), most probably in Italian, and the book became quite celebrated; between 1535 and 1607 twenty-five editions appeared, and between 1551 and 1660 it was translated into French, Latin, Spanish and Hebrew. Reactions were sometimes mixed. Ronsard presented a copy of the book to Charles IX and wrote an ode on the occasion, 'Au roi Charles lui donnant un Leone Hebrieu' (Ronsard, *Oeuvres complètes*, ed. de la Pléiade, (Paris, 1950), vol. I, p. 61); but he also wrote another poem (*ibid.* vol. II, p. 674) on Leo Hebraeus, which ends thus:

> Je n'aime point les Juifs, ils ont mis en la croix
> Ce Christ, ce Messias, qui nos pechez efface,
> Des Prophetes occis, ensanglanté la place,
> Murmuré contre Dieu qui leur donna les loix.
> Fils de Vespasian, grand Tite, tu devois,
> Destruisant leur cité, en destruire la race,
> Sans leur donner ni temps, ni moment, ni espace
> De chercher autre part autres divers endroits.
> Jamais Leon Hebrieu des Juifs n'eust prins naissance,
> Leon Hebrieu, qui donne aux Dames cognoissance
> D'un amour fabuleux, la mesme fiction:
> Faux, trompeur, mensonger, plein de fraude et d'astuce,
> Je croix qu'en luy coupant la peau de son prepuce
> On lui coupa le coeur et toute affection.

The *Dialoghi d'Amore* were written in a secular language and represent a
book of profane philosophy. This is not a work of Jewish philosophy, but
a book of philosophy written by a Jew.

Three dialogues between Philo and Sophia present the theme of love; here
is an extract:

Since the beginning and end of the circle is the most high Creator, the first half is
the descent from Him to the lowest and most distant point from His supreme
perfection. And first in order of descent comes the angelic nature with its ordered
degrees from greater to less; then follows the heavenly, ranging from the heaven
of the Empyrean, which is the greatest, to that of the moon, which is the least; and
finally the circle passes to our sphere, the lowest of all, to wit, first matter, the least
perfect of the eternal substances and the farthest removed from the high perfection
of the Creator. For as He is pure actuality so it is pure potentiality. And it is the
terminating point of the first half of the circle of being, which descends from the
Creator through successive degrees, from greater to less, to first matter, the least
of all. At this point the circle begins to turn through its second half, ascending from
lesser to greater, as I have already described, to wit, from first matter to the elements, thence to the compounds, from these to the plants and the animals, and
finally to man. In man it ascends from the vegetative to the sensitive soul and finally
to the intellect, and in intellectual activities from one less intelligible object to
another more so, until it reaches the supreme act of intellection, which has as its
object the Divinity; and this is final union, not only with the angelic nature, but
through its medium with the most high Divinity itself . . . The whole of the first half
circle consists of the love of the superior for the inferior less beautiful than itself,
and of successive procreation. And the producer is more beautiful than what he
produces, and it is love which causes him to procreate and impart his beauty; and
so it is from the highest creature down to first matter, the least of all creation,
because love of the greater for the less is the means and cause of generation. In
the other half circle, on the contrary, from first matter to the highest good, since
it ascends the steep of perfection from inferior to superior, love must be of the
less for the more beautiful to acquire greater beauty and to attain to union with it.
And so the circle passes from one degree to another above it until the created intellect is united to the highest beauty and comes to enjoyment of the supreme good
by means of the final love of it, which is the cause of the active union of the universe
with its Creator, in which its ultimate perfection consists.

(Trans. F. Friedberg-Sealy and J. H. Barnes, *The Philosophy of Love*, pp. 450-3)

The universe described is very close to the medieval world. Other passages,
however, are often more of the 'Renaissance', like the following:

You have heard that the soul is the mean between the intellect and the body, and
I am speaking not only of the soul of the world, but also of our copy of it. Our
soul has, therefore, two faces, like those of the moon turned towards the sun and
the earth respectively, the one being turned towards the intellect above it, and the
other towards the body below. The first face looking towards the intellect is the
understanding with which the soul reasons of universals and spiritual knowledge,
extracting the forms and intellectual essences from particular and sensible bodies,
ever transforming the corporeal world into the intellectual. The second face turned
towards the body is sense, which is particular knowledge of corporeal things, to

which is added the materialness of the corporeal things known. These two faces have contrary or opposed motions; and as our soul with its upper face or understanding makes the corporeal incorporeal, so the lower face, or sensible cognition, approaching the objects of sense and mingling with them, draws the incorporeal to the corporeal. Corporeal beauty is recognized by our soul by these two forms of knowledge with one or other face, that is sensible and corporeal or rational and intellectual. For each of these two forms of knowledge of corporeal beauty there arises a corresponding manner of love in the soul – for sensible cognition, sensual love, and for rational cognition, spiritual love. There are many who hold that the face of the soul turned towards the body is luminous and that turned towards the intellect is dark: and this is because their soul is sunk in the body to which it cleaves, and the body is rebellious and hardly overcome by the soul . . . There are others, however, who can more truly be called men, for the face of their soul which is turned towards the intellect is no less luminous than that which is turned towards the body, and in some it is even more brilliant. These make rational cognition the true end of their sensible knowledge, and only value sensible beauty perceived by the lower face in so far as rational beauty can be culled from it by the upper face, which is true beauty, as I have told you. And though they allow their spiritual soul to remain with the lower face towards the body, the sensible forms are immediately raised by contrary motion to the upper, rational face which draws from them the intelligible forms and species, recognising this to be the true beauty in them and leaving the corporeal and the sensible as the rude husk of the incorporeal or its shadow and image. And as the one form of knowledge is the end of the other, so the one form of love is the end of the other, that is the intellectual of the sensual; for these men love sensible beauty in so far as a knowledge of it causes them to know and love the spiritual and non-sensible.

(*Ibid.* pp. 394–6)

The theme of cosmic love in Leo Hebraeus was perhaps borrowed from an *Epistle on Love* by Avicenna, and he himself says that these theories are those of the Arabs. But, as in the case of Elijah Delmedigo and Averroes, the medieval ideas were profoundly transformed, not in themselves, but in the use made of them; love was one of the aspects of the relation between God and the universe and the universe towards God; suddenly it became the principal active agent in the world and everything was ordered around it.

Together with the Neoplatonism of which the *Dialoghi* are such a fine example, astrology also continued to flourish. Cosmic love involved not only the relations between the superior and the inferior but also analogies, resemblances, influences. The value placed on sympathetic magic was for Christians reinforced by the accessibility of hermetic texts, and by Marsilio Ficini's translation of the *Corpus* of Hermes Trismegistus. The quest for texts and for oriental wisdom led people to read not only Greek works but also some in Hebrew. Humanists studied Greek and Hebrew, and in Hebrew especially the Kabbalah, the esoteric wisdom of which promised a revelation of the secrets of the universe.

We have remarked that the Hebrew Middle Ages were poor in alchemist texts. In the fifteenth century, however, works on magic began to be translated into Hebrew from Arabic or Latin: *Picatrix*, was translated three times. Judah ben Nissim Ibn Malkah, in the thirteenth century, and in the fourteenth Nissim of Marseilles, Samuel Ibn Motot, Samuel Sarsa, and to a certain extent Moses of Narbonne, were close to a certain kind of theoretical magic, but not to its practice. Magic was always marginal to the official philosophy. In the Jewish Middle Ages practical magic was a popular superstition scorned by cultivated people, but astrology, firmly established on the basis of astronomy, was admitted by the great majority of scholars.

At the period of the Renaissance magic achieved right of entry among the philosophers, and its status was that of a natural science, like alchemy or astrology.

Johanan Alemanno (*ca.* 1435 – after 1504), who was also one of Pico della Mirandola's teachers (M. Idel affirms that he was the most erudite of all the Renaissance humanists), declared that natural magic was inferior to the Kabbalah, which provides the keys to a 'divine' magic.

A certain short text seems to me to illustrate the revolution that took place in Jewish thought at the end of the fifteenth century. This is a letter written at Naples in 1490, and, like most letters written during the Renaissance, intended for publication. David Messer Leon asked *Jacob ben David Provençal* if the rabbis of the Talmud loved or hated the sciences and philosophy. At that time the game of 'loves and hates' was a literary exercise; one wrote for or against women, for or against love, etc. Jacob Provençal was a rabbi and a Talmudist; he presented himself as spokesman of the tradition, and, as such, he declared that he hated philosophy.

But, he said, one must distinguish between theoretical philosophy, which the rabbis of the Talmud refused, and practical philosophy. Theoretical philosophy is that of Aristotle, it is deceitful appearance and subterfuge, it denies temporal creation and is opposed to the divine *Torah*.

Practical philosophy, on the other hand, is praiseworthy. In fact, all the sciences are included in the *Torah* (written or oral), even if at present we have recourse to foreign books. To despise the sciences would be to despise the *Torah*, gift of God. The rabbis never refused to admit a true thing verified by experience, nor true knowledge, whatever the language in which it was written, for the *Torah* is truth and everything that is truth is the *Torah*.

These true sciences are neither philosophy nor logic, but the knowledge of natural things: first medicine, judiciary astrology and alchemy, and secondly the practical arts, agriculture and metalwork; in short, everything that belongs to nature.

During the Middle Ages it was philosophical truth that one discovered in the *Torah*; in the Renaissance, it was natural science.

Jacob Provencal was not very conversant with philosophy. But *Yehiel Nissim of Pisa*, who wrote in 1538, had an admirably wide knowledge of the philosophical texts. In his *Minḥat Kenaot* (*Offering of Jealousy*) he demonstrates the superiority of religion over philosophy. This is not because philosophy is dangerous and may lead men astray from religion, it is because philosophy cannot offer any certitude. It does not respond to questions that the man and the Jew may ask, for the opinions of different philosophers are opposed to each other. One can achieve definite knowledge regarding the sciences of nature or physics, but not concerning metaphysics, and this incertitude is harmful. And, adds Yehiel Nissim, 'let him who wishes to understand for himself the philosophical beliefs and opinions, of the ancients and of the moderns, of the Christian philosophers, their demonstrations and arguments, let him read the commentaries on Aristotle and in particular those of the greatest of contemporary philosophers: Agostino Nifo da Sessa [Aristotelian philosopher, 1473–1545?]' (*Offering of Jealousy*, pp. 71–2, cited in R. Bonfil, *The Rabbinate in Renaissance Italy*, p. 184).

As Bonfil remarks, for Yehiel Nissim, a devotee of the orthodox religion, philosophy is no longer a redoubtable adversary, as it was during preceding centuries. It is true that Aristotelian philosophy disintegrated from within; in the fifteenth century, as in the sixteenth and seventeenth, it was no longer possible to realize the great dream of the medieval philosophers – to dominate all Creation by the force of human thought and to unite with the Intellect to approach the Creator. However, the Aristotelian edifice still held firm, and, as with all ideologies that are about to give way, it was more and more obstinately defended as more and more breaches appeared. It was difficult to see how, if this structure crumbled, reason and religion could continue to exist. Moreover, the universities taught Aristotle and, as today, the university professors liked to teach what they had learnt.

Like their Christian colleagues, Jewish thinkers had been brought up in an Aristotelian culture; like them they cited the authorities, like them they discussed the great questions that the learned world debated, that of the soul and that of the Active Intellect. Thus for instance *Obadiah Sforno* (*ca.* 1470 – *ca.* 1550) in his *Or Amim* (*The Light of the Peoples*), published in Hebrew at Bologna in 1537, and in Latin in the same town in 1548.

For Jewish writers, the basic text remained the *Guide of the Perplexed*, which is the only work of philosophy frequently found in book lists of the fifteenth to the seventeenth centuries. It was generally accompanied by commentaries, not those of Joseph Caspi or Moses Narboni, but that of Efodi, more elementary, and emphasizing the agreement between philosophy and religion.

Moses ben Abraham Provençal (1503–75) composed yet another commentary on the twenty-five propositions at the beginning of Book II of the *Guide*. In the seventeenth century, Maimonides is still the principal source of inspiration. *Joseph Solomon Delmedigo* (1591–1626) often cites him, and often criticizes him.

Another book that was still read was the *Kuzari* of Judah Halevi. *David Ibn Yahya*, who taught in Rome *ca.* 1532, still read Al-Ghazālī's *Intentions of the Philosophers*. On Saturdays he studied alternately the *Guide of the Perplexed* and the *Kuzari*.

Judah ben Joseph Moscato (ca. 1530 – *ca.* 1593) wrote a commentary on the *Kuzari* called *Kol Yehudah* (*The Voice of Judah*) which had a great success; among other sources he cites Philo, in Greek.

Medieval philosophy had a profound and enduring impact on Jewish thought. Maimonides, in the orthodox interpretation, is still the *Guide*; Abraham Ibn Ezra's biblical commentary became a classic; like the *Kuzari*, it has not ceased to be read and studied to our day. Thus, the three schools of thought of the medieval world: universalist philosophy with Maimonides, Jewish particularism with Judah Halevi, and Neoplatonism allied to astrology with Abraham Ibn Ezra, have remained alive in traditional Jewish thought and are still part of the Jewish cultural heritage.

BIBLIOGRAPHY

Under individual philosophers, each bibliography is arranged in the following sections:

(1) the author's works; translations into English or other European languages;
(2) the most important studies published before 1978, and a more exhaustive list of books and articles appearing since that date.

A comprehensive guide to a more complete bibliography may be found in:

Kirjath Sepher (*Kiryat Sefer*), a Quarterly Bibliographical Review published by the Jewish National and University Library Jerusalem (1923–)
and

Index of Articles on Jewish Studies, also published by the Jewish National and University Library (1966–).

Abbreviations

AHDLMA	*Archives d'histoire doctrinale et littéraire du Moyen Age*
BJRL	*Bulletin of the John Rylands Library*
E.J.	*Encyclopaedia Judaica*, Jerusalem, 1971
HTR	*Harvard Theological Review*
HÜb	M. Steinschneider, *Die hebraeischen Übersetzungen des Mittelalters und die Juden als Dolmetscher*
HUCA	*Hebrew Union College Annual*
JAAR	*Journal of the American Academy of Religion*
JJS	*Journal of Jewish Studies*
JQR	*Jewish Quarterly Review*
JSS	*Journal of Semitic Studies*
JTS	*Journal of Theological Studies*
MGWJ	*Monatsschrift für Geschichte und Wissenschaft des Judentums*
PAAJR	*Proceedings of the American Academy for Jewish Research*
REI	*Revue des études islamiques*
REJ	*Revue des études juives*

Introduction

GENERAL INTRODUCTION TO JEWISH TRADITION AND HISTORY

Abrahams, I. *Jewish Life in the Middle Ages*. 2nd ed. C. Roth. New York. 1969.

Baron, S. W. *A Social and Religious History of the Jews*. New York, 1958–. Sixteen volumes have so far appeared.

Carmi, T. (ed. and trans.). *The Penguin Book of Hebrew Verse*, 1981.

Ginzberg, L. *The Legends of the Jews*, Philadelphia, 1956.

On Jewish Law and Lore. Philadelphia, 1955.

Kobler, F. *Letters of Jews through the ages*. Philadelphia, 1952.

Steinschneider, M. *Jewish Literature from the Eighth to the Eighteenth Century*. London, 1857; 2nd. ed. New York, 1965.

An Introduction to the Arabic Literature of the Jews. London, 1901.
Trachtenberg, J. *Jewish Magic and Superstition*. Philadelphia, 1961.
Urbach, E. E. *The Sages, their concepts and beliefs*. Trans. from the Hebrew by I. Abrahams. 2 vols., Jerusalem, 1975.

GENERAL WORKS AND COLLECTED ARTICLES ON JEWISH MEDIEVAL PHILOSOPHY

Altmann, A. (ed.). *Jewish Medieval and Renaissance Studies*. Cambridge (Mass.), 1967.
Nahon, G., and Touati, Ch. (eds.). *Hommage à Georges Vajda*. Louvain, 1980.
Reinharz, J., and Schwetschinski, D. (eds.), with the collaboration of Bland, K. P. *Mystics, Philosophers and Politicians; Essays in Jewish Intellectual History in Honor of Alexander Altmann*. Durham (North Carolina), 1982.
Stein, S., and Loewe, R. (eds.). *Studies in Jewish Religious and Intellectual History, presented to Alexander Altmann*. Alabama, 1979.
Twersky, I. (ed.). *Studies in Medieval Jewish History and Literature*. [Vol. I.] Cambridge (Mass.), 1979; [vol. II.] 1984.

Altmann, A. *Studies in religious philosophy and mysticism*. London, 1969.
Biblical and other studies. Cambridge (Mass.), 1963.
Essays in Jewish Intellectual History. London, 1981.
Bettan, I. *Studies in Jewish Preaching*. Cincinnati, 1939.
Bleich, J. D. 'Providence in late Medieval Jewish Philosophy'. Ph.D. diss. New York University, 1974.
Davidson, H. A. 'John Philiponus as a source of medieval Islamic and Jewish Proofs of creation'. *Journal of the American Oriental Society* 89 (1969), 357–91.
Guttmann, J. *Philosophies of Judaism*. Trans. D. W. Silverman, introd. R. J. Z. Werblowsky. London, 1964.
Dat u-Mada (Religion and Science). Jerusalem, 1955 (in Hebrew).
Efros, I. 'The Problem of Space in Jewish Medieval Philosophy'. *JQR* n.s. 6 (1916), 495–554; 7 (1916) 61–87, 223–51.
Heinemann, I. *Ta'amei ha-miṣvot be-sifrut Israel (The Reasons of the Commandments in Hebrew Literature)*. Jerusalem, 1954–6 (in Hebrew).
Husik, I. *A History of Medieval Jewish Philosophy*. New York, 1916.
Philosophical Essays, Ancient, Mediaeval and modern. Ed. M. C. Nahon and L. Strauss. Oxford, 1952.
Jacobs, L. *Principles of the Jewish Faith*. New York, 1964.
Kaufmann, D. *Die Sinne – Beiträge zur Geschichte der Physiologie und Psychologie im Mittelalter*. Jahresbericht der Landes-Rabbinerschule in Budapest. Budapest, 1884.
Mehqarim be-sifrut ha 'ivrit shel yemei he-binayim (Studies in Hebrew Literature of the Middle Ages). Jerusalem, 1962 (in Hebrew).
Klatzkin, J. A. *Ozar ha-Munahim ha-pilosofi'im ve-antologia pilosofit (Thesaurus of Philosophical Terms and Philosophical Anthology)*. Berlin, 1926–34 (in Hebrew).
Lasker, D. L. *Jewish Philosophical Polemics against Christianity in the Middle Ages*. New York, 1977.
Maccoby, H. *Judaism on Trial, Jewish–Christian Disputation in the Middle Ages*. London–Toronto, 1982.
Munk, S. *Mélanges de philosophie juive et arabe*. Paris, 1857; repr. 1955.
Neubauer, A., and Renan, E. 'Les Rabbins français du commencement du quatorzième siècle'. In *Histoire littéraire de la France*, vol. XXVII, Paris, 1877, pp. 431–776.
Pines, S. *Bein maḥshevet Israel lemaḥshevet ha'amim (Studies in the History of Jewish Philosophy; the Transmission of Texts and Ideas)*. Jerusalem, 1977 (in Hebrew).

Renan, E. *Les écrivains juifs français du XIVe siècle.* Paris, 1893. (= *Histoire littéraire de la France,* vol. XXI, pp. 351–789.)

Rosenberg, S. 'Logic and Ontology in Jewish Philosophy in the 14th Century'. Ph.D. diss. Hebrew University, Jerusalem, 1974 (in Hebrew with an English summary).

(The following articles by S. Rosenberg are all in Hebrew)

'Signification of Names in Medieval Jewish Logic'. *Iyyun* 27 (1977), 105–44.

'Possible and Assertoric in Medieval Logic'. *Iyyun* 28 (1978), 55–76.

'Necessary and Possible in Medieval Logic'. *Iyyun* 28 (1978), 103–55.

'Ontological Categories and Some Jewish Philosophers: Substance and Accident'. *Iyyun* 30 (1981), 3–25.

'Ontological Categories and Some Jewish Philosophers: On the Quadruple Root of Accident'. *Iyyun* 31 (1982) 58–87.

'*Barbara Celarent* in Hebrew Logical Tradition'. *Tarbiz* 48 (1979), 74–98.

Sirat, C. *Les théories des visions surnaturelles dans la pensée juive du Moyen-Age.* Leyden, 1969.

Hagut ha-pilosofit bimei ha-binayim (Jewish Philosophical Thought in the Middle Ages). Jerusalem, 1975 (in Hebrew).

Schechter, S. *Studies in Judaism.* New York, 1970.

Steinschneider, M. *Gesammelte Schriften,* vol. I. Berlin, 1925.

Die hebraeischen Übersetzungen des Mittelalters und die Juden als Dolmetscher. Berlin, 1893; repr. Graz, 1956. (*HÜb*).

Strauss, L. *Persecution and the art of writing.* Glencoe (Ill.), 1952; repr. 1976.

Vajda, G. *Introduction à la pensée juive du Moyen Age.* Paris, 1947.

L'Amour de Dieu dans la théologie juive du Moyen Age. Paris, 1957.

Wolfson, H. A. *Studies in the History of Philosophy and Religion.* Cambridge (Mass.), 1973 and 1977.

Philo

Works:

In ten volumes and two supplementary volumes, in the Loeb Classical Library, Cambridge (Mass.).

Studies:

Lieberman, S. *Hellenism in Jewish Palestine.* New York, 1962.

Tcherikover, V. *Hellenistic Civilization and the Jews.* Philadelphia–Jerusalem, 1959.

Wolfson, H. A. *Philo. Foundations of Religious Philosophy in Judaism, Christianity and Islam.* Cambridge (Mass.), 1947.

Sandmel, S. *Philo of Alexandria, an introduction.* New York, 1979.

On the theory of the ancient Jewish sources of pagan philosophy, cf.:

Steinschneider, M. *Jewish Literature, from the Eighth to the Eighteenth Century.* New York, 1965, p. 275.

Malter, H. 'Shem Tob ben Joseph Palquera'. *JQR* n.s. 1 (1910/11) 151–81; repr. in *The Works of Rabbi Shem Tov Falaquera,* 3 vols., Jerusalem, 1970, vol. I.

ON EARLY MYSTICISM

Gruenwald, I. 'A Preliminary Critical Edition of Sefer Yeẓira'. *Israel Oriental Studies* I (Tel-Aviv, 1971) 132–77.

'Some Critical Notes on the First Part of Sefer Yeẓira'. *REJ* 132 (1973), 475–512.

The Book of Creation. Trans. I. Friedman. New York, 1977.

Scholem, G. G. *Jewish Gnosticism, Merkabah Mysticism and Talmudic Tradition.* New York, 1960.
Kabbalah. Jerusalem, 1974.
Major Trends in Jewish Mysticism. Jerusalem, 1941; paperback repr. New York, 1961.

The Mutakallimūn and other Jewish thinkers inspired by Muslim theological movements

THE KALĀM

Nader, A. N. *Le système philosophique des Mu'tazila.* Beirut, 1956.
Peters, J. R. I. M. *God's Created Speech.* Leyden, 1976.
Pines, S. 'Philosophy' in *The Cambridge History of Islam,* vol. IIB, Cambridge, 1970, pp. 780–823.
Beitrage zur islamischen Atomenlehre. Berlin, 1936.
Wolfson, H. A. *The Philosophy of the Kalam.* Cambridge (Mass.) and London, 1976.
Repercussions of the Kalam in Jewish Philosophy. Cambridge (Mass.), 1979.

THE RABBANITES

David Al-Mukammis

E.J., s.v. 'Al-Mukammis, David Ibn Marwan Al-Raqi Al-Shirazi'

Works:

A unique manuscript in Leningrad (Bibliothèque Saltykov–Schedrin, Firkovič collection 2, no. 4 817) contains the greater part of the '*Ishrūn Maqāla (The Twenty Chapters*). Fragments in Hebrew translation are included in the *Commentary on the Book of Creation (Perush Sefer Yeẓira*) by Judah ben Barzillai of Barcelona (published Berlin, 1885), pp. 65, 77, 151.
    In her Ph.D. thesis, 'Dawūd ibn Marwān al-Muqammis and his '*Ishrūn Maqāla*', Hebrew University, Jerusalem, 1983, S. Stroumsa gives in an appendix a critical edition of the text.

Studies:

Vajda, G. 'A propos de la perpétuité de la rétribution d'outre-tombe en théologie musulmane'. *Studia islamica* 11 (1959), 29–38.
    'La finalité de la création selon un théologien juif du IXe siècle'. *Oriens* 15 (1962), 51–85.
    'Le pari de Pascal dans un texte judéo-arabe du IXe siècle'. In *Mélanges d'histoire des religions offerts à H. C. Puech,* Paris, 1974, pp. 569–71.
    'Le problème de l'unité de Dieu d'après Dāwūd Ibn Marwān Al-Muqammiṣ'. In A. Altmann (ed.), *Jewish Medieval and Renaissance Studies,* Cambridge (Mass.), 1967, pp. 49–73.
    'La prophétologie de Dāwūd Ibn Marwān Al-Raqqī al-Muqammiṣ, théologien juif arabophone du IXe siècle'. *Journal Asiatique* (1977) 227–35.

Saadiah Gaon

E.J., s.v. 'Saadiah b. Joseph Gaon'

Works:

(1) *Amānāt wal-i 'tiqādāt.* The Arabic text in Arabic characters, published by S. Landauer, Leyden, 1880.
The same text in Hebrew characters with a translation into modern Hebrew, published by J. Kafih. Jerusalem, 1970.
Sefer ha-Emunot weha-De'ot. The Hebrew translation of the *Amānāt* by Judah Ibn Tibbon. First printed in Constantinople, 1562, and frequently reissued.

The Book of Beliefs and Opinions. An English translation of the *Amānāt*, published by S. Rosenblatt. New Haven, 1948.

The Book of Doctrines and Beliefs. An abridged translation of the *Amānāt*, with an introduction, published by A. Altmann, in *Three Jewish Philosophers.* New York, 1969.

(2) *Tafsīr Kitāb al-Mabādī.* The Arabic text in Arabic characters, published by M. Lambert with a French translation entitled *Commentaire sur le Sefer Yesira par le Gaon Saadya.* Paris, 1891.

The same text in Hebrew characters with a translation into modern Hebrew, *Perush Sefer Yeẓira*, published by J. Kafih, Jerusalem, 1972.

The medieval Hebrew translation, probably made by Moses ben Joseph of Lucerna in the eleventh century has not been published. Fragments of other translations are quoted by Judah ben Barzillai of Barcelona and Berakhia ha-Naqdan. On these and other translations in manuscript, cf. Malter, H. *Saadia Gaon; his Life and Works.* New York, 1929. New ed. 1969.

(3) Biblical commentaries

Les Oeuvres complètes de Saadia b. Josef al Fayyoumi. Ed. J. and H. Derenbourg. Paris, 1893–. Thirteen volumes were planned, but only vols. I, III, V, VI and IX appeared.

A new edition of the Arabic text in Hebrew characters, with a translation in modern Hebrew, has been undertaken by J. Kafih. The following have appeared:

The Song of Songs, Ruth, Ecclesiastes, Esther, Lamentations. Jerusalem 1962.

Psalms. Jerusalem, 1966.

Job. Jerusalem, 1973.

Proverbs. Jerusalem, 1976.

(4) Davidson, I. *Saadia's Polemic Against Hiwi al-Balkhī.* New York, 1915.

Studies:

Malter, H. *Saadia Gaon; his Life and Works.* New York, 1929. (Lists bibliography up to 1929.)

Cohen, B. (ed.). *Saadia Anniversary Volume.* PAAJR, 1943. (Lists bibliography 1920–42.)

Finkelstein, L. (ed.). *Rav Saadia Gaon; Studies in his honor.* New York: Jewish Theological Seminary, 1944.

Rosenthal, E. I. J. (ed.). *Saadya Studies.* Manchester, 1943.

Ventura, M. *La Philosophie de Saadia Gaon.* Paris, 1934.

Altmann, A. 'Saadya's Conception of the Law'. *BJRL* 28 (1944) 320–9.

'Saadya's Theory of Revelation; its Origin and Background'. In Rosenthal (ed.), *Saadya Studies*, pp. 4–25.

Diesendruck, Z. 'Saadya's Formulation of the Time Argument for Creation'. In *Jewish Studies in Memory of George Kohut.* Ed. S. W. Baron and A. Marx. New York, 1935.

Efros, I. 'Saadya's Theory of Knowledge'. *JQR* 33 (1942–3) 133–70.

'Saadya's Second Theory of Creation in its Relation to Pythagorism and Platonism'. In *Louis Ginzberg Jubilee Volume*, New York, 1945, pp. 133–42 (English section).

Fleisher, E. 'A Fragment from Hivi al-Balkhi's Criticism of the Bible.' *Tarbiz* 51 (1981) 49–56 (in Hebrew).

Fox, M. 'On the rational commandments in Saadia's Philosophy: a reexamination'. In *Proceedings of the Sixth World Congress of Jewish Studies*, vol. III, Jerusalem, 1977 pp. 33–43.

Goldman, E. 'The Ethical Theory of R. Saadiah Gaon'. *Daat* 2–3 (1978–9) 7–28 (in Hebrew).

Guttmann, J. *Die Religionsphilosophie des Saadia.* Göttingen, 1882.

Heller, B. 'La version arabe et le commentaire des Proverbes du Gaon Saadia'. *REJ* 37 (1898) 72–85, 226–51.

Heschel, A. J. 'The Quest for Certainty in Saadia's Philosophy'. *JQR* 33 (1942–3) 213–64.
'Reason and Revelation in Saadia's Philosophy'. *JQR* 39 (1944) 391–408.
Kasher, H. 'The Guarantee of Truth According to Saadiah and Maimonides'. *Daat* 4 (1980) 35–40 (in Hebrew).
Marmorstein, A. 'The Doctrine of Redemption in Saadya's Theological System'. In Rosenthal (ed.), *Saadya Studies*, pp. 4–25.
Ratsaby, Y. 'The Commentary on the Pentateuch of Rav Saadiah', *Sinai* 91 (1982) 196–222, with a list of manuscript fragments.
Rosenthal, J. 'Hiwi al-Balkhi'. *JQR* 38 (1938) 317–42, 419–30; 39 (1939) 79–94.
Schweid, E. 'The Ethical–Religious Doctrine of Saadiah Gaon'. *Jerusalem Studies in Jewish Thought* 3 (1982) 15–32 (in Hebrew).
Vajda, G. 'A propos de l'attitude religieuse de Hiwi al-Balkhi'. *REJ* 99 (1935) 88–91.
'Autour de la théorie de la connaissance chez Saadia'. *REJ* 126 (1967) 135–89, 375–97.
'Notes critiques sur le Kitāb al Amanāt'. *REJ* 9 (109) (1948–9) 68–102.
'Sa'adya, commentateur du Livre de la Création'. *Annuaire de l'Ecole Pratique des Hautes Etudes, section des Sciences religieuses* (1959/60) 1–35.
'Saadia Gaon et l'amour courtois'. In *Mélanges d'islamologie dédiés à la mémoire de A. Abel*, vol. II, Brussels, 1975, pp. 415–20.
Wolfson, H. A. 'The Kalam Problem of Nonexistence and Saadia's Second Theory of Creation'. In his *Studies in the History of Philosophy and Religion*, vol. II, Cambridge (Mass.), 1977, pp. 338–58.
'Atomism in Saadia'. *Ibid.* pp. 359–26.
'Arabic and Hebrew Terms for Matter and Element with Especial Reference to Saadia'. *Ibid.* pp. 377–92.
'Saadia on the Trinity and Incarnation'. *Ibid.* pp. 393–414.

Hai Gaon

E.J., s.v. 'Hai ben Sherira'.
Kaufman, D. 'An Answer of Hai Gaon on the problem of God's Foreknowledge'. In his *Mehqarim be-sifrut ha'ivrit shel yemei ha-binayim*, Jerusalem, 1962, pp. 1–10 (in Hebrew).

Samuel ben Hofni

E.J., s.v. 'Samuel ben Hophni'.

Study:
Sirat, C. *La Théorie des visions surnaturelles*, Leyden, 1969, pp. 32–5.

Aaron ben Sargado

E.J., s.v. 'Aaron ben Joseph ha-Kohen Sargado'.

Study:
Sirat, C. *La Théorie des visions surnaturelles*, pp. 35 ff.

THE KARAITES

Ankori, Z. *Karaïtes in Byzantium*. New York, 1959.
Ben-Shammai, H. 'The Attitude of Some Early Karaites toward Islam', in I. Twersky (ed.), *Studies in Medieval Jewish History and Literature*. Vol. II. Cambridge (Mass.), 1984, pp. 3–40.
'Studies in Karaite Atomism'. To be published in *Jerusalem Studies in Arabic and Islam* 6.

Birnbaum, P. (ed.). *Karaite Studies*. New York, 1971. A collection of earlier essays. See especially S. A. Poznanski, 'The Anti-Karaite Writings of Sa'adiah Gaon' and 'The Karaite Literary Opponents of Sa'adiah Gaon'; and W. Bacher, 'Qirqisani the Karaite and his Work on Jewish Sects'.

Mann, J. *Texts and Studies in Jewish History and Literature*. Philadelphia, 1931 and 1935.

Nemoy, L. *Karaite Anthology*. New Haven, 1932.

'The Epistle of Sahl ben Maṣliaḥ'. *PAAJR* 38–39 (1970–1), 145–77.

Pinsker, S. *Lickute Kadmoniot. Zur Geschichte des Karaismus und der Karaischen Literatur*. Vienna, 1860; repr. Jerusalem, 1968.

Vajda, G. 'Two Epitomes of Karaite Theology: *Sefer Meshivat Nefesh* and *Pereq Zidduq Haddin*'. In *Studia Orientalia Memoriae D. H. Baneth Dedicata*, Jerusalem, 1979, pp. 103–10 (in Hebrew).

'L'homélie du Karaite Samuel al-Maghribī sur les Dix Commandements'. In J. A. Emerton and S. C. Reif (eds.), *Interpreting the Hebrew Bible; Essays in Honour of E. I. J. Rosenthal*, Cambridge, 1982, pp. 251–65.

Wieder, N. *Judean Scrolls and Karaism*. London, 1962.

Daniel ben Moses al-Qumīsī

E.J., s.v. 'Daniel ben Moses al-Qumīsī'

Works:

Commentarius in librium duodecim prophetarum quem composuit Daniel al-Kumisi, primum edidit. Published by I. D. Markori, Jerusalem, 1957 (in Hebrew).

Solomon ben Jeroham

E.J., s.v. 'Solomon ben Jeroham'

Works:

Davidson, I. *The Book of the Wars of the Lord*. New York, 1959.

Marwick, L. *The Arabic Commentary of Salmon ben Yeruham the Karaite on the Book of Psalms, Chapters 42–72*. Philadelphia, 1956.

Riese, M. I. 'The Arabic Commentary of Solomon ben Jeruham the Karaite on Ecclesiastes'. Ph.D. thesis. Yeshiva University, New York, 1973.

Vajda, G. *Deux commentaires karaïtes sur l'Ecclésiaste*. Leyden, 1971, pp. 8–114.

A partial French translation is contained in: 'Le Psaume VIII commenté par Salmon b. Yeruhim'. In A. I. Katsh and L. Nemoy (eds.), *Essays on the Occasion of the Seventieth Anniversary of the Dropsie University (1909–1979)*, Philadelphia, 1980, pp. 441–8.

Jacob al-Kirkisānī

E.J., s.v. 'Kirkisānī, Jacob al-'

Works:

Kitāb al-Anwār wa'l-Marāqib. Ed. by L. Nemoy. 5 vols. New York, 1939–43.

Nemoy, L. 'Corrections and Emendations to al-Qirqisani's Kitāb al-Anwār'. *JQR* 50 (1959 60), 371–83.

Chapters from Kirkisānī's works are published in vol. II of H. Ben-Shammai, 'The Doctrines of Religious Thought of Abu Yūsuf Ya'qūb al-Qirqisānī and Yefet ben 'Eli'. Ph.D. thesis, Jerusalem, 1977.

Bibliography to pages 37–55

Translations of parts of *Kitāb al-Anwār* are found in

Ben-Shammai, H. 'Qirqisānī on the Oneness of God', *JQR* 73, 2 (1982), 105–11.
and
  'Hebrew in Arabic Script, Qirqisānī's View', *Studies in Judaica, Karaitica and Islamica*,
  Tel-Aviv, 1982, pp. 115–26.
Nemoy, L. 'Al-Qirqisani's Account of the Jewish Sects and Christianity'. *HUCA* 7 (1930),
  317–97.
  'A Tenth Century Criticism of the Doctrine of the Logos (John 1, 1). *Journal of Biblical
  Literature* 64 (1945), 515–29.
Karaite Anthology, New Haven, 1932, pp. 42–68.
Vajda, G. 'Etudes sur Qirqisānī', *REJ* 106 (1941–5), 87–123, 137–40; 107 (1946–7), 52–98;
  108 (1948), 64–91; 120 (1961), 211–57; 122 (1963), 7–74.

Study:

Ben-Shammai, H. 'The Doctrines of Religious Thought of Abū Yūsuf Ya'qūb al-Qirqisānī
  and Yefet ben 'Eli' (see above).

Japheth ben Ali ha-Levi

E.J., s.v.'Japheth b. Ali ha-Levi'

Works:

Most of the biblical commentaries have not been published.
The Commentary on Numbers is quoted according to MS F. 12, Trinity College, Cambridge,
110(Cat. Loewe no. 25).
The Commentary on Psalms is quoted according to Paris, Bibliothèque nationale, MS
hébr. 287.
Birnbaum, P. *The Arabic Commentary of Yefet b. Ali, the Karaite, on the Book of Hosea*.
  Philadelphia, 1942.
Hirschfeld, H. (ed.). *Jefet b. Ali's Arabic Commentary on Nahum*. London, 1911.
Margoliouth, D. S. (ed. and trans.). 'A Commentary on the Book of Daniel by Jephet Ibn
  Ali, the Karaite'. *Anecdota Oxoniensa*, vol. I, 3 'Semitic Studies'. Oxford, 1889.
Schorstein, N. *Der Commentar des Karäers Jephet ben 'Ali zum Buche Rüth*. Berlin, 1903.
  Fragments of the biblical commentaries are given by H. Ben-Shammai in 'The Doctrines
of Religious Thought of Abū Yūsuf Ya'qūb al-Qirqisānī and Yefet ben 'Eli', Jerusalem, 1977.
  A French translation of many passages of the *Commentary on Ecclesiastes* is given in
G. Vajda, *Deux commentaires karaïtes sur l'Ecclesiaste*, Leyden, 1971, pp. 115–238.

Study:

Birnbaum, P. 'Yefet b. Ali and his Influence on Biblical Exegesis'. *JQR* 32 (1941–2), 51–70,
  159–74, 251–71

Yūsuf al-Baṣīr

E.J., s.v. 'Baṣîr, Joseph b. Abraham'

Works and Studies:

A list of manuscripts and partial editions is given in many studies by G. Vajda, who also
gives French translations.

Vajda, G. 'La démonstration de l'unité divine d'après Yūsuf al-Baṣīr'. In *Studies in Mysticism
  and Religion Presented to G. Scholem*, Jerusalem, 1967, pp. 285–315.
  'De l'universalité de la Loi morale selon Yūsuf al-Baṣīr'. *REJ* 128 (1969) 133–201.

'La réfutation de la métensomatose d'après le théologien karaïte Yūsuf al-Baṣīr'. In *Philomathes Merlan Memorial Volume*, The Hague, 1971, pp. 281–90.

'Le problème de la vision de Dieu d'après Yūsuf al-Baṣīr'. In *Islamic Philosophy and the classical tradition (Mélanges R. Walzer)*, Oxford, 1972, pp. 473–89.

'Le problème de la souffrance gratuite selon Yūsuf al-Baṣīr'. *REJ* 131 (1972) 269–322.

'Le libre arbitre de l'homme et la justification de son assujettissement à la loi divine; Traduction et commentaire des chapitres xxvii et xxxii du Kitāb al-Muḥtawi de Yūsuf al Baṣīr'. *Journal asiatique* (1974) 305–67.

'La Parole créée de Dieu d'après le théologien karaïte Yūsuf al-Baṣīr'. *Studia islamica* 39 (1974) 59–76.

'Le problème de l'assistance bienveillante de Dieu, du "mieux" et de la nécessité de la loi révélée selon Yūsuf al-Baṣīr; traduction et commentaire du Kitāb al Muḥtawi (chapitres xxxiv–xxxvi)'. *REJ* 134 (1975) 31–74.

'Les problèmes des sanctions divines, du repentir et questions connexes selon Yūsuf al-Baṣīr'. *REJ* (1978) 279–365.

'L'examen rationnel, préalable de la foi, dans l'oeuvre du théologien karaïte Yūsuf al-Baṣīr'. *AHDLMA* (1981) 7–35.

'La volonté et l'autarcie divines selon Yūsuf al-Baṣīr'. *REJ* 140 (1981) 5–99.

'The Opinions of the Karaite R. Yafeth b. Ali on the Destruction of the World in the End of Days'. In *American Academy for Jewish Research Jubilee Volume*, Jerusalem, 1980, pp. 85–95 (in Hebrew).

Jeshua ben Judah

E.J., s.v. 'Jeshua b. Judah'

For a list of the manuscripts, see Schreiner, M. *Studien über Jeshua ben Jehuda*. Berlin, 1900.

Judah Hadassi

E.J., s.v. 'Hadassi, Judah (ha-Avel) ben Elijah'

The edition of *Eshkol ha-Kofer*, Eupatoria, 1836, is very incomplete and should be compared with the manuscripts.

Jacob ben Reuben

E.J., s.v. 'Jacob b. Reuben'

Only a small part of the *Sefer ha-Osher* (*The Book of Riches*) has appeared in print: *Mivḥar Yesharim*, Eupatoria, 1836.

Aaron ben Elijah of Nicomedia

E.J., s.v. 'Aaron ben Elijah'

Works:

Eẓ Hayyim. Ed. Delizsch. Leipzig, 1841; Eupatoria, 1847.

Charner, M. 'The Tree of Life by Aaron ben Elijah of Nicomedia; First Half (Chapter 1–178)'. Ph.D. thesis. Columbia University, 1949.

Study:

Blumberg, H. 'Aaron ben Eliyah's Refutation of Maimonides' Theories of Attributes'. *Journal of Hebraic Studies* 2 (1969) 25–39.

The Neoplatonists

Isaac ben Solomon Israeli

E.J., s.v. 'Israeli, Isaac ben Solomon'

Works:

A list of manuscripts and editions is to be found in A. Altmann and S. M. Stern, *Isaac Israeli, a Neo-platonic philosopher of the early tenth century*. Oxford, 1958. The first part of the book contains a translation of I. Israeli's works. The *Book on the Elements* is given only in excerpt. The second part is a study of I. Israeli's philosophy, by A. Altmann.

Studies:

Altmann, A. 'Isaac Israeli's Chapter on the Elements', *JJS* 7 (1956–7) 31–57.
　'Creation and Emanation in Isaac Israeli, a Reappraisal'. In his *Essays in Jewish Intellectual History*, London, 1981, pp. 1–15.
Stern, S. M. 'Isaac Israeli and Moses Ibn Ezra'. *JJS* 7 (1956–7) 83–9.
　'Ibn Hasday's Neoplatonist – A Neoplatonic Treatise and His Influence on Isaac Israeli and the Longer Version of the Theology of Aristotle'. *Oriens* 8–14 (1961) 58–120.
Wolfson, H. A. 'The Meaning of *Ex-Nihilo* in Isaac Israeli'. In his *Studies in the History of Philosophy and Religion*, vol. I, Cambridge (Mass.), 1973, pp. 222–33.
　'Isaac Israeli on the Internal Senses'; and 'Notes on Isaac Israeli's Internal Senses'. *Ibid.* pp. 315–43.

Dunash Ibn Tamim

E.J., s.v. 'Dunash Ibn Tamim'

About a third of the original Arabic text of the *Commentary on the Book of Creation* was found in the Cairo Genizah. The four known Hebrew translations are unpublished (for a first list of manuscripts, cf. M. Steinschneider, *HÜb*, § 227, p. 394). The articles cited below contain translations of parts of the text.

Goldziher, I. 'Mélanges judéo-arabes'. *REJ* 52 (1906) 187–90.
Vajda, G. 'Quelques notes sur le commentaire kairouanais du Sefer Yesira'. *REJ* 105 (1939) 132–40.
　'Le commentaire Kairouanais'. *REJ* 107 (1946–7) 99–156; 110 (1949–50) 67–92; 112 (1953) 5–23.
　'Nouveaux fragments arabes du commentaire de Dunash b. Tamim sur le "Livre de la Création"'. *REJ* 113 (1954) 37–61.
　'Notes sur divers manuscrits hébraïques'. *REJ* 119 (1961) 159–61.
　'La structure du corps humain, d'après le commentaire de Dunash b. Tamim sur le "Livre de la Création"'. *Journal of Semitic Studies* 23, 1 (1978) 88–94.

Solomon ben Judah Ibn Gabirol

E.J., s.v. 'Gabirol, Solomon ben Judah Ibn'

Works

(1) *Mekor Hayyim* (*Fountain of Life*). Fragments of the original Arabic text in S. Pines, 'Sefer arugat ha-bosem, haqetaïm, mi-tokh Sefer Meqor Hayyim'. *Tarbiz* 27 (1948) 218–33 (in Hebrew).
The Hebrew fragments by Shem Tov Falaquera published and translated into French by A. Munk: 'La Source de Vie'. In *Mélanges de philosophie juive et arabe*, Paris, 1857; repr. 1955.

Latin version: C. Boeumker. *Avencebrolis Fons Vitae*. Münster, 1892.

In English: *The Fountain of Life*, trans. H. E. Wedeck, London, 1963 (Book III).

Also in English: trans., in typescript, A. B. Jacob, Philadelphia, 1954.

(2) *Iṣlāḥ al-'akhlāq* (*Tikkun Middot ha-Nefesh*) (*The Improvement of Moral Qualities*). The Arabic original published with an English trans. by S. Wise as *The Improvement of Moral Qualities*. New York, 1902.

The Hebrew version first published Constantinople, 1550.

(3) *Keter Malkhut* is found in prayerbooks. A critical edition with an English trans.: *The Royal Crown* in I. Davidson, *Selected Religious Poems of Solomon Ibn Gabirol*. Philadelphia, 1924.

Quotations on pp. 70–80 from B. Lewis' trans., *The Kingly Crown*. London, 1961.

A beautiful translation by R. Loewe is not yet in print. I thank him for giving me the opportunity to quote part of it.

Studies:

Brunner, F. *Platonisme et aristotélisme – la critique d'Ibn Gabirol par St Thomas d'Aquin*. Louvain, 1965, with an important bibliography.

'Sur la philosophie d'Ibn Gabirol'. *REJ* 128 (1969) 317–37.

Kaufman, D. 'The Pseudo-Empedocles as a Source of Salomon Ibn Gabirol'. In his *Mehqarim be-sifrut ha'ivrit shel yemei ha-binayim*, Jerusalem, 1962, pp. 78–165 (in Hebrew).

Loewe, R. 'Ibn Gabirol's Treatment of Sources in the Keter Malkhut'. In A. Altmann (ed.), *Jewish Medieval and Renaissance Studies*, Cambridge (Mass.), pp. 183–94.

Pines, S. '*And he called out to nothingness and it was split*, a note on a passage in Ibn Gabirol's *Keter Malkhut*'. *Tarbiz Anniversary Volume*, vol. III (1980–1) 339–97 (in Hebrew).

Schlanger, J. *La philosophie de Salomon Ibn-Gabirol*. Leyden, 1968.

Baḥya Ibn Paquda

E.J., s.v. 'Baḥya (Baḥye) Ben Joseph Ibn Paquda'

Works:

The Arabic text published in Arabic letters by A. S. Yahuda. *Al-Hidāja 'ilā Farā'iḍ al-Qulūb des Bachja Ibn Joséf Ibn Paqūda*. Leyden, 1912.

The Hebrew version, *Sefer Ḥovot ha-Levavot*, by Juda Ibn Tibbon, first published Naples, 1489.

An English translation, *Duties of the Hearts*, published by M. Hyamson. Jerusalem, 1962.

Studies:

Eisenberg, Y. 'Reason and Emotion in "Duties of the Heart".' *Daat* 7 (1981) 5–35.

Vajda, G. *La théologie ascétique de Baḥya Ibn Paquda*. Cahiers de la Société Asiatique 7, Paris, 1947.

'Le dialogue de l'âme et de la raison dans les Devoirs des Coeurs de Baḥya Ibn Paquda'. *REJ* 102 (1937) 93–104.

'Questiones de anima'

Goldziher, I. *Kitāb Ma'ānī al-nafs*. Berlin, 1902.

Hebrew translation: *Les Réflexions sur l'Ame par Bahya ben Joseph Ibn Pakouda, traduites de l'arabe en hébreu*. With a summary in French. I. Broydé, Paris, 1896.

Studies:

Plessner, M. 'The aims of the "Questiones de Anima", and its place in the history of Jewish Thought'. *Kiryat Sefer* (1972–3) 491–8 (in Hebrew).

Halkin, A. S. 'Studies in Kitāb Ma'ānī al-nafs'. In *Arabic and Islamic Studies*, Bar Ilan University, 1973, pp. 81-94 (in Hebrew).

Joseph ben Jacob Ibn Ẓaddik

E.J., s.v. 'Ẓaddik, Joseph b. Jacob Ibn'

Works:

Ha-Olam ha-katan, ed. A. Jellinck. Leipzig, 1854.
Horovitz, S. *Der Mikrokosmos des Josef Saddik*. Breslau, 1903. With a German translation.

Studies:

Vajda, G. 'La philosophie et la théologie de Joseph Ibn Çaddiq'. *AHDLMA* (1949) 93-181.
Wolfson, H. A. 'Joseph Ibn Saddik on divine attributes'. *JQR* 55, (1965) 277-98.

Nethanel ben al-Fayyumi

E.J., s.v. 'Nethanel ben Al-Fayyumi'

Works:

'*The Bustān al-Ukūl*' by *Natanaël Ibn al-Fayyumi*. With an English translation, *The Garden of Wisdom*, ed. D. Levine. New York, 1908; repr. 1966.

Study:

Pines, S. 'Nathanael ben Al-Fayyumi et la théologie ismaélienne'. *Revue de l'Histoire Juive en Egypte* 1 (1947) 5-22.

ASTROLOGY

Texts:

Ptolemy. *Tetrabiblos*, ed. and trans. into English by F. E. Robbins. Loeb Classical Library. Cambridge, Mass., 1971.

Studies:

The astrological History of Māshā' allāh. Ed. and trans. E. S. Kennedy and D. Pingree. Cambridge, Mass. 1971.
Bouché-Leclerc, A. *L'Astrologie grecque*. Paris, 1899; repr. Brussels, 1963.
Sarton, E. A. L. *Introduction to the history of science*. Baltimore, 1927-48 (esp. vol. II).
Pines, S. 'The Semantic distinction between the terms *Astronomy* and *Astrology* according to Al-Bīrūni'. *Isis* 55 (1914) 343-9.

ASTROLOGY AND ISRAEL

E.J. s.v. 'Astrology'

Studies:

Halkin, A. *Moses Maïmonides' Epistle to Yemen*. New York, 1952; introd., pp. xxi, xxvi.
Marx, A. 'The Correspondence between the Rabbis of Southern France and Maimonides about Astrology'. *HUCA* 3 (1926) 311-58.
Trachtenberg, J. *Jewish Magic and Superstition*. New York, 1939.
Vajda, G. *Juda b. Nissim Ibn Malka, philosophe juif marocain*, Paris, 1954, pp. 102-31.

Bibliography to pages 97–112

Abraham bar Ḥiyya

E.J., s.v. 'Abraham bar Ḥiyya'

Works:

Megillat ha-Megalleh. Ed. A. Poznanski with introd. and notes by J. Guttmann. Berlin, 1924.
Hegyon ha-Nefesh ha-Azuvah. Ed. G. Wigoder. Jerusalem, 1971.
  English translation: G. Wigoder, *Meditation of the Sad Soul.* New York, 1969.
The Letter on astrology published by Z. Schwartz in *Festschrift Adolf Schwartz*, Vienna, 1917, pp. 23–36.

Studies:

Guttmann, J. 'Über Abraham bar Chijjas "Buch der Enthüllung"'. *MGWJ* 47 (1903) 446–68, 545–69.
Levey, M. 'The Encyclopaedia of Abraham Savasorda: A Departure in Mathematical Methodology'. *Isis* 43 (1952) 257–64.
  'Abraham Savasorda and his Algorism – A Study in Early European Logistic'. *Osiris* 11 (1954) 50–64.
Millás Vallicrosa, J. M. *Estudios sobre la historia de la ciencia espanola*, Barcelona, 1949, pp. 219–26.
Scholem, G. 'Reste neuplatonischer Spekulation in der Mystik der deutschen Chassidim und ihre Vermittlung durch Abraham bar Chijja'. *MGWJ* 75 (1931) 172–91.
Stitskin, L. D. *Judaism as a Philosophy – The Philosophy of Abraham bar Hiyya.* New York, 1960.
Vajda, G. 'Les idées théologiques et philosophiques d'Abraham ben Hiyya'. *AHDLMA* 15 (1946).
  'Le système des Sciences exposé par Abraham Bar Hiyya et une page de Juda ben Barzilai'. *Sefarad* 22 (1962) 60–8.

Abraham Ibn Ezra

E.J., s.v. 'Ibn Ezra, Abraham'

Works:

Commentary on the Torah. Critical ed. by A. Wieser. Jerusalem, 1976.
The other biblical commentaries are included in *Mikra'ot Gedolot.*
For the editions and manuscripts of Abraham Ibn Ezra, see M. Friedlaender, *Essays on the Writings of Abraham Ibn Ezra*, below.
All the short treatises have been reprinted in 4 vols.: *Kitvei Rav Abraham Ibn Ezra.* Jerusalem, 1970.
The Beginning of Wisdom, an Astrological Treatise by Abraham Ibn Ezra. Ed. and trans. F. Cantera, Baltimore, 1939.
The Astrological works of Abraham Ibn Ezra; a literary and linguistic Study with special Reference to the old French Translation of Hagin. Ed. and trans. R. Levy. Baltimore–Paris, 1927.

Studies:

Friedlaender, M. *Essays on the Writings of Abraham Ibn Ezra.* London, 1877. Repr. Jerusalem, 1964.
Greive, H. *Studien zum jüdischen Neoplatonismus. Die Religionsphilosophie des Abraham Ibn Ezra.* Berlin–New York, 1973.
Lipchitz, A. 'The theory of Creation of Rabbi Abraham Ibn Ezra'. *Sinaï* 84 (1979) 105–25 (in Hebrew).

Bibliography to pages 104–131

Orschansky, G. *Abraham Ibn Ezra als Philosoph.* Breslau, 1900.
Olitzky, M. 'Die Zahlensymbolik des Abraham Ibn Ezra'. In *Jubelschrift für Israel,* Hildesheimer, 1890, pp. 99–106.
Rosin, D. 'Die Religionsphilosophie Abraham Ibn Ezra'. *MGWJ* 42 (1898) 17–33, 58–73, 108–15, 154–61, 200–14, 241–52, 305–15, 345–62, 394–407, 444–52; 43 (1899) 22–31, 75–91, 125–33, 168–84, 231–240.

Judah Halevi and Abu-l-Barakāt

Judah Halevi

E.J., s.v. 'Judah Halevi'

Goitein, S. D. 'The Biography of Rabbi Judah Ha-Levi in the Light of the Cairo Geniza Documents'. *PAAJR* 2 (1959) 41–56.
'Did Yehuda Halevi arrive in the Holy Land?' *Tarbiz* 46 (1977) 245–50 (in Hebrew).
On the Khazars, see Dunlop, D. M. *The History of the Jewish Khazars.* Princeton 1954. Repr. 1967.

Works:

Kitāb al-Radd wa-'l Dalīl fī 'l-Din al-Dhalīl. Ed. D. H. Banett and H. Ben-Shammaï. Jerusalem, 1977.
The *Kuzari* (Hebrew version) was first published at Fano, 1506.
English translation: Hirschfeld, H. *Book of Kuzari.* New York, 1946.
This is the translation included by I. Heinemann in *Three Jewish Philosophers.* New York, 1969.
A new translation based on the critical edition of 1977 is due to be published shortly. It is quoted here thanks to L. V. Berman's kindness.

Studies:

Alony, N. 'The Kusari – An Anti-arabiyyeh Polemic'. In *Eshel Beer-Sheva,* vol. II, Jerusalem, 1980, pp. 119–44 (in Hebrew).
Davidson, H. 'The Active Intellect in the *Cuzari* and Hallevi's Theory of Causality.' *REJ* 131 (1972) 351–96.
Goldziher, J. 'Le Amr Ilahi (ha-inyan ha-elohi) chez Judah Halévi'. *REJ* 50 (1905) 32–41.
Motzkin, A. L. 'On Halevi's Kazari as a platonic dialogue'. *Interpretation* 9.1 (1980) 111–24.
Pines, S. 'La longue recension de la théologie d'Aristote dans ses rapports avec la doctrine ismailéienne'. *REI* (1955) 7–20.
'Note sur la doctrine de la prophétie et la réhabilitation de la matière dans le Kuzari'. In *Mélanges de philosophie et de littérature juives,* Paris, 1957, pp. 253–60.
'Amr', s.v. *Encyclopédie de l'Islam,* vol. I (1960), pp. 462–3.
'Shi'ite Terms and Conceptions in Judah Halevi's *Kuzari'. Jerusalem Studies in Arabic and Islam* 2 (1980) 165–251.
Silman, Y. 'The Distinctiveness of Book III of the *Kuzeri'.* In *Eshel Beer-Sheva* vol. I, Jerusalem, 1976, pp. 94–119 (in Hebrew).
'Historical Reality in the Kusari'. *Daat* 2–3 (1978–9) 29–42 (in Hebrew).
'Between Theory of God and Theory of Man in the Kuzari', *Daat* 4 (1980) 7–34 (in Hebrew).
Strauss, L. 'The Law of Reason in the Kuzari'. *PAAJR* 3 (1943) 47–96.
Ventura, M. *Le Kalām et le péripatétisme d'après le Kuzari.* Paris, 1934.
Wienner, M. 'Judah Halevi's Concept of Religion and a Modern Counterpart.' *HUCA* 23 (1951) 669–82.
Wolfson, H. A. 'Maimonides and Halevi: A Study in Typical Jewish Attitudes toward Greek Philosophy in the Middle Ages'. In his *Studies in the History of Philosophy and Religion,* vol. II, Cambridge (Mass.), 1977, pp. 120–60.

'Hallevi and Maimonides on Design, Chance and Necessity'. *Ibid.* vol. II, pp. 1–59.
'The Platonic, Aristotelian and Stoic Theories of Creation in Halevi and Maimonides'. *Ibid.* vol. I, pp. 234–49.
'Hallevi and Maimonides on Prophecy'. *Ibid.* vol. II, pp. 60–119.
'Juda Halevi on Causality and Miracle'. *Ibid.* vol. II, pp. 415–32.

Abu-l-Barakāt

E.J., s.v. 'Hibat Allah, Abu Al-Barakāt (Nathanel) Ben Ali (Eli) Al-Baghdādī'

Translations and studies:

Pines, Shlomo. *Studies in Abu'l-Barakāt al-Baghdādī; Physics and Metaphysics.* Collected Works, I. Jerusalem, 1979.

Aristotelianism

Pinès, S. 'A Tenth Century Philosophical Correspondence'. *PAAJR* 24 (1955) 103–6.

Abraham Ibn Daud

E.J., s.v. 'Ibn Daud, Abraham ben David Halevi'

Works:

Emunah Ramah. The Hebrew translation by Solomon ben Labi published by S. Weil, *Das Buch Emunah Ramah.* With a German translation. Frankfort-am-Main, 1982.
The translation by Samuel Ibn Motot found in several manuscripts; cf. *HÜb*, 211–13, pp. 369 ff.

Study:

Horovitz, S. 'Die Psychologie des Aristotelikers Abraham Ibn Daud'. *Jahresberichte des jüdisch-theologischen Seminars Breslau* (1912) 212–86.

Maimonides

E.J., s.v. 'Maimonides, Moses'

Biography:

Yellin, D. and Abrahams, I. *Maimonides, His Life and Works*, repr. with notes by J. I. Dienstag, New York, 1972.
Goiten, S. D. 'Moses Maimonides, Man of Action, a Revision of the Master's Biography in Light of the Geniza Documents'. In G. Nahon and Ch. Touati (eds.), *Hommage à Georges Vajda*, Louvain, 1980, pp. 155–67.

Works:

(1) *Mishneh Torah.* The edition of Constantinople, 1509, reproduced with annotation by S. Liebermann, Jerusalem, 1964.
   With an English translation, by M. Hyamson: *Mishneh Tora: The Book of Knowledge.* Jerusalem, 1962.
(2) The Introductions to the *Commentary on the Mishnah*, in their medieval Hebrew translations, published by M. D. Rabinowitz, Jerusalem, 1961. English translations: *Ethical Writings of Maimonides.* Trans. R. L. Weiss, and C. E. Butterworth. New York, 1975.

The Eight Chapters of Maimonides on Ethics. Trans. J. I. Gorfinckel. New York, 1912; repr. 1966.

(3) 'Maïmonides' Arabic Treatise on Logic'. Ed. E. Efros. *PAAJR* 34 (1966), supplementing a previous publication in *PAAJR* 8 (1938).

(4) Letters. The *Letters* in Arabic, written in Hebrew letters with a modern Hebrew translation. Ed. J. Kafih. Jerusalem, 1962.

Moses Maimonides' Epistle to Yemen. The Arabic original and the three Hebrew versions, ed. from Mss with introd. and notes by A. S. Halkin and English trans. by B. Cohen. New York, 1952.

Letters of Maimonides. Trans. and ed. with introd. and notes by L. D. Stitskin. New York, 1977.

'Maimonides' *Treatise on Resurrection;* The Original Arabic and Samuel Ibn Tibbon's Hebrew Translation and Glossary'. Ed. J. Finkel. *PAAJR* 9 (1939).

'Epistle on Resurrection, trans. Al-Harizi'. Ed. A. S. Halkin. *Kobets al yad* 9 (19) (1980) 129–50.

The first Letter on Astrology: see 'The Correspondence between the Rabbis of Southern France and Maimonides about astrology'. Ed. and trans. A. Marx. *HUCA* 3 (1926) 311–58.

The second Letter on Astrology, trans. into English by R. Lerner: 'Maïmonides' Letter on Astrology'. *History of Religions* 8 (1968) 143–68.

The letter to Samuel Ibn Tibbon. An ed. of the two Hebrew versions by A. Marx, 'Texts by and about Maimonides'. *JQR* n.s. 25 (1934) 371–428.

Epistle on the fixed term of life. Ed. and trans. into Hebrew by M. Schwartz. Tel-Aviv University, 1979.

(5) *Le Dalalat Al-Hayarin.* The Arabic text, ed. S. Munk. In *Le Guide des Egarés.* Paris, 1856–66; repr. with notes and variants by I. Yoël. Jerusalem, 1931.

Moreh ha-Nevukhim. Printed before 1480.

The most useful ed. is Vilna 1904, with the commentaries of Efodi, Shem Tov ben Shem Tov, Crescas and Abrabanel.

A modern Hebrew trans. published by Eben Shemuel. Jerusalem, 1959.

The Guide of the Perplexed. Trans. S. Pines. Chicago, 1963.

Studies:

On Maimonides and Thomas Aquinas: *Studies in Maimonides and St Thomas Aquinas.* Ed. J. I. Dienstag. New York, 1975. (This includes the most important studies up to 1975, with an annotated bibliography on 'The relationship of St Thomas Aquinas to the philosophy of Maimonides', pp. 334–45.)

Ahad ha-am. 'Shilton ha-sekhel'. In *Kol Kitvei Ahad ha-am,* Tel-Aviv, 1947, pp. 355–69 (in Hebrew).

Altmann, A. 'Das Verhältnis Maimunis sur jüdischen Mystik'. *MGWJ* 80 (1936) 305–30.

Maimonides's 'Four Perfections'. In his *Essays in Jewish Intellectual History,* London, 1981, pp. 65–76.

'Maimonides and Thomas Aquinas: Natural or Divine Prophecy?' *Ibid.* pp. 77–96.

Berman, L. V. 'Ibn Bajjah and Maimonides, a Chapter in the History of Political philosophy'. Ph.D. diss. Hebrew University, Jerusalem, 1959 (in Hebrew with English summary).

'The Structure of the Commandments of the *Torah* in the Thought of Maimonides'. In S. Stein and R. Loewe (eds.), *Studies in Jewish Religious and Intellectual History, presented to Alexander Altmann,* Alabama, 1979, pp. 51–66.

'The Structure of Maimonides' *Guide of the Perplexed*'. In *Proceedings of the Sixth World Congress of Jewish Studies,* vol. III, Jerusalem, 1977, pp. 7–13.

'Maimonides on the fall of man'. *Association for Jewish Studies Review* 5 (1980) 1–15.

Bland, K. P. 'Moses and the Law According to Maimonides'. In J. Reinharr and D. Schwetschinski (eds.), *Mystics, Philosophers and Politicians; Essays in Jewish Intellectual History in Honor of Alexander Altmann*, Durham (North Carolina), 1982, pp. 49–66.

Blidstein, G. J. 'The Concept of Joy in Maimonides'. In *Eshel Beer-Sheva*, vol. II, Jerusalem, 1980, pp. 145–63 (in Hebrew).

Breslauer, S. D. 'Philosophy and imagination; the Politics of Prophecy in the view of Moses Maimonides'. *JQR* 70 (1980) 153–71.

Davidson, H. 'Maimonides' Secret Position on Creation.' In I. Twersky (ed.), *Studies in Medieval Jewish History and Literature* (vol. I). Cambridge (Mass.), 1979, pp. 16–40.

Diesendruck, Z. 'Maimonides' Lehre von der Prophetie'. In *Jewish Studies in Memory of Israël Abraham*, New York, 1927, pp. 74–134.

'Die Teleologie bei Maimonides'. *HUCA* 5 (1928) 415–534.

Efros, I. *Philosophical Terms in the Moreh Nebukhim*. New York, 1924; repr. 1966.

Fackenheim, E. 'The Possibility of the Universe in al-Farabi, Ibn Sina and Maimonides'. *PAAJR* 16 (1947) 39–70.

Faur, J. *Studies in the Mishneh Torah – Book of Knowledge*. Jerusalem, 1978 (in Hebrew).

Galson, M. 'The Purpose of the Law according to Maimonides'. *JQR* 69 (1978) 27–51.

Giladi, A. 'A short note on the possible origin of the title *Moreh hanevukhim*'. *Tarbiz* 48 (1979) 346–7 (in Hebrew).

Goldmann, S. 'The halakhic Foundation of Maimonides' Thirteen Principles'. In *Essays presented to Chief Rabbi Israel Brodie*, London, 1967, pp. 111–18.

Guttmann, J., *et al. Moses ben Maimon, sein Leben, seine Werke, und sein Einfluss*. Leipzig, 1908–14.

Hartman, D. *Maimonides, Torah and Philosophic quest*. Philadelphia, 1976.

Harvey, W. Z. 'Maimonides and Spinoza on the Knowledge of Good and Evil'. *Iyyoun* 28 (1978) 167–85 (in Hebrew).

'The Return of Maimonideanism'. *JSS* 42 (1980) 249–68.

'A Third Approach to Maimonides' Cosmogony–prophetology Puzzle'. *HTR* 74, 3 (1981) 287–301.

Heineman, I. 'Maimuni und die arabischen Einheitslehrer'. *MGWJ* 79 (1935) 102–48.

Hyman, A. 'Maimonides' Thirteen Principles'. In A. Altmann (ed.), *Jewish Medieval and Renaissance Studies*, Cambridge (Mass.), 1967, pp. 119–44.

Ivry, A. L. 'Maimonides on Possibility'. In J. Reinharr and D. Schwetschinski (eds.), *Mystics, Philosophers and Politicians* (see above), pp. 67–84.

Jacobs, L. *Principles of the Jewish Faith*. New York, 1964.

Kaplan, L. 'Maimonides on the Miraculous Element in Prophecy'. *HTR* 70 (1977) 233–56.

Kellner, M. M. 'Maimonides, Crescas and Abravanel on Exod. 20.2'. *JQR* 69 (1979) 129–57.

Klein-Braslavy, S. *Maimonides' Interpretation of the Story of Creation*. Jerusalem, 1978 (in Hebrew).

Kraemer, J. L. 'Alfarabi's *Opinions of the Virtuous City*'. In *Studia Orientalia, Memoriae D. H. Baneth Dedicata*, Jerusalem, 1979, pp. 323–43.

Macy, J. 'A Study in Medieval Jewish and Arabic Political Philosophy: Maimonides' *Shemonah Peraqim* and Al-Fārābī's *Fuṣūl al- Madanī*'. Ph.D. diss. Hebrew University, Jerusalem, 1982.

Marx, A. 'Texts about Maïmonides'. *JQR* 9 (1935) 371–428.

Motzkin, A. L., 'On the interpretation of Maïmonides'. *The Independent Journal of Philosophy* 2 (1979) 39–46.

Nuriel, A. 'The Question of a created or primordial world in the Philosophy of Maimonides'. *Tarbiz* 33 (1964) 372–87 (in Hebrew).

'Maimonides and the Concept of Faith'. *Daat* 2–3 (1978–9) 43–7 (in Hebrew).

'Providence and Governance in More ha- Nevukhim'. *Tarbiz* 49 (1980) 346–55 (in Hebrew).

'The Torah speaketh in the language of the sons of man in the *Guide of the Perplexed'*. In M. Hallamish and A. Kasker (eds.), *Religion and Language, Philosophical Essays*, Tel-Aviv, 1981, pp. 97–103 (in Hebrew).

'Maimonides on chance in the world of generation and passing away'. *Jerusalem Studies in Jewish Thought* 2, 1 (1982–3) 33–42 (in Hebrew).

Nutkiewicz, M. 'Maimonides on the Ptolemaic System: the limits of our knowledge'. *Comitatus* 9 (1978) 63–72.

Pines, S. s.v. 'Maimonides'. *Encyclopaedia of Philosophy*, vol. v (1967), p. 129–34.

Introd. to *Livre de la Connaissance*. Trans. by V. Nikiprowetzky and A. Zaoui. Paris, 1961.

Introd. to *The Guide of the Perplexed*, Chicago, 1963, pp. lvi-cxxxiv.

'The Limits of Human Knowledge according to Al-Farabi, Ibn Bajja and Maïmonides'. In I. Twersky (ed.), *Studies in Medieval Jewish History and Literature*, [vol. 1] (see above), pp. 82–109.

'Les limites de la métaphysique selon al-Farabi, Ibn Bajja et Maïmonide; sources et antithèses de ces doctrines chez Alexandre d'Aphrodise et chez Themistius'. *Miscellanea Mediaevalia* 13.1 (1981) 211–25.

Rawidowicz, S. 'Philosophy as a Duty'. In I. Epstein (ed.), *Moses Maimonides*, London, 1935, pp. 177–88.

Reines, A. J. *Maimonides and Abrabanel on Prophecy*. Cincinnati, 1970.

Rosenberg, S. 'On Biblical Interpretation in the *Guide of the Perplexed'. Jerusalem Studies in Jewish Thought* 1 (1981) 85–157 (in Hebrew).

Rosenthal, E. 'Maimonides' Conception of State and Society'. In I. Epstein (ed.), *Moses Maimonides* (see above), pp 191–206.

Rosin, D. *Die Ethik Maimonides*. Breslaw, 1876.

Roth, L. *Spinoza, Descartes and Maimonides*. Oxford, 1924.

Stern, M. S. 'Al-Ghazzali, Maimonides and Ibn Paquda on repentance; a comparative mode'. *JAAR* 47 (1979) 589–607.

Strauss, L. *Philosophie und Gesetz*. Berlin, 1935.

'Quelques remarques sur la science politique de Maïmonide et de Farabi', *REJ* 100 (1936) 1–37.

'Der Ort der Vorschungslehre nach der Ansicht Maimunis'. *MGWJ* 81 (1937) 35–105.

'Maimonides' Statement on Political Science'. *PAAJR* 22 (1953) 115–30.

'The Literary Character of the Guide for the Perplexed'. In his *Persecution and the art of writing*, Glencoe (Ill.), 1976, pp. 38–94.

'How to begin to study the *Guide of the Perplexed'*. Preface to the *Guide* (Pines trans., 1963), pp. xi–lvi.

Touati, C. 'Les deux théories de Maimonides sur la Providence'. In S. Stein and R. Loewe (eds.), *Studies in Jewish Religious and Intellectual History* (see above), pp. 331–43.

Twersky, I. 'Some Non-Halakic Aspects of the *Mishneh Torah'*. In A. Altmann (ed.), *Jewish Medieval and Renaissance Studies* (see above), pp. 95–118.

Introduction to the Code of Maimonides (Mishneh Tora). New Haven–London, 1980.

Wolfson, H. A. 'Maimonides on the Internal Senses'. In his *Studies in the History of Philosophy and Religion*, Cambridge (Mass.), 1973, vol. I, pp. 344–70.

'The Amphibolous Terms in Aristotle, Arabic Philosophy and Maimonides'. *Ibid.* vol. I, pp. 455–77.

'Note on Maimonides' Classification of the Sciences'. *Ibid.* vol. I, pp. 551–60.

'The Aristotelian Predicables and Maimonides' Division of Attributes'. *Ibid.* Cambridge (Mass.), 1977, vol. II, pp. 191–94.

'Maimonides on Negative Attributes'. *Ibid.* vol. II, pp. 195–230.

'Maimonides on the Unity and Incorporeality of God'. *Ibid.* vol. II, pp. 433–57.

Bibliography to pages 205–208

The Thirteenth Century

Halkin, S. H. *After Maimonides; An Anthology of Writings by His Critics, Defenders and Commentators.* Jerusalem, 1979 (in Hebrew).

Averroes

Works:

Fasl al-Maqāl (The Decisive Treatise). G. Hourani (ed. and English trans.). *On the Harmony of Religion and Philosophy.* London, 1961.

    Golb, M. 'The Hebrew Translation of Averroes' Fasal al-Maqāl'. *PAAJR* 25 (1956) 91–113; 26 (1957) 41–64.

Studies on Averroes' influence:

Steinschneider, M. *HÜb, s.v.* Averroës.

Nogales, S. G. 'Bibliografia sobre las obras de Averroès'. In *Multiple Averroes; Actes du Colloque international organisé à l'occasion du 850e anniversaire de la naissance d'Averroès*, Paris, 1978, pp. 351–87.

Wolfson, H. A. 'The Twice-revealed Averroes'. In his *Studies in the History of Philosophy, and Religion*, vol. I, Cambridge (Mass.), 1973, pp. 371–401.

    'Plan for the Publication of a *Corpus Commentariorum Averrois in Aristotelem*'. *Ibid.* pp. 430–54.

IN ISLAMIC COUNTRIES

Blumenthal, D. R. 'Was there an Eastern Tradition of Maimonidean Scholarship?' *REJ* 138 (1979) 57–68.

Joseph ben Judah of Ceuta

Work:

A Treatise as to Necessary Existence; The Procedure of Things from the Necessary Existence; The Creation of the World. Ed. J. L. Magnes. Berlin, 1904.

Joseph ben Judah Ibn Aknin

E.J., s.v. 'Aknin, Joseph b. Judah b. Jacob Ibn'.

Works:

Sefer ha-Mussar. Ed. W. Bacher. Berlin, 1910.

Tibb al-nufus. Ed. and German trans. by M. Güdemann. In *Das jüdische Unterrichtswesen während der spansich-arabischen Periode.* Vienna, 1873, pp. 43–138, and appendix, pp. 1–57.

Inkishāf al-asrār waṭuhūr al-anwār. Ed. and Hebrew trans. by A. S. Halkin. Jerusalem, 1964.

Studies:

Halkin, A. S. 'Classical and Arabic Material in Ibn Aknin's Hygiene of the Soul'. *PAAJR* 14 (1944) 25–147.

    'Ibn Aknin's Commentary on the Song of Songs'. In *Alexander Marx Jubilee Volume.* New York, 1950, pp. 389–424.

Munk, S. 'Notice sur Joseph ben-Iehouda'. *Journal Asiatique* 14 (1842) 5–70.

Neubauer, A. 'Joseph B. Aqnin'. *MGWJ* 14 (1970) 348–55, 395–401, 445–8.

Al-Tabrizi

The Hebrew translation by Isaac ben Nathan was first published in Venice, 1574, and repr. in vol. I of the complete works of Abrabanel, Jerusalem, 1967.
The second translation is still in manuscript. Cf. *HÜb*, § 208, pp. 361–3.

Sa'd ben Manṣur Ibn Kammūna

E.J., s.v. 'Ibn Kammūna, Sa'd Ibn Manṣur'

Works:

List of manuscripts and editions given in the facsimile of the Arabic text ed. by L. Nemoy, *Treatise on the Immortality of the Soul*. New Haven, 1944.
English translation. Nemoy, L. 'Ibn Kammuna's *Treatise on the Immortality of the Soul*'. In *I. Goldziher Memorial Volume*, vol. II, Jerusalem, 1958, pp. 83–99.

Study:

Nemoy, L. 'New Data for the Biography of Sa'ad Ibn Kammunah'. *REJ* 123 (1964) 507–10.

Abraham ben Maimonides and his pietist circle

On manuscripts and editions, see the Introduction and notes by P. Fenton to *The Treatise of the Pool, Al-Maqāla al Hawdiyya; 'Obadyāh b. Abraham b. Moses Maimonides*. London, 1981.

Abraham ben Moses Maimonides

E.J., *s.v.* 'Abraham ben Moses Maimonides'

Works:

(1) *Milhamot Adonaï*. Ed. R. M. Margalioth. Jerusalem, 1953.
(2) *Commentary on Genesis and Exodus*. Ed. and Hebrew trans by E. J. Wiesenberg. London, 1959.
(3) *Kifāyat al'Abidīn*. Ed. of Arabic fragments by S. Eppenstein. In *Festschrift zu Israel Lewy's siebzigsten Geburtstag*, Breslau, 1911, Hebrew part, pp. 33–59.
    The High Ways to Perfection of Abraham Maimonides. Ed. and trans. S. Rosenblatt. 2 vols. New York and Baltimore, 1927 and 1938.

Studies:

Cohen, G. D. 'The Soteriology of R. Abraham Maimuni'. *PAAJR* 25 (1967) 75–98; 36 (1968) 33–56.
Goitein, D. S. 'Abraham Maïmonides and his Pietist Circle'. In A. Altmann (ed.), *Jewish Medieval and Renaissance Studies*, Cambridge (Mass.), 1967, pp. 145–67.

Abraham he-Hasid

Fenton, P. 'Some Judeo-Arabic Fragments of Rabbi Abraham he-Ḥasid, the Jewish Sufi'. *JSS* 26 (1981) 47–72.

Perakim behaṣlaḥa

De Beatitudine Capita Duo R. Mosi b. Maïmon Adscripta. Ed. H. S. Davidowitz and D. H. Baneth. Jerusalem, 1939.

Bacher, W. 'The Treatise on Eternal Bliss attributed to Moses Maimuni'. *JQR* 9 (1896/7) 270–89. Bacher believed that the text was by Maimonides. Cf. Vajda, G. *REJ* 107 (1947) 212–13.

Vajda, G. 'Une Citation non signalée du Chapitre sur la Béatitude attribué à Moïse Maïmonide'. *REJ* 130 (1971) 305–6.

Work by an unknown author

Rosenthal, F. 'A Judeo-Arabic work under sufic influence'. *HUCA* 15 (1940) 433–84.
Fenton, P. 'A Jewish Sufi on the Influence of Music'. *Yuval* 4 (1982) 124–30.

PROVENCE

Neubauer, A., and Renan, E. 'Les Rabbins français du commencement du quatorzième siècle'. In *Histoire littéraire de la France*, vol. XXVII, Paris, 1877, *passim*.

Renan, E. *Les écrivains juifs français du XIVe siècle*. Paris, 1893. (= *Histoire littéraire de la France*, vol. XXI, pp. 351–789.)

Ravitzky, A. 'The Thought of R. Zerahiah b. Isaac b. Shealtiel Hen and the Maimonidean–Tibbonian Philosophy in the 13th century'. Ph.D. diss. Hebrew University of Jerusalem, 1977 (in Hebrew, summary in English).

Vajda, G. *Recherches sur la Philosophie et la Kabbale dans la pensée juive du Moyen-Age*. Paris, 1962.

Vicaire, M. H., and Blumenkranz, B. (eds.). *Juifs et Judaïsme de Languedoc XIIIe – début XIVe sièle*. Toulouse, 1977.

On the influence of Maimonides on Christian authors, see G. Vajda, 'Un abrégé chrétien du Guide des Egarés de Moïse Maïmonide'. *Journal Asiatique* (1960) 115–36.

On contacts between Jewish and Christian philosophy, see: Pines, S. 'Scholasticism after Thomas Aquinas and the teachings of Hasdai Crescas and his Predecessors'. In *Proceedings of the Israel Academy of Sciences and Humanities*, vol. I, 10, Jerusalem, 1967, pp. 1–101.

Judah ben Saul Ibn Tibbon

E.J., s.v. 'Tibbon, Judah ben Saul Ibn'

Work:

A Father's Admonition. Ed. and trans., in I. Abrahams, *Hebrew Ethical Wills*, 1st ed., Philadelphia, 1926, pp. 51–99.

The portrait of Faraj

Durrieu, Paul. 'Un portrait de Charles 1er d'Anjou'. *Gazette archéologique* 11 (1886) 192–201 and plate 23.
Kaufman, D. 'Un portrait de Faradj (Mosé b. Salem) le traducteur'. *REJ* 19 (1889) 152–4.

Samuel ben Judah Ibn Tibbon

E.J., s.v. 'Tibbon, Samuel ben Judah ibn'

Works:

The Glossary of Unusual Words to be found in the Guide of the Perplexed is printed in most editions of the *Moreh ha-nevukhim*.
Ma'amar Yikkawu ha-mayim (*Let the waters be gathered*). Ed. M. L. Bisliches, Pressburg, 1827.

A few important passages ed. on the basis of manuscripts and trans. into French in
G. Vajda, *Recherches sur la Philosophie et la Kabbale dans la pensée juive du Moyen-Age*,
Paris, 1962, pp. 12–32.

Perush Kohelet, a Commentary on Ecclesiastes. Parma, Bibliotheca palatina, MS de Rossi
272.

Studies:

Diesendruck, Z. 'Samuel and Moses Ibn Tibbon on Maimonides' Theory of Providence'.
HUCA 11 (1936) 341–66.

Ravitzky, A. 'The Thought of R. Zerahiah b. Isaac b. Shealtiel Hen and the Maimonidean–
Tibbonian Philosophy in the 13th century', Ph.D. diss., Hebrew University of Jerusalem, 1977, pp. 5–21. With a list of manuscripts of minor and attributed works.

'Samuel Ibn Tibbon and the esoteric character of the *Guide of the Perplexed*'. *Association
of Jewish Studies Review* 6 (1981) 87–123.

Sermoneta, J. 'The critics of Samuel Ibn Tibbon on Maimonides' Theory of Intelligences'.
In *Proceedings of the Sixth World Congress of Jewish Studies*, vol. III, Jerusalem, 1977,
pp. 315–19 (in Hebrew).

Vajda, G. 'An Analysis of the *Ma'amar yiqqawu ha-Mayim* by Samuel b. Judah Ibn Tibbon'.
JJS 10 (1959) 137–49.

David ben Joseph Kimḥi

E.J., s.v. 'Kimhi, David'

Works:

The commentaries on the Bible are printed in all the classical editions. The first editions are
of the fifteenth century.

Philosophical commentaries. On Genesis 2: 7–5: 1: in L. Finkelstein, *The Commentary of
David Kimhi on Isaiah*, New York, 1926; repr. 1966, appendix I, pp. liii–lxxiv.

On Ezekiel 1: in e.g., *Rabbinical Bible*, published Bragadin, Venice, 1618, fols. 615b–617a;
or Warsaw, 1902.

Studies:

Talmage, F. E. 'R. David Kimhi as polemicist'. *HUCA* 38 (1967) 213–35.

'David Kimhi and the Rationalist tradition'. *HUCA* 39 (1968) 177–218; also in *Studies in
Honor of I. E. Kiev*, New York, 1971, pp. 453–78.

David Kimhi, the Man and the Commentaries. Cambridge (Mass.), 1975.

The dispute concerning philosophical studies:

E.J., s.v. 'Maimonidean Controversy'

Nahmanides. *Commentary on the Torah*, trans. C. B. Chavel, New York, 1971, pp. 226–8.

Chavel, C. B. *Ramban, his life and teachings*. New York, 1960.

Writings and Discourses by Ramban. New York, 1978.

Sarachek, J. *Faith and Reason; the Conflict over the Rationalism of Maimonides*. New York,
1935; repr. 1970.

Septimus, B. *Hispano-Jewish Culture in Transition; the Career and Controversies of Ramah*.
Cambridge (Mass.), 1982.

Silver, D. J. *Maimonidean Criticism and the Maimonidean Controversy*. Leyden, 1965.

Touati, Ch. 'Les deux conflits autour de Maïmonide'. In M. H. Vicaire and B. Blumenkranz
(eds.), *Juifs et Judaïsme de Languedoc XIIIe – début XIVe siècle*, Toulouse, 1977,
pp. 173–84.

'Croyances vraies et croyances nécessaires'. In G. Nahon and Ch. Touati (eds.), *Hommage à Georges Vajda*, Louvain, 1980, pp. 169–82.

Twersky, I. *Rabad of Posquières, a Twelfth-Century Talmudist*. Cambridge (Mass.), 1962.

Jacob ben Abba Mari Anatoli

E.J., s.v. 'Anatoli, Jacob ben Abba Mari ben Samson'

Work:

Malmad ha-Talmidim (*Incentive to the pupils*), Lyck, 1866.

Studies:

Bettan, I. 'Jacob Anatolio: a Thirteenth century Liberal'. In *Studies in Jewish Preaching*, Cincinnati, 1939, pp. 49–88.

Gordon, M. L. 'The Rationalism of Jacob Anatoli'. Ph.D. diss. Yeshiva University, New York, 1974.

Sermoneta, G. 'Federico II e il pensiero ebraico nell 'Italia del suo tempo'. In *Federico II e. l'arte del duecento italiano*, Gulatina, 1980, pp. 183–97.

Isaac ben Yedaya

Studies:

Saperstein, M. 'The Works of R. Isaac b. Yedaiah: Philosophical Interpretation of the Aggadah in 13th Century Southern France'. Ph.D. diss. Harvard University, 1977.

'The Earliest Commentary on the Midrash Rabbah'. In I. Twersky (ed.), *Studies in Medieval Jewish History and Literature*, [vol. I], Cambridge (Mass.), 1979, pp. 283–306.

'R. Isaac b. Yedaya, a Forgotten Commentator on the Aggada'. *REJ* 138 (1979) 17–45.

Decoding the Rabbis. A thirteenth-century Commentary on the Aggadah, Cambridge (Mass.), 1980.

Moses ben Samuel Ibn Tibbon

E.J., s.v. 'Tibbon, Moses ben Samuel Ibn'

Works:

Perush Shir-ha-Shirim (*A Commentary on the Song of Solomon*). Lyck, 1874.

I am preparing an edition of the *Sefer Pea* and other works.

Study:

Sirat, C. 'La Pensée philosophique de Moïse Ibn Tibbon'. *REJ* 138 (1979) 505–15.

Ruah Hen (Spirit of Grace)

Numerous editions exist, the last published being, Warsaw, 1826; repr. Jerusalem, 1970.

Study:

Sirat, C. 'Le Livre *Rouah Hen*'. In *Proceedings of the Sixth World Congress of Jewish Studies*, vol. III, Jerusalem, 1977, pp. 117–23.

Gershom ben Solomon of Arles

E.J., s.v. 'Gershom b. Solomon'

Works:

Sha'ar ha-Shamayim (*The Gate of the Heavens*). Numerous editions exist, the last being Warsaw, 1876; repr. Jerusalem, 1968.

English translation: F. S. Bodenheim, *The Gate of Heaven*, Jerusalem, 1953.

Studies:

Kopf, L. 'The words in vernacular language in *The Gate of Heaven*', *Tarbiz* 24 (1955) 150–66, 274–89, 410–25 (in Hebrew).

Lay, J. 'L'astronomie et la métaphysique de Rabbi Gershom ben Salomon d'Arles'. M.A. thesis. University of Paris III, 1978.

Shem Tov ben Joseph Falaquera

E.J., s.v. 'Falaquera, Shem Tov ben Joseph'

Works:

The texts that are not cited below have been reprinted in *The Works of Rabbi Shem Tov Falaquera*. 3 vols. Jerusalem, 1970.

Moreh ha-moreh (*The Guide to the Guide*). Ed. M. Bisliches, Pressburg, 1837; repr. in *Three Ancient Commentators of the Guide of the Perplexed*. Jerusalem, 1961 (in Hebrew).

Shelemut ha-Ma'asim (*The Perfection of Actions*) and Fragments of Bible Commentary preserved in Samuel Zarza's *Mekor Hayyim* to be published in the forthcoming book by R. Jospe, *The life* (see below).

De'ot ha-Pilosofim (*Opinions of the Philosophers*). Parma, Bibliotheca palatina, MS De Rossi 164.

Sefer Ha-Mebaqqesh; Falaquera's Book of the Seeker. Eng. trans. by M. H. Levine. New York, 1976.

'Sefer ha-nefesh; Shem Tov Ibn Falaquera's Psychology'. Crit. ed. and trans. R. Jospe. Ph.D. diss. Brandeis University, 1978. To be published in his forthcoming book, *The Life* (see below).

'Epistola dialogi – une traduction latine de l'Igeret ha-Vikuah de Shemtov ibn Falaquera'. Ed. E. Dahan. *Sefarad* 39 (1979) 47–85, 237–64.

Studies:

Harvey, S. 'Averroes on the Principles of Nature; The Middle Commentary on Aristotle's Physics, I–II'. Ph.D. diss., Harvard University, 1977, pp. 472–9.

Jospe, R. *The Life and Philosophy of Shem Tov Ibn Falaquera*, forthcoming. Includes a biography of Falaquera, a survey of his philosophy and editions of works already mentioned.

Malter, H. 'Shem Tob ben Joseph Palquera'. *JQR* n.s. I (1910/11) 151–81; repr. in *The Works of Rabbi Shem Tov Falaquera*, vol. I.

Isaac Albalag

E.J., s.v. 'Albalag, Isaac'

Work:

Tikkun ha-De'ot. Ed. G. Vajda. Jerusalem, 1973.
    French translation and study in G. Vajda. *Isaac Albalag – Averroiste juif, traducteur et commentateur d'Al-Ghazali*. Paris, 1960.

Study:

Touati, C. 'Vérité philosophique et vérité prophétique, chez Isaac Albalag'. *REJ* 121 (1962) 35–47.

Levi ben Abraham ben Hayyim of Villefranche de Conflent

E.J., s.v. 'Levi ben Abraham ben Hayyim'

Works:

A list of manuscripts given in C. Sirat. 'Les différentes versions du *Liwyat Hen* de Levi b. Abraham'. *REJ* 122 (1963) 167–77.

436

The polemic against the Christians published by M. Steinschneider, in *Yeshurun, Kovak* 8 (1872) 1–13.

Studies:

Baeck, L. 'Zur Characteristik des Levi ben Abraham ben Chajjim'. *MGWJ* 44 (1900) 24–41, 59–71, 156–67, 337–44, 417–23.

Falbel, N. 'On a heretic argument in Levi ben Abraham ben Chaiim's critique of Christianity'. In *Proceedings of the Seventh World Congress of Jewish Studies: History of the Jews in Europe*, Jerusalem, 1981, pp. 29–45.

PHILOSOPHERS OF SOUTHERN SPAIN

Baer, Y. *A History of the Jews in Christian Spain*. Philadelphia, 1966.
On the Kabbalah and its history. Scholem, G. G. *Major Trends in Jewish Mysticism*. Jerusalem, 1941.
On the Kabbalah and its symbolism. London, 1965.
Kabbalah. Jerusalem, 1974.
On *Gematria, Notarikon*, cf. *E.J.*, s.v.
Kraus, P. *Jabīr Ibn Ḥayyān; essai sur l'histoire des idées scientifiques dans l'Islam*. Cairo–Paris, 1935.

Judah ben Solomon ha-Cohen Ibn Malkah

E.J., s.v. 'Matkah, Judah ben Solomon ha-Kohen'

Work:

Midrash ha-Ḥokhmah (*The Exposition of Science*); one complete copy in the Vatican, MS heb. 338; but the best copy is in Oxford, Bodleian Library, Mich. 551 (Cat. no. 1321), and is almost complete.

Parts of this work have been published. *Otot Hashamayim, hu Sefer Mishpete Hakokhavim Umishpete Hanolad*. Ed. J. Spiro. Warsaw, 1886.

'The Commentary of Judah ben Solomon Hakohen ibn Matqah to Genesis, Psalms and Proverbs'. Ed. D. Goldstein, *HUCA* 52 (1981) 203–52.

Sirat, C. 'L'explication des Lettres selon Juda b. Salomon ha-Cohen'. In *La lettre hébraïque et sa signification*, Paris, 1981, pp. 39–42.

Studies:

Goldstein, D. 'The Citations of Judah ben Solomon ha-Cohen in the Commentary to Genesis of Rabbenu Bahya ben Asher'. *JJS* 26 (1975) 105–112.

Sirat, C. 'Judah b. Salomon ha-Cohen, philosophe, astronome et peut-être kabbaliste de la première moitié du XIIIe siècle'. *Italia* 2 (1977) 39–61.

'La *qabbale* d'après Juda b. Salomon ha-Cohen'. In G. Nahon and Ch. Touati (eds.) *Hommage à Georges Vajda*, Louvain, 1980, pp. 191–202.

Isaac ben Abraham Ibn Latif

E.J., s.v. 'Latif, Isaac b. Abraham ibn'

Works:

Most of the printed works have been reproduced in two volumes, *The Works of Rabbi Isaac Ibn Latif*, Jerusalem, 1970.

The full list of works in S. O. Heller-Wilensky. 'Isaac Ibn Latif, Philosopher or Kabbalist?' In A. Altmann (ed.), *Jewish Medieval and Renaissance Studies*, Cambridge (Mass.), 1967, pp. 185–223.

Study:

Heller-Wilensky, S. O. 'The Problem of the Authorship of the book: *Sha'ar ha-Shamayim*, ascribed to Abraham Ibn Ezra', *Tarbiz* 32 (1963) 277–95 (in Hebrew).

Judah ben Nissim Ibn Malkah

E.J., s.v. 'Malkah, Judah ben Nissim Ibn'

Work:

A Hebrew Abridgment of R. Judah ben Nissim Ibn Malka's Commentary on the Book of Creation. Ed. G. Vajda. Ramat-Gan, 1974.

Studies:

Vajda, G. *Juda b. Nissim Ibn Malka, philosophe juif marocain*. Paris 1954.
  'La doctrine astrologique de Juda b. Nissim Ibn Malka'. In *Homenaje a Millás-Vallicrosa*, vol. II, Barcelona, 1956, pp. 483–500.

Abraham ben Samuel Abulafia

E.J., s.v. 'Abulafia, Abraham Ibn Samuel'

Studies:

Idel, M. 'Abraham Abulafia's Works and Doctrine'. Ph.D. diss. Hebrew University, Jerusalem, 1976 (in Hebrew with an English summary). With a list of works, manuscripts and printed books on pp. 1–80, together with full bibliography.
  'Music and Prophetic Kabbalah'. *Yuval* 4 (1982) 150–69.
  'Was Abraham Abulafia influenced by the Cathars?' *Iyun* 30 (1981) 133–40 (in Hebrew).

Moses ben Joseph ha-Levi of Seville

E.J., s.v. 'Moses ben Joseph Ha-Levi'

Studies:

Vajda, G. 'Un champion de l'avicennisme; le Problème de l'identité de Dieu et du Premier moteur d'après un opuscule judéo-arabe inédit du XIIIe siècle'. *Revue Thomiste* 48 (1948) 480–504.
  'The Doctrine of R. Moses b. Joseph Halevi on Providence'. *Melilah* 5 (1955) 163–8 (in Hebrew).
Wolfson, A. H. 'Averroes' Lost Treatise on the Prime Mover'. *Studies in the History of Philosophy and Religion*, Cambridge (Mass.), 1973, vol. I, pp. 402–29.

THE ITALIAN PHILOSOPHERS

Barzilay, I. E. *Between Reason and Faith. Anti-Rationalism in Italian Jewish Thought*, 1250–1650, The Hague, 1967, pp. 11–51.
Ravitsky, A. 'The Thought of R. Zerahiah b. Isaac b. Shealtiel Hen and the Maimonidean-Tibbonian Philosophy in the 13th century', Ph.D. diss., Hebrew University of Jerusalem, 1977, *passim*.
  'Possible and Contingent Existence in the Exegesis of Maimonides in the 13th century', *Daat* 2–3 (1978–9) 67–97 (in Hebrew).
Sermoneta, G. (or J.). 'La Dottrina dell'intelletto et la "fede filosofica" di Jehudah e Immanuel Romano'. *Studi Medievali*, 3rd series, 6, 2 (1965) 1–76.

Bibliography to pages 266–271

'The Scholastic literature in Rabbi Joseph Taitazak's *Parat Yosef*'. *Sefunot* 11 (1971–8) 136–85 (in Hebrew).
'Per una storia del Tomismo ebraico'. In *S. Tommaso vella storia del pensiero*, Naples, 1980, vol. II, pp. 354–9.
Steinschneider, M. *Letteratura italiana dei Giudei*. Rome, 1864.
'Die italienische Literatur'. *MGWJ* 42 (1898) 263–5, 315–22, 418–24, 466–72, 517–22; 43 (1899) 32–6, 91–6.

Moses ben Solomon of Salerno

Works:

Ta'anot (*Argumentations*). Published in S. Simon. *Mose ben Salomo von Salerno und seine philosophischen Auseinandersetzungen mit den Lehren des Christentums*, Breslau, 1931.
Sermoneta, G. (ed.). *Un glossario filosofico ebraico–italiano del XIII secolo*. Rome, 1969.
The *Commentary* on the *Guide of the Perplexed* is preserved in a dozen manuscripts, listed in Steinschneider, *HÜb*, p. 433.

Study:

Sermoneta, J. 'Moses ben Solomon of Salerno and Nicholaus of Giovinazo on Maimonides' *The Guide of the Perplexed*'. *Iyun* 20 (1970) 212–40 (in Hebrew; English summary, pp. 298–9).

Zerahiah ben Shealtiel Gracian of Barcelona

E.J., s.v. 'Gracian, Zerahiah ben Isaac ben Shealtiel.'

Works:

Imrei Da'at (*The Commentary on Proverbs*). Ed. I. Schwartz. Vienna, 1871.
Tikvat Enoch (*The Commentary on Job*). Ed. I. Schwartz. Berlin, 1868.
The letters were published in *Otsar Nehmad* 2 (1857) 229–45.

Study:

Ravitzky, A. 'The Thought of R. Zerahiah b. Isaac b. Shealtiel Hen and the Maimonidean–Tibbonian Philosophy in the 13th century', Ph.D. diss., Hebrew University of Jerusalem, 1977, which lists other works still in manuscript.

Hillel ben Samuel of Verona

E.J., s.v. 'Hillel ben Samuel'

Work:

Hillel ben Samuel of Verona; Sefer Tagmulei ha-Nefesh (*Retributions of the Soul*). Ed. G. Sermoneta. Jerusalem, 1981.

Study:

Sermoneta, J. 'On the third dissertation: *the Fall of the Angels*'. In *Studies in honour of J. Friedman*, Jerusalem, 1974, pp. 155–203 (in Hebrew).

Judah ben Moses ben Daniel Romano

E.J., s.v. 'Romano, Judah ben Moses ben Daniel'

Works:

The *Commentary on Genesis, Chapters on Prophecy* and various exegeses: Vatican, MS ebreo Urbinate 38.

Ben Porat exists in several manuscripts.

Romano's translation of Thomas Aquinas' *De ente et essentia: Sancti Thomae de Aquino Opusculum de ente et essentia.* Ed. G. Sermoneta. Jerusalem, 1978.

Study:

Sermoneta, G. 'Jehudah ben Moseh ben Daniel Romano, traducteur de Saint Thomas'. In G. Nahon and Ch. Touati (eds.), *Hommage à Georges Vajda.* Louvain, 1980, pp. 231–62.

'R. Yehudah Romano on Prophecy'. *Daat* 8 (1982) 53–86 (in Hebrew).

Immanuel ben Solomon of Rome

E.J., s.v. 'Immanuel (ben Solomon) of Rome'

Works:

Maḥbarot Immanuel. Ed. D. Yarden. Jerusalem, 1957.

The beginning of the *Commentary on Genesis* was published by F. M. Tocci, *Il commento di Emanuele Romano al Capitolo I della Genesi,* Rome 1963.

(I have used Parma, Bibliotheca palatine, MS de Rossi 404.)

The Book of Proverbs, with the Commentary of Immanuel of Rome, Naples, *ca.* 1487, was reprinted Jerusalem, 1981, with an introd. by D. Goldstein, together with a list (pp. 7–8) of the manuscripts where the other biblical commentaries are preserved.

Study:

Goldstein, D. 'Longevity, the Rainbow and Immanuel of Rome'. *HUCA* 43 (1971/2) 243–50.

The Fourteenth Century

Pines, S. 'Scholasticism after Thomas Aquinas and the teachings of Hasdai Crescas and his Predecessors'. In *Proceedings of the Israel Academy of Sciences and Humanities,* vol. I, 10, Jerusalem, 1967, pp. 1–101; the Hebrew version of this paper, printed in *Bein maḥshevet Israel lemaḥshevet ha'amim* (Jerusalem, 1977), pp. 174–262, was much expanded.

'Saint-Thomas et la pensée juive médiévale, quelques notations'. In *Aquinas and Problems of his time,* Louvain-La Haye, 1976, pp. 118–29.

Renan, E. *Les écrivains juifs français du XIVe siècle.* Paris, 1893. (= *Histoire littéraire de la France,* vol. xxi, pp. 351–789.)

Rosenberg, S. 'Logic and Ontology in Jewish Philosophy in the 14th Century'. Ph.D. diss. Hebrew University, Jerusalem, 1974.

Shatzmiller, J. 'Contacts et échanges entre savants juifs et chrétiens à Montpellier en 1300'. In M. H. Vicaire and B. Blumenkrantz (eds.), *Juifs et Judaïsme de Languedoc XIIIe– début XIVe Siècle.* Toulouse, 1977.

Steinschneider, M. *HÜb,* pp. 461–500, 616–49, 775–843, 948–70, 971–87.

Touati, C. 'L'inerrance prophétique dans la Théologie du Moyen-Age'. *Revue de l'Histoire des Religions* 174 (1968) 168–87.

Yedayah ha-Penini

E.J., s.v. 'Jedaiah ben Abraham Bedersi'

Behinat Olam (Examination of the World). First printed in Manua, before 1480.

Works:

The Letter of Apology was printed in *She'elot u-Tchuvot . . . Rabbenu Shelomo ben Adret,* Hanover, 1610, 65 d – 67 a (416–18).

The Commentary on the *Aggadot of Psalms. Erlauterungen der Psalmen Haggada von Jedaja Penini*. Ed. S. Buber. Cracow, 1891; first printed Venice, 1599.

Studies:

Halkin, A. S. 'Yedaiah Bedershi's Apology'. In A. Altmann (ed.), *Jewish Medieval and Renaissance Studies*, Cambridge (Mass.), 1967, pp. 165–84.

Pines, S. 'Individual forms in the thought of Yedaya Bedarsi'. In *H. A. Wolfson Jubilee Volume*, Jerusalem, 1965, pp. 187–201 (in Hebrew).

Renan, E. *Les écrivains juifs français du XIVe siecle*, Paris, 1893, pp. 13–56 (359–402).

Nissim ben Moses of Marseille

E.J., s.v. 'Nissim ben Moses of Marseilles'

Work:

Sefer ha-Nissim (*Book of Miracles*). Introduction published by H. Schorr, *Hehalutz* 7 (1865) 102–44.

Studies:

Halkin, A. S. 'Rabbi Nissim of Marseille, thinker from the fourteenth century'. In *Proceedings of the Fifth World Congress of Jewish Studies*, vol. III, Jerusalem, 1972, pp. 143–9.

'Nissim ben Moscheh on Providence'. In G. Nahon and Ch. Touati (eds.), *Hommage à Georges Vajda*, Louvain, 1980, pp. 219–25.

Gersonides

E.J., s.v. 'Levi ben Gershom (Ralbag)'

Biography:

Shatzmiller, J. 'Gersonides and the Community of Orange in the Middle-Ages.' In *Research on the History of Israel and Erets Israel*, vol. II, Haifa, 1972, pp. 111–26 (in Hebrew).

Works:

Milḥamot Adonai (*The Wars of the Lord*). Riva di Trento, 1560; repr. Jerusalem, n.d.; also Leipzig, 1866. These editions are very faulty.

A list of manuscripts is given by C. Touati in the French translation of Books III and IV, *Les Guerres du Seigneur*, Paris, 1968, pp. 31–6.

English translations. Book III in N. M. Samuelson, *Gersonides on God's Knowledge*, Toronto, 1977.

Book IV in J. D. Bleich, *Providence in the Philosophy of Gersonides*, New York, 1973.

Book VI, part 2, Chapter I in J. J. Staub, *The Creation of the World according to Gersonides*. Chico (Ca.), 1982.

The Biblical Commentaries are printed in the rabbinical bibles.

To 'aliyot, the *Lessons* of these commentaries, were printed separately, Riva di Trento, 1570.

The commentaries on Aristotle and Averroes. List of manuscripts in Steinschneider, *HÜb* s.v. 'Levi ben Gerson'.

Only one commentary published, 'Gersonides' Commentary on Averroes' Epitome of *Parva Naturalia*, II, 3'. Annotated critical ed. by A. Altmann, in *American Academy for Jewish Research Jubilee Volume*, Jerusalem, 1950, pp. 1–31.

Astronomy. 'The astronomical Tables of Levi ben Gerson'. Ed. and trans. B. R. Goldstein. The Connecticut Academy of Arts and Sciences, 1974.

Studies:

Feldman, S. 'Gersonides' Proofs for the Creation of the Universe'. *PAAJR* 35 (1967) 113–37.

'Platonic Themes in Gersonides' Cosmology'. In *Salo Wittmayer Baron Jubilee Volume*, American Academy for Jewish Research, Jerusalem, 1975, pp. 383–405.

'Gersonides on the possibility of conjunction with the Agent Intellect'. *Association of Jewish Studies Review* 3 (1978) 99–120.

Goldstein, B. R. 'Astronomical and Astrological themes in the philosophical works of Levi ben Gerson'. *Archives internationales d'Histoire des Sciences*, 26, 99 (1976) 221–4.

Kellner, M. M. 'Gersonides, Providence and the Rabbinic Tradition'. *Journal of the American Academy of Religion* 42 (1974) 673–85.

'Gersonides and his cultured despisers: Arama and Abravanel'. *The Journal of Medieval Renaissance Studies* 6 (1976) 269–196.

'Maimonides and Gersonides on Mosaic Prophecy'. *Speculum* 52 (1977) 62–79.

'Gersonides on Miracles, the Messiah and Resurrection', *Daat* 4 (1980) 5–34 (in Hebrew).

'R. Levi Ben Gerson: A Bibliographical Essay'. *Studies in Bibliography and Booklore* 12 (1979) 13–23.

Rudavsky, T. M. 'Individuals and the Doctrine of Individualism in Gersonides'. *The New Scholasticism* 56 (1982) 30–50.

Touati, C. *La pensée philosophique et théologique de Gersonide*, Paris 1973. With bibliography until 1972.

'Les idées philosophiques et théologiques de Gersonide dans ses commentaires bibliques'. *Revue des Sciences religieuses* 28 (1954) 335–67.

Wolfson, H. A. 'Maimonides and Gersonides on Divine Attributes as Ambiguous Terms', repr. in his *Studies in the History of Philosophy and Religion*, vol. II, Cambridge (Mass.) 1977, pp. 231–46.

Abner of Burgos and the question of free will and providence

E.J., s.v. 'Abner of Burgos'

Altmann, A. 'Free Will and Predestination in Saadia, Bahya and Maimonides'. In his *Essays in Jewish intellectual History*, London, 1981, pp. 35–64.

Baer, I. *A History of the Jews in Christian Spain*, Philadelphia, 1961, vol. I, pp. 327–54 and index.

'Abner of Burgos' *Minhath Kenaoth* and its influence on Hasdai Crescas'. *Tarbiz*, 11 (1940) 188–206 (in Hebrew).

Baudry, L. *La Querelle des futurs contingents*. Paris, 1950.

Sirat, C. 'Deux philosophes juifs répondent à Abner de Burgos à propos du libre-arbitre humain et de l'omniscience divine'. In *Mélanges offerts à André Neher*, Paris, 1975, pp. 87–94.

Isaac Pulgar (Pollegar)

E.J., s.v. 'Pollegar, Isaac ben Joseph ibn'

Work:

Ezer ha-dat (*The Support of the Faith*). Ed. G. S. Belasco. London, 1906.

Ezer hadat (*A defence of Judaism*), ed. and annotated J. S. Levinger. Tel Aviv, 1984.

Study:

Pines, S. 'Some topics dealt with in Pulgar's treatise *Ezer ha-dat*; parallels in Spinoza', *Jerusalem Studies in Jewish Thought* (forthcoming).

Joseph Caspi (*En Bonafoux de l'Argentière*)

E.J., s.v. 'Kaspi, Joseph ben Abba Mari'

Works:

Adney Kesef, Ed. I. Last, London, 1911
'*Amudey Kesef U-Maskiyyoth Kesef, Sheney Perushim 'al Sefer Ha-Moreh Le Ha-Ramban.* Ed. S. Werblumer. Frankfurt s/Main, 1848; reprinted in *Three Ancient Commentators on the Guide of the Perplexed*, Jerusalem, 1961.
Sefer Ha-Musar. Ed. and trans. into English by I. Abrahams. In *Hebrew Ethical Wills*, Philadelphia, 1926, 1926, vol. I, pp. 127–61.
'Sharshoth Kesef, The Hebrew Dictionary of Roots, by Joseph Ibn Kaspi'. Excerpts published by I. Last, *JQR* o.s. 19 (1907) 651–87.
Tam Ha Kesef. Ed. I. Last. London, 1913.
'*Asarah Keley Kesef: Zehn Schriften des R. Josef Ibn Kaspi (Ten Books by Joseph Caspi).* Ed. I. Last. Pressburg, 1903.
Mishné Kesef: Zwei Schriften des R. Josef Ibn Kaspi (Two Books by Joseph Caspi). Ed. I. Last. Vol. I, '*Tirath Kesef*', Cracow, 1906; vol. II, '*Mazrefla Kesef*', Pressburg, 1905.
The manuscripts are described and analysed in E. Renan *Les écrivains juifs français du XIVe siècle*, Paris, 1893, pp. 131–201 (477–547); and B. Mesch, *Studies in Joseph Ibn Caspi.* Leyden, 1975.

Studies:

Herring, B. F. (ed. and trans.). *Gevia Kesef: A Study in Medieval Jewish Bible Commentary.* New York, 1982.
Mesch, B. 'Principles of Judaism in Maimonides and Joseph ibn Caspi'. In J. Reinhart and D. Schwetschinski (eds.), *Mystics, Philosophers and Politicians; Essays in Jewish Intellectual History in Honor of Alexander Altmann*, Durham (North Carolina), 1982 pp. 85–98.
Pines, S. 'The resurrection of the Jewish State according to Ibn Caspi and Spinoza'. *Iyyun* 14 (1963) 289–317 (in Hebrew).
Rosenberg, S. 'Logic, Language and Exegesis of the Bible in the Works of Joseph Ibn Kaspi'. In M. Hallamish and A. Kasher (eds.), *Religion and Language; Philosophical Essays*, Tel-Aviv, 1981, pp. 104–13.
Twersky, I. 'Joseph Ibn Kaspi, portrait of a Medieval Jewish Intellectual'. In his *Studies in Medieval Jewish History and Literature*, [Vol. I], Cambridge (Mass.), 1979, pp. 231–57.

Kalonymus ben Kalonymus ben Meir

Renan, E. *Les écrivains juifs français du XIVe siècle*, Paris, 1893, pp. 71–114 (417–61).
Rosenberg, S. 'Logic and Ontology in Jewish Philosophy in the 14th Century'. Ph.D. diss., Hebrew University, Jerusalem, 1974, pp. 85–6.
Shatzmiller, J. 'The Small Epistle of Excuse from Kalonymos ben Kalonymos'. *Sefunot* 10 (1966) 9–52 (in Hebrew).

Todros Todrosi

Renan, E. *Les écrivains juifs français du XIVe siècle* (see above) pp. 224–7 (570–3).
Rosenberg, S. 'Logic and Ontology in Jewish Philosophy in the 14th Century' (see above), pp. 86–8.

Samuel ben Judah ben Meshullam ben Isaac of Marseille

Renan, E. *Les écrivains juifs français du XIVe siècle* (see above), pp. 207–21 (554–67).

Rosenberg, S. 'Logic and Ontology in Jewish Philosophy in the 14th Century' (see above), pp. 89–90.

Berman, L. V. 'Greek into Hebrew: Samuel b. Judah of Marseilles, Fourteenth Century Philosopher and Translator'. In A. Altmann (ed.), *Jewish Medieval and Renaissance Studies*, Cambridge (Mass.), 1967, pp. 289–320.

Shemariah ben Elijah the Cretan

E.J., s.v. 'Shemariah ben Elijah ben Jacob'

'*Mikhtav al-Hiddush ha-'olam* (*The Epistle on the Creation of the World* by Shemaryah b. Elijah)', ed. C. Sirat. In *Eshel Beer-Sheva*, vol. II, Jerusalem, 1980, pp. 199–227 (in Hebrew). With a list of works, printed and in manuscript.

Rosenberg, S. 'Logic and Ontology in Jewish Philosophy in the 14th Century' (see above), pp. 94–9.

Moses ben Joshua Narboni

E.J., s.v. 'Moses ben Joshua of Narbonne'

Works:

'Iggeret Shiur Qoma, Moses Narboni's Epistole in Shi'ur Qoma'. Ed. and English trans. by A. Altmann. In his *Jewish Medieval and Renaissance Studies*, Cambridge (Mass.), 1967, pp. 225–88.

Ma'amar habehira (*Treatise on Free Will*). Ed. and French trans. by M. R. Hayoun, 'L'épitre du libre-arbitre de Moïse de Narbonne'. *REJ* 141 (1982) 139–67.

'*Pirkei Moshé le Moshe Narboni*' (*The Chapters of Moses*). Ed. C. Sirat. *Tarbiz* 39 (1970) 287–306.

French trans. by C. Sirat, in 'Moïse de Narbonne et l'astrologie'. *Proceedings of the Fifth World Congress of Jewish Studies*, vol. III, Jerusalem, 1972, pp. 61–72.

Ma'amar bi-Shelemut ha-nefesh; Treatise on the Perfection of the Soul. Ed. A. L. Ivry. Jerusalem, 1977.

The Epistle on Conjunction with the Active Intellect by Ibn Rushd with the Commentary of Moses Narboni. Ed. and trans. K. P. Bland. New York, 1981.

Commentary on the Guide of the Perplexed. Ed. J. Goldenthal. Vienna, 1852; reprinted in *Three Ancient Commentators on the Guide of the Perplexed*, Jerusalem, 1961.

The first fifty chapters of this Commentary, new ed. and French trans. by M. R. Hayoun: *Le Commentaire de Narboni sur les cinquante premiers chapitres du Guide de Maimonide.* Paris, 1983.

'The Commentary on Maimonides' Vocabulary of Logic'. Ed. M. R. Hayoun. *Daat* 10 (1983), 75–92.

The Commentary on Lamentations. Ed. M. R. Hayoun (in preparation).

A list of manuscripts of unpublished works is found in Renan, E. *Les écrivains juifs français du XIVe siècle*, Paris, 1893, pp. 320–35 (666–81).

Studies:

Rosenthal, E. I. J. 'Political Ideas in Moshe Narboni's Commentary on Ibn Ṭufail's Ḥayy b. Yaqẓān'. In G. Nahon and Ch. Touati (eds.), *Hommage à Georges Vajda*, Louvain, 1980, pp. 227–34.

Touati, C. 'Dieu et le monde selon Moïse Narboni'. *AHDLMA* 23 (1956) 80–102.

Vajda, G. 'Comment le philosophe juif Moïse de Narbonne, commentateur d'Ibn Ṭufayl, comprenait-il des paroles extatiques (*Šaṭaḥāt*) des Soufis?' In *Actas del Primer Congreso de Estudios Arabes e islamicos*, Madrid, 1964, pp. 129–35.

Joseph ben Abraham Ibn Waqar

E.J., s.v. 'Ibn Waqar, Joseph b. Abraham'

Studies:

Vajda, G. *Recherches sur la philosophie et la Kabbale dans la pensée juive du Moyen-Age*, Paris–La Haye, 1962, pp. 115–297, 385–91.
'The Commentary of Rabbi Joseph Ibn Waqar on the Book of Creation'. *Ozar Yehudei Sefarad* 5 (1962) 17–20 (in Hebrew).
Sed-Rajna, G. 'The Commentary on the prayers by Joseph Ibn Waqar'. *Ozar Yehudei Sefarad* 9 (1966) 11–23 (in Hebrew).

With a few exceptions, the authors listed below have not yet received systematic study. I have encountered them in the course of my readings in manuscripts and printed books, and the bibliography that follows is thus far from exhaustive. Neither text nor bibliographical indications are anything more than suggestions for future research.

Solomon ben Abraham Paniel

Work:

Or Eynayim (*Light of the Eyes*). Cremona, 1557; repr. Jerusalem, 1967.

Solomon ben Hanokh Al-Kostantini

Works:

Sefer Megalleh Amukot (*The Revealer of Hidden Things*), finished in 1352, Vatican MS ebreo 59.
Other manuscripts listed in M. Steinschneider, *Die Handschriften Verzeichnisse der Königlichen Bibliothek zu Berlin*, Berlin, 1897, pp. 62–3.

'Sefer Ma'ayan Ganim'

Sefer Ma'ayan Ganim (*Source of Gardens*). Philosophical commentary on Genesis and Exodus, Vatican MS ebreo 274.

Eleazar Ashkenazi ben Nathan Ha-Bavli

Work:

Zafenath Paneach, Commentary on the Pentateuch. Ed. S. Rappaport, Johannesburg, 1965 (edition based on a photostatic copy of part of the book, the only surviving trace of the unique copy made by Ephraïm b. Shabbataï ha-Melamed in Crete, 1399).

Hayyim ben Israel of Toledo

Work:

'Trattato del Paradiso di Hajjim Israel' [=*Ma'amar Gan-Eden*]. Ed. P. Perreau, In *Jubelschrift zum...Dr L. Zunz*, Berlin, 1884, pp. 141–2, and in Hebrew, pp. 20–42.

Hanokh ben Solomon Al-Kostantini

Work:

Les Visions divines. Ed. and French trans. by C. Sirat. Paris-Jerusalem, 1976.

Bibliography to page 343

Abba Mari ben Eligdor
Study:
Renan E. *Les écrivains juifs français du XIVe siècle*, Paris, 1893, pp. 202–6 (548–52).

Judah ben Benjamin Ibn Roqques
Work:
Teshuvot al ha-nevuah (Questions on prophecy). Jewish Theological Seminary, New York, no. 2383, MS ENA 82.

Judah ben Solomon Campanton
Work:
Arba'ah Kinyanim. The first half of the work published by E. H. Golomb, *Judah ben Salomon Campanton and his Arba'ah Kinyanim*, Philadelphia, 1930. With a list of manuscripts.

Moses Cohen Ibn Crispin of Toledo
Work:
Most contained in Paris, Bibliothèque nationale, MS héb. 719.
Study:
Vajda, G. 'A propos de l'averroisme juif'. *Sefarad* 12 (1952) 3–29.

Elhanan ben Moses Kalkish
Work:
Even Sapir (*The Sapphire*). Paris, Bibliothèque nationale, MS héb. 727–8.

Moses ben Isaac Ibn Waqar
Work:
Matok la-Nefesh (*Sweetness for the Soul*). Ed. of the surviving chapters by E. Kupffer, in *Kovetz al-Yad* 9 (19), Jerusalem, 1980, pp. 297–331.

Samuel Sarsa
Works:
Mikhlol Yofi (*The Fullness of Beauty*). Paris, Bibliothèque nationale, MS héb. 729–30.
Mekor Hayyim (*The Fountain of Life*). (A commentary on the biblical commentary of Abraham Ibn Ezra.) Mantua, 1549.

En Solomon Astruc of Barcelona
Works:
Most found in Florence, Biblioteca Ambrosiana, MS ebreo 32.

David ben Yom Tov Ibn Bilia
E.J., s.v. 'Ibn Bilia, David ben Yom-Tov'
Work:
Yesodot ha-maskil. Ed. and French trans. by E. Ashkenazi. *Principles des hommes intelligents*, Metz, 1849, pp. 1–19.

Bibliography to pages 343–344

Study:

Allony, N. 'David Ibn Bilia and his works'. *Areshet* (1944) 377–86 (in Hebrew).

Judah ben Isaac Cohen

Work:

Paris, Bibliothèque nationale, MS héb. 956, fols. 129v–132v.

Study:

Vajda, G. 'La question disputée de l'essence et de l'existence vue par Juda Cohen, philosophe juif de Provence'. *AHDLMA* 44 (1977) 127–147.

Judah Ibn Mosconi

Works:

A list of manuscripts found in M. Steinschneider, *Magazin für die Wissenschaft des Judenthums* 3 (1876) 41–51, 94–100, 140–53, 190–206.

The introd. to his commentary on the biblical commentary of Abraham Ibn Ezra published in *Otsar Tov*, Berlin, 1878, pp. 1–10.

Nehemiah Kalomiti

Work:

Milhemet Emet, The War of Truth by Nehemiah Kalomiti. Ed. with English summary by P. Doron. New York, 1978.

Abraham Avigdor (Bonet) ben Meshullam ben Solomon

Study:

Renan, E. *Les écrivains juifs français du XIVe siècle*, Par is, 1893, pp. 371–5 (717–21.)

Moses ben Judah Nagah

Work:

Ahavat Ta'anugim (*Love of Pleasures*), Oxford, Bodleian Library, MS Opp. 141 (Cat. 1291) and Bodl. Or. 45 (Cat. 1292)

Elijah ben Eliezer ha-Yerushalmi

Study:

Rosenberg, 'The Book of Logic by Elyahu ben Eliezer Hayerushalmi'. *Daat* 1 (1978) 63–71; 2–3 (1979) 127–38; 7 (1981) 73–92 (in Hebrew).

Joseph Bonfils ben Eliezer ben Joseph the Spaniard

Work:

Sophnath Pane'ah. Ed. D. Herzog. Heidelberg, 1911.

Samuel Ibn Motot

Study:

Vajda, G. 'Recherches sur la synthèse philosophico-kabbalistique de Samuel Ibn Motot'. *AHDLMA* 27 (1960) 29–63. With a list of manuscripts.

Bibliography to pages 344–346

Shem Tov ben Isaac Ibn Shaprut of Tudela

Works:

Two commentaries on the biblical commentary of Abraham Ibn Ezra. Paris, Bibliothèque nationale, MS héb. 852.

Pardes Rimonim (Commentary on the *aggadot* of the Talmud). Ed. Sabionetta, 1554; repr. Jerusalem, 1968.

His Hebrew translation of the Gospel of St Matthew appeared in a bilingual ed., Basle, 1537.

A list of works found in M. Steinschneider, *Catalogus Librorum hebraicorum in Biblioteca bodleiana*, no. 7125, col. 2548–58.

Solomon Franco

Work:

Commentary on the biblical commentary of Abraham Ibn Ezra. Oxford, Bodleian Library, MS Hunt 559 (Cat. 1258).

The Fifteenth Century
SPANISH JEWS BETWEEN JUDAISM AND CHRISTIANITY

Baer, Y. *A History of the Jews in Christian Spain*. Philadelphia, 1966.

Lasker, D. J. *Jewish Philosophical Polemics against Christianity in the Middle Ages*. New York, 1977.

Rosenberg, S. 'Logic and Ontology in Jewish Philosophy in the 14th century'. Hebrew University, Jerusalem, 1974.

Schechter, S. 'The Dogmas of Judaism'. In his *Studies in Judaism*, New York, 1970, pp. 73–104.

David of Rocca Martino

Work:

Zekhut Adam. Ed. Y. Bril. In *Jen Lebanon*. Paris, 1966.

Studies:

Renan, E. *Les écrivains juifs français du XIVe siècle*, Paris, 1893, pp. 314–19 (660–5). [The reasons given here for placing him in the fourteenth century do not seem to me convincing.]

Lasker, D. J. 'Averroistic Trends in Jewish–Christian Polemics in the Late Middle Ages'. *Speculum* 55 (1980) 294–304.

The Shem Tov family

Study:

Guttman, J. 'Die Familie Shem Tob in ihren Beziehungen zur Philosophie'. *MGWJ* 57 (1913) 177–95, 326–36.

Shem Tov Ibn Shem Tov

E.J., s.v. 'Ibn Shem Tov, Shem Tov'

Work:

Sefer ha-Emunot (*Book of Beliefs*). Ferrara, 1956; repr. Jerusalem, 1969.

448

Bibliography to pages 346–357

Solomon Ha-Levi of Burgos

E.J., s.v. 'Pablo de Santa Maria'

Studies:

Serrano, L. *Los conversos Pablo de Santa Maria y Alfonso de Cartagena*. Madrid, 1942.
Cantera y Burgos, F. *La conversion del celebre talmudista Salomon Levi*. Santander, 1933.
   Alvar Garcia de Santa Maria y su familia de conversos. Madrid, 1952.

Joshua Lorki

Work:

The *Letter* published in *Divré Hakhamim*, ed. E. Ashkenazi, Metz, 1849, pp. 41–6. With a
   French translation by 'B.H.', pp. 19–28.

Ephraim ben Israel al-Naqawa

Work:

Shaar Kevod Elohim. Ed. with a commentary, 'Petah ha-Shaar', by A. Baliah. Tunis, 1902.

Study:

Sirat, C. 'La pensée philosophique d'Ephraïm al-Naqawa'. *Daat* 5 (1980) 5–21.

Judah ben Samuel Ibn Abbas

Work:

Ya'ir Nativ (*He who lights the Way*). Oxford, Bodleian Library, MS Bodl. Or. 44 (Cat.
   Neubauer 1280).

Isaac ben Moses Levi (*Efodi*)

E.J., s.v. 'Duran, Profiat'

Works:

Alteca Boteca. 1st ed. Constantinople, *ca.* 1557.
   Ma'aseh Efod (*Making of the Ephod*). Vienna, 1865; pp. 181–7, commentary on some
      passages of the commentary on the Torah by Abraham Ibn Ezra; pp. 191–7, letter to
      En Joseph Abram.
Commentary on the Guide of the Perplexed. 1st ed. Venice, 1551; printed in the classical
   editions of the *Guide of the Perplexed*.
Commentary on the Book of the Name by Abraham Ibn Ezra. Paris, Bibliothèque nationale,
   MS héb. 831, fols. 319r-324v.

A list of other manuscripts is given in Renan, E. *Les écrivains juifs français du XIVe siècle*,
   Paris, 1893, pp. 395–407 (741–53).

Abraham ben Judah Leon of Candie

Work:

Arba'ah Turim (*Four Rows*). Vatican, MS ebreo 399.

Ḥasdai Crescas

E.J., s.v. Crescas, Hasdai.

Works:

Biṭṭul 'Iqqarrey ha-Noṣrim (*Refutation of Christian Dogmas*). Ed. E. Deinard. Kearny, N.J., 1904.
Or Adonai (*The Light of God*). Ferrara, 1540; repr. Jerusalem, 1963.
All the passages dealing with physics are critically edited and translated into English in H. Wolfson, *Crescas' Critique of Aristotle*, Cambridge (Mass.), 1929.

Studies:

Baer, Y. 'Abner of Burgos' *Minhath Kenaoth* and its influence on Hasdai Crescas', *Tarbiz* 11 (1940) 188–206 (in Hebrew).
Davidson, H. 'The Principle that a finite Body Can Contain Only Finite Power'. In S. Stein and R. Loewe (eds.), *Studies in Jewish Religious and Intellectual History, presented to Alexander Altmann*, Alabama, 1979, pp. 75–92.
Feldman, S. 'The theory of eternal Creation in Hasdai Crescas and some of his Predecessors'. *Viator* 11 (1980) 1289–320.
Guttmann, J. 'The Problem of Free-Will in Hasdai Crescas; Thought and the Muslim Aristotelians'. In his *Dat u-Maddah*, Jerusalem, 1955, pp. 149–68 (in Hebrew).
Harvey, W. Z. 'The term *hitdabbekut* in Crescas' definition of time'. *JQR* 71 (1980) 44–7.
'Kabbalistic elements in Crescas' *Light of the Lord*'. *Jerusalem Studies in Jewish Thought* 2, 1 (1982–3) 75–109.
Joel, M. *Don Chasdai Creskas' religionsphilosophische Lehren*. Breslau, 1886; Hebrew trans., Tel-Aviv, 1928.
Klein-Braslavy, S. 'The Influence of R. Nissim Girondi on Crescas' and Albo's Principles'. In *Eshel Beer Sheva*, vol. 11, Jerusalem, 1980, pp. 177–97 (in Hebrew).
'Gan-Eden et Gehinnom dans le système de Hasdaï Crescas'. In G. Nahon and Ch. Touati (eds.), *Hommage à Georges Vajda*, Louvain, 1980, pp. 263–79.
Ravitzky, A. 'Crescas' Theory on Human Will: Development and Sources'. *Tarbiz* (1981) 445–69.
Touati, Ch. 'Hasdaï Crescas et ses paradoxes sur la liberté'. In *Mélanges d'Histoire des Religions offerts à Henri-Charles Puech*, Paris 1974, pp. 573–8.
Waxman, M. *The Philosophy of Don Hasdai Crescas*. New York, 1920.
Wolfson, H. A. *Crescas' Critique of Aristotle*. Cambridge (Mass.), 1929.
'Crescas on the Problem of Divine Attributes'. In his *Studies in the History of Philosophy and Religion*, vol. 11, Cambridge (Mass.), 1977, pp. 247–337.
'Studies in Crescas'. *Ibid.* pp. 458–78.
'Emanation and Creation *ex-nihilo* in Crescas'. *Ibid.* pp. 623–9 (in Hebrew).

'Mesharet Moshe'

Mesharet Moshe (*Moses' Servant*) has been published as *Kalonymi Apologia Mosis Maimonidis*. Ed. J. Goldenthal. Leipzig, 1845.

Elijah ben Moses Bashyatchi

E.J., s.v. 'Bashyazi'

Work:

'Adderet Eliyahu. 1st ed. Constantinople, 1540–1.

Studies:

Ankori, Z. *Karaites in Byzantium*, New York, 1959, s.v. 'Elijah Bashyachi'.
Nemoy, L. *Karaite Anthology*, New Haven, 1932, pp. 236–70, 378–85.

Simon ben Zemaḥ Duran

E.J., s.v. 'Duran, Simeon b. Zemah'

Works:

Ohev Mishpat (*Lover of Justice*). Venice, 1589.
Magen Avot (*Shield of the Fathers*). Leghorn, 1785.
Keshet u-Magen (*The Arrow and the Shield*). Leghorn, 1780; repr. Jerusalem, 1970.

Studies:

Arieli, N. 'The Philosophy of Rashbaz, Shimon Ben Zemah Duran'. Ph.D. diss. Hebrew University, Jerusalem, 1976 (in Hebrew, with English summary).
Bleich, J. D. 'Duran's View of the Nature of Providence'. *JQR* 69 (1979) 208–25.
Guttman, J. 'Die stellung des Simon ben Zemah Duran in der Geschichte der jüdischen Religionsphilosophie'. *MGWJ* 52 (1908) 46–79; 53 (1909) 46–79, 199–208.
Leibowitz, J. 'R. Simon b. Zemah Duran and his Conception of Metabolism'. In *Magen Avot*, *Koroth* 7, 8/10 (1979) clxix-clxxix.
Spiro, S. J. 'The Principles of Judaism according to Rabbi Simon ben Semah Duran'. Ph.D. diss. Yeshiva University, 1970.

On the Disputation of Tortosa:

Pacios Lopez, A. *La Disputa de Tortosa*, 2 vols. Madrid–Barcelona, 1957.
Posnanski, A. 'Le Colloque de Tortose et de San Mateo', *REJ* 74 (1922) 17–39 and 160–83; 75 (1922) 74–88 and 187–204; 76 (1923) 37–46.

Joseph Albo

E.J., s.v. 'Albo, Joseph'

Work:

Sefer ha-Ikkarim (*Book of Principles*). Critical ed. with English trans. by I. Husik. Philadelphia, 1929.

Studies:

Guttmann, J. 'Towards a Study of the Sources of the Book of Principles'. In his *Dat u-Maddah*, Jerusalem, 1955, pp. 169–81 (in Hebrew).
Harvey, W. Z. 'Albo's discussion of time'. *JQR* 70 (1980) 210–38.
Husik, I. 'Joseph Albo, the last of the Jewish Philosophers'. *PAAJR* 1 (1930) 61–72.
Lasker, D. J. 'Joseph Albo's Theory of Verification'. *Daat* 5 (1980) 5–12 (in Hebrew).
Schweid, E. 'Joseph Albo's System of Dogmas as distinct from that of Maimonides'. *Tarbiz* 33 (1964) 74–84 (in Hebrew).

Joseph ben Shem Tov Ibn Shem Tov

E.J., s.v. 'Ibn Shem Tov, Joseph ben Shem Tov'

Works:

Kevod Elohim (*The Glory of God*). Ferrara, 1556.
Commentary on *Alteca Boteca*. Constantinople 1570–8.
Short Commentary on Averroes' 'Epistle on the Possibility of Conjunction'. Ed. S. Regev, who also gives lists of the other works. *Jerusalem Studies in Jewish Thought* 2 (1982) 38–93 (in Hebrew).

Isaac ben Shem Tov Ibn Shem Tov

E.J., s.v. 'Ibn Shem Tov, Isaac ben Shem Tov'

A list of Works, lost and extant, is given by Wolfson, H. A. 'Isaac Ibn Shem-Tob's Unknown Commentaries on the *Physics* and his other unknown works'. In his *Studies in the History of Philosophy*, vol. II, Cambridge (Mass.), 1977, pp. 479–90.

Shem Tov ben Joseph ben Shem Tov

E.J., s.v. 'Ibn Shem Tov, Shem Tov ben Joseph ben Shem Tov' (an article by Warren Harvey)

Abraham ben Shem Tov Bibago

E.J., s.v. 'Bibago, Abraham b. Shem Tov'

Work:

Derekh Emunah (*The Way of Faith*). Constantinople, 1522; repr. Jerusalem, 1970.

Studies:

Lazaroff, A. *The Theology of Abraham Bibago; the Defense of the Divine Will, Knowledge and Providence in Fifteenth-Century Spanish Jewish Philosophy*. University of Alabama Press, 1981.
    'The Absolute Freedom of the Divine will in the Philosophy of Abraham Bibago'. In *Mystics, Philosophers and Politicians*, pp. 119–40.
Nuriel, A. 'The Philosophy of Abraham Bibago'. Ph.D. diss. Hebrew University, Jerusalem, 1975 (in Hebrew with an English summary).
    'Israel and the nations in the thought of R. Abraham Bibago'. In *Bein Israel la'amim*, Jerusalem, 1978, pp. 37–42.
    'Allan Lazaroff: The Theology of Abraham Bibago'. Book-review, *Tarbiz* 52 (1983) 154–66.
Steinschneider, M. 'Abraham Bibagos Schriften'. *MWGJ* 33 (1833) 79–96, 125–44.

Isaac ben Moses Arama

E.J., s.v. 'Arama, Isaac b. Moses'

Work:
Akedat Izhak. Salonica, 1522.

Studies:

Bettan, I. *Studies in Jewish Preaching*, Cincinnati, 1939, pp. 130–91.
Heller Wilensky, S. *The Philosophy of Isaac Arama*. Jerusalem–Tel-Aviv, 1956 (in Hebrew).
    'Isaac Arama on the Creation and the Structure of the World'. *PAAJR* 22 (1953) 131–50.
Pearl, C. *The Medieval Jewish Mind*. London, 1971.

Abraham ben Isaac Shalom

E.J., s.v. 'Shalom, Abraham ben Isaac ben Judah ben Samuel'

Work:
Neve Shalom. Constantinople, 1539; Venice 1574; repr. Jerusalem, 1967.

Study:
Davidson, H. A. *The Philosophy of Abraham Shalom*. Berkeley–Los Angeles, 1964.

Isaac Abrabanel

E.J., s.v. 'Abrabanel, Isaac ben Judah'

Works:

All Abrabanel's works have been published:

Commentary on the Torah. 1st ed. Venice, 1579.
Commentary on the Early Prophets. Pesaro, 1511/12.
Commentary on the later Prophets. Pesaro, 1520.

These commentaries are generally found in the classic editions of *Mikraot Gedolot*:

Atarat Zekenim (*The Crown of the Ancients*). 1st ed. Sabionetta, 1557; with *Zurat ha-yesodot* (*The Form of the Elements*), Warsaw, 1894.
Shamayim hadashim (*New Skies*). Rodelheim, 1828.
Mifalot Elohim (*The Works of God*). Venice 1592.
Rosh Amanah (*The Principle of Faith*). Constantinople, 1505; Tel-Aviv, 1958.
   English transl. by M. M. Kellner, *Principles of Faith*, London and Toronto, 1982.

All these treatises and his answers to the questions on the *Guide of the Perplexed* (1st ed., Venice, 1574), *Yeshuot Meshiḥo* (*The Messiah and Salvation*) were reprinted under the title *Ketavim al Maḥshevet Israel*, Jerusalem, 1967.

   The *Commentary* on the *Guide of the Perplexed* is published in the standard edition of the *Guide*.

Studies:

Baer, I. 'Don Isaac Abrabanel and his conception of History'. *Tarbiz* 8 (1937) 241–59 (in Hebrew).
Barzilay, I. *Between Reason and Faith*, The Hague–Paris, 1967, pp. 72–132.
Guttmann, J. *Die Religionsphilosophischen Lehren des Isaak Abravanel*. Breslau, 1916.
Kellner, M. M. 'Rabbi Isaac Abravanel on Maimonides' principles of faith'. *Tradition* 18 (1980) 343–56.
Mihaly, E. 'Isaac Abrabanel on the Principles of Faith'. *HUCA* 26 (1955) 481–522.
Natanyahu, B. *Don Isaac Abravanel, Statesman and philosopher*. Philadelphia, 1953.
Reines, A. J. *Maïmonides and Abrabanel on Prophecy*. Cincinnati, 1970.
Sarachek, J. *Don Isaac Abravanel*. New York, 1938.
Trends, J. B., and Loewe, H. (eds.). *Isaac Abravanel; six lectures*. Cambridge, 1937.

THE LAST PHILOSOPHERS IN NORTH AFRICA, PROVENCE AND TURKEY

Samuel ben Saadiah Ibn Danan

Works:

To be found in the John Rylands Library, Manchester, M.S. 30/6.

Study:

Rosenberg, S. 'Logic and Ontology in Jewish Philosophy in the 14th Century', Hebrew University, Jerusalem, 1974, p. 56.

Moses ben Shem Tov Ibn Habib

Works:

To be found in M. Steinschneider, *Catalogus Librorum hebraeorum in Biblioteca bodleiana*, Berlin, 1931, no. 6445, col. 1786.

453

Study:

Rosenberg, S. 'Logic and Ontology in Jewish Philosophy' (see above), p. 56.

Salomon ben Menahem Prat Maimon and his students

Renan, E. *Les écrivains juifs français du XIVe siècle*, Paris, 1843, pp. 407–13 (753–9). With a list of manuscripts.

Abraham Farissol

E.J., s.v. 'Farissol, Abraham ben Mordecai'

Study:

Ruderman, D. B. *The World of a Renaissance Jew; the Life and Thought of Abraham ben Mordecai Farissol*. Cincinnati, 1981.

Mordecai ben Eliezer Comtino

E.J., s.v. 'Comtino, Mordecai ben Eliezer' (article by E. Kupfer)

JEWISH THOUGHT IN YEMEN

Blumenthal, D. R. 'An Illustration of Philosophic Mysticism from fifteenth century Yemen'. In G. Nahon and Ch. Touati (eds.), *Hommage à Georges Vajda*, Louvain, 1980, pp. 291–308.
Goitein, S. D. 'About the Jews of Yemen.' Introd. to *From the Land of Sheba*. New York, 1973.
Tobi, Y. 'The Jews of Yemen'. In *Bibliography of Jewish History* vol. II. Jerusalem, 1975.
Kafih, J. 'An Epistle of Defence from Yeman'. *Kobez al-Jad* 15 (1951) 39–63 (in Hebrew).
Ratzaby, Y. 'The Literature of Yemenite Jews'. *Kirjath Sefer* 28 (1952–3) 255–80, 394–409; 33 (1957–8) 111–17; 34 (1958–9) 109–116 (in Hebrew).
  The Yemenite Jews; Literature and Studies, Bibliography 1935–1975, supplement to *Kirjath Sefer* 50 (1976) (in Hebrew).
Rosenthal, F. 'From the "Unorthodox" Judaism of Medieval Yemen'. In G. Nahon and Ch. Touati (eds.), *Hommage à Georges Vajda* (see above), pp. 279–90.

Nethanel ben Isaiah

Work:

Maor ha-Afela. Hebrew trans. of *Nūr al-Ẓalām*, by J. Kafih. Jerusalem, 1957.

Study:

Vajda, G. 'Une copie peu connue du Nūr-al-Ẓalām de l'auteur yéménite Nathanael fils d'Isaïe'. *REJ* 130 (1971) 307–9.

Hōter ben Solomon

Works edited with an English translation:

Blumenthal, D. R. *The Commentary of R. Ḥōṭer ben Shelōmō to the Thirteen Principles of Maimonides*. Leyden, 1974.
  The Philosophic Questions and Answers of Ḥōṭer ben Shelōmō. Leyden, 1982.
  'The rationalistic Commentary of R. Ḥōṭer ben Shelōmō to Pirkei de Rabbi Eliezer'. *Tarbiz* 48 (1979) 99–106 (in Hebrew).

454

Studies:

Blumenthal, D. R. 'Ezechiel's vision seen through the eyes of a philosophic mystic [Ḥōṭer ben Shelōmō]'. *JAAR* 48 (1979) 417–27.
  'An Example of Ismaili Influence in post-Maimonidean Yemen'. In *Studies in honor of . . . Goitein*, Jerusalem, 1981, pp. 155–74 (in Hebrew).

JEWISH PHILOSOPHERS IN ITALY OF THE QUATTROCENTO

Altmann, A. 'Ars Rhetorica as Reflected in Some Jewish Figures of the Italian Renaissance'. In his *Essays in Jewish Intellectual History*, London, 1981, pp. 97–118.
Bonfil, R. *The Rabbinate in Renaissance Italy*, Jerusalem, 1979, especially pp. 173–206 (in Hebrew).
Cassuto, U. *Gli Ebrei a Firenze nell' eta del Rinascimento*. Florence, 1918.
Idel, M. 'The Magical and Neoplatonic Interpretation of the Kabbalah in the Renaissance'. *Jerusalem Studies in Jewish Thought* 4 (1982) 60–112 (in Hebrew).
  'The Magical and Theurgic Interpretation of Music in Jewish Sources from the Renaissance to Hassidism'. *Yuval* 4 (1982) 33–52 (in Hebrew).
Pines, S. 'Medieval Doctrines in Renaissance Garb? Some Jewish and Arabic Sources of Leone Ebreo's Doctrines'. In B. D. Cooperman (ed.), *Jewish Thought in the Sixteenth Century*. Cambridge (Mass.)–London, 1983.
Roth, C. *The Jews in the Renaissance*. Philadelphia, 1959.
Steinschneider, M. *La Literatura ebraica*. Rome, 1884.

Judah ben Yehiel Messer Leon

E.J., s.v. 'Judah ben Jehiel'. With a list of printed works.

Works:

A list of manuscripts may be found in the article by U. Cassuto in the German *Encyclopaedia Judaica*, s.v. 'Judah ben Jehiel'.

Studies:

Husik, I. *Judah Messer Leon's Commentary on the Vetus Logica*. Leyden, 1906.
Carpi, D. 'Notes on the Life of Rabbi Judah Messer Leon'. In *Studi sull'Ebraismo italiano in memoria di C. Roth*. Rome, 1974.

David ben Judah Messer Leon

E.J., s.v. 'Leon, Messer David ben Judah'

Works:

A list of printed books and manuscripts is to be found in H. Tirosh-Rothschild, 'The Philosophy of David ben Yehuda Messer Leon'. Ph.D. diss. Hebrew University, Jerusalem, 1978 (in Hebrew with a summary in English).
Carpi, D. 'Notes on the Life of Rabbi Judah Messer Leon.' In *Studi sull' Ebraismo italiano in memoria di C. Roth*. Rome, 1974, pp. 39–62.
Schechter, S. 'Notes sur Messer David Léon tirées de manuscrits'. *REJ* 24 (1892) 118–38.
Tirosh-Rothschild, H. 'The Conception of the Torah in the Work of Messer David ben Judah Leon'. *Jerusalem Studies in Jewish Thought* 2 (1982), 94–117 (in Hebrew) with a list of surviving and lost works.

Elijah ben Moses Abba Delmedigo

E.J., s.v. 'Delmedigo, Elijah ben Moses Abba'

Work:

Behinat ha-dat (*Examination of Religion*). Ed. I. Reggio. Vienna, 1833.

Study:

Geffen, D. 'Insights into the Life and Thought of Elijah del Medigo based on his published and unpublished works'. *PAAJR* 41–2 (1973–4) 69–86.

Judah ben Isaac Abrabanel (*Leo Hebraeus*)

E.J., s.v. 'Abrabanel, Judah'

Work:

The Philosophy of Love. Trans. F. Friedberg–Sealy and J. H. Barnes. London, 1937.

Studies:

Damiens, S. *Amour et Intellect chez Léon l'hébreu*. Toulouse, 1971. With a bibliography.
Genot, J. 'Philosophie et Poétique dans l'oeuvre d'Immanuel de Rome'. Ph.D. diss. Université de Paris III, 1977.
Idel, M. 'The Sources of the Circle Images in Dialoghi d'Amore'. *Iyyun* 28 (1978) 156–66 (in Hebrew).
Pines, S. 'Medieval Doctrines in Renaissance Garb? Some Jewish and Arabic Sources of Leone Ebreo's Doctrines'. In B. D. Cooperman (ed.), *Jewish Thought in the Sixteenth Century*, Cambridge (Mass.)–London, 1983, pp. 365–98.

Johanan Alemanno

Works:

A list of printed works and manuscripts is given by U. Cassuto in the German *Encyclopaedia Judaica;* s.v. 'Alemann, Johanan ben Isak'.

Studies:

Idel, M. 'The Study Programme of R. Yohanan Alemanno'. *Tarbiz* 48 (1979) 303–31 (in Hebrew).
Perles, F. 'Les savants juifs à Florence à l'époque de Laurent de Médicis'. *REJ* 12 (1886) 244–57.
Rosenthal, E. I. J. 'Some observations on Yohanan Alemanno's Political Ideas'. In S. Stein and R. Loewe (eds.), *Studies in Jewish Religious and Intellectual History, presented to Alexander Altmann*, Alabama, 1979, pp. 249–61.

Jacob ben David Provençal

E.J., s.v. 'Provençal, Jacob ben David'

Works:

'The Letter on the Study of Sciences'. Ed F. Ashkenazi. In *Divre Hakhamin*, Metz, 1849, pp. 63–75.

Yehiel Nissim of Pisa

E.J., s.v. 'Pisa, da'

Work:

Minchath Kenaoth (*Offering of Jealousy*). Ed. D. Kaufman. Berlin, 1898.

Studies:

Bonfil, R. *The Rabbinate in Renaissance Italy*, Jerusalem, 1979, pp. 183–90.

Cassuto, U. 'La Famiglia da Pisa et Ancora sulla Famiglia da Pisa'. *Rivista Israelitica* 7 (1910) 9–19, 72–86, 146–50; 10 (1913) 48–57.

Kaufmann, D. 'La famille de Yehiel de Pise'. *REJ* 26 (1893) 85–110, 220–39; 27 (1893) 276 and 318; 29 (1894) 142–7; 31 (1895) 62–73; 32 (1896) 130–40.

Obadiah Sforno

E.J., s.v. 'Sforno, Obadiah ben Jacob'

Study:

Bonfil, R. 'The doctrine of the Human Soul and its Holiness in the thought of R. Obadiah Sforno'. In *Eshel Beer-Sheva*, vol. I, Jerusalem, 1976, pp. 200-57 (in Hebrew).

Moses ben Abraham Provençal

E.J., s.v. 'Provençal, Moses ben Abraham'

Study:

Bonfil, R. 'The Commentary of Moses Provençal on the twenty-five propositions preceding book II of the Guide of the Perplexed'. *Kiryat Sefer* 50 (1975) 156–76 (in Hebrew).

Joseph Solomon Delmedigo

E.J., s.v. 'Delmedigo, Joseph Solomon'

Study:

Barzilay, I. *Yoseph Shlomo Delmedigo* (*Yashar of Candia*). Leyden, 1974.

David Ibn Yahya

E.J., s.v. 'Ibn Yahya, David b. Joseph'

Study:

Marx, A. 'Glimpses of the life of an Italian Rabbi of the First Half of the sixteenth century'. *HUCA* I (1924) 605–24.

Judah ben Joseph Moscato

E.J., s.v. 'Moscato, Judah b. Joseph'

Work:

Kol Yehudah (*The Voice of Judah*). Venice, 1594.

Studies: Bettan, I. *Studies in Jewish Preaching*, Cincinnati, 1939, pp. 192–225.

'The Sermons of Judah Moscato'. *HUCA* 6 (1929) 297–326.

GENERAL INDEX

INDEX OF ANCIENT WORKS
QUOTED IN THE TEXT

476

Index of Ancient Works Quoted